AN A–Z OF
Health and
Safety Law

AN **A–Z** OF

Health and Safety Law

SECOND EDITION

PETER CHANDLER

KOGAN
PAGE

INFORMATION AND THE LAW

Every effort has been made to ensure the accuracy of the information and guidance given in this book. However, no legal responsibility can be accepted by the author or the publishers for the accuracy of that information and guidance. In the final analysis, it is for the courts and tribunals to give an authoritative interpretation of the law as laid down in Acts of Parliament and their attendant statutory instruments, regulations and orders.

First published in 1995
2nd Edition published in 1997

Apart from any fair dealing for the purposes of research or private study, or criticism or review, as permitted under the Copyright, Designs and Patents Act 1988, this publication may only be reproduced, stored or transmitted, in any form or by any means, with the prior permission in writing of the publishers or, in the case of reprographic reproduction, in accordance with the terms of licences issued by the Copyright Licensing Agency. Enquiries concerning reproduction should be sent to the publishers at the undermentioned address.

Kogan Page Limited
120 Pentonville Road
London N1 9JN

© Peter Chandler 1995 & 1997

British Library Cataloguing in Publication Data
A CIP record for this book is available from the British Library

ISBN 0 7494 2444 3

Typeset from the author's disk
Printed and bound in Great Britain by
Biddles Ltd, Guildford and Kings Lynn

Table of Contents

Table of Statutes, Regulations & Orders

Part I: Statutes

Part II: Regulations & Orders

Preface

Since this book first appeared in April 1995, the transitional period for implementation of the so-called 'Six-Pack' of health and safety regulations has expired. So too have many of the related and outdated provisions of statutory regulations and orders made under, or saved by, the Factories Act 1961 — ranging from the Gut Scraping & Tripe Dressing Welfare Order 1906 to the Woodworking Machines Regulations 1974 . Since 1 January 1996 (or, in the case of the PUWER Regulations 1992, 1 January 1997), *every* employer in *every* place of work must now comply with his (or her) duties under that new generation of EC-prompted health and safety legislation. This 2nd edition of the *A-Z of Health & Safety Law* has accordingly been stripped of all reference to that outdated legislation (save for those few provisions which remain in force).

All new health and safety legislation, brought into force since April 1995 has, where appropriate, also been included in this 2nd edition. For example, under the Health & Safety (Consultation with Employees) Regulations 1996, which came into force on 1 October 1996, employers are nowadays duty-bound to consult employees directly (or their elected representatives) on matters affecting their health and safety at work. Before October 1996, the only people who had the statutory right to be consulted on such matters were trade union-appointed safety representatives — an anomaly which (following pressure from the European Commission) has now happily been corrected.

Other new legislation, brought into force on 3 March 1997, requires employers to review their risk assessments before employing young persons under the age of 18 — given that people of that age (to paraphrase the Health & Safety (Young Persons) Regulations 1997) are usually inexperienced, perhaps a little immature, and somewhat casual [maybe a little cavalier] in their approach to workplace hazards and risks. Likewise, before employing a child aged 16 or under, a putative employer must in future provide one or other of the child's parents (or a guardian) with comprehensible and relevant information about the health and safety risks associated with the job on offer and about the preventive and protective measures which have been put into place to eliminate or minimise those risks.

Finally, there is the controversial 'Working Time Directive' (93/104/EC), which was introduced by the European Commission as *a health and safety measure* under Article 118a of the Treaty of Rome. The UK Government (which fought a long, hard but unsuccessful battle to have it overturned) is now duty-bound to implement the Directive by bringing-in the appropriate national legislation. The Directive's provisions (minimum annual holidays, rest breaks, a maximum *average* working week of 48 hours, restrictions on night work and shiftworking, etc.) already apply to UK civil servants and the like who are employed by 'emanations of the State'. Employees in the private sector must either await implementing legislation or (if the Government is dilatory in introducing that legislation) refer the matter for determination by the European Court of Justice. The Directive's implications are reviewed in three new sections in the handbook, titled: *Holidays, Annual*, *Meal & rest breaks* and *Working hours*.

My thanks to my publishers and, as always, to my family for their tolerance and support.

Peter Chandler
April 1997

| ABRASIVE WHEELS |

Key points

- The "hardware provisions" of the Abrasive Wheels Regulations 1970 (summarised elsewhere in this section) were revoked on 1 January 1996 by the Provision and Use of Work Equipment Regulations 1992 (SI 1992/2932). All that now remains of the 1970 Regulations are regulations 2 and 9, discussed below. These continue to apply to all workplace abrasive wheels, regardless of the date on which they were purchased or acquired.

- The Provision & Use of Work Equipment Regulations 1992 are reviewed elsewhere in this handbook in the sections titled **Fencing and guarding, Machinery safety**, and **Work equipment**.

HEALTH & SAFETY AT WORK ETC. ACT 1974

- Section 2 of the Health & Safety at Work etc. Act 1974 imposes a general duty on every employer to ensure, so far as is reasonably practicable, the health, safety and welfare at work of all his employees — which duty extends to the provision and maintenance of plant and equipment that are safe and without risks to health.

- People and organisations who (or which) design, manufacture, import or supply any article (such as an abrasive wheel) for use at work have a like duty under section 6 of the 1974 Act to ensure, so far as is reasonably practicable, that the article in question is so designed and constructed that it will be safe and without risks to health when it is being set, used or maintained by a person at work. Furthermore, the manufacturer, supplier etc. must provide the purchaser of any such article with adequate information about the use for which the article is designed or has been tested and about any conditions necessary to ensure that it will be safe and without risks to health not only while it is being set, used or maintained but also when it is being disposed of (*ibid*; section 6(1)(c)).

• Any person who fails to discharge a duty to which he (or she) is subject, by virtue of sections 2 to 6 of the 1974 Act, is guilty of an offence and liable, on summary conviction, to a fine of up to £20,000 or, if convicted on indictment, to a fine of an unlimited amount. The penalty for contravening any health and safety Regulations, including the Abrasive Wheels Regulations 1970 (summarised in this section) is a fine of up to £2,000 or, where a conviction is obtained on indictment, a fine of an unlimited amount (*ibid*; section 33). Any person injured as direct consequence of his (or her) employer's (or the manufacturer or supplier's) negligent failure to comply with his statutory duty to provide safe plant or equipment may sue for damages in the ordinary courts, as to which, please turn to the sections titled **Defective equipment** and **Insurance, Compulsory** elsewhere in this handbook.

ABRASIVE WHEELS REGULATIONS 1970

Meaning of 'abrasive wheel'

• Regulation 2 of the 1970 Regulations defines 'abrasive wheel' as meaning —

(a) a wheel, cylinder, disc or cone which consists of abrasive particles held together by mineral, metallic or organic bonds (whether natural or artificial);

(b) a mounted wheel or point consisting of abrasive particles, etc. (as in (a) above) permanently mounted on the end of a mandrel or quill, and a wheel or disc having in either case separate segments of abrasive material;

(c) a wheel or disc in either case of metal, wood, cloth, felt, rubber or paper and having any surface consisting wholly or partly of abrasive material; and

(d) a wheel, disc or saw to any surface of which is attached a rim or segments consisting in either case of diamond abrasive particles,

and which is, or is intended to be, power-driven and which is for use in any grinding or cutting operation.

Training and appointment of persons to mount abrasive wheels

- No employee may mount an abrasive wheel unless he (or she) has received suitable and sufficient instruction in hazards arising from the use of abrasive wheels and the precautions which should be observed; the methods of marking abrasive wheels as to type and speed; the methods of storing, handling and transporting abrasive wheels; methods of testing and inspecting abrasive wheels to check for damage; the functions of components used with abrasive wheels, including flanges, washers, bushes and nuts used in mounting (including knowledge of the correct and incorrect methods of assembling all components, and correct balancing of abrasive wheels); the proper method of dressing an abrasive wheel; the adjustment of the rest to an abrasive wheel; and the requirements of the 1970 Regulations (*ibid*; Regulation 9). He must also be familiar with, and understand, the particulars contained in Training and Advisory Leaflets SHW 11 and SHW 12, (see *FURTHER INFORMATION* below).

- Once trained, the operator's name must be entered in a register (Form F2346: *Abrasive Wheels Register*) together with details of whichever of the following class or description of abrasive wheels may be mounted by the person appointed:

  1. Straight-side wheels not exceeding 250 mm in diameter.
  2. Straight-side wheels exceeding 250 mm in diameter (including relieved and/or recessed wheels).
  3. Tapered wheels.
  4. Bonded abrasive discs.
  5. Cylinder wheels.
  6. Cup wheels (including dish wheels and saucer wheels).
  7. Cone wheels.
  8. Depressed centre wheels.
  9. Cutting-off wheels.

Note: These requirements do not apply to persons employed to mount mounted wheels or points or to persons employed to mount wheels or discs of metal, wood, cloth, felt, rubber or paper; or wheels, discs or saws with diamond abrasive particles.

The *Abrasive Wheels Register* (F2346) (ISBN 0 7176 0817 4, price £3.50) referred to above can be purchased from HSE Books (at the address given on page 328)

FURTHER INFORMATION

- The following HSE publications and forms are also available from HSE Books at the address on page 328.

Forms and notices

F2345
Abrasive wheels placard (paper version)
ISBN 0 7176 0423 3   £2.00 + VAT

F2346
Abrasive wheels register
ISBN 0 11 880792 7   £2.00 + VAT

F2347
Dangers arising from use of abrasive wheels
ISBN 0 7176 0431 4   £3.00 + VAT

F2347
Abrasive Wheels Regulations — cautionary card (encapsulated version)
ISBN 0 7176 0785 2   £7.50 + VAT

F2350
Mounted wheels and points — notice
ISBN 0 7176 0511 6   £3.00 + VAT

F2351
Maximum permissible speed — certificate of exemption
ISBN 0 7176 0518 3   £1.50 + VAT

Guidance

HS(G) 17
Safety in the use of abrasive wheels [1992]
ISBN 0 7176 0466 7   £7.00

See also **Fencing & guarding, Machinery safety** and **Work equipment** elsewhere in this handbook.

| ABSTRACTS & NOTICES |

Key points

- With the coming into force, in October 1989, of the Health & Safety Information for Employees Regulations 1989 (SI 1989/682) every employer must now display a poster on his premises titled: *Health & Safety Law: What You Should Know* . Furthermore, the poster must be displayed in a place where it can be easily seen and read by employees during their normal working hours. Alternatively, employers must issue each of their employees with a leaflet, also titled *Health & Safety Law: What You Should Know*. It is important to bear in mind that the poster (or leaflet) must be displayed (or issued to employees) in *every* premises (other than domestic premises) in which people are employed to work. The penalty for non-compliance is a fine of up to £2,000.

  Note: Employers in factories and on construction sites, and in offices, shops and railway premises should no longer display the once-familiar abstracts of the Factories Act 1961 (Forms F1, F2 or F3) or of the Offices, Shops & Railway Premises Act 1963 (Form OSR 9). These are no longer relevant (or available).

- An employer must state (in the spaces provided on the poster) the name and address of the enforcing authority (e.g., the HSE or the local authority Environmental Health Department) for the area or district in which his premises are situated, and the address also of the HSE's Employment Medical Advisory Service. The same information should either accompany the alternative leaflet or be readily available to employees on request.

DISPLAY OF REGULATIONS, ABSTRACTS AND NOTICES

- Many of the 50 and more sets of special safety Regulations made under (or saved by) the Factories Act 1961 have long since been overtaken by modern legislation. Many of these have been revoked; others (although still in force) have been 'mutilated' beyond recognition. For example, all that now remains of the Vitreous Enamelling Regulations 1908 is the citation and Regulation 7, which cautions that "No child .... shall be employed in any enamelling process".

Abstracts and notices

- With the coming into force of the Health & Safety Information for Employees (Modifications & Repeals) Regulations 1995 (SI 1995/2923) and the repeal of section 139 of the Factories Act 1961, employers need no longer display a great many abstracts and notices which for so long were a feature of the normal factory environment. However, the following should continue to be displayed, where appropriate:

RESIDUAL LEGISLATION ON THE DISPLAY OF NOTICES & POSTERS

Form No.	Regulations
F999 (Placard) ISBN 0 11 881450 8 £2.00 + VAT	Horizontal Milling Machines Regs 1928 (SR & O 1928/548)
F2345 (Paper placard) ISBN 0 7176 0423 3 £3.00 + VAT	Abrasive Wheels Regulations 1970 (SI 1970/535)
F2345 (Encapsulated placard) ISBN 0 7176 0784 4 £7.50 + VAT	*ditto*
F2347 *Dangers arising from use of abrasive wheels* (Cautionary card - paper version) ISBN 0 7176 0431 4 £3.00 + VAT	*ditto*
F2347 *Dangers arising from use of abrasive wheels* (Cautionary card - encapsulated version) ISBN 0 7176 0785 2 £7.50 + VAT	*ditto*

F2350
Mounted wheels and points
(Notice)
ISBN 0 7176 0511 6
£3.00 + VAT

ditto

F2440
(Notice)
ISBN 0 7176 0434 9
£2.98 + VAT

Highly Flammable Liquids & Liquefied
Petroleum Gases Regulations 1972
(SI 1972/918)

F2470
(Paper version)
ISBN 0 7176 0433 0
£3.00 + VAT

Woodworking Machines Regulations 1974
(SI 1974/903)

F2470
(Encapsulated version)
ISBN 0 7176 0782 8
£9.50 + VAT

ditto

Health & Safety Law:
What you should know
(Encapsulated poster)
ISBN 0 11 701573 3
£3.20 + VAT
(Discounts for quantity)

Health & Safety (Information for Employees)
Regulations 1989
(SI 1989/682)

Health & Safety Law:
What you should know
(Welsh version)
ISBN 0 11 701424 9
£3.20 + VAT
(Discounts for quantity)

ditto

Health & Safety Law:
What you should know
(Leaflet)
ISBN 0 7176 0818 2
£4.95 per pack of 50 leaflets

ditto

MISC 046
(Emergency procedures
 for an electric shock)
ISBN 0 7176 1123 X
£7.50

Optional (1996)

The notices & posters listed above are available from HSE Books at the
address given on page 328 of this handbook.

Other repeals

• Section 46(9) of the Offices, Shops & Railway Premises Act 1963
(which required the owners or occupiers of the relevant premises
to post up copies of exemption certificates) and section 2(4) of

the Petroleum (Consolidation) Act 1922, which contained similar requirements, have also been repealed.

See also **Safety signs & signals** elsewhere in this handbook.

ACCESS TO PREMISES & WORKSTATIONS

Key points

- An employer has a common law as well as statutory duty to provide safe means of access to (and egress from) his place of business. Employees must be able to get to and from their place of work and to their desks, chairs, workbenches, machines or assembly lines without first having to negotiate compacted snow, ice or potholes on pathways (or in an unlit company car park), damaged or crumbling steps or staircases, frayed carpets, loose floor boards, unlit passageways, stacked materials, trailing cables, fork trucks, blocked doorways, slippery floors or gangways, and the like. Obstructions, such as boxes, pallets, filing cabinets, stacked materials and machinery, and cramped working conditions, are not acceptable — the more so if an employee has to evacuate his workstation easily and quickly in the event of a fire or similar emergency.

  Note: The space around every 'workstation' (and the means of access to it) must be clear and unobstructed and be sufficient to enable the employee both to move about with ease and to manoeuvre and position any materials safely. He (or she) should be able to stand upright and to carry out his duties without undue bending or stretching (Regulation 11, Workplace (Health, Safety & Welfare) Regulations 1992 [SI 1992/3004] Paragraph 82 of the accompanying Approved Code of Practice states that "workstations, including seating and access to workstations, should be suitable for any special needs of the individual worker, including workers with disabilities". See also Chronically Sick & Disabled Persons Act 1970 (later in this section) and **Disabled persons** and **Room dimensions & space** elsewhere in this handbook.

- If any employee is injured as a direct consequence of his (or her) employer's refusal or failure to comply with his common law (and implied contractual duty) to provide safe means of access to his place of work (or to his workstation) he may pursue a civil action for damages in the ordinary courts. In the meantime, depending on the severity of the employee's injuries (see **Accidents at work** elsewhere in this handbook), his employer will have had to report the accident to the "relevant enforcing authority" and can expect to receive a visit from a health and safety inspector. As is explained in the next paragraph, this may lead to a caution (reinforced, if necessary, by an improvement or prohibition notice) or criminal prosecution.

- Although an employer can insure (indeed *must* insure) against any civil liability for injuries or diseases sustained by his employees in the course of their employment, he cannot insure himself against the consequences of his criminal acts. For further particulars, see **Insurance, Compulsory** and **Offences & penalties** elsewhere in this handbook.

Note: Any employee who is dismissed, selected for redundancy, or otherwise victimised (e.g., denied a promised promotion or pay rise) for questioning his (or her) employer's safety policies, or for complaining about his cramped working conditions, or for demanding safe means of access to and from his place of work, may complain to an industrial tribunal and will be awarded a substantial amount of compensation if his complaint is upheld. Such a complaint may be presented regardless of the employee's age or length of service at the material time. For further particulars, please turn to the section titled **Dismissal in health and safety cases** elsewhere in this handbook.

Health & Safety at Work etc. Act 1974

- An employer's general statutory duty (as distinct from his common law duty) to provide *and* maintain safe means of access to, and egress from, the workplace is laid down in section 2(2)(d) of the Health & Safety at Work, etc. Act 1974 — reinforced by related and more specific provisions in the Management of Health & Safety at Work Regulations 1992 (SI 1992/2051) and the Workplace (Health, Safety & Welfare) Regulations 1992 (*q.v.*). If an employer fails to comply with that statutory duty he may be prosecuted, with the attendant heavy penalties if he is convicted. In practice, an HSE or local authority inspector will ordinarily warn the owner or occupier of business premises to 'put his house in order'. If that fails, the inspector may serve an improvement or (in serious cases) a prohibition notice on the occupier (usually the employer) or the owner (if the owner is primarily responsible for the common parts of a building shared by a number of employers) effectively ordering him to implement specific changes, within specified time limits, or face prosecution. For further particulars, see **Improvement Notices, Inspectors, Powers of**, and **Prohibition Notices**, elsewhere in this handbook.

Note: Failure to comply with the terms of an improvement or prohibition notice is a very serious offence. The penalty, on summary conviction, is a fine of a maximum £20,000 and, on conviction on indictment, a fine of an unlimited amount (and, in some situations, imprisonment for a term of up to two years).

- An employer's general duty under section 2 of the 1974 Act is arguably more stringent in the case of employees who are disabled. If there is a dangerous occurrence or other emergency (such as a fire, explosion or bomb warning), the people responsible for evacuating the employer's premises should already have the names and locations of every disabled employee and should have well-established procedures for moving such people or helping them move speedily to a place of safety. In the absence of such procedures, any resultant accident involving a disabled employee will almost certainly invite a very thorough investigation and possible criminal proceedings under the 1974 Act.

Management of Health & Safety at Work Regulations 1992

- Regulation 3 of the Management of Health & Safety at Work Regulations 1992 (*q.v.*) imposes a duty on every employer (whatever the nature of his business) to make a "suitable and sufficient" assessment of the risks to which his employees are exposed while they are at work, and of the risks facing persons not in his employ (e.g., customers, clients, guests, contractors, tradesmen and others) who may be affected by the way in which he conducts his business or maintains his premises. The risk assessment must be repeated as often as prudence demands (either as a matter of course, dependent on the nature of the employer's business, or on an *ad hoc* basis, if there is a perception that issues of safety are not being treated as seriously as they should be). Paragraph 16(d) of the accompanying Approved Code of Practice says that the risk assessment should (amongst other things) identify groups of workers, including disabled persons, who might be particularly at risk

- If an employer has five or more people in his employ, he must keep a written (or computerised) record not only of the significant findings of the assessment but also of the names or job titles of those of his employees who are especially at risk. Following a reported accident, or during the course of a routine health and safety inspection, an inspector might well demand to see the risk assessment log as evidence of the employer's compliance with his duties under the 1992 Regulations.

- In the present context, a risk assessment exercise may well highlight relevant housekeeping problems, e.g., confusion about who is responsible for the cleanliness of floors, passages and staircases, or for removing obstructions (such as discarded pallets, tools or packaging), or for repairing damaged floors and floor coverings, or for mopping-up spillages, replacing faulty light bulbs; and so on.

- If a "risk assessment" exercise indicates that current arrangements (if any) for dealing with such hazards are unsatisfactory, the employer should:

  (a)   make good any structural damage (uneven floor surfaces, potholes in car parks, loose handrails on staircases, etc.);

  (b)   replace damaged floor coverings (loose tiles, frayed carpet), install additional lighting, etc.

  (c)   post temporary warning signs to remain in position until the work in (a) or (b) is completed;

  (d)   introduce a system of routine inspection and maintenance (by whom, when, how often and to what standards) to ensure that the risks identified by the assessment are eliminated or minimised.

When carrying out his risk assessment, an employer should involve the 'competent person' (or persons) appointed by him in compliance with Regulation 5 of the Management of Health & Safety at Work Regulations 1992 (*q.v.*)(see **Competent persons**, elsewhere in this handbook) and should also involve safety representatives, members of the safety committee, managers and supervisors.

Workplace (Health, Safety & Welfare) Regulations 1992

- The floors, stairs, steps, passages and gangways in premises covered by the Workplace (Health, Safety & Welfare) Regulations 1992 (SI 1992/3004) must be of sound const
  and properly maintained. They must be
  from obstructions and from any subst
  persons to slip. The open sides of staircase
  substantial hand-rails—as well as secure
  persons falling through the gap between th
  steps of the staircase. Here too, a prosecu

health and safety inspector considers floors, stairs, steps and passageways to be unsafe and potential sources of injury.

- Regulation 17 of the 1992 Regulations imposes a duty on employers to provide a sufficient number of pedestrian walkways, corridors and traffic routes in factories, offices, shops, warehouses, schools, hospitals (indeed, in any premises made available as a place of work) to enable people to move about safely. When designing, rearranging or organising traffic routes employers should not (says the accompanying Approved Code of Practice) overlook the needs of people with impaired sight, or who are hard of hearing, or who are in wheelchairs or using crutches or other walking aids. Traffic routes used by people in wheelchairs should be wide enough to allow unimpeded access and be provided with ramps where necessary. Buzzers, hooters, flashing lights, safety signs, etc. will give warning of approaching traffic to people with impaired sight or hearing. For the same reason, corridors, gangways and pedestrian walkways should avoid dangerous features or obstructions, such as pillars or low ceilings.

Fire Precautions Act 1971

- By section 9A of the Fire Precautions Act 1971, shop and office premises must be provided with such means of escape in case of fire for the use of employees as may reasonably be required. See also **Fire certificate** and **Fire precautions** elsewhere in this handbook.

Occupiers' Liability Act 1957

- By section 2 of the Occupiers' Liability Act 1957 (as amended), the occupier of business premises owes a duty to all his visitors to see to it that they are reasonably safe in using those premises for the purposes for which they are invited or permitted by the occupier to be there. The occupier must be prepared for children to be less careful than adults, but has a right to expect tradesmen, sub-contractors and the like to be more conscious of special risks than clientele, customers and residents. By section 2 of the Unfair Contract Terms Act 1977, the owner or occupier of premises cannot indemnify himself against liability for injury or death simply by posting a notice, or presenting his clients or customers with a contract clause, purporting to exclude or restrict his liability for death or personal injury arising from his own negligence or that of his employees. See **Occupier of premises** elsewhere in this handbook.

Chronically Sick & Disabled Persons Act 1970

- Section 8A of the Chronically Sick & Disabled Persons Act 1970 (inserted by the eponymous (Amendment) Act 1976) imposes a duty on the owners and developers of proposed new offices, shops, railway premises, factories, and other commercial and industrial premises, to consider the needs of disabled persons when designing the means of access to (and within) those premises, including the means of access to parking facilities, toilets cloakrooms and washing facilities.

- Although the owners or developers of premises intended for use as offices, shops, factories, workshops, etc. cannot be prosecuted for failing to comply with their duties under the 1970 Act, there is nothing to prevent a disabled person denied ready access to such premises (or injured as a direct consequence of the owner or developer's breach of his statutory duty under the 1970 Act) from pursuing a civil action for damages. In any event, when granting planning permission for new offices, shops, factories, etc. (or for the conversion of existing buildings), local authorities are duty-bound to draw the attention of the person to whom planning permission has been granted to the relevant provisions of the 1970 Act and to the Code of Practice for Access for the Disabled to Buildings (per section 29A, Town & Country Planning Act 1971).

Disability Discrimination Act 1996

- Under the Disability Discrimination Act 1995 (which came into force on 2 December 1996), employers are obliged in certain circumstances to make appropriate adjustments to their premises if any physical features of those premises place disabled persons at a substantial disadvantage in comparison with persons who are not disabled (*ibid*; section 6). A similar duty devolves on 'providers of services' (such as hoteliers, restaurateurs, cinema owners, bankers, and the like). Indeed, subject to the written consent of the lessor (which must *not* be unreasonably withheld) the 1995 Act overrides any term in a lease which purports to prevent the lessee (or occupier) of premises held under a lease from making any alterations to those premises.

- Although the link between the 1995 Act and health and safety legislation may be tenuous (given that the primary aim of the 1995 Act is to make it unlawful to discriminate against disabled persons in employment and other areas), there *is* a link insofar as any adjustments to premises to accommodate disabled persons must necessarily involve consideration of health and safety factors.

Construction (Health, Safety & Welfare) Regulations 1996

- Similar provisions relating to the safety of the means of access to (and egress from) construction sites and places of work on such sites are to be found in The Construction (Health, Safety & Welfare) Regulations 1996 (SI 1996/1592), reviewed elsewhere in this handbook in the section titled **Construction work**.

  See also **Car parks**, **Fire Precautions** and **Occupier of premises** elsewhere in this handbook.

ACCIDENT BOOK

Key Points

- Every employee who has an accident at work (or who contracts a work-related industrial disease), which could prompt a claim for Industrial Injuries Disablement Benefit (either immediately or at some later date), must report the matter to his or her employer (either in writing or by word of mouth) as soon as reasonably possible after the accident occurred (or after the disease in question was first diagnosed) (Regulation 24, Social Security (Claims & Payments) Regulations 1979 (SI 1979/628, as amended).

- To that end, every employer, who normally employs 10 or more persons at the same time on or about the same premises, must keep readily accessible a means (whether in an accident book or on computer) by which an injured employee can record the relevant particulars (*ibid*; Regulation 25, as amended by the Social Security (Claims & Payments) Amendment (No. 3) Regulations 1993 [SI1993/2113].

- Furthermore, every such entry in an accident book (or equivalent record, computerised or otherwise) must be maintained for a period of at least three years from the date on which that entry was made.

- The prescribed form of accident book is Form BI 510, copies of which are available from The Stationery Office (see page 328). Where fewer than 10 persons are employed, the employer must nonetheless maintain some form of record of every accident reported to him by an injured employee. On balance, the sensible course would be for *every* employer to maintain an accident book (or computerised record) of all accidents and industrial diseases reported to him, regardless of the number of persons he employs at any one time.

- The particulars to be entered in the accident book (or alternative record) are as follows:

  (a) Full name, address and occupation of injured person.
  (b) Date and time of accident.
  (c) Place where accident happened.
  (d) Cause and nature of injury.
  (e) Name, address and occupation of person giving notice, if other than the injured person.

  Every entry in an accident book should be signed by the person making that entry or (if he or she is unable to do so) by some other person acting on the employee's behalf.

Purpose of accident book

- As was explained above, the purpose of the accident book (or alternative record) is to provide a record of any injury (or sustained by an employee which could give rise to a claim for Industrial Injuries Disablement Benefit. The accident book (or other form of record) is also acceptable for the purposes of the Reporting of Injuries, Diseases & Dangerous Occurrences Regulations 1995 (discussed in the next section).

Duty of Injured Employee

- If the employer keeps an accident book (in whatever form, computerised or otherwise) on his premises, it will be sufficient for the injured employee to enter the relevant particulars in that book — or have a colleague (or first aid attendant) do so on his or her behalf. In practice, most employers insist that particulars of every accident and injury (however minor) must be reported and recorded — the purpose being to identify problem areas and to enable them (their safety officers, safety representatives, representatives of employee safety, safety committee and/or 'designated competent persons') to instigate the appropriate corrective action.

Note: Regulation 6 of the Management of Health & Safety at Work Regulations 1992 (SI 1992/2051) imposes a duty on *every* employer in *every* workplace to appoint one or more 'competent persons' to assist him to do what needs to be done "to comply with the requirements and prohibitions imposed upon him by or under the relevant statutory provisions". See **Competent persons** elsewhere in this handbook. See also **Safety committees** and **Safety representatives**.

- If an employee neglects to report or record particulars of his (or her) accident, he may have difficulty in proving a later claim for Industrial Injuries Disablement Benefit, particularly if his claim is not presented until some weeks or months after the date of the accident (e.g., in the case of a minor cut which later turns septic; or of a back injury which does not incapacitate the employee for work until some months after his accident).

Obligations of Employer

- An employer has a duty in law to investigate the circumstances of every accident reported to him. If he discovers any discrepancy between the facts as reported or recorded by the injured employee and the circumstances found by him as a result of his investigation, he must record that discrepancy in writing (either alongside the relevant entry in the accident book or alternative record, or elsewhere (e.g., in the employee's personal file)(*ibid*; Reg. 25).

- Should an employee subsequently submit a benefit claim to the Department of Social Security (DSS.), the employer must furnish such information and particulars as may be required by the DSS to progress the employee's claim. The injured employee will not receive any payment in respect of his claim until that information is made available.

  See also **Accidents at work** and **Industrial injuries** elsewhere in this handbook.

| ACCIDENTS AT WORK |

Key points

- The Reporting of Injuries, Diseases & Dangerous Occurrences Regulations 1995 (SI 1995/3163), which came into force on 1 April 1996, impose a duty on every employer to notify and report to the "relevant enforcing authority" any accident arising out of or in connection with his business or work activities if the accident —

    (a)   results in the death of, or major injury to, *any* person, whether employee or member of the general public); or

    (b)   results in an *employee* being incapacitated for work for more than three consecutive days (excluding the day on which the accident occurred, but including any days which would not have been working days).

    Note: For most employers, the "relevant enforcing authority" is either the nearest area office of the Health & Safety Inspectorate (see page 368) or, in the case of commercial premises (offices, shops, department stores, supermarkets, hotels, restaurants, etc.) the local authority (usually the Environmental Health Department) for the area or district in which the premises are situated.

- Clearly, the purpose of the 1995 Regulations is to alert the health and safety inspectorate to fatalities, major injuries and 'lost-time accidents' arising out of the conduct of an employer's business and to give inspectors an opportunity to investigate the causes. If an investigation reveals a failure on the part of an employer (owner, manager or whomever) to comply with his or her statutory duties under health and safety legislation, the organisation, as well as the responsible person, is likely to be prosecuted under the Health & Safety at Work, etc. Act 1974 (see *Offences & penalties* below).

    Note: The term "accident" includes an act of non-consensual physical violence done to a person at work; or an act of suicide which occurs on, or in the course of the operation of, a railway, tramway, trolley vehicle system or guided transport system.

- Specified *dangerous occurrences,* gas incidents, and cases of occupational disease must likewise be notified and reported. These are discussed elsewhere in this handbook in the sections titled **Dangerous occurrences** and **Diseases, Reportable**.

Notification and reporting of fatalities and major injuries

- If an employee, tradesman, member of the public, client, visitor (or whomever) dies or sustains a major injury or condition, as a result of an accident at work, the person having control of the relevant premises (employer, owner or manager) must *immediately* notify the enforcing authority by the quickest practicable means (e.g., by telephone, fax or e.mail) and must send a follow-up report within the next 10 days (using Form F2508) (*ibid*; regulations 3(1) & 10(1)).

  Note: This rule does not apply to an accident causing death or major injury to a person arising out of the conduct of any operation on (or any examination or other medical treatment of) of that person which is administered by (or conducted under the supervision of) a registered medical practitioner or a registered dentist (*ibid*; regulation 10(1)).

- The requirement to report fatal accidents and major injuries also applies to an accident arising out of (or in connection with) the movement of a vehicle on the road if, but only if, the person killed or injured:

  (a) dies or is injured as a result of exposure to a substance being carried by the vehicle; or

  (b) was, at the time of the accident, engaged in (or was killed or injured as a result of the activities of another person engaged in) work connected with the loading or unloading of any article or substance onto or off the vehicle; or

  (c) was, at the time of the accident, engaged in (or was killed or injured as a result of the activities of another person engaged in) work on or alongside a road — being work concerned with the construction, demolition, alteration, repair or maintenance of the road or its markings or equipment; or of the verges, fences, hedges or other boundaries of the road; or of pipes or cables on, under or over (or adjacent to) the road; or of buildings or structures adjacent to or over the road; or

  (d) was killed or injured as a result of an accident involving a train (e.g., a collision at a level crossing).

- If a conveyor of flammable gas (through a fixed pipe distribution system), or a wholesale filler, importer or supplier of liquefied petroleum gas (in refillable containers) learns of a death or major injury arising out of (or in connection with) the gas he (or she) has distributed, filled imported or supplied, he must immediately notify the Health & Safety Executive of the incident (by telephone, Fax or other means), and must send a follow-up report in writing (using Form 2508G) to the Executive within the next 14 days (*ibid*; regulation 6).

Subsequent death of employee

• If an employee injured at work dies of his injuries within one year of the date on which the relevant accident occurred, his (former) employer must notify the enforcing authority in writing as soon as receives news of the death — whether or not he had previously notified or reported the accident (*ibid*; regulation 4).

Meaning of 'major injury'

• The major injuries and conditions which must be notified and reported are:

(a)   any fracture, other than to the fingers, thumbs or toes;

(b)   any amputation;

(c)   disclocation of the shoulder, hip, knee or spine;

(d)   loss of sight (whether temporary or permanent);

(e)   a chemical or hot metal burn to the eye, or any penetrating injury to the eye;

(f)   any injury resulting from an electric shock or electrical burn (including any electrical burn caused by arcing or arcing products) leading to unconsciousness or requiring resuscitation or admittance to hospital for more than 24 hours;

(g)   any other injury leading to hypothermia, heat-induced illness or to unconsciousness; or which requires resuscitation; or which leads to admittance to hospital for more than 24 hours;

(h)   loss of consciousness caused by asphyxia or by exposure to a harmful substance or biological agent;

(i)   the absorption of any substance by inhalation, ingestion or through the skin, resulting either in acute illness requiring medical treatment or loss of consciousness;

(j)   acute illness which requires medical treatment where there is reason to believe that this resulted from exposure to a biological agent or its toxins or infected material..

It is important to stress that it is the person having control of the premises at which the relevent accident or injury occurred who is duty bound not only to notify the "relevant enforcing authority" but also to send to follow-up written report — whether or not the injured party is an employee or a member of the general public (including a tradesman, contractor, visitor, customer, client or passer-by (as to which, see the next section titled **Accidents to customers, visitors etc**).

'Lost-time' accidents

• If an accident or incident involving an employee does not produce the type of major injury or condition referred to in the preceding paragraph, but nonetheless incapacitates that employee for work for more than three consecutive days (excluding the day of the accident, but including any days which would not have been working days), his employer need not report the accident immediately. But, he must complete Form F2508 and send it to the enforcing authority within the next ten days.

Duty to maintain records

• An employer (or person having control of the relevant premises) must maintain a record of all "notifiable accidents" occurring on his premises; which records must include the following particulars:

(a)   date and time of the accident;

(b)   the full name and occupation of the person (or persons) injuredfollowing particulars of the person killed or injured;

(c)   the nature of the injury or condition;

(d)   place where the accident happened; and

(e)   a brief description of the circumstances.

Any form of record will suffice — so long as it includes the particulars described above. Furthermore, it must be kept available for inspection by an HSE or local authority health and safety inspector for a period of at least three years from the date of the last entry in it. See also **Accident book** elsewhere in this handbook.

Offences & Penalties

- Any employer or responsible person, who fails to comply with duties under the 1995 Regulations, is guilty of an offence and is liable, on summary conviction, to a fine of up to £2,000 and, on conviction on indictment, to a fine of an unlimited amount (sections 15 & 33(1)(c), Health & Safety at Work, etc. Act 1974).

- Regulation 11 of the 1995 Regulations allows that it shall be a defence in proceedings for the person prosecuted to prove that he failed to notify and/or report a fatality or major injury because he (or she) was not aware that the accident, incident or event in question had occurred, and that he had taken all reasonable steps to have all such events brought to his notice.

Further information

- The following publications are available from HSE Books at the address given on page 328.

  L73
  A guide to RIDDOR 95 [1996]
  ISBN 0 7176 1012 8   ££6.95

  A guide to RIDDOR (on diskette) plus electronic versions of forms F2508/F2508A
  ISBN 0 7176 1080 2   £19.50

  HS(G) 96
  The costs of accidents at work [1993]
  ISBN 0 7176 0439 X   £8.50

F2508/F2508A
Report of an injury, dangerous occurrence or case of disease [1996]
ISBN 0 7176 1078 0
Each pad contains 16 F2508 forms and 4 F2508A forms
    1 – 9 pads each cost £4.95 + VAT
    10 and more pads each cost £4.50 + VAT

F2508G
Report of flammable gas incidents and dangerous gas fittings [1996]
ISBN 0 7176 1114 0   £4.95 + VAT per pad of 20 forms.

Leaflets

HSE.31
Everyone's guide to RIDDOR 95
ISBN 0 7176 1077 2   £5.00 per pack of 10 leaflets

HSE 32
RIDDOR 95 – Information for doctors
(Free leaflet)

See also **Accidents to customers, visitors etc; Dangerous occurrences; Industrial injuries; Insurance, Compulsory; Occupier of premises; Safety representatives.**

ACCIDENTS TO CUSTOMERS, VISITORS ETC.

Key points

- By section 2 of the Occupiers' Liability Act 1957, the occupier of business premises owes a "common duty of care" to any person (whether customer, client, guest, tradesman, child, or otherwise) who has a lawful reason for being on his premises at a particular time. "The common duty of care is a duty to take such care as in all the circumstances of the case is reasonable to see that the visitor will be reasonably safe in using the premises for the purposes for which he is invited or permitted to be there" (*ibid*; section 2 (2)). A breach of that duty of care could lead to a civil action for damages in the ordinary courts. See **Insurance, Compulsory** and **Occupier of premises** elsewhere in this handbook.

Health & Safety at Work, etc. Act 1974

- The common law duty of care owed by the occupier of business premises is reinforced by an employer's statutory duty (and criminal liability) under the Health & Safety at Work, etc. Act 1974 to provide and maintain a safe place of work; safe means of access to (and egress from) that place of work; safe plant and systems of work; safe use, handling, storage and transport of articles and substances; a safe and healthy working environment; and trained, informed, competent and safety-conscious employees (*ibid*; section 2). It is an employer's duty also to ensure, so far as is reasonably practicable, that persons not in his employment (tradesmen, contractors, customers, clients, visitors, etc.), who may be affected by the way in which he conducts his business, are not thereby exposed to risks to their health and safety. That same duty extends to self-employed persons (ibid; section 3).

- A successful prosecution under the 1974 Act could lead to a fine of an unlimited amount and/or imprisonment for a term of up to two years (as to which, see **Offences & penalties** elsewhere in this handbook).

Reporting of Injuries, Diseases & Dangerous Occurrences Regs 1995

- Under The Reporting of Injuries, Diseases & Dangerous Occurrences Regulations 1995 (SI 1995/3163) the person having control of business premises must formally notify the *relevant enforcing authority* of any accident which results in the death of, or *major injury* to, *any* person (whether employee or member of the general public) so long as the death or injury was connected with, or attributable to, the work being carried on at the premises at the material time, or to the way in which the business or undertaking was being managed, or to the equipment, materials or substances in use on the premises, or to the condition of the premises when the accident or incident occurred. See also the section titled **Accidents at work**.

- If, for example, a visitor to a factory (or a customer in a department store, or a guest in an hotel), sustains a *major injury* when he (or she) trips and falls down an unlit staircase, the person having control of the premises at that time must notify the local enforcing authority immediately and must send a follow-up report within the next 10 days — given that the injuries sustained by the visitor (customeer or guest) appear to have been directly attributable both to the manner in which the occupier or owner of those premises conducted his business, and to the condition of his premises at the material time (*ibid;* Regulation 2(2) (c)). See *Notification procedure* below.

Meaning of 'major injury'

- The following injuries and conditions constitute *major injuries* within the meaning of the 1995 Regulations:

  (a) any fracture, other than to the fingers, thumbs or toes;

  (b) any amputation;

  (c) disclocation of the shoulder, hip, knee or spine;

  (d) loss of sight (whether temporary or permanent);

  (e) a chemical or hot metal burn to the eye, or any penetrating injury to the eye;

  (f) any injury resulting from an electric shock or electrical burn (including any electrical burn caused by arcing or arcing products) leading to unconsciousness or requiring resuscitation or admittance to hospital for more than 24 hours;

  (g) any other injury leading to hypothermia, heat-induced illness or to unconsciousness; or which requires resuscitation; or which leads to admittance to hospital for more than 24 hours;

  (h) loss of consciousness caused by asphyxia or by exposure to a harmful substance or biological agent;

  (i) the absorption of any substance by inhalation, ingestion or through the skin, resulting either in acute illness requiring medical treatment or loss of consciousness;

  (j) acute illness which requires medical treatment where there is reason to believe that this resulted from exposure to a biological agent or its toxins or infected material..

It is important to stress that it is the person having control of the premises where the death or major injury occurred who is duty bound both to notify the "relevant enforcing authority" and to send the follow-up written report.

Enforcing authority

- For industrial premises (factories, workshops, building sites, docks, etc.) the *relevant enforcing authority* is the nearest area office of the Health & Safety Executive. For commercial premises (such as offices, shops, supermarkets, department stores, hotels, restaurants, and the like), the relevant "enforcing authority" is the local authority for the area in which those premises are situated, viz; a district council, a London borough council, the Common Council of the City of London, the sub-treasurer of the Inner Temple, the Under-Treasurer of the Middle Temple or the Council of the Isles of Scilly; or, in Scotland, an islands or district council (*vide* The Health and Safety (Enforcing Authority) Regulations 1989 (SI 1989/1903).

Notification Procedure

- The occupier of business premises is duty-bound to inform the relevant enforcing authority *immediately* or as soon as is reasonably practicable (either by telephone or Fax) if a member of the public is killed or sustains a major injury while on his premises — if (as was explained earlier) there is any evidence or suspicion that the accident was attributable to the activities or processes carried on in those premises or to the condition of the premises at the material time.

Keeping a record

The owner or occupier must also keep a written record of the accident, either in the accident book (Form BI 510) or in some other form. A simple exercise book will suffice, so long as it contains the following particulars:

(a) date and time of the accident or dangerous occurrence;

(b) the full name and occupation of the person affected;

(c) the nature of the injury or condition;

(d)   place where the accident or dangerous occurrence happened; and

(e)   a brief description of the circumstances.

The record book must be kept available for inspection by an inspector of the enforcing authority and must not be discarded or destroyed until a period of at least three years has elapsed from the date of the last entry in it.

- The occupier must also complete form F2508 and send it to the enforcing authority within the next 10 days. Copies of the form are available from HSE Books (see *FURTHER INFORMATION* below).

Offences and Penalties

- A person who contravenes any requirement of the Reporting of Injuries, Diseases & Dangerous Occurrences Regulations 1995 (*q.v.*) is guilty of an offence and liable, on summary conviction, to a fine of up to £2,000 or, on conviction on indictment, to a fine of an unlimited amount (section 33(1)(c), (3)(a) and (3)(b)(ii), Health and Safety at Work, etc., Act 1974).

FURTHER INFORMATION

- The following are available from HSE Books at the address given on page 328.

L73
A guide to RIDDOR 95 [1996]
ISBN 0 7176 1012 8   ££6.95

A guide to RIDDOR (on diskette) plus electronic versions of forms F2508/F2508A
ISBN 0 7176 1080 2   £19.50

HS(G) 96
The costs of accidents at work [1993]
ISBN 0 7176 0439 X   £8.50

F2508/F2508A
Report of an injury, dangerous occurrence or case of disease [1996]
ISBN 0 7176 1078 0

Each pad contains 16 F2508 forms and 4 F2508A forms
    1 – 9 pads each cost £4.95 + VAT
    10 and more pads each cost £4.50 + VAT

F2508G
Report of flammable gas incidents and dangerous gas fittings [1996]
ISBN 0 7176 1114 0   £4.95 + VAT per pad of 20 forms.

Leaflets

HSE 31
Everyone's guide to RIDDOR 95
ISBN 0 7176 1077 2   £5.00 per pack of 10 leaflets

HSE 32
RIDDOR 95 – Information for doctors
(Free leaflet)

See also **Accident book, Accidents at work, Dangerous occurrences,** and **Diseases, Reportable,** elsewhere in this handbook.

ACCOMMODATION FOR CLOTHING

Key points

- The Workplace (Health, Safety & Welfare) Regulations 1992 (SI 1992/3004), as amended by the Construction (Health, Safety & Welfare) Regulations 1996 (SI 1996/1592), came into force for all workplaces on 1 January 1996.

- Regulation 23 of the 1992 Regulations imposes a duty on employers to provide "suitable and sufficient" accommodation for the storage of street clothing (such as hats, jackets, topcoats, scarves, etc) removed by employees before they start work. An employer must also provide "suitable and sufficient" accommodation for any special clothing worn by his employees during their duty hours — uniforms, coveralls, caps, safety shoes, and other items of protective clothing or equipment — which is not taken home at the end of the working day or shift.

Meaning of "suitable and sufficient"

- Employers must set aside an area where employees can hang the overcoats, jackets, scarves, etc., which they remove before they start work. Although it is not usually necessary to provide a dedicated cloakroom for office or shop workers, such facilities as *are* provided must be warm, dry and well-ventilated. There must be at least one separate coat hook or peg, and sufficient hanging space, for use by every employee. The accommodation must also be secure. Security in an office may not be a problem, as topcoats, jackets, scarves, etc., are often stored in open view (especially in a small office with just a handful of employees). But security could be a problem in large offices, and in shops, department stores, hotels, hospitals, factories and warehouses, etc; in which case, the employer will have little choice but to provide lockable lockers — the more so if employees are required to leave any cash or valuables in the cloakroom during the working day. "Food workers", for example, are not permitted to wear items of jewellery while handling open food.

- In many industries, employees have to strip to their underwear or remove more than their outer clothing in order to don uniforms, aprons, coveralls, safety footwear, caps and other types of protective clothing and equipment. In those circumstances, the employer must provide separate and secure changing rooms for male and female employees. By "secure" is meant secure from the risk of theft (e.g., by the provision of a lockable locker for each employee).

- Furthermore, if work clothing is likely to become dirty, damp or contaminated during the working day, the employer must provide one area for the storage of work clothing and another area (not necessarily in a separate room) for the storage of street (or personal) clothing. Both areas must be clean, warm and dry, and sufficiently well-ventilated to ensure that damp clothing dries out before the end of the same (or the beginning of the next) working day or shift (Regulation 23).

- Employees who work in industries which expose them to hazardous substances, such as lead or asbestos, must be able to change out of and into their street clothing in one room and into and out of their boiler suits or overalls in another room. Ideally, the two rooms should be situated on either side of the washroom and shower facilities (which, of course, must also be provided for the use of employees), the object being to further minimise the risk of cross-contamination by requiring workers to wash or take a shower after they have changed out of their work clothes and before they change back into their street clothes at the end of their working day or shift. For further information, please turn to the sections titled, respectively, **Asbestos at work, Changing Rooms, Dangerous chemicals, Hazardous substances, Ionising radiation,** and **Lead at work.**

- See also **Construction work** for information about the provision and maintenance of welfare facilities for workers on construction sites.

Offences & penalties

- The penalty for any infringement of health and safety regulations is a fine of up to £2,000; or, if a conviction is obtained on indictment, a fine of an unlimited amount. As to which, see **Offences & penalties** elsewhere in this handbook.

AGRICULTURE

Key points

- Although the issue of health and safety on farms and other agricultural holdings is not covered in any depth in this handbook, it is as well to point out that farmers (as employers or self-employed persons) share the same duties and responsibilities as employers in the industrial and commercial sectors. They have a general and overriding duty under the Health & Safety at Work etc. Act 1974 to provide a safe and healthy working environment, safe plant, machinery and equipment, safe means of access to and from the workplace, and a duty also to inform, instruct, train and supervise the people they employ to ensure that they carry out their duties without risk of injury to themselves or to their colleagues. Farmers also owe a duty to visitors and members of the general public (and, especially, children) who may be affected by the way in which they carry out their work, the machinery and implements they employ, and in their storage, handling, transport and distribution of hazardous substances.

- Statutes and Regulations for securing the safety, health and welfare of persons employed in agriculture, and for the avoidance of accidents to children, have, to a large extent, been supplanted by more recent and all-embracing legislation affecting every employer, whatever the nature of his business or undertaking. However, there remain —

  (a)   the Agriculture (Poisonous Substances) Act 1952 — whose only remaining provision empowers a health and safety inspector to secure and remove a sample of any substance or thing which he (or she) believes may be poisonous;

  (b)   the Agriculture (Safety, Health & Welfare Provisions) Act 1956 (sections 7 & 9) — which empowers the Secretary of State to make Regulations prohibiting children from riding on or driving agricultural vehicles, machinery or implements; and requires a coroner to adjourn an inquest into the death of a person killed while engaged in agricultural operations unless a health and safety inspector is present to watch the proceeding;

  (c)   the Agriculture (Ladders) Regulations 1957 (SI 1957/1385);

  (d)   the Agriculture (Avoidance of Accidents to Children) Regulations 1958 (SI 1958/366);

  (e)   the Agriculture (Circular Saw) Regulations 1959 (SI 1959/427, as amended by SI 1976/1247);

  (f)   the Agriculture (Safeguarding of Workplaces) Regulations 1959 (SI 1959/428, as amended by SI 1976/1247);

  (g)   the Agriculture (Threshers & Balers) Regulations 1960 (SI 1960/1199);

  (h)   the Agriculture (Field Machinery) Regulations 1962 (SI 1962/1472, as amended by SI 1976/1247) and

  (i)   the Agriculture (Tractor Cabs) Regulations 1974 (SI 1974/2034, as amended by SI 1990/1075).

The term "agriculture" includes dairy-farming; the production of any consumable produce which is grown for sale or for consumption or for other use for the purposes of a trade or business; and the use of land as grazing, meadow or pasture land, or as orchard, osier land or woodland, or for market gardens or nursery grounds.

FURTHER INFORMATION

• The following HSE publications are available from HSE Books at the address given on page 328.

Guidance Notes

Farm wise: Your guide to health and safety [1992]
ISBN 0 11 882107 5   £3.50

Farm wise: Your guide to health and safety (Welsh version) [1995]
ISBN 0 7176 0839 5   £3.50

Tractor action — a safety training guide [1995]
ISBN 0 7176 0839 5   £11.50

The occupational zoonoses [1993]
ISBN 0 1188 6397 5   £5.00

Bovine spongiform encephalopathy: Background and general occupational guidance [1996]
ISBN 0 7176 1212 0   £5.50

COP 24
Preventing accidents to children in agriculture. Approved Code of Practice & guidance notes [1988]
ISBN 0 11 883997 7   £2.75

EH 66
Grain dust [1993]
ISBN 0 11 882101 6   £2.50

GS 17
Safe custody and handling of stock bulls on farms and at artificial insemination centres [1982]
ISBN 0 11 883552 1   £2.50

GS 48
Training and standards of competence for users of chain saws in agriculture, arboriculture and forestry [1990]
ISBN 0 11 885575 1   £2.50

HS(G) 86
Veterinary medicines. Safe use by farmers and other animal handlers [1992]
ISBN 0 11 886361 4   £3.50

HS(G) 89
Safeguarding agricultural machinery: moving parts [1992]
ISBN 0 11 882051 6   £4.00

RP 28
Grain dust: some of its effects on health
by R F Howarth
ISBN 0 11 885953 6   £5.00

Contract Research Reports (CRR)

CRR 7
A review of agricultural tractor noise test procedures and measured levels [1988]
ISBN 0 11 885927 7   £20.00

CRR 18
A survey of exposure to noise in agriculture [1989]
ISBN 0 11 885944 £55.00

CRR 23
A study to assess the effect of ageing on the acoustic performance and structural integrity of type-approved agricultural tractor cabs [1990]
ISBN 0 11 885973 0   £20.00

CRR 25
Noise measurement techniques for tractor-operated machinery [1991]
ISBN 0 11 885975 7   £20.00

CRR 43
Causes of damage to power take-off shaft guards [1992]
ISBN 0 11 886377 0 £20.00

CRR 44
Rops test criteria for 40km/h agricultural and forestry tractors [1992]
ISBN 0 11 886378 9   £20.00

CRR 52
Braking and overturning stability of all-terrain vehicles with trailed and mounted loads and review of guidelines [1993]
ISBN 0 11 882149 0   £20.00

CRR 56
An ergonomic evaluation of agricultural crop sprayers [1993]
ISBN 0 11 882145 8   £45.00

CRR 74
An investigation into the possible chronic neuropsychological and neurological effects of occupational exposure to organophosphates in sheep farmers [1995]
ISBN 0m7176 0929 4   £35.00

Free Safety Leaflets (Telephone: 01787 881165)

AIS3	*Controlling grain dust on farms (Rev)*
AIS4	*Safe use of big round balers*
AIS5	*Leptospira Hardjo (bovine leptospirosois) and human health*
AIS6	*Safe use of combine harvesters*
AIS7	*Deer farming*
AIS8	*Working safely near overhead power lines*
AIS9	*Preventing access to effluent storage and similar areas on farms*
AIS10	*Use of ATVs fitted with spray equipment*
AIS11	*Selecting and using equipment for All Terrain Vehicles (ATVs)*
AIS12	*Safe working on glasshouse roofs*
AIS13	*Safe use of potato harvesters*
AIS14	*Airborne soil dust in potato and bulb grading*
AIS15	*Silage clamp hazard: nitrogen dioxide*
AIS16	*Guidance on storing pesticides for farmers and other professional users*
AIS17	*Keeping cattle in fields with public access*
AIS18	*Controlling the risk of steel framed farm buildings collapsing during erection*
AIS19	*Occupational health risks from cattle and other animals*

AIS20	*Health hazards from whole body vibration caused by mobile agricultural machinery*
AIS21	*The safe use of rotary flail hedgecutters*
AS5	*Farmer's lung*
AS7	*Guns (Rev)*
AS8	*Noise*
AS10	*Accidents to children*
AS15	*Farm forestry operations*
AS16	*Checking tractor trailers*
AS17	*Electricity on the farm*
AS20	*Safe use of chain saws (Rev)*
AS22	*Prevention of tractors overturning*
AS23	*Handling loads in agriculture (Rev)*
AS24	*Power take off shafts*
AS27	*Agricultural pesticides (Rev)*
AS28	*COSHH in agriculture*
AS29	*Sheep dipping (Rev)*
AS30	*COSHH in forestry (Rev)*
CAT18	*Agricultural films catalogue*
IACL25a	*Agriculture: health carry card*
IACL31	*The professionals: help with health and safety on the farm*
INDG84	*Leptospirosis: are you at risk?*
INDG85	*Bovine spongiform (BSE)*
INDG125	*Stacking, transporting and handling bales in agriculture*
INDG140	*Grain dust*
INDG145	*Avoiding back strain/chain saws*
INDG177	*Health and safety for gamekeepers*
INDG185	*Tractor action: a step by step guide*
MISC049	*Shock horror: key facts: safe working near overhead power lines in agriculture*

AIR CONDITIONING

Key points

- Although sophisticated air conditioning systems are commonplace in many large office buildings and in 'high tech' workplaces, they are not a legal requirement. The Workplace (Health, Safety & Welfare) Regulations 1992 (SI 1992/3004) simply require employers to take steps to ensure that every enclosed workplace under their control is ventilated by "a sufficient quantity of fresh or purified air". In other words, stale air, and air which is hot or humid, must be replaced at a reasonable rate. If this can be achieved in factories, offices, shops, department stores, schools, workshops, etc. by other means, well and good (*ibid*; Regulation 6).

  Note: The 1992 Regulations apply to *every* premises or part of premises (other than domestic premises) which are made available to any person as a place of work (viz; schools, hospitals, mortuaries, hotels, guest houses, nursing homes, leisure centres, prisons; and so on)

- The approved Code of Practice, accompanying the 1992 Regulations (see L24, page 97), states that the fresh air supply rate per employee (or occupant) in a workplace should be between 5 and 8 litres a second — determined by factors such as the floor area per person, the processes and equipment involved, and the nature of the work (*Is it light or strenuous?*).

- Employers must take steps to protect employees from uncomfortable draughts and do all that is practicable to eliminate or minimise impurities and offensive smells and odours (whether generated internally or introduced from outside the workplace). Air inlets for ventilation systems should be located away from exhaust ventilation outlets or areas in which vehicles manoeuvre. Where necessary, they should also be filtered to remove particulates.

- In humid factories and other workplaces where a close, humid atmosphere must be maintained at all times (e.g., mushroom growing), employers must allow their workers to take adequate rest breaks in a well-ventilated area. See **Humid Factories** elsewhere in this handbook.

- If an air conditioning system *is* installed, it must be fitted with filters to remove impurities, and with fresh air inlets which allow fresh air to be added to recirculated air to avoid it becoming unhealthy. All air conditioning systems must be regularly and properly cleaned, tested and maintained. If part of the function of an air conditioning system (e.g., a dilution ventilation system) is to reduce concentrations of dusts or fumes in the atmosphere, it must also be fitted with a device to give visible or audible warning of a breakdown.

Air inlets for ventilation systems

- Air inlets for ventilation systems (whose purpose it is to 'top up' recirculated air with fresh air) must be kept open. However, they should not be sited close to a flue, or to an exhaust ventilation system outlet, or to an area in which heavy goods vehicles manoeuvre, or at a place where they may draw in excessively contaminated air. See also the sections titled **Confined spaces**, **Legionnaire's disease** and **Ventilation** elsewhere in this handbook. See also **Offences & penalties**.

ALTERATIONS & EXTENSIONS

Key points

- The occupier of business premises (factory, workshop, office, shop, warehouse, etc.) may be unwittingly prevented from complying with his duties under health and safety legislation (e.g., his duty to provide a rest-room for pregnant employees and nursing mothers, and the like) because of a term in his lease or tenancy agreement preventing him from effecting any structural alterations.

- In premises to which the Factories Act 1961 or the Offices, Shops & Railway Premises Act 1963 applies, the occupying employer may apply to the county court (or to the sheriff, in Scotland) for an order setting aside or modifying that term. The court may also order the owner (or any other party having an interest in those premises) to pay the whole or part of the costs of those alterations, either directly or by reducing the amount of rent payable by the occupier (*vide* sections 169 and 73, respectively, of the 1961 and 1963 Acts).

Fire Precautions

- Similar difficulties may be encountered when the occupier of business premises applies to his local fire authority for a fire certificate. If, having inspected the premises, the fire authority are not satisfied that there are suitable and sufficient fire exits (to give but one example), they will serve a notice on the applicant informing him of the steps that must be taken before a fire certificate will be issued — which steps may well include structural alterations. If the applicant is prevented from making those alterations by virtue of a restrictive clause in his lease (or agreement), he too may apply to the county court (or sheriff) for an order setting aside or modifying that clause. The court may also order the lessor (or owner) to pay the whole or part of the expenditure necessarily incurred by the applicant, and may modify the terms of the lease or agreement relating to the premises so far as concerns rent payable in respect of the premises (section 28, Fire Precautions Act 1971).

- In small factories, offices and shops, which do not require a fire certificate, the owner or occupier nonetheless has a duty in law to provide those premises "with such means of escape in case of fire for the persons employed to work therein as may reasonably be required in the circumstances of the case" (*ibid*; section 9A). If, yet again, the occupier's lease prevents him from carrying out any structural alterations to ensure compliance with his duty under the 1971 Act, the matter may be referred to the county court (or sheriff) for a resolution of the difficulty.

- Section 8 of the 1971 Act cautions that, so long as a fire certificate is in force with respect to any premises, the occupier must not —

    (a)   make a material extension of, or material structural alteration to, the premises; or

    (b)   make a material alteration in the internal arrangements of the premises or in the furniture or equipment with which the premises are provided; or

    (c)   keep explosive or highly flammable materials of any kind anywhere under, in or on the relevant building in a quantity or aggregate quantity greater than the prescribed maximum without first giving notice of his proposals to the fire authority. Any occupier/owner who fails to comply with this requirement is guilty of an offence and liable, on summary conviction, to a fine of up to £400 or, on conviction on indictment, to a fine of an unlimited amount and/or imprisonment for a maximum term of two years (*ibid;* section 8 (8)). See also **Fire certificate** and **Fire precautions** elsewhere in this handbook.

Workplace (Health, Safety & Welfare) Regulations 1992 (SI 1992/3004)

- In many workplaces, employers will have to carry out structural alterations in order to comply with their duties under the Workplace (Health, Safety & Welfare) Regulations 1992. Some employers will have to install showers or baths; others will have to upgrade their washrooms, toilets and changing rooms. Most will have to decide what needs to be done in order to comply with their duty to provide rest rooms (or the equivalent) for the use of employees who are pregnant or have recently given birth.

- The responsibility for installing or upgrading shared facilities (e.g., in an office building occupied by two or more tenant employers) will usually devolve on the owner. In other premises, it will devolve on the occupier or lessee. Much will depend on what is written into the lease or tenancy agreement. But, in every case, it is the responsibility of the employer to ensure that the workplace he owns or occupies complies with the 1992 Regulations (whether or not is also his responsibility to carry out any necessary structural alterations)(*ibid;* Regulation 4). Tenants should cooperate with one another, and with the landlord or owner, to the extent necessary to ensure that the Workplace Regulations 1992 are fully complied with and that areas of responsibility are clearly defined.

Disability Discrimination Act 1995

- Under the Disability Discrimination Act 1995 (which came into force on 2 December 1996), employers are obliged in certain circumstances to make appropriate adjustments to their premises if any physical features of those premises place disabled persons at a substantial disadvantage in comparison with persons who are not disabled (*ibid;* section 6). A similar duty devolves on 'providers of services' (such as hoteliers, restaurateurs, cafe proprietors, cinema owners, bankers, and the like). Indeed, subject to the written consent of the lessor (which must *not* be unreasonably withheld) the 1995 Act overrides any term in a lease which purports to prevent the lessee (or occupier) of premises held under a lease from making any alterations to those premises.

• Although the link between the 1995 Act and health and safety legislation may be tenuous (given that the primary aim of the 1995 Act is to make it unlawful to discriminate against disabled persons in the field of employment and other areas), there *is* a link insofar as any adjustments to premises to accommodate disabled persons must necessarily involve consideration of health and safety factors.

Chronically Sick & Disabled Persons Act 1970

• Section 8A of the Chronically Sick & Disabled Persons Act 1970 (inserted by the eponymous (Amendment) Act 1976) imposes a duty on the owners and developers of proposed new offices, shops, railway premises, factories, and other commercial and industrial premises, to consider the needs of disabled persons when designing the means of access to (and within) those premises, including the means of access to parking facilities, toilets cloakrooms and washing facilities.

• Although the owners or developers of premises intended for use as offices, shops, factories, workshops, etc. cannot be prosecuted for failing to comply with their duties under the 1970 Act, there is nothing to prevent a disabled person denied ready access to such premises (or injured as a direct consequence of the owner or developer's breach of his statutory duty under the 1970 Act) from pursuing a civil action for damages. In any event, when granting planning permission for new offices, shops, factories, etc. (or for the conversion of existing buildings), local authorities are duty-bound to draw the attention of the person to whom planning permission has been granted to the relevant provisions of the 1970 Act and to the Code of Practice for Access for the Disabled to Buildings (per section 29A, Town & Country Planning Act 1971).

ASBESTOS AT WORK

Key points

- The use of asbestos at work is regulated by —

  o the **Asbestos (Licensing) Regulations 1983** (SI 1983/1649) relating to the issue of licences for work with asbestos insulation or asbestos coatings.

  o the **Asbestos Products (Safety) Regulations 1985** (SI 1985/2042)

  o the **Control of Asbestos at Work Regulations 1987** (SI 1987/2115) as amended by the Control of Asbestos at Work (Amendment) Regulations 1992 (SI 1992/3068) — implementing Directive 91/382/EEC which amended Council Directive 83/477/EEC on the protection of workers from the risks related to exposure to asbestos at work and Council Directive 90/394/EEC on the protection of workers from the risks related to carcinogens at work;

  o the **Control of Asbestos in the Air Regulations 1990** (SI 1990/556);

  o the **Asbestos (Prohibitions) Regulations 1992** (SI 1992/3067) – implementing Council Directive 91/659/EEC on restrictions relating to the marketing and use of dangerous substances and preparations; and

REQUIREMENTS AND PROHIBITIONS

- An employer (or self-employed person) who intends to engage in work in which he or one or more of his employees is liable to be exposed to asbestos must write to his nearest area office of the Health & Safety Executive (HSE) at least 28 days beforehand informing them of his intentions, unless —

  (i)   he is already licensed under Regulation 3(1) of the Asbestos (Licensing) Regulations 1983 to undertake work with asbestos insulation or asbestos coating; or

  (ii) the extent to which his employees are liable to be exposed to asbestos dust arising out of or in connection with that work (or with any product containing asbestos) is not expected to exceed the *action level.*

When writing to the HSE, the employer must supply

(a) his name, address and telephone number;

(b) the name, address and telephone number of his usual place of business;

(c) a brief description of the type of asbestos to be used or handled (chrysotile or amphibole), the maximum quantity of asbestos to be held on the premises at any one time, the activities or processes involved, and (where applicable) the products to be manufactured; and

(d) the date on which the work is to begin.

Note: In determining whether an employee's exposure to asbestos dust exceeds the *action level* or any *control limit*, the employer must take no account of any respiratory protective equipment worn by the employee at the material time.

Risk assessment

• Before beginning any work which exposes or is likely to expose any of his employees to asbestos dust, or to any product containing asbestos, an employer must either identify (by analysis or otherwise) the type of asbestos in question or assume that the asbestos is not chrysotile alone and treat it accordingly. Furthermore, he must assess the nature and degree of the exposure which may occur while the work is being carried out and set out the steps he intends to take to prevent or minimise that exposure. The risk assessment must be reviewed regularly and, if necessary, repeated if the employer has any reason to believe that the previous or initial assessment is no longer valid or if there is a significant change in the work to which the previous assessment relates (*ibid*; Regulations 4 & 5).

• If the work consists of (or includes) the removal of asbestos from any building, structure, plant, or installation, or from a ship which is being re-fitted or demolished, the employer, must first produce a suitable written plan detailing how the work is to be carried out. Amongst other things, the plan must give details of the nature and probable duration of the work, the location of the place where the work is to be carried out, the methods to be applied where the work involves the handling of asbestos or materials containing asbestos, and the characteristics of the equipment to be used for the protection and decontamination of the people carrying out the work and for the protection of other persons on or near the worksite (*ibid*; Regulation 5A).

Information, instruction and training

• An employer must see to it those of his employees who work with (or are liable to be exposed to) asbestos dust in the course of their employment receive adequate information, instruction and training about the risks associated with that work and the precautions to be observed; and that supervisors, managers and others responsible for directing, controlling or overseeing that work on their employer's behalf are familiar with his and their obligations under the 1987 Regulations (*ibid*; Regulation 7).

Control measures and air monitoring

• An employer's first duty under the 1987 Regulations is to prevent the exposure of his employees to asbestos dust (e.g., by installing exhaust ventilation equipment at source) or, if that is not reasonably practicable, to reduce that exposure to the lowest possible level. If the control measures adopted by an employer do not reduce the exposure of an employee to below both the *control limits* (see **Table 1** on page 46) which apply to that exposure, he must provide that employee with suitable respiratory protective equipment (see *Note* below). In other words, respiratory protective equipment should be made available only as a last resort, and then only in conjunction with other control measures introduced by an employer to prevent or minimise the exposure of his employees to asbestos (*ibid*; Regulation 8).

Note: Respiratory protective equipment will be suitable if it complies with any enactment (whether in an Act or instrument) which implements in Great Britain any provision on design or manufacture with respect to health or safety in any relevant Community directive listed in Schedule 1 to the Personal Protective Equipment at Work Regulations 1992 (SI 1992/2966) which is applicable to that item of equipment (*ibid*; Regulation 8(3A)).

• As a matter of routine, an employer must monitor the exposure of his employees to asbestos if monitoring is appropriate for the protection of their health. Records (or suitable summaries) of air monitoring must be retained for at least 40 years, in the case of employees whose exposure to asbestos exceeds the action level and for a minimum of five years in every other case.

- An employer must ensure that his employees use or apply the control measures, protective clothing and equipment, and other equipment or facilities provided for their protection. It is his duty also to maintain those measures, equipment and facilities in a clean and efficient state, in efficient working order, and in good repair. Exhaust ventilation equipment must be regularly examined and tested by a competent person. Furthermore, particulars of all cleaning, maintenance, tests and examinations must be entered into a log and kept for at least five years (*ibid;* Regulations 8, 9(1) & 10). See also **Cleanliness of premises** elsewhere in this handbook.

- Employers must do all that is reasonably practicable to prevent the spread of asbestos from any place where work with asbestos is carried. For example, protective clothing must be removed before meal breaks and at the end of the working day or shift. Protective clothing and footwear must be kept in a changing room separate from that in which employees remove or change into their street clothing — and ideally situated opposite sides of the washroom and shower facilities. Protective clothing must never be removed from the workplace, except for cleaning or disposal as asbestos waste, when it must be packed in sealed containers (see *Provision and cleaning of protective clothing* below).

- Raw asbestos and waste materials containing asbestos must not be stored, received into or despatched from any place of work, or distributed (except in a totally enclosed distribution system) within any place of work, unless it is in a suitable and sealed container labelled in accordance with the Chemicals (Hazard Information & Packaging for Supply) Regulations 1994 (SI 1994/3247) or, if it is to be conveyed by road, in a road tanker or tank container, in accordance with the Carriage of Dangerous Goods (Classification, Packaging & Labelling) & Use of Transportable Pressure Receptacles Regulations 1996 (SI 1996/2092). In any other case, it must be labelled in accordance with Schedule 2 to the 1987 Regulations, as illustrated below.

- No product containing asbestos (being an article or substance for use at work) may be supplied by any person unless it is labelled in accordance with Schedule 2 to the 1987 Regulations. However, a product component containing asbestos need not be labelled if it is too small to allow a label to be affixed to it (*ibid*; Regulation 19), but see also *PROHIBITED ASBESTOS* below.

Alternatives to asbestos

• If asbestos is ordinarily used in a manufacturing process or in the installation of any product, the employer should investigate the practicability of using a less hazardous substance. If an intrinsically safe or less hazardous substitute *is* available and does the job as well as asbestos, it must be used (*ibid*; Regulation 8(1A)).

Accidents and emergencies

• If there is an unforeseen escape of asbestos dust into the workplace at a concentration likely to exceed any applicable *control limit*, the employer must ensure that only those persons who are responsible for carrying out repairs and other necessary work are permitted in the affected area and that they wear appropriate respiratory protective equipment and protective clothing for so long as they remain in that area. Furthermore, the employer must immediately inform his employees and other persons affected by the event that the applicable control limit has (or is liable to have) been exceeded (*ibid*; Regulation 8(4)).

Health records and medical surveillance

• An employer must keep a health record containing particulars approved by the HSE for every employee whose work exposes him (or her) to asbestos (unless the exposure does not exceed the *action level* [see **Table 1**]). He must allow the employee to inspect the record on request, provided the employee gives reasonable notice, and must keep a copy of that record for at least 40 years from the date of the last entry in it.

• Every employee whose work exposes him (or her) to asbestos above the action level must present himself for examination (during normal working hours) by an employment medical adviser or appointed doctor. If medical examinations are to take place on the employer's premises, he *must* provide suitable facilities. The first examination must take place within two years of his first exposure to asbestos and the second and subsequent examinations at specified intervals (not exceeding two years) thereafter — or for so long as his exposure to asbestos continues. The employee must cooperate with the medical adviser or doctor and give him as much information about his state of health and physical condition as may reasonably be required. The employer must keep all resultant medical certificates on file for at least four years and must give a copy of every certificate to the employee himself as soon as it is issued. The cost of all such medical examinations must be borne by the employer. At the present time (April 1997), the basic fee for a medical examination is £42.13. The fee for an X-Ray is £45.23; and, for a laboratory test, £27.17 (*per* the Health & Safety (Fees) Regulations 1995 [SI 1995/2646, as amended by SI 1996/2094]).

Designated areas

- An employer must designate as an "asbestos area" any area under his control in which one or more of his employees is exposed or is likely to be exposed to asbestos in excess of the *action level* and as a "respirator zone", any area in which the concentration of asbestos dust exceeds or is likely to exceed any *control limit*. Asbestos areas and respirator zones must be clearly and separately identified as such by the posting of notices indicating (in the case of a respirator zone) that the exposure of an employee who enters it is likely to exceed the relevant control limit and that respiratory protective equipment must be worn.

- The employer must take steps to ensure that no employee enters, or remains in, an asbestos or respirator zone unless specifically authorised to do so.

Duties of employees

- Employees are duty-bound to cooperate with their employers and make full and proper use of any control measure, personal protective clothing and equipment or other thing or facility provided by their employer to prevent or minimise their exposure to asbestos dust. If an employee discovers any defect in any such equipment or control measure, he must inform his employer immediately. (*ibid*; Regulation 9(2)).

Table 1
DEFINITIONS
Control of Asbestos at Work Regulations 1987

Asbestos

"Asbestos" means chrysotile and any of the following forms of amphibole asbestos, viz; crocidolite ("blue asbestos"), amosite ("brown asbestos"), fibrous actinolite, fibrous anthophyllite, fibrous tremolite and any mixture containing any of those minerals. It is as well to point out that it is illegal to import crude, fibre, flake, powder or waste amphibole asbestos into the UK or to supply or use amphibole asbestos or any mixtures containing amphibole asbestos.

Action level

"Action level" means one of the following cumulative exposures to asbestos over a continuous 12-week period when measured or calculated by a method approved by the Health & Safety Commission, namely —

(a) where the exposure is solely to chrysotile, 96 fibre-hours per millilitre of air; or

(b) where the exposure is to any other form of asbestos either alone or in mixtures including mixtures of chrysotile with any other form of asbestos, 48 fibre-hours per millilitre of air; or

(c) where both types of exposure occur separately during the 12-week period concerned, a proportionate number of fibre-hours per millilitre of air.

Control limit

"Control limit" means one of the following concentrations of asbestos in the atmosphere when measured or calculated by a method approved by the Health & Safety Commission, namely —

(a) for chrysotile —

  (i) 0.5 fibres per millilitre for air averaged over any
  continuous period of 4 hours,
  (ii) 1.5 fibres per millilitre of air averaged over any
  continuous period of 10 minutes;

(b) for other forms of asbestos either alone or in mixtures, including mixtures containing chrysotile —

  (i) 0.2 fibres per millilitre of air averaged over any
  continuous period of 4 hours; or

  (ii) 0.6 fibres per millilitre of air averaged over any
  continuous period of 10 minutes

Note: An employee who is disciplined, victimised or dismissed for reporting a defect in plant or equipment provided in the interests of his health and safety has every right to present a complaint to an industrial tribunal, regardless of his age or length of service at the material time. If his complaint is upheld, the tribunal will order the employer to either reinstate or re-engage the employee and/or to pay a substantial amount of compensation, as to which see Dismissal or victimisation in health and safety cases, elsewhere in this handbook.

No smoking, eating or drinking

- Employees must not eat, drink or smoke in any area designated as an asbestos area or a respirator zone.

Provision and cleaning of protective clothing

- As was indicated earlier, employees who are exposed to asbestos dust must be provided with adequate and suitable protective clothing (see *Note* below), unless no significant amount of asbestos dust is likely to be deposited on the clothes they would normally wear at work. All such protective clothing must either be disposed of as asbestos waste or adequately cleaned at suitable intervals in a suitably equipped laundry. Protective clothing which has to be sent away for cleaning and further use must be packed in suitable containers labelled in accordance with Schedule 2 to the 1987 Regulations (see opposite). Protective clothing intended for disposal as asbestos waste must likewise be packed in a suitable container labelled in accordance with either of the Chemicals (Hazard Information & Packaging for Supply) Regulations 1994 (SI 1994/3247, as amended by SI 1996/1092 and SI 1996/2092), or the Carriage of Dangerous Goods (Classification, Packaging & Labelling) & Use of Transportable Pressure Receptacles Regulations 1996 (SI 1996/2092) (*ibid*; Regulations 11 & 18).

Note: Protective clothing provided in pursuance of Regulation 11(1) will be suitable only if it complies with an enactment which implements in Great Britain a provision on design or manufacture with respect to health or safety in any relevant Community Directive listed in Schedule 1 to the Personal Protective Equipment at Work Regulations 1992 (q.v.) which is applicable to that item of protective clothing (*ibid*; Regulation 8(3A)).

Welfare facilities

- Employees who are exposed to asbestos must be provided with adequate and suitable washing and changing facilities. If protective clothing is required, there must be two changing rooms — one for the storage of personal clothing and the other for the removal and storage of protective clothing. If respiratory protective equipment is provided, a third room must be set aside for the storage of that equipment (*ibid*; Regulation 14 & 17). Employees who work in a designated asbestos or respirator zone must have access to a place (such as a restroom or mess hall in which they can take their rest breaks and meals)(*ibid*; Regulation 14(4)).

PROHIBITED ASBESTOS

• With the coming into force of the Asbestos (Prohibitions) Regulations 1992 (*q.v.*) it is unlawful to import amphibole asbestos (in any form) into the UK and unlawful also for any person (acting in the course of a trade, business or other undertaking, whether for profit or not) to supply amphibole asbestos or any product to which amphibole asbestos has intentionally been added. Furthermore, it is unlawful for any person to use amphibole asbestos or any product containing amphibole asbestos in the manufacture or repair of any other product. Nor may any person use a product containing amphibole asbestos (other than in connection with its disposal), unless the product in question was in use before 1 January 1986 (if it contains crocidolite or amosite) or 1 January 1993 (if it contains any other form of amphibole asbestos other than crocidolite or amosite).

Table 2
Asbestos (Prohibitions) Regulations 1992 (SI 1992/3067)
PRODUCTS CONTAINING CHRYSOTILE WHICH ARE PROHIBITED

1. Materials or preparations intended to be applied by spraying.

2. Paints or varnishes.

3. Filters for liquids.

4. Road surfacing material where the fibre content is more than 2%.

5. Mortars, protective coatings, fillers, sealants, jointing compounds, mastics, glues and decorative products in powder form, and decorative finishes.

6. Insulating or soundproofing materials which, when used in their intended form, have a density of less than $1g/cm^3$.

7. Air filters and filters used in the transport, distribution and utilisation of natural gas and town gas.

8. Underlays for plastic floor and wall coverings.

9. Textiles finished in the form intended to be supplied to the end user unless treated to avoid fibre release, except that this prohibition shall not apply to diaphragms for electrolysis processes until after 31 December 1998.

10. Roofing felt (after 1 July 1993).

- The 1992 Regulations also prohibit asbestos spraying (that is to say, the spraying of any material containing asbestos to form a continuous surface coating) and the supply and use (other than the disposal) of any of the products containing chrysotile listed in **Table 2** above (unless those products were in use before 1 January 1993).

Offences & penalties

- A person guilty of an offence under the Control of Asbestos at Work Regulations 1987 (and related legislation) is liable, on summary conviction, to a fine of up to £2,000 or, if convicted on indictment, to a fine of an unlimited amount. If the offence consists of a failure by an employer (or self-employed person) to discharge a duty to which he is subject by virtue of sections 2 to 6 of the Health & Safety at Work etc. Act 1974, the penalty is either a fine of up to £20,000 or a fine of an unlimited amount (*ibid*; section 33(3)).

- If an employer carries out any work which exposes, or is likely to expose, any of his employees to asbestos dust exceeding the action level, either without the benefit of a licence issued by the HSE, or in contravention of any condition or restriction attached to such a licence, the penalty on summary conviction is a fine of up to £2,000 or, if convicted on indictment, imprisonment for a term not exceeding two years and/or a fine of an unlimited amount (*ibid*; section 33(3)(a) & (b)(i)).

  See also the sections titled **Accommodation for clothing, Canteens & rest rooms, Cloakrooms & changing rooms, Meals for employees, No smoking!, Protective clothing & equipment,** and **Washing facilities** elsewhere in this handbook.

FURTHER INFORMATION

- The following publications are available from HSE Books at the address given on page 328.

Legislation

L11
A guide to the Asbestos (Licensing) Regulations 1983 [1991]
ISBN 0 11 885684 7   £3.50

L27
The Control of Asbestos at Work. Control of Asbestos at Work Regulations 1987: Approved code of practice [2nd Edition, 1993]
ISBN 0 11 882037 0   £5.00

L28
Work with asbestos insulation, asbestos coating and asbestos insulating board. Control of Asbestos at Work Regulations 1987: Approved code of practice [2nd Edition, 1993]
ISBN 0 11 882038 9   £5.00

Guidance

EH 10 (Rev)
Asbestos - exposure limits and measurement of airborne dust concentrations [1995]
ISBN 0 7176 0907 3   £5.00

EH 46 (Rev)
Man-made mineral fibres [1990]
ISBN 0 11 885571 9   £2.50

EH 47 (Rev)
Provision, use and maintenance of hygiene facilities for work with asbestos insulation and coatings [1990]
ISBN 0 11 885567 0   £2.50

EH 50
Training operatives and supervisors for work with asbestos insulation and coatings [1988]
ISBN 0 11 885400 3   £2.50

EH 51
Enclosures provided for work with asbestos insulation, coatings and insulating board [1989]
ISBN 0 11 885408 9   £2.50

EH57
The problems of asbestos removal at high temperatures [1993]
ISBN 0 11 885586 7   £2.50

MDHS 39/4
Asbestos Fibres in Air. Light microscope methods for use with the Control of Asbestos at Work Regulations [1995]
ISBN 0 7176 1113 2   £5.00

MDHS 77
Asbestos in bulk materials: Sampling & identification by Polarised Light Microscopy (PLM) [1994]

ISBN 0 7176 0677 5   £11.50

Free leaflets (Telephone 01787 881165)

(Note: Orders for more than a single copy of some free publications are subject to a charge)

INDG 107
Asbestos and you
ISBN 0 7176 1241 4   £5 per pack of 15 leaflets (etc.)

INDG 187
Asbestos dust — the hidden killer! Essential advice for building maintenance, repair and refurbishment workers.
ISBN 0 7176 1208 2   £5.00 per pack of 10 leaflets (etc.)

INDG 188
Asbestos alert (pocket card) *for building maitenance, repair and refurbishment workers*

INDG 223
Managing asbestos in workplace buildings
ISBN 0 7176 1179 5   £5.00 per pack of 10 leaflets (etc.)

Sector guidance

Effects on health of exposure to asbestos
by R Doll and J Peto [1985]
ISBN 0 11 883803 2   £5.00

B

BATHS OR SHOWERS FOR EMPLOYEES

Key points

- An employer must provide showers or baths (connected to a supply of hot and cold [or warm] running water) for those of his employees whose work is either particularly strenuous or dirty, or whose duties involve exposure to harmful or offensive substances or materials which could promote dermatitis and other skin conditions. The facilities must include a sufficient supply of soap and clean towels (to be replenished or replaced as often as circumstances require), and must be kept in a clean and orderly condition. The number of showers provided must be sufficient to enable the people wanting to use them to do so without undue delay (Regulation 21, Workplace (Health, Safety & Welfare) Regulations 1992 [SI 1992/3004], as amended).

- Separate showers and baths must be provided for men and women, unless the numbers involved are too few to justify separate facilities — in which case the shower or bathroom (designed for use by one person at a time) must be capable of being locked or otherwise secured from the inside and not communicate directly with toilets or washrooms routinely used by persons of the opposite sex.

- Showers fed by both hot and cold water should be fitted with thermostatic mixers (or similar devices) to prevent accidental scalding. In the interests of decency, all entrances and exits to washrooms should be suitably screened to ensure that passers-by cannot see into communal shower or bathing areas when the doors are open. Windows should likewise be frosted, or obscured by blinds or curtains, unless they are set too high in the wall for people to be able to see into the washrooms (toilets or changing rooms).

- Washrooms and shower-rooms should communicate directly with changing rooms and toilets. They should be clean and comfortably warm (never cold), and be well-lit and ventilated. The plumbing, taps, shower roses, drains, heating system, and other fittings, should be inspected and tested at regular intervals and (if found to be damaged) repaired as quickly as possible.

• The following Regulations, made under section 15 of the Health & Safety at Work etc. Act 1974, also contain provisions relating to washing facilities, showers and baths. These remain in force alongside the 1992 Regulations. These are: the Control of Lead at Work Regulations 1980 (SI 1980/1248); the Ionising Radiations Regulations 1985 (SI 1985/1333); the Control of Asbestos at Work Regulations 1987 (SI 1987/2115); and the Control of Substances Hazardous to Health Regulations 1994 (SI 1994/3246).

For further details, please turn to the sections titled **Hazardous substances**, **Ionising radiations**, and **Lead at work** elsewhere in this handbook. See also **Washing facilities** and **Toilet facilities**.

C

CANTEENS & REST ROOMS

Key points

• Although employers are not legally-bound to provide staff or works canteens serving hot and cold meals or drinks, they *are* required to provide suitable "eating facilities" for use by employees who routinely take their meals in the workplace. People are entitled to eat their meals or sandwiches out of the public gaze seated at a table, desk or other suitable surface on which to place their food. If there is no vending machine nearby, they must have access to a conveniently-situated kettle (provided by their employer) for preparing hot drinks.

Note: But, under the Work in Compressed Air Regulations 1996 (SI 1996/1656), "The compressed air contractor shall ensure that there are provided and maintained for the use of any person engaged in work in compressed air .... suitable drinks for consumption during or after decompression; suitable food and drinks for consumption by any person receiving therapeutic recompression or decompression; and ... " (Reg. 18).

- Furthermore, if there is no nearby shop or snack-bar selling hot food, the employer must also provide suitable facilities (such as an electric hob, mini-cooker or microwave oven) for heating or warming food. This is particularly important in workplaces in which people work unsociable hours or in areas (such as industrial estates and the like) where sandwich shops, snack bars, etc. are either closed, inaccessible or non-existent. These provisions (expanded-on below) are to be found in Regulation 25 of the Workplace (Health, Safety & Welfare) Regulations 1992 (SI 1992/3004) — supplemented by paras 227 to 236 of the accompanying Approved Code of Practice (as to which, see L24 on page 97).

- For office and shop workers, "suitable and sufficient" means a chair on which to sit and a desk or suitable surface on which to place their food. This is not a problem for the average office worker who can take his (or her) meals and rest breaks while seated at his desk — so long as he has access to a kettle or vending machine and his desk is not in an area frequented or overlooked by customers or members of the public. If his desk or workbench *is* overlooked, a separate eating area must be provided.

- Separate eating facilities must also be provided if considerations of health, safety or hygiene mean that factory workers and the like must not eat or drink in work areas in which there is a risk of food and drink becoming contaminated (e.g., by dusts, fumes, vapours, hazardous substances, chemicals or water) (see **Table 1** overleaf).

- The canteen, mess-room or rest area (or whatever) must be large enough to accommodate the number of people likely to use it at any one time and must be equipped with a sufficient number of tables and chairs with backrests. It must be well-ventilated, heated and lit, and must be be placed in the charge of a responsible person whose job it is to keep it in a clean and hygienic condition. If a rest room (see below) doubles as a mess-room or eating area, it must also be furnished with a vending machine or kettle (and a nearby supply of fresh running water), a small cooker and hob (or a microwave oven) in or on which employees can, if they wish, heat up the food they bring with them to work.

Table 1
REGULATIONS PROHIBITING EATING, DRINKING SMOKING ETC. IN WORKROOMS

Work in Compressed Air Regulations 1996 (SI 1996/1656)

"No person shall consume alcohol or have with him any acoholic drink when in compressed air" (Reg. 17(2)).

Control of Lead at Work Regulations 1980 (SI 1980/1248)

"Every employer shall take such steps as are adequate to secure that —

(a) so far as is reasonably practicable, his employees do not eat, drink or smoke in any place which is, or is liable to be, contaminated by lead;

(b) suitable arrangements are made for such employees to eat, drink or smoke in a place which is not liable to be contaminated by lead.

(2) An employee shall not eat, drink or smoke in any place which he has reason to believe to be contaminated by lead.

(3) Nothing in this Regulation shall prevent the provision and use of drinking facilities which are not liable to be contaminated by lead where such facilities are required for the welfare of employees who are exposed to lead" (Reg. 10)

Ionising Radiations Regulations 1985 (SI 1985/1333)

"No employee shall eat, drink, smoke, take snuff or apply cosmetics in any area which the employer has designated as a controlled area .... except that an employee may drink from a drinking fountain so constructed that there is no contamination of the water" (Reg. 6(6)).

Control of Asbestos at Work Regulations 1987 (SI 1987/2115)

"Every employer shall take suitable steps to ensure that —

(a) his employees do not eat, drink or smoke in any area designated as an asbestos area or a respirator zone; and
(b) in such a case, arrangements are made for such employees to eat or drink in some other place" (Reg 14(4)).

Table 1 (Continued)

Workplace (Health, Safety & Welfare) Regulations 1992 (SI 1992/3004)	Rest facilities provided in accordance with Regulation 25(1) must "include suitable facilities to eat meals where food eaten in the workplace would otherwise be likely to become contaminated" e.g., cement works, clay works, foundries, potteries, tanneries and laundries; premises in which glass bottles and pressed glass articles, sugar, oil cake, jute and tin or terne plates are manufactured; and workplaces in which glass bevelling, fruit preserving, gut scraping, tripe dressing, herring curing and the cleaning or repairing of sacks is carried on (*ibid*; Regulation 25(3) and para. 231 of the accompanying Approved Code of Practice).
Control of Substances Hazardous to Health Regulations 1994 (SI 1994/3246)	If risk assessment shows that it is not reasonably practicable to prevent exposure to carcinogens by using an alternative process, the employer must (amongst other measures) prohibit eating, drinking and smoking in areas that may be contaminated by carcinogens (Reg. 7(3)(e)).

- If employees are required (by law) or expected (by their employer) to remove contaminated work clothing during rest breaks, or before eating or drinking, the canteen or mess-room should be located as near as possible to cloakrooms and washrooms.

Rest rooms

- Regulation 25 also requires employers to provide suitable and sufficient rest rooms or rest areas in which workers can 'put up their feet' during rest breaks — bearing in mind that there are a great many workplaces (including shops, department stores, factories, warehouses, restaurants, cafeterias, hotels, schools, hospitals, and the like) in which employees spend most of their duty hours on their feet. In those circumstances, the employer must provide a separate rest area furnished with chairs, benches or seats which employees can use (out of sight of the public) if the work they do allows them the occasional opportunity to sit down or if (as is often the case in factories) they are frequently required to leave their work areas and wait around until they can return. As was suggested earlier, a works or staff canteen can double as a rest room. This is acceptable so long as employees are not obliged to purchase food or drink in order to use the canteen during rest periods.

Smoking and smokers

- Regulation 25(3) points out that non-smokers must be able to take their meals and rest-breaks without being discomforted by other people's tobacco smoke. There are two options available to employers. They must either provide separate rest rooms or areas for smokers and non-smokers, or ban smoking altogether in those areas.

- A useful HSE publication IND(G)63 titled *Passive smoking at work* (ISBN 0 7176 0882 4) is available from HSE Books (free of charge for a single leaflet, or for £5.00 per pack of 10 leaflets. Further quantity discounts for bulk purchases). For ordering details, please turn to page 328 of this handbook.

Pregnant employees and nursing mothers

- Regulation 25(4) of the 1992 Regulations states that suitable rest facilities must be provided for employees who are pregnant or nursing mothers. This requirement is discussed elsewhere in this handbook in the section titled **Pregnant employees & nursing mothers**.

Meaning of "workplace"

- It is as well to emphasise that the 1992 Regulations apply to *every* workplace, that is to say, every premises (or part of premises), other than domestic premises, which are made available to one or more persons as a place of work. In addition to factories, warehouses, offices and shops, the term also embraces schools, colleges, universities, hospitals, advice centre, hotels, guest houses, bed and breakfast establishments, launderettes, cinemas, theatres, amusement arcades, leisure centres, premises in which self-employed people work or do business, and so on. The list is almost endless.

See also **Seats for employees** elsewhere in this handbook.

CAR PARKS

Key points

- If an unattended or unsupervised car park at any commercial or industrial premises (factory, office, school, hospital, shop, hotel, guest house, department store, etc.) is provided for the use of staff, customers, patrons or visitors, the owner or occupier of those premises will not normally be liable for loss of, or damage to, motor vehicles and their contents. Liability will only arise in exceptional circumstances if the loss or damage was clearly occasioned by the neglect or wilful act of the proprietor or a member of his staff.

- If, on the other hand, a car park is supervised or attended, access is restricted, a parking fee is levied, or a vehicle and its contents are entrusted to the care of a doorman or attendant, a *contract of bailment is* said to come into existence. The motorist has temporarily given up custody of his vehicle, and the proprietor of the establishment, as *bailee,* assumes responsibility for its safekeeping. If the vehicle or its contents are subsequently lost or damaged, the proprietor will be answerable and could face a civil action for damages.

- To protect himself against litigation, the proprietor may impose certain conditions, either in a form of words on the back of a parking ticket or by exhibiting a notice warning motorists that (sic) "The Management does not accept liability for loss or damage to motor vehicles or their contents". However, a term or notice, which excludes or restricts liability for negligence, will be valid only in so far as it satisfies the requirement of reasonableness (section 2 (2), Unfair Contract Terms Act 1977). Furthermore, where a contract term or notice purports to exclude or restrict liability for negligence, a person's agreement to or awareness of it is not of itself to be taken as indicating his voluntary acceptance of any risk (*ibid;* section 2(3)).

Safety of Car Parks

- By section 2 of the Occupiers' Liability Act 1957, the occupier of "premises" (which expression includes a car park) owes a duty to all his visitors to take such care as is reasonable to see that they will be reasonably safe in using those premises for the purposes for which they are invited or permitted by the occupier to be there. See also **Accidents to customers, visitors etc.** elsewhere in this handbook.

- Thus, if a car park is in a poor state of repair (e.g., if it has an uneven or slippery surface, is littered with dangerous obstructions, or is poorly-lit at night), the owner may be sued for damages by any motorist or pedestrian who is injured as a direct consequence of such neglect. Once again, the owner may not exclude or restrict his liability for negligence simply by posting a notice in the car park warning motorists that they use the facility at their own risk. If negligence is proven, the owner will be liable to pay damages.

- The civil liability of the occupier of premises (including a car park or forecourt) is reinforced by a corresponding criminal liability imposed by section 3 of the Health and Safety at Work, etc. Act 1974, viz. "it shall be the duty of every employer to conduct his undertaking in such a way as to ensure, so far as is reasonably practicable, that persons not in his employment who may be affected thereby are not thereby exposed to risks to their health and safety". The same duty attaches to a self-employed person in relation to persons (other than his employees) (*ibid*; section 3 (2)). This means, in effect, that the owner or occupier of the premises in question may be prosecuted by the relevant "enforcing authority" for keeping an unsafe car park — by, for example, failing to fill-in a pothole or drainage excavation, or by neglecting to remove or cover an oil spillage — any or all of which could pose a hazard to persons using the car park. The penalty on summary conviction is a fine of a maximum £20,000; and, on conviction on indictment, a fine of an unlimited amount (*ibid*; section 33 (3)).

- Similar provisions are to be found in the Workplace (Health, Safety & Welfare) Regulations 1993 (SI 1992/3004) which state that the surface of every traffic route in a workplace must be suitable for its intended purpose. It must have no hole or slope, or be uneven or slippery, and must be supplied with effective drainage (*ibid*; Reg. 12). The term "workplace", as used in the Regulations, includes any private road or other place (including a car park or parking facilities and any connected walkways) which is used as a means of access to or egress from the workplace itself. See also Access to premises elsewhere in this handbook.

CARE, COMMON DUTY OF

Key points

- An employer has a common law, as well as statutory, duty to take reasonable care for health and safety of his employees. He must provide them with a safe working environment (including safe means of access to and from his premises), safe tools, appliances and equipment, and protection against any hazards associated with their employment.

- An employee who is injured in the course of his employment may sue his employer for damages. To succeed in such an action, he (or she) will need to prove negligence on the part of his employer and that he was injured as a direct result of that negligence.

- An employer cannot deny negligence on grounds only that he was not in breach of a statutory duty; for example, that he was under no obligation in law to guard a particular machine, or to provide an employee with this or that item of protective clothing or equipment. Liability at common law will still exist if the employer should have known of a particular hazard and did nothing to protect his employees from the possible consequences.

- If, on the other hand, an employer has complied with a statutory duty to guard a particular machine (indeed, any duty under a particular statute or set of Regulations), he may be able to claim in his defence that he had fulfilled his common law duty of care to an injured employee.

- An injured employee may sue his employer on two counts: (a) that he was negligent and in breach of his common law duty of care, and (b) that he was in breach of a duty imposed by statute. Nowadays, an employer must insure against civil liability for damages arising out of personal injury sustained by his employees. The subject is dealt with elsewhere in this handbook in the section titled **Insurance, Compulsory**. See also **Accidents at work** which deals with the statutory duty of an employer to notify and report all 'lost-time' accidents, serious injuries and fatalities sustained by employees in the course of their employment.

Criminal Liability

- Under section 2 of the Health and Safety at Work etc. Act 1974, an employer is duty-bound to do all that is reasonably practicable to protect the health, safety and welfare at work of his employees. If he needlessly or recklessly exposes his employees to danger, he may be prosecuted — whether or not an accident has occurred. The penalty, on summary conviction, is a fine of up to £20,000 and, on conviction on indictment, a fine of an unlimited amount. If he foolishly ignores the requirements of an improvement or prohibition notice, he is not only likely to pay a very heavy fine, but could be sent to prison for a term of up to two years. Unlike his liability for damages at common law (see above), an employer cannot insure against his criminal liabilities under the 1974 Act.

- Regulation 5 of the Provision & Use of Work Equipment Regulations 1992 (SI 1992/2932) reminds employers that, when selecting work equipment (machines, vehicles, tools, plant, appliances, etc.) they must be mindful of the circumstances in which that equipment is to be used. As the accompanying Approved Code of Practice points out, a machine which is inherently safe could pose a serious risk to employees if used in the wrong environment, e.g., a petrol-driven generator operating in a confined space, or an electric drill used in an flammable atmosphere. A breach of the 1992 Regulations attracts the same penalties as a breach of the 1974 Act. For further information (notably the duties of manufacturers and suppliers in relation to the manufacture and supply of machinery), please turn to the sections titled, respectively, **Fencing and guarding**, **Machinery Safety** and **Work equipment**.

Duty to customers, clients, etc.

- In addition to his duty of care towards his own employees, the occupier of premises owes a like duty to persons invited or permitted to be on his premises (such as guests, customers, patrons, clients, tradesmen, etc.). This "common duty of care" has been codified by the Occupiers' Liability Act 1957. In short, the owner or occupier of business premises may well be sued for damages if a member of the public is injured as a direct consequence of his negligence. Furthermore, he runs the risk of being prosecuted under the 1974 Act for failing to take all reasonably practicable steps to safeguard the interests of those members of the general public who have a valid or legitimate reason for being on or near his premises (*vide* section 3, Health & Safety at Work, etc. Act 1974). If a customer, client, tradesman (or whomever) is killed or seriously injured while visiting or present in a shop, factory, warehouse, restaurant, office block , department store, or wherever, and the accident is (or appears to be) directly attributable to the manner in which that business was conducted, the owner or occupier must report the matter to the health and safety inspectorate immediately — as to which, see **Accidents to customers, visitors, etc.** elsewhere in this handbook.

See also **Dangerous machines, Defective equipment, Insurance, Compulsory, Occupier of premises** and **Health & safety at work.**

CEILINGS & WALLS

Key points

- The walls and ceilings in every workplace (except those parts which cannot be safely reached using a 5-metre ladder) must be cleaned at regular intervals and be repainted (or resurfaced) as often as may be necessary, given the nature of the work and the processes carried on in the relevant workroom (Regulation 9, Workplace (Health, Safety & Welfare) Regulations 1992 [SI 1992/3004]).

- Except in parts which are normally visited for short periods only, or where any soiling is likely to be light, interior walls and ceilings should be painted, tiled or otherwise treated so that they can be kept clean, and the surface treatment renewed when it can no longer be cleaned properly.

- The cleaning methods used must not expose any person to substantial quantities of dust, including flammable or explosive concentrations of dusts, or to health or safety risks arising from the use of harmful cleaning agents (as laid down in the Control of Substances Hazardous to Health Regulations 1994, SI 1994/3246).

See also the sections titled **Cleanliness of premises** and **Hazardous substances,** elsewhere in this handbook.

CELLULOID & CINEMATOGRAPH FILM

Key points

- In spite of technological advances over the past 60 and more years and the determination of the Health & Safety Commission to do away with a great deal of outdated health and safety legislation, the following Regulations, made under or saved by the Factories Act 1961 (itself a mere shadow of its former self) have survived intact and are still in force. These are:

    o   the Celluloid (Manufacture etc.) Regulations 1921
        (SR & O 1921/1825);

    o   the Manufacture of Cinematograph Film Regulations 1928
        (SR & O 1928/82); and

    o   the Cinematograph Film Stripping Regulations 1939
        (SR & O 1939/571).

    Celluloid is a highly flammable material and extremely dangerous if not handled correctly. As most people reading this handbook are unlikely to come into contact with celluloid, and those who do will be well aware of its properties and the precautions that must be taken, the following is a summary only of the principal requirements of the Regulations listed above.

1.   Celluloid (Manufacture, etc.) Regulations 1921

- The 1921 Regulations apply to factories or workshops in which celluloid is manufactured or in which any manufacturing processes involving the use of celluloid is carried on — including the manufacture of cinematograph film.

- Stocks of celluloid must always be stored away from the workrooms in which it is manufactured, manipulated or used and, if those stocks exceed 50 kilograms, must be kept in a fire-resistant chamber or room. The storeroom must not be situated a place which is likely to impede fire escape routes out of the factory should a fire occur in the storeroom itself.

- The amount of celluloid or cinematograph film kept in a workroom at any one time must be as small as is practicable consistent with production requirements. Finished articles made wholly or partly of celluloid must be removed from the workshop without delay and "kept in a suitable place". A saw may be used for cutting celluloid if its cutting edge is kept constantly wet. Although it is unlikely that sealing wax or solder is nowadays used to seal tins or packages containing celluloid, the Regulations caution that such activities must be carried out safely and away from rooms in which celluloid is manufactured or used. Celluloid waste must not be permitted to accumulate on the floor of any workroom, but must be collected automatically, as it is created, and placed in suitable receptacles. At the end of every working day or shift, the waste material must be removed from workrooms and deposited in a receptacle provided with a lid or cover and marked "Celluloid Waste". Every workroom and storeroom must be equipped with suitable fire extinguishers and unobstructed means of escape. Unless workrooms are equipped with sliding doors, all doors must be constructed so as to open outwards. Most of these latter requirements (although still in force) have long since been overtaken by the Fire Precautions Act 1971 and Regulations made under that Act.

- For obvious reasons, employees and visitors must not be allowed to smoke in (or take matches or lighters into) any room in which celluloid or products containing celluloid are manufactured, manipulated or stored. A competent person must be appointed to oversee and enforce compliance with the 1921 Regulations and to carry out his employer's instructions to that same end.

2. *Manufacture of Cinematograph Film Regulations 1928*

- The rules relating to the manufacture and storage of cinematograph film are similar. to those relating to the manufacture and storage of celluloid. "Cinematograph film" means any film, including uncoated raw base, which contains nitro-cellulose or some other nitrated product "which is intended for use in a cinematograph or other similar apparatus" (such as a film projector).

- Cinematograph film which is not being actually used,

manipulated, manufactured or repaired must be kept in a room or chamber or similar enclosure constructed of fire-resisting material — except that a quantity not exceeding 20 reels or 37 kilograms in weight, whichever is the greater, may be kept in *any* room so long as each reel of film is kept in its own sealed metal container fitted with a secure metal lid.

Note: "Fire-resisting material" means properly constructed brickwork at least 100 mm in thickness; concrete at least 75 mm thick; oak or teak at least 50 mm thick; wire-mesh-embedded glass at least 6 mm thick; or any other material approved in writing by the Chief Inspector of Factories.

- The ceiling of every room in which cinematograph film is (or is to be) manufactured, repaired, manipulated or used must be constructed of fire-resting material unless the room is on the top floor of the building or is situated in a single-storey building. The walls floor, doors and, where possible, the fittings in the room must likewise be constructed of fire-resisting material and the furniture and equipment in the room, so arranged as to provide an unobstructed means of escape in the event of a fire. The room must be equipped with a sufficient number of fire-extinguishers and its own intercommunicating fire alarm. Doors must be self-closing: and all doors and windows constructed to open outwards.

- Storerooms provided in accordance with the 1928 Regulations must not be used for any purpose other than the storage of cinematograph film or film waste. Not may any single storeroom contain more than 1 tonne or 560 reels of film (each in its own tin), whichever is the greater.

- Storerooms, as distinct from workrooms, must be constructed *entirely* of fire-resisting materials (except as regards the gas relief space referred to below); must be clearly marked with the words "Film Store"; must be adequately ventilated; must be fitted with self-closing doors, fire extinguishers and an efficient water-sprinkling system; must be kept locked when not in use; and (most important) must either comprise a single-storey building, or be situated on the roof or top floor of a building or in some other position approved by the Chief Inspector of Factories (or the HSE). Part of the wall or roof of a single-storey storeroom (or one located on the top floor or roof of a building) must be constructed of ordinary sheet glass lightly fixed in position so as to provide a gas relief space in the event of an explosion or fire — but not so that an outburst of flame through the space would endanger the safety of the building itself or of any adjacent premises. The area of the gas relief space must not be less than 200 square centimetres or more than 260 square centimetres for every 100 kilograms of cinematograph film stored in the room. The gas relief space should be protected against external breakage by a strong wire mesh fitted on the outside of the glass.

- Waste and scrap film must be collected from the floors and benches of workrooms at frequent intervals and deposited in a strong metal receptacle with a self-closing lid clearly marked with the words *Film Waste*. The receptacle (which must never contain any material liable to ignite spontaneously or to ignite or decompose cinematograph film) must either be transferred to a storeroom at the end of each day's work or be removed from the premises.

- Employees must not smoke (or be permitted to smoke) in any workroom or storeroom in which cinematograph is present or likely to be present, and must deposit matches, lighters, tobacco, cigarettes, etc, in a receptacle provided for that purpose outside the room in question, to be collected when they leave the room.

- A competent person must also be appointed to 'police' and enforce compliance with the Regulations and his employer's written instructions concerning the Regulations. See also **Competent persons** elsewhere in this handbook.

3. *Cinematograph Film Stripping Regulations 1939*

- The 1939 Regulations contain virtually the same provisions as those listed in the Cinematograph Film Regulations 1928. The term "film stripping" refers to the process by which emulsion is removed from cinematograph film and all incidental activities including the unpacking, sorting, unwinding, winding, decolouring, washing, grading and packing of cinematograph film before and after the emulsion is removed.

- Most of the activities described in the previous paragraph must be carried on in separate workrooms. Sorting and/or rewinding of film for washing purposes must be carried on in one room, washing in another, drying in yet another; and so on. Loose unwound film must not be placed (or be allowed to remain) on the floor of any workroom and must not be carried from one part of the factory to another unless it is a suitable tray or container.

If carried on forklift trucks or similar, the film must be enclosed in covered containers. Drying must be carried out in carefully-controlled conditions, away from any possible source of ignition and in a drying room in which the temperature must never exceed 38 degrees Celsius.

- The gas relief space in a storeroom (otherwise constructed and equipped in the same way as a room used for the storage of cinematograph film, but situated at least six metres away from any building in which persons are regularly present) must not be less than one square metre for every 15 cubic metres of space in the storeroom, and must be so constructed as to protect any glass from external breakage and to prevent the projection of articles from within the room in the event of a fire or explosion.

General duty of employers

- Employers in every industry, business or undertaking (as well as self-employed persons) must be aware of their general duty (and criminal liability) under the Health & Safety at Work etc. Act 1974 to do all that they reasonably can to ensure the health, safety and welfare at work of their employees. They must also be conscious of their statutory as well as common law duty to do all that needs to be done to protect the health and safety of persons not in their employ (such as visitors, customers, passers-by, and the like) who may be affected by the way in which they conduct their businesses or undertakings.

- Employers are reminded also that they must not only comply with their duties and obligations under the relevant industry-specific legislation (such as that summarised in this section) but also with their all-embracing but no less specific duties under legislation such as the Management of Health & Safety at Work Regulations 1992 and the Workplace (Health, Safety & Welfare) Regulations 1992 — not to mention the Provision & Use of Work Equipment Regulations 1992, the Manual Handling Operations Regulations 1992, the Health & Safety (Display Screen Equipment) Regulations 1992, the Personal Protective Equipment at Work Regulations 1992; and so on.

See also **Health surveillance, Medical examinations** and **Offences & penalties** elsewhere in this handbook.

| CERTIFICATE OF FITNESS |

Key points

- A health and safety (or factory) inspector may take the view that the employment of a young person in a factory, or in a particular process or kind of work in a factory, is prejudicial to his health or the health of other persons. If this is so, he will serve written notice on the occupier of the factory informing him of his views, and requiring him to discontinue the employment of that young person in the factory (or in the process or kind of work, as the case may be) at the end of the period named in the notice (which shall not be less than one nor more than seven days after the service of the notice).

- The occupier may not continue to employ that young person unless the appointed doctor or an employment medical adviser has personally examined the young person and certified that he is fit for employment in the factory (or in the process or kind of work) (section 119, Factories Act 1961).

- From 3 March 1997, employers are no longer required to notify the local careers offices when they engage a young person under 18 to work in a factory. This requirement, laid down in section 119A of the Factories Act 1961 was repealed by the Employment Act 1989 (Commencement No. 2) Order 1997 [SI 1997/134]).

The Management of Health & Safety at Work Regulations 1992

- Restrictions on the employment of young persons under 18 are to be found in the Management of Health & Safety at Work Regulations 1992 (SI 1992/2051), regulation 13D(1) of which imposes a duty on every employer to ensure that young persons under 18 employed by him are protected at work from any risks to their health and safety which are a consequence of their lack of experience, of absence of awareness of existing or potential risks or the fact that young persons have not yet fully matured.

  Note: Regulation 13D was inserted by regulation 2(6) of the Health & Safety (Young Persons) Regulations 1997 (SI 1977/135) which came into force on 3 March 1997.

- Regulation 13(D)(2) cautions that no employer may employ a young person under 18 for work which —

(a)   is beyond his physical or psychological capacity;

(b)   involves harmful exposure to agents which are toxic or carcinogenic, cause heritable genetic damage or harm to the unborn child or which in any other way chronically affect human health;

(c)   involves harmful exposure to radiation;

(d)   involves the risk of accidents which it may reasonably be assumed cannot be recognised or avoided by young persons owing to their insufficient attention to safety or lack of experience or training; or for work

(e)   in which there is a risk to health from extreme cold or heat, noise, or vibration;

unless the work is necessary for the young person's training in circumstances in which he (or she) is supervised by a competent persons and the risks associated with that work are reduced to the lowest level that is reasonably practicable. A failure to comply with these requirements could prompt the intervention of a health and safety inspector or of an employment medical adviser (let alone criminal prosecution under the Health & Safety at Work etc, Act 1974).

For particulars of other legal restrictions on the employment of young persons, please turn to the section titled **Women & young persons, Employment of** elsewhere in this handbook.

Diver's Fitness Register

•   The Diving Operations at Work Regulations 1981 (SI 1981/399) state that no person may be employed under water as a diver unless (a) he is certified as fit for that employment, and (b) he has undergone a medical examination within the previous six months and has similarly been pronounced fit. Such medical examinations must be undertaken by an Employment Medical Adviser or appointed doctor and must include chest examination by radiography. A declaration of fitness for employment as a diver must be entered in a Diver's Fitness Register maintained by the employer and handed to the diver on the termination of his employment.

See also **Health surveillance** and **Risk assessment** elsewhere in this handbook.

CHAINS, ROPES & LIFTING TACKLE

Key points

- Chains, ropes and lifting tackle (which latter includes chain slings, rope slings, rings, hooks, shackles and swivels) may not be used to raise or lower persons, goods, equipment or whatever unless they are of good construction, sound materials, adequate strength and free from patent defect (section 26, Factories Act 1961).

Safe working loads, etc.

- A table showing the safe working loads of every kind and size of chain, rope or lifting tackle in use within a factory must be prominently displayed in the storeroom in which these items are kept when not in use. However, in the case of lifting tackle, it will be sufficient if the safe working load of that tackle is plainly marked upon it (including, in the case of a multiple sling, the safe working load at different angles of the legs).

Six-monthly examinations (Section 26(1)(d))

- All chains, ropes and lifting tackles in use in a factory must be thoroughly examined by a competent person at least once every six months. Furthermore, a record containing the particulars prescribed by Part V of Schedule 1 to the Lifting Plant & Equipment (Records of Test & Examination etc.) Regulations 1992 [SI 1992/195]) must be kept for all such chains, ropes or lifting tackles (see **Table 1** overleaf) (*ibid*; section 26(1)(d)).

Initial examination (Section 26(1)(e))

- Nor may any chain, rope or lifting tackle (except a fibre rope or a fibre rope sling) be taken into use for the first time in a particular factory unless —

(a)   it has been tested and thoroughly examined by a competent person; and

(b)   a record of that test and thorough examination and of the results thereof — containing the particulars required by the Lifting Plant & Equipment (Records of Test & Examination etc.[*q.v.*]) has been obtained and the particulars in that record are kept available for inspection (*ibid*; section 26(1)(e)).

Annealing and other heat treatment

•   Every chain and item of lifting tackle, except a rope sling, must be annealed at least once in every 14 months or, in the case of chains or slings of half-inch bar or smaller, or chains used in connection with molten metal or molten slag, once in every six months. On the other hand, chains and lifting tackle, which are not in regular use, need be annealed only when necessary (*ibid*; section 26(1)(f)). The dates of annealing or other heat treatment must be entered into the record described in **Table 1** opposite.

Note: By Certificate of Exemption No. 1, the following are exempted from the requirement to be annealed:

1.   Chains made of malleable cast iron.
2.   Plate link chains.
3.   Chains, rings, hooks, shackles and swivels made of steel or of   any non-ferrous metal.
4.   Pitched chains working on sprocket or pocketed wheels.
5.   Rings, hooks, shackles and swivels permanently attached to pitched chains, pulley blocks or weighing machines.
6.   Hooks and swivels having screw-threaded parts or ball-bearings or other case-hardened parts.
7.   Socket shackles secured to wire ropes by white metal capping.
8.   Bordeaux connections.
9.   Any chain or lifting tackle which has been subjected to the heat treatment known as 'normalising'instead of annealing.

Construction work

•   Similar provisions are to be found in Part IV of the Construction (Lifting Operations) Regulations 1961 (SI 1961/1581); as to which, see **Construction work** elsewhere in this handbook.

See also **Hoists & lifts** and **Lifting Machines**.

Table 1
PARTICULARS OF CHAINS, ROPES
& LIFTING TACKLE
required to be kept under section 26(1)(g) of the
Factories Act 1961

1. Description, identification mark and location of every chain, rope, chain sling, rope sling, ring, hook, shackle and swivel.

2. The safe working load or loads and (where relevant)   corresponding radii of that equipment.

3. Details and date of completion of the initial test and examination of each item of equipment, as required by section 26(1)(e)).

4. Details and date of completion of each thorough examination made under section 26(1)(e)).

5. Details of any defect found and, where appropriate, a statement of the time by when each defect will be rectified.

6. Date of making of the record required to be obtained under section 26(1)(e), and an identifying number.

7. Latest date by which the next thorough examination made under section 26(1)(d) should be carried out.

8. Name and address of the owner of the equipment referred to.

9. Name and address of the person responsible for the initial test and examination made under section 26(1)(e) or of the six-monthly or more frequent examinations made under section 26(1)(d).

10. Name and address of the person who authenticates the record.

11. A number or other means of identifying the record.

CHILDREN, EMPLOYMENT OF

Key points

- A child is a person who is not over 'compulsory school age' (construed in accordance with section 8 of the Education Act 1996). In Scotland, a child is a person who is not over school age, construed in accordance with section 31 of the Education (Scotland) Act 1980. In short, a child is a person who has not yet lawfully left school.

- If an employer (or would-be employer) is in any doubt concerning the true age of an employee (or job applicant), he may apply to the registrar or superintendent registrar of births, deaths and marriages for a certified copy of the employee's birth certificate.

Legal restrictions on the employment of children

- Enactments which regulate or prohibit the employment of children are:

  (a) Employment of Women, Young Persons & Children Act 1920, as amended

  (b) Children & Young Persons Act 1933 (as amended)

  (c) Children & Young Persons (Scotland) Act 1937 (as amended)

  (d) Children & Young Persons Act 1963

  (e) Employment of Children Act 1973

- See also **Table 1** (on page 78 below) which contains provisions (made under or saved by the Factories Act 1961) limiting or prohibiting the employment of children or young persons in specified hazardous industries and activities.

Children & Young Persons Acts

The Children & Young Persons Acts 1933 & 1937 state that "no child shall be employed —

  o   so long as he (*or she*) is under the age of thirteen years; or o   before the close of school hours on any day on which he (*or she*) is required to be at school; or

o   before seven o'clock in the morning or after seven o'clock in the evening on any day; or

o   for more than two hours on any day on which he (*or she*) is required to attend school; or

o   for more than two hours on any Sunday; or

o   to lift, carry or move anything so heavy as to be likely to cause injury to him (*or her*)".

Most local (or education) authorities require employers to notify the local education department when they propose to employ a person under the age of 16. An employer must also obtain the consent of the child's parent or guardian.

Note: Under the Employment of Children Act 1973the power of local authorities (or, in Scotland, education authorities) to make by-laws regulating the employment of children is replaced by a power of the Secretary of State for Employment to make cognate regulations. To date, the Secretary of State has not exercised that power.

Other prohibited occupations

•   Many local authorities prohibit the employment of children in the following occupations:

o   in the kitchen of any hotel, cook shop, fried fish shop, restaurant, snack bar or cafeteria.

o   as a marker or attendant in any billiards or pools saloon, licensed gaming house or registered club.

o   in, or in connection with, the sale of alcohol, except where alcohol is sold exclusively in sealed containers.

o   in collecting or sorting rags, scrap metal or refuse.

o   as a fairground attendant or assistant.

o   in any slaughterhouse.

o   in, or in connection with, any racecourse or race-track, or other place where any like sport is carried on.

o   in any heavy agricultural work.

o   in, or in connection with, the sale of paraffin, turpentine, white spirit, methylated spirit or petroleum spirit.

o   touting or selling from door to door.

o   as a window cleaner.

Even if employed in a legitimate occupation, a child must not be required to lift, carry or move anything so heavy as to be likely to cause injury to him (*per* sections 18 & 28, respectively, of the Children & Young Persons Acts 1933 & 1937). Copies of local authority by-laws (including applications for a permit to employ a child) are available on request from the relevant local authority for the district in which the would-be employer conducts his business.

Industrial undertakings

• Section 1(1) of the Employment of Women, Young Persons & Children Act 1920 prohibits the employment of any child in an "industrial undertaking", which latter includes particularly:

o   Mines and quarries

o   Industries in which articles are manufactured, altered, cleaned, repaired, ornamented, finished, adapted for sale, broken up or demolished, or in which materials are transformed;

o   Construction, reconstruction, maintenance, repair, alteration or demolition of any building, railway, harbour, dock, pier, canal, inland waterway, road, tunnel, bridge, viaduct, sewer, drain, well, gaswork, waterwork or other work of construction, including the preparation for or laying the foundations of any such work or structure.

o   Transport of passengers or goods by road, rail or inland waterway, including the handling of goods at docks, quays, wharves and warehouses, but excluding transport by hand.

The 1920 Act cautions that the relevant local authority (in Scotland, the education authority) must be consulted if the employer is in any doubt about the lines or divisions between industry, commerce and agriculture.

Information to parents

- Before employing a child, a would-be employer must provide one or other of the child's parents (or a person who has parental responsibility for the child) with relevant and comprehensible information about any health and safety risks associated with the job in question. That information must include particulars about the preventive and protective measures the employer proposes to adopt (or has already put in place) to eliminate or minimise those risks (Regulation 8(2), Management of Health & Safety at Work Regulations 1992 (SI 1992/2051), as amended by The Health & Safety (Young Persons) Regulations 1997 (SI 1997/135), which came into force on 3 March 1997.

Offences & penalties

- If a child is employed in contravention of any of the statutes or bye-laws discussed above, the employer (or, as appropriate, the parent or guardian) will be guilty of an offence and liable, on summary conviction, to a fine of up to £200, rising to £500 if convicted on a second or subsequent occasion. The penalty for an offence under health and safety legislation restricting or prohibiting the employment of children (notably the legislation listed in **Table 1** overleaf) is a fine of up to £2,000 or a fine of an unlimited amount if a conviction is obtained on indictment. If the offence constitutes a failure on the part of an employer to discharge a duty to which he is subject under sections 2 to 6 of the Health & Safety at Work etc. Act 1974, the fine on summary conviction could be as much as £20,000.

  See also **Certificate of fitness** and **Women & young persons, Employment of elsewhere in this handbook.**

(Text continues overleaf)

Table 1

FACTORY LEGISLATION PROHIBITING THE EMPLOYMENT OF CHILDREN

Lead Paint Manufacture Regulations 1907 (SR & O 1907/17) Regulation 3	"No....child may be employed in manipulating lead colour"
Yarn (Dyed by Lead Compounds) Heading Regulations 1907 (SR & O 1907/6166) Regulation 2	"No person under school-leaving age shall be employed" in the heading of yarn dyed by means of a lead compound.
Vitreous Enamelling Regulations 1908 (SR & O 1908/1258) Regulation 7	"No child shall be employed in any enamelling process" (that is to say, in crushing, grinding, sieving, dusting or laying on, brushing or woolling off, spraying, or any other process for the purposes of vitreous covering and decoration of metal or glass).
Tinning of Metal Hollow-ware, Iron Drums & Harness Furniture Regulations 1909 (SR & O 1909/720) Regulation 2	"No person under school-leaving age shall be employed in tinning" (that is to say, the dipping and wiping of any metal in the process of coating it with a mixture of tin and lead, or lead alone, where hydrochloric acid or any salt of that acid is used)
Lead Smelting & Manufacture Regulations 1911 (SR & O 1911/752) Regulation 10	"No person under 16 years of age, and no female, shall be employed in any lead process".
Indiarubber Regulations 1922 (SR & O 1922/329) Regulation 1(a)	"No person under 16 years of age, and no female under 18 years of age shall be employed in any lead process"
Pottery (Health & Welfare) Special Regulations 1950 (SI 1950/65) Regulation 6(4)	"No young person under sixteen years of age shall be employed or work in any process included in Part II of the First Schedule to the Regulations", namely, the following processes when carried on in factories other than leadless glaze factories: (i) dipping or other process

Pottery Regulations 1950 (Continued)	carried on in the dipping house; (ii) the application of majolica or other glaze by blowing, painting or any other process except dipping; (iii) drying after the application of glaze by dipping, blowing or any other process; (iv) ware-cleaning after the application of glaze by dipping, blowing or any other process; (v) glost placing; and (vi) any other process in which glaze is used or in which pottery articles treated with glaze are handled before glost firing.

IMPORTANT NOTE

The Regulations listed above specifically prohibit the employment on children in processes involving work with lead. There are also statutes and Regulations which prohibit the employment of young persons under the age of 18 in certain activities and processes. As the expression "young person" includes a "child", the reader should also consult the section titled **Women and young persons** elsewhere in this handbook.

CLAY WORKS & POTTERIES

Key points

- The Clay Works (Welfare) Special Regulations 1948 (SI 1948/1547) — which (as the name suggests) were primarily concerned with the provision of first aid facilities, shelters, washrooms, protective clothing, changing rooms and cloakroom accommodation, and canteens and messrooms for workers employed in clay works — have, for the most part, been revoked and supplanted in recent years by related provisions in

    (a) the Health & Safety (First-Aid) Regulations 1981 (SI 1981/917)

    (b) the Personal Protective Equipment at Work Regulations 1992 (SI 1992/2966); and

    (c) the Workplace (Health, Safety & Welfare) Regulations 1992 (SI 1992/3004).

- All that remain of the 1948 Regulations is the citation and Regulation 2 which simply defines "clay works" as meaning a factory in which clay, shale, sand, lime or similar materials are made into bricks, tiles, blocks, slabs, pipes, stilts and spurs, nozzles or similar articles.

Potteries

The Pottery (Health & Welfare) Special Regulations 1950 (SI 1950/65) have to a large extent been revoked and superseded by the Control of Lead at Work Regulations 1980 (SI 1980/1248). The only substantive survivors are Regulation 6 (supported by Schedule 1) and Regulation 16 which deal, respectively, with the employment of women and young persons in certain lead-based processes and the maximum dry-bulb temperatures in workrooms. These are discussed elsewhere in this handbook in the sections titled **Women and young persons, Employment of** and **Temperature in workrooms.**

FURTHER INFORMATION

- The following publications are available from HSE Books at the address given on page 328:

L60
Consolidation of COSHH in the potteries [1995]
ISBN 0 7176 0849 2   £5.00

HS(G) 72
Control of respirable silica dust in heavy clay and refractory processes [1992]
ISBN 0 11 885679 0   £4.00

Picking up the pieces: prevention of musculoskeletal disorders in the ceramics industry [1996]
ISBN 0 7176 0872 7   £8.50

Safe operation of ceramic kilns [1993]
Research paper ISBN 0 7176 0630 9   £6.50

Silica and lead: control of exposure in the pottery industry [1992]
ISBN 0 11 882044 3   £6.00

Free leaflets (Telephone 01787 881165)

IACL40   *Precautions for kiln wreck clearance*
IACL55   *Ceramics workplace inspection*
IACL56   *Ceramics: personal protective equipment*
IACL57   *Asbestos in kilns and dryers*
IACL62   *COSHH assessment in potteries*
IACL100 *Health surveillance in the ceramics industry*

CLEANLINESS OF PREMISES

Key Points

- Section 2 of the Health & Safety at Work etc. Act 1974 imposes a general duty on every employer to provide and maintain a working environment for his employees that is, so far as is reasonably practicable, safe, without risks to health and adequate as regards facilities and arrangements for their welfare at work. Non-compliance with this general duty is an offence, the penalty for which is a fine of up to £20,000 or, if the offender is convicted on indictment, a fine of an unlimited amount (*ibid*; section 33(1)(a) and (1A)).

- Section 2 of the 1974 Act is reinforced by related and more specific duties imposed by:

  o   the Workplace (Health, Safety & Welfare) Regulations 1992 (SI 1992/3004 (made under section 15 of the 1974 Act) with an accompanying Code of Practice approved and issued by the Health & Safety Commission under section 16(1)(*ibid*);

  o   the Control of Lead at Work Regulations 1980 (SI 1980/1248);

  o   the Control of Asbestos at Work Regulations 1987 (SI 1987/2115, as amended);

  o   the Control of Substances Hazardous to Health Regulations 1994 (SI 1994/3246);

o   the Food Safety Act 1990, and Regulations made under that Act;

o   the Public Health Acts 1936 and 1961; and

o   the Prevention of Damage by Pests Act 1949.

ALL WORKPLACES

• The walls, windows, skylights, ledges, ceilings and floors in every workplace and in every part of a workplace — office, shop, factory, warehouse, restaurant, school, hospital, hotel, and the like; indeed in any premises (other than domestic premises) made available to a person as a place of work — must be cleaned as often as circumstances and common sense demand. The owner or occupier of any workplace who fails to comply with this duty, imposed by Regulation 9 of the Workplace (Health, Safety & Welfare) Regulations 1992 (*q.v.*) is guilty of an offence under the 1974 Act and liable on summary conviction to a fine of up to £2,000 or, if convicted on indictment, a fine of an unlimited amount (*ibid*; section 33(1)(c) and (3)(b)(ii)).

• Furthermore, the surfaces of walls, floors and ceilings must be capable of being kept clean. This means that they must be painted or tiled or otherwise treated with a suitable non-absorbent material, and must be repainted or resurfaced as often as may be necessary (*ibid*). According to paragraph 70 of the accompanying approved Code of Practice, Regulation 9 does not apply to those parts of a wall or ceiling which cannot be safely reached using a five-metre ladder.

• A factory floor need not be as clean as an office or shop floor; nor a shop floor cleaner than a kitchen floor. The degree of cleanliness required is a matter of common sense and will be largely dictated by the type of activity going on in the workplace in question. The Food Safety (General Food Hygiene) Regulations 1995 (SI 1995/1763) lay down strict guidelines for the standard of cleanliness in food manufacturing companies, supermarkets, food stores, hotels, restaurants, pubs, schools, hospitals and in related catering establishments; while the risks posed by dangerous chemicals and hazardous substances will determine the standard and frequency of cleaning in pharmaceutical and chemical works and in premises where there is a likelihood of exposure to lead or asbestos. Spillages of oil, water and other liquids must be mopped-up as they occur, and waste materials cleared away. Any unexpected discharges from drains or toilets, whether caused by blockages or faulty plumbing, must be investigated promptly and resolved.

- Particular attention should be paid to walkways, corridors, halls, staircases, and the like. Frayed carpeting should be removed or repaired and cracked or uneven tiles replaced or made good. Windows and skylights must be cleaned regularly, as must canteens, rest rooms, changing rooms, washrooms, and toilets.

- Waste materials must be removed promptly from floors and placed in suitable receptacles, and the drains tested and examined regularly to ensure that they are working efficiently.

See also the sections titled **Floors, passageways & stairs**, **Food safety & hygiene** and **Window cleaning** elsewhere in this handbook.

Furniture, furnishings and fittings

- Every workplace (including furniture, furnishings and fittings) must be kept sufficiently clean. The standard of cleanliness required, and the frequency of cleaning, will depend on the use to which the workplace is put and the risks posed by a failure to clean. A factory harbouring accumulations of dangerous or explosive dusts, or a premises in which food is processed or handled, will need to be cleaned more often than the walls, ceiling, desks, chairs, windows, curtains and floor coverings in a large office. In the final analysis it will be for a local authority or HSE-appointed health and safety inspector (in the case of industrial premises) to determine whether the standard of cleanliness in a particular workplace is sufficient to comply with the relevant statutes and Regulations (Regulation 9).

- The Workplace (Health, Safety & Welfare) Regulations 1992 apply to all workplaces, that is to say "any premises or part of premises which are not domestic premises and are made available to any person as a place of work", including "any place within the premises to which such person has access while at work; and any room, lobby, corridor, staircase, road or other place used as a means of access to or egress from the workplace".

- In short, the Workplace Regulations apply not only to factories, offices, shops, supermarkets, department stores, warehouses, building sites, and the like, but also to every school, hospital, hotel, museum, library, restaurant, cafeteria, pub, leisure centre, car park, laundrette, roadside snack bar — indeed, to any place or premises (other than a private house) in which one or more persons (including self-employed persons) either work or are employed to work.

- The penalty for failing to comply with the requirements of the 1992 Regulations is a fine, on a summary conviction, of up to £2,000; and, on conviction on indictment, a fine of an unlimited amount. Under normal circumstances, it is unlikely that proceedings will be instituted against the occupier until he has first been cautioned by a health and safety inspector and been given an opportunity to put matters to rights (See also **Improvement notices** and **Prohibition notices** elsewhere in this handbook)

PREVENTION OR CONTROL OF EXPOSURE TO SUBSTANCES HAZARDOUS TO HEALTH

- If a risk assessment exercise carried out in a workplace shows that it is not reasonably practicable to prevent exposure to a carcinogen by using an alternative substance or process, the employer in question must (inter alia) provide appropriate hygiene measures including the regular cleaning of walls and surfaces (Reg. 7(3)(f), Control of Substances Hazardous to Health Regulations 1994 (*q.v.*))

MINIMISING EXPOSURE TO METALLIC LEAD AND ITS IONIC COMPOUNDS

- In factories and workshops in which lead, lead alloys or compounds of lead are used or manipulated (in a form which is liable to be inhaled, ingested or otherwise absorbed) the employer must take adequate steps to secure the cleanliness of all areas (including washrooms, changing rooms and eating or drinking areas) in which lead is liable to be present (Regulation 11, Control of Lead at Work Regulations 1980 (*q.v.*)).

- The accompanying Approved Code of Practice states (see COP2 on page 92 below) that the floors, inside walls, ceilings, workbenches in 'lead factories', and external surfaces of machinery and other fixtures, should have smooth and impervious surfaces to facilitate cleaning. Floors and workbenches should be washed-down or vacuum-cleaned at least once a day (using a mobile or fixed vacuum cleaner equipped with high-efficiency filters). Inside walls and ceilings must likewise be cleaned as often as the degree of contamination dictates; and accumulations of lead dust, from overhead ledges and other fixtures, removed as often as may be necessary to prevent lead deposits being dislodged or becoming airborne.

- Dry brushes or brooms must *never* be used to remove deposits of lead dust. When wet-cleaning methods are employed, care should be taken to ensure that wet sludge is not left on the floor where it can attach itself to the wheels of fork-lift trucks (or similar) and be transferred to lead-free areas in the same premises where it can create a substantial amount of airborne dust when it dries.

- Employers in 'lead factories' must introduce and enforce a clear, and written procedure for the routine cleaning of their premises. The procedure must (a) nominate the person appointed to take charge of the cleaning team, (b) identify those parts of the factory or workshop (including changing rooms, etc.) which must be cleaned (c) state how often and when those parts are to be cleaned, and (d) indicate precisely which cleaning methods must be employed and which must not (paras 60 & 61 of the Approved Code of Practice).

PROTECTION FROM RISKS ASSOCIATED WITH EXPOSURE TO ASBESTOS

- Similar provisions are to be found in the Control of Asbestos at Work Regulations 1987 (*q.v.*) — Regulation 13 of which states that every part of a workplace (including machines and other fixtures) in which work with asbestos is carried out must be kept in a clean state and must be thoroughly cleaned *after* work with asbestos has been completed.

- Where a manufacturing process which gives rise to asbestos dust is carried out in a building (or in a part of a building), the employer must ensure that building (or part) is so designed and constructed as to facilitate cleaning. Furthermore, it must be equipped with an adequate and suitable vacuum-cleaning system "which shall, where reasonably practicable, be a fixed system" (*ibid*; Reg. 13(2)).

FOOD PREMISES

- Regulation 4 and Schedule 1 (Chapter I) of The Food Safety (General Food Hygiene) Regulations 1995 (SI 1995/1763) impose a duty on the proprietor of a food business to ensure that premises under his (or her), in which food or drink intended for human consumption is prepared, processed, manufactured, packaged, stored, handled and offered for sale (or supply) are kept clean and maintained in good repair and condition. To that end, the layout, design, construction and size of food premises must —

  (a)   permit adequate cleaning and/or disinfection;

  (b)   be such as to protect against accumulations of dirt, contact with toxic materials, the shedding of particles into food, and the formation of condensation or undesirable mould on surfaces;

  (c)   permit good food hygiene practices, including protection against cross contamination between and during operations, by foodstuffs, equipment, materials, water, air supply or personnel, and external sources of contamination such as pests; and

  (d)   provide, where necessary, suitable temperature conditions for the hygienic processing and storage of products.

- A "food business" is somewhat broadly defined as any trade or business for the purposes of which any person engages in the handling of food intended for human consumption. The expression "food" includes drink, chewing gum and other products of like nature and use, and articles and substances used as ingredients in the preparation of food or drink or of such products. The Regulations clearly apply to all food manufacturers; and to enterprises, such as supermarkets, grocery stores, hotels, clubs, boarding-houses, restaurants, cafeterias, sandwich bars, public houses, wine bars, schools, hospitals, hot dog stalls, ice cream vans, etc. in which food and/or drink are sold or supplied for human consumption.

- Persons guilty of an offence under the 1990 Act (and its attendant Regulations) are liable to a fine of up to £20,000 and, in some cases, imprisonment for up to two years. For further particulars, please turn to the section titled **Food safety & hygiene** elsewhere in this handbook.

Closure of Food Premises

- If a person is convicted of an offence under The Food Safety (General Food Hygiene) Regulations 1995 (*q.v.*), and the offence includes the carrying on of a food business at unsanitary premises (or at any premises whose condition is such that food is exposed to risk of contamination), the court may decide that the business puts public health at risk; in which event, it must issue a prohibition order, i.e., an order prohibiting the preparation, storage, exposure or sale of food on the premises until such time as the measures specified in the order have been carried out and the local authority is satisfied that the premises are once again suitable for use as a food business. Furthermore, if an enforcement officer believes that a food business poses an imminent risk to health, he (or she) may close it by issuing an emergency prohibition notice without prior reference to a court. He will then apply to the court for an emergency prohibition order, giving the owner or manager of the offending premises a minimum of just 24 hours' notice of his intention to do so.

- To have a prohibition order or emergency prohibition order lifted, the proprietor or manager of the food business concerned must apply to the enforcement authority for a certificate stating that enough has been done to ensure that the business can operate once again without putting the health of customers and the public at risk. The enforcing authority have 14 days within which to consider the application and a further three days within which to convey their decision to the applicant. If they decide not to issue the certificate, the proprietor or manager of the food business may lodge an appeal with a magistrates' court (or, in Scotland, with the Sheriff).

FILTHY OR VERMINOUS PREMISES OR ARTICLES

- If a local authority are satisfied that any premises are in such a filthy or unwholesome condition as to be prejudicial to health, or are verminous, they may give notice to the owner or occupier of the premises requiring him to take such steps as may be specified in the notice to remedy the condition of the premises by cleansing and disinfecting them; and the notice may require, among other things, the removal of wallpaper or other wall-coverings, or, in the case of verminous premises, the taking of such steps as may be necessary for destroying or removing vermin. The notice may also require the interior surfaces of premises used for human habitation, or as shops or offices, to be papered, painted or distempered (section 83 (1), Public Health Act 1936, as amended by section 35, Public Health Act 1961).

- Any person, who fails to comply with the requirements of such a notice served on him by the local authority, is guilty of an offence and liable to a fine of up to £200 and to further fines if the offence continues after conviction. (*ibid*; section 83 (3)).

INFESTATION OF FOOD

- The Prevention of Damage by Pests Act 1949 (in Northern Ireland, the Destruction of Rats and Mice Act (NI) 1919) empowers local authority inspectors to enter and inspect infested premises; to order the destruction of infested food; to prohibit or restrict the sale or storage of food on infested premises; or to require the carrying out of structural alterations (or the application of any form of treatment) for preventing or remedying infestation on such premises (*ibid*; sections 14 and 15).

- Any infestation of food by insects and mites (or of food wrappings, storerooms or food vehicles) must be reported to the Ministry of Agriculture, Fisheries and Food (MAFF) (or, in Scotland, the Department of Agriculture and Fisheries (*ibid*; section 13).

- Any person who fails to report infestation, or who does not comply with any directions given by inspectors, is guilty of an offence and liable, on summary conviction to a fine of a maximum £500 in the case of a first offence and up to £1,000 for a second or subsequent offence (*ibid*; section 17).

OTHER INFORMATION

- A useful booklet titled *The Food Safety Act 1990 & You* (REF. PB 2507) summarises the legal duties of employers, managers and owners of food businesses under the 1990 Act. Copies of that and other food safety publications can be obtained by contacting MAFF Publications, London SE99 7TP, or by telephoning 0645 556000. For other general enquiries, the MAFF Helpline Number on 0645 335577.

See also the sections titled **Cloakrooms & changing rooms** (next section), **Toilet facilities** and **Washing facilities** elsewhere in this handbook.

CLOAKROOMS & CHANGING ROOMS

Key points

- Separate changing rooms for men and women must be provided if employees routinely strip to their underwear (or beyond) or remove more than their outer clothing before donning special work clothing (such as uniforms, coveralls, protective clothing, etc.). See also the section titled **Protective clothing & equipment** elsewhere in this handbook.

- Changing rooms should be constructed and arranged to ensure privacy. They must be large enough to accommodate the number of people likely to use them at any one time (without overcrowding or unreasonable delay). They should be within convenient walking distance of workrooms and eating facilities, and should either contain or communicate directly with washrooms, bathrooms, showers and toilet facilities. They must be kept clean, warm, dry, well-lit and ventilated, and must contain a sufficient number of seats or benches, as well as hooks or pegs. If work clothing is likely to become damp, badly soiled or contaminated with a hazardous substance (including lead or asbestos, sugar or flour dust [which can cause dermatitis], cutting oils, etc.) employees must be able to store their personal clothing in one part of the changing room (or in an adjoining room) and their work clothing in another, so that there is no risk of contact between the two (Regs 23 & 24, Workplace (Health, Safety & Welfare) Regulations 1992 [SI 1992/3004]'. See also the sections titled **Accommodation for clothing, A work, Construction work,** and **Lead at work** elsew handbook.

- In the interests of security, the employer must either restrict access to the changing room during working hours (or employ a full-time attendant) or provide each employee with a lockable locker. In short, he must provide suitable security for employees'personal clothing and effects *(ibid;* Regulation 23(2)(a)*).*

- The responsibility for policing and enforcing compliance with the 1992 Workplace Regulations rests with the relevant "enforcing authority'. The penalties for non-compliance can be severe; as to which, please turn to the sections titled **Inspectors, Powers of** and **Offences & penalties** elsewhere in this handbook.

CODES OF PRACTICE & GUIDANCE

Key points

- Section 16 of the Health & Safety at Work etc. Act 1974 empowers the Health & Safety Commission, with the consent of the Secretary of State for Employment, to approve, issue and (from time to time) revise such codes of practice (whether prepared by it or not) as are suitable "for the purposes of providing practical guidance with respect to the requirements of any provision of sections 2 to 7 [of the Act] or of any of the *existing statutory provisions*". Nowadays, approved codes of practice are invariably issued and come into force at the same time as the Health & Safety Regulations they complement — the most recent and all-embracing of which are the so-called 'six-pack' of Regulations, comprising:

  o the Management of Health & Safety at Work
     Regulations 1992 (SI 1992/2051) — summarised elsewhere in this handbook in the section **Health & Safety at work.**

  o the Health & Safety (Display Screen Equipment)
     Regulations 1992 (SI 1992/2792) — discussed in the section titled **Visual Display Units (VDUs);**

  o the Manual Handling Operations Regulations 1992 (SI 1992/2793)(see **Manual Handling of Loads);**

o the Provision & Use of Work Equipment Regulations 1992 (SI 1992/2932)(see **Work Equipment**);

o the Personal Protective Equipment at Work Regulations 1992 (SI 1992/2966)(see **Protective Clothing & Equipment**); and

o the Workplace (Health, Safety & Welfare) Regulations 1992 (SI 1992/3004)(discussed throughout this handbook).

These Regulations (all of which stem from recent European Directives) are modernising Regulations in the sense that they have 'done away with' a number of outdated statutes and Regulations (many of which latter were made under, or saved by, the Factories Act 1961 or the Offices, Shops & Railway Premises Act 1963). Another important feature of modernising health and safety legislation is that it applies to *every* workplace, that is to say to every premises (or part of premises), other than domestic premises, made available to a person as a place of work. They also apply to self-employed persons.

Legal status of a code of practice

• A failure on the part of any person to observe any provision of an approved code of practice does not of itself render that person liable to any proceedings; but in any proceedings before an industrial tribunal or the Central Arbitration Committee (or, as appropriate, in any criminal proceedings in relation to an alleged offence under the Health and Safety at Work, etc. Act 1974), any code of practice issued under the relevant legislation shall be admissible in evidence, and if any provision of such a code appears to the tribunal or Committee or court to be relevant to any question arising in the proceedings, it shall be taken into account in deciding that question.

• In other words, the codes of practice listed in this section have much the same status as the Highway Code under road traffic laws. A motorist will not be prosecuted for a breach of the Highway Code. He may, however, be prosecuted under the Road Traffic Act 1972; in which event, his failure to observe any relevant provisions of the Highway Code will be admissible in evidence in proceedings before the magistrates' court.

HSE PUBLICATIONS

- The approved codes of practice listed below (carrying the prefix COP or HS(R)) are gradually being superseded by the 'L' series (also listed). HSE publications in the 'L' series explain or interpret legislation. All of the following publications are available from HSE Books at the address given on page 328. When ordering, readers should quote the series number (e.g., COP6, HS(R)28, L46) and the accompanying ISBN number.

Approved codes of practice

Note: The list below does not include codes of practice specific to railways, mines, quarries or offshore installations.

COP 2
Control of lead at work: approved code of practice [Revised June 1985] (in support of SI 1980/1248)
ISBN 0 7176 1046 2   £3.90

COP 6
Plastic containers with nominal capacities up to 5 litres for petroleum spirit: Requirements for testing and marking or labelling (in support of SI 1982/830) [1982]
ISBN 0 11 883643 9   £2.00

COP 7
Principles of good laboratory practice: Notification of New Substances Regulations 1982 (in support of Sl 1982/1496) [1982]
ISBN 0 11 883658 7   £2.50

COP 14
Road tanker testing: examination, testing and certification of the carrying tanks of road tankers and of tank containers used for the conveyance of dangerous substances by road (in support of SI 1981/1059) [1985]
ISBN 0 11 883811 3   £2.80

COP 15
Zoos: safety, health and welfare standards for employers and persons at work: approved code of practice and guidance note [1985]
ISBN 0 11 883823 7   £3.50

COP 18
Dangerous substances in harbour areas: The Dangerous Substances in Harbour Area Regulations 1987: approved code of practice [1987]
ISBN 0 11 883857 1   £4.00

COP 20
Standards of training in safe gas installation: approved code of practice [1987]
ISBN 0 7176 0603 1   £6.00

COP 23
Exposure to Radon: the Ionising Radiations Regulations 1985: Approved code of practice [1988]
ISBN 0 11 883978 0   £2.00

COP 24
Preventing accidents to children in agriculture: Approved Code of Practice and guidance notes [1988]
ISBN 0 11 883997 7   £2.75

COP 25
Safety in docks: Docks Regulations 1988: Approved Code of Practice with Regulations and guidance [1988]
ISBN 0 11 885456 9   £7.50

COP 26
Rider operated lift trucks — operator training: Approved Code of Practice and supplementary guidance [1988]
ISBN 0 7176 0474 8   £3.75

COP 37
Safety of pressure systems. Pressure systems and Transportable Gas Containers Regulations 1989: Approved Code of Practice. [1990]
ISBN 0 11 885514 X   £4.50

COP 38
Safety of transportable gas containers. Pressure Systems and Transportable Gas Containers Regulations 1989: Approved Code of Practice [1990]
ISBN 0 11 885515 8   £4.00

COP 42
First aid at work. Health and Safety (First-Aid) Regulations 1981:

Approved Code of Practice   [1990]
ISBN 0 7176 0426 8   £3.00

Other codes of practice

Code of safe practice at fairs: amusement device log book [1993]
ISBN 0 7176 0959 6   £3.00

*Code of safe practice at fairs: record of daily inspection of
passenger carrying devices* [1984]
ISBN 0 7176 1020 9   £3.00

Code of safe practice at fairs: technical annex [1988]
ISBN 0 11 885919 6   £3.50

HS(R) Series

HS(R)4 (Rev)
Guide to the OSRP Act 1963 [1989]
ISBN 0 11 885463 1   £3.25

HS(R) 17
*Guide to the Classification and Labelling of
Explosives Regulations 1983* [1983]
ISBN 0 11 883706 0   £3.25

HS(R)21 (Rev)
*A guide to the Control of Industrial Major Accident Hazards
Regulations 1984* [1990]
ISBN 0 11 885579 4   £5.00

HS(R)25
*Memorandum of guidance on the Electricity at Work
 Regulations 1989* [1989]
ISBN 0 11 883963 2   £4.00

HS(R)26
*Guidance on the legal and administrative measures taken to
implement the European Community Directives on Lifting and
Mechanical Handling Appliances and Electrically Operated Lifts*
[1987]
ISBN 0 11 883962 4   £3.50

HS(R)27
*Guide to the Dangerous Substances in Harbour Areas Regulations
1987* [1988]
ISBN 0 11 883991 8   £3.00

HS(R)28
*Guide to the Loading and Unloading of Fishing Vessels
Regulations 1988* [1988]
ISBN 0 11 885457 7   £2.50

HS(R)29
*Guide to the notification and marking of sites in accordance with the
Dangerous Substances (Notification and Marking of Sites)
Regulations 1990* [1990]
ISBN 0 11 885435 6   £3.50

HS(R)30
*Guide to the Pressure Systems and Transportable Gas
Containers Regulations 1989* [1990]
ISBN 0 7176 0489 6   £4.50

'L' Series

L1
A guide to the Health and Safety at Work etc Act 1974 [4th
Edition, 1990]
ISBN 0 7176 0441 1   £4.00

L2
Power presses. The Power Presses Regulations 1965 and 1972
[1991]
ISBN 0 11 885534 4   £3.50

L5
*The Control of Substances Hazardous to Health Regulations 1994
(COSHH): Approved Code of Practice*
ISBN 0 7176 0819 0   £6.75

L6
*Diving operations at work. The Diving Operations at Work
Regulations 1981 as amended by the Diving Operations at
Work (Amendment) Regulations 1990* [1991]
ISBN 0 11 885599 9   £4.25

L7 (see also COP 23)
Dose limitation - restriction of exposure: Additional guidance on
Regulation 6 of the Ionising Radiations Regulations 1985:
Approved code of practice, Part 4 [1991]
ISBN 0 11 885605 7   £2.25

L8
The prevention or control of legionellosis (including legionnaires
disease): Approved code of practice [1991]
ISBN 0 7176 0457 8   £3.00

L9
The safe use of pesticides for non-agricultural purposes:
Approved code of practice [1991]
ISBN 0 11 885673 1   £4.00

L10
A guide to the Control of Explosives Regulations 1991 [1991]
ISBN 0 11 885670 7   £3.00

L11
A guide to the Asbestos (Licensing) Regulations 1983 [1991]
ISBN 0 11 885684 7   £3.50

L13
A guide to the Packaging of Explosives for Carriage Regulations
1991 [1991]
ISBN 0 11 885728 2   £3.00

L16
Design and construction of vented non-pressure road tankers used for
the carriage of flammable liquids. Road Traffic (Carriage of Dangerous
Substances in Road Tankers and Tank Containers) Regulations 1992:
Approved code of practice [1993]
ISBN 0 11 886300 2   £4.00

L19
Design and construction of vacuum operated road tankers used for the
carriage of hazardous wastes. Road Traffic (Carriage of Dangerous
Substances in Road Tankers and Tank Containers) Regulations 1992.
Approved code of practice [1993]
ISBN 0 7176 0564 7   £4.00

L20
A guide to the Lifting Plant and Equipment (Records of Test and Examination etc) Regulations 1992 [1992]
ISBN 0 7176 0488 8   £3.00

L21
Management of Health and Safety at Work Regulations 1992: Approved code of practice [1992]
ISBN 0 7176 041 2 8   £5.00

L22
Work equipment. Provision and Use of Work Equipment Regulations 1992. Guidance on Regulations 1992]
ISBN 0 7176 0414 4   £5.00

L23
Manual handling. Manual Handling Operations Regulations 1992. Guidance on Regulations [1992]
ISBN 0 7176 0411 X   £5.00

L24
Workplace health, safety and welfare. Workplace (Health, Safety and Welfare) Regulations 1992: Approved code of practice and guidance [1992]
ISBN 0 7176 0413 6   £5.00

L25
Personal Protective Equipment at Work Regulations 1992. Guidance on Regulations [1992]
ISBN 07176 0415 2   £5.00

L26
Display screen equipment work. Health and Safety (Display Screen Equipment) Regulations 1992. Guidance on Regulations [1992]
ISBN 0 7176 0410 1   £5.00

L21 -26 Also available as a pack (6 vols.)
ISBN 0 7176 0420 9   £30.00

L27
The Control of Asbestos at Work. Control of Asbestos at Work Regulations 1987: Approved code of practice [2nd Edition, 1993] ISBN 0 11 882037 0   £5.00

L28
Work with asbestos insulation, asbestos coating and asbestos insulating board. Control of Asbestos at Work Regulations 1987: Approved code of practice [2nd Edition, 1993]
ISBN 0 11 882038 9   £5.00

L29
A guide to the Genetically Modified Organisms (Contained Use) Regulations 1992
ISBN 0 11 882049 4   £5.00

L31
A guide to the Public Information for Radiation Emergencies Regulations 1992 [1993]
ISBN 0 11 886350 9   £5.00

L49
Protection of outside workers against ionising radiations [1993]
ISBN 0 7176 0681 3   £5.00

L51
Carriage of Dangerous Goods by Rail Regulations 1994
ISBN 0 7176 0698 8   £8.95

L55
Preventing asthma at work
ISBN 0 7176 0661 9   £6.25

L56
The Gas Safety (Installations & Use) Regulations 1994: Approved Code of Practice
ISBN 0 7176 0797 6   £5.75

L58
The protection of persons against ionising radiation arising from any work activity (1994)
ISBN 0 7176 0508 6   £6.00

L60
Consolidation of COSHH in the potteries [1995]
ISBN 0 7176 0849 2   £5.00

L62
The Approved Code of Practice on Regulation 6

Safety data sheets for substances and preparations dangerous for supply
ISBN 0 7176 0859 X £3.95

L63
The Approved Guide
Approved guide to the classification and labelling of substances and preparations dangerous for supply
ISBN 0 7176 0860 3 £6.50

L64
Safety signs & signals. The Health & Safety (Safety Signs & Signals) Regulations 1996. Guidance on the Regulations [1996]
ISBN 0 7176 0870 0 £8.50

L67
Control of vinyl chloride at work (1994 edition). Control of Substances Hazardous to Health Regulations 1994. Approved Code of Practice [1995]
ISBN 0 7176 0894 8 £3.95

L73
A guide to RIDDOR 95 [1996]
ISBN 0 7176 1012 8 £6.95

A guide to RIDDOR 95 plus electronic versions of forms F2508/F2508A on diskette [1996]
ISBN 0 7176 1080 2 £19.50

L76
Approved supply list and database — CHIP 96 [1996]
ISBN 0 7176 1116 7 £17.00

L80
A guide ot the Gas Safety (Management) Regulations 1996 [1996]
ISBN 0 7176 1159 0 ££8.50

L81
The design, construction and installation of gas service pipes. The Pipelines Safety Regulations 1996. Approved Code of Practice & guidance [1996]
ISBN 0 7176 1172 8 £6.50

L82
A guide to the Pipelines Safety Regulations 1996 [1996]
ISBN 0 7176 1182 5 £9.00

L86
Control of substances hazardous to health in fumigation operations:
Approved Code of Practice: COSHH '94 [1996]
ISBN 0 7176 1195 7 £8.50

L87
Safety representatives and safety committees (The Brown Book) 3rd
Edition. Approved Code of Practice and guidance on the regulations
[1996]
ISBN 0 7176 1220 1 1 – 9 copies: £5.75 each copy. 100+
copies: £4.00 each copy.

L88
Approved requirements and test methods for the classificiation and
packaging of dangerous goods for carriage [1996]
ISBN 0 7176 1221 X £12.75

L89
Approved vehicle requirements [1996]
ISBN 0 7176 1222 8 £5.50

L90
Information approved for the carriage of dangerous goods by road and
rail other than explosives and radioactive material [1996]
ISBN 0 7176 1223 6 £13.50

L91
Suitability of vehicles and containers and limits on quantities for the
carriage of explosives: Carriage of Explosives by Road Regulations
1996 — Approved Code of Practice [1996]
ISBN 0 7176 1224 4 £6.50

L92
Approved requirements for the construction of vehicles for the carriage
of explosives by road [1996]
ISBN 0 7176 1225 2 £5.00

L93
Approved tank requirements: the provision for bottom loading and
vapour recovery systems of mobile containers carrying petrol [1996]

ISBN 0 7176 1226 0   £6.50

L94
Approved requirements for the packaging, labelling and carriage of radioactive material by rail   [1996]
ISBN 0 7176 1227 9   £7.75

L95
A guide to the Health & Safety (Consultation with Employees) Regulations 1996   [1996]
ISBN 0 7176 1234 1   £8.00

L96
A guide to the Work in Compressed Air Regulations 1996   [1996]
ISBN 0 7176 1120 5   £10.50

COMMON PARTS OF PREMISES

Key points

Owners of premises

- The owner of any premises used as a workplace has a responsibility to ensure that the premises are structurally sound and in a good state of repair— unless, under the terms of the lease or letting agreement, that duty devolves on the occupier or lessee. In short, he must determine which provisions of the Workplace (Health, Safety & Welfare) Regulations 1992 (SI 1992/3004) are his responsibility and which are those of his tenants (Reg. 4).

- If there are a number of employers occupying a building, chances are that certain areas, facilities and systems (lobby, reception area, lifts, washrooms, toilets, plumbing, electricity supply, ventilation, lighting, heating etc.) are the responsibility of the owner (or landlord), whereas day-to-day matters such as cleanliness, hygiene, removal of obstructions and spillages, space for workstations, seating, etc. are the responsibility of the tenant employers.

What is important is that tenants should cooperate with one

other, and with the landlord or owner, to agree their joint and several responsibilities under the 1992 Regulations.

• Many buildings (notably office buildings) are occupied by several tenants. Responsibility for the common parts of such buildings rests with the owner or landlord. He (or she) must see to it that there is safe means of access to (and egress from the building, that the lobby, staircases, landings and corridors comply with the Regulations; that toilets and washrooms are suitable and sufficient for the number of people likely to use them; that lifts, escalators, air conditioning plant, electricity circuits, lighting systems (including emergency lighting), hot and cold water systems are in good working order; that windows and skylights are cleaned regularly; that floors are kept in a good state of repair; that the common parts (including walls, ceilings and floors) are kept clean; and so on (Reg. 4).

• If the owner of a building provides work equipment (such as a photocopier) for use by his tenants or keeps tools and appliances (e.g., vacuum cleaners, floor polishers, power tools, hammers, screwdrivers, spanners) on the premises, either for his own use or for that of his employees, he must also comply with his duties under the Provision & Use of Work Equipment Regulations 1992 (SI 1992/2932). He will also have responsibilities under the Management of Health & Safety at Work Regulations 1992 (SI 1992/2051); and, if hazardous substances are kept on the premises (in the form of cleaning materials, scouring agents, etc.) must comply with his duties under the Control of Substances Hazardous to Health Regulations 1994 (SI 1994/3246).

• Tenant employers who are uncertain about their precise responsibilities under the Workplace Regulations should examine the terms of their leases and talk to the landlord or owner. The latter are not usually responsible for the routine cleaning and maintenance of areas occupied by tenants, nor for the cleaning-up of spillages, the removal of obstructions, the cramped conditions within work areas, damaged three-pin plugs, the replacement of faulty light bulbs, the suitability of seating, etc.

• Where tenants have a joint responsibility in relation to their obligations under the Regulations, they should cooperate with one another to develop a plan of action (perhaps a roster). Nor should a tenant in his capacity as an employer lose sight of his duty under the Management of Health & Safety at Work Regulations 1992 to appoint a 'competent person' (see next section) whose job it is to assist him to do what has to be done to comply with his duties under health and safety legislation. In a small branch office, occupied by a manager, his (or her) secretary, a cat and a pot plant, the employer (who will be situated elsewhere) may appoint the manager or the secretary as the competent person — but competent he (or she) must be.

See also **Alterations & extensions** elsewhere in this handbook.

COMPETENT PERSONS, APPOINTMENT OF

Key points

- With the coming into force on 1 January 1993 of the Management of Health & Safety at Work Regulations 1992 (SI 1992/2051) *every* employer must nowadays appoint one or more 'competent persons' to help him understand and come to terms with his duties under health and safety legislation (*ibid*; Regulation 6(1)). Other legislation, which has long since required the appointment of competent persons, is listed in the **Table 1** on page 107.

- An employer who pays 'lip service' to Regulation 6(1) by appointing just anybody to be the 'competent person' within his organisation is taking a risk. Health & Safety inspectors may prosecute unless satisfied that the person appointed is familiar with the requirements and prohibitions imposed by contemporary health and safety legislation and has the time, knowledge, capabilities, inclination and interest to carry out his (or her) assigned tasks. An inspector will also need to be satisfied that the 'competent person' has the confidence and 'ear' of his employer; and that what he says has to be done *is* done.

- There is no need for an employer to recruit 'competent persons' from outside his business or undertaking. Nor need he appoint someone to fill the role on a full-time basis, although this might well be advisable in larger organisations which have never employed full-time safety officers and have been less than energetic about health and safety issues. The function of the 'competent person' is to provide competent advice and assistance. In most organisations, that advice and assistance can be provided by one or more existing employees, so long as the person(s) appointed satisfies the criteria described above and is allowed sufficient time away from his normal duties to carry out his health and safety functions. If there is no suitable candidate, an employer may have no choice but to seek help or support from outside the organisation (see next paragraph). See also *Procedures for serious and imminent danger* later in this section.

• If an employer is a sole trader or a member of a partnership, he can appoint himself (or one of his partners) to be the 'competent person' — so long as he is familiar (or acts speedily to familiarise himself) with his duties and obligations under the 1992 Regulations and has the qualities "properly to undertake the measures he needs to take to comply with the requirements and prohibitions imposed upon him by or under the relevant statutory provisions"(see *Note* below). Indeed, there is nothing in law to prevent him or, for that matter, any employer (large or small), from enlisting help or support from an external consultancy or firm which specialises in health and safety matters (so long as he is prepared to listen to what the consultant has to say and act upon his recommendations).

Note: The expression "relevant statutory provisions" means Part I of the Health & Safety at Work etc. Act 1974 and statutes and Regulations made under or saved by that Act.

• Many large organisations engaged in recognisably hazardous activities (pharmaceuticals, chemicals, etc.) have entire departments with specific health and safety responsibilities. The role of the safety department is to conduct routine safety audits (or 'risk assessment' exercises), monitor safe working practices and safe systems of work, inspect plant and equipment, investigate accidents, carry out (or organise) health surveillance and medical examinations, conduct induction and follow-up training courses; and so on. In every such department, there will already be several 'competent persons' (many of them highly skilled and technically qualified) answerable to the Board of Directors and to the Health & Safety Inspectorate.

• A trade union-appointed safety representative or a *representative of employee safety* (see below) may be ideally qualified to be the 'competent person' in the organisation in which he (or she) works, but should not be asked, or be expected, to wear two hats. Although there is undoubtedly a degree of overlap, the first duty of a safety representative is to look after the interests of the people he was appointed or elected to represent. The first duty of a 'competent person' is to help his employer come to terms with his duties and responsibilities under health and safety legislation. The notion that the safety representative (or, as appropriate, the *representative of employee safety*) and the 'competent person' should not be one and the same person. is reinforced by the Safety Representatives & Safety Committees Regulations 1977 (SI 1977/500), Regulation 4A(1) of which states that an employer must (amongst other things) consult safety representatives about his arrangements for appointing the competent person required by Regulation 6(1) of the 1992 Regulations. If there is no trade union involvement (and no trade union-appointed safety representatives), the employer must either consult the employees themselves or one or more *representatives of employee safety* elected by those employees to represent their interests in matters affecting their health and safety at work.

- Paragraph 37 of the Approved Code of Practice (see below), which accompanies the 1992 Regulations, cautions that appointing a competent person, setting-up a safety department, or hiring the services of an external consultant, does *not* absolve an employer from his general duty under section 2 of the Health & Safety at Work etc. Act 1974 "to ensure, so far as is reasonably practicable, the health, safety and welfare at work of all his employees". If an employer is prosecuted for failing to comply with that duty, he cannot argue in mitigation that he was unaware of the extent of his duties and responsibilities or that he was wrongly advised by his safety advisers, or by external consultants or by the competent person or persons appointed by him to help him discharge those duties and responsibilities.

  HSE publication L21: *Management of Health and Safety at Work Regulations 1992: Approved code of practice* [1992] ISBN 0 7176 041 2 8 is available from HSE Books (see page 328) price £5.00.

Procedures for serious and imminent danger

- Regulation 7 of the 1992 Regulations requires employers to develop emergency procedures for dealing with situations (such as a fire, dust explosion, bomb scare, or a spillage of flammable or hazardous substances) which could present serious and imminent danger to the health and safety of their employees. To that end, every employer must nominate a sufficient number of capable, responsible and experienced employees ('competent persons') whose collective responsibility it is to oversee the evacuation of all personnel from the premises and to move them to a place of safety when any such situation arises.

- An office building or shop will not normally be as hazardous as a warehouse or building site; nor a sausage factory as hazardous as a major chemical plant. Most employers will be familiar with the risks facing their employees, given their knowledge of the industry in which they are engaged and the processes carried on in that industry. They will also be aware of the quantities of explosive, flammable or hazardous substances stored, produced, used or manipulated on the premises either as part of the production process itself or intended for sale or transfer to customers or other sites. But employers will never be entirely certain that they have anticipated every risk unless and until they have complied with their duty under Regulation 3 of the 1992 Regulations to make a suitable and sufficient assessment of every risk to which their employees are or may be exposed while they are at work and of the risks to the health and safety of people who are not in their employment (customers, clients, visitors, tradesmen, neighbours or passers-by) arising out of, or in connection with, the way in which they conduct their businesses.

- The emergency evacuation procedures referred to earlier must be committed to writing and circulated to every employee. They must also be issued to 'agency temps', to self-employed tradesmen and contractors' employees carrying out cleaning, repair or maintenance work on the premises, and to any external health and safety consultant appointed as the 'competent person' for the business in question. Emergency procedures should also form part of the induction training given to every new employee before he (or she) starts work (as required by Regulation 11, *ibid.*). Employers may wish to reinforce that training by requiring new and existing employees to take part in exercises to familiarise them with the emergency procedures and to test their effectiveness.

- Emergency procedures should ensure that, wherever possible, persons at work who are exposed to serious and imminent danger are informed of the nature of the hazard confronting them and of the steps which have been taken (or are about to be taken) to protect them from it. If this is not possible, given the suddenness and urgency of the situation, they should also make it plain to employees that, in the absence of any guidance or instructions (and in the light of their knowledge and the technical means at their disposal) they should stop work of their own initiative and immediately proceed to a place of safety. Finally, the procedures must make it plain to employees that they must not re-enter the building or resume work until the 'All Clear' has been sounded.

OTHER LEGISLATION REQUIRING THE APPOINTMENT OF COMPETENT PERSONS

• **Table 1** below lists a number of pre-1974 Regulations and orders (still in force) which require employers to appoint one or more competent persons to 'police' compliance with those Regulations and to ensure that their instructions are carried out.

Table 1 LEGISLATION REQUIRING THE APPOINTMENT OF COMPETENT PERSONS	
Celluloid (Manufacture etc.) Regulations 1921 (SR & O 1921/1825)	"11.— (i) A *competent person* shall be appointed in writing to exercise supervision with regard to the requirements of these Regulations and to enforce the observance of them and of any directions given by the occupier with a view to carrying out the Regulations."
Manufacture of Cinematograph Film Regulations 1928 (SR & O 1928/82)	Regulation 13 (text as per previous item)
Kiers Regulations 1938 (SR & O 1938/106)	"19. The occupier shall appoint a *competent person* to supervise the working of each set of kiers in accordance with these Regulations and to control the entry of persons into those kiers. Each person so appointed shall be known as the authorised person for that set of kiers. The occupier may appoint a second competent person to act as a deputy in the absence of the first
	(Continued overleaf)

Table 1 (Continued)	
	authorised person, and may also appoint a particular person to perform specified duties in connection with the completion of operation and blowing down of the kiers. The name of every person appointed in pursuance of this Regulation shall be stated in a notice affixed near the kiers concerned. "20. The authorised person shall take all reasonable steps to secure that all valves, taps, disconnecting arrangements, pumps, notices, signs and other appliances in connection with the kiers under his supervision are properly manipulated and used in accordance with these Regulations."
Cinematograph Film Stripping Regulations 1939 (SR & O 1939/571)	Regulation 15 (text as for first item in this column)
Work in Compressed Air Regulations 1996 (SI 1996/1656)	"5. "The principal contractor for any project shall appoint as the compressed air contractor in respect of the work in compressed air included in that project a contractor *competent* to execute or to supervise the execution of such work"
Power Presses Regulations 1965 (SI 1965/1441)	Unless undergoing training and working under the immediate supervision of a *competent person* appointed under paragraph (1), "no person shall set, re-set, adjust or try out the tools on a power press, or install or adjust any safety device thereon, being installation or adjustment preparatory to production or die proving, or carry out an inspection or test of any safety device thereon ....., unless he (a) has attained the age of eighteen; (b) has been trained in accordance with the Schedule to these Regulations; (c) is competent to carry out those duties; and (d) has been appointed by the occupier of the factory to carry out those duties .... ; and every such appointment shall be made by signed and dated entry in, or by signed and dated certificate attached to, a register (form F2198) kept for the purposes of this Regulation" (Reg. 4(1)).
	(Continued opposite)

Table 1 (Cont.)

Abrasive Wheels Regulations 1970 (SI 1970/535)	Unless undergoing training in the work of mounting abrasive wheels and working under the immediate supervision of a *competent person* appointed under paragraph (1), "no person shall mount any abrasive wheel unless he has been trained in accordance with the Schedule to these Regulations; is competent to carry out that duty; and has been appointed by the occupier of the factory to carry out that duty in respect of the class or description of abrasive wheel to which the abrasive wheel belongs; and every such appointment shall be made by a signed and dated entry in, or signed and dated certificate attached to, a register (form F 2346) kept for the purposes of this Regulation."
Carriage of Explosives by Road Regulations 1996 (SI 1996/2093)	A *competent person* must be in attendance with a vehicle carrying explosives whenever the driver is not present, except in specified circumstances or when certain types of explosives are being carried (Reg. 20)
Pressure Systems & Transportable Gas Containers Regulations 1989 (SI 1989/2169)	The user of an installed system and the owner of a mobile system must have a written scheme for the periodic examination of the system by a *competent person* or of specified parts of the system (*ibid*; Regs 8 & 9)

COMPRESSED AIR, WORK IN

Key points

- The duties of employers and contractors in relation to the health and safety of employees who work in compressed air are explained in the Work in Compressed Air Regulations 1996 (SI 1996/1656), which came into force on 16 September 1996.

- As the Regulations are complicated, and replete with technical detail, it is impossible to do justice to them in a handbook of this size or scope (but see *FURTHER INFORMATION* below). Suffice to say that they contain comprehensive rules relating to the appointment of a competent contractor to execute or supervise work in compressed air; require specified information to be notified in writing to the Health & Safety Executive(HSE) and to specified hospitals and other bodies; require safe and supervised systems of work; impose requirements with regard to the provision, use and maintenance of adequate and suitable plant and equipment; provide that a contract medical adviser be appointed to advise on matters relating to the health of compressed air workers; require compression and decompression to be carried out safely in accordance with HSE-approved procedures; impose requirements for the making and maintenance of records; require adequate medical facilities; impose requirements with regard to the preparation of adequate emergency arrangements (and suitable fire precautions); prohibit smoking and the possession of smoking materials in compressed air; require adequate instruction, information and training; prohibit persons working in compressed air if impaired by drink or drugs and prohibit the consumption of alcohol in compressed air; impose requirements for the provision and maintenance of suitable welfare facilities; impose a requirement (in specified circumstances) for badges to be supplied to persons who have worked in compressed air; etc.

FURTHER INFORMATION

- The following publications are available from HSE Books at the address on page 328:

L96
A guide to the Work in Compressed Air Regulations 1996 [1996]

ISBN 0 7176 1120 5   £10.50

*Dangerous substances: Compressed air. Worker's health and
exposure record* [1996].
ISBN 0 7176 1245 7   ££10.00

HS(G)39 (Rev)
Compressed air safety (1990)
ISBN 0 7176 0498 5   £5.00

CONFINED SPACES

Key points

- No person may enter or remain inside any chamber, tank, vat, pit, pipe, flue, or similar confined space in which dangerous fumes are liable to be present unless he (or she) has been authorised to do so by a responsible person and is wearing a respirator or other suitable breathing apparatus. Furthermore, he must wear a belt with a rope securely attached, the free end of which is being held by a person keeping watch outside who is capable of pulling him out at a moment's notice (section 30, Factories Act 1961).

- No person may enter or remain in any confined space in which the proportion of oxygen to air is liable to have been substantially reduced unless he is wearing a suitable breathing apparatus or the space has been and remains adequately ventilated and a responsible person has tested and certified it as safe for entry without breathing apparatus. Nor may any work be permitted inside a boiler furnace or flue until it has been sufficiently cooled by ventilation or otherwise to make the work safe for the persons employed (*ibid*; section 30(9) & (10).

- Even if a confined space has been certified by a responsible person as safe to enter for a specified period, without the need for a respirator, no person may enter or remain in that space unless forewarned when that period will expire. A confined space should not be certified as being safe for entry unless and until —

  (a)   effective steps have been taken to prevent the ingress of dangerous fumes;

(b)   any sludge or other deposit liable to give off dangerous fumes has been removed and the space contains no other material liable to give off dangerous fumes; and

(c)   the space has been adequately ventilated and tested for dangerous fumes and has an adequate supply of air for breathing.

People whose work takes them into confined spaces (or who routinely keep watch outside) should be trained and practised in the use of breathing apparatus and rope harnesses, and should be familiar with basic resuscitation techniques.

•   Although section 30 of the 1961 Act makes no mention of the importance of written procedures, the Health & Safety Executive (HSE) has long since urged employers to devise a permit-to-work (or similar) system as a means of avoiding (or minimising the risk of) injury to persons who are routinely (or occasionally) required to work in confined spaces. In short, no person should be allowed to enter a confined space, for whatever reason, without a written authorisation signed by his immediate supervisor or other competent person on a form which specifies the work to be done and the procedures to be followed.

•   Employers must provide a sufficient number of suitable respirators of a type approved by the Health & Safety Executive (HSE) for the use of persons working in confined spaces. Belts and ropes and other rescue equipment, (including suitable reviving apparatus and oxygen), must also be kept 'on standby'. All respirators and rescue equipment must be maintained in good condition and must be thoroughly examined by a competent person at least once every month, or more often if the apparatus and equipment in question is in regular or constant use. A written report of every such examination, signed by the competent person and containing the particulars specified in the Breathing Apparatus etc. (Report of Examination) Order 1961 (SI 1961/1345), must be kept on file and must be produced for inspection at the request of a health and safety (or factory) inspector. The particulars to be included in the report are:

(a)   the name of the occupier of the factory;

(b)   the address of the factory;

(c)   in the case of breathing or reviving apparatus, particulars of the type of apparatus and of its distinguishing number or mark, together with a description sufficient to identify the apparatus and the name of the maker;

(d)   in the case of a belt or rope, the distinguishing number or mark and a description sufficient to identify the belt or rope;

(e)   the date of the examination and the name of the person by whom it was carried out;

(f)   the condition of the apparatus, belt or rope, and particulars of any defect found during the examination;

(g)   in the case of a compressed oxygen apparatus, a compressed air apparatus or a reviving apparatus, the pressure of oxygen or of air, as the case may be, in the supply cylinder.

- Unless there is other adequate means of egress, every confined space must be provided with a rectangular, oval or circular manhole which is not less than 460 mm long and 410 mm wide or (if circular) not less than 460 mm in diameter. In the case of a tank wagon and other mobile plant, the manhole must be at least 410 mm long and 360 mm wide or (if circular) at least 410 mm in diameter (*ibid*; section 30(2)).

OTHER LEGISLATION

- Every employer, in every work situation, has an overriding duty under section 2 of the Health & Safety at Work etc. Act 1974 to provide and maintain plant and *systems of work* that are, so far as is reasonably practicable, safe and without risks to health. A failure to comply with that general duty is a criminal offences, the penalty for which is a heavy fine and the possibility of imprisonment; as to which, see *Offences & penalties* below.

Control of Substances Hazardous to Health Regulations 1994

- Although the Control of Substances Hazardous to Health Regulations 1994 (SI 1994/3246) contain no specific reference to the risks associated with work in confined spaces, they do impose a duty on employers to take such steps as are necessary to prevent or control the exposure of their employees to any natural or artificial substance which is hazardous to health — including vapours and fumes given off by such substances and by dusts of any kind (when present at a substantial concentration in air) (*ibid*; Regulations 2 & 7).

Kiers Regulations 1938

- Regulation 19 of the Kiers Regulations 1938 (SR & O 1938/106) requires the occupier of a factory in which kiers are present to appoint a competent person (and, if need be, a second person to act as his or her deputy) to supervise the working of each set of kiers and to control the entry of persons into those kiers. Regulations 21 to 26 warn that no person may enter or remain in a kier if there is any hot liquor or water present in the kier or kier system at a temperature in excess of 40° Celsius. Nor may a person enter or remain in a kier unless the competent person has seen to it that every steam pipe, valve, external connecting pipe, puffer pipe and associated pump has been closed, locked, isolated, disconnected, closed off or secured, as the case may be, and that the kier itself isolated from every other kier or vessel in the system. Warning signs must be posted outside a kier and must not be removed until the competent person is satisfied that there are no persons remaining inside it; and so on.

See also **Construction work** (next section).

Offences & penalties

- A failure to comply with the requirements summarised above is an offence, the penalty for which is a fine of up to £2,000; or, if a conviction is obtained on indictment, a fine of an unlimited amount. If the offence is tantamount to a failure on the part of an employer (or self-employed person) to discharge a duty to which he is subject by virtue of sections 2 to 6 of the Health & Safety at Work etc. Act 1974, the penalty on summary conviction is a fine of up to £20,000 (*ibid*; section 33(1A)). See also **Improvement notices** and **Prohibition notices** elsewhere in this handbook.

FURTHER INFORMATION

The following publications are available from HSE Books (see page 328):

GS5   *Entry into confined spaces* [1995]
            ISBN 0 7176 0787 9   £5.00
CIS15   *Confined spaces (Free leaflet)*

CONSTRUCTION WORK

Key points

- Employers engaged in construction work have the same general duty as other employers to do all that they reasonably can to ensure the health, safety and welfare at work of the people they employ. They have the same duty to visitors and members of the public who may be put at risk when construction work is being undertaken in or adjacent to public streets and highways or in the areas in which they live. Self-employed workers share that same general duty of care. These provisions are to be found in sections 2 to 5 of the Health & Safety at Work etc. Act 1974 summarised elsewhere in this handbook in the section titled **Health & safety at work.**

- 'Construction work', as defined by regulation 2(1) of the Construction (Design & Management) Regulations 1994 (SI 1994/3140), means "the carrying out of any building, civil engineering or engineering construction work" including:

  (a) the construction, alteration, conversion, fitting out, commissioning, renovation, repair, upkeep, redecoration or other maintenance (including cleaning which involves the use of water or an abrasive at high pressure or the use of substances classified as corrosive or toxic for the purposes of regulation 5 of the Carriage of Dangerous Goods (Classification, Packaging & Labelling) & Use of Transportable Pressure Receptacles Regulations 1994 [SI 1996/2092]), de-commissioning, demolition or dimantling of a structure (see *Meaning of 'structure'* below),

  (b) the preparation for an intended structure, including site clearance, exploration, investigation (but not site survey) and excavation, and laying and installing the foundations of the structure,

  (c) the assembly of prefabricated elements to form a structure or the disassembly of prefabricated elements which, immediately before such disassembly, formed a structure,

  (d) the removal of a structure or part of a structure or of any product or waste resulting from demolition or dismantling of a structure or from disassembly of prefabricated elements which, immediately before such disassembly, formed a structure, and

(e)   the installation, commissioning, maintenance, repair or removal of mechanical, electrical, gas, compressed air, hydraulic, telecommunications, computer or similar services which are normally fixed within or to a structure,

but does not include the exploration for, or extraction of, mineral resources or activities preparatory thereto carried out at a place where such exploration or extraction is carried out.

Meaning of 'structure'

- For these purposes, the word "structure" means —

  (a)   any building, steel or reinforced concrete structure (not being a building), railway line or siding, tramway line, dock, harbour, inland navigation, tunnel, shaft, bridge, viaduct, waterworks, reservoir, pipe or pipe-line (whatever, in either case, it contains or is intended to contain), cable, aqueduct, sewer, sewage works, gasholder, road, airfield, sea defence works, river works, drainage works, earthworks, lagoon, dam, wall, caisson, mast, tower, pylon, underground tank, earth retaining structure, or structure designed to preserve or alter any natural feature, and any other structure similar to the foregoing, or

  (b)   any formwork, falsework, scaffold or other structure designed or used to provide support or means of access during construction work, or

  (c)   any fixed plant in respect of work which is installation, commissioning, de-commissioning or dismantling, and where any such work involves a risk of a person falling more than two metres.

Legislation specific to 'construction work'

- The following Regulations (made under or saved by the Health & Safety of Work etc. Act 1974) apply particularly to building operations and works of engineering construction (referred to, collectively, as 'construction work'):

1. The Construction (Design & Management) Regulations 1994 (SI 1994/3140)(in force from 31 March 1995); and

2. The Construction (Health, Safety & Welfare) Regulations 1996 (SI 1996/1592);

Note: The 1996 Regulations, above came into force on 2 September 1996, at which time The Construction (General Provisions) Regulations 1961, The Construction (Working Places) Regulations 1966, the Construction (Health & Welfare) Regulations 1966, and the Construction (Health & Welfare) (Amendment) Regulations 1974, were revoked.

3. The Construction (Lifting Operations) Regulations 1961 (SI 1961/1581); and

4. The Construction (Head Protection) Regulations 1989 (SI 1989/2209);

the provisions of each of which are summarised in this section.

• As employers (and self-employed persons) building contractors, civil engineers, and the like, must also comply with their duties under:

5. The Electricity at Work Regulations 1989 (SI 1989/635);

6. The Noise at Work Regulations (SI 1989/1790);

7. The Management of Health & Safety at Work Regulations 1992 (SI 1992/2051);

8. The Manual Handling Regulations (SI 1992/2793);

9. The Provision & Use of Work Equipment Regulations 1992 (SI 1992/2932);

10. The Personal Protective Equipment at Work Regulations 1992 (SI 1992/2966);

11. The Workplace (Health, Safety & Welfare) Regulations 1992 (SI 1992/3004) (but see *Note* below); and

12. The Control of Substances Hazardous to Health

Regulations 1994 (SI 1994/3246);

and with any other legislation summarised in this handbook which is not industry-specific (e.g., the duty of every employer to provide suitable and sufficient first aid facilities and to report injuries, diseases and dangerous occurrences).

Note: The provisions of The Workplace (Health, Safety & Welfare) Regulations 1992 (SI 1992/3004) do *not* apply to any workplace on a construction site which is set aside for purposes other than construction work (*ibid*; regulation 3(1)(b)). The term 'construction site' means aby place where the principal work activity being carried out is construction work (as defined above).

FACTORIES ACT 1961

- Provisions of the 1961 Act, which continue to apply to 'construction work' are:

Section 34	Steam boilers (restrictions on entry). See **Pressure systems** elsewhere in this handbook.
Section 38	Steam boilers (supplementary provisions).
Section 140	Duty to maintain a General Register (Form F36) (see *FURTHER INFORMATION* at the end of this section).
Section 141	Duty to preserve prescribed records and registers for at least two years

Note: Section 140 of the 1961 Act will be complied with, so far as 'construction work' is concerned, if the General Register (Form F36) is kept in the contractor's office.

- Reports of the statutory inspections of lifting appliances, cranes, jib cranes and hoists, must be kept in the site office. All other reports, certificates and documents, required under the Regulations (summarised in the following pages) must be kept either on site or at the office of the contractor or employer for whom they were made or obtained, or at the office of the owner of the plant or equipment to which a particular certificate of test and examination relates.

1. Construction (Design & Management) Regulations 1994

Notice of construction work

- Particulars of any project which includes (or is intended to include) construction work must be sent to the Health & Safety Executive (HSE) before work on that project begins. The person responsible for notifying the HSE is the "planning supervisor" appointed by the client in compliance with Regulation 6 of the Construction (Design & Management) Regulations 1994 (*q.v.*). Under the 1994 Regulations, 'the client' is the person or organisation on whose behalf the building work is being carried out. However, the HSE need not be notified of proposed building work if the construction phase of the project is not expected to last for more than 30 days or is unlikely to involve more than 500 person/days (*ibid*; Reg. 7).

- The information to be sent to the HSE must contain the particulars listed in **Table 1** on page 121.

Competence of planning supervisor, designers and contractors

- The client (ie; the person for whom the proposed building work is to be carried out) must appoint a "planning supervisor" in respect of a building project and a "principal contractor" to carry out or manage the related construction work. There is nothing to prevent the "planning supervisor" and the "principal contractor" being one and the same person. Indeed, if the client is himself competent to carry out construction work (and intends to do so), he may appoint himself to either or both of those positions.

- However, Regulation 8 of the 1994 Regulations cautions that the person appointed must not only be competent (in every sense of the word) but also familiar with any and all health and safety legislation applicable to the site and the work that is to be carried out on it. To that end, the client must also be satisfied that the planning supervisor and principal contractor intend to allocate whatever resources are necessary to enable them to comply with their duties under that legislation.

- The designer (i.e; person responsible for designing the project in all its phases) must also be competent at what he (or she) does and familiar with the requirements of health and safety legislation. When preparing his design, he must ensure that the design considerations include adequate regard to the need —

(a) to avoid foreseeable risk to the health and safety of each and every worker or self-employed person likely to be employed or working on the site and to the health and safety of other persons (such as members of the public, visitors or passers-by) who may be affected by that work;

(b) to combat at source risks to the health and safety of those workers and other persons; and to give priority to associated health and safety protective measures.

Furthermore, the design for the building or structure (or whatever) must include adequate information about any aspect of the project or structure or materials (including articles or substances) which might affect the health and safety of any person working on the site or of any person who may be affected by such work. The designer must also cooperate with the planning supervisor and with any other designer who is preparing a design in connection with the same project so far is necessary to enable each of them to comply with the requirements and prohibitions imposed by or under the relevant health and safety legislation.

Requirements on planning supervisor

• Apart from his (or her) duty to notify the Health & Safety Executive about proposed construction work (see above) it is the planning supervisor's job to ensure that the design for the project satisfies the necessary health and safety requirements and that, if there is more than one designer working on different aspects or phases of the project, that they cooperate with one another to that same end.

• The planning supervisor must also be in a position to advise the client and any contractor working on the site about health and safety issues. Of particular importance is the his (or her) duty to prepare a health and safety file for the site. The file must be prepared before building work begins and must include information supplied by the designer about those aspects of the project, structure or materials (including machinery, tools, appliances, hoists, lifts, scaffolding, potentially hazardous substances, and so on) which could affect the health and safety of workers and mebers of the public. The file must be used as a

Table 1
WRITTEN PARTICULARS OF CONSTRUCTION WORK
to be notified to the Health & Safety Executive
by the "planning supervisor" in accordance with Regulation 7 and
Schedule 1 to The Construction (Design & Management)
Regulations 1994

1. Date on which notification sent.
2. Exact address of the construction site.
3. Name and address of the client or clients (see *Note* below).
4. Type of project.
5. Name and address of the planning supervisor.
6. A declaration signed by or on behalf of the planning supervisor that he/she has been appointed as such.
7. Name and address of the principal contractor.
8. A declaration signed by or on behalf of the principal contractor that he/she has been appointed as such.
9. Date planned for the start of the construction phase.
10. Planned duration of the construction phase.
11. Estimated maximum number of people at work on the construction site.
12. Planned number of contractors on the construction site.
13. Name and address of any contractor or contractors already chosen.

Note: The term "client" in this context means any person for whom a project (which includes or is intended to include construction work) is carried out, whether it is carried out by another person or is carried out in-house. A client may appoint an agent or another client to act as the only client in respect of a project, but must not do so unless reasonably satisfied that the person appointed has the competence to perform the duties imposed on him by the Construction (Design & Management) Regulations 1994.

A person appointed to act as agent or the only client in respect of a project must make a written declaration to that effect, stating his name and address (ie; the address where documents may be served) and the address of the construction site. Once signed, the declaration must be sent to the nearest local office of the Health & Safety Executive.(HSE). When the HSE receives the declaration, it will serve notice on the person by whom it was made advising him of the date on which the declaration was received (reminding him that the requirements and prohibitions imposed by the 1994 Regulations apply to him from that date and for so long as he continues to act as agent for the person who appointed him.

source of reference and must be reviewed and updated if and when new or unexpected materials, equipment or substances are introduced to the site. Once the construction work is completed, the planning supervisor must hand the health and safety file to the client (*ibid*; Regulation 14).

- Specifically, the health and safety plan referred to in the previous paragraph must include the following information:

  (a)   a general description of the construction work comprised in the project;

  (b)   details of the time within which it is intended that the project, and any intermediate stages, will be completed;

  (c)   details of risks to the health or safety of any person carrying out the construction work so far as such risks are known to the planning supervisor or are reasonably foreseeable;

  (d)   any other information which the planning supervisor knows or could ascertain by making reasonable enquiries and which it would be necessary for any would-be contractor to have if he were asked either to attest to his competence or his ability (and determination) to allocate resources sufficient to enable him to comply with his duties under relevant health and safety legislation;

  (e)   information likely to be required by the principal contractor and any sub-contractors to enable them to monitor compliance with the relevant health and safety legislation (in the light of the risks associated with the project; and

Other requirements

- The principal contractor on a building site or on works of engineering construction is responsible for ensuring that other contractors (including sub-contractors) are aware of their duties and responsibilities under health and safety legislation; that they comply with those duties; and that they provide their employees with whatever instruction and training is needed to enable them to carry out their duties safely and responsibly.

- The principal contractor must also be mindful of the needs of his own employees and those of any self-employed persons working on the site. They too must receive any necessary information and instruction about health and safety issues and be encouraged to approach him for advice on matters connected with the project which could foreseeably put them at risk. He must also set up arrangements for the co-ordination of the views of all employees working on the site (perhaps through their appointed safety representatives or shop stewards) to enable him to identify and deal with any concerns they may have about health and safety issues.

- Sub-contractors must cooperate with one another and with the principal contractor. They must obey the principal contractor's reasonable instructions on health and safety issues and comply with any and all rules and safety procedures laid down in the site safety plan prepared by the planning supervisor. Every contractor and sub-contractor on site must provide the principal contractor with information about any notifiable injury or death or dangerous occurrence reportable under the Reporting of Injuries, Diseases & Dangerous Occurrences Regulations 1995 (SI 1995/3163) and with any related information which would enable him to identify the cause and take the appropriate corrective action.

- Finally, an employer must not allow any employee of his to work on a construction site (in whatever capacity) unless and until he has been given —

  (a)   the name of the planning supervisor for the project;

  (b)   the name of the principal contractor for the project; and

  (c)   a copy of the health and safety plan or such part of that plan as is relevant to the construction work which the employee in question is required or expected to carry out.

A self-employed person is also prohibited from starting work on a construction site unless he (or she) too has been given the information referred to in (a), (b) and (c) above.

Construction (Health, Safety & Welfare) Regulations 1996

- The Construction (Health, Safety & Welfare) Regulations 1996, which came into force on 2 September 1996, impose requirements with respect to the health, safety and welfare of persons at work carrying out "construction work" (defined below), and of others who may be affected by that work.

  Note: The 1996 Regulations revoke and (to a large extent) replace the Construction (General Provisions) Regulations 1961 (SI 1961/1580), the Construction (Working Places) Regulations 1966 (SI 1966/94) and the Construction (Health & Welfare) Regulations 1966 (SI 1966/95).

- It is the duty of every employer whose employees are carrying out construction work (and of every self-employed person carrying out construction work) to comply with the provisions of the 1996 Regulations insofar as they affect him (or her) or any person at work under his control or relate to matters which are within his control. Any person (other than a particular employer or self-employed person), who controls the way in which work is carried out on a construction site, must also comply with the 1996 Regulations insofar as they relate to matters which are within his control.

Duties of employees

- Employees engaged on construction work must comply with their duties under the 1996 Regulations (e.g., by using and operating plant, equipment and vehicles safely; by reporting any defects which may endanger health and safety; by wearing the appropriate personal protective equipment; and so on). Employees must likewise cooperate with their employers in their efforts to comply with their duties under those Regulations.

- The following is a consolidation and summary of the principal provisions of the 1996 Regulations. Further practical guidance is to be found in HSE publication HS(G)150 (*Health & Safety in Construction*) and in related HSE publications and leaflets listed at the end of this section.

SAFE PLACE OF WORK

- Every employer working on a construction site is duty bound to take all reasonably practicable steps to ensure that the site itself, the workplaces he controls on that site, and the means of access to (and egress from) those workplaces, do not present a risk to the health and safety of the people he employs. Workers must have sufficient space in which to work, with due regard to the type of work on which they are engaged. No person, whether worker or otherwise (other than a person whose job it is to make that part safe) should be allowed access to any part of a construction site which is intrinsically unsafe (Reg. 5).

- A construction site and every place of work on that site must, so far as is reasonably practicable, be kept in good order and in a reasonable state of cleanliness. The site perimeters must be delineated with suitable signs, and the site itself so arranged that its extent is readily identifiable.

- Timber and materials with projecting nails must never be used in any situation in which they are likely to cause injury. They must be removed promptly and stacked or stored in a safe place. Loose materials, which are not required for immediate use, must not be placed or allowed to remain on any platform, gangway, or floor so as to restrict the free passage of workers. Such materials should be removed, stacked or stored so as to leave an unobstructed passage. Building materials must be correctly and safely stacked — but must never be stacked in such a way as to be likely to topple over or to overload any floor, roof or working platform.

Training

- Construction workers (such as young people new to the industry), who do not have the training, technical know-how or experience needed to avoid risks to their health and safety when carrying out a particular work activity, must not be allowed to carry out that activity unless working under the direction of, or closely supervised by, persons who have that training, knowledge or experience (Reg. 28).

Plant and equipment

- All plant and equipment (machines, tools, appliances or vehicles) must be maintained in good working order and be repaired as often as need be to ensure that (when properly used) it does not present a risk to the health and safety of construction workers whose job it is to operate or use that plant and equipment (Reg. 27).

Traffic routes on construction sites

- Traffic routes on construction sites must be so organised and situated as to ensure, so far as is reasonably practicable, that pedestrians and vehicles can move safely about the site without posing a risk to other persons. Every traffic route must be large enough to accommodate the persons or vehicles using it, and must be suitably signposted. Doors and gates used by pedestrians, and which open directly onto any vehicular traffic route, must be so positioned and kept separate from that traffic route as to provide pedestrians with a clear view of approaching vehicles or plant.

- Every loading bay must have at least one exit point for the exclusive use of pedestrians. If it is unsafe for pedestrians to use an entrance or exit gate primarily intended for vehicles, one or more unobstructed doors must be provided in the immediate vicinity of that gate and be clearly marked as being for the exclusive use of pedestrians (Reg. 15).

Doors and gates

- Sliding, powered or upward-opening doors, gates or hatches must be fitted with suitable safety devices to ensure (a) that they do not come off their tracks; (b) that they do not fall back once opened; or (c) that they do not cause injury by trapping people as they close. Power-operated doors, gates and hatches must be capable of being operated manually, unless they are designed to open automatically when there is a power failure. These requirements do not apply to any door, gate or hatch which forms part of any mobile plant and equipment (Reg. 16).

Vehicles

- Suitable and sufficient steps must be taken to prevent or control the unintended movement of any vehicle. When any such vehicle is being driven, operated or towed about a construction, the driver or person having control of that vehicle must carry out his job in a safe and responsible way and must warn any persons who are liable to be put at risk from the movement of the vehicle.

- No person may ride (or be required or permitted to ride) on any vehicle being used for the purposes of construction work other than in a seat or cabin designated for that purpose. Nor should any person remain (or be permitted or required to remain) on such a vehicle while loose material is being loaded or unloaded, unless there is a designated safe and secure place on the vehicle for just such a person. Suitable measures must be taken to prevent any vehicle engaged in excavating, handling or tipping materials from falling into any excavation or pit, or into water, or from overrunning the edge of any embankment or earthwork. If a railed vehicle becomes derailed, suitable plant and equipment must be provided and used either to replace the vehicle on its track or otherwise move it safely (Reg. 17).

Fresh air

- Every enclosed place of work on a construction site (tunnel, excavation, shaft or other confined space), and every approach to such a place must have a sufficient supply of fresh or purified air for the benefit of any person working or present in that place. Any plant or machinery used to generate or introduce a supply of fresh or purified air must be fitted with a reliable device designed to give a visible or audible warning of any failure of the plant (Reg. 23).

Temperature and weather protection

- The temperature during working hours in any indoor place of work must, so far as is reasonably practicable, be comfortable for the persons working there. People working out of doors must be protected, so far as is reasonably practicable, from exposure to the vagaries of the weather — having regard to the type of work on which they are engaged and any protective clothing or equipment provided for their use (Reg. 24).

Fire prevention, emergency routes, exits, etc.

- Suitable and sufficient steps must be taken to prevent any risk of injury to construction workers arising from fire, explosion or flooding, or from any substance liable to cause asphyxiation.

- Construction sites must be provided with a sufficient number of suitably signposted emergency routes and fire exits leading as directly as possible to identified safe areas. All such routes and exits must be kept clear and unobstructed and must, where necessary, be equipped with emergency or secondary lighting to enable them to be used at any time. When providing emergency routes and exits, the person having control of the construction site must pay due regard to the type of work being carried on at the site; its characteristics and size; the number of places of work on the site; the plant and equipment being used; the number of persons likely to be present on the site at any one time; and the physical and chemical properties of any substances or materials on (or likely to be on) the site.

• Fire-fighting equipment, fire detectors, and alarm systems must be provided and suitably located on every construction site. All such equipment and applicancesmust be readily accessible, clearly signposted, properly maintained, and examined and tested at regular intervals. People at work on construction sites should know how to use fire-fighting equipment and should not be permitted to engage in any activity which poses a fire risk (however small) without having first been instructed as to the measures to be taken to prevent that risk (Regs 18 & 19).

Emergency procedures

• On every construction site, suitable and sufficient arrangements must be put in place for dealing with any foreseeable emergency. Those arrangements (including emergency evacuation porocedures and the names and duties of the persons responsible for implementing and overseeing those procedures) must be made known to all persons present on site and must be tested (e.g., by practice drills) at regular intervals (Reg 20).

ACTION TO PREVENT PERSONS FALLING

• If any person engaged on construction work (or any authorised visitor) is liable to fall a distance of two or more metres from any working platform, the person responsible for that platform must do whatever needs to be done to prevent that person from falling.Reg. 6).

Note: The term "working platform" means any platform used as a place of work or as a means of access to (or egress from) that place. It includes any scaffold, suspended scaffold, cradle, mobile platform, trestle, gangway, run, gantry, stairway and crawling ladder. Working platforms must ordinarily be erected and made available whenever work cannot be safely done on or from the ground, or from part of a building or other permanent structure.

• In short, contractors, sub-contractors, and self-employed persons engaged in construction work must take sufficient and suitable steps to prevent workers (or themselves) falling a distance of two or more metres, whether from a working platform or into any excavation (such as an earthwork, trench, well, shaft or tunnel). Working platforms must be fitted with strong, rigid and secure guard-rails, toe-boards, barriers or other similar means of protection (see next paragraph). If guard-rails and toe-boards are *not* a practicable proposition — given the nature or duration of the work to be carried out — any worker likely to fall a distance of two metres or more *must* be equipped with, and *must* wear or use, suitable "personal suspension equipment" (e.g; a securely anchored safety harness or belt, a boatswain's chair, abseiling equipment, etc). Otherwise, the employer or responsible person must install some other suitable sufficient and reliable apparatus (such as a safety net or sheet) which is designed to arrest such a fall (*ibid*).

- Any working platform from which a person is liable to fall a distance of two or more metres must be equipped with a strong and secure barrier or with guard-rails and toe-boards. The topmost guard-rail should be at least 910 millimetres above the surface of the platform. The gap between it and the next guard-rail (and between other guard-rails) must not exceed 470 millimetres Toe-boards must be at least 510 millimetres high. The combination of barriers, guard-rails and toe-boards on a working platform must be designed not only to prevent people from falling a distance of two or more metres, but also to prevent materials and objects falling on to persons walking or working below that platform (*ibid*).

Personal suspension equipment

- Personal suspension equipment (safety belts, harnesses, boatswain's chairs, and the like), must be strong enough to support the weight of the person wearing them (including the weight of any tools and appliances that person may be carrying or using at the time). They must also be continuously attached or anchored to a secure structure which is itself capable of safely bearing the weight of the worker in question (and the tools or equipmen he or she is using or carrying at the time) (*ibid*).

Safety nets or sheets

- If personal suspension equipment is inappropiate or impracticable, given the nature or duration of the work to be carried out, safety nets (or safety sheets) and similar must be installed beneath the working platform or place (such as a fragile roof) from or through which a worker is liable to fall a distance of two or more metres. Furthermore, they must be strong enough (as must their anchorage points) to arrest the fall and support the weight of any such worker. Safety nets may only be removed, and then only briefly, to permit the access of workmen and materials (*ibid*).

Disposal of waste materials

• Scaffolding, tools, waste materials, etc. must always be lowered to the ground from any height, and must never be thrown, tipped or shot down where they are liable to cause injury. If proper lowering is impracticable (e.g., during demolition work), steps must be taken to ensure that workers and passers-by are not exposed to risk from falling or flying debris.

Roof work

• If construction work is to take place on a fragile roof or other surface, through which a person is liable to fall a distance of two or more metres, suitable and sufficient crawling ladders or boards must be provided for that person's use. These must be well-constructed, properly supported and securely fixed or anchored to the surface or (if the roof is sloping) over the roof ridge. Unless the work to be done on a sloping roof is not extensive, barriers must also be provided at the lower edge of the roof to prevent any person falling from that edge. Alternatively, the work should be undertaken from a properly secured and supported working platform equipped with guard-rails and toe-boards. Crawling boards or ladders need not be used if adequate handholds and footholds are afforded by the battens or other similar members to the extent that work on the roof is as safe as it would be if crawling boards or ladders had been provided. Work on a sloping roof having a pitch of more than 30 degrees, or on a roof which is otherwise unsafe by reason of bad weather or the poor condition of the surface of the roof, may only be undertaken by competent and experienced workmen (*ibid*).

• Although this is no longer a statutory requirement, common sense dictates that warning notices be posted on all fragile roofs and other surfaces through which any person is liable to fall a distance of two or more metres.

STABILITY & SAFETY OF WORKING PLATFORMS

- Working platforms (such as scaffolds) must be strong, rigid, stable and secure, and must be incapable of being accidentally displaced (either while in use or while being dismantled). The platform itself should be *at least* 600 millimetres wide (wider, if necessary) so as to facilitate the free and safe movement of workers, equipment and materials. The working surface of any such platform must be level and free of projections or substances likely to cause workers to trip or slip. Gaps in the surface (or floor) of the platform, and between the platform and any adjacent structure, should be as narrow as need be to prevent falls of people, tools or materials (Schedules 1 & 2).

- Experienced and competent workmen only may be employed to erect, add to, alter or dismantle working platforms. Furthermore, every working platform must be inspected by a competent person (a) before being taken into use for the first time; (b) after any substantial addition, dismantling or other alteration; (c) after any event likely to have affected its strenght or stability; and (d) at regular intervals (not exceeding seven days) since the last inspection (as to which see *REPORTS* below and **Tables 2 & 3** on pages 134 and 137, respectively.

- Working platforms must be properly maintained, and fixed or secured in such a way as to prevent any possibility of accidental displacement. Partly-erected or dismantled platforms must not be used in any circumstances. Access to such platforms must be effectively blocked, and a notice posted warning that they must not be used.

- Working platforms must never be overloaded or subjected to violent shocks during the placement or movement of building materials. Wherever possible, loads must be evenly distributed. Materials should not be stored on such platforms unless needed for work within a reasonable time.

- The standards (or uprights) of working platforms must be either vertical or slightly inclined towards the building or other structure supporting it. A sufficient number of uprights must be used to ensure that the platform is stable. The foot of every upright must rest on an adequate base plate to prevent slipping or sinking. Ledgers must be as nearly as possible horizontal and securely fastened to the uprights. The putlogs or other supports on which a platform rests must be securely fastened to the ledgers or uprights. Where one end of a putlog is supported by a wall, it must extend on to the wall sufficiently to provide an adequate supporting surface.

- Working platforms must be securely supported or suspended and sufficiently and properly strutted or braced to prevent collapse. They must be rigidly connected to the building or structure unless so designed and constructed as to ensure stability without such connection. Any platform which can be moved on wheels or skids must be inherently stable or adequately weighted at the base. It must be adequately secured to prevent accidental movement and be incapable of being moved other than by the application of force at or near the base.

Inspections of working platforms, safety harnesses, etc.

- Working platforms (and their components) and all items of personal suspension equipment must be inspected by a competent person (a) *before* being taken into use for the first time; (b) *after* any substantial addition, dimsmantling or other alteration; (c) *after* any event likely to have affected its strength or stability; and (d) at regular intervals thereafter (not exceeding seven days since the last inspection).

- If the person carrying out the inspection is not satisfied that construction work can safely be carried out on a working platform or that personal suspension equipment is unsound, the platform and/or the equipment must not be used until the defects identified by the inspection have been satisfactorily remedied (Reg. 29). See also *Reports* below.

LADDERS AND SAFETY

- Every ladder and folding step-ladder used in construction work must be stoutly constructed and properly maintained. Ladders must not be used if one or more rungs are missing, or if the rungs are secured only by means of nails, spikes or similar. The rungs of a ladder must be properly fixed to the stiles or sides. If the tenon joints of a ladder are not secured by wedges, reinforcing ties must be used. The grain in wooden stiles or sides, and in the rungs, must run lengthways. These rules do not apply to crawling ladders or crawling boards used on sloping roofs (Schedule 5).

- When in use, a ladder or folding step-ladder must be securely fixed near to its upper resting place or, in the case of a vertical ladder, near to its upper end. If such fixing is impracticable, the ladder must be fixed at or near to its lower end. A ladder must have a firm footing and never be permitted to stand on loose bricks or rubble. Where necessary, it should be secured to prevent undue swaying or sagging. It must be equally and properly supported on each stile or side. If it is impracticable to secure either end of the ladder, a person must be stationed at the foot of a ladder, when it is in use, to prevent it slipping. Unless a ladder is used only for the purposes of access from one place to another, the above requirements do not apply to a ladder which is not more than three metres long, always provided that it is securely positioned when in use.

- The upper portion of a ladder must extend at least 1.05 metres above the landing place or the highest rung to be reached by any person using the ladder. If this is not practicable or possible, other adequate handholds must be made available. Each rung of the ladder must provide an adequate foothold for the user.

- Ladders or a run of ladders rising a vertical distance of more than nine metres must be provided with an intermediate landing stage. The distance between successive landing stages must never exceed nine metres. Each landing stage must be of adequate dimensions and, if a person is liable to fall a distance of more than two metres, must be fitted with guard-rails and toe-boards positioned in the manner described above.

EARTHWORKS, SHAFTS, ETC.

- To ensure that people do not become trapped or buried, all reasonably practicable steps must be taken to prevent the collapse or dislodgement of loose earth, stones and rocks from the sides, and, where appropriate, the roof of any excavation, earthwork, trench, well, shaft, tunnel or underground working. To that end, all such excavations, trenches, wells, etc. must be sufficiently supported (using appropriate equipment) as the work progresses.

- Adequate precautions must be taken to prevent any person, vehicle, plant and equipment, or any accumulation of earth or other material, from falling into an excavation. Nor should any vehicles, material, plant or equipment be placed or moved near any excavation if doing so is likely to cause the excavation to collapse (Reg. 12).

Table 2
Regulation 29(1)
The Construction (Health, Safety & Welfare) Regulations 1996
(SI 1996/1592)
PLACES OF WORK REQUIRING INSPECTION

Column 1 *Place of work*	**Column 2** *Time of inspection*
1. Any working platform (or part thereof) or any personal suspension equipment provided in accordance with the Regulations.	(a) Before being taken into use for the first time; (b) after any substantial addition, dismantling or other alteration; and (c) after any event likely to have affected its strength or stability.
2. Any excavation which is supported (shored-up or timbered) to prevent danger from an accidental collapse or dislodgement of rock, earth, etc.	(a) Before any person carries out any work at the start of every shift; (b) after any event likely to have affected the strength or stability of the excavation (or of any part of the excavation); and (c) after any accidental fall of rock or earth or other material.
3. Cofferdams and caissons	(a) Before any person carries out work at the start of every shift; and (b) after any event likely to have affected the strength or stability of the cofferdam or caisson (or any part thereof).

- Excavations, earthworks, trenches, etc., which are supported or timbered, must be inspected by a *competent person* (a) at the beginning of each shift and (b) after any event (including any accidental fall of rock or earth, or other material) likely to have affected the strength or stability of the excavation or any part of that excavation (see **Table 2** above)

- The results of those daily inspections may, if the contractor chooses, be entered on factory form F91 (Part 1, Section B), although this is no longer a statutory requirement. If the person carrying out the inspection is not satisfied that construction work can safely start (or continue), work on or inside that excavation must be suspended until the defects identified by the inspection have been satisfactorily put to rights. See also *REPORTS* and **Table 3** below.

Note: Form F91 and other forms referred to in this section are available from HSE Publications. (See *FURTHER INFORMATION* at the end of this section).

- The job of erecting, modifying or dismantling timbering and other supports used to secure excavations, shafts, earthworks, etc. should be handled only by experienced and competent workmen. Routine examination of these supports should also be undertaken by a competent person.

- Every excavation, shaft or tunnel must be provided with suitable and efficient means of escape against the possibility of flash flooding.

COFFERDAMS AND CAISSONS

- Cofferdams and caissons must be designed and constructed so as to be safe and watertight, and may only be erected, altered or dimantled by competent and experienced workers. Furthermore, they must be inspected by a *competent person* (a) *before* any person carries out any work at the start of every shift, and (b) after any event likely to have affected the strength or stability of the cofferdam or caisson or of any part thereof. If the person carrying out the inspection is not satisfied that construction work can safely start (or continue), no person may work in the relevant cofferdam or caisson until the defects identified by the inspection have been satisfactorily put to rights (Reg. 13). See **Table 2** opposite and *REPORTS* and **Table 3** below (page 137).

EXPLOSIVES

- Explosives must not be handled or used on a construction site except by or under the immediate control of a competent person who is familiar with explosives and aware of the dangers connected with their use. Steps must be taken to ensure that people are moved to a safe distance, *before* a charge is fired, to ensure that they are not exposed to risk from the explosion itself or from any flying debris (Reg. 11).

LIGHTING

- Adequate lighting (preferably natural light) must be provided and maintained in all work areas and their approaches, and in places where lifting and lowering operations are carried on. The colour of any artificial lighting must not adversely affect or change the perception of any safety sign or signal propvided for health and safety purposes. Where appropriate, emergency (or secondary) lighting , must also be provided in any place where the failure of the primary lighting would pose a risk to the health and safety of persons working or present in that place (Reg. 25).

COLLAPSE OF WEAKENED STRUCTURES

- All practicable precautions must be taken (e.g., by the use of temporary guys, stays, supports and fixings) to avoid danger to employees from the collapse of any part of a building or other structure during any temporary state of weakness or instability in that building or structure.

- If construction work is likely to reduce or weaken the security or stability of any part of a building or other structure, steps must be taken (either by shoring or otherwise) to prevent danger to any employee from the collapse of that building or structure, or from the fall of any part of that structure.

- The demolition or dismantling of any structure (building, tunnel, shaft, bridge, viaduct waterworks, earthworks, etc), which gives rise to a risk of danger to any person, must not only be properly planned but must be carried out in a way which, so far as is reasonably practicable, will prevent such a risk (Reg. 9).

- The Register and Certificates (F2202 referred to earlier, as well as the General Register Form F36), must be preserved either on the site of the operations or works or at the contractor's office. These registers, etc. must at all reasonable times be open to inspection by a health and safety inspector.

REPORTS

- Where, in the circumstances described in Table 2 above (and in the accompanying text), a *competent person* is required to carry out an inspection, he (or she) must prepare a report including the particulars set out in **Table 3** opposite *before* the end of the working period within which the inspection was completed. Furthermore, he must, within 24 hours of completing his inspection, hand or send the report (or a copy of it) to the person on whose behalf the inspection was carried out.

Table 3

Regulation 30

The Construction (Health, Safety & Welfare) Regulations 1996
(SI 1996/1592)

PARTICULARS TO BE INCLUDED IN A REPORT OF INSPECTION

1 Name and address of the person on whose behalf the inspection was carried out.

2. Location of the place of work inspected.

3. Description of the place of work or part of that place inspected (including any plant and materials, if any).

4. Date and time of the inspection.

5. Details of any matter indentified that could give rise to a risk to the health or safety of any person.

6. Details of any action taken as a result of any matter identified in paragraph 5 above.

7. Details of any further action considered necessary.

8. Name and position of the person making the report.

Notes

A. A report need not be prepared in respect of any mobile tower scaffold unless it remains erected in the same place for a period of seven days or more.

B. A report of an inspection, carried out after any substantial addition, dismantling or other alteration to any working platform or personal suspension equipment, need not be prepared more than once in any 24-hour period

C. A report of an inspection of any supported or timbered excavation, or of any cofferdam or caisson, before (in either case) any person carries out any work at the start of every shift, need not be prepared more than once in any 24-hour period.

D. No report need be prepared in respect of any working platform or alternative means of support from which a person is liable to fall a distance of two metres or less

- The report (or a copy of it) must be kept in the site manager's office for so long as construction work continues on that site. Once the work is completed, it must be kept for a further period of three months (starting with the date on which the work was completed) at the office of the person on whose behalf the inspection was carried out. Every such report must be kept available for inspection by an inspector of the relevant enforcing authority. If the inspector asks for a copy of any such report (or for extracts), the copy or extract must be sent or handed to the inspector on request (*ibid*; Reg. 30).

WELFARE FACILITIES

- Every employer and every self-employed person on a construction site must see to it that his (or her) workers are provided with (or have ready access to) suitable and sufficient sanitary conveniences, washing facilities (including showers, if required by the nature of the work or for health reasons), changing rooms, facilities for storing both street clothes and working clothes. There must also be a place in which workers can rest or eat their meals, and an adequate and readily-accessible supply of wholesome drinking water. The person in overall control of a construction site is duty-bound to ensure, so far as is reasonably practicable, that every employer and self-employed person working on the site provides the welfare facilities described above (Reg. 22).

Sanitary facilities

- Rooms containing sanitary facilities (toilets, urinals, etc.) must be provided at *readily accessible places*; must be adequately ventilated and lit; and must be kept in a clean and orderly conditions. Separate facilities must be provided for men and women, except where and so far as each convenience is in a separate room, the door of which is capable of being secured from the inside. For reasons of hygiene, toilet blocks must be situated adjacent to a washroom (as to which, see next paragraph) (Schedule 6, paras 1 to 3).

Washing facilities

- Adequate and suitable washing facilities must be provided at *readily accessible places* in the immediate vicinity of every sanitary facility, whether or not such facilities are situated elsewhere on the same construction site. Showers must be provided if required by the nature of the work or for health reasons. If a dedicated shower-room is provided as an entirely separate facility, it need not be located adjacent to a toilet block.

- Washing facilities must also be situated in the vicinity of any changing rooms (see below). Again, this rule applies even if washing facilities are available elsewhere on the same site. On a 'smallish' site, the sensible option would be to locate washing facilities, toilet blocks and changing rooms together, in a central position — always provided that they are conveniently accessible to persons wishing to use them. On a larger site, it may well be necessary to provide more than one amenity block (incorporating toilets, washrooms, showers, changing rooms and locker-rooms).

- Washing facilities (basins, showers, foot-troughs, etc.) must be equipped with a supply of clean hot and cold, or warm, (preferably) running water, as well as with soap or soap dispensers, towels and/or other suitable means of drying. The facilities, and the rooms containing them, must be sufficiently well-ventilated and lit, and must be kept in a clean and orderly condition.

- Unless washbasins are provided for washing the face, hands and forearms only, separate washing facilities must be provided for men and women. Men and women may, however, use the same washing facilities if the room in which they are provided is intended to be used by only one person at a time, and the door to that room is capable of being secured from the inside.

Drinking water

- On every construction site, an adequate supply of wholsesome drinking water must be provided (or made available) at readily accessible and suitable places. For safety and hygiene reasons, the supply must be conspicuously marked by an appropriate sign indicating that the water is drinking water.

- Unless the drinking water is delivered by a fountain or jet from which persons can drink easily, the person having control of the site (or the relevant employer) must see to it that a sufficient number of cups or other drinking vessels is also provided.

Accommodation for clothing

- Suitable and sufficient 'accommodation for clothing' (i.e; a cloakroom or similar) must be provided:

  (a) for the storage of clothing (jackets, shirts, overcoats, shoes, etc.) which workers do not wear during their normal working hours; and

  (b) for the storage of special clothing (overalls, aprons, work boots, helmets etc.) which is not taken home at the end of a working day or shift.

  Every such cloakroom must also include or allow for facilities for drying clothing. Although the site manager (or employer) is not obliged to provide lockable lockers for the safekeeping of workers' valuables, a cloakroom might well be held not to be 'suitable and sufficient' in the absence of any such facility or equivalent arrangement.

Facilities for changing clothing

- One or more 'suitable and sufficient' changing rooms must be provided for the use of construction workers who have to wear special clothing for the purposes of their work and who cannot be reasonably be expected (for reasons of health or propriety) to change elsewhere. For reasons of propriety also, separate changing rooms must be provided for men and women.

Rest rooms

- Suitable, sufficient and readily accessible rest rooms (or rest areas) must be provided or made available for workers on construction sites. The rooms or areas must include suitable arrangements to protect non-smokers from discomfort caused by tobacco smoke and, where necessary, must include suitable and separate rest facilities for any worker who is either pregnant or a nursing mother.

General

- A contractor or employer has a duty in law to provide safe access to (and egress from) the workplace and to (and from) any and all welfare facilities (washrooms, toilets, rest rooms, etc.) provided in accordance with the 1966 Regulations. Nor should he (or she) lose sight of his overriding duty and criminal liability under section 2(1)(3) of the Health and Safety at Work etc. Act 1974 to provide and maintain a working environment for employees that is, so far as is reasonably practicable, safe, without risks to health, and adequate as regards facilities and arrangements for their welfare at work.

2. Construction (Lifting Operations) Regulations 1961

- The 'Lifting Operations' Regulations deal with the construction, examination and use of hoists and lifts, other types of lifting appliances and gear, mobile cranes, plant and equipment, and scaffolds used in construction work.

Definitions

- For these purposes:

  o A *hoist* is a lifting machine, whether worked by mechanical power or not, with a carriage, platform or cage, the movement of which is restricted by a guide or guides, but does not include a lifting appliance used for the movement of trucks or wagons on a line of rails.

  o A *lifting appliance* is a crab, winch, pulley block or gin wheel used for raising or lowering, and any hoist, crane, sheer legs, excavator, dragline, piling frame, aerial cableway, aerial ropeway or overhead runway.

  o The term *lifting gear* means a chain sling, rope sling, or similar gear, and a ring, link, hook, plate clamp, shackle, swivel or eye-bolt.

  o A *mobile crane* is any crane (other than a crane mounted on rails) which is capable of travelling under its own power.

  o The expression *plant and equipment* includes any plant, equipment, gear, machinery, apparatus or appliance, or any part of such plant or equipment.

o   A *scaffold* is any temporary structure used in connection with construction work which enables persons to obtain access to (or which facilitates the movement of materials to or from) any place at which such work is performed, and includes any working platform, working stage, gangway, run, ladder or step ladder (other than an independent ladder or step ladder which does not form part of such a structure), together with any guard rail, toe board or other safeguards and all fixings, but does not include a lifting appliance or a structure used merely to support such an appliance or to support other plant and equipment.

Note: A *suspended scaffold*, on the other hand, is a scaffold suspended by ropes or chains and capable of being raised or lowered by such means (but does not include a boatswain's chair or similar appliance).

*   The obligations and duties imposed by the Regulations may be summarised as follows:

LIFTING APPLIANCES

*   Every lifting appliance (including its working gear and any other plant or equipment used to anchor or fix it) must be of good mechanical construction, sound material, adequate strength and free from patent defect. It must be examined at least once a week by the driver or other competent person, and a report of each such examination entered on Factory form F91 (Part 1, Section C) — which latter must be kept available for inspection by a health and safety inspector (Reg. 10).

*   Lifting appliances must not be used unless they are adequately and securely supported. Every part of a stage, scaffold, framework or other structure, and every mast, beam, pole, or other article of plant or equipment, must be of good construction and adequate strength. The framework of crabs and winches (other than jack rolls), including their bearers, must be of metal. Anchoring and fixing arrangements must be adequate and secure, as must any temporary attachment or connection of a rope, chain or other plant or equipment, used in the erection or dismantling of a lifting appliance. Any jib or boom separated from a crane during dismantling must be clearly marked so as to indicate the crane of which it is a part.

- An unobstructed passageway, at least 600 mm wide, must be maintained between any part of a lifting appliance having a travelling or slewing motion and any guard-rails, fencing or other fixture on a stage, gantry or other place where the lifting appliance is in use. If this presents problems, or is totally impracticable, the employer or contractor must take reasonable steps to ensure the safety of employees when the lifting appliance is being operated (Reg. 12).

- Platforms for crane drivers and signallers must be of sufficient size, close-planked or plated, and easily accessible. If the crane driver or signaller is liable to fall a distance of more than two metres, the platform he or she uses must be equipped with guard-rails and toe-boards. The guard-rails must be at least 910 mm above the platform. The toe boards must be at least 200 mm deep and so placed as to prevent the fall of persons, materials and tools. The space between the top of the toe board and the bottom of the lowest guard-rail must not exceed 700 mm (Reg. 13(1)).

- The driver of any power-driven lifting appliance must be provided with an enclosed and weatherproof cabin, so constructed as to allow easy access to those parts within the cabin which need periodic inspection or maintenance. The cabin must be capable of being heated during cold weather and must present the driver with a clear and unrestricted view of the work on which he or she is engaged (Reg. 14).

Note: These requirements do not apply in cases where the driver is indoors and protected from the weather. Nor do they apply to a hoist, other than a hoist operated only from one position alongside the winch; or to a lifting appliance mounted on wheels and having a maximum safe working load of one tonne or less. A machine which incorporates a lifting appliance, where the primary purpose of that machine is not that of a lifting appliance, is also excluded, as are lifting appliances used only occasionally or for short periods at a time.

- Drums or pulley rounds used in connection with lifting appliances must be of suitable diameter and designed for the chains or ropes wound on them. A chain or rope which terminates at the winding drum must be properly secured to the drum itself. Furthermore, at least two turns of the chain or rope must remain on the drum in every operating position of the lifting appliance (Reg. 15).

- Crane, crabs and winches (other than jack rolls) must be equipped with efficient brakes (or equivalent safety devices) to prevent suspended loads falling from them and to control such loads as they are being lowered. Levers, handles, switches and other controls must be incapable of accidental movement or displacement. Amendments proposed by the Health & Safety Commission in November 1994 and expected to be incorporated in new Information for Employee Regulations in 1995 will mean that levers, handles, switches and related operating controls on lifting appliances will no longer need to be marked to indicate their purpose and mode of operation. The marking of such controls is now the responsibility of the manufacturer (Reg. 16).

- An person liable to fall a distance of more than two metres while examining, repairing or lubricating a lifting appliance, must be afforded safe means of access to, and egress from, the working area (including suitable handholds and footholds, where appropriate) (Reg. 17).

- Pulley blocks and gin wheels must be securely fixed to their poles and beams. The latter must adequately and properly secured and be strong enough to support their pulley blocks or gin wheels and loads with safety (Reg. 18).

- Precautions must be taken to ensure the stability of lifting appliances used on slopes or on soft or uneven surfaces. Cranes must be securely anchored and adequately weighted with a suitable ballast. The rails and sleepers on which a crane is mounted must never be used as anchorage points. The appliances used for the anchorage or ballasting of a crane must be examined by a competent person on each occasion before the crane is erected (Reg. 19).

- Every crane erected on a construction site must be tested by a competent person (*before* it is taken into use) to ensure that it is securely anchored or adequately weighted. The same rule applies when a crane is moved or repositioned or if there is any change in the arrangements made to anchor or weight it. The test will consist of the imposition either:

  (a) of a load of 25 per cent above the maximum load to be lifted by the crane as erected (at the positions where there is the maximum pull on each anchorage), or

  (b) of a lesser load arranged to provide an equivalent test of the anchorage or ballasting arrangements.

A record of every such test and of the test results (containing the particulars required by the Lifting Plant & Equipment (Records of Test & Examination etc.) Regulations 1992 [SI 1992/195]) must be made as soon as the test has been completed. Although there is no longer a prescribed form for this purpose (the employer being free to devise his own form or store the required information on computer), the record of the test results must contain the particulars listed in **Table 4** overleaf. The Health & Safety Executive have published a form (F2531) for this purpose but its use is not mandatory. The form is available from HSE Books (as to which, see *FURTHER INFORMATION* at the end of this section).

- If the person who tested the crane considers that the maximum load which it may safely lift is less than its safe working load, he must make a note of that finding in the test record and must see to it that a loading diagram, indicating a modified safe working load, is affixed to the crane in a position where it can readily be seen by the crane driver. If removable weights are used to stabilise a crane, a diagram or notice showing the position and amount of such weights must also be affixed to the crane where it can be readily seen. The Health & Safety Executive will be reviewing the latter requirements in their proposed Consultative Document on Lifting Appliances planned for 1997 (Reg. 19(5) & (6)).

- A crane must not be used or erected in weather conditions likely to endanger its stability. After exposure to such weather conditions, the crane must not be re-used until the anchorage arrangements and ballast have been examined by a *competent person* and any necessary steps have been taken to ensure its stability (Reg. 19(7)).

- In the case of rail-mounted cranes, the rails must be supported on a firm surface. They must have an even running surface, be well-supported, and be of adequate section. They must be joined by fish plates or double chairs; be securely fastened to sleepers or bearers; be laid in straight lines or in curves of such radii that the crane can be moved freely and without danger of derailment; and be provided with adequate stops or buffers on each rail at each end of the track. Rails and equipment must be properly maintained. Sprags, scotches or stocks must be available and used where necessary, or the crane itself provided with effective brakes for the travelling motion. A rail-mounted travelling crane must be equipped with guards designed to remove any loose or dangerous materials from the track (Reg. 20).

Table 4
PARTICULARS REQUIRED IN RECORDS TO BE MADE FOLLOWING A TEST, TEST AND EXAMINATION OR TEST AND THOROUGH EXAMINATION OF LIFTING PLANT AND EQUIPMENT
as prescribed by the Lifting Plant & Equipment (Records of Test & Examination etc.) Regulations 1992 (SI 1992/195)

1. Description, date of manufacture, identification mark and location of the equipment referred to.

2. The safe working load (or loads) and (where relevant) corresponding radii, jib lengths and counterweights.

3. Details of the test, test and examination or test and thorough examination carried out.

4. Date (or dates) of completion of the test, test and examination or test and thorough examination.

5. A declaration that the information is correct and that the equipment has been tested, tested and examined or tested and thoroughly examined in accordance with the appropriate legal provisions, and that it is found free from any defect likely to affect safety.

6. Name and address of the owner of the equipment referred to.

7. Name and address of the person declaring that the test, test and examination or test and thorough examination has been carried out.

8. Date on which the record of the test, test and examination or test and thorough examination was carried out.

9. A number or other means of identifying the record.

Note: If a Scotch derrick crane is mounted on more than one bogie, trolley or wheeled carriage, the crane sleepers or land ties and, if necessary, the bogies, trolleys or wheeled carriages must be properly connected. The rails on which bogies, trolleys or wheeled carriages move must be level (*ibid*).

- An effective interlocking arrangement, between the derricking clutch and the pawl sustaining the derricking drum, must be provided and maintained on every crane with a derricking jib operated through a clutch. The interlocking arrangement must be designed to ensure that the clutch cannot be disengaged unless the pawl is in effective engagement with the derricking drum, and the pawl cannot be disengaged unless the clutch is in effective engagement with the derricking drum. These requirements do *not* apply to a crane in which the hoisting drum and the derricking drum are independently driven, or where the mechanism driving the derricking drum is self-locking (Reg. 22).

- A crane's hoisting mechanism must not be used for any purpose other than raising or lowering a load vertically, unless doing so does not impose undue stress on any part of the crane structure or mechanism, and does not endanger the stability of the crane. However, all such operations must be supervised by a competent person. A crane with a derricking jib must not be used with the jib at a radius exceeding the maximum radius required to be specified for the jib in the record (see **Table 4** opposite) of the results of any test and thorough examination (Reg. 23).

- Lifting appliances (as defined above) may only be operated by trained and competent persons (or by persons undergoing training under the supervision of a qualified trainer). Unless supervised by a competent person, no employee under the age of 18 may be employed either to give signals to the operator of any lifting appliance or to operate a lifting appliance himself (or herself) (Reg. 26).

- Unless he (or she) has a clear and unrestricted view of the load, the person operating a lifting appliance must not do so unless one or more competent persons have been stationed at strategic places to give the necessary signals. Signallers are not necessary in the case of a hoist, or an aerial cable way or ropeway, or (in a case other than a hoist) where the lifting appliance can raise or lower loads vertically only, without any horizontal or slewing motion. In the latter instance, effective arrangements must, however, be made by means of a signalling system, position indicators, or otherwise, for giving the driver or operator as much information as he needs for safe working. Efficient and effective signalling arrangements must be available between the driver of an aerial cable way or ropeway and persons employed at a loading or unloading point (*ibid*).

- Signals given for the movement or stopping of a lifting appliance must be distinctive in character and readily visible (or audible, as the case may be) to (or by) the person for whom they are intended. Devices used for giving sound, colour or light signals must be properly maintained and protected from accidental interference (Reg. 27).

Testing and examination of cranes, etc.

- Cranes, crabs and winches must be tested and thoroughly examined by a competent person at least once every four years. Pulley blocks, gin wheels or sheer legs must not be used in the raising or lowering of loads weighing one tonne or more unless they too have been thoroughly tested and examined. Nor may any of these items be used (or brought back into use after undergoing any substantial alterations or repairs) until thoroughly tested and examined by a competent person, nor until a record has been obtained of the result of every such test and thorough examination, containing the particulars listed in **Table 2** on page 134. The record of every test and through examination must be kept available for inspection on demand by a health and safety inspector (Reg. 28).

- A lifting appliance must not be used unless it has been thoroughly examined by a competent person within the previous 14 months or in the period since it has undergone any substantial alteration or repair (Reg. 28(3)). A written or computer record of the results of that thorough examination (see **Table 5** on page 150 below) must also be obtained from the person who carried out the examination before the appliance can be used or returned to use. Form F2530 may be used for this purpose (as to which, see *FURTHER INFORMATION* at the end of this section).

- A record of the results of every prescribed test and/or thorough examination of a crane, crab, winch or lifting appliance must be made within 28 days. Furthermore, if any such test or examination reveals that the plant or equipment in question cannot be used with safety unless certain repairs are carried out immediately, or within a specified time, the person authenticating the resultant record must send a copy of the particulars in the record to a health and safety inspector at his nearest local office of the Health & Safety Executive (*ibid*; Reg. 28(7).

Marking of safe working loads

- The safe working load (or safe working loads) and a means of identification must be plainly marked:

    (a)   on every crane, crab or winch, and

    (b)   on every pulley block, gin wheel, sheer legs, derrick pole, derrick mast or aerial cable way used in the raising or lowering of any load weighing one tonne or more.

    Similarly, every crane of variable operating radius (including a crane with a derricking jib) must:

    (c)   have plainly marked upon it the safe working load at various radii of the jib, trolley or crab, and, in the case of a crane with a derricking jib, the maximum radius at which the jib may be worked; and

    (d)   be fitted with an accurate indicator, clearly visible to the driver. showing the radius of the jib, trolley or crab, at any time, and the safe working load corresponding to that radius.

    Note: In a consultative document titled *Proposals for Reform of Health & Safety Poster and Notice Requirements*, the Health & Safety Executive has indicated (November 1994) that it intends to review the requirement for the marking of safe working loads on cranes, winches, pulleys, etc. and will very likely propose the revocation of that requirement in a consultative document on lifting equipment planned for 1997.

Indication of safe working load of jib cranes

- No jib crane with a fixed or a derricking jib (other than a mobile crane, see below) may be used unless it has been tested and thoroughly examined fitted with an approved type of automatic safe load indicator. The indicator must be tested by a competent person before the crane is brought into use, and inspected at weekly intervals thereafter whilst the crane is in use. The results of every test and inspection must be entered on form F91 (Part 1, Sections C & E) (as to which, see *FURTHER INFORMATION* at the end of this section) and kept available for inspection at any time by a health and safety inspector (Reg. 30).

Table 5
PARTICULARS REQUIRED IN RECORDS TO BE MADE
FOLLOWING THE THOROUGH EXAMINATION OF A
LIFTING APPLIANCE
as prescribed by the Lifting Plant & Equipment
(Records of Test & Examination etc.) Regulations 1992
(SI 1992/195)

1. Description, identification mark and location of the equipment referred to.

2. Date of the last thorough examination and number of the record of such thorough examination.

3. The safe working load (or loads) and (where relevant) corresponding radii.

4. The date of the most recent test and examination or test and thorough examination and the date and number of other identification of the record of it.

5. Details of any defects found and, where appropriate, a statement of the time by when each defect shall be rectified.

6. Date of completion of the thorough examination.

7. Latest date by which the next thorough examination should be carried out.

8. A declaration that the information is correct and that the equipment has been thoroughly examined in accordance with the appropriate provisions and is found free from any defect likely to affect safety, other than any recorded by virtue of item 5 above.

9. Name and address of the owner of the equipment.

10. Name and address of the person responsible for the thorough examination.

11. Date the record of the thorough examination is made.

12. Name and address of the person who authenticates the record.

13. A number or other means of identifying the record.

- A mobile crane, with either a fixed or a derricking jib, must likewise be fitted with an automatic safe load indicator before it is brought into use. The indicator must be tested before the crane is first brought into use, and on each occasion after it has been wholly or partially dismantled or after each erection, alteration or removal of the crane likely to affect the proper operation of the indicator. The indicator must, in any event, be inspected by a competent person, at least once a week, while the crane is in use (*ibid.*). The prescribed form of record is again F91 (Part 1, Sections C & E).

Note: These requirements do not apply (a) to any guy derrick crane (being a crane of which the mast is held upright solely by means of ropes with the necessary fittings and tightening screws; (b) to any hand crane (which is being used solely for erecting or dismantling another crane); or (c) to any crane having a maximum safe working load of one tonne.

Load not to exceed safe working load

- Cranes, crabs, winches, pulley blocks, gin wheels, sheer legs, derrick poles and derrick masts (or any of their parts) must never be loaded beyond their safe working loads, except when being tested by a competent person (Reg. 31).

- If a crane, crab, winch (other than a piling winch), sheer legs or aerial cable way is used to raise a load equal to, or slightly lower than, its safe working load, the lifting must be halted, after the load has been raised a short distance and before the operation is proceeded with, to determine whether the load can be wholly sustained by the appliance. If more than one lifting appliance is required to raise or lower one load, the plant or equipment used must be arranged and fixed in such a way that none of the appliances used is at any time loaded beyond its safe working load or likely to become unstable. At any event, a competent person must be present to supervise the lifting operation (Reg. 32).

- The jib of a Scotch derrick crane must not be erected between the back stays of the crane. Nor may a Scotch derrick crane be used to move any load lying in the angle between those back stays. Measures must be taken to prevent the foot of the king post of the crane from being lifted out of its socket or support whilst the crane is in use. If the guys of a guy derrick crane cannot be fixed at approximately equal inclinations to the mast, so that the angles between adjacent pairs of guys are approximately equal, other measures must be instituted to ensure the safety and stability of the crane (Reg. 33).

CHAINS, ROPES AND LIFTING GEAR

- Chains, ropes and lifting gear (as defined earlier in this section) used in raising or lowering, or as means of suspension, must be strong and well-made and free from patent defect. Each must be tested and examined by a competent person before being brought into use and at six-monthly intervals thereafter. A report of the result of every such test and examination must be made (containing the particulars listed in **Table 6** opposite) and kept available for inspection by a health and safety inspector (Reg. 34).

- (Except in the case of a fibre rope or a fibre rope sling) all chains, rope and lifting gear must be clearly marked with their safe working loads and identification numbers. A rope or rope sling need not be marked with its safe working load if that information is contained in the record of the six-monthly thorough examination of the rope or rope sling in question (as to which, see *Examination of chains, ropes and lifting gear* below).

- A wire rope must not be used in raising or lowering, or as a means of suspension, if in any length of 10 diameters the total number of visible broken wires exceeds 5 per cent of the total number of wires in the rope.

- No chain rope or lifting gear may be loaded beyond its safe working load other than under supervised test conditions, and then only to the extent authorised by the person carrying out the tests.

Testing of chains, rings, etc. altered or repaired by welding

- If a chain, ring, link, hook, plate clamp, shackle, swivel or eye bolt has been lengthened, altered or repaired by welding, it must be tested and thoroughly examined before being brought back into use either for the purposes of raising or lowering or as a means of suspension. The report of the result of every such test and thorough examination (containing the particulars listed in **Table 4** on page 146) must also be obtained *before* the chain, ring, link etc. is returned to use. These requirements do not, however, apply to chains attached to the buckets of draglines and excavators.

Hooks

- Any hook used for raising or lowering, or as a means of suspension, must either be provided with an efficient device to prevent the displacement of the sling or load from the hook, or be of such shape as to reduce the risk of any such displacement.

Table 6
PARTICULARS OF CHAINS, ROPES
& LIFTING TACKLE
required to be kept under section 26(1)(g) of the Factories Act 1961

1. Description, identification mark and location of every chain, rope, chain sling, rope sling, ring, hook, shackle and swivel.

2. The safe working load or loads and (where relevant) corresponding radii of that equipment.

3. Details and date of completion of the initial test and examination of each item of equipment, as required by section 26(1)(e)).

4. Details and date of completion of each thorough examination made under section 26(1)(e)).

5. Details of any defect found and, where appropriate, a statement of the time by when each defect will be rectified.

6. Date of making of the record required to be obtained under section 26(1)(e), and an identifying number.

7. Latest date by which the next thorough examination made under section 26(1)(d) should be carried out.

8. Name and address of the owner of the equipment referred to.

9. Name and address of the person responsible for the initial test and examination made under section 26(1)(e) or of the six-monthly or more frequent examinations made under section 26(1)(d).

10. Name and address of the person who authenticates the record.

11. A number or other means of identifying the record.

Slings

- Any sling used for raising or lowering on a lifting appliance must be attached to the appliance in such a way as to prevent any damage to any part of the sling or to any part of the lifting gear supporting it. A double or multiple sling may be used for raising or lowering only if the upper ends of the sling legs are connected by means of a strong shackle, ring or link, or if the safe working load of any sling leg is not exceeded as a result of the angle between the sling legs.

- Packing or other suitable means must be used to prevent the edges of a load from coming into contact with any sling, rope or chain, where this could cause danger.

Knotted chains, etc.

- A load must never be raised, lowered or suspended on a chain or wire rope which has a knot tied in any part of the chain or rope under direct tension. Nor may a chain be used to raise, lower or suspend a load if it has been shortened or joined to another chain by means of bolts and nuts inserted through the links.

Examination of chains, ropes and lifting gear

- All chains, ropes and lifting gear in regular use must be thoroughly examined by a competent person at least once every six months. A record of every such thorough examination (see **Table 5** on page 150) must be made as soon as the examination has been completed (Reg. 40).

Annealing of chains and lifting gear

- All chains and lifting gear (other than those described below) must be effectively annealed, or subjected to an appropriate form of heat treatment, at least once every 14 months (or, in the case of chains or slings of half-inch bar or smaller, once every six months). Chains and lifting gear, which are used only irregularly, need only be annealed, etc. when strictly necessary. Particulars of all annealing and heat treatments may be recorded on Factory form F91 (Part 2, Section K) (although this is no longer a statutory requirement) or be kept in some other form signed by the competent person under whose supervision the annealing was carried out (Reg. 41).

Note: Requirements for the annealing or heat treatment of chains and other forms of lifting gear do not apply to :

(a) chains made of malleable cast iron;

(b) plate link chains;
(c) the following when made of steel or of any non-ferrous metal: chains, rings, links, hooks, plate clamps, shackles, swivels and eye bolts;
(d) pitched chains working on sprocket or pocketed wheels;
(e) rings, links, hooks, shackles and swivels — if permanently attached to pitched chains, pulley blocks or weighing machines;
(f) hooks, eye-bolts and swivels which have ball bearings, or screw-threaded or case-hardened parts;
(g) socket shackles secured to wire ropes by white metal cappings;
(h) Bordeaux connections; and
(i) Linden Alimac hoist (rack and pinion hoist).

(*ibid*; Reg. 41 and Schedule 2)

Hoists

- Enclosures and gates on hoists must be at least two metres high, unless a lesser height is sufficient to prevent any person falling down the hoistway, and there is no risk of any person coming into contact with any moving part of the hoist itself. However, no enclosure or gate may be less than 910 mm high. The gates fitted to hoist enclosures must be kept closed unless the hoist is at a loading or unloading stage (Reg. 42).

- A hoist must be equipped with an efficient device designed to support the platform or cage (together with its safe working load) should the hoist ropes or any part of the hoisting gear fail. Suitable devices must also be fitted to ensure that the platform or cage does not over-run the hoist's highest point of travel.

- The construction and installation of a hoist should be such that the hoist can only be operated from one position (but see below). If the operator of a hoist does not have a clear and unrestricted view of the platform or cage throughout its travel, effective arrangements must be made for the operator to receive signals from each landing stage at which the hoist is used to enable him to stop the platform or cage at the appropriate level.

- The winch on a winch-operated hoist must be constructed in such a way that the brake is applied when the control lever (handle or switch) is not held in the operating position. The winch must not be a winch fitted with a pawl and ratchet gear on which the pawl has to be disengaged before the platform or cage can be lowered.

- The safe working load of each hoist must be plainly marked on the platform or cage and must never be exceeded except when being tested by a competent person. Passenger-carrying hoists must display a sign clearly indicating the maximum number of persons that may be carried in safety at any one time. Every non-passenger-carrying hoist must display a prominent notice forbidding the carriage of passengers.

- Any hoist which has been manufactured or substantially altered or substantially repaired must not be returned to use unless it has been tested and thoroughly examined by a competent person. Nor may it be returned to use until that competent person has completed and submitted a written (or computer-stored) record of the results of that test and thorough examination. The record in question *must* contain the particulars listed in **Table 2** on page 134 above.

- A hoist used for carrying people must not be used for that purpose unless, since it was last erected or the height of travel was last altered (whichever occurred later), it has been tested and thoroughly examined by a competent person. Nor may it be used until the person who carried out the test and thorough examination has completed and submitted a record of the results of such test and thorough examination. Every hoist must be thoroughly examined by a competent person at least once every six months, and *must* be taken out of use if more than six months have elapsed since it was last examined. A record of the results of every such thorough examination (containing the particulars listed in **Table 5** on page 150) must be made and submitted within 28 days.

- If any test or examination of a hoist reveals that it is in urgent need of repair and cannot continue to be used with safety until those repairs are carried out, the person responsible for authenticating the record containing the results of that test or examination must send a copy of the particulars entered in that record to his nearest local office of the Health & Safety Executive (Reg. 46(3)).

Carrying persons by means of lifting appliances

- Power-driven lifting appliances must not be used to raise, lower or carry people other than on the driver's platform of a crane or on a hoist or approved suspended scaffold. In the absence of a hoist or approved suspended scaffold a person may be carried in a power-driven lifting appliance if, but only if:

(a)   the appliance can be operated from one position only;

(b)   the winch used in connection with the appliance is fitted with a braking device that operates automatically when the control lever or handle is not being held in the operating position; and

(c)   the person is carried in a suitable chair or cage, or a skip or similar which is at least 910 mm deep and equipped with suitable means for preventing the occupant falling out, and which does not contain materials or tools liable to interfere with his (or her) hand-hold or foothold, or otherwise endanger him.

In exceptional circumstances, a person may be raised, lowered or carried on an aerial cable way or aerial ropeway provided that requirements (b) and (c) above are complied with (Reg. 47).

- No person may be carried in a hoist unless it is provided with a cage, which latter must be so constructed as to prevent any person falling out of it when the cage gate or gates are shut, or from being trapped between any part of the cage and any fixed structure or other moving part of the hoist, or from being struck by articles or materials falling down the hoist way. Furthermore, the cage itself must be equipped with efficient interlocking devices designed to prevent the cage gates being opened except when the cage is at a landing place, and to prevent the cage from moving until the gate (or gates) are closed. Every gate in the hoist way enclosure of a hoist must also be fitted with efficient interlocking devices to secure that the gate cannot be opened except when the cage is at the landing place, and that the cage cannot be moved away from the landing place until the gate is closed. A passenger-carrying hoist must also be equipped with efficient automatic devices designed to ensure that the cage comes to rest at a point above the lowest point of travel of the cage (Reg. 48).

Secureness of loads

- Every part of a load must be securely suspended or supported during raising and lowering operations, and must be adequately secured to prevent danger from slipping or displacement. Steps must be taken to prevent a moving load from coming into contact with any other object. Containers used for raising or lowering stone, bricks, tiles, slates or other objects must be so enclosed, constructed or designed as to prevent the accidental spillage of their contents. This latter requirement does not, however, apply to grabs, shovels and similar excavating receptacles if effective steps are taken to prevent danger to persons from falling objects (Reg. 49).

• Loose materials and other goods must not be placed directly on the platform of a hoist, unless the platform is enclosed or steps have been taken to prevent those items falling from the platform. Hand trucks and wheelbarrows must similarly be scotched or secured on the platform (*ibid*).

• A load must never be left suspended from a lifting appliance unless there is a competent person in charge of the appliance at the time (*ibid*).

Suspended scaffolds (not power-operated)

• Suspended scaffolds, which are *not* raised or lowered by power-driven lifting appliances, must be provided with adequate and suitable chains or ropes and winches. They must be suspended from suitable outriggers, joists, runways or rail tracks, or from some other equally safe anchorage. The winch or other lifting appliance used to raise or lower a suspended scaffold must be provided with a brake or other similar device which comes into operation immediately the winding handle or lever is released. The winch must be protected from the weather and corroding dusts, etc. The outriggers must be of adequate length and strength. They must be installed horizontally and fitted with adequate stops at their outer ends, and must be properly spaced — having regard to the construction of the scaffold and of the runway, joist or rail track on which it is carried.

• Where counterweights are used, they must be securely attached to the outriggers and must be at least three times heavier than the collective weights of the runway (joists or tracks), the suspended scaffold, the persons on the scaffold and any materials carried on the scaffold. Runways, joists and rail tracks must be properly secured to the building or structure itself or, if outriggers are used, to the outriggers.

- Suspension ropes or chains must be securely attached to the outriggers or to the winches, as appropriate. Ropes and chains must be kept in tension. If winches are used, two turns of each suspension rope must be left wound on the winch drums when the scaffold is at its lowest position. The length of each suspension rope must be clearly marked on its winch. Sound and strong materials only may be used in the construction of suspended scaffolds. Metal scaffolds must be free from corrosion and other patent defects. Arrangements must be made to prevent undue tipping, tilting, swinging or horizontal movement whilst the scaffold is in use as a working platform. Wire ropes only should be employed for the raising, lowering or suspension of a scaffold. Fibre ropes and pulley blocks may be used only if the work to be done can be carried out with safety using a cradle or a light-weight suspended scaffold.

- The platform of every suspended scaffold must be closely boarded, planked or plated. The platform itself must be at least 600 mm wide (if used for footing only and not for the deposit of any material), or at least 800 mm wide (if also used for depositing material). The platform must never be used for the support of any higher scaffold. The space between the platform and the working face of the building from which it is suspended must be as small as possible. If, however, workmen sit at the edge of the platform, the space may be a maximum 300 mm wide. If a suspended scaffold is carried on fibre ropes and pulley blocks (see above), the ropes must not be spaced more than 3.20 metres apart. Furthermore, the platform of a light-weight scaffold or cradle (used only for light work, where the use of fibre ropes and pulley blocks can be justified with complete safety) must never be less than 430 mm wide.

- Boatswain's chairs, cages, skips, etc. which are raised and lowered other than by power-driven lifting appliances, must be intrinsically strong and sound, and well-supported on strong and properly-installed and supported outriggers. Suitable means must be provided to prevent any occupant falling out, and measures taken to prevent spinning or tipping in a manner dangerous to the occupant. A skip or other receptacle must be at least 910 mm deep. Boatswain's chairs, cages or skips must be installed and used under the direct supervision of a competent person. They should not be used in circumstances where a suspended scaffold could be used, unless the work to be done is of such short duration as to make the use of a suspended scaffold unreasonable or not reasonably practicable.

- Chains, wire ropes, lifting gear, metal tubes, and other means of suspension for slung scaffolds, must be suitable and strong enough for their intended use, properly and securely fastened to safe anchorage points, kept vertical and taut, and so placed as to ensure the stability of the scaffold. Ropes, other than wire ropes, must never be used for the suspension of a slung scaffold. Chains or wire ropes used to support a slung scaffold must not be permitted to come into contact with any edge or ledge liable to cause fraying or damage. Steps must also be taken to prevent undue horizontal movement of the working platform.

- Cantilever or jib scaffolds must not be used unless they are adequately supported, fixed and anchored, have outriggers of adequate length and strength and, where necessary, are sufficiently and properly strutted or braced to ensure rigidity and stability.

- No figure or bracket scaffold should be used if supported or held by dogs, spikes or similar fixings liable to pull out of the stone work, brickwork or other surface in which they are gripped or fixed.

- No part of a building or other structure may be used to support a scaffold, ladder, folding step-ladder or crawling ladder, unless that part of the building is sufficiently stable and strong to support the load. Neither should gutters be used for this purpose unless they and their fixings are of adequate strength. In the case of overhanging eaves, gutters must not be used unless, in addition, they have been specially designed as walkways.

Trestle scaffolds

- Trestles and supports used to construct trestle scaffolds must be strong, sound, well-built and properly maintained. A trestle scaffold must not be used if the working platform is to be more than 4.50 metres above floor (or ground) level, nor if constructed with more than one tier where folding supports are used. A trestle scaffold must not be erected on a scaffold platform unless the width of the platform is such as to leave sufficient clear space for the transport of materials along the scaffold, and unless the trestles or supports are firmly secured and braced (Reg. 21(2)(a)).

Tests and examinations

- No scaffold, boatswain's chair, cage, skip, or similar, may be brought into use unless (in addition to satisfying the relevant requirements of the Construction (Lifting Operations) Regulations 1961):

  (a)   it has been inspected by a competent person within the previous seven days;

  (b)   it has been inspected by a competent person since exposure to weather conditions likely to have affected its strength of stability or to have displaced any part;

  (c)   a report has been made of the results of every such inspection on Factory form F91 (Part 1, Section A) and signed by the person making the inspection.

  Note: Inspection is not required if a scaffold has been in position for less than seven days, nor is a signed report on Factory form F91 necessary in the case of a ladder scaffold, a trestle scaffold or any scaffold whose working platform is less than 2 metres above ground or floor level (Reg. 22(1)).

- If a different group of workmen is to use a scaffold erected for an earlier or other group of workmen, their employer must take steps, either personally or by a competent agent, to satisfy himself that the scaffold is stable and soundly-constructed, and that it complies with the safeguards specified in these Regulations.

Reports, certificates, etc.

- All reports or records and certificates of test and examination referred to in the preceding paragraphs must be kept (or, if stored on computer, be capable of being inspected and copied) at the office of the contractor or employer for whom those inspections, tests or examinations were carried out. These reports, etc. must be kept and made available for inspection by a health and safety inspector on demand. If asked to do so, the employer or contractor must send copies of (or extracts from) any such reports, certificates or record to his nearest area office of the Health & Safety Executive (Reg. 50).

5. Construction (Head Protection) Regulations 1989

- Under the 1989 Regulations, which came into force on 30 March 1990, every employer carrying out (or having control of) building, demolition or engineering works must issue each of his employees with suitable head protection (hard hats or helmets constructed to British Standard 5240) and must see to it that they wear their helmets while they are at work or walking about the site — *unless*, in his judgement, there is no foreseeable risk of injury to the head other than by falling. However, it is for an employer to decide whether hard hats should be issued, and his right also to promulgate written rules about the wearing of hard hats and to discipline or remove any person who refuses to wear a hard hat in defiance of those rules. However, by virtue of section 11 of the Employment Act 1989, hard hats or helmets need not be worn by Sikhs who are wearing turbans at the time.

  Note: Signs on construction sites concerning the wearing of hard hats will usually read SAFETY HELMETS MUST BE WORN IN THIS AREA, as to which, please turn to the section titled Safety and warning signs elsewhere in this handbook.

- Hard hats selected for use on a building site or works of engineering construction must be designed to provide protection against all foreseeable risks of injury to the head and must be capable of being adjusted to fit the individuals to whom they are issued. Self-employed persons, who are not under the control of another employer or self-employed person or of an employee, must also provide suitable, adjustable hard hats for their own use, and must wear them at all times, unless there is no foreseeable risk of injury to the head other than by falling.

- Every person working on a building site, who has been issued with a hard hat and instructed to wear it, must obey his (or her) employer's rules and wear the hard hat properly. If he loses or damages his hard hat, he must report the matter immediately to his employer (usually the site foreman) and obtain a replacement before returning to work (*ibid*; Regs. 6 & 7).

- Section 9 of the Health & Safety at Work etc. Act 1974 reminds employers that they cannot lawfully charge employees for hard hats (or for any other form of protective clothing or equipment) made available for their use in compliance with health and safety legislation. Nor may an employer charge an employee for replacing a hard hat which has been damaged, lost or stolen.

However, there is nothing to prevent an employer taking the appropriate disciplinary action against an employee whom he reasonably believes to be deliberately damaging or losing his helmet as a ploy to avoid having to wear it.

Duty to visitors

- Although the 1989 Regulations do not require contractors and others in charge of a building site (or similar) to issue hard hats to visitors who are being shown about a site, they must not lose sight of their general duty under section 3 of the 1974 Act "to ensure, so far as is reasonably practicable, that persons not in [their] employment who may be affected thereby are not thereby exposed to risks to their health or safety". In view of the fact that an employer could be prosecuted for failing to criminal prosecution for failing to discharge that duty (whether or not an accident has occurred) it is accepted practice nowadays for visitors to building sites to be required to wear hard hats and to be denied admission unless they do. See also **Occupier of premises** elsewhere in this handbook.

OFFENCES AND PENALTIES

- It is an offence to contravene any of the requirements of the Regulations summarised in the preceding pages. The penalty on summary conviction is a fine of up to £2,000 and, on conviction on indictment, a fine of an unlimited amount. If the offence consists of a failure to discharge a duty under one or other of sections 2 to 6 of the 1974 Act (*q.v.*), the penalty on summary conviction is a fine of up to £20,000 and, on conviction on indictment, a fine of an unlimited amount.

INFORMATION FOR EMPLOYEES

- Under the Health & Safety Information for Employees Regulations 1989 (SI 1989/682), every employer (including every contractor on a building site) is required to display a poster titled *Health & Safety Law: What you should know* in a prominent position (e.g., in the site office or mess-room) where it can be easily seen and read by his employees. Alternatively, he must issue each employee with a leaflet which contains the same information. Copies of the poster and leaflet (ISBN 0 11 701424 9) are available from HSE Publications (see *FURTHER INFORMATION* below).

FURTHER INFORMATION

- The following forms, HSE publications and sector guidance booklets and leaflets are available from HSE Books at the address given on page 328).

Forms

F36
General register for building operations etc
ISBN 0 7176 0452 7   £3.00

F91 (Part 1) (*No longer a statutory requirement*)
Building ops etc: records of inspections, examinations and special tests
ISBN 0 7176 0438 1   £3.75

F91 (Part 1) (Section A) (*No longer a statutory requirement*)
Record of inspections of scaffolding
ISBN 0 7176 0437 3   £3.00

F91 (Part 1) (Section B) (*No longer a statutory requirement*)
Record of weekly thorough examination of excavations etc
ISBN 0 7176 0612 0   £3.50

F91 (Part 1) (Section C & E)
Building ops etc records of weekly inspections, examination and special tests of lifting appliances
ISBN 0 7176 0931 6   £3.50

F91 (Part 2) (Section K) (*No longer a statutory requirement*)
Record of reports on heat treatment of chains & lifting gear
ISBN 0 11 886359 2   £3.50

F2202
Register and certificates of shared welfare arrangements (*No longer a statutory requirement*)
ISBN 0 7176 0443 8   £3.95

F2526
Certificate of thorough test and examination of lifting plant
ISBN 0 11 885479 8   £2.50 for 25 copies

F2527
Report of thorough examination of lifting plant
ISBN 0 7176 0513 2   £2.50

F2530
Record of thorough examination of lifting plant
ISBN 0 7176 0468 3   £3.50 per pad of 10 forms
(Reductions available for purchases in quantity)

F2531
Record of test and examination of lifting plant
ISBN 0 7176 0453 5   £3.50 per pad of 10 forms
(Reductions available for purchases in quantity)

Legislation

HS(G) 150
Health & safety in construction
ISBN 0 7176 1143 4   £7.95

Construction (Head Protection) Regulations 1989 [1989]
ISBN 0 11 885503 4   £2.25

Designing for health & safety in construction (1995)
ISBN 0 7176 0807 7

Guidance

CS 6
Storage and use of LPG on construction sites [1981]
ISBN 0 11 883391 X   £2.50

EH 35 (Rev)
Probable asbestos dust concentrations at construction processes
[1989]
ISBN 0 11 885421 6   £2.50

EH 36 (Rev)
Work with asbestos cement [1990]
ISBN 0 11 885422 4   £2.50

EH 52
Removal techniques and associated waste handling for asbestos
insulation, coatings and insulating board [1989]

ISBN 0 11 885409 7   £2.50

GS 7 (Rev)
Accidents to children on construction sites [1989]
ISBN 0 11 885416 X   £2.50

GS 15
General access scaffolds [1982]
ISBN 0 11 883545 9   £2.50

GS 28/1
Safe erection of structures. Part 1: initial planning and design
[1984]
ISBN 0 11 883584 X   £2.50

GS 28/2
Safe erection of structures. Part 2: site management and procedures
[1985]
ISBN 0 11 883605 6   £2.50

GS 28/3
Safe erection of structures. Part 3: working places and access
[1986]. ISBN 0 11 883530 0   £2.50

GS 28/4
Safe erection of structures. Part 4: legislation and training [1986]
ISBN 0 11 883531 9   £2.50

GS 29/1 (Rev)
Health and safety in demolition work. Part 1: preparation and
planning [1988]
ISBN 0 11 885405 4   £2.50

GS 29/3
Health and safety in demolition work. Part 3: techniques [1984]
ISBN 0 11 883609 9   £2.50

GS 29/4
Health and safety in demolition work. Part 4: health hazards [1985]
ISBN 0 11 883604 8   £2.50

GS 31
Safe use of ladders, step ladders and trestles [1984]
ISBN 0 11 883594 7   £2.50

GS 42
Tower scaffolds [1987]
ISBN 0 11 883941 1   £2.50

GS 49
Pre-stressed concrete [1991]
ISBN 0 11 885597 2   £2.50

GS 51
Facade retention [1992]
ISBN 0 11 885727 4   £2.50

PM 17
Pneumatic nailing and stapling tools [1979]
ISBN 0 11 883192 5   £2.50

PM 46
Wedge and socket anchorages for wire ropes [1985]
ISBN 0 11 883611 0   £2.50

HS(G) 32
Safety in falsework for in situ beams and slabs [1987]
ISBN 0 11 883900 4   £4.00

HS(G) 46
*A guide for small contractors. Site safety and concrete
construction* [1989]
ISBN 0 11 885475 5   £2.50

HS(G)47
Avoiding danger from underground services [1989]
ISBN 0 7176 0435 7   £3.25

HS(G) 58
Evaluation and inspection of buildings and structures [1990]
ISBN 0 11 885441 0   £3.00

HS(G) 66
*Protection of workers and the general public during the
development of contaminated land* [1991]
ISBN 0 11 885657 X   £3.00

HS(G)141
Electrical safety on construction sites [1995]

ISBN 0 7176 1000 4   £8.75

HS(G) 150
Health & safety in construction [1996]
ISBN 0 7176 1143 4   £7.95

Managing health and safety in construction: principles and application to main contractor/sub contractor projects [1987]
ISBN 0 11 883918 7   £3.50

Remedial timber treatment in buildings: a guide to good practice and the safe use of wood preservatives [1991]
ISBN 0 11 885987 0   £4.00

CRR 45/1992
Research into management [1992]
ISBN 0 11 886383 5   £30.00

CRR 51/1993
Improving safety on construction sites by changing personnel behaviour
ISBN 0 11 882148 2   £30.00

Free leaflets (Telephone 01787 881165)

CIS8	*Safety in excavations*
CIS14	*Small lifting appliances*
CIS15	*Confined spaces*
CIS17	*Construction site health and safety checklist Rev 1996*
CIS18	*Provision of welfare facilities at fixed construction sites. (Rev)*
CIS19	*Safe use of mobile cranes*
CIS24	*Chemical cleaners*
CIS26	*Cement*
CIS27	*Solvents*
CIS28	*Personal protective equipment: principles, duties and responsibilities*
CIS29	*Head protection*
CIS30	*Personal protective equipment: hearing protection*
CIS31	*Personal protective equipment: eye and face protection*
CIS32	*Personal protective equipment: respiratory protection*
CIS33	*Personal protective equipment: general and specialist clothing*
CIS34	*Personal protective equipment: gloves*

CIS35   *Personal protective equipment: safety footwear*
CIS36   *Silica in construction*
CIS39   *CDM Regulations 1994: the role of the client*
CIS40   *CDM Regulations 1994: the role of the planning supervisor*
CIS41   *CDM Regulations 1994: the role of the designer*
CIS42   *CDM Regulations 1994: the pre-tender health and safety plan*
CIS43   *CDM Regulations 1994: health and safety plans during the construction phase*
CIS44   *CDM Regulations 1994: the health and safety file*
CIS45   *Establishing exclusion zones when using explosives in demolition*
INDG127   *Noise in construction (Rev)*
INDG212   *Glazing and workplace health and safety*
INDG220   *A guide to the Construction (Health, Safety & Welfare) Regs 1996 (ISBN 0 7176 1161 2) (for pack of 10 leaflets: £5.00)*

- See also the sections titled **Access to premises, Asbestos at work, Compressed air, Confined spaces, Hoists & lifts, Lifting appliances, Machinery safety, Offences & penalties, Pressure systems, Protective clothing & equipment,** and **Work Equipment.**

D

DANGEROUS CHEMICALS & PREPARATIONS
(Classification, packaging, labelling & transport)

Key points

- The manufacturers, importers and suppliers of substances have a
  duty to do all that they reasonably can to ensure that they will
  be safe and without risks to health when used, handled,
  processed stored or transported by persons at work. A failure to
  discharge that duty is an offence under the Health & Safety at
  Work etc. Act 1974 for which the penalty, on summary
  conviction, is a fine of up to £20,000. If a manufacturer, importer
  or supplier is convicted on indictment, there is no upper limit on
  the fine which the court may impose (*ibid*; sections 6(4) and
  33(1A).

  Note: A substance is any natural or artificial substance, whether in solid or
  liquid form or in the form of a gas or vapour.

- The manufacturer of a substance (e.g., a chemical or a
  preparation which includes one or more chemicals) must identify
  the hazardous properties of that substance and take such steps
  as are reasonably practicable to eliminate or minimise the risks to
  persons who will use, handle, process, store or transport that
  substance in the course of their employment. If a manufacturer
  has neither the knowledge nor resources to carry out the
  appropriate research, tests and examinations, he must arrange
  for some other person or organisation (such as an approved
  laboratory service) to do so on his behalf. If the manufacturer is
  based overseas (i.e., outside the European Economic
  Community), and there is some uncertainty as to whether the
  substance in question has been correctly analysed or tested, that
  responsibility devolves on the importer or supplier (*ibid*; section
  6(5)).

  Note: It should be noted that there are strict rules within the European
  Community concerning the manufacture and supply of dangerous substances.
  Those rules have been imported into UK legislation (see below), but are not
  necessarily mirrored by manufacturers outside the EEC.

- It is the responsibility also of manufacturers, importers and suppliers to provide purchasers and end-users with adequate information about any risks to health and safety to which the inherent properties of a particular substance may give rise. When doing so, they must include adequate information about the results of any relevant tests which have been carried out on (or in connection with) the substance and about any conditions necessary to ensure that it will be safe and without risks to health when used, handled, processed, stored or transported by persons at work. If that information is subsequently revised or updated, the manufacturer, importer or supply must lose not time in relaying that new information to the persons to whom the substance was supplied (*ibid*; section 6(4)(d)).

- The importer or supplier of a substance intended for use or distribution within the EEC is not required to repeat any testing, examination or research carried out by the manufacturer (or by a person or organisation who or which has done so on the manufacturer's behalf). However, he may have to satisfy the Health & Safety Executive (through one or other of its inspectors) that it was reasonable for him to rely on the results of those tests, examinations or research (*ibid*).

SUPPORTING HEALTH AND SAFETY REGULATIONS

- The general duty of care imposed on all manufacturers, importers and suppliers of dangerous substances by the 1974 Act has been reinforced in recent years by requirements and prohibitions imposed by a raft of subordinate legislation (most of which implement related EC Directives). The Regulations in question (in order of appearance) are as follows:

  Notification of Installations Handling Hazardous Substances Regulations 1982 (SI 1982/1357).

  These prohibit the undertaking of any activity in which there is, or is liable to be, at any one time, a notifiable quantity of a hazardous substance (as defined in Schedule 1 to the Regulations) unless the Health & Safety Executive (HSE) is informed in writing (giving the particulars prescribed by Schedule 2) at least three months beforehand. Etc. For the relevant HSC publications, see *FURTHER INFORMATION* at the end of this section.

  Dangerous Substances in Harbour Areas Regulations 1987 (SI 1987/37).

These lay down rules for the carriage, loading, unloading and storage of dangerous substances in harbours and harbour areas (enforced, where appropriate, by the HSE or by the relevant statutory harbour authority). Etc. For the relevant HSC publications, see *FURTHER INFORMATION* at the end of this section.

Dangerous Substances (Notification & Marking of Sites) Regulations 1990 (SI 1990/304).

These Regulations require the notification and marking of sites in which the total quantity of dangerous substances present on the site is 25 tonnes or more. Signs bearing the exclamation mark (!) (or an exclamation mark accompanying the legend DANGEROUS SUBSTANCES) must be displayed at the entrance to the site (or at other approved places throughout the site) in order to give adequate warning to fireman. Etc. For the relevant HSC publications, see *FURTHER INFORMATION* at the end of this section.

Notification of New Substances Regulations 1993 (SI 1993/3050).

Persons responsible for placing a new substance on the market (that is to say, a substance which does not appear in the European Inventory of Existing Commercial Chemical Substances [EINECS]) in a quantity of one tonne or more per year must notify the appointed competent authority (i.e., in Great Britain, the Secretary of State for the Environment and the HSE acting jointly) at least 60 days before placement is intended to occur. Etc. For the relevant HSC publications, see *FURTHER INFORMATION* at the end of this section.

Chemicals (Hazard Information & Packaging for Supply) Regulations 1996 (SI 1996/1092) — or 'CHIP 2' Regulations, (printed in bold to indicate that they are) summarised later in this section.

These Regulations, which revoked and re-enacted with amendments the Chemicals (Hazard Information & Packaging) Regulations 1993 (SI 1993/1746), came into force on 31 January 1995 (subject to certain transitional provisions). As indicated above, these Regulations are summarised in the principal text below.

Carriage of Dangerous Goods by Rail Regulations 1996 (SI 1996/2089).

These Regulations impose requirements and prohibitions in relation to the suitability and maintenance of, and the carriage of dangerous goods by rail in, wagons and large containers in bulk, in small containers and in tanks, packages, tank containers and tank wagons; the segregation, marking and labelling of dangerous goods; etc. They also require safety systems and procedures to be drawn up, including an action plan for dealing with any emergency on a train, at a railway facility or on a railway track. They also cover the provision of information, instruction and training to train crews; the loading, stowage, unloading and cleaning of containers, tank containers, tank wagons, etc; the safe marshalling and formation of trains carrying dangerous goods; etc. For the relevant HSC publications, see *FURTHER INFORMATION* at the end of this section.

Carriage of Dangerous Goods (Classification, Packaging & Labelling) & Use of Transportable Pressure Receptacles Regulations 1996 (SI 1996/2092).

The Regulations impose requirements and prohibitions in relation to the classification, packaging and labelling of dangerous goods for carriage by road or on a railway. They repeal and re-enact, with modifications, the Carriage of Dangerous Goods by Road and Rail (Classification, Packaging & Labelling) Regulations 1994 (SI 1994/669). For example, they now cover the carriage of certain environmentally hazardous substances to which the 1994 Regulations did not apply. The Regulations provide, inter alia, for HSC approval of documents containing requirements relating to the design, construction, modification, repair, testing, examination, filling and marking of transportable pressure receptacles (the Approved Requirements); the conduct of safety checks; the maintenance of specified records; and so on.

Note: The current edition of the *European Agreement concerning the International Carriage of Dangerous Goods by Road* (ADR), the *Convention concerning International Carriage by Rail* (COTIF) (CMND. 5897), and the current edition of the *United Nations Recommendations on the Transport of Dangerous Goods* (9th revised edition) (ISBN 9 21 139048 X) may be obtained from The Stationery Office (formerly HMSO) at the address given on page 328 of this handbook. The current edition of the *International Maritime Dangerous Goods Code* (Volumes I to IV) (ISBN 92 801 1316 X) may be obtained from the International Maritime Organisation, 4 Albert Embankment, London SE1 7SR. The current edition of the *Technical Instructions for the Safe Transport of Dangerous Goods by Air & Supplement 1995/96* (Doc 9284-AN/905 may be obtained from the Civil Aviation Authority, Printing & Publishing Services, Greville House, 37 Gratton Road, Cheltenham, Gloucestershire GL50 2BN. The approved documents referred to in the previous paragraph may be obtained from HSE Books (at the address given on page 328); from Rymans the Stationer, and from other booksellers. See also *FURTHER INFORMATION* at the end of this section.

Carriage of Dangerous Goods by Road (Driver Training) Regulations 1996 (SI 1996/2094)

The operator of any vehicle registered in the UK, which is engaged in the carriage of dangerous goods, must ensure that the driver of any such vehicle has successfully completed an approved tanker/tank container (or related ' package') training course and holds a vocational training certificate (valid for five years), which he (or she) must keep in the cabin throughout the journey, to be produced for inspection on demand, The driver must understand the danger to which he may be exposed and the action to be taken in the event of an emergency. Etc. For the relevant HSC publications, see *FURTHER INFORMATION* at the end of this section.

Carriage of Dangerous Goods by Road Regulations 1996 (SI 1996/2095)

Persons or organisations responsible for the design, manufacture, importation, supply, modification or repair of vehicles or tank containers — used, or intended to be used, for the carriage of specified dangerous goods — must ensure that such vehicles and containers comply with the 'approved vehicle' and the 'approved vehicle and tank requirements' as published (and routinely updated) by the Health & Safety Commission. For their part, the operators of such vehicles must comply with the requirements of the 'approved carriage list' relating to the marking of vehicles and containers; tank pressures; provisions in the Regulations (and approved lists and guidance) relating to the carriage of flammable, toxic, or corrosive solids, spontaneously combustible substances, oxidising agents, organic peroxides, and the like; and must not carry such goods without first obtaining a declaration from the consignor concerning the designation of the goods to be carried, their classification, UN number, the mass and volume of those goods, information about prescribed control or emergency procedures; etc. The Regulations deal also with the loading and unloading of vehicles, the information to be displayed on vehicles, tanks and containers; the carriage, accessibility and use of respiratory protective equipment, the supervision of parked vehicles, damage to vehicles; and so on. For the relevant HSC publications, see *FURTHER INFORMATION* at the end of this section.

and, bearing in mind that the manufacturers, importers and suppliers of dangerous chemicals and substances are invariably employers in their own right:

the Control of Substances Hazardous to Health Regulations 1994 (SI 1994/3246, as amended by SI 1994/3247)).

The 1994 COSHH Regulations are discussed elsewhere in this   handbook in the section titled **Hazardous substances.**

Also relevant are the

Workplace (Health, Safety & Welfare) Regulations 1992 (SI 1992/3004).

The latter are discussed throughout this handbook under the relevant subject heads (see **Table of Statutes, Regulations & Orders** on page *ix* above). Although a little out of place in this section, the Workplace Regulations contain rules relating to the disposal of hazardous substances and rules for the protection of employees who work in the vicinity of tanks or open vessels containing dangerous substances.

The Approved Code of Practice which accompanies the 1992 Regulations cautions (in para. 102) that the methods used by employers or self-employed persons to drain toxic, corrosive and highly flammable liquids away from the floor of any workplace must not lead to the contamination of drains, sewers, watercourses or ground water supplies. Nor should they put people or the environment at risk. Maximum concentration levels are specified in the Environmental Protection (Prescribed Processes & Substances) Regulations 1991, and in the Surface Waters (Dangerous Substances) (Classification) Regulations 1989 and 1992. In some cases, consent for discharges are required under the Environmental Protection Act 1990, the Water Resources Act 1991, and the Water Industry Act 1991.

Every tank, pit, sump, silo, vat, kier or vessel containing a dangerous substance must be adequately protected to prevent a person falling into it. Such vessels or structures must either be securely fenced to a height of at least 1100 millimetres above their highest point (915mm, if installed before December 31, 1992) or be securely covered (*ibid*; Regulation 13).

Overhead pipelines containing flammable or hazardous chemicals must be shielded if they pass over traffic routes used by goods vehicles, forklift trucks and the like (*ibid*; Regulation 17).

Comment

• This section simply summarises the principal provisions of the **Chemicals (Hazard Information & Packaging for Supply) (or 'CHIP 2') Regulations 1994** (highlighted in bold above) — as these are likely to be of more immediate interests to the readers of this handbook. Any attempt to review the requirements and prohibitions imposed by the other Regulations listed above (many of which contain lengthy technical data) would be well beyond the scope of a book of this size.

• There are, however, a number of helpful and comprehensive publications (including codes of practice and guidance notes) produced by the Health & Safety Executive which give practical advice on matters affecting the storage, transport, loading and unloading of dangerous substances. There is a list of those publications at the end of this section, and a supplementary list of 'general interest' publications. See *FURTHER INFORMATION* below. Copies of the Regulations listed above may be purchased from The Stationery Office (formerly HMSO) by quoting the relevant SI numbers also given above (as to which, see page 328).

CHEMICALS (HAZARD INFORMATION & PACKAGING FOR SUPPLY) REGULATIONS 1994

• When an employer takes delivery of a dangerous chemical or preparation for use at work he has a right to expect that it has been correctly classified, packaged and labelled by the manufacturer, importer or supplier and the right also to be provided with an accompanying 'safety data sheet'. These requirements are to be found in the Chemical (Hazard Information & Packaging for Supply) Regulations 1994 — nowadays referred to as the CHIP 2 Regulations — which came into force (subject to one or two transitional provisions) on 31 January 1995.

Note: The acronym CHIP 2 is used by the Health & Safety Executive both for the sake of convenience and to distinguish the 1994 Regulations from their predecessor, the Chemicals (Hazard Information & Packaging) Regulations 1993 (or CHIP), which they have revoked and re-enacted with amendments.

- The CHIP 2 Regulations apply to every chemical element or compound which is classified as dangerous for supply and to every product or preparation which contains one or more such elements or compounds (referred to collectively as substances and preparations dangerous for supply) *EXCEPT* —

  (a)   radioactive substances within the meaning of the Ionising Radiations Regulations 1985 (SI 1985/1333);

  (b)   substances or preparations intended for use as animal feeding stuffs which are in a finished state intended for the final user;

  (c)   cosmetic products (including aerosol dispensers containing cosmetic products);

  (d)   substances or preparations which are intended for use as medicinal products;

  (e)   substances or preparations which are controlled drugs within the meaning of the Misuse of Drugs Act 1971 (excluding drugs which are excepted by section 4(1) of that Act);

  (f)   substances or preparations which are dangerous because they contain disease-producing micro-organisms (but are not otherwise dangerous for supply);

  (g)   munitions and preparations supplied with a view to producing practical effect by explosion or a pyrotechnic effect;

  (h)   substances or preparations intended for use as a food as defined by section 1 of the Food Safety Act 1990;

  (i)   (subject to Council Regulation EC/2455/92 on the export notification and information exchange of dangerous substances) substances which are intended for export to a country outside the EEC;

(j)   pesticides approved under the Food & Environment Protection Act 1985;

(k)   substances or preparations transferred from one part of a factory (warehouse or other place of work) to another place of work within that same factory (etc.);

(l)   substances labelled in accordance with the provisions of paragraph (7) of Regulation 6 of the Notification of New Substances Regulations 1993;

(m)   substances, preparations and mixtures in the form of wastes, which are covered by Council Directives 91/156/EEC and 91/689/EEC;

(n)   any plant protection product which has been approved under the Plant Protection Products Regulations 1995 (SI 1995/887).

Also excluded are quantities or samples of substances and preparations dangerous for supply which have been held or taken by customs officials or health and safety inspectors.

1.   *Classification of substances and preparations dangerous for supply*

- The expression substance dangerous for supply means a substance listed in Part I of the *Approved Supply List* (see *CHIP on supply* below) or any other substance which is in one or more of the categories of danger specified in Column 1 of Schedule 1 to the 1994 Regulations (see **Table 1** on page 182). A preparation dangerous for supply means a preparation, that is to say, a mixture or solution of two or more substances, which is also in one or more of the categories of danger specified in that part of Schedule 1.

- Before selling or offering to sell a substance or preparation dangerous for supply, the manufacturer or importer must classify it by reference to column 2 of Part V of the *Approved Supply List*. If the substance is a new substance within the meaning of Regulation 2(1) of the Notification of New Substances Regulations 1993 (*q.v.*), which has been notified in accordance with Regs 4 or 6(2) of those Regulations, he must classify it in accordance with that notification.

- Any other substance dangerous for supply (which is not listed in Part I of the *Approved Supply List* and is not a new substance as defined in the previous paragraph) must be classified by placing it in one or more of the categories specified in column 1 of Part I of Schedule 1 to the CHIP 2 Regulations (see **Table 1** on page 182) which corresponds to the properties of the substance specified in the entry opposite that category in column 2, and must be assigned the appropriate risk phrase by using the criteria set out in the approved classification and labelling guide.

- Dangerous or hazardous chemicals are classified in the *Approved Supply List* by their physico-chemical properties (explosive, oxidising, extremely flammable, highly flammable or flammable) by the risks they pose to health (very toxic, toxic, harmful, corrosive, irritant, sensitizing, carcinogenic, mutagenic, toxic for reproduction); and by the danger they present to the environment. The *Approved Supply List* also gives the appropriate risk phrase and safety phrase for every substance or preparation identified in the *List* as dangerous for supply.

- If a manufacturer or supplier has wrongly classified a chemical, or a product or preparation containing a chemical, the label on the receptacle in which it is packaged (and on any associated packaging) will also be wrong (or non-existent) as will be the accompanying safety data sheet (if one is provided at all). In such a case, he not only risks prosecution and a heavy fine under the 1974 Act but could also be sued for damages by any person injured as a direct consequence of his negligence.

2. *Safety data sheet*

- Once he has correctly classified the dangerous substance or preparation he intends to sell or supply, the manufacturer, supplier or importer will need to prepare a safety data sheet which must accompany every purchase and delivery of that product. The safety data sheet must be provided free of charge (as must every revision of the sheet) and must contain the following obligatory information:

  1. Identification of the substance or preparation and of the name and address of the supplier or importer.
  2. Composition/information on ingredients.
  3. Hazards identification.
  4. First-aid measures.
  5. Fire-fighting measures.
  6. Accidental release measures.

7.   Handling and storage.
8.   Exposure controls/personal protection.
9.   Physical and chemical properties.
10. Stability and reactivity.
11. Toxicological information.
12. Ecological information.
13. Disposal considerations.
14. Transport information.
15. Regulatory information.
16. Other information.

The purpose of the safety data sheet is to enable the purchaser or recipient of the relevant product or preparation to comply with *his* duties under the CHIP 2 Regulations (if he intends to incorporate it in a product or preparation which he *too* will be selling-on) and to comply also with his obligations under the Control of Substances Hazardous to Health Regulations 1994 (*q.v.*), namely: to prevent or minimise any risks to the health and safety of those of his employees who are liable to be exposed to that product or preparation in the course of their employment.

• The safety data sheet *must* be kept up to date and must be revised whenever there is any significant new information regarding risks to human health or the environment. The sheet must clearly show the date on which it was first introduced or last revised. If it has been revised, it must be clearly marked with the word REVISION.

• Safety data sheets need not accompany dangerous chemicals (or preparations containing such chemicals) which are sold or intended for sale to members of the public through normal retail outlets (such as hardware shops, DIY stores, supermarkets, and the like). Such products must, nonetheless, be correctly labelled to identify their hazardous properties.

Note: Any small businessman or self-employed person who purchases a dangerous chemical or a product containing a dangerous chemical from a retail or wholesale outlet (whether a 'High Street' shop, DIY store or 'cash and carry' outlet) for use in his business (e.g., a proprietary scouring agent, oven cleaner, or whatever) may contact the manufacturer or supplier of that product and ask to be supplied with a safety data sheet. The latter must be forwarded or supplied on request and without charge.

3. Labelling

• Every receptacle (that is to say the bottle, jar, drum, box, or similar container) which contains *and* is in immediate contact with a dangerous chemical, or a preparation which incorporates such a chemical, must be correctly labelled. This rule applies regardless of whether the chemical or preparation is intended for sale to a member of the public in a shop or is supplied to an employer for use in connection with his trade or business. If, as often happens, jars, bottles, etc. are packaged in quantity in their own individual boxes which are then packaged in quantity in an 'outer container', each of the jars or bottles must be labelled as well as the individual boxes and the outer container. The only (obvious) situation in which labels are not needed is when a chemical or preparation in question is supplied from a tanker or through a pipeline.

- The label for a substance dangerous for supply must contain the following particulars:

    1. the name, full address and telephone number of a person in a Member State of the EEC who is responsible for supplying the substance; whether he be its manufacturer, importer or distributor;

    2. the name of the substance, being the name or one of the names for the substance listed in Part I of the *Approved Supply List* or, if it is not so listed, an internationally recognised name; and

    3. the following particulars, namely —

        (a)   the indication or indications of danger and the corresponding symbol or symbols (if any),
        (b)   the risk phrases (set out in full),
        (c)   the safety phrases (set out in full),
        (d)   the EEC number (if any) and, in the case of a substance dangerous for supply listed in Part I of the *Approved Supply List*, the words EEC Label; and
        (e)   in respect of a substance which is required to be labelled (or would be so required, but for certain exceptions) as:

            (i)   Carcinogenic of category 1 or 2;
            (ii) Nutagenic of category 1 or 2; or
            (iii) Toxic for reproduction, of Category 1 or 2,

            the labelling phrase *'Restricted to professional users'*

- For every preparation which is, or may be, dangerous for supply, the label must contain the following particulars:

1. the name, full address and telephone number of a person in a Member State of the EEC who is responsible for supplying the preparation, whether he be its manufacturer, importer or distributor;

2. the trade name or other designation of the preparation;

3. the following particulars, namely —

    (a) identification of the constituents of the preparation which result in the preparation being classified as dangerous for supply,
    (b) the indication or indications of danger and the corresponding symbol or symbols (if any),
    (c) the risk phrases (set out in full),
    (d) the safety phrases (set out in full),
    (e) in the case of a pesticide, the modified information specified in para. 5 of Part I of Schedule 6 to the CHIP 2 Regulations (not discussed here), and
    (f) in the case of a preparation intended for sale to the general public, the nominal quantity (nominal mass or nominal volume); and

4 (in the case of a preparation which contains at least one substance which *may* be dangerous for supply and which is present in a concentration equal to or in excess of 1% by weight) the words *Caution — This preparation contains a substance not yet fully tested*; and

5. in respect of a preparation containing such a substance, which is required to be labelled (or would be so required, but for certain exceptions) as —

    (a) Carcinogenic of category 1 or 2;
    (b) Nutagenic of category 1 or 2; or
    (c) Toxic for reproduction, of Category 1 or 2,

    the labelling phrase Restricted to professional users

Comment

- As was indicated earlier in this section, the above is an outline only of the principal provisions of the CHIP 2 Regulations. As might be expected, they also contain many detailed requirements relating, inter alia, to the construction and suitability of the receptacles containing dangerous substances and preparations, the size and positioning of labels, the fitting of replaceable closures (including child-proof safety caps), the methods of marking and the colour and nature of the markings on labels; and so on — all of which are beyond the scope of a book of this size. The Health & Safety Executive (HSE) has published a number of supporting documents, available either from the Stationery Office or from HSE book; as to which, see *FURTHER INFORMATION* at the end of this section.

See also the sections titled **Asbestos at work, Celluloid & cinematograph film, Dangerous occurrences, Explosives, Hazardous substances, Ionising radiation, Lead at work,** and **Highly flammable liquids** elsewhere in this handbook.

Table 1 **Classification of substances and preparations** **dangerous for supply** **CATEGORIES OF DANGER**		
(1) *Category of danger*	(2) *Property* (See Note 1)	(3) *Symbol letter*
PHYSICO-CHEMICAL PROPERTIES		
Explosive	Solid, liquid, pasty or gelatinous substances and preparations which may react exothermically without atmospheric oxygen thereby quickly evolving gases, and which under defined test conditions detonate, quickly deflagrate or upon heating explode when partially confined.	E
Oxidising	Substances and preparations which give rise to a highly exothermic reaction in contact with other substances, particularly flammable substances.	O

Table 1 (Cont.)		
Extremely flammable	Liquid substances and preparations having an extremely low flash point and a low boiling point and gaseous substances and preparations which are flammable in contact with air at ambient temperature and pressure. (See Note 2.)	F+
Highly flammable	The following substances and preparations. namely —	F
	(a) substances and preparations which may become hot and finally catch fire in contact with air at ambient temperature without any application of energy .	
	(h) solid substances and preparations which may readily catch fire after brief contact with a source of ignition and which continue to burn or to be consumed after removal of the source of ignition.	
	(c) liquid substances and preparations having a very low flash point, or	
	(d) substances and preparations which, in contact with water or damp air, evolve highly flammable gases in dangerous quantities. (See Note 2)	
Flammable	Liquid substances and preparations having a low flash point (See Note 2.)	None

HEALTH EFFECTS

Very toxic	Substances and preparations which in very low quantities cause death or acute or chronic damage to health when inhaled, swallowed or absorbed via the skin .	T+
Toxic	Substances and preparations which in low quantities cause death or acute or chronic damage to health when inhaled, swallowed or absorbed via the skin.	T
Harmful	Substances and preparations which may cause death or acute or chronic damage to health when inhaled, swallowed or absorbed via the skin.	Xn

Table 1 (Cont.)		
Corrosive	Substances and preparations which may, on contact with living tissues, destroy them.	C
Irritant	Non-corrosive substances and preparations which, through immediate, prolonged or repeated contact with the skin or mucous membrane, may cause inflammation.	Xi
Sensitising	Substances and preparations which, if they are inhaled or if they penetrate the skin, are capable of eliciting a reaction by hypersensitization such that on further exposure to the substance or preparation, characteristic adverse effects are produced	
Sensitising by inhalation		Xn
Sensitising by skin contact	(	Xi
Carcinogenic (see *Note* 3 below)	Substances and preparations which, if they are inhaled or ingested or if they penetrate the skin, may induce cancer or increase its incidence.	
Category 1 Category 2 Category 3		T T Xn
Mutagenic (See *Note* 3 below)	Substances and preparations which, if they are inhaled or ingested or if they penetrate the skin, may induce heritable genetic defects or increase their incidence.	
Category 1 Category 2 Category 3		T T Xn
Toxic for reproduction (See *Note* 3 below	Substances and preparations which, if they are inhaled or ingested or if they penetrate the skin, may produce or increase the incidence of non-heritable adverse effects in the progeny and/or an impairment of male or female reproductive functions or capacity.	
Category 1 Category 2 Category 3		T T Xn

Table 1 (Cont.)
Dangerous for the environment (See *Note* 4 below)   Substances which, were they to enter into the environment, would present or might present an immediate or delayed danger for one or more components of the environment.   N

Notes

1. As further described in the approved classification and labelling guide.
2. Preparations packed in aerosol dispensers must be classified as flammable in accordance with the additional criteria set out in Part II of this Schedule.
3. The categories as specified in the approved classification and labelling guide.
4(a). In certain cases specified in the approved supply list and in the approved classification and labelling guide, substances classified as dangerous for the environment do not require to be labelled with the symbol for this category of danger.
4(b). The category of danger does not apply to preparations.

FURTHER INFORMATION

• The CHIP 2 Regulations are available from The Stationery Office (see page 328). Telephone 0171 873 9090 and ask for a copy of SI 1994/3247 (ISBN 0 11 043877 9), price £6.75 net.

• The following subject-specific list of HSE publications below is as comprehensive as space allow. Any that have been omitted are to be found in the 1997 Price list for HSC/E publications, which is available free of charge from HSE Books by telephoning 01787 881165 (Fax numbers: 01787 313995/370769).

L16
Design and construction of vented non-pressure road tankers used for the carriage of flammable liquids. Road Traffic (Carriage of Dangerous Substances in Road Tankers and Tank Containers) Regulations 1992: Approved code of practice [1993]
ISBN 0 11 886300 2   £4.00

L19
Design and construction of vacuum operated road tankers used for the carriage of hazardous wastes. Road Traffic (Carriage of Dangerous Substances in Road Tankers and Tank Containers) Regulations 1992. Approved code of practice [1993]
ISBN 0 7176 0564 7   £4.00

L51
Carriage of Dangerous Goods by Rail Regulations 1994
ISBN 0 7176 0698 8   £8.95

L62
Safety data sheets for substances and preparations dangerous for supply. Guidance on regulation 6 of the CHIP Regulations 1994. Approved Code of Practice.
ISBN 0 7176 0859 X   £3.95

L63
The Approved Guide
Approved guide to the classification and labelling of substances and preparations dangerous for supply [1995]
ISBN 0 7176 0860 3   £6.50

L76
Approved supply list and database — CHIP 96 [1996]
ISBN 0 7176 1116 7   £17.00
HS(G) 126

L88
Approved requirements and test methods for the classification and packaging of dangerous goods for carriage [1996]
ISBN 0 7176 1221   £12.75

L89
Approved vehicle requirements [1996]
ISBN 0 7176 1222 8   £5.50

L90
Information approved for the carriage of dangerous goods by road and rail other than explosives and radioactive material [1996]
ISBN 0 7176 1223 6   £13.50

L91
Suitability of vehicles and containers and limits on quantities for the

carriage of explosives: Carriage of Explosives by Road Regulations 1996 — Approved Code of Practice. [1996]
ISBN 0 7176 1224 4   £6.50

L92
Approved requirements for the construction of vehicles for the carriage of explosives by road [1996]
ISBN 0 7176 1225 2   £5.00

L93
Approved tank requirements: the provision for bottom loading and vapour recovery systems of mobile containers carrying petrol [1996]
ISBN 0 7176 1226 0   £6.50

L94
Approved requirements for the packaging, labelling and carriage of radioactive material by rail [1996]
ISBN 0 7176 1227 9   £7.75

Other codes of practice & legal guides

COP 7
Principles of good laboratory practice: Notification of New Substances Regulations 1982 (in support of Sl 1982/1496)
ISBN 0 11 883658 7   £2.50

COP 14
Road tanker testing: examination, testing and certification of the carrying tanks of road tankers and of tank containers used for the conveyance of dangerous substances by road (in support of SI 1981/1059)
ISBN 0 11 883811 3   £2.80

COP 18
Dangerous substances in harbour areas: The Dangerous Substances in Harbour Area Regulations 1987: approved code of practice [1987]
ISBN 0 11 883857 1   £4.00

Leaflet packs (Telephone 01787 881165)(Single copies supplied freee of charge)

IND(G) 181D (Packs of 10 leaflets)
The Complete Idiot's Guide to CHIP 2 [1995]
ISBN 0 7176 0901 4

1 pack: £5.00 (discounts for multiple packs)

IND(G) 182 (Packs of 10 leaflets)
Why do I need a safety data sheet? [1995]
ISBN 0 7176 0895 6
1 pack: £3.50 (discounts for multiple packs)

IND(G) 186 (Packs of 10 leaflets)
Read the label [1995]
ISBN 0 7176 0898 0
1 pack: £3.50 (discounts for multiple packs)

IND(G)234 (packs of 10 leaflets)
Are you involved in the carriage of dangerous goods by road or rail?
[1996]
ISBN 0 7176 1258 9
1 pack: £5.00 per pack (discounts for multiple packs)

Other Guidance Notes

GS 40
*Loading and unloading of bulk flammable liquids and gases at
harbours and inland waterways* [1986]
ISBN 0 7176 1230 9   £5.00

HS(G) 40
Chlorine from drums and cylinders [1987]
ISBN 0 7176 1006 3   £2.50

HS(G) 71
Storage of packaged dangerous substances [1992]
ISBN 0 11 885989 7   £4.00

HS(G) 78
*Container packing: guidance for those packing and
transporting dangerous goods in CTUs for carriage by sea*
[1992]
ISBN 0 11 885734 7   £4.00

HS(G) 110
Seven steps to successful substitution of hazardous substances [1994]
ISBN 0 7176 0695 3   £6.50

HS(G)126
Chip 2 for everyone   [1995]
ISBN 0 7176 0857 3   £6.75

HS(G)162
*The carriage of dangerous goods explained: Guidance for operators,
drivers and others involved in the carriage of dangerous goods (Part
4)*   [1996]
ISBN 0 7176 1251 1   £10.95

HS(G)163
*The carriage of dangerous goods explained: Guidance for rail
operators and others involved in the carriage of dangerous goods
(Part 3)* [1996]
ISBN 0 7176 1256 2   £7.50

HS(G)164
*The carriage of dangerous goods explained: Guidance for
consignors, rail operators and others involved in the carriage of
dangerous goods* [1996]
ISBN 0 7176 1257 0   £8.95

HS(G)166
*Formula for health and safety: Guidance for small to medium-
sized firms in the chemical manufacturing industry*   [1996]
ISBN 0 7176 0996 0   £8.95

HS(R)27
*Guide to Dangerous Substances in Harbour Areas Regulations
1987* [1988]
ISBN 0 11 883991 8   £3.00

HS(R)29
*Guide to the notification and marking of sites in accordance with the
Dangerous Substances (Notification & Marking of Sites) Regulations*
ISBN 0 11 885435 6   £3.50

CS 9
Bulk storage and use of liquid carbon dioxide: hazards and procedures
[1985]
ISBN 0 11 883513 0   £2.50

CS 18
Storage and handling of ammonium nitrate [1986]

ISBN 0 11 883937 3   £2.50

CS 21
Storage and handling of organic peroxides [1991]
ISBN 0 11 885602 2   £2.50

CS22
Fumigation [1996]
ISBN 0 7176 1218 X   £5.00

Free leaflets (Telephone: 01787 881165)

HSE8	*Misuse of oxygen: fire and explosion in the use and misuse of oxygen*
INDG66	*VCM and you*
INDG197	*Working with sewage: the health hazards (a pocket card for employees)*
INDG198	*Working with sewage: the health hazards (a guide for employers)*
INDG230	*Storage and safe handling of ammonium nitrate*
MSA7	*Cadmium and you*
MSA8	*Arsenic and you*
MSA9	*Cyanide and you*
MSA13	*Benzene and you*
MSA14	*Nickel and you*
MSA15	*Silica dust and you*
MSA16	*Chromium and you*
MSA17	*Cobalt and you*
MSA18	*Beryllium and you*
MSA19	*PCBs and you*
MSA21	*MbOCA and you*
MSB4	*Skin cancer by pitch and tar*
MSB5	*Skin cancer by oil*
INDG98	Permits to work in the chemical industry
INDG155	*Prepare for emergency*
INDG186	*Read the label: how to find out if chemicals are dangerous* (ISBN 0 7176 0898 0). Free for a single copy. £3.50 per pack of 10 leaflets (plus further quantity discounts)..

There are also a number of useful Guidance Notes (regrettably, too numerous to include here) in the HSC/E's *Environmental Hygiene (EH)* series. For a full list of those Guidance Notes, the interested reader is commended to HSE Book's Price List for

1997, which (as indicated earlier) is available free of charge from HSE Books by telephoning 01787 881165.

DANGEROUS MACHINES
(*Prescribed dangerous machines*)

Key Points

- Machines prescribed as *dangerous* by the Offices, Shops & Railway Premises Act 1963 must *not* be operated by people of whatever age or sex without comprehensive instruction and on-the-job training, or close supervision.

- It is perhaps as well to point out that, although a great deal of pre-1974 legislation on machinery safety has been repealed or revoked (most recently by the Provision & Use of Work Equipment Regulations 1992 [SI 1992/2932]), section 19 of the 1963 Act summarised in this section has survived intact and will continue to be enforced by local authority-appointed health and safety inspectors.

Note: Sections 20 and 21 of the Factories Act 1961, and the Dangerous Machines (Training of Young Persons) Order 1954 (SI 1954/921), were repealed and revoked, respectively, by the Health & Safety (Young Persons) Regulations 1997 (SI1997/135) which came into force on 3 March 1997.

Employer's duty under the 1963 Act

- Section 19 of the 1963 Act states that *no* person employed in premises to which that Act applies may operate any *prescribed dangerous machine* unless the employer has seen to it that the employee has been fully instructed as to the dangers arising in connection with that machine (and the precautions to be observed) and that he (or she):

  (a) has received sufficient training in work at the machine; or

  (b) is under adequate supervision by a person who has a thorough knowledge and experience of the machine

Prescribed dangerous machines

- The machines prescribed as dangerous by the Prescribed Dangerous Machines Order 1964 (SI 1964/171) — and listed in **Table 1** opposite — are to be found, for the most part, in the kitchens of hotels, restaurants, cafeterias, schools, hospitals, and the like; and behind delicatessen counters in supermarkets and grocery shops. Others are to be found in butcher shops, print works, shoe and furniture repair shops, etc. All have been prescribed as 'dangerous' by the 1964 Order.

Employer's overriding duty

- Although the 1964 Order is specific as to what constitutes a dangerous machine, employers should not lose sight of their overriding duty under section 2(2)(a) of the Health and Safety at Work etc. Act 1974 (reinforced by the Provision & Use of Work Equipment Regulations 1992 [SI 1992/2932]) to provide and maintain plant and systems of work that are, so far as is reasonably practicable, safe and without risks to health; and, furthermore, to provide such information, instruction, training and supervision as is necessary to ensure ... the health and safety at work of his employees (*ibid*; section 2(2)(c)).

- Putting an inexperienced employee to work on any machine without even a modicum of training and instruction is the height of folly and could lead to a criminal prosecution under the 1974 Act (whether or not an accident or injury has occurred). The employer who fails to discharge his duty under section 2 of the 1974 Act is guilty of an offence and liable, on summary conviction, to a fine of up to £20,000; or, if he is convicted on indictment, to a fine of an unlimited amount (*ibid.*, section 33(1)(a) and (1A)).

Training of supervisors

- Supervisors and other persons responsible for overseeing the use of machines and other types of work equipment must receive adequate health and safety training, including training in the safe use of machines and other work equipment (tools, appliances, etc.). They must also be aware of the risks associated with the use of that equipment (especially in the hands of inexperienced or untrained workers) and of the precautions taken to eliminate or minimise those risks (*per* Regulation 9(2), Provision & Use of

Work Equipment Regulations 1992 (*q.v.*)).

Table 1
OFFICES, SHOPS & RAILWAY PREMISES ACT 1963
Prescribed Dangerous Machines

No person (regardless of age) may operate any of the following machines without prior safety instruction supplemented by 'on-the-job' training and/or competent supervision.

The following machines when worked with the aid of mechanical power —

1. Worm-type mincing machines
2. Rotary knife bowl-type chopping machines
3. Dough brakes, dough mixers
4. Food mixing machines when used with attachments for mincing, slicing, chipping or any other cutting operation, or for crumbing
5. Pie and tart making machines
6. Vegetable slicing machines
7. Wrapping and packing machines
8. Garment presses
9. Opening or teasing machines used for upholstery or bedding work
10. Corner staying machines
11. Loose knife punching machines
12. Wire stitching machines
13. Machines of any type equipped with a circular saw blade
14. Machines of any type equipped with a saw in the form of a continuous band or strip
15. Planing machines, vertical spindle moulding machines and routing machines, being, in any case, machines used for cutting wood, wood products, fibre-board, plastic or similar material

The following machines (whether worked with the aid of mechanical power or not)

16. Circular knife slicing machines used for cutting bacon and other foods (whether similar to bacon or not)
17. Potato chipping machines
18 Platen printing machines, including such machines when used for cutting and creasing

FURTHER INFORMATION

- The following HSE publications are available from HSE Books at the Address given on page 328.

HS(G)31
Pie and tart machines [1986]
ISBN 0 11 883891 1   £3.50

PM 33
Safety of bandsaws in the food industry [1983]
ISBN 0 11 883564 5   £2.50

PM 35
Safety in the use of reversing dough brakes [1983]
ISBN 0 11 883576 9   £2.50

See also the sections titled **Fencing & guarding, Machinery safety** and **Work equipment** elsewhere in this handbook.

DANGEROUS OCCURRENCES
(Reportable under RIDDOR 1995)

Key points

- By Regulation 3(1) of The Reporting of Injuries, Diseases & Dangerous Occurrences Regulations 1995 (SI 1995/3163), every notifiable dangerous occurrence must —

    (a)   be reported immediately to the *relevant enforcing authority;* and

    (b)   be followed-up by a written report on form F2508 within 10 days of the date on which the incident occurred.

- For factories, warehouses, construction sites, etc. the *relevant enforcing authority* is the health and safety inspectorate. For offices, shops, department stores, hotels, inns, guest houses, catering establishments (including restaurants, public-houses, clubs, etc.), schools, hospitals, etc., it is the local authority for the district in which the premises are situated (viz. a district council, a London borough council, the Common Council of the City of London, the Sub-Treasurer of the Inner Temple, the Under-Treasurer of the Middle Temple, the Council of the Isles of Scilly, or, in Scotland, an islands or district council).

See also the paragraph headed *Control of Industrial Major Accident Hazards* at the end of this section.

NOTIFIABLE DANGEROUS OCCURRENCES

• The following are notifiable dangerous occurrences, viz;

Lifting machinery etc.

• 1. The collapse of, the overturning of, or the failure of any load bearing part of —

(a) any lift, hoist, crane, derrick or mobile powered access platform, access cradle or window-cleaning cradle;

(b) any excavator;

(c) fork lift truck; or

(c) any pile driving frame or rig having an overall height, when operating, of more than 7 metres.

Pressure systems

• The failure of any closed vessel (including a boiler or boiler tube) or of any associated pipework, in which the internal pressure was above or below atmospheric pressure, where the failure has the potential to cause the death of any person.

Freight containers

• The failure of any freight container in any of its load-bearing parts while it is being raised, lowered or suspended.

   Note: Freight container means a container as defined in regulation 2(1) of the Freight Containers (Safety Convention) Regulations 1984.

Overhead electric lines

• Any unintentional incident in which plant or equipment either comes into contact with an uninsulated overhead electric line in which the voltage exceeds 200 volts; or causes an electrical discharge from such an electric line by coming into close proximity to it.

Electrical short circuit

- Electrical short circuit or overload attended by fire or explosion which results in the stoppage of the plant involved for more than 24 hours or which has the potential to cause the death of any person.

Explosives

- (1) Any of the following incidents involving explosives —

  (a) the unintentional explosion or ignition of *explosives* other than one (i) caused by the unintentional discharge of a weapon where, apart from that unintentional discharge, the weapon and *explosives* functioned as they were designed to do; or (ii) where a fail-safe device or safe system of work functioned so as to prevent any person from being injured in consequence of the explosion or ignition;

  (b) a misfire (other than one at a mine or quarry or inside a well or one involving a weapon) except where a fail-safe device or safe system of work functioned so as to prevent any person from being endangered in consequence of the misfire;

  (c) the failure of the shots in any demolition operation to cause the intended extent of collapse or direction of fall of a building or structure;

  (d) the projection of material (other than at a quarry) beyond the boundary of the site on which the *explosives* are being used, or beyond the *danger zone*, in circumstances such that any person was, or might have been, injured by that projection;

  (e) any injury to a person (other than at a mine or quarry, or one otherwise reportable under these Regulations) involving first-aid or medical treatment resulting from the explosion
  or   discharge of any *explosives* or detonator.

Note: The word explosives means any explosive of a type which would, were it being transported, be assigned to Class 1 within the meaning of the Classification & Labelling of Explosives Regulations 1983; and danger zone means the area from which persons have been excluded or forbidden to enter to avoid being endangered by any explosion or ignition of explosives.

Biological agents

- Any accident of incident which resulted, or could have resulted, in the release or escape of a biological agent likely to cause severe human infection or illness.

Malfunction of radiation generators, etc.

- Any incident in which —

  (a) the malfunction of a *radiation generator* or its ancillary equipment, used in fixed or mobile industrial radiography, the irradiation of food, or the processing of products by irradiation, causes it to fail to de-energise at the end of the intended exposure period; or

  (b) the malfunction of equipment used in fixed or mobile industrial radiography, or gamma irradiation, causes a radioactive source to fail to return to its safe position by the normal means at the end of the intended exposure period.

  Note: The term radiation generator has the same meaning as in regulation 2 of the Ionising Radiations Regulations 1985.

Breathing apparatus

- Any incident in which breathing apparatus malfunctions while in use, or during testing immediately prior to use (in such a way, in the latter instance, that had the malfunction occurred while the apparatus was in use, it would have posed a danger to the health or safety of the user).

  Note: The above does not apply to an incident involving breathing apparatus in use in a mine. Nor does it apply to breathing apparatus while it is being maintained or tested as part of a routine maintenance procedure.

Diving operations

- Any of the following incidents in relation to a diving operation —

  (a) the failure or the endangering of any lifting equipment associated with the diving operation, or of life support equipment, including control panels, hoses and breathing apparatus, which puts a diver at risk;

(b)   any damage to, or endangering of, the dive platform, or any failure of the dive platform to remain on station, which puts a diver at risk;

(c)   the trapping of a diver;

(d)   any explosion in the vicinity of a diver; or

(e)   any uncontrolled ascent or any omitted decompression which puts a diver at risk.

Collapse of scaffolding

- A collapse or partial collapse of —

   (a)   any scaffold which is more than 5 metres high which results in a substantial part of the scaffold falling or overturning; or the complete or partial collapse of a scaffold erected over (or adjacent to water) in circumstances such that there would be a risk of drowning to a person falling from the scaffold into the water.

   (b)   the suspension arrangements (including any outrigger) of any slung or suspended scaffold, which causes a working platform or cradle to fall.

Train collisions

- Any unintended collision of a train with any other train or vehicle (other than one otherwise reportable under Part IV of Schedule 3 to the 1995 Regulations) which caused, or might have caused, the death or, or major injury to, any person.

   Note: For the meaning of the expression major injury, please turn to the sections of this handbook titled **Accidents at Work** and **Accidents to Customers, Visitors, etc.**

Wells

- Any of the following incidents in relation to a well (other than a well sunk for the purpose of the extraction of water) —

   (a)   a blow-out (that is to say, an uncontrolled flow of well-fluids from a well);

(b) the coming into operation of a blow-out prevention or diversion system to control a flow from a well where normal control procedures fail;

(c) the detection of hydrogen sulphide in the course of operations at a well, or in samples of well-fluids from a well where the presence of hydrogen sulphide in the reservoir being drawn on by the well was not anticipated by the responsible person before that detection;

(d) the taking of precautionary measures additional to any contained in the original drilling programme following failure to maintain a planned minimum separation distance between wells drilled from a particular installation; or

(e) the mechanical failure of any *safety critical element* of a well.

Note: For the purposes of (e) above, the *safety critical element* of a well is any part of a well whose failure would cause, or contribute to, or whose purpose is to prevent or limit the effect of, the unintentional release of fluids from a well or a reservoir being drawn on by the well.

Pipeline or pipeline works

- The following incidents in respect of a pipeline or pipeline works —

(a) the uncontrolled or accidental escape of anything from, or inrush of anything into, a pipeline, which has the potential to cause the death of, or major injury or damage to the health of, any person, or which results in the pipeline being shut down from ore than 24 hours;

(b) the unintentional ignition of anything in a pipeline or of anything which, immediately before it was ignited, was in a pipeline;

(c) any damage to any part of a pipeline which has the potential to cause the death of, major injury or damage to the health of any person, or which results in the pipeline being shut down for more than 24 hours;

(d) any substantial and unintentional change in the position of a pipeline requiring immediate attention to safeguard the integrity or safety of a pipeline;

(e)   any unintentional change in the subsoil or seabed in the vicinity of a pipeline which has the potential to affect the integrity or safety of a pipeline;

(f)   any failure of any pipeline isolation device, equipment or system, which has the potential to cause the death of, major injury or damage to the health of, any person, or which results in the pipeline being shut down from more than 24 hours; or

(g)   any failure of equipment involved with pipeline works which has the potential to cause the death of, major injury or damage to the health of, any person.

Fairground equipment

- The following incidents on fairground equipment in use or under test —

    (a)   the failure of any load-bearing part;
    (b)   the failure of any part designed to support or restrain passengers; or
    (c)   the derailment or the unintended collision of cars or trains.

Carriage of dangerous substances by road

- Any incident involving a *road tanker* or *tank container* used for the *carriage* of a *dangerous substance* in which —

    (a)   the road tanker or vehicle carrying the tank container (overturns or turns on its side;

    (b)   the tank carrying the dangerous substance is seriously damaged;

    (c)   there is an uncontrolled release or escape of the dangerous substance being carried; or

    (d)   there is a fire involving the dangerous substance being carried.

Note: The words carriage, dangerous substance, road tanker and tank container have the same meanings as in the Carriage of Dangerous Goods by Road

Regulations 1996 (SI 1996/2095).

- Any incident involving a vehicle used for the *carriage* of a *dangerous substance*, other than a vehicle to which the preceding paragraph applies, where there is —

  (a) an uncontrolled release or escape of the dangerous substance being carried in such a quantity as to have the potential to cause the death of, or major injury to, any person; or

  (b) a fire which involves the dangerous substance being carried.

  Note: In the paragraph above, carriage and dangerous substance have the same meaning as in the Carriage of Dangerous Goods by Road Regulations 1996 (SI 1996/2095).

OTHER REPORTABLE DANGEROUS OCCURRENCES

- The following dangerous occurrences are also reportable *except* in relation to offshore workplaces:

Collapse of a building or structure

- Any unintended collapse or partial collapse of —

  (a) any building or structure (whether above or below ground) under construction, reconstruction, alteration or demolition which involves a fall of more than 5 tonnes of material; or

  (b) any floor or wall of any building (whether above or below ground) used as a place of work; or

  (c) any false-work.

Explosion or fire

- An explosion or fire occurring in any plant or premises which results in the stoppage of that plant or, as the case may be, the suspension of normal work in those premises for more than 24 hours, where the explosion or fire was due to the ignition of any material.

Escape of flammable substances

- The sudden, uncontrolled release —

  (a) (inside a building) of 100 kilograms or more of a *flammable liquid*; of 10 kilograms or more of a flammable liquid at a temperature above its normal boiling point; or of 10 kilograms or more of a *flammable gas*; or

  (b) in the open air, of 500 kilograms or more of any of the substances referred to in (a).

  Note: The terms flammable liquid and flammable gas mean, respectively, a liquid and a gas so classified in accordance with regulation 5(2), (3) or (5) of the Chemicals (Hazard Information & Packaging for Supply) Regulations 1994 (SI 1994/3247); as to which, see **Dangerous chemicals** elsewhere in this handbook.

Escape of substances

- The accidental release or escape of any substance in a quantity sufficient to cause the death, major injury or any other damage to the health of, any person.

REPORTING PROCEDURE

- Regulation 3(1)(*ibid.*) states that the enforcing authority must be notified immediately of any notifiable dangerous occurrence in their area. This usually means a telephone call to the nearest office of the enforcing authority (as defined earlier in this section), or direct to the homes of inspectors who are on 24-hour call. If there is no 24-hour call service, and the incident occurs at a weekend or at night, or at any other time when the enforcing authority's offices are closed, the information should reach the authority as soon as is reasonably practicable. Early notification will enable inspectors to make a prompt investigation of the circumstances, if they consider such an investigation to be necessary.

- A written report of the dangerous occurrence must be despatched to the enforcing authority within 10 days. The prescribed form is F2508 (ISBN 0 7176 1078 0), copies of which are available from HSE Books (price £4.95 per pad, or £4.50 each for 10 and more pads) at the address given on page 328.

RECORD OF DANGEROUS OCCURRENCES

- An employer must not only report every dangerous occurrence but must keep a written record of every such occurrence — which record must be kept for at least three years from the date on which it was made (*ibid*; Regulation 7). A legible copy of every completed form F2508 will suffice for this purpose.

Offences and penalties

- A person who fails to report a notifiable dangerous occurrence or who neglects to maintain a written record of all such occurrences is guilty of an offence and liable, on summary conviction, to a fine not exceeding £2,000 (or, on conviction on indictment, to a fine of an unlimited amount (section 33(3), Health and Safety at Work, etc., Act 1974). See also **Accidents at work** and **Diseases, Reportable**, elsewhere in this handbook.

CONTROL OF INDUSTRIAL MAJOR ACCIDENT HAZARDS

- Under the Control of Industrial Major Accident Hazards Regulations 1984 (SI 1984/1902, as amended), any manufacturer having control of installations, in which specified processes (such as alkylation, esterification, sulphonation, distillation, etc.) are used for the production, processing or treatment of organic or inorganic chemicals, must be able to demonstrate to the relevant enforcing authority that he has identified major accident hazards, has taken appropriate steps to prevent or limit the consequences of any major accident, and has provided suitable information, training and equipment for those of his employees who are working on the site. He must also report any major accident to the Health & Safety Executive (HSE) which, in its turn, is duty-bound to relay that information to the Commission of the European Communities.

- The manufacturer is also required to prepare and keep up to date an on-site emergency plan detailing how major accidents will be dealt with on the site. The local authority for the district in which the installation is situated is also duty-bound to prepare and keep up to date an off-site emergency plan on the basis of the information to be supplied to it by the manufacturer after consulting him, the HSE and "any other appropriate person". The manufacturer must also inform persons outside the installation, who may be affected by a major accident occurring on the premises, of the nature of the hazard, and of the safety measures and steps to be taken should such an accident occur. Details of HSE publications which explain the requirements and prohibitions imposed by the 1984 Regulations are to be found at the end of the section titled **Managing health & safety at work** elsewhere in this handbook.

FURTHER INFORMATION

- The following publications are available from HSE Books, For more details, please turn to page 328 of this handbook.

  L73
  A guide to RIDDOR 95 [1996]
  ISBN 0 7176 1012 8   ££6.95

  A guide to RIDDOR (on diskette) plus electronic versions of forms F2508/F2508A
  ISBN 0 7176 1080 2   £19.50

  F2508/F2508A
  Report of an injury, dangerous occurrence or case of disease [1996]
  ISBN 0 7176 1078 0
  Each pad contains 16 F2508 forms and 4 F2508A forms
    1 – 9 pads each cost £4.95 + VAT
    10 and more pads each cost £4.50 + VAT

  F2508G
  Report of flammable gas incidents and dangerous gas fittings [1996]
  ISBN 0 7176 1114 0   £4.95 + VAT per pad of 20 forms.

Free Leaflets (Telephone 01787 881165)

  HSE.31
  Everyone's guide to RIDDOR 95
  ISBN 0 7176 1077 2   Single copy free; £5.00 per pack of 10 leaflets (Further quantity discounts)

Also available from HSE Books at the address given on page 328 is the following publication, which will be of interest only to employers in the education sector:

Guidance on a voluntary scheme for the collection, collation and analysis of injury, disease and dangerous occurrence data in

the education sector [1986]
ISBN 0 11 883855 5   £2.90

DEFECTIVE EQUIPMENT
(Injury to Employees)

Key points

- If an employee is injured in the course of his employment in consequence of a defect in any machine or appliance provided by his employer and the defect is attributable wholly or partly to the fault of a third party (usually the manufacturer or supplier of the machine or appliance in question) the employer will nonetheless be held liable for the employee's injuries and may face an action for damages in the ordinary courts (section 1, Employer's Liability (Defective Equipment) Act 1969).

- Any attempt by an employer to exclude or restrict his liability in such circumstances (either by the inclusion of an escape clause in an employee's contract of employment or by the posting of a notice adjacent to a particular machine or appliance, or by any other method) is null and void. In other words, whether or not the injured employee had previously agreed to any such contract term etc; he (or she) may still sue his employer for damages in the ordinary courts.

- It is up to the employer to seek his own remedy from the manufacturer or supplier of the defective machine or appliance (*ibid*; section 1(1)(h)). Clearly he is better placed than an injured employee to locate a manufacturer or supplier who may be based overseas or have since gone out of business.

- The expression injury includes loss of life, any impairment of a person's physical or mental condition, and any disease (*ibid*; section 1(3)).

  See also **Care, Common duty of, Dangerous machines, Fencing & Guarding, Insurance, Compulsory** and **Machinery safety** elsewhere in this handbook.

DISABLED PERSONS

Key points

- An employer's general duty under section 2 of the Health & Safety at Work etc. Act 1974 to ensure, so far as is reasonably practicable, the health, safety and welfare at work of all his employees, is arguably more stringent in the case of employees who are disabled. If there is a dangerous occurrence or other emergency (such as a fire, explosion or bomb warning), the people responsible for evacuating the employer's premises should already have the names and locations of every disabled employee and should have well-established procedures for moving such people or helping them move speedily to a place of safety. In the absence of such procedures, any resultant accident involving a disabled employee will almost certainly invite a very thorough investigation and possible criminal proceedings under the 1974 Act.

Duty to persons other than employees

- Section 3 of the 1974 Act also imposes a duty on employers and self-employed persons to conduct their undertakings in such a way as will ensure, so far as is reasonably practicable, that persons not in their employ (visitors, customers, clients, trades people, and members of the public) are not needlessly exposed to risks to their health and safety. An employer's criminal liability under the 1974 Act is reinforced by his duty under the Occupiers' Liability Act 1957 (as amended) to take such steps as are necessary to ensure that his visitors are reasonably safe in using those premises for the purposes for which they are invited or permitted to be there — as to which, please turn to the section titled **Occupier of premises** elsewhere in this handbook.

- That same general duty clearly applies to all employees and to all visitors (whether they are able-bodied or otherwise); the more so as contemporary legislation (see next paragraph and below) requires employers (trade organisations and the providers of services) to make such alterations or adjustments to their premises as may be necessary to facilitate access to and from those premises by disabled persons.

Management of Health & Safety at Work Regulations 1992

- Regulation 3 of the Management of Health & Safety at Work Regulations 1992 (SI 1992/2051) requires every employer in every workplace to make a suitable and sufficient assessment of the risks to which his employees are exposed while they are at work. Paragraph 16(d) of the accompanying Approved Code of Practice says that the risk assessment should (amongst other things) identify groups of workers, including disabled persons, who might be particularly at risk

Workplace (Health, Safety & Welfare) Regulations 1992

- Regulation 17 of the Workplace (Health, Safety & Welfare) Regulations 1992 (SI 1992/3004) imposes a duty on employers to provide a sufficient number of pedestrian walkways, corridors and traffic routes in factories, offices, shops, warehouses, schools, hospitals (indeed, in any premises made available as a place of work) to enable people to move about safely. When designing, rearranging or organising traffic routes employers should not (says the accompanying Approved Code of Practice) overlook the needs of people with impaired sight, or who are hard of hearing, or who are in wheelchairs or using crutches or other walking aids. Traffic routes used by people in wheelchairs should be wide enough to allow unimpeded access and be provided with ramps where necessary. Buzzers, hooters, flashing lights, safety signs, etc. will give warning of approaching traffic to people with impaired sight or hearing. For the same reason, corridors, gangways and pedestrian walkways should avoid dangerous features or obstructions, such as pillars or low ceilings.

- Traffic routes in existence in workplaces before January 1, 1993, must be modified or adapted before January 1, 1996 if they do not already comply with the 1992 Regulations. In the meantime, employers owe it to their employees to inform them about any inherently unsafe features, bearing in mind their overriding duty under section 2(2)(d) of the Health & Safety at Work etc. Act 1974 to provide a safe place of work, and safe means of access to and egress from that place of work.

Washrooms and toilets

- When designing and building washrooms and toilets for use by employees, employers must ensure that they too are accessible to and suitable for use by workers with disabilities, particularly those in wheelchairs. The transitional arrangements for facilities built or brought into first use before 31 December 1992 expired on 31 December 1995. Nowadays, all washrooms and toilets must accommodate the needs of disabled workers (Regs 20 & 21, Workplace (Health, Safety & Welfare) Regulations 1992 [*q.v.*]).

Chronically Sick & Disabled Persons Act 1970

- Section 8A of the Chronically Sick & Disabled Persons Act 1970 (inserted by the eponymous (Amendment) Act 1976) imposes a duty on the owners and developers of proposed new offices, shops, railway premises, factories, and other commercial and industrial premises, to consider the needs of disabled persons when designing the means of access to (and within) those premises, including the means of access to parking facilities and sanitary conveniences.

- Although the owners or developers of premises intended for use as offices, shops, factories, workshops, etc. cannot be prosecuted for failing to comply with their duties under the 1970 Act, there is nothing to prevent a disabled person denied ready access to such premises (or injured as a direct consequence of the owner or developer's breach of his statutory duty under the 1970 Act) from pursuing a civil action for damages. In any event, when granting planning permission for new offices, shops, factories, etc. (or for the conversion of existing buildings), local authorities are duty-bound to draw the attention of the person to whom planning permission has been granted to the relevant provisions of the 1970 Act and to the Code of Practice for Access for the Disabled to Buildings (per section 29A, Town & Country Planning Act 1971).

Disability Discrimination Act 1995

- The Disability Discrimination Act 1995 (which came into force on 2 December 1996) is not safety-specific. Nonetheless, it does caution employers (with 20 or more people on the payroll), trade organisations and the providers of services that, if any physical feature of the premises they occupy places a disabled person at a substantial disadvantage relative to persons who are not disabled, or makes it impossible or unreasonably difficult for such persons to make use of such a service, it is their duty to take such steps as are reasonable —

(a)   to remove the feature;
(b)   alter it so that it no longer has that effect;
(c)   provide a reasonable means of avoiding the feature; or
(d)   provide a reasonable alternative method of making the
        service in question available to disabled persons.

(*ibid*; sections 6(1), 15(1) & 21(2))

•   Any attendant adjustment or alteration to business or
    commercial premises (which terms include hotels, boarding
    houses, restaurants, cafeterias, schools, hospitals, cinemas,
    gymnasia; etc.) may well satisfy the needs of the Disability
    Discrimination Act 1995, but could fall foul of the Health &
    Safety at Work, etc. Act 1974, the Fire Precautions Act 1971,
    and related legislation — if issues of safety are not also taken
    into account.

Alterations to premises occupied under leases

•   If an employer, trade organisation or provider of services,
    occupies leasehold premises — on terms which do not allow the
    lessee (or occupier) to make a particular alteration to those
    premises — the lease in question shall have effect by virtue of the
    relevant provisions of the 1995 Act, as if it provided for the
    occupier to be entitled to make the alteration with the written
    consent of the lessor (which consent must not be unreasonably
    withheld, although the lessor is entitled to make his [or her]
    consent subject to reasonable conditions) (*ibid*; sections 16 & 27).

DISEASES, REPORTABLE
(*under RIDDOR 1995*)

Key points

•   An employer must complete Form F2508A and send it forthwith
    to the *enforcing authority* as soon as he is aware that one of his
    employees has contracted a *reportable disease*. A disease is
    reportable (a) if it is one of those listed below and (b) if the
    person who contracted it is (or was) engaged in the work activity

(or was exposed to the substances) referred to in the accompanying text.

Note: For industrial undertakings (factories, workshops, railway premises, docks, container depots, wharves, quays, construction, electrical or engineering works, building sites, garages, laundries, radio and TV repair shops, gas installations, water and sewage works, dry cleaners, and the like, the *enforcing authority* is the Health & Safety Executive. The same is true of premises in which flammable, toxic, oxidizing, corrosive or explosive substances or petroleum spirit are sold or stored for retail or wholesale distribution. For offices, shops, wholesale outlets, department stores, supermarkets, warehouses, restaurants, cafeterias, canteens, pubs, hotels, guest houses, bed and breakfast establishments, the enforcing authority will be the relevant district council, London borough council or (in Scotland) the appropriate islands or district council. For the most part, it is the main activity carried on at a particular premises (rather than any ancillary or minor activity) which determines the identity of the enforcing authority for those premises. For example, the Health & Safety Executive will be the enforcing authority for a factory as well as for the offices and administrative buildings attached to that factory. Likewise, the local authority will be the enforcing authority for a large office block as well as for the small maintenance workshop in the basement of the same building.

• An employer's (or self-employed person's) duty to inform the enforcing authority of all reportable diseases is to be found in Regulation 5 of the Reporting of Injuries, Diseases & Dangerous Occurrences Regulations 1995 (SI 1995/3163). A person who fails to comply with that duty is guilty of an offence under the Health & Safety at Work etc. Act 1974 and is liable, on summary conviction, to a fine of up to £2,000 or, on conviction on indictment, to a fine of an unlimited amount (*ibid*; section 33(1)(c)). However, in any proceedings for an offence under the 1995 Regulations (*q.v.*), it will be a defence for an employer to prove that he was not aware of the fact that one of his employees had contracted a reportable disease, so long as he can also satisfy the court that he had put in place a procedure for ensuring that all reportable diseases (including reportable accidents and dangerous occurrences) were brought to his notice without delay (*ibid*; Regulation 11).

REPORTABLE DISEASES

The reportable diseases listed below are to be found in Schedule 3 to the 1995 Regulations (Crown copyright acknowledged).

Conditions due to physical agents and the physical demands of work

• The following — due to (and caused by) work with ionising radiation:

(a) inflammation, ulceration or malignant disease of the skin
(b) malignant disease of the bones
(c) blood dycrasia

- Cataract due to work involving exposure to electromagnetic radiation (including radiant heat.

- The following — due to work involving breathing gases at increased pressure (including diving):

  (a) decompression illness
  (b) barotrauma resulting in lung or other organ damage
  (c) dysbaric osteonecrosis

- Cramp of the hand or forearm due to repetitive movements (such as prolonged periods of handwriting, typing or other repetitive movements of the fingers, hand or arm).

- Subcutaneous cellulitis of the hand (usually referred to as *beat hand*) resulting from physically demanding work causing severe or prolonged friction or pressure on the hand.

- Bursitis or subcutaneous cellulitis arising at or about the knee (or elbow) due to severe or prolonged external friction or pressure at or about the knee (or elbow) — commonly referred to as *beat knee* or *beat elbow*.

- Traumatic inflammation of the tendons of the hand or forearm (or of the associated tendon sheaths), resulting from physically demanding work, frequent or repeated movements, constrained postures, or extremes of extension or flexion of the hand or wrist.

- Carpal tunnel syndrome, occasioned by work with hand-held vibrating tools.

- Hand-arm vibration syndrome associated with activities involving:

  (a) the use of chain saws, brush cutters or hand-held (or hand-fed) circular saws in forestry or woodworking;

  (b) the use of hand-held rotary tools in grinding material, or in sanding or polishing metal;

(c)   the holding of material being ground, or of metal being sanded or polished, by rotary tools;

(d)   the use of hand-held percussive metal-working tools, or the holding of metal being worked upon by such tools in connection with riveting, caulking, chipping, hammering, fettling or swaging;

(e)   the use of hand-held powered percussive drills or hand-held powered percussive hammers in mining, quarrying or demolition, or on roads or footpaths (including road construction); or

(f)   the holding of material being worked upon by pounding machines in shoe manufacture.

Infections due to biological agents

- Anthrax caused by work involving the handling infected animals (or of their products or packaging containing infected material); or due to work on infected sites.

- Brucellosis occasioned by work involving contact with brucella-infected animals or animal carcases (including any parts or products of such animals or carcases); or by work with laboratory specimens or vaccines of, or containing, brucella.

- Avian chlamydiosis caused by work involving contact with birds infected with chlamydia psittaci, or the remains or untreated products of such birds.

- Ovine chlamydiosis caused either by work involving contact with sheep infected with chlamydia psittaci, or by work involving contact with the remains or untreated products of such sheep.

- Hepatitis caused by work involving contact with human blood (or human blood products) or with any source of viral hepatitis.

- Legionellosis due to work on or near workplace cooling systems using water; or work on workplace hot water service systems which are likely to be a source of contamination.

- Leptospirosis occasioned by work in places which are, or are liable to be, infested by rats, field mice, voles or other small animals; or by work at dog kennels involving the care or handling of dogs; or by work involving contact with bovine animals (or their meat products) or pigs (or their meat products).

- Lyme disease contracted by people (such as forestry workers, rangers, dairy farmers, gamekeepers, and other persons engaged in countryside management) whose work involves exposure to ticks.

- Q fever developed by people whose work involves contact with animals, their remains or their untreated products.

- Rabies contracted by people whose work involves contact with infected animals.

- Streptococcus suis due to work involving contact with pigs infected with streptococcus suis, or with the carcases, products or residues of pigs so affected.

- Tetanus occasioned by work involving contact with soil likely to be contaminated by animals.

- Tuberculosis attributed to work with persons, animals, human or animal remains, or with any other material which might be a source of infection.

- Any infection reliably attributable to work with micro-organisms; work with live or dead human beings (in the course of providing any treatment or service, or in conducting any investigation involving exposure to blood or body fluids); or work with animals or any potentially infected material derived from any of the above.

Conditions due to substances

- Poisoning of a person at work by one or other of the following substances:

  (a) acrylamide monomer
  (b) arsenic or one of its compounds
  (c) benzene or a homologue of benzene
  (d) beryllium or one of its compounds
  (e) cadmium or one of its compounds
  (f) carbon disulphide

(g)   diethylene dioxide (dioxan)
(h)   ethylene oxide
(i)   lead or one of its compounds
(j)   manganese or one of its compounds
(k)   mercury or one of its compounds
(l)   methyl bromide
(m)   nitrochlorobenzene, or a nitro- or amino- or chloro-
        derivative of benzene or of a homologue of benzene
(n)   oxides of nitrogen
(o)   phosphorus or one of its compounds

while engaged in any activity.

• Cancer of a bronchus or lung due to work in or about a building
  where nickel is produced by decomposition of a gaseous nickel or
  where any industrial process which is ancillary or incidental to
  that process is carried on; or work involving exposure to
  bis(chloromethyl) ether or any electrolytic chromium processes
  (excluding passivation) which involves hexavalent chromium
  compounds, chromate production or zinc chromate pigment
  manufacture.

• Primary carcinoma of the lung, where there is accompanying
  evidence of silicosis, contracted by persons engaged in glass
  manufacture, sandstone tunnelling or quarrying, the pottery
  industry, metal ore mining, slate quarrying or production, clay
  mining, the use of siliceous materials as abrasives, foundry work,
  granite tunnelling or quarrying, or stone cutting or masonry.

• Cancer of the urinary tract occasioned by workers engaged in the
  manufacture of auramine or magenta, or by workers exposed to
  any of the following substances:

  (a)   beta-naphthylamine or methylene-bis-orthochloroaniline;

  (b)   diphenyl substituted by at least one nitro or primary
        amino group or by at least one nitro and primary
        amino group (including benzidine);

  (c)   any of the substances mentioned in (b) if further ring
        substituted by halogeno, methyl or methoxy groups,
        but not by other groups;

  (d)   the salts of any of the substances mentioned in (a) to

(c) above;

- Bladder cancer contracted by persons engaged in work involving exposure to aluminium smelting using the Soderberg process.

- Angiosarcoma of the liver occasioned by:

    (a)   work in or about machinery or apparatus used for the polymerization of vinyl chloride monomer, a process which, for these purposes, comprises all operations up to and including the drying of the slurry produced by the polymerization and the packaging of the dried product; or

    (b)   work in a building or structure in which any part of the process described in (a) takes place.

- Peripheral neuropathy contracted by workers using or handling (or exposed to) the fumes of (or vapour containing) n-hexane or methyl n-butyl ketone.

- Chrome ulceration of

    (a)   the nose or throat; or of
    (b)   the skin of the hands or forearm

    while engaged in work involving exposure to chromic acid or of any other chromium compound.

- Folliculitis, acne or skin cancer contracted while engaged in work involving exposure to mineral oil, tar, pitch or arsenic.

- Pneumoconiosis (excluding asbestosis) contracted while engaged in:

    (a)   the mining, quarrying or working of silica rock or the working of dried quartzose sand or of any dry deposit or dry residue of silica or of any dry admixture containing such materials (including any activity in which any of the aforesaid operations are carried out incidentally to the mining or quarrying of other materials or to the manufacture of articles containing crushed or ground silica rock);

(b)   the handling of any of the materials specified in sub-paragraph (a) above in (or incidental to) to any of the operations mentioned in that paragraph, or substantial exposure to the dust arising from such operations;

(c)   the breaking, crushing or grinding of flint or the working or handling of broken, crushed or ground flint or materials containing such flint, or substantial exposure to the dust arising from any such operations;

(d)   sand blasting by means of compressed air, with the use of quartzose sand or crushed silica rock or flint, or substantial exposure to the dust arising from such sand blasting;

(e)   work in a foundry or the performance of, or substantial exposure to, the dust arising from, any of the following operations:

(i) the freeing of steel castings from adherent siliceous substance; or

(ii) the freeing of metal castings from adherent siliceous substance by blasting with an abrasive propelled by compressed air, steam or a wheel; or by the use of power-driven tools.

(f)   the manufacture of china or earthenware (including sanitary earthenware, electrical earthenware and earthenware tiles) and any activity involving substantial exposure to the dust arising from such activity;

(g)   the grinding of mineral graphite or substantial exposure to the dust arising from such grinding;

(h)   the dressing of graphite (or any igneous rock) by masons, the crushing of such materials, or substantial exposure to the dust arising from such operations;

(i)   the use (or preparation for use) of an abrasive wheel, or substantial exposure to the dust arising from such use (or preparation);

(j)   work underground in any mine in which one of the objects of the mining operation is the getting of any material;

(k)   the working or handling above ground at any coal or tin mine of any minerals extracted from that mine, or any operation incidental to such activities;

(l)   the trimming of coal in any ship, barge or lighter, or in any dock or harbour, or at any wharf or quay;

(m)   the sawing, splitting or dressing of slate, or any operation incidental to such activities;

(n   the manufacture (or work incidental to the manufacture) of carbon electrodes by an industrial undertaking for use in the electrolytic extraction of aluminium from aluminium oxide, and any activity involving substantial exposure to the dust arising from that process; and

(o)   boiler scaling or substantial exposure to the dust arising from that activity.

- Byssinosis contracted by a person working in a room in a factory in which raw or waste cotton or flax is spun or manipulated, or in which cotton or flax is woven.

- Mesothelioma, lung cancer or asbestosis due to:

(a)   the working or handling of asbestos or any admixture of asbestos;

(b)   the manufacture or repair of asbestos textiles or other articles containing or composed of asbestos;

(c)   the cleaning of any machinery or plant used in any of the operations referred to in (b) and of any chambers, fixtures and appliances for the collection of asbestos dust; or

(d)   substantial exposure to the dust arising from any of the foregoing operations.

- Cancer of the nasal cavity or associated air sinuses contracted by a person engaged in:

(a)   work in or about a building where wooden furniture is manufactured; or

(b)   work in a building used for the manufacture of footwear (or components of footwear) made wholly or partly of leather or fibre board; or

(c)   work at a place used wholly or mainly for the repair of footwear made wholly or partly of leather or fibre board; or

(d)   work in or about a factory building where nickel is produced by decomposition of a gaseous nickel compound which necessitates working in or about a building or buildings where that process or any other incidental or ancillary industrial process is carried on.

- Occupational dermatitis caused by work involving exposure to any of the following:

(a)   epoxy resin systems;

(b)   formaldehyde and its resins;

(c)   metalworking fluids;

(d)   chromate (haxavalent and derived from trivalent chromium);

(e)   cement, plaster or concrete;

(f)   acrylates and methacrylates;

(g)   colophony (rosin) and its modified products;

(h)   glutaraldehyde;

(i)   mercaptobenzothiazole, thiurams, substituted paraphenylene-diamines and related rubber processing;

(j)   biocides, anti-bacterials, preservatives or disinfectants

(k)   organic solvents;

(l) antibiotics and other pharmaceuticals and therapeutic agents;

(m) strong acids, strong alkilis, strong solutions (e.g. brine) and oxidising agents (including domestic bleach or reducing agents);

(n) hairdressing products — including, in particular, dyes, shampoos, bleaches and permanent waving solutions

(o) soaps and detergents;

(p) plants and plant-derived material including, in particular, daffodil, tulip and chrysanthemum families, the parsley family (carrots, parsnips, parsley and celery), garlic and onion, hardwoods, and the pine family;

(q) fish, shell-fish or meat;

(r) sugar or flour; or

(s) any other known irritant or sensitizing agent including, in particular any chemical bearing the warning may cause sensitization by skin contact or irritating to the skin.

- Extrinsic alveolitis due to exposure to moulds or fungal spores or heterologous proteins during work in —

  (a) agriculture, horticulture, forestry, cultivation of edible fungi or malt-working;

  (b) loading, unloading or handling stored mouldy vegetable matter or edible fungi;

  (c) caring for or handling birds; or

  (d) handling bagasse.

- Occupational asthma contracted while engaged in work involving exposure to any of the following agents:

  (a) isocyanates;

  (b) platinum salts;

(c)   fumes or dusts arising from the manufacture, transport or use of hardening agents (including epoxy resin curing agents) based on phthalic anhydride, tetrachlorophthalic anhydride, trimellitic anhydride or triethylene-tetramine;

(d)   fumes arising from the use of rosin as a soldering flux;

(e)   proteolytic enzymes;

(f)   animals, including insects and other anthropods used for the purposes of research or education, or in laboratories;

(g)   dusts arising from the sowing, cultivation, harvesting, drying, handling, milling, transport or storage of barley, oats, rye, wheat or maize; or the handling, milling, transport or storage of meal or flour made from meal;

(h)   antibiotics;

(i)   cimetidine;

(j)   wood dust;

(k)   ispaghula;

(l)   castor bean dust;

(m)   ipecacuanha;

(n)   azodicarbonamide;

(o)   animals including insects and other anthropods (whether in their larval forms or not) used for the purposes of pest control or fruit cultivation, or the larval forms of animals used for the purposes of research or education, or in laboratories;

(p)   glutaraldehyde;

(q)   persulphate salts or henna;

(r) crustaceans or fish or products arising from these in the food processing industry;

(s) reactive dyes;

(t) soya bean;

(u) tea dust;

(v) green coffee bean dust;

(w) fumes from stainless steel welding;

(x) any other sensitizing agent, including in particular any chemical bearing the warning may cause sensitization of the skin.

FURTHER INFORMATION

• The following publications are available from HSE Books. For more details, please turn to page 328 of this handbook.

L73
A guide to RIDDOR 95 [1996]
ISBN 0 7176 1012 8   ££6.95

A guide to RIDDOR (on diskette) plus electronic versions of forms F2508/F2508A
ISBN 0 7176 1080 2   £19.50

F2508/F2508A
Report of an injury, dangerous occurrence or case of disease [1996]
ISBN 0 7176 1078 0
Each pad contains 16 F2508 forms and 4 F2508A forms
    1 – 9 pads each cost £4.95 + VAT
    10 and more pads each cost £4.50 + VAT

Free Leaflets (Telephone 01787 881165)

HSE.31
Everyone's guide to RIDDOR 95
ISBN 0 7176 1077 2   Single copy free; £5.00 per pack of 10 leaflets (Further quantity discounts)

Also available from HSE Books at the address given on page 328 is the following publication, which will be of interest only to employers in the education sector:

Guidance on a voluntary scheme for the collection, collation and analysis of injury, disease and dangerous occurrence data in the education sector [1986]
ISBN 0 11 883855 5　£2.90

See also **Accidents at work, Accident Book** and **Dangerous occurrences** elsewhere in this handbook.

DISMISSAL OR VICTIMISATION *(in health and safety cases)*

Key points

- It is inadmissible and unfair for an employer to recruit or 'designate' an employee either as a safety officer or 'competent person' and then to victimises, dismiss or select that same employee for redundancy for carrying out (or proposing to carry out) his or her legitimate duties (sections 44 & 100, Employment Rights Act 1996).

- *Note:* Regulation 6 of the Management of Health & Safety at Work Regulations 1992 (SI 1992/2051) requires an employer to appoint one or more competent persons to assist him in undertaking the measures he needs to take to comply with the requirements and prohibitions imposed upon him by or under the relevant statutory provisions (that is to say, under the Health & Safety at Work etc. Act 1974 and statutes and regulations made under or saved by that Act). For further particulars, please turn to the section titled **Competent persons** elsewhere in this handbook.

- The same rule applies if an employee is victimised (ie; subjected to any detriment) dismissed or selected for redundancy —

  (a)　for performing (or proposing to perform) his functions as an appointed *safety representative* or as a *member of a safety committee* (under the Safety Representatives & Safety Committees Regulations 1977 [SI 1977/500]);

  (b)　for performing (or proposing to perform) his functions as a *representative of employee safety*, having been elected as such by his or her fellow-employees (under the provisions of the Health & Safety (Consultation with Employees) Regulations 1996 [SI 1996/1513]).

- Any employee designated, appointed or elected to represent the interests of fellow-employees on issues affecting (or likely to affect) their health and safety at work, has the legal right to carry out his (or her) functions without being victimised or threatened with dismissal for doing so. If such a person *is* dismissed for that reason, he may pursue a complaint of unfair dismissal regardless of his (or her) age or length of service at the time his employment ended.

- It is *also* automatically unfair to victimise, dismiss or select an employee for redundancy:

  (a) for bringing to the employer's attention, by reasonable means, circumstances connected with his (or her) work which he reasonably believed to be harmful or potentially harmful to health or safety (in a situation in which there either *is* no safety representative or safety committee or *representative of employee safety,* or it was not reasonably practicable to contact or involve such persons) ;

  (b) for leaving (or proposing to leave) his (or her) place of work in circumstances of danger (which he reasonably believed to be serious and imminent and which he could not reasonably have been expected to avert) *or* for refusing to return to that place of work or to the dangerous part of that place of work while the danger persisted;

  (c) for taking (or proposing to take) *appropriate* steps to protect himself or other persons from a danger which he reasonably believed to be serious and imminent.

  Whether the steps which an employee took (or proposed to take) under (c) above were *appropriate* is to be judged by all the circumstances including, in particular, his (or her) knowledge and the facilities and advice available to him at the material time (*ibid;* section 100(2)).

- However, sections 44(3) and 100(3) point out that subjecting an employee to a detriment or dismissing him (or her) for acting as he did under (c) above will *not* be treated as having been unreasonable or unfair if the employer can satisfy an industrial tribunal that it was (or would have been) so negligent of the employee to do what he did (or proposed to do) that *any* reasonable employer would have reacted in the same way.

Complaints

- The procedure for presenting a complaint to an industrial tribunal, and the time limits for doing so, are explained in Employment Department booklet PL 712 (Rev 8), copies of which are available free of charge from offices of the Employment Service. Complaints should normally be presented on Form IT1 (available from Job Centres and offices of the Employment Service) and be lodged with the Secretary of the Tribunals within three months either of the effective date of termination or the date on which the punishment or act of victimisation occurred.

Applications for Interim relief

- Any safety officer, safety representative, representative of employee safety, 'competent' person, 'designated' person, or member of a safety committee bringing a complaint of unfair dismissal to an industrial tribunal, in the circumstances described above, may apply to the tribunal for *interim relief* (briefly, a direction to his [or her] employer or former employer ordering him to reinstate or re-engage him pending the determination of his complaint at the subsequent full tribunal hearing).

- An application for interim relief *must* be submitted to an industrial tribunal within seven days of the effective date of termination of the employee's contract of employment.

- An industrial tribunal must hear an application for interim relief as quickly as possible, but not before sending the employer a copy of the employee's application and giving the employer at least seven days' advance written notice of the date, time and place for the hearing.

- If, on hearing the employee's application for interim relief, the tribunal agrees that there is a likelihood that the complaint will be upheld at a full tribunal hearing (which may not take place until several weeks or months later), it will order the employer to reinstate or re-engage the employee until the date set for the full hearing. If the employer fails to attend the interim hearing or has made it clear that he has no intention of reinstating or re-engaging the employee, the tribunal will make an order for the continuation of the employee's contract of employment. This means, in effect, that the employer must continue to pay the employee his or her normal wages or salary (less any reduction in respect of payments already made) until the employee's complaint is finally heard and decided. A failure to comply with the terms of a 'continuation order' will likewise attract an award of compensation which, if need be, will be enforced by the ordinary courts.

Compensation for unlawful dismissal or selection for redundancy

- If an industrial tribunal decides that an employee has been dismissed or selected for redundancy, contrary to section 100 of the Employment Rights Act 1996, it will order the employer either to reinstate or re-engage the complainant or pay a substantial amount of compensation (*ibid*; Part X, Chapter II).

   Note: Employees with no special health and safety responsibilities, who have been dismissed (or selected for redundancy) either for highlighting health and safety issues or for abandoning (or refusing to return to) their place of work in circumstances of serious and imminent danger, will qualify for the *basic* award of compensation (current [March, 1997] minimum: £2,770; maximum: £6,300), the *compensatory* award (Max: £11,300) and, in the appropriate circumstances, an *additional* award (Max: £5,460). Employees, such as safety officers, safety representatives and members of a safety committee, who have been dismissed or selected for redundancy for carrying out (or proposing to carry out) their official or designated functions, will receive the *basic* and *compensatory* awards of compensation plus a *special* award of compensation (as an alternative to the *additional* award). The *special* award will be £13,775 (or two years' pay, whichever is the greater, subject to a maximum of £27,500). These figures are reviewed (but not necessarily adjusted) once every year.

Compensation in victimisation cases

- In victimisation cases (where, for example, an employee has been unfairly disciplined or penalised for challenging or questioning his employer's lack of commitment to health and safety matters), the compensation awarded will be such as the tribunal considers just and equitable in all the circumstances, having regard to the infringement complained of and to any loss sustained by the employee attributable to the act or failure which infringed his or her statutory rights (*ibid*; sections 48 & 49).

   See also **Safety committees and Safety representatives**.

DIVING OPERATIONS AT WORK

Key points

• Because of its industry-specific nature, it is not proposed to conduct an 'in depth' (!) review of legislation dealing with the health and safety aspects of diving operations. Suffice to say that a diving contractor, in his capacity as employer, is as much bound by the provisions of the Health & Safety at Work etc. Act 1974 as is any other employer or self-employed person. Recent legislation, notably the Management of Health & Safety at Work Regulations 1992 (SI 1992/2051) and the Workplace (Health, Safety & Welfare) Regulations 1992 (SI 1992/3004) also apply to diving operations (as they do to all work situations, other than in relation to the master or crew of a sea-going ship) and must be taken into account — as must the Mineral Workings (Offshore Installations) Act 1971 and the Offshore Installations (Operational Safety, Health & Welfare) Regulations 1976 (SI 1976/1019).

• Regulations of particular interest are the Diving Operations at Work Regulations 1981 (SI 1981/399), as amended by the Diving Operations at Work (Amendment) Regulations 1990 (SI 1990/996).

Meaning of 'diver'

• The 1981 Regulations do not define the word diver, but state instead that a person is deemed *not* to be a diver if he (or she) —

   (a)   is in a submersible chamber or craft or in a pressure-resisting diving suit, and is not exposed to a pressure exceeding 300 millibars above atmospheric pressure during normal operation, or

   (b)   uses no underwater breathing apparatus or uses only snorkel type apparatus;

   (c)   is taking part in the diving operation in a capacity other than as an employee or self-employed person; or

   (d)   is on duty as a member of the armed forces and is engaged in operations or operational training.

- According to the *Explanatory Note* accompanying the 1981 Regulations, their purpose is to ensure that a diving contractor is put in charge of all diving operations. His role is to provide safe and suitable plant and equipment, to make rules laying down the procedures to be followed during all diving operations and to appoint a diving supervisor to exercise immediate control over those operations. The Regulations also assign duties to the diving supervisor (who must have certain qualifications and experience) and impose obligations both on the divers themselves and on all persons who exercise any control over diving operations. Divers must have certificates of training in the type of diving to be undertaken, and must be certified medically fit to dive.

- A failure to comply with the provisions of the Diving Operations at Work Regulations 1981 is an offence under the 1974 Act for which the penalty on summary conviction is a fine of up to £2,000; or, if the offender is convicted on indictment, a fine of an unlimited amount.

Dangerous occurrences during diving operations

- Under the provisions of regulation 2(1) of, and Schedule 2 (paragraph 10) to, the Reporting of Injuries, Diseases & Dangerous Occurrences Regulations 1995 (SI 1995/3163), any of the following incidents in relation to a diving operation must be reported to the enforcing authority without delay (to be followed-up by a written report within the next 10 days). The incidents in question are —

  (a) the failure or the endangering of any lifting equipment associated with the diving operation, or of life support equipment, including control panels, hoses and breathing apparatus, which puts a diver at risk;

  (b) any damage to, or endangering of, the dive platform, or any failure of the dive platform to remain on station, which puts a diver at risk;

  (c) the trapping of a diver;

  (d) any explosion in the vicinity of a diver; or

  (e) any uncontrolled ascent or any omitted decompression

which puts a diver at risk.

The prescribed reporting procedure is explained in more detail in the section titled **Dangerous occurrences** elsewhere in this handbook.

FURTHER INFORMATION

• The following HSE forms and publications are available from HSE Books at the address given on page 328.

Explanatory & interpretative

L6
Diving operations at work. The Diving Operations at Work Regulations 1981 as amended by the Diving Operations at Work (Amendment) Regulations 1990 [1991]
ISBN 0 11 885599 9   £4.25

Free leaflets (Telephone 01787 881165)

INDG 108 (Free leaflet)
Advice to divers

INDG 156
Diving directory

Standards for assessing divers

Part I
Basic air diving [1992]
ISBN 0 11 885905 6   £4.00

Part II
Mixed gas diving [1992]
ISBN 0 11 885906 4   £4.00

Part III
Air diving where no surface compression chamber is required on site [1992]
ISBN 0 11 885907 2   £4.00

Part IV
Air diving with self-contained equipment where no surface compression chamber is required on site [1992]

ISBN 0 11 885908 0   £4.00

See also the section titled **Compressed air** elsewhere in this handbook.

DOCK WORKS

Key points

- Because of their industry-specific nature, the following is a summary only of the principal provisions of the Docks Regulations 1988 (SI 1988/1655, as amended by SI 1992/195). The Health & Safety Commission (HSC) has published the full text of the Regulations with their accompanying Approved Code of Practice, copies of which can be purchased from HSE Books — as to which see *FURTHER INFORMATION* at the end of this section).

Meaning of dock operations

- The term dock operations means —

  (a)   the loading or unloading of goods on or from a ship at any dock premises (that is to say, any dock, wharf, jetty, quay or other place at which ships load or unload goods or embark or disembark passengers, including neighbouring land or water and any part of a ship used or occupied for dock operations); and

  (b)   the following incidental activities which take place on dock premises, namely: the mooring, fuelling and provisioning of a ship; the storing, sorting, inspecting, checking, weighing or handling of goods; and the movement of goods, passengers and vehicles

  but does not include a fish-loading process, within the meaning of the Loading & Unloading of Fishing Regulations 1988 (SI 1988/1656), or the loading or unloading of persons or goods from a pleasure craft.

Requirements & prohibitions

- There must be safe means of access (and egress from) dock premises. Dock operations must be planned and executed to avoid danger. Fencing must be provided at specified places. Rescue, life-saving and fire-fighting equipment must be made available and properly maintained. Ships' hatches must be safe, and ramps and car-decks operated safely.

- Only authorised employees may operate lifting appliances or powered vehicles. Lifting plant must be of good design and construction, properly installed and maintained, operated safely, and tested and examined at regular intervals. Certificates and reports of all such tests and examinations must be kept on file and copies made available for inspection by any employer or self-employed person using or wishing to use or hire lifting plant. In specified circumstances, copies of such certificates and reports must be forwarded to the Health & Safety Executive.

- There are also rules relating to work in confined spaces; the wearing of protective helmets and high-visibility clothing; the cleanliness and accessibility of welfare amenities (washrooms, toilets and changing rooms); and so on.

FURTHER INFORMATION

- The following publications are available from HSE Books at the address given on page 328 of this handbook.

  COP 25
  Safety in docks: Docks Regulations 1988: Approved code of practice with Regulations and guidance [1988]
  ISBN 0 11 885456 9   £7.50

Prescribed form

  F.35
  General register for docks etc
  ISBN 0 11 883640 4   £2.00

DOORS & OTHER OPENINGS

Key points

- Doors and gates in workplaces must be suitably constructed and, where appropriate, be fitted with any necessary safety devices. See also *Doors and gates on construction sites* below.

- A sliding door or gate must be fitted with a stop or other type of device to prevent it coming off its track. Upward opening doors or gates must likewise be fitted with devices (such as counter balances or ratchet mechanisms) to prevent them falling back. Automatic (or self-closing) doors and gates must be fitted with detectors or sensitive leading edges to prevent people being struck or trapped as they pass through. If a door or gate is designed to swing in both directions, it must incorporate a transparent panel at eye level to give warning of approaching people or vehicular traffic. The same applies to conventionally hinged doors in corridors and walkways and to doors on main traffic routes (as, for example, in a factory or depot)(Regulation 18, Workplace (Health, Safety & Welfare) Regulations 1992 (SI 1992/3004).

Control switches for automatic doors, etc.

- Automatic doors and gates (including swing doors, sliding doors and upward-moving doors) provided for use in a workplace must be capable of being operated manually in the event of a power failure or similar emergency. Control switches or devices for overriding automatic doors and gates must be clearly identifiable and readily accessible. Normal 'Stop/Start' or 'On/Off' controls will usually suffice. But the employer must see to it that those control switches and devices are tested regularly and maintained in good working order. If tools are necessary for the manual opening of automatic doors and gates, they must be readily available at all times. Furthermore, the employer must satisfy himself that no person opening an automatic door manually is put at risk if the power supply is restored while he is doing so (*ibid*).

Note(1): The expression workplace means any premises (or part of premises), other than domestic premises, which are made available to a person as a place of work. Nowadays, health and safety legislation applies not only to the traditional factories, offices, shops and railway premises but to *every* workplace (including hospitals, schools, cinemas, theatres, the residential areas of hotels, guest houses, bed-and-breakfast establishments, snooker halls, leisure centres, and so on, and so on. The list is endless. If a person is employed to work in a place (other than in the house or flat in which he or she lives), that is his workplace. If a self-employed person works in his (or her) garage or shed, that is his workplace, even if he works alone.

Note (2): The rule about power-operated doors being capable of being opened manually, in the event of a power failure, does not apply to lift doors and other doors and gates which are there to prevent falls or access to areas of potential danger.

• All the devices and controls referred to above must be routinely inspected, tested, adjusted, lubricated, cleaned and, if need be, repaired by a competent person to ensure that they remain in good working order and in keeping with the manufacturer's or supplier's instructions. Particulars of all tests and inspections should be entered in a maintenance log kept for that purpose.

• The minimum fire resistance of doors is usually specified in the fire certificate issued in accordance with the Fire Precautions Act 1971 and Regulations made under that Act. Further advice on these matter can be obtained from the fire authority or local council. See also **Fire certificate** and **Fire Precautions** elsewhere in this handbook.

Glass doors and partitions

• All transparent or translucent surfaces in doors and gates (including door and gate side panels) must consist of a suitable safety material or be adequately protected against breakage — unless those surfaces are above shoulder level.

• All transparent or translucent parts in windows, walls and partitions must likewise consist of a suitable safety material or be protected against breakage — unless those parts are above waist level (*ibid*; Regulation 18).

Note: These rules do not apply to narrow panes up to 250mm wide measured between glazing beads.

The expression 'safety materials' includes

o   materials which are inherently robust, such as polycarbonates or glass blocks;

o   'safety glass' complying with British Standard BS 6206:1981 (*Specification for impact performance requirements for flat safety glass and safety plastic for use in buildings)*; and

o   ordinary annealed glass which meets the thickness criteria in the table below.

Nominal Thickness	Maximum Size
8mm 10mm 12mm 15mm	1.10 m x 1.10 m 2.25 m x 2.25 m 3.00 m x 4.50 m Any size

- If safety glass or its equivalent is not used, steps must be taken to prevent people injuring themselves by inadvertently walking into or colliding with a transparent wall, door or partition. To prevent this happening, the owner or occupier of the premises must erect suitable screens or barriers (perhaps guard rails).

- Even if safety glass *is* used in a wall or partition, there remains the risk of injury if people are not aware that there is a barrier in front of them. The danger is particularly acute if the floor is at the same level on either side of the invisible barrier. To prevent accidents, glass walls, doors and partitions should include features (such as mullions, transoms, heavy tinting) to make the surface apparent. Another solution is to mark or etch the otherwise transparent surface with horizontal lines or patterns at waist or shoulder level (even lower if children are about) so that pedestrians are not deluded into thinking there is nothing in front of them.

Doors & gates on construction sites

- To prevent the risk of injury to any person, every permanent or temporary door, gate and hatch on a construction site must either incorporate or be fitted with suitable safety devices (Regulation 16(1), Construction (Health, Safety & Welfare) Regulations 1996 [SI 1996/1592]).

- A door, gate or hatch on a building site will not satisfy regulation 16(1) unless —

(a) any sliding door, gate or hatch has a devise to prevent it coming off its track during use;

(b) any upward-opening door, gate or hatch has a device to prevent it falling back;

(c) any powered door, gate or hatch has suitable and effective features to prevent any person being trapped (and injured) by it;

(d) where necessary for reasons of health and safety, any powered door, gate or hatch can be operated manually unless it opens automatically if the power fails.

Regulation 16(1) does not, however, apply to any door, gate or hatch forming part of any mobile plant and equipment.

Note: The term construction site means any place where the principal work activity being carried out is construction work; as to which, see **Construction work** elsewhere in this handbook.

See also **Access to premises, Fire precautions, Inspectors, Powers of** and **Offences & penalties** elsewhere in this handbook.

DRAINS & EFFLUVIA

Key points

- Every floor in a workplace must have effective means of drainage where necessary (Regulation 12(2)(b), Workplace (Health, Safety & Welfare) Regulations 1992 (SI 1992/3004) and, adds paragraph 71 of the accompanying Approved Code of Practice, workplaces must be kept free from offensive waste matter or discharges, for example, leaks from drains or sanitary conveniences.

Smells and effluvia

- If a local authority is satisfied that any smell or other effluvia arising on industrial, trade or business premises is prejudicial to health or a nuisance to, local residents, it may serve an abatement notice on the occupier of the premises in question requiring him to abate the nuisance and to execute such works and take such steps as may be necessary for that purpose. If a person on whom an abatement notice is served, without reasonable excuse, contravenes or fails to comply with any requirement or prohibition imposed by the notice, he is guilty of an offence and liable, on summary conviction, to a fine of up to £20,000 (Part III, Environmental Protection Act 1990).

- Section 17 of the Public Health Act 1961 adds that a medical officer of health or public health inspector may serve written notice on the occupier of any premises requiring him to remedy any stopped-up drain, private sewer, water-closet or soil pipe within 48 hours of the service of the notice. If the notice is not complied with, the local authority may themselves carry out the work and recover the cost from the occupier or owner of the premises.

FOOD PREMISES

- In premises in which food or drink intended for human consumption is prepared, processed, manufactured, packaged, stored, handled or offered for sale or supply (whether for profit or not), there must be an adequate number of flush lavatories — each of which must be connected to an effective drainage system. Lavatories situated in, or regularly used in connection with, any food premises must be kept clean and in efficient order, and must be so placed that no offensive odours are allowed to penetrate into any food room. Lavatories must not lead directly into rooms in which food or drink is handled (Chapter I, Schedule I to the Food Safety (General Food Hygiene) Regulations 1995 [SI 1995/1763]).

- Chapter II (*ibid.*) adds that the floor surfaces of rooms in which foodstuffs are prepared, treated or processed (excluding the floors of dining rooms and movable or temporary premises [such as marquees, market stalls and mobile sales vehicles]) must be maintained in a sound condition and be easy to clean and, where necessary, disinfect. Where appropriate, such floors must also allow adequate surface drainage.

Food waste

- Food waste and other refuse must not be allowed to accumulate in food rooms, except so far as is unavoidable for the proper functioning of the business. Food waste must be deposited in closable containers, which latter must be kept in sound condition and be easy to clean and disinfect. Adequate provision must be made for the removal and storage of food waste, which must be kept in a refuse store which must be kept clean and so designed as to protect against access by pests (*ibid*; Chapter VI).

Offences & penalties

- Any person guilty of an offence under the 1995 Regulations is liable to a fine of up to £5,000. If convicted on indictment, the penalty is a fine of an unspecified amount and/or imprisonment for a term not exceeding two years (*ibid*; regulation 6).

TOILETS AND URINALS

- Toilet accommodation and washing facilities provided and maintained in accordance with Regulations 20 and 21 of the Workplace (Health, Safety & Welfare) Regulations 1992 (SI 1992/3004), and paragraphs 192 to 211 of the accompanying Approved Code of Practice, must be adequately ventilated to eliminate offensive odours. Water closets and urinals must be connected to a suitable drainage system and be fitted with effective flushing mechanisms. Chemical water closets used in remote workplaces (without access to main drains or running water) must be provided with a suitable deodorising agent and be emptied and recharged regularly.

See also **Cleanliness of premises, Effluent, Disposal of, Floors, passageways & stairs, Food safety & hygiene, Toilet facilities,** and **Washing facilities** elsewhere in this handbook.

DRINKING WATER

Key points

- Employers must provide an adequate and readily accessible supply of wholesome drinking water for their employees. The water should normally be obtained from a public or water supply. It is very important that the taps delivering drinking water are clearly identified as such so as to distinguish them from water which is non-drinkable or unsuitable for drinking (Regulation 22, Workplace (Health, Safety & Welfare) Regulations 1992 [SI 1992/3004]).

  Note: The 1992 Workplace Regulations do not impose any additional requirements (so far as drinking water is concerned) on employers who previously complied with their duties under the relevant (but since repealed) provisions of the Factories Act 1961 or the Offices, Shops & Railway Premises Act 1963. The point about the 1992 Regulations is that they apply not only to factories, offices and shops but to *all* workplaces — that is to say, any premises (or part of premises), other than domestic premises, which are made available to any person as a place of work — including, for the first time, schools, hospitals, the residential areas of hotels, private hotels, B & B establishments, guest houses, clubs, places of entertainment, leisure complexes, and so on.

- Storage cisterns, tanks or vessels connected to the mains water supply and used to supply drinking water via a connecting pipe and tap must be well-covered, kept clean, and tested and disinfected as often as necessary. Refillable containers or flasks should *not* be used to supply drinking water unless water cannot be obtained directly from a mains supply (as will often be the case on temporary or remote construction sites). If flasks *are* used, they should be suitably enclosed to prevent contamination and must be refilled as often as necessary, and the water in them discarded and replaced at least once every day.

- Although taps or fountains delivering drinking water should be conveniently accessible, they should *not* be sited in workrooms where there is a risk of the water (or the taps, sink or bowl from or into which it is delivered) being contaminated by hazardous substances such as lead or asbestos dust.

Table 1
Health & Safety Legislation
PROHIBITING EATING, DRINKING OR SMOKING
or taking snuff or applying cosmetics
in contaminated & other areas

Control of Lead at Work Regulations 1980 (SI 1980/1248)

10. – (1) Every employer shall take such steps as are adequate to secure that —

(a) so far as is reasonably practicable, his employees do not eat, drink or smoke in any place which is or is liable to be contaminated by lead;

(b) suitable arrangements are made for such employees to eat, drink or smoke in a place which is not liable to be contaminated by lead.

(2) An employee shall not eat, drink or smoke in any place which he has reason to believe to be contaminated by lead.

(3) Nothing in this Regulation shall prevent the provision and use of *drinking facilities* which are not liable to be contaminated by lead where such facilities are required for the welfare of employees who are exposed to lead.

Ionising Radiations Regulations 1985 (SI 1985/1333)

No employee shall eat, drink, smoke, take snuff or apply cosmetics in any area which the employer has designated as a controlled area .... except that an employee may drink from a drinking fountain so constructed that there is no contamination of the water (*ibid*; Regulation 6(6)).

Control of Asbestos at Work Regulations 1987 (SI 1987/2115)

Every employer shall take suitable steps to ensure that —

(a) his employees do not eat, drink or smoke in any area designated as an asbestos area or respirator zone; and

(b) in such a case, arrangements are made for such employees to eat or drink in some other place (*ibid*; Regulation 14(4).

Table 1 (Cont.)	
Workplace (Health, Safety & Welfare) Regulations 1992 (SI 1992/3004)	Rest facilities provided in accordance with Regulation 25(1) must include suitable facilities to eat meals where food eaten in the workplace would otherwise be likely to become contaminated e.g., cement works, clay works, foundries, potteries, tanneries and laundries; premises in which glass bottles and pressed glass articles, sugar, oil cake, jute and tin or terne plates are manufactured; and workplaces in which glass bevelling, fruit preserving, gut scraping, tripe dressing, herring curing and the cleaning or repairing of sacks is carried on (*ibid*; Regulation 25(3) and para. 231 of the accompanying Approved Code of Practice).
Control of Substances Hazardous to Health Regulations 1994 (SI 1994/3246)	To prevent or control exposure to substances hazardous to health, the employer should (inter alia) prohibit eating, drinking or smoking in contaminated areas [*ibid*; Regulation 7(3)(e)].
Work in Compressed Air Regulations 1996 (SI 1996/1656)	" (1) The compressed air contractor shall ensure that no person works in compressed air where the compressed air contractor has reason to believe that person to be under the influence of drink or a drug to such an extent that his capacity to carry out any task for which he is responsible is impaired. (2) No person shall consume alcohol or have with him any alcoholic drink when in compressed air." (*ibid*; Regulation 17) "The compressed air contractor shall ensure that there are provided and maintained for the use of any person engaged in work in compressed air ... (b) suitable drinks for consumption during or after decompression; (c) suitable food and drinks for consumption by any person receiving therapeutic recompression or decompression .... " (*ibid*; Regulation 18).

- Indeed, in certain premises which are subject to the Regulations listed in **Table 1** above, employees must not be permitted to drink (eat or smoke) in workrooms, production departments, and other area likely to be contaminated with dangerous dusts, fumes or vapours.

- Unless drinking water is delivered by means of a fountain, employers must provide (and maintain) a sufficient supply of disposable or non-disposable drinking cups or tumblers. If non-disposable cups, mugs or tumblers are made available, there must be a basin or sink nearby (with taps connected to the mains supply) in which they can be washed or rinsed as and when necessary.

Suitable eating facilities

- Although employers are not legally-bound to provide staff or works canteens serving hot and cold meals or drinks, they *are* required to provide suitable eating facilities for use by employees who routinely take their meals in the workplace. People are entitled to eat their meals or sandwiches out of the public gaze seated at a table, desk or other suitable surface on which to place their food. If there is no vending machine nearby, they must have access to a conveniently-situated kettle (provided by their employer) for preparing hot drinks (*ibid*; Regulation 25); as to which, see **Canteens & restrooms** elsewhere in this handbook.

FOOD PREMISES

- A supply of potable (that is to say, drinkable) water, sufficient in quantity to enable compliance with the Food Safety (General Food Hygiene) Regulations 1995 (SI 1995/1763), must be provided at all food premises in which food or drink intended for sale or sold for human consumption is prepared, stored or presented. This potable water must be used whenever necessary to ensure that foodstuffs are not contaminated. Where appropriate, ice must be made from potable water and must be used whenever necessary to ensure foodstuffs are not contaminated. It must be made, handled and stored under conditions which protect it from all contamination.

- Steam used directly in contact with food must not contain any substance which presents a hazard to health, or is likely to contaminate the product. Water unfit for drinking, which is used for the generation of steam, refrigeration, fire control and other similar purposes not related to food, must be conducted in separate systems, readily identifiable and having no connection with, nor any possibility of reflux into, the potable water systems. See also **Food safety & hygiene**.

Offences & penalties

- A person who refuses or fails to comply with his duties under the legislation summarised above is guilty of an offence and liable on summary conviction to a fine of up to £2,000; or, if convicted on indictment, a fine of an unlimited amount. The penalty for a single offence under the Food Safety Act 1990 (and Regulations made under that Act) could be as high as £5,000 and/or, in the appropriate circumstances, imprisonment for a period of up to six months (or two years, given the nature of the offence).

See also **Offences & penalties** elsewhere in this handbook.

DUSTS, FUMES & VAPOURS

Key points

- Every employer has a duty under the Health & Safety at Work etc. Act 1974 to provide and maintain a working environment for his employees that is (so far as is reasonably practicable) safe and without risks to health (*ibid*; section 2(2)(e)). A failure to discharge that duty is a criminal offence for which the penalty on conviction is a fine of up to £20,000 or, if the offender is convicted on indictment, a fine of an unlimited amount (*ibid*; section 33). Any employee who is injured, as a direct consequence of his (or her) employer's negligence in failing to provide a safe and healthy working environment, may pursue a civil action for damages in the ordinary courts. If his employer has already been successfully prosecuted for a breach of his statutory duty under the 1974 Act, his chances of success will be so much the higher.

- This section of the handbook is concerned primarily with the safety of the working environment and the measures which employers must take to prevent or minimise the exposure of their employees to dangerous dusts, fumes, gases and vapours. The duties of the occupiers of premises in relation to the emission of noxious or offensive substances into the atmosphere are reviewed elsewhere in this handbook in the section titled **Emissions of noxious or offensive substances**

COSHH REGULATIONS 1994

- An employer's general duty under the 1974 Act — to provide a safe and healthy working environment — is reinforced by his more specific duties under a variety of Regulations made under (or saved by) section 15 of the 1974 Act. The latter have been complemented, in some instances, by codes of practice approved and issued by the Health & Safety Commission under section 16 of that Act. See *FURTHER INFORMATION* below.

- Until October 1989, section 63 of the Factories Act 1961 imposed a duty on factory employers to take all practicable measures to protect employees from inhaling dusts, fumes and other impurities given off in connection with any process. Section 63 was repealed in that month by the Control of Substances Hazardous to Health Regulations 1988 (SI 1988/1657) which extended that same duty to every employer in every workplace. The 1988 Regulations have since been revoked and replaced (on 16 January 1995) by the Control of Substances Hazardous to Health Regulations 1994 (SI 1994/3246, as amended by SI 1994/3247). For convenience, the 1994 Regulations are referred to in this section as the COSHH Regulations 1994 or, simply, COSHH.

- An employer's first duty under COSHH is to assess the risks to his employees arising out of their exposure to one or more substance hazardous to health (including carcinogenic and biological substances or agents). Having completed his assessment, his next task is to eliminate any identified risks altogether or, if that is not reasonably practicable, to do what he can to adequately control the exposure of his employees to the substance or substances which give rise to those risks. Measures to control the exposure of an employee to a substance for which there is a maximum exposure limit (in Schedule 1 to the COSHH Regulations 1994) will not be considered *adequate* if the level of exposure has not been reduced below that maximum exposure limit (as to which, see **Hazardous substances** elsewhere in this handbook).

Note: The expression substance hazardous to health includes dust of any kind when present at a substantial concentration in air (*ibid*; Reg. 2(1)). See also **Dangerous chemical and preparations** elsewhere in this handbook.

- If exposure to a hazardous substance cannot be entirely

eliminated and there is no possibility of replacing it with one which is relatively harmless yet equally effective, the employer must, inter alia, totally enclose the related process and handling systems; use plant, processes and systems of work which minimise the generation of, or suppress and contain, spills, leaks, dust, fumes and vapours of carcinogens; regularly clean walls and work surfaces; provide adequate washing facilities for all affected employees; and prohibit eating, drinking and smoking in contaminated areas (*ibid*; Reg. 7(3)(b)). If those measures do not prevent (or provide adequate control of) exposure to the substance or substances in question, then, *in addition to* those measures, the employer must provide every affected employee with suitable respiratory protective equipment or some other form of personal protective equipment (*ibid*; Regulation 7(4)).

• Respiratory protective equipment must not only be suitable for the purpose but must also comply with Regulations in the UK which implement one or other of the Community directives applicable to that item of personal protective equipment listed in Schedule 1 to the Personal Protective Equipment at Work Regulations 1992 (SI 1992/2966) which is .If there are no Regulations specific to respiratory protective equipment, it must be of a type (or conform to a standard) approved by the Health & Safety Executive (*ibid*; Reg. 7(5) & (8)).

OTHER LEGISLATION

• Control measures for the elimination or removal of noxious, harmful or toxic fumes and dusts in certain hazardous trades, industries and processes, are laid down in the following Regulations and Orders:

(a) **Magnesium (Grinding of Castings & Other Articles) Special Regulations 1946** (SI 1946/2107) which state that adequate appliances must be used for the interception and safe removal of the dust generated when any power-driven abrasive wheel, disc, buff, mop, brush, dolly or band is used to grind or polish castings or other articles consisting wholly or mainly of magnesium (Reg. 6).

(b) **Highly Flammable Liquids and Liquefied Petroleum Gases Regulations 1972** (SI 1972/917)). These stipulate that, except in the case of tanks and vessels which have been emptied and made free of vapour, all openings (other than those necessary for venting) in cupboards, bins, tanks and vessels which have at any time been used for storing highly flammable liquids shall be kept closed except as necessary for the use, operation or maintenance of these cupboards, bins, tanks and vessels (Regulation 5(2)). Suitable steps must be taken to prevent the escape of vapours from highly flammable liquid into the general atmosphere of any workplace (Reg. 10).

(c)   **Control of Lead at Work Regulations 1980** (SI 1980/1248, as modified by SI 1990/305), requiring the provision of such control measures (e.g., total enclosure, an effective exhaust ventilation system, ductwork with an airflow of adequate conveying velocity, or fans or air movers of a suitable type) for materials, plant and processes as will adequately control the exposure of employees to lead otherwise than by the use of respiratory protective equipment or protective clothing (Reg. 6).

(d)   **Control of Asbestos at Work Regulations 1987** (SI 1987/2115, as amended by SI 1992/3068) which impose a duty on every employer to prevent the exposure of his employees to asbestos or, if that is not reasonably practicable, to reduce that exposure to the lowest level reasonably practicable by measures other than the use of respiratory protective equipment (Reg. 8(1)). If it is not reasonably practicable to reduce the exposure of an employee to below both the *control limits* which apply to that exposure (see **Asbestos at work** elsewhere in this handbook), then, in addition to the measures required by paragraph (1), the employer must provide that employee with suitable respiratory protective equipment which will reduce the concentration of asbestos in the air inhaled by the employee to a concentration which is below those control limits (Reg. 8(2). Where practicable, the prevention of exposure to asbestos should be achieved by substituting for asbestos a substance which, under the conditions of its use, does not create a risk to the health of employees or creates a lesser risk than that created by asbestos (Reg. 8(1A).

For further particulars, please turn to the sections titled Asbestos at work, **Clay works & potteries, Dangerous chemicals,**

Hazardous substances, Health surveillance, and **Lead at work** elsewhere in this handbook. For a list of useful HSE publications, please see *FURTHER INFORMATION* below.

DANGEROUS OCCURRENCES

- The accidental release or escape of any substance or agent, in a quantity sufficient to cause the death, major injury or any other damage to the health of any person, is a 'notifiable dangerous occurrence' within the meaning of the **Reporting of Injuries, Diseases & Dangerous Occurrences Regulations 1995** (SI 1995/3163) and, as such, must be reported to the 'enforcing authority' without delay. The same is true of a major injury, such as loss of consciousness caused by asphyxia or by exposure to a harmful substance or biological agent; or acute illness (requiring medical treatment) or loss of consciousness resulting from the absorption of any substance by inhalation, ingestion or through the skin. Also reportable is any acute illness which requires medical treatment, where there is reason to believe that this resulted from exposure to a biological agent or its toxins or infected material.

- The sudden, uncontrolled release inside a building of 100 kilograms or more of a flammable liquid; or of 10 kilograms or more of a flammable liquid (at a temperature above its normal boiling point); or of 10 kilograms or more of a flammable gas; or, in the open air, of 500 kilograms or more of any of the substances referred to here, is also a dangerous occurrence which must be notified immediately (by telephone or Fax) — to be followed-up by a written report within the next 10 days. For further particulars, including the correct reporting procedure, please turn to the sections titled **Accidents at work, Accidents to Customers, visitors, etc** and **Dangerous occurrences** elsewhere in this handbook. See also **Ventilation of premises.**

   Note: The terms flammable liquid and flammable gas mean, respectively, a liquid and a gas so classified in accordance with regulation 5(2), (3) or (5) of the Chemicals (Hazard Information & Packaging for Supply) Regulations 1994 (SI 1994/3247); as to which, see **Dangerous chemicals** elsewhere in this handbook.

FACTORIES ACT 1961

- Section 30 of the Factories Act 1961 (which is still in force) cautions that a person must not enter or remain in any confined space in which dangerous fumes are liable to be present, unless he is equipped with suitable breathing apparatus, safety harness and ropes, or until the area has been thoroughly cleared of fumes (and the source sealed off) and certified safe for entry. See **Confined spaces** elsewhere in this handbook.

- Section 31(4) *(ibid)* adds that no plant, tank or vessel, which contains or has contained any explosive or inflammable substance, may be subjected to any welding, brazing, soldering or cutting operation (or any other operation involving the application of heat) until all practicable steps have been taken to remove the substance and fumes arising from it (or to render those fumes non-explosive or non-inflammable). Nor may any explosive or inflammable substance be re-admitted to the plant, tank or vessel until the metal has cooled sufficiently to prevent any risk of igniting the substance.

Dusts and dust explosions

- If dust given off from any grinding, sieving or other process is of a character liable to explode on ignition, all practicable steps must be taken to prevent such an explosion by enclosing the plant used in the process; by removing or preventing any accumulation of dust that may escape in spite of the enclosure; and by excluding or enclosing all possible sources of ignition. The plant itself should also be capable of withstanding the pressure likely to be produced by any such explosion. Otherwise, all practicable steps must be taken to restrict the spread and effects of such an explosion, by equipping the plant with chokes, baffles and vents, or other equally effective appliances (section 31(1) and (2), Factories Act 1961).

FURTHER INFORMATION

- The following publications are available from HSE Books at the address given on page 328. Further lists of related HSE publications are to be found in the sections titled **Asbestos at work, Hazardous substances** and **Lead at work**.

Occupational exposure limits

EH 40/97
Occupational exposure limits [1997]
ISBN 0 7176 1315 1   £6.95

EH40/95
Workplace air and biological monitoring database product: instrument enhanced — developed by HSE using d-Base lll. Available on 3.5 and 5.25 inch diskettes (both sorts provided as part of package) [1995]
ISBN 0 7176 0902 2   £220.00 + VAT.

Guidance notes

EH 54
Assessment of exposure to fume from welding and allied processes [1990]
ISBN 0 7176 0570 1   £2.50

EH 55
The control of exposure to fume from welding brazing and similar processes [1990]
ISBN 0 11 885439 9   £2.50

EH 65/12
Portland cement dust: criteria document for an OEL [1994]
ISBN 0 7176 0763 1   £10.00

EH65/22
Softwood dust: criteria document for an OEL [1996]
ISBN 0 7176 1087 X   £10.00

EH66
Grain dust [1993]
ISBN 0 11 882101 6   £2.50

EH 67
Grain dust in maltings (maximum exposure limits) [1993]
ISBN 0 11 886357 6   £2.50

HS(G) 37
Introduction to local exhaust ventilation [1993]
ISBN 0 7176 1001 2   £4.50

HS(G) 72
Control of respirable silica dust in heavy clay and refractory processes [1992]
ISBN 0 11 885679 0   £4.00

HS(G) 73
Control of respirable crystalline silica in quarries [1992]
ISBN 0n 11 885680 4   £4.00

HS(G) 74
Control of silica dust in foundries [1992]
ISBN 0 11 885677 4   £4.00

HS(G) 103
Safe handling of combustible dusts: precautions against explosions
ISBN 0 7176 0725 9   £6.00

Methods for the determination of hazardous substances

MDHS 3
Generation of Test Atmospheres of Organic Vapours by the Syringe Injection Technique. Portable apparatus for laboratory and field use [1984]
ISBN 0 11 885632 4   £2.50

MDHS 4
Generation of Test Atmospheres of Organic Vapours by the Permeation Tube Method. Apparatus for laboratory use [1986]
ISBN 0 11 885647 2   £2.50

MDHS 14/2
General Methods for sampling & gravimetric analysis of respirable and total inhalable dust [1997]
ISBN 0 7176 1295 3   £5.00

MDHS 38
Quartz in Respirable Airborne Dusts. Laboratory method using infra-red spectroscopy (KBr disc technique) [1984]
ISBN 0 11 885629 4   £2.50

MDHS 39/4
Asbestos fibres in air. Light microscopic methods for use with the Control of Asbestos at Work Regulations (Rev) [1995]
ISBN 0 7176 1113 2   ££5.00

MDHS 70
General methods for sampling airborne gases and vapours [1990]
ISBN 0 7176 0608 2   £3.50

MDHS 71
Analytical quality in workplace air monitoring [1991]
ISBN 0 7176 1263 5   £5.00

MDHS 76(
*Cristobalite in respirable airborne dust. Laboratory method using
 X-ray diffraction* [1994]
ISBN 0 7176 0634 1   £2.50

Note: a supplementary list of MDHS publications is to be found in the
section titled **Hazardous substances**.

Rubber industry

*Control of fume at extruders, calendars and vulcanising
operations* [1994]

*COSHH in the rubber industry: Guidance on the Control of
Substances Hazardous to Health Regulations 1988* [1992]
ISBN 0 11 885610 3   £5.00

Dust control in powder handling and weighing [1989]
ISBN 0 11 885495 X   £6.50

Dust and fume control at rubber mixing and milling [1996]
ISBN 0 7176 0992 8   £8.50

Free leaflets (Telephone: 01787 881165)

INDG 140	*Grain dust*
MSA 15	*Silica dust and you*
IACL95	*Safe to breathe: dust and fume control in the rubber industry*

E

EFFLUENT, DISPOSAL OF

Key points

Drains and drainage

- Consistent with their general duty under section 2 of the Health & Safety at Work etc. Act 1974 — to provide a safe and healthy working environment — employers must not only keep the workplaces they control free from offensive waste matter or discharges, but must also deal swiftly with leaks (or overflows) from drains and toilets.

- In workplaces where floors are likely to become wet — e.g. laundries, tanneries, textile factories, potteries, food processing plants, etc.— there must be a network of drains and channels with the floor sloping slightly towards a drain to ensure the rapid and efficient removal of excess water and waste liquids. The covers on all drains and channels should not present a tripping hazard and should be as near flush to the surrounding floor surfaces as possible (Regulation 9 & 12, Workplace (Health, Safety & Welfare) Regulations 1992 [SI 1992/3004]).

Flammable, toxic and corrosive liquids

- The method used to drain and contain highly flammable liquids must not result in the contamination of drains, sewers, watercourses or ground water supplies. Nor should it put people or the environment at risk (*ibid*; Regulation 12).

- Maximum concentration levels for toxic, corrosive or highly flammable liquids are specified in the Environmental Protection (Prescribed Processes & Substances) Regulations 1991 (SI 1991/472, as amended), and in the Surface Waters (Dangerous Substances) (Classification) Regulations 1989 and 1992.

See also **Drains & effluvia** elsewhere in this handbook.

ELECTRICITY AT WORK

Key points

- The Electricity at Work Regulations 1989 (SI 1989/635) came into force on April 1, 1990, and apply to every work situation in which electricity is used or is available for use, and to every appliance and every item of plant, machinery or equipment which is (or is designed to be) powered by electricity.

Duties of Employers

- The Regulations impose a duty on each and every employer (whatever the nature of his business) to take steps to ensure, so far as is reasonably practicable:

   (a)   that the electrical systems, equipment and appliances under his control are not only soundly constructed but also that they are maintained (by personnel who are competent and experienced) in such a way as to pose no danger to his employees when properly used;

   (b)   that the work activities of his employees — including the operation, use and maintenance of electrical systems, appliances and equipment, and work near any such equipment — are carried out in such a manner as not to give rise to danger;

   (c)   that electrical equipment which is, or could be, exposed to mechanical damage, the effects of weather (natural hazards, temperature or pressure), or to wet, dirty, dusty or corrosive conditions, are constructed or protected in such a way as to prevent any risk of injury arising from such exposure; and

   (d)   that suitable means are available for cutting off or isolating the supply of electricity to any electrical equipment when there is an imminent risk of injury.

Working space, access and lighting

- Regulation 15 of the 1989 Regulations states that all working areas and rooms in which powered machinery, tools, systems, and the like, are used or located, must be well lit, easily accessible and sufficiently spacious — the intention being to ensure that people working in (or passing through) any such room or area are not at risk when exposed to or using such equipment.

Competent persons only

• Finally, the Regulations stress that no person should be allowed to carry out any activity which requires a technical knowledge or experience of electricity unless the person in question *has* that technical knowledge or experience. Persons unfamiliar with electrical appliances and equipment should *never* be permitted to tinker or tamper with them and should certainly *not* be permitted to attempt any repairs. New recruits and inexperienced employees should *never* be asked to operate or use any electrically-powered machine or appliance unless they have received sufficient instruction and on-the-job training (reinforced, if need be, by adequate supervision) to ensure that they use that equipment responsibly and safely — without risks to themselves or other persons. If an employer does not have a competent electrician or electrical engineer in his employ, he should secure the services of a qualified electrician to carry out all routine maintenance and emergency repairs.

Practical implications

• In practical terms, employers would be well-advised to make an inventory of all situations, circumstances and locations within their premises in which electrical energy is generated, provided, transmitted, transformed, conducted, distributed, controlled or used. An employer (through his competent and trained appointees) should know the location, state of repair and maintenance record of every circuit board, fuse box, switch, socket, power point, transformer and cable under his control. He should likewise maintain a detailed record of all electrically-powered machines, equipment and appliances and be able to tell at a glance when such equipment was purchased, serviced or repaired. If he has not already done so, he should introduce and enforce a regular inspection and maintenance programme, to include checks for damage caused by exposure to the weather or to wet, dirty, dusty or corrosive conditions.

- So far as employees are concerned, the employer should make it clear to them that they must not, under any circumstances, tamper with or attempt to repair any switch, socket, plug, wiring or cable; that they must promptly report all electrical failures and any damage (or suspected damage, however insignificant) to electrical equipment, machines, tools and appliances. No employee should be set to work with any machine or other portable or fixed electrical appliance unless he or she has been sufficiently trained in the safe use of that appliance and the procedure to be followed in the event of a malfunction or related emergency. Such training should form part of the employer's regular induction (or refresher) training programme and should be fully documented.

Offences and penalties

- The 1989 Regulations were made under the Health & Safety at Work etc. Act 1974 and are enforced by health and safety inspectors. Conviction for an offence under the Regulations could result in a fine of up to £2,000 or, if convicted on indictment, a fine of an unlimited amount. If an employer contravenes any requirement or prohibition imposed by an improvement or prohibition notice served on him by an HSE or local authority inspector, he could be ordered to pay a fine of up to £20,000 and may be sent to prison for up to six months. If convicted on indictment, there is no limit on the fine that may be imposed. Furthermore, he could be sent to prison for up to two years (*ibid*; section 33(1)(g) and (2A)).

FURTHER INFORMATION

- The Health & Safety Executive has published a *Memorandum of Guidance on the Electricity at Work Regulations 1989* (HS(R)25)), copies of which are available from HSE Books (see page 328), price £4.00 (ISBN 0 11 883963 2). Although the 50-page booklet does not have the force of a Code of Practice, it is designed to assist employers in meeting their obligations under the Regulations. It also includes a comprehensive list of complementary HSE and HSC publications as well as other Guidance Notes on electrical safety.

- The following useful publications are also available from HSE Books:

HS(G) 85
Electricity at work: safe working practices [1993]
ISBN 0 7176 0442 X   £3.50

HS(G) 87
Safety in the remote diagnosis of manufacturing plant and equipment [1995]
ISBN 0 7176 0932 4   £12,00

HS(G) 107
Maintaining portable and transportable electrical equipment [1994]
ISBN 0 7176 0715 1   £5.00

HS(G) 118
Electrical safety in arc welding
ISBN 0 7176 0704 6   £5.25

HS(G) 141
Electrical safety on construction sites [1995]
ISBN 0 7176 1000 4   £8.75

GS 23 (Rev)
Electrical safety in schools [1990]
ISBN 0 11 885426 7   £2.50

GS 38
Electrical test equipment for use by electricians (Rev) [1995]
ISBN 0 7176 0845 X   £3.50

GS 50
Electrical safety at places of entertainment [1991]
ISBN 0 11 885598 0   £2.50

PM 29 (Rev)
Electrical hazards from steam/water pressure cleaners etc [1995]
ISBN 0 7176 0813 1   £4.00

PM 38
Selection and use of electric handlamps [1992]
ISBN 0 11 886360 6   £2.50

Safe use of electric induction furnaces [1987]
ISBN 0 11 883909 8   £9.00

Leaflet packs

IND(G) 236L
Maintaining portable electrical equipment in offices and other low-risk environments [1994]
ISBN 0 7176 1272 4
£5 per single pack (Discounts for multi-pack purchases)

IND(G) 237L
Maintaining portable electric equipment in hotels and tourist accommodation [1996]
ISBN 0 7176 1273 2
£5 per single pack (Discounts for multi-pack purchases)

See also **Dangerous machines, Health & safety at work** and **Machinery safety** elsewhere in this handbook.

EMISSIONS OF NOXIOUS OR OFFENSIVE SUBSTANCES

Key points

- Persons having control of premises to which section 1(1)(d) of the Health & Safety at Work etc. Act 1974 applies must use the best practicable means for preventing the emission into the atmosphere of any substance deemed to be noxious or offensive. Furthermore, they must render harmless and inoffensive such substances as may be so emitted(*ibid*; section 5). A failure to discharge this duty is a criminal offence for which the penalty is a fine of up to £20,000 or, if the offender is convicted in indictment, a fine of an unlimited amount (*ibid*; section 33).

- The premises to which section 1(1)(d) (and, hence, section 5) applies are those listed in **Table 1** overleaf. The substances which are deemed to be noxious or offensive are those listed in **Table 2** on page 257. These provisions are to be found in the Health & Safety (Emissions into the Atmosphere) Regulations 1983 (SI 1983/943, as amended by SI 1989/319).

- Under the Control of Industrial Air Pollution (Transfer of Powers of Enforcement) Regulations 1987 (SI 1987/180), section 5 of the

1974 Act is enforced not by the Health & Safety Executive but by the Pollution Inspectorate of the Department of the Environment.

Control of asbestos in the air

• Regulation 2 of the Control of Asbestos in the Air Regulations 1990 (SI 1990/556) states that the occupier of any workplace in which asbestos is used, and from which asbestos is discharged into the air through discharge outlets, must ensure that the concentration of asbestos so discharged does not exceed 0.1 milligrams of asbestos per cubic metre of air. To that end, he must measure the concentrations of asbestos discharged from his premises at least once in every period of six months.

Note: The sampling and analysis procedures to be used for measuring the concentration of asbestos discharged into the air are those described in the Annex to Council Directive 87/217/EEC (as to which, see OJ No. L85 of 28.3.87, page 40). Copies of the Official Journal (OJ) of the European Community are to be found in most EC Information Centres and good reference libraries.

Table 1
LIST OF WORKS
Prescribed classes of premises for the purposes of section 1(1)(d) of the Health & Safety at Work etc, Act 1974

Acetylene works	Gas and coke works
Acrylates works	Hydrochloric acid works
Aldehyde works	Hydrofluoric acid works
Aluminium works	Hydrogen cyanide works
Amines works	Iron works and steel works
Ammonia works	Large combustion works
Anhydride works	Large glass works
Arsenic works	Large paper pulp works
Asbestos works	Lead works
Benzene works	Lime works
Beryllium works	Magnesium works
Bisulphite works	Manganese works
Bromine works	Metal recovery works
Calcium works	Mineral works
Carbon disulphide works	Nitrate & chloride of iron works
Carbonyl works	Nitric acid works
Caustic soda works	Paraffin oil works
Cement works	Petrochemical works
Ceramic works	Petroleum works
Chemical fertiliser works	Phosphorus works
Chlorine works	Picric acid works
Chromium works	Producer gas works
Copper works	Pyridine works

Table 1 (Cont.)

Di-isocyanate works	Selenium works
Electricity works (in which	Smelting works
solid or gaseous fuel is burned)	Sulphate of ammonia works and
Fibre works	chloride of ammonia works
Fluorine works	Sulphide works
Gas liquor works	Sulphuric acid (Class I) works

Important

These are general descriptions only. For more details, the reader should consult Schedule 1 to the Health & Safety (Emissions into the Atmosphere) Regulations 1983 (SI 1983/943), as amended by the eponymous (Amendment) Regulations 1989 (SI 1989/319). Copies of these Regulations are available from The Stationery Office (see page 328).

- Any person undertaking activities involving the working of products containing asbestos must ensure that those activities do not cause significant environmental pollution by asbestos fibres or dust emitted into the air. The same duty applies to building contractors and other persons or organisations engaged in the demolition of buildings, structures or installations containing asbestos and the removal of asbestos from such premises and installations (*ibid*; Reg. 4).

Table 2
Substances deemed to be noxious or offensive for the purposes of section 5(1) of the Health & Safety at Work etc. Act 1974

Acetic acid or its anhydride;

Acetylene;

Acrylates;

Acrylic acid;

Aledehydes;

Amines;

Ammonia or its compounds;

(Continued overleaf)

Table 2 (Cont.)

Arsenic or its compounds;

Asbestos;

Bromine or its compounds;

Carbon disulphide;

Carbon dioxide;

Carbon monoxide;

Chlorine or its compounds;

Cyanogen or its compounds;

Di-isocyanates;

Ethylene and higher olefines;

Fluorine or its compounds;

Fumaric acid;

Fumes or dust containing aluminium, antimony, arsenic, beryllium, cadmium, calcium, chlorine, chromium, copper, gallium, iron, lead, magnesium, manganese, mercury, molybdenum, nickel, phosphorus, platinum, potassium, selenium, silicon, silver, sodium, sulphur, tellurium, thallium, tin, titanium, tungsten, uranium, vanadium, zinc or their compounds;

Fumes or vapours from benzene works, paraffin oil works, petrochemical works, petroleum works, or tar works and bitumen works;

Glass fibres;

Hydrocarbons;

Hydrogen chloride;

Hydrogen sulphide;

Iodine or its compounds;

Isocyanates;

Lead or its compounds;

Maleic acid or its anhydride;

Mercury or its compounds;

Metal carbonyls;

Mineral fibres;

Nitric acid or oxides of nitrogen;

Nitriles;

Phenols;

Phosphorus or its compounds;

(Continued)

Table 2 (Cont.)

Phthalic acid or its anhydride;

Products containing hydrogen from the partial oxidation of hydrocarbons;

Pyridine or its homologues;

Smoke, grit and dust;

Styrene;

Sulphuric acid or sulphur trioxide;

Sulphurous acid or sulphur dioxide;

Vinyl chloride;

Volatile organic sulphur compounds.

Environmental protection

- Part III of the Environmental Protection Act 1990 empowers a local authority to serve an abatement notice on the owner or occupier of any industrial, trade or business premises from which any dust (other than dust emitted as an ingredient of smoke) is emitted — if that dust is prejudicial to health or a nuisance. A failure to comply with the terms of an abatement notice is an offence for which the penalty, on summary conviction, is a fine of up to £20,000 (*ibid*; sections 79 & 80).

See also **Dangerous chemicals & preparations, Dusts, Fumes & Vapours** and **Hazardous substances** elsewhere in this handbook.

EMPLOYMENT MEDICAL ADVISORY SERVICE

Key points

- The Employment Medical Advisory Service (EMAS) was established by the Employment Medical Advisory Service Act 1972, and came into being on 1 February 1973. The Service was continued under the amending provisions of Part II of the Health and Safety at Work etc Act 1974, while responsibility for maintaining the Service was transferred from the Employment Department to the Health and Safety Commission.

- EMAS is staffed by doctors and nurses ('employment medical advisers') whose job it is to monitor health hazards and medical problems in all branches of industry, and to advise the Secretary of State for Employment, the Health and Safety Commission, Careers Officers, School Medical Officers, young people (and their parents), employers, employees, trade unions, and the like, on precautions and environmental controls required to minimise health risks in employment.

- EMAS doctors and nurses have powers similar to those enjoyed by HSE inspectors. They may enter an employer's premises at any reasonable time to investigate suspected instances of occupational disease; may demand to see and inspect registers and other documents; and may interview managers and employees in all aspects of the working environment. EMAS also advises employers on the suitability of first-aid facilities and on the names of organisations which offer EMAS-approved first-aid training courses.

- The address of the nearest office of EMAS (which is usually the same as that of the local office of the Health & Safety Executive) must appear on the poster titled *Health & Safety Law: What you should know*, which every employer must display in his workplace. Alternatively, it must accompany the leaflet of the same title distributed to employees (as an alternative to the poster). For further details, please turn to the section titled **Abstracts and notices** elsewhere in this handbook.

Medical examinations

- An employment medical adviser who is of the opinion that an employee's health has been, or is likely to be, impaired because of the type of work he (or she) does or because of the substances to which he is exposed, may serve written notice on the employer in question requiring him to permit the medical examination of that employee during normal working hours.

- The medical examination may be conducted either on the employer's premises (in which event, the occupier must provide suitable facilities) or elsewhere at a time and place nominated by the employment medical adviser.

- If a medical examination reveals that an employee is unsuited on health grounds to the type of work he (or she) has been doing, the employer may be left with no choice but to dismiss the employee or transfer him either to lighter duties or to work which will not damage (or further damage) his health. But see *Suspension from work on medical grounds* below.

Note: It is not the function of an employment medical adviser or appointed doctor to provide medical treatment. If medical treatment is considered necessary, the employee will be encouraged to talk to his or her GP.

- In the event of a dismissal (and a complaint to an industrial tribunal), it will be for the employer to show that he had acted reasonably and fairly in treating the medical report as a sufficient reason for dismissing the employee. A tribunal will take into account the size and administrative resources of the employer's business and will come to its decision in accordance with equity and the substantial merits of the case. Although every case is different, experience shows that the dismissal of a long-serving employee on health grounds is more difficult to justify (a) if the employee's health has been affected by the type of work in which he has been engaged and/or (b) if the employer has made no attempt to explore the possibility of transferring the employee to more amenable work (if such work was available at the time). These provisions are to be found in Part X of the Employment Rights Act 1996 (notably sections 98 to 107).

- An employee is not obliged to submit to a medical examination. But, if he (or she) refuses to cooperate, his employer will (as we have seen) be put in the invidious position of having either to dismiss him on medical grounds or transfer him to less hazardous duties. In some hazardous industries and trades, the medical examination of employees is compulsory. Any employee who unreasonably refuses to submit to such an examination may be lawfully dismissed for breach of a statutory duty, and will have scant chance of success on complaint to an industrial tribunal. See also **Health surveillance** elsewhere in this handbook.

Suspension from work on medical grounds

- In certain trades and industries in which employees are exposed to ionising radiations, lead dust or any one of a number of prescribed hazardous substances (where health surveillance and medical examinations are a legal requirement), an employment medical adviser or appointed doctor may direct that an employee be suspended from work on medical grounds until such time as it is safe for him (or her) to return.

- An employee who is suspended from work in such circumstances has a legal right to be paid his (or her) normal wages or salary for a period of up to 26 weeks or until he returns to work (whichever occurs sooner) — unless he unreasonably refuses an offer of suitable alternative employment made to him by his employer. If an employer's response to a suspension order is to dismiss the employee, the employee may present a complaint of unfair dismissal to an industrial, so long as he had worked for his employer for at least one month. These provisions are to be found in sections 64 and 65 of the Employment Rights Act 1996. For further particulars, please turn to the section titled **Suspension on medical grounds** elsewhere in this handbook.

Fees for medical examinations

- By the Health and Safety (Fees) Regulations 1995 (SI 1995/2646, as amended by SI 1996/2094), an employer is required to pay a fee to the Health and Safety Executive for the first and subsequent medical examinations of persons employed in prescribed hazardous trades and industries. At present (April, 1997), the prescribed basic fee for a medical examination is £42.13, with an additional fee of £45.23 and £27.17, respectively, for X-Rays and laboratory tests.

Young persons

- One of the functions of EMAS is to advise young people, their parents, Careers Officers and School Medical Officers on the health aspects of work in various industries.

- Factory employers are no longer duty-bound to notify their local Careers Offices when they employ young persons under 18 to work in their factories. Section 119A of the Factories Act 1961 (which contained this requirement) was repealed on 3 March 1997 by the Employment Act 1989 (Commencement No. 2) Order 1997 (SI 1997/134).

- Section 119A has been overtaken by the 'health surveillance' provisions of the Management of Health & Safety at Work Regulations 1992 (SI 1992/2051), Regulation 5 of which requires every employer to ensure that his employees are provided with such health surveillance as is appropriate having regard to the risks to their health and safety which are identified by the assessment. For further particulars, please turn to the section titled **Health surveillance** elsewhere in this handbook.

- For further information on the activities of EMAS, please refer to the sections in this handbook titled **Certificate of fitness** and **Health Surveillance**, elsewhere in this handbook.

EXPLOSIVES, MANUFACTURE & USE OF

Key points

- Because of the specialist nature of the subject and its relatively limited appeal in a book of this type, it is not intended here to give a detailed analysis of the workings of the Explosives Acts 1875 and 1923 or, indeed, the Fireworks Act 1951. Persons engaged in the manufacture, importation, keeping, transportation and sale of explosives must be in possession of licences issued by the Explosives Inspectorate and/or the local authorities responsible for enforcing those statutes and will be familiar with the general rules

FURTHER INFORMATION

- The following publications are available from HSE Books at the address given on page 328.

  Guide to the Explosives Acts 1875 and 1923
  ISBN 0 11 880796 X   £14.95

Codes of practice

COP 27
Explosives at quarries. Quarries (Explosives) Regulations 1988:
Approved code of practice [1989]
1989 ISBN 0 11 885462 3   £3.00

HS(R) 17
Guide to the Classification and Labelling of
Explosives Regulations 1983 [1983]
ISBN 0 11 883706 0   £3.25

Guidance notes

HS(G) 36
Disposal of explosives waste and the decontamination of explosives
plant [1987]
ISBN 0 11 883926 8   £3.00

L10
A guide to the Control of Explosives Regulations 1991 [1991]
ISBN 0 11 885670 7   £3.00

L13
A guide to the Packaging of Explosives for Carriage Regulations
1991 [1991]
ISBN 0 11 885728 2   £3.00

List of authorised explosives 1992: Explosives Acts, 1875 and 1923
[Rev. 1992]
ISBN 0 11 886396 7   £7.75

Classified and authorised explosives [1995]
ISBN 0 7176 0772 0   £11.00

Supplement No. 1 to the list of classified and authorised explosives
1994 (Quote MISC039 when ordering) [1996]
ISBN 0 7176 1134 5   £12.50

Guide to general fire precautions in explosives factories and
magazines (Fire Certificate [Special Premises] Regulations 1976
[1990]
ISBN 0 7176 0793 3   £6.50

Safe handling of combustible dusts: precautions against explosions
[1994]
ISBN 0 7176 0725 9   £6.00

Free leaflets (Telephone 01787 881165)

INDG 115
An introduction to the Control of Explosives Regulations

See also the sections titled **Dangerous Chemicals, Dangerous Occurrences, Highly flammable liquids** and **Hazardous substances** elsewhere in this handbook.

F

FALLS & FALLING OBJECTS

Key points

* Regulation 13 of the Workplace (Health, Safety & Welfare) Regulations 1992 (SI 1992/3004) imposes a duty on employers in *every* workplace to take suitable and effective measures — without relying solely on information, instruction, training and supervision or the provision of personal protective equipment — to prevent any person falling a distance likely to cause him (or her) injury. It also requires employers to take such steps as are necessary to prevent a person being struck by a falling object.

FALLS

* If a person is likely to fall a distance of two metres or more from the edge of any platform, scaffold or teagle opening, or runs the risk of falling into any tank, pit, vat, kier, or similar vessel containing a dangerous substance, the edges, apertures and vessels in question must be securely fenced or covered.

Note: The expression dangerous substance means any substance likely to scald or burn; any poisonous or corrosive substance; any fume, gas or vapour likely to overcome a person; or any granular or free-flowing substance, or any viscous substance, which is of a nature and quantity likely to cause danger to any person.

- If covers are used (over pits, vats, kiers, etc.), they must be capable of supporting all loads likely to be imposed upon them, and any traffic which is liable to pass over them. They must be of a type which cannot be readily detached or removed, and should not be capable of being easily displaced.

- If fencing (instead of covers) is installed around vats, kiers and similar vessels, it must be securely fixed and structurally sound. Kiers are vessels commonly used for boiling or bleaching textiles. As they can be extremely dangerous, employers must take suitable measures to prevent people falling into them. Any kier installed after 31 December 1992, must either be securely covered or be fenced to a height of at least 1100 mm — unless the sides of the kier extend to at least 1100 mm above the highest point from which people could fall in. A kier in use before January 1, 1993, should be fenced to a height of at least 915 mm or, in the case of open or atmospheric kiers, 840 mm.

- Fencing at teagle doorways and openings in floors, and at any edge where a person is liable to fall a distance of two metres or more, must likewise be at least 1100 mm high and must be filled-in with upstands or toeboards to prevent people or objects falling over or through it.

Removal of fencing or covers

- There will clearly be occasions when fencing at an opening or edge has to be removed to facilitate the transfer of goods or materials from one level to another. Secure handholds must be provided where workers have to position themselves at an unfenced opening or edge. If the work necessarily requires an employee to position himself at an unguarded edge, as little of the adjacent fencing or rails as possible should be removed, and should be replaced as soon as possible.

- The same applies to the covers over tanks, vats, kiers, and the like. These must be kept securely in place except when they have to be removed for inspection purposes or in order to gain access. These too must be replaced as soon as possible.

- When fencing or covers cannot be provided, or have to be removed, the employer must devise and adopt a suitable and rigorously-enforced 'permit to work' system. This means, in effect, that nominated employees, who are necessarily familiar with the dangers and have received appropriate instruction and training, must nonetheless obtain written authorisation and follow certain rules before they are allowed to work in high-risk situations.

Teagle openings

- A teagle opening is a door-sized (or larger) opening in a wall, usually several metres above street level, from the top of which protrudes a beam with a rope and pulley or electric hoist attached. Teagle openings are commonly used for hoisting or lowering goods.

- Any person working at a teagle opening clearly runs the risk of falling. To prevent this happening, the opening should be fenced as far as possible, with handholds on both sides. If that is impracticable, given the size and nature of the goods being raised or lowered, or the width of the opening itself, a safe system of work should be devised and enforced. Such a system typically restricts such work to competent and experienced workers (who have received the necessary information, instruction and training) insists on the presence of at least one other person both to oversee the work and provide assistance if needed, and demands that workers wear safety harnesses with lines attached to secure anchorage points.

- The approved Code of Practice accompanying the 1992 Regulations states that safety lines must be short enough to prevent injury even if an employee does stumble or fall over an edge. Indeed, if an employee can do his work without having to go too near to a dangerous edge, the length of the line and the position of the anchorage point should be such as to prevent him doing so.

- All 'permit-to-work' systems should be fully documented and records kept of all occasions when employees work in high risk situations.

FALLING OBJECTS

- Employers are duty bound to take 'suitable and effective measures' to prevent any person in the workplace being struck and injured by a falling object. Although it is undoubtedly sensible to forewarn employees (and others, including visitors) about the possibility of their being struck by objects falling from on high, and to issue them with safety helmets, that is not what the Regulations require. Regulation 13 makes it clear that employers must do whatever needs to be done to prevent objects falling in the first place.

- In short, fencing which is designed to prevent people falling off an edge or through a floor opening (or teagle doorway) must also be sufficient to prevent objects falling off the same edge or through the same floor opening or doorway. This means the fencing must be fitted with strong and stable upstands or toeboards to prevent objects — such as tools, spare parts, wooden planks, iron bars, rubble, cleaning materials, and the like — falling onto people working or passing below.

Note: On premises subject to the provisions of the Construction (Head Protection) Regulations 1989 (SI 1989/2209), employers must provide their employees with suitable safety helmets or hard hats (constructed to British Standard 5240) and must insist that they wear them whenever there is a risk of head injury. Employees (including self-employed persons) must wear hard hats when instructed to do so by their employer or by the person having control of the relevant construction site. However, by virtue of section 11 of the Employment Act 1989, the duty to wear suitable head protection does not apply to Sikhs who are wearing turbans.

Articles falling from (or ejected by) work equipment

- Regulation 12 of the Provision & Use of Work Equipment Regulations 1992 (SI 1992/2932) warns employers that they must take all reasonably practicable steps to prevent articles or substances falling from (or being ejected by) any item of work equipment (such as scaffolding, an overhead travelling crane, high-rise storage racks; and so on). Factory employers may choose to issue their employees with hard hats (a legal requirement on building sites), but that is not the answer. What Regulation 12 requires is for employers to tackle the problem at source, by taking steps to prevent objects falling from work equipment in the first place. If they do not take those steps, they are guilty of an offence and run the risk of being prosecuted under the Health & Safety at Work etc. Act 1974 — section 2 of which imposes a general duty on every employer to provide and maintain safe plant and systems of work.

See also **Construction work** elsewhere in this handbook.

FENCING & GUARDING OF MACHINERY

Key points

- Every employer has a duty under section 2(2)(a) of the Health & Safety at Work etc. Act 1974 to provide and maintain plant and systems of work that are, so far as is reasonably practicable, safe and without risks to health.

- The manufacturers, designers, importers and suppliers of machinery for use at work have a like duty to ensure that every machine they design, produce, sell or supply is so designed and constructed that it will be safe and without risks to health at all times when it is being set, used, cleaned or maintained by a person at work (*ibid*; section 6(1)(a).

- Any person who fails to discharge a duty to which he is subject under sections 2 to 7 of the 1974 Act is guilty of an offence and liable to a fine of up to £20,000 or, if convicted on indictment, a fine of an unlimited amount (*ibid*; section 33(1)(a) and (1A).

SUPPLY OF MACHINERY (SAFETY) REGULATIONS 1992

- The general duties of manufacturers under the 1974 Act are reinforced by their more specific duties under the Supply of Machinery (Safety) Regulations 1992 (SI 1992/3073, as amended by SI 1994/2063). The Regulations do not apply to machinery first supplied or put into service in the EEC before 1 January 1993 or to machinery intended for export to a country outside the EEC. But, for most other relevant machinery (see *Note* below), the Regulations came into force on 1 January 1993; and, for the remainder, on 1 January 1995. The Regulations contain transitional provisions for specific types of machinery (notably roll-over protective structures, falling-object protective structures and industrial trucks supplied or put into service for the first time before 1 July 1995) but, for all intents and purposes, the Regulations are now fully 'up and running'.

Note: The term relevant machinery means all types of machinery other than 'Regulation 9' machinery, 'Regulation 10' machinery or 'Schedule 5' machinery, discussed elsewhere in this handbook in the section titled **Machinery safety**.

- Regulation 11 of the Supply of Machinery (Safety) Regulations cautions that a relevant machine must not be sold or supplied within the UK (or, indeed, anywhere within the EEC) unless:

(a)   it complies with Annex 1 of Council Directive 89/392/EEC of 14 June 1989 (as amended) on the approximation of the laws of the Member States relating to machinery (which contains detailed requirement for the fencing and guarding of machinery); and

(b)   the appropriate *conformity assessment procedure* has been carried out.

Furthermore, the machinery must either have been issued with an EC declaration of conformity and have the 'CE marking' fixed to it (*ibid*; Reg. 25)(see example on page 328) or, if intended for incorporation in other machinery, must have been issued with an EC declaration of incorporation. The machinery must also be safe. In other words, when properly installed and maintained, and used for the purposes for which it is intended, it must not present a risk to the health and safety of persons using it (or to that of people in the immediate vicinity) or be the cause or occasion of damage to property.

• A person guilty of an offence under Regulations 11 and 25 of the Safety of Machinery (Supply) Regulations 1992 is liable on summary conviction to imprisonment for a term not exceeding three months and/or to a fine of up to £5,000 (level 5 on the standard scale) (*ibid*; Regs 29 & 30).

For further particulars, please turn to the section titled **Machinery safety** elsewhere in this handbook.

PROVISION & USE OF WORK EQUIPMENT REGULATIONS 1992

• The acronym PUWER is used in the paragraphs below to refer to the Provision & Use of Work Equipment Regulations 1992 (SI 1992/2932, as amended).

• Nowadays, any employer or self-employed person who is contemplating acquiring a new (or 'newish') machine for use in his business or undertaking should first satisfy himself that the machine he is buying, leasing or hiring carries the CE marking and has been issued with an EC Declaration of Conformity or (where appropriate) with an EC Declaration of Incorporation. If the machine *does* comply with the Supply of Machinery (Safety) Regulations 1992 or with any other Regulations implementing a relevant Community directive (see *Note* below), Regulations 11 to 24 of PUWER summarised below will apply to that machine to the extent only that those other Regulations do not (*ibid*. Reg. 10).

Note: HSE publication L22 (see *FURTHER INFORMATION* at the end of this section) contains a list of UK Regulations implementing relevant Community Directives on machinery design and supply.

- Any employer who buys or hires a second-hand machine first supplied or put into service in the EEC before 1 January 1993 — which does *not* comply with the Supply of Machinery (Safety) Regulations 1992 or with any related regulations implementing Community Directives — must not install or use that machine in his premises or in connection with his trade or business unless it complies with Regulations 11 to 24 of PUWER, summarised below.

- A machine installed or made available for use in a particular workplace before 1 January 1993, and still in use in that same workplace, must now comply with Regulations 11 to 24 of PUWER (which came into force for all such machines on 1 January 1997). By now, all pre-1993 machines must either have been modified or adapted to comply with PUWER or have been replaced.

Fencing and guarding under PUWER

- It is not proposed to examine the 'machinery safety' provisions of PUWER in any great detail — not only because of the limitations of space in a book which is already quite long (*pace* Kogan Page Ltd.) but also because the Health & Safety Executive (HSE) have published their own comprehensive and eminently readable guidelines on PUWER as well as a raft of other literature on aspects of machinery safety. See *FURTHER INFORMATION* at the end of this section.

- In summary, Regulations 11 to 24 of PUWER require employers:

  (a) to take steps designed either to prevent any person coming into contact with any dangerous part of a machine (including any rotating stock-bar) or to stop the movement of that dangerous part before any part of a person enters the danger zone;

(b)   to take measures to protect any person using a
      machine from being injured by any article or substance
      ejected by or falling from that machine;

(c)   to insulate, shield or guard those parts of a machine
      which are very hot or very cold so as to prevent
      any person being burned, scalded or seared by coming
      into contact with one or other of those parts;

(d)   to take steps (e.g., by fitting temperature-controlled
      interlocking doors or lids, catchpans, spillways, etc.)
      to prevent people being injured by coming into contact
      with (or being splashed by) very hot or very cold
      articles or substances present in or being processed by
      a machine;

(e)   to fit every machine with a starting control (so that
      the machine cannot be started other than by a
      deliberate action on that control) as well as controls
      whose purpose it is to change the speed, pressure or
      other operating conditions of the machine where the
      risks to health and safety after the change are greater
      than such risks before the change;

(f)   to ensure that all machines are provided with one or
      more readily-accessible stop controls capable of
      bringing the machine to a complete stop.

Machines should not eject articles and substances or
unintentionally discharge any gas, dust, liquid or vapour. Nor
should their parts be prone to rupture or disintegration, or be
liable to overheat or catch fire.

• Regulation 11(2) of PUWER states that the fencing and guarding
  required by paragraph (a) above will ordinarily consist of one or
  more fixed guards enclosing every dangerous part of a machine
  and every rotating stock-bar. If fixed guards are impracticable,
  other types of guards and protection devices (such as
  interlocking movable guards, adjustable or automatic guards,
  and similar) will have to be considered. If these too are
  inappropriate, the machine may have to be equipped with
  photo-electric or mechanical-trip devices designed to halt a
  dangerous moving part before the operator can come into contact

with it. Pressure-sensitive mats and two-handed controls should also be considered.

- Certain types of machines (e.g., woodworking machines, bacon slicers, bandsaws, etc.) simply will not do the job they are designed to do when guards are fitted. In such circumstances, so much of the blade or cutting edge as can be enclosed should be enclosed and the machine operators provided with jigs, holders, push-sticks or similar protection devices to prevent them coming into contact with that part of the machine. There are other machines, of course, whose dangerous parts cannot be guarded at all. One obvious example is the chain saw; another is the hand-held power tool (such as an electric drill). For machines such as these, it devolves on the employer to give his employees as much information, instruction, training and supervision as they need to enable them to operate those machines safely (*ibid*; Regulation 11(1)(d)). An employer would be well-advised to keep a written record of all such training (names, dates, times etc.) in case an inspector comes to call.

- Fencing, guards and other protection devices fitted to a machine must —

   (a)   be suitable for the purpose for which they are provided;

   (b)   be of good construction, sound material and adequate strength; and

   (c)   be maintained in an efficient state, in efficient working order and in good repair;

   Furthermore, they must

   (d)   not give rise to any increased risk to health and safety;

   (e)   not be easily bypassed or disabled;

   (f)   be situated at a sufficient distance from the danger zone (that is to say, the zone in and around a machine in which a person is liable to be injured by coming into a dangerous part of that machine or by a rotating stock bar);

(g)   not unduly restrict the view of the operating cycle of the machinery, where such a view is necessary; and must

(h)   be so constructed and adapted that they allow maintenance work to be carried out and parts and replacement parts to be fitted, while at the same time restricting access only to the area where the work is to be carried out and, if possible, without having to dismantle the guard or protection device.

- An employer's first priority under PUWER is to take effective measures either to prevent access to the dangerous parts of the machines installed or used in his premises or to bring those dangerous parts to an immediate halt when any person enters a danger zone. It is no longer enough to instruct and train employees in safe working methods. Nor is it enough to issue them with protective clothing and equipment (e.g., safety goggles, helmets, ear defenders, waterproof or chain-mail aprons). Protective clothing serves a purpose, but should only be issued and used when fencing or guarding and other precautions taken to protect employees from coming into contact with the dangerous parts of a machine are not wholly effective; or if there is still a risk, however small, of vapours, dusts, substances or articles falling from or being ejected by the machine; or if (as we have seen) the machine in question cannot be guarded effectively without rendering them inoperable.

Suitability of work equipment

- Since 1 January 1993, every machine, tool or appliance provided for use in a workplace (whether purchased, leased or hired before that date or afterwards) must be so constructed or adapted as to be suitable for the purposes for which it is used or provided. When selecting a machine, an employer must have regard both to the working conditions in which it is to be used and to the risks to the health and safety of persons working with, or in the vicinity of, that machine (*ibid*; Reg. 5). For example, an electric power drill should not be used in an environment in which flammable fumes or vapours are likely to be present. Nor should an internal combustion engine be used in a confined space if there is no provision for venting harmful exhaust gases into the open air.

Maintenance

- All work equipment (including machines) must be maintained in an efficient state, in efficient working order and in good repair. If a machine has a maintenance log, it must be kept up to date and made available for inspection by an HSE or local authority inspector (*ibid*; Reg. 6).

- If a machine (e.g., an exhaust ventilation system) is not properly maintained or is not operating efficiently or is not cleaned at regular intervals, it will in time present a risk not only to the health and safety of the persons operating but also to persons situated or working nearby. The HSE's guidance notes accompanying the 1992 Regulations caution employers to develop written procedures for the routine lubrication, cleaning, inspection and testing of machines (and machine guards, controls, etc.) and for the periodic replacement or refurbishment of machine components before they reach the end of their useful life.

Information and instructions

- Every employee who uses or operates a machine (of whatever type) in the course of his employment must receive as much information and instruction as is necessary to ensure that he does so without risk to his own health and safety or that of other persons (including members of the public). If appropriate, every machine operator should be provided with (or have ready access to) a copy of the manufacturer's operating or training manuals, warning labels and placards. Employers should also see to it that supervisors, foremen and chargehands whose job it is to oversee machine operations and safe working practices are themselves familiar with the machines installed or used in their respective departments or areas of responsibility and that they too receive the necessary information and instruction before they take up their appointments (*ibid*; Reg. 8).

- If there is an accident or dangerous occurrence, and there is evidence that the employees concerned were untrained or inexperienced, or supervised by people ill-equipped to provide the necessary safety advice and guidance, the employer could well be prosecuted under the 1974 Act, with the attendant heavy penalties if he is convicted. See **Accidents at Work** elsewhere in this handbook.

Training

- An inexperienced employee should not be asked to use or operate any machine unless he (or she) has first received adequate health and safety training, including training in safe working methods, the risks associated with work on that machine, and the precautions to be taken to eliminate or minimise those risks. Nor should supervisors or foremen be appointed or transferred to oversee machine operations unless they too receive the necessary formal or 'on the job' training and instruction (*ibid*; Reg. 9).

MANAGEMENT OF HEALTH & SAFETY AT WORK REGULATIONS 1992

- Regulation 3 of the Management of Health & Safety at Work Regulations 1992 (*q.v.*) imposes a duty on every employer in *every* workplace to make a suitable and sufficient assessment of the risks to which his employees are exposed while they are at work and the risks facing people who are not in his employment (e.g., contractors' employees, visitors and members of the general public) who may be affected by the way in which he conducts his business. The assessment must be repeated if there is reason to believe that it is no longer valid or there has been a significant change in the matters (e.g., the acquisition of new plant and machinery) to which it relates. That same duty applies to self-employed persons (e.g., a builder using electrically-operated power tools on a building site or a tradesman working in the corridor of a block of flats).

Safety of new or expectant mothers

- The 'risk assessment exercise' necessarily carried out by *every* employer must include an assessment of the risk to the health and safety of new or expectant mothers (or to that of their unborn babies) arising out of their working conditions, the type of work in which they are engaged (e.g., manual handling of loads, noise, vibration hot or humid conditions, etc.), or their exposure to physical, biological or chemical agents. If there *is* a risk, the employer must either transfer a pregnant employee or new mother to suitable alternative employment or suspend her from work on full pay until that risk has passed (*ibid*; Regulation 13A). See also the sections titled **Pregnant**

employees & nursing mothers and **Suspension on maternity grounds** elsewhere in this handbook.

Note: The expression new or expectant mother means an employee who is pregnant; who has given birth within the previous six months; or who is breastfeeding.

Safety of young persons under 18

- The 1992 Regulations also contains provisions relating to the employment of school leavers and young persons under 18. Regulation 13D(1) reminds employers that young persons under 18 may not be fully matured, are likely to be inexperienced, and are inclined to be somewhat cavalier in their approach to (and acceptance of) health and safety risks in the workplace.

  Note: Regulation 13D was inserted by regulation 2(6) of the Health & Safety (Young Persons) Regulations 1997 (SI 1977/135) which came into force on 3 March 1997. The new Regulations give effect in Great Britain to Articles 6 and 7 of Council Directive 94/33/EC (OJ No. L216, 20.8.94, p. 12) on the protection of young people at work.

- From 3 March 1997, employers may not employ any young person under 18 without first reviewing their risk assessments to determine the particular risks facing young persons in the light of their relative immaturity, lack of experience, and unfamiliarity with the workplace. When doing so, an employer must also take particular account of the fitting and layout of the workplace; the machines, plant and equipment in use in the workplace; the amount of training young persons can expect to receive before they are put to work; and the risks they are likely to face if to be engaged in work involving (amongst other things) the handling of equipment for the production, storage or application of compressed liquefied or dissolved gases; or in work involving high-voltage electrical hazards; or in work the pace of which is determined by machinery and involving payments by results. See also **Women & young persons, Employment of** elsewhere in this handbook.

Purpose of risk assessment

- The purpose of the risk assessment exercise (or safety audit) prescribed by Regulation 3 is to enable an employer to identify the measures he needs to take to comply with the requirements and prohibitions imposed upon him by existing health and safety legislation. A 'hit and miss' approach to accident prevention is no longer acceptable.

- Every employer with five or more people 'on the payroll' must keep a written or computerised record of the significant findings of his risk assessment exercise, including the names (or job titles) of those of his employees identified in that record as being especially at risk. An employer who fails to carry out the assessment, or does so in a desultory or half-hearted fashion, or who fails to provide the necessary documentation when asked to do so by a health and safety inspector, is guilty of an offence and is liable to be prosecuted under the Health & Safety at Work etc. Act 1974. The penalty on conviction is a fine of up to £2,000 or, if the conviction is obtained on indictment, a fine of an unlimited amount.

  Note: It should be borne in mind that the term workplace nowadays applies to every premises (or part of premises), other than domestic premises, which are made available to a person as a place of work. A school is a workplace — as is a hospital, cinema, theatre, guest house, bed-and-breakfast establishment, swimming baths, leisure centre; indeed, every place in which one or more persons are employed. The list is endless.

- An employer who has carried out a thorough assessment of the risks facing his employees in the course of their employment will be able to produce a document which (*inter alia*) lists every machine and every item of plant and equipment installed or used in his premises. Alongside each machine in the list should be a statement about its age and condition, the last occasion on which it was repaired or maintained, and information also about any defects (such as a tendency to overheat, loose fittings, missing guards, inadequate fencing, faulty stop/start controls and so on) which must be put to rights, and quickly.

- In large, well-run organisations, the head of the maintenance department will already have that information at his fingertips and will have long since developed an efficient maintenance and accident-prevention programme. In the smaller organisation (such as a workshop, cafeteria, laundry, school, printing works, etc.), the employer, who is not mechanically-minded or who is lax about maintaining machines which are well beyond their 'use-by' dates, would be well-advised to seek professional advice and to enter into a maintenance contract for each and every machine on his premises.

- It is as well to add that every employer is now required to appoint a competent person to advise him on health and safety legislation and the practical implications of that legislation (*ibid*; Regulation 6). The person appointed may be the employer himself, or his Safety Officer or an external consultant. But the person appointed must be truly competent — an issue which is explored at greater length elsewhere in this handbook in the section titled **Competent persons.**

See also the sections titled **Abrasive wheels, Dangerous Machines, Dangerous occurrences, Horizontal milling machines, Machinery safety, Power presses** and **Work equipment** elsewhere in this handbook.

FURTHER INFORMATION

• The following publications are available from HSE Books at the address given on page 328. A more complete listing of HSE publications is to be found in the HSE Books Price List for 1997, a copy of which will be sent free of charge by telephoning 01787 881165.

Codes of practice & guidance on Regulations

L21
Management of Health and Safety at Work Regulations 1992: Approved code of practice [1992]
ISBN 0 7176 0412 8   £5.00

L22
Work equipment. Provision and Use of Work Equipment Regulations 1992. Guidance on Regulations [1992]
ISBN 0 7176 0414 4   £5.00

L25
Personal Protective Equipment at Work Regulations 1992. Guidance on Regulations [1992]
ISBN 07176 0415 2   £5.00

Guidance notes

PM 1
Guarding of portable pipe-threading machines [1984]
ISBN 0 11 883590 4   £2.50

PM 35
Safety in the use of reversing dough brakes   [1983]
ISBN 0 11 883576 9   £2.50

PM 40
Protection of workers at welded steel tube mills [1984]
ISBN 0 11 883588 2   £2.50

PM 41
Application of photo-electric safety systems to machinery   [1984]
ISBN 0 11 883593 9   £2.50

PM 65
Worker protection at crocodile (alligator) shears [1986]
ISBN 0 11 883935 7   £2.50

PM 66
Scrap baling machines [1986]
ISBN 0 7176 1264 3   £5.00

PM 73
Safety at autoclaves [1990]
ISBN 0 7176 1197 3   £2.50

HS(G) 42
Safety in the use of metal cutting guillotines and shears [1988]
ISBN 0 11 885455 0   £2.75

HS(G) 43
Industrial robot safety [1988]
ISBN 0 7176 1237 6   £9.50

HS(G) 44
Drilling machines: guarding of spindles and attachments   [1988]
ISBN 0 7176 0616 3   £4.00

HS(G) 83
Training woodworking machinists [1992]
ISBN 0 11 886316 9   £4.00

FIRE CERTIFICATE

Key points

- A fire certificate is compulsory for any premises which are put to a use designated by the Secretary of State by an order made under section 1 of the Fire Precautions Act 1971 (as modified by the Fire Safety & Safety of Place of Sport Act 1987).

- However, the Secretary of State (in this instance, the Home Secretary) may not designate any premises as requiring a fire certificate unless they are used —

  (a) as sleeping accommodation, or for any purpose involving the provision of sleeping accommodation;

  (b) as (or as part of) an institution providing treatment or care;

  (c) for the purposes of entertainment, recreation or instruction, or for the purposes of any club, society or association;

  (d) for the purposes of teaching, training or research;

  (e) for any purpose involving access to the premises by members of the public, whether on payment or otherwise; or

  (f) as a place of work

- To date, 'designation orders' have been made relating to factories, offices, shops and railway premises (SI 1989/76) and for certain hotels and boarding houses (SIs 1972/238/382). Special conditions apply in the case of premises in which large quantities of highly flammable liquids, explosives or prescribed dangerous chemicals are processed, manufactured, used or stored (SI 1976/2003). Premises which do not require a fire certificate or which have been exempted by the fire authority under section 5A of the 1971 Act must nonetheless be provided with such means of escape in case of fire and such means for fighting fire as may reasonably required in the circumstances of the case(*ibid*; section 9A) — all of which requirements are summarised in the text below.

HOME OFFICE GUIDES

- The Home Office has published a number of useful guides to the 1971 Act, details of which appear at the end of the next section on page 297. The following is little more than a summary of the principal provisions of the Act. Readers uncertain about their legal obligations should not hesitate to contact their local fire authority for advice.

FACTORIES, OFFICES, SHOPS AND RAILWAY PREMISES

- A fire certificate is required for any factory, office, shop or railway premises in which: (a) more than 20 persons are employed at any one time; or (b) more than 10 persons are employed elsewhere than on the ground floor.

- If a factory, office or shop, etc occupies only part of a building in which there are other factories, offices and shops, a fire certificate will nonetheless be required if the total number of people employed in the building exceeds 20, or if 10 or more of that total are employed elsewhere than on the ground floor.

- When a building is in multiple occupation, it is the owner (or owners) of the building who will be held responsible if the building is used without a fire certificate being in force. The occupiers (or lessees) of premises within that building must, however, check that a fire certificate has been issued (or, at the very least, applied for) before putting those premises to a designated use. Special conditions for smaller premises (i.e., a building in which not more than 20 or, as appropriate, 10 persons are employed at any one time) are described below.

- The meaning of the expressions 'factory premises', 'office premises', 'shop premises' and 'railway premises' are as given in the Factories Act 1961 and the Offices, Shops and Railway Premises Act 1963. To avoid confusion, it must be remembered that 'shop premises' includes not only 'shops' in the everyday sense of the word, but any building (or part of a building) in which a retail or wholesale trade or business is carried on, and to which members of the public are invited to resort; or in which goods are kept for sale wholesale. Thus, barbers and hairdressers, auction sale rooms, lending libraries, betting shops, laundries (including self-service laundrettes), warehouses (other than factory warehouses, or warehouses on docks, wharves or quays), fish and chip shops, fast food shops, cafeterias, restaurants, tea and coffee houses, public houses, inns, coke and coal merchants' premises, and so on, are all 'shop premises' for the purposes of the Fire Precautions Act 1971 and the Offices, Shops and Railway Premises Act 1963.

HOTELS AND BOARDING HOUSES

- By virtue of the Fire Precautions (Hotels and Boarding Houses) Order 1972 (SI 1972/238 and [for Scotland] SI 1972/382), every hotel, motel, inn, residential club, boarding house, lodging house and hostel, which provides sleeping accommodation for six or more persons (whether guests or staff), or which provides any form of sleeping accommodation for guests or staff above the first floor or at basement level, must have a fire certificate.

- Should the proprietor (occupier, owner, landlord, manager, etc) of a hotel or boarding house, etc be in any doubt concerning his obligations under the 1971 Act, he should contact his local fire authority for advice.

SMALL & EXEMPTED PREMISES

- Exempted premises and premises which do not otherwise require a fire certificate must nonetheless be provided with such means of escape in case of fire and such means for fighting fire as may reasonably be required. A failure to comply with this requirement is an offence for which the penalty on summary conviction is a fine of up to £5,000 (*ibid*; section 9A).

Codes of practice

- Section 9B of the 1971 Act empowers the Secretary of State (the Home Secretary) to prepare and issue codes of practice for the purpose of providing practical guidance on how to comply with the duty imposed by section 9A of the Act (see previous paragraph) (*ibid*; section 9B).

- The Home Office has published a code of practice titled *Code of Practice for Fire Precautions in Factories, Offices, Shops & Railway Premises not required to have a fire certificate;* as to which, see *HOME OFFICE PUBLICATIONS* at the end of this section.

- A failure on the part of a person to observe any provision of a code of practice does not of itself render him liable to any criminal or civil proceedings. However, if, in any such proceedings it is alleged that there has been a contravention of the duty imposed by section 9A of the 1971 Act, a failure to observe a provision of the relevant code of practice may be relied on as tending to establish liability; and compliance with such a code, as tending to negative liability (*ibid*; section 9C).

IMPROVEMENT & PROHIBITION NOTICES

- If, in the opinion of the fire authority, the duty imposed by section 9A of the 1971 Act (as regards the adequacy of the means of escape and/or the means of fighting fire) has been contravened in respect of any premises to which that section applies, it may serve an improvement notice on the occupier of those premises instructing him to 'set matters to rights' within the period specified in the notice. A person on whom such a notice has been served has 21 days within which to lodge an appeal against the notice — which will have the effect of suspending the notice until the appeal is heard. The procedure for lodging an appeal is explained in the notice itself (*ibid*; sections 9D & 9E)

- In a more serious case where employees and/or members of the public are considered to be especially at risk in the event of a fire, the fire authority may serve a prohibition notice on the occupier of the premises in question. A prohibition notice comes into effect *immediately* and prohibits or restricts the use of the premises until the matters specified in the notice have been remedied. Unlike an appeal against an improvement notice, an appeal against the service or contents of a prohibition notice does not have the effect of lifting the notice. In short, the occupier must comply with a prohibition notice pending the outcome of his appeal (*ibid*; sections 10 & 10A).

- A failure to comply with the terms of an improvement or prohibition notice is a serious offence, the penalty for which, on summary conviction, is a fine of up to £20,000 or, on conviction on indictment, a fine of an unspecified amount and/or imprisonment for a term not exceeding two years (*ibid*; sections 9F & 10B)

SPECIAL PREMISES

• Certain types of premises have been designated 'special premises' by virtue of the Fire Certificates (Special Premises) Regulations 1976 (SI 1976/2003, as amended by SI 1985/1333). In such cases, a fire certificate is compulsory irrespective of the size of the premises or the number of persons employed in those premises at any one time. Those premises are:

1. Manufacturing premises in which the total quantity of any highly flammable liquid under pressure greater than atmospheric pressure, and above its boiling point at atmospheric pressure, may exceed 50 tonnes.

2. Premises in which expanded cellular plastics are manufactured, where the quantities manufactured are normally of, or in excess of, 50 tonnes per week.

3. Any premises at which there is stored, or storage facilities exist for, 100 or more tonnes of liquefied petroleum gas (unless intended for use either as a fuel or for the production of an atmosphere for the heat treatment of metals).

4. Any premises at which there is stored, or storage facilities exist for, 100 or more tonnes of liquefied natural gas, unless such gas is intended solely for use as a fuel at the premises.

5. Any premises at which there is stored, or storage facilities exist for, 100 or more tonnes of liquefied flammable gas consisting predominantly of methyl acetylene, unless kept solely for use as a fuel at the premises.

6. Premises at which oxygen is manufactured and at which there are stored, or storage facilities exist for, quantities of liquid oxygen of, or in excess of, 135 tonnes.

7. Any premises at which there are stored, or storage facilities exist for, 50 or more tonnes of chlorine, except when the chlorine is kept solely for the purposes of water purification.

8. Premises at which artificial fertilisers are manufactured and at which there are stored, or storage facilities exist

for, 250 or more tonnes of ammonia.

9.   Any premises at which there are in process,
     manufacture, use or storage, or there are facilities provided
     for such processing, manufacture, use or storage of,
     quantities of any of the materials listed below in, or in
     excess of, the quantities specified:

phosgene	5 tonnes
ethylene oxide	20 tonnes
carbon disulphide	50 tonnes
acrylonitrile	50 tonnes
hydrogen cyanide	50 tonnes
ethylene	100 tonnes
propylene	100 tonnes

any highly flammable liquid not otherwise specified 4000
tonnes

10.   Explosives factories or magazines which are required to be
      licensed under the Explosives Act 1875.

11.   Any building on the surface at any mine within the
      meaning of the Mines and Quarries Act 1954.

12.   Any premises consisting of a site for which a licence is
      required in accordance with section I of the Nuclear
      Installations Act 1965, or for which a permit is required in
      accordance with section 2 of that Act (including premises
      occupied by the United Kingdom Atomic Energy Authority,
      or by, or on behalf of, the Crown, notwithstanding that
      they are exempt from the licensing provisions of the 1965
      Act).

13.   Any premises containing any machine or apparatus in
      which charged particles can be accelerated by the
      equivalent of a voltage of not less than 50 megavolts
      (except where the premises are used as a hospital).

14.   Premises to which Regulation 26 of the Ionising
      Radiations Regulations 1985 (SI 1985/1333) applies;

15.   Any building, or part of a building, constructed for
      temporary occupation during building operations or works

of engineering construction, or already in existence when further such operations or works begin, and which is used for any process or work ancillary to any such operations or works.

Enforcement in the case of 'special premises' is the province of the Health & Safety Executive, *not* the fire authority.

• Once a fire certificate has been issued, the occupier of 'special premises' must display a notice, in a position where it may be easily seen and read, informing his employees —

(a)   that a fire certificate has been issued;
(b)   where it, or a copy of it, may be inspected; and

specifying the date on which the notice was posted.

The procedure for applying for a fire certificate in respect of 'special premises' is described below.

APPLICATION FOR A FIRE CERTIFICATE

• For premises other than 'special premises', an application for a fire certificate must be submitted to the local fire authority on form FP I (Rev) 1993 which will be supplied on request by the authority. The application should be signed by the occupier of the premises, unless the premises are held under a lease and consist of part of a building, all parts of which are in the same ownership, or consist of part of a building in which different parts are owned by different people. In such cases, application should be made by or on behalf of the owner(s) of the building. However, the occupier of such premises should check that a fire certificate is in force or that an application has been made for one. A person who puts his premises to a designated use without having applied for a fire certificate is guilty of an offence and liable on summary conviction to a fine of up to £400; or, if he is convicted on indictment, a fine of an unlimited amount and/or imprisonment for a term of up to two years (*ibid*; section 7(1) &

Special premises

In the case of 'special premises' the occupier of the premises must apply direct to the nearest local office of the Health & Safety Executive (HSE). There is no prescribed form of application for a fire certificate in such cases, although the following information must be supplied:

1. Address of the premises.

2. Description of the premises by reference to the list set out under *Special premises* above.

3. Nature of the processes carried on, or to be carried on, on the premises.

4. Nature and approximate quantities of any explosive or highly flammable substance kept, or to be kept, on the premises.

5. Maximum number of persons likely to be on the premises at any one time.

6. Maximum number of persons likely to be in any building of which the premises form part at any one time.

7. Name and address of the occupier of the premises.

8. Name and address of any other person who has control of the premises.

9. If the premises consist of part of a building, the name and postal address of the person or persons having control of the building or any part of it.

Procedure

•   On receipt of an application for a fire certificate, the fire authority (or the HSE, in the case of 'special premises') may require the applicant to furnish plans of his premises and, in some instances, plans of the remainder of the building or any adjoining premises. If the plans are not provided within specified time limits, the application for a fire certificate will be deemed to have been withdrawn, in which event, it will be an offence for the occupier to use those premises for the intended purpose.

•   Subsequent to the receipt of plans, the fire authority or inspectorate will inspect the premises to assess the adequacy of the fire precautions. If they are not satisfied, they will write to the applicant specifying the steps that need to be taken before a fire certificate is issued.

- During the period in which the fire authority is considering an application for a fire certificate, the owner or occupier of the premises in question must ensure that the means of escape in case of fire with which those premises are provided can be safely and effectively used at all material times; that the fire fighting appliances are maintained in efficient working order; and that the persons employed in those premises receive instruction and training in what to do in case of fire. A failure to comply with these requirements is an offence, the penalty for which, on summary conviction is a fine of up to £5,000 (*ibid*; sections 5(2A) and 7(3A)).

Right of appeal

- If an applicant is aggrieved by any of the requirements laid down by the fire authority or inspectorate, or by a refusal to issue a fire certificate, or by any inclusion in, or omission from, a fire certificate, he may appeal to a magistrates' court (in Scotland, the sheriff). Such an appeal must be lodged within 21 days of the date on which notice was served on him by the fire authority or relevant health and safety inspectorate.

Power of fire authority to grant exemptions

- In some circumstances, the fire authority has the power to exempt a particular premises from the need to have a fire certificate — given the size of the premises, the nature of the risk, the number of persons present in the premises at any one time; and so on (*ibid*; section 5A). The notice granting the exemption may include a statement specifying the greatest number of persons who can safely be in the premises at any one time. It is an offence, during the currency of an exemption granted in this way, for the owner or occupier

  (a) to allow more people into the premises than the maximum number specified in the statement;

  (b) to carry out any structural alterations to the premises or to alter the internal arrangements (in a way which undermines of otherwise affects the means of escape from those premises); or

(c) to begin to keep explosive or highly inflammable material of any prescribed kind anywhere under, in or on the building which constitutes or comprises the premises (in a quantity or aggregate quantity greater than the prescribed maximum)

without first informing the fire authority about his intentions.

A failure to comply with this requirement is a serious offence, the penalty for which is a fine of up to £20,000. If the offender is convicted on indictment, the penalty is a fine (for which there is no prescribed upper limit) and/or imprisonment for a term not exceeding two years (*ibid*; section 8A)

CONTENTS OF A FIRE CERTIFICATE

- A fire certificate will specify:

    1. the means of escape which are provided in case of fire;

    2. the correct fire evacuation procedure;

    3. the type, number and location of fire fighting appliances, sprinkler systems, etc; and

    4. the type and locations of the warning system and fire alarm points;

It will normally do so by means of, or reference to, a plan or photographs of the premises. A fire certificate may also impose conditions:

    5. for securing that the means of escape in case of fire which are provided are properly maintained and kept free from obstruction;

    6. for securing that fire fighting appliances and systems are routinely and regularly maintained, tested and examined, and that suitable records are kept;

    7. for securing that employees receive appropriate instruction and training in what to do in case of fire,

and that records are kept of instruction and training given for that purpose;

8. for limiting the number of persons who may be on the premises, or in part of the premises, at any one time;

9. as to other precautions to be observed in relation to the risk to persons in case of fire.

Duties of occupier

- The occupier of the premises will normally be held responsible for a contravention of any requirement or condition contained in the fire certificate. However, in the case of factory, office, shop or railway premises, which are held under a lease or agreement, it is the owner(s) of the building who will be liable, in relation to the maintenance of means of escape, etc., unless the premises are 'special premises' as discussed earlier.

- The fire certificate will be sent to the applicant or occupier, as the case may be. If the applicant is the owner of the building, a copy will also be sent to the occupier of the premises, and must be kept on the premises for so long as the fire certificate is in force.

Alterations to premises

- So long as a fire certificate is in force, the fire authority (or, in the case of 'special premises' the relevant factory or related health and safety inspectorate) may inspect the premises at any reasonable time to ascertain whether there have been any change of conditions affecting the adequacy of the means of escape, fire evacuation procedures, fire fighting appliances, instruction and training, and so on.

- Structural alterations of any kind must never be undertaken until the fire authority (or relevant inspectorate) have first been notified and have given their approval. The same applies to any proposed material alterations in the internal arrangements of the premises or in the furniture or equipment with which the premises are provided. If it is intended to keep explosive or highly flammable materials on the premises, the fire authority must also be given advance notification. By section 8 of the Fire Precautions Act 1971, it is an offence to carry out any such alterations or proposals without advance notification and approval. The penalty for non-compliance is a fine of up to £400 or, if the offender is convicted on indictment, a fine of an unlimited amount or imprisonment for a term not exceeding two years, or both (*ibid*; section 8(8)).

Other enactments

- Premises, such as public houses, restaurants and clubs, which are required to obtain a licence or registration under the Licensing Act 1964 (or the Licensing (Scotland) Act 1976), will not be granted a Justices' Licence or Certificate of Registration, as appropriate, unless the district council is satisfied with the general suitability of the premises including the provision of adequate means of escape in case of fire.

- It must also be remembered that planning permissions will be subject to the requirements of the relevant Buildings Regulations (which include minimum fire precautions); while new buildings (particularly those to which members of the public are to be admitted) must comply with the requirements of the Chronically Sick and Disabled Persons Acts 1970 and 1976.

    See also **Fire precautions** (next section).

FIRE PRECAUTIONS

Key points

- Section 2(2)(c) and (d) of the Health and Safety at Work etc. Act 1974, imposes a duty on every employer :

    (a)   to provide his employees with such information, instruction, training and supervision as is necessary to ensure their health and safety at work.

    (b)   to maintain his place of business in a condition that is safe and without risks to health, and to provide safe means of access to, and egress from, his premises.

    An employer who fails to discharge that duty is guilty of an offence and liable, on summary conviction, to a fine of up to £20,000.

- In the context of fire prevention, the practical implications are clear. Fire escape routes must not only be provided and maintained, but must be kept free from obstruction at all times. Exit doors must be kept unlocked and unfastened (or, at the very least, be capable of being opened quickly and easily) so long as any employee remains on the premises. Fire fighting appliances must be maintained in efficient working order and be conveniently accessible in case of fire. There must be a secure and efficient method for sounding the fire alarm, capable of being heard throughout the employer's premises. Where necessary, a system of emergency lighting should be installed. Every employee must be familiar with fire evacuation procedures and the precautions to be taken to prevent an outbreak of fire. Fire drills should be conducted at frequent intervals, as well as competent and comprehensive training sessions in the use of fire fighting appliances. See also *Proposed new Regulations* below.

Safety policy statement

- Section 2(5) of the 1974 Act states that every employer of five or more persons must prepare a written statement of his general policy with respect to the health and safety at work of his employees. This statement must include details of the arrangements he has made for carrying out that policy. Fire prevention and evacuation procedures must, of necessity, feature prominently in every such policy statement.

FIRE PRECAUTIONS ACT 1971

- A fire certificate is compulsory for every workplace in which 20 or more persons are employed at any one time (or in which 10 or more persons are employed elsewhere than on the ground floor); and for every hotel and boarding house (or similar) which provides any form of sleeping accommodation (whether for staff or guests) above the first floor or below ground level, or sleeping accommodation for more than six persons (staff as well as guests) in total.

- In such cases, the duties of the occupier are very clearly laid down in the fire certificate itself. If the occupier contravenes any requirement or condition of the fire certificate, he is guilty of an offence and liable, on summary conviction, to a fine of up to

£400 or, if the offender is convicted on indictment, a fine for which there is no prescribed upper limit and/or imprisonment for up to two years (*ibid*; section 7(5)). See also *Improvement and prohibition notices* in the previous section (titled Fire certificate).

- In smaller factories, offices, shops and railway premises, where a fire certificate is not compulsory (and in premises which have been exempted under section 5A of the 1971 Act), the occupier must nonetheless comply with section 9A (*ibid*.) which imposes a duty on him to provide adequate means of escape in case of fire and adequate facilities for fighting fire. The penalty for non-compliance with section 9A is a fine of up to £5,000 (level 5 on the standard scale) (*ibid*; section 9A(3).

Proposed new Regulations

- In September 1994, the Home Office published draft proposals for Regulations to be titled *Fire Precautions (Places of Work) Regulations 199(?)*. At the time of writing (April 1977), consultations were still in progress. However, once the new Regulations appear, every employer will be required to carry out a 'fire risk assessment' and to draw up plans for the controlled evacuation of his premises in the event of an emergency. Both the risk assessment and the emergency plan will have to be repeated and, if need be, revised at regular intervals. If there are five or more employees in the workplace, the findings of the risk assessment must be documented and must identify the employees who are at risk. Responsible persons will have to be appointed to activate the emergency plan. Depending on the size of the workplace and the nature of the activities carried on there, employers will be duty-bound to provide and maintain safe and effective means of escape in the event of fire, fire-detection and warning systems, a sufficient number of fire fighting appliances, and emergency lighting. They will also be expected to provide induction and 'refresher' training sessions for new recruits and existing employees. Fire drills will have to be conducted and assessed at regular intervals (at least once a year, if five or more persons are employed); records kept; and so on.

STORAGE OF FLAMMABLE SUBSTANCES

- Rules relating to the storage of flammable substances are to be found in —

    (a)   the Petroleum (Consolidation) Act 1928 (as amended);

(b) the Highly Flammable Liquids & Liquefied Petroleum Gases Regulations 1972 (SI 1972/917);

(c) the Dangerous Substances (Notification & Marking of Sites) Regulations 1990 (SI 1990/304); and

(d) the Notification of Installations Handling Hazardous Substances Regulations 1982 (SI 1982/1357).

SPECIAL REGULATIONS

• The following special Regulations, Orders, etc lay down fire prevention measures to be taken in the hazardous trades, industries and processes to which they relate:

1. **Celluloid (Manufacture, etc) Regulations 1921** (SI 1921/1825): storage and manipulation of celluloid; the provision of receptacles for celluloid waste; the appointment of a competent person to supervise compliance with the Regulations; etc.

2. **Cinematograph Film Stripping Regulations 1939** (SI 1939/571): the use of fire-resisting materials used in the construction of rooms used for stripping or drying; the frequent collection and removal of film scrap; the construction and location of storerooms and the provision of gas-relief spaces, etc; arrangements for the temporary reception of smoking materials, matches and similar articles outside the premises; etc.

3. **Highly Flammable Liquids and Liquefied Petroleum Gases Regulations 1972** (SI 1972/917): marking of storerooms, tanks, vessels, etc; precautions against spills and leaks; prevention of escape of vapours and dispersal of dangerous concentrations of vapours; explosion pressure relief of fire-resisting structures; prevention and removal of solid residues; prohibition on smoking; and control of ignition and burning of highly flammable liquids; etc.

4. **Magnesium (Grinding of Castings and Other Articles) Special Regulations 1944** (SI 1944/2107): precautions against causing sparks; interception and removal of dust; disposal of magnesium dust; prohibition of smoking, open lights and fires, etc.

5. **Manufacture of Cinematograph Film Regulations 1928**
   SI 1928/82): separate storage of cinematograph film reels;
   collection and storage of waste and scrap; use of
   fire-resisting materials in the construction of workrooms;
   the reception of smoking materials, matches, etc;
   outside workrooms; flameproofing of light-fittings; etc.

6. **Testing of Aircraft Engines and Accessories Special
   Regulations 1952** (SI 1952/1689): flameproofing of
   electrical apparatus; construction of rooms; use of heat-
   treated safety glass in windows; separation of work;
   drainage of tanks and pipework; provision of control
   valves; earthing of magnetos; etc.

The penalty for non-compliance with the provisions of those
Regulations is a fine of up to £2,000 or, if the offender is
convicted on indictment, a fine of such amount as the court
considers appropriate.

FURTHER INFORMATION

HSE publications

• The following HSE publications are available from HSE Books at
  the address given on page 328.

HS(G) 64
*Assessment of fire hazards from solid materials and the precautions
required for their safe storage and use: a guide for manufacturers,
suppliers, storekeepers and users* [1991]
ISBN 0 11 885654 5   £3.00

*Guide to general fire precautions in explosives factories and
magazines. (Fire Certificate (Special premises) Regulations 1976).*
[Rev. 1990]
ISBN 0 11 885965 X   £6.50

Guidance on permit-to-work systems in the petroleum industry
[1991]
ISBN 0 11 885688 X   £2.50

CS 15
Cleaning and gas freeing of tanks containing flammable residues
[1985]

ISBN 0 11 883518 1   £2.50

GS 40
Loading and unloading of bulk flammable liquids and gases at harbours and inland waterways [1986]
ISBN 0 7176 1230 9   £5.00

HS(G) 50
The storage of flammable liquids in fixed tank (up to 10,000 m³ total capacity) [1990]
ISBN 0 11 885532 8   £4.50

HS(G) 51
The storage of flammable liquids in containers [1990]
ISBN 0 7176 0481 0   £4.50

HS(G) 52
The storage of flammable liquids in fixed tanks (exceeding 10,000 m³) total capacity) [1991]
ISBN 0 11 885538 7   £4.50

L16
Design and construction of vented non-pressure road tankers used for the carriage of flammable liquids. Road Traffic (Carriage of Dangerous Substances in Road Tankers and Tank Containers) Regulations 1992: Approved code of practice [1993]
ISBN 0 11 886300 2   £4.00

Home Office publications

The following Home Office publications are available from The Stationery Office (see page 328 for details) below:

Guide to fire precautions in existing places of work that require a fire certificate: Factories, offices, shops and railway premises (Revised December 1993)
ISBN 0 11 341079 4   £8.50

Fire safety at work (Reprinted May 1993)
ISBN 0 11 340905 2   £4.25

Guide to fire precautions in premises used as hotels and boarding houses which require a fire certificate
ISBN 0 11 341005 0   £7.50

Fire safety management in hotels and boarding houses
(November 1991)
ISBN 0 11 340980 X   £4.50

Code of practice for fire precautions in factories, offices, shops and railway premises not required to have a fire certificate
(April 1989)
ISBN 0 11 340904 4   £3.50

Other relevant Home Office guides are:

Draft guide to fire precautions in residential care premises
(January 1983)
ISBN 0 86 252084 3 (Free)

Guide to fire precautions in existing places of entertainment and like premises (Reprinted October 1994)
ISBN 0 11 340907 9   £9.95

Assessment of fire hazards from solid materials and the precautions required for their safe storage and use
(November 1991)
ISBN 0 11 885654 5   £3.00

Fire safety in the printing industry (December 1992)
ISBN 0 11 886375 4   £6.00

For further information, contact:

Home Office
Fire Safety Division (Room 711)
Horseferry House
Dean Ryle Street
LONDON
SW1P 2AW
Telephone: 0171 217 8734

FIRST AID

Key points

- The legal duty of employers to provide adequate and appropriate first-aid equipment and facilities for the benefit of employees who are injured or become ill at work, and to appoint suitable persons to administer first-aid treatment, is laid down in the Health & Safety (First Aid) Regulations 1981 (SI 1981/917, as amended by SI 1989/1671)).

- The 1981 Regulations came into force on 1 July 1982. A revised Approved Code of Practice (replacing the original 1982 code) came into effect on 2 July 1990. The Regulations and Code of Practice apply to *all* employers (and, indeed, to all self-employed persons) irrespective of the type of trade or industry in which they happen to be engaged.

- Accordingly, adequate and appropriate first-aid equipment and facilities must be provided in every business or undertaking in which persons are employed.

- It should be pointed out that employers are not duty-bound to provide first-aid facilities for the benefit of visitors or members of the public (customers, guests, patrons, etc.) in supermarkets, shops, hotels, restaurants, pubs, and the like — although it is unlikely that any responsible employer would willingly deny first-aid treatment to a member of the general public in an emergency.

  Note: Although he is not obliged to provide first-aid facilities for the benefit of guests, customers, patrons of visitors, an employer does have a duty in law to notify the relevant enforcing authority if a member of the general public sustains a major injury or is killed while visiting his premises — the more so if the accident which led to the injury or fatality was directly attributable to the manner in which he conducted his business activities. For further information, including details of the correct procedure to be followed in such cases, please see **Accidents to clients, customers, etc.** elsewhere in this handbook. See also **Occupier of premises**.

FIRST-AID EQUIPMENT AND FACILITIES

- The criteria for deciding precisely what constitutes adequate and appropriate first-aid equipment and facilities are:

  (a) the number of persons employed in a particular

establishment;

(b)   the type of business carried on in that establishment;

(c)   the size of the establishment and the distribution of employees; and

(d)   the location of the employer's business (e.g. whether situated in a remote and relatively inaccessible part of the country or within easy distance of a hospital with accident and emergency facilities).

Paragraph 23 of the Code of Practice on First Aid (see *FURTHER INFORMATION* below) points out that every establishment in which people are employed should be equipped with at least one first-aid box or similar container. In some establishments (such as a large inner-city hotel employing several hundred people), a fully-equipped first-aid room would be more appropriate. However, in general, an employer need only provide a first-aid room as such if he has 400 or more workers in his employ *(ibid.,* para 13). For further particulars, see *First-Aid Room* below.

First-aid boxes

- One first-aid box will ordinarily suffice in a workplace employing fewer than 150 persons. However, more than one may be appropriate in establishments where relatively few employees are dispersed over a wide area (such as is in a multi-storey office building or sprawling factory complex).

- The important consideration is that every employee should have reasonably rapid access to first-aid. Furthermore, as we shall see, every first-aid box or container must be placed in a clearly identified and readily accessible location.

- A first-aid box should be of solid construction and designed to protect the contents from dust and damp. Each box should (ideally) be wall-mounted and marked with a white cross on a green background. In areas where corrosive or irritant substances (e.g., acids, cleaning fluids, de-scaling agents, and similar) are employed or there are concentrations of dusts and fumes, the first-aid box should be convenient to a supply of tap water. If this is not a practicable proposition, sterile water or sterile normal saline — in disposable containers each holding at least 300 ml—should be kept available nearby for eye irrigation. Soap and disposable towels should also be ready to hand for use both by an injured employee and the person administering first-aid treatment (e.g., when cuts have to be cleaned before a dressing is applied).

Contents of first-aid boxes

- First-aid boxes should contain a sufficient quantity of suitable first-aid materials and nothing else. Advice on the contents of first-aid boxes is given in the *Guidance Notes* for the 1981 Regulations. A list of those contents and the quantities required in each case (determined by the number of persons employed in the particular establishment, or, if more than one box, the number of employees served by each box) is given in **Table 1** (page 303).

- The person in charge of each first-aid box — whether a trained first-aider or appointed person (see *FIRST-AID ATTENDANTS* below) must check the contents at regular intervals and replenish missing items as soon as possible. If a first-aid box is used relatively infrequently, he (or she) must replace any item which may have deteriorated with the passage of time.

- In large establishments employing more than 150 persons, where trained first-aiders are employed, the management should provide appropriate carrying equipment — such as stretchers, carrying chairs, wheel chairs and wheeled carriages — for the use of first-aiders. In addition, paragraph 9 of the *Guidance Notes* recommends that blankets be stored alongside such equipment, and in such a way as to keep them free from dust and dampness.

First-aid room

- As was mentioned earlier, a fully-equipped and staffed first-aid room is not generally necessary in any establishment employing fewer than 400 persons. If such a room *is* made available, it should normally be placed in the charge of an occupational health nurse or trained first-aider. First-aid room provided for the benefit of both staff and members of the public (as in a large hotel or department store) need only be staffed by a trained first-aider.

Note: Regulation 25 of the Workplace (Health, Safety & Welfare) Regulations 1992 (SI 1992/3004) imposes a duty on employers in every workplace to provide suitable facilities in which employees who are pregnant or have recently given birth may rest. Such facilities, says the accompanying approved code of practice, should be conveniently situated to sanitary facilities and, where necessary, should include the facility to lie down. Although there is no reason why a first-aid room should not be made available for the use of pregnant women and nursing mothers, the general tenor of the Regulations is that such employees should be able to rest without the risk of being disturbed.

- Apart from the conduct of routine medical examinations, a first-aid room should not be used for any purpose other than the first-aid treatment of sick or injured employees. It should be well-ventilated, lit and heated, and should be cleaned daily. Ideally, it should be situated adjacent to toilets, with doorways wide enough to accommodate stretchers and wheel chairs. The room itself should be clearly identified as such (i.e., with a white cross on a green background and the legend First-aid room on the outer door). A further notice in the room itself — or on the outer wall near the door — should give the names and locations of the nearest first-aiders, their telephone contact numbers, and the hours of the day (or night) during which each is on call. It follows that there should be a telephone in the room itself, or nearby.

- Paragraph 27(k) of the Code of Practice cautions that, if any part of the employer's establishment is not within easy reach of the first-aid room (viz; if the room cannot be reached within approximately three minutes), a first-aid box should be provided in that part of the establishment.

Contents of First-Aid Rooms

- Advice on the facilities and equipment to be provided in first-aid rooms is given in the Guidance Notes for the 1981 Regulations. See **Table 2** on page 305.

FIRST-AID ATTENDANTS

- The Health & Safety (First-Aid) Regulations 1981 allow that a trained first-aider is not absolutely essential in low-hazard establishments (such as offices, shops, hotels, and the like) where fewer than 150 people are employed at any one time.

Table 1
Health & Safety (First-Aid) Regulations 1981

CONTENTS OF FIRST-AID BOXES OR CONTAINERS

First-aid boxes should contain a sufficient quantity of suitable first-aid materials and nothing else. Contents should be replenished as soon as possible after use. Items should not be used after the expiry date shown on packets. It is therefore essential that first-aid equipment be checked frequently, to make sure there are sufficient quantities and all items are usable.

Every first-aid box should contain a sufficient quantity of each of the following:

(a) one Guidance Card [IND(G)4] *
(b) twenty individually-wrapped sterile adhesive dressings (assorted sizes) appropriate to the work environment (which may be colour-coded for the catering industry);
(c) two sterile eye pads, with attachment;
(d) six individually wrapped triangular bandages;
(e) six safety pins;
(f) six medium sized individually wrapped sterile unmedicated wound dressings (approx. 10 cm x 8 cm);
(g) two large sterile individually wrapped unmedicated wound dressings (approx. 13 cm x 9 cm); and
(h) three extra large sterile individually wrapped unmedicated wound dressings (approx. 28 cm x 17.5 cm).

If tap water is not readily available, sterile water (or sterile normal saline), in disposable containers (each holding at least 300 ml), should be kept near each first-aid box for the purposes of eye irrigation.

* See *FURTHER INFORMATION* on page 307.

- If the numbers employed in a particular workplace do *not* exceed 150, the employer need only appoint one or more responsible persons (hence the expression appointed person used earlier in this section) —

(a) to take charge of the situation (e.g. to call an ambulance) if a serious injury or major illness occurs;

(b) to administer elementary first-aid (e.g., treatment of minor cuts and burns);

(c) to maintain or make entries in the Accident Book (Form Bl 510) (see *Accident Book* below); and

(d) to check and replenish the contents of first-aid boxes

as and when required.

The number of persons appointed in any establishment to take charge of first-aid facilities and arrangements will be determined by the number of employees and the employer's statutory duty to provide coverage at all times when employees are at work. Thus, if there is a system of shift-working in operation, there must be at least two appointed persons on duty on each of those shifts (one of whom will provide coverage if the other is temporarily absent).

- Whatever the strict legal position, it makes sense to employ at least one *trained* first-aider in every workplace—especially in establishments (such as small workshops, garages, laundries, hotels, restaurants, and the like) where there is an ever-present risk of injury from hazardous substances, dust, machines, machine tools, slippery or greasy floors, steam, and the like.

- In organisations in which there are 150 or more employees, the employer must appoint at least one trained first-aider (in the ratio of one first-aider to every 150 persons employed) to administer first aid when required and to take charge in an emergency. Furthermore, where a trained first-aider is absent from duty, in temporary and exceptional circumstances, the employer must nominate a person (who need not himself hold a certificate in first aid) to take charge during the first-aider's absence. It must again be emphasised that, when deciding just how many trained first-aiders are needed, the employer must ensure that there is adequate coverage at all times when employees are at work. If there are two shifts, there must be two trained first-aiders (plus two persons nominated by the employer to take charge if one or other of those first-aiders is temporarily absent from work).

Recruitment and selection of first-aiders

- When recruiting or selecting personnel to go on first-aid courses, an employer should bear in mind the requirements of the course and the qualities likely to make a good first-aider. It is essential that he selects reliable people who will remain calm in an emergency. Furthermore, a first-aider should *not* be employed in a job which prevents him (or her) leaving his post and going rapidly to the scene of an emergency. He must be someone who is within easy reach and can be summoned instantly.

Table 2
CONTENTS OF FIRST-AID ROOMS

Guidance on the furnishing and maintenance of first-aid rooms is given in HSE publication COP 42 (*First aid at work. Health & Safety (First-Aid) Regulations 1981. Approved code of practice* [1990] ISBN 0 7176 0426 8, available from HSE Books, price £3.00.

A first-aid room should be clearly identified as such (i.e. with a white cross on a green background, accompanied by the words First-aid room). The name(s) and location(s) of the nearest first-aider(s) (and also of appointed persons- see text) should be attached by notice to (or alongside) the outer door of the room, together with the times of the day when each is on duty. It follows that a first-aid room should be equipped with a telephone or other effective means of communication.

A first-aid room should contain the following equipment and facilities:

(a)   a sink with running hot and cold water always available;
(b)   drinking water when not available on tap, and disposable cups;
(c)   soap;
(d)   paper towels;
(e)   smooth-topped working surfaces;
(f)   a suitable store for first-aid materials;
(g)   first-aid equipment equivalent in range and standard, and quantities, to those listed in Table 1 (page 303);
(h)   suitable refuse containers lined with disposable plastic bags;
(i)   a couch (with a waterproof surface) and frequently cleaned pillow and blankets;
(j)   clean protective garments for use by first-aiders;
(k)   a chair;
(l)   an appropriate record book (see **Accident book** elsewhere in this handbook); and
(m)   a bowl.

Corridors, lifts and doors, etc, which lead to the first-aid room, should allow access for a stretcher, wheelchair or carrying chair. Consideration should also be given to the possibility of providing some form of emergency lighting.

Training of first-aiders

- A first-aider is a person who has been trained in first-aid by an organisation approved by the Health & Safety Executive for the purposes of the 1981 Regulations. A first-aid certificate should be renewed after three years, with a refresher course lasting at least one full day.

- The following well-known organisations are just three of a vast number of organisations which provide HSE-approved first-aid training courses. The names of others can be obtained by contacting the Employment Medical Advisory Service ordinary located at the nearest area office of the Health & Safety Executive (see pages 368 to 372).

> St. John Ambulance Association;
> St. Andrew's Ambulance Association;
> British Red Cross Society.

INFORMATION AND INDUCTION TRAINING

- Regulation 4 of the 1981 Regulations states that an employer should inform his employees of the arrangements that have been made in connection with the provision of first aid, including the location of equipment, facilities and personnel. Thus, an employer must see to it that every employee in his establishment knows the location of his nearest first-aid box and the name of the person (whether trained first-aider or appointed person) in charge of that box. This information must be part of any induction training given to new employees at the time of their joining the establishment. If an employee is transferred to another job or department within the same establishment, he must be told of the first-aid facilities and arrangements for that other job or in that other department.

- There must be at least one notice posted in a conspicuous position in *every* workplace giving the location(s) of the nearest first-aid equipment and facilities, and the name(s) and location(s) of the people in charge of those facilities.

Note: Such notices should be in English. However, if persons of a different nationality are well represented in a particular establishment, a version in the language of that group may be displayed alongside the English version. Every such notice should comply with the requirements of the Health & Safety (Safety Signs & Signals) Regulations 1996 (SI 1996/341), viz; a square or oblong sign on a green background with symbols in white (to indicate a safe condition). First-aid signs, which satisfy the requirements of the 1996 Regulations, are available from organisations such as:

The Royal Society for the
Prevention of Accidents
(RoSPA)
Cannon House
The Priory
BIRMINGHAM
B4 6BS
Telephone: 0121 2002461

Signs & Labels Limited
Lathan Close
Bredbury Industrial Estate
STOCKPORT
Cheshire
SK6 2SD
Telephone: 0161 4946125

Chancellor Formecon
Gateway
CREWE
Cheshire
CW1 1YN
Telephone: 01270 500800

Stocksigns Limited
Ormside Way
Holmethorpe Industrial Estate
Redhill
SURREY RH1 2LG
Telephone: 01737 764764
Facsimile: 01737 763763

and a great many others (Yellow Pages?) all of whom will provide their catalogues and price lists on request.

Accident Book

- An Accident Book (Form BI 510, available from The Stationery Office, see page 328), or an equivalent computerised record containing the same particulars, must be maintained on every premises in which 10 or more persons are normally employed at the same time. Where fewer than 10 persons are employed, the employer must nonetheless maintain some form of record of every accident sustained by (or reported to him) an injured employee. For further particulars, see **Accident book** elsewhere in this handbook.

FURTHER INFORMATION

- The following publications are available from HSE Books at the address given on page 328.

Codes of practice

COP 42
First aid at work. Health and Safety (First-Aid) Regulations 1981: Approved code of practice [1990]
ISBN 0 7176 0426 8   £3.00

Guidance notes

INDG4
First aid at work: general guidance for inclusion in first aid boxes [1987]
ISBN 0 7176 0440 3   £4.50 per pack for 1 - 3 packs; £3.75 per pack for 4 - 19 packs; £3.50 per pack for 20 + packs.

Free leaflets (Telephone 01787 881165)

INDG129
Mental stress at work: first-aid measures

See also **Accidents at work, Accident book, Accidents to clients, customers, etc, Care, Common duty of, Dangerous machines, Dangerous occurrences, Health & safety at work, Insurance, Compulsory,** and **Occupier of premises,** elsewhere in this handbook.

FLOORS, PASSAGEWAYS & STAIRS

Key points

- Employers have a common law as well as statutory duty to provide and maintain the workplaces under their control in a condition that is safe and without risks to health. An employee who is injured (e.g., by tripping on a frayed carpet and tumbling headlong down a flight of stairs) can sue his employer for damages in the ordinary courts. The employer who has steadfastly ignored a health and safety inspector's strictures about the maintenance and repair of floors and floor coverings runs the risk of being prosecuted under section 2 of the Health & Safety at Work etc. Act 1974. An employer can (indeed must) insure himself against liability for bodily injury or diseases sustained by his employees in the course of his employment. But he cannot insure himself against his criminal liabilities under the 1974 Act. If he is successfully prosecuted under section 2 he could be ordered to pay a fine of up to £20,000. If the prosecution arises out of his failure to comply with the terms of an improvement notice served on his by an HSE or local authority inspector, he will not only be liable to pay a heavy fine, but could be sent to prison for six months (possibly two years)(*ibid*; section 33(1)(g) & (2A)).

- Modern health and safety legislation nowadays applies to every workplace, that is to say, to every premises (or part of premises), other than a private dwelling, which is made available to a person as a place of work. In short, the term is no longer restricted to factories, warehouses, building sites, offices and shops but to premises such as schools, hospitals, hotels, cinemas, bed-and-breakfast establishments, guest houses, retirement homes, leisure centres; and so on. It also applies to a workshop used by a self-employed person who works alone. The list is virtually endless. Also included are those parts of premises (such as a storeroom, washroom, toilet, works canteen) to which an employee has access while at work, not to mention an adjoining staff car park, the reception area or lobby, steps, staircases, corridors, gangways, and so on.

- The provisions of the Factories Act 1961 and of the Offices, Shops & Railway Premises Act 1963 (and of Regulations made under, or saved by, those Acts) relating to the condition and maintenance of floors and walkways have, for the most part, been repealed and replaced by related provisions in the Workplace (Health, Safety & Welfare) Regulations 1992 (SI 1992/3004) which came into full force for all workplaces on 1 January 1996.

Construction and strength of floors

- According to the Workplace Regulations 1992, every floor in a workplace must be suitable for its intended use. It must be structurally sound and strong enough to support the weight of any load placed (or likely to be placed) upon it and of any traffic passing over it. It must be free from holes or slopes and must not have an uneven or slippery surface. Furthermore, every floor (other than an office floor) must be provided with effective drainage if liable to get wet. Floors must be kept free of obstructions which may present a hazard or impede access, and must be cleaned as often as circumstances require (Reg. 12).

Floor coverings

- The floor coverings in every workplace must be capable of being kept clean and must be suitable for the type of traffic using the floors and the activities carried on in the relevant workroom. People should not have to work standing for long periods on cold floors. Unless the employer provides special footwear, he must fit a suitable insulated floor covering or provide insulated duckboards (*ibid*).

- The accompanying Approved Code of Practice (see *FURTHER INFORMATION* below) points out that carpets are not an appropriate covering for absorbent floors, such as untreated concrete or timber, the more so if the floors themselves are likely to be contaminated by oil or other difficult-to-remove substances. The surfaces of such floors should be sealed or coated with a suitable non-slip floor paint (or similar).

Damaged and sloping floors

- Any damage to a floor must be made good as quickly as possible. While cleaning or repairs are being carried out, warning notices, cones or temporary fencing must be placed to alert pedestrian traffic to any danger (*Warning! Slippery floor*). See **Safety signs & signals** elsewhere in this handbook.

- If a sloping floor is unavoidable, it must not be steeper than is strictly necessary and must be fitted with a non-slip covering supplemented by hand rails where necessary (the more so if used, or intended for use, by disabled persons).

Cleanliness of floors and their coverings

- All floor coverings (including carpets) must be cleaned regularly. The cleaning method used must not expose anyone to substantial amounts of dust or to health and safety risks arising from the use of cleaning agents (Reg. 9).

- Frayed or damaged carpet in workrooms, corridors and stairs present a safety hazard and should be repaired or replaced quickly. Until repairs are completed and the danger removed, the area should be roped-off or screened to prevent accidents.

Holes in floors

- Holes, bumps and uneven surfaces in floors (resulting from damage or wear and tear, or the temporary removal of floor boards or surface coverings) should be made good as quickly as possible.

- In the meantime, the occupier or owner of the premises must take steps to prevent accidents, e.g., by erecting barriers accompanied by conspicuous notices warning people to 'steer clear' until repairs are effected.

- Purpose-built holes in floors, traffic routes and production areas must be securely fenced or covered when not in use (see also *Covers on tanks, pits, etc.* below).

Footwear, Slip-resistant

- An employer's first priority is not to provide his employees with safety footwear but to ensure that all floor surfaces in the workplace under his control are safe. If floors are liable to become wet or slippery, he must apply a slip-resistant coating and keep them free from slippery substances and loose materials (particularly on the floor surfaces around machinery).

- If, in spite of such precautions, a floor still presents slipping hazards, the employer may then exercise his second option which is to provide his employees with suitable slip-resistant shoes or boots and insist that they wear them. All footwear necessarily provided in the interests of safety must be supplied (and, as necessary, replaced) free of charge.

Cover on tanks, pits, etc.

- Tanks, pits, holes, sumps, silos, vats and kiers must be securely fenced or covered (a) if they contain dangerous substances or (b) if a person is likely to fall a distance of two or more metres. If covers are used, they must be capable of supporting the weight of any load likely to be imposed on them and any traffic liable to pass over them. They must be of a type which can neither be easily displaced nor readily detached and removed (Reg. 13).

- Secure fencing or covers must also be provided at any place, regardless of the distance a person might fall, if there are any sharp or dangerous surfaces which increase the risk of serious injury. See also the section titled **Falls & falling objects** elsewhere in this handbook.

Duckboards on floors

- An employer should provide duckboards or other types of floor coverings in workrooms where workers would otherwise have to stand for long periods on cold floors. The only other solution would be to provide each worker with a pair of suitably-insulated boots or shoes (Reg. 7). See also **Protective clothing & equipment** elsewhere in this handbook.

Obstructions on floors

- Obstructions on floors and traffic routes (including corridors, steps, staircases and emergency exit routes) can cause persons to trip, slip or fall. All such obstructions must be removed as soon as they occur or are reported. Spillages must be wiped away, frayed carpet and loose tiles replaced or repaired, trailing cables made safe, waste materials and stacked boxes, etc., removed. If spillages cannot be cleared away or damaged areas made good immediately, the area in question must be screened or roped-off to prevent pedestrian or vehicular access, and warning signs posted (Regs 12 & 17).

Moving walkways and escalators

- All floors and traffic routes in workplaces must be kept free of obstructions which may present a hazard or impede access. This is particularly important on or near stairs, steps, escalators and moving walkways, not to mention emergency escape routes (Regs 12 & 17).

- Moving walkways are not yet a common feature in factories and offices. Escalators are to be found in some new office blocks and have long since been a feature in railway stations, airports and modern department stores and shopping malls — all of which are 'workplaces' within the 1992 Workplace Regulations. Moving walkways and escalators must be inspected, tested, adjusted, lubricated and cleaned at regular intervals (with all details entered in a running log). They must not present a safety hazard to employees or members of the public, must be maintained in efficient working order, and must be kept free from spillages and obstructions (notably at entry and exit points and at adjacent corners or junctions).

- Escalators and moving walkways must not only function safely, they must also be equipped with any necessary safety devices and be fitted with one or more readily-accessible and easily identifiable emergency stop controls.

Note: The relevant British Standard for escalators and passenger walkways is BS 5656:1993 *'Safety rules for the construction and installation of escalators and passenger conveyors'* (available from the British Standards Institution. 389 Chiswick High Road. London. W4 4AL (Telephone: 0181 996 7000).

FOOD PREMISES

- Food premises, to which The Food Safety (General Food Hygiene) Regulations 1995 (SI 1995/1763) apply must be kept clean and must be maintained in good repair and condition. The floor surfaces in rooms where food is prepared, treated or processed must likewise be maintained in sound condition.

Furthermore they must be easy to clean and, where necessary, disinfect. In short, such floors must be covered (or coated) with an impervious, non-absorbent, washable and non-toxic material — unless the proprietor of the relevant food business can satisfy the food authority (environmental health officers) that the material covering the floors of food rooms in his (or her) premises is suitable. Where appropriate, floors must allow adequate surface drainage (*ibid;* Schedule 1, Chapter II, para. 1(a)).

Note: The above requirements do not apply to dining areas, or to movable or temporary premises (such as marquees, market stalls, mobile sales vehicles), or to premises used occasionally for catering purposes, or to the floors surrounding vending machines.

- The term food premises means any premises used for the purposes of a food business; that is to say, a business (including a canteen, club, school, hospital or institution — whether carried on for profit or not — and any undertaking carried on by a public or local authority) in the course of which commercial operations with respect to food (or food sources) are carried out (section 1, Food Safety Act 1990). For further particulars, please turn to the section titled **Food safety & hygiene** elsewhere in this handbook.

FURTHER INFORMATION

- The following HSE publications are available from HSE Books at the address given on page 328:

Code of practice

- L24
  Workplace health, safety and welfare: Workplace (Health, Safety & Welfare Regulations 1992: Approved code of practice and guidance [1992]
  ISBN 0 7176 0413 6   £5.00

Guidance

  PM45
  Escalators: periodic thorough examination [1984]
  ISBN 0 11 883595 5   £2.50

FOOD POISONING

Key points

- The provisions described in this section are directly applicable to workplaces, such as food manufacturing companies, staff and works canteens and other catering establishments (restaurants, cafeterias, tea and coffee shops, snack and sandwich bars, hot dog stalls, pubs, clubs, school and hospital canteens, hotels, guest houses, bed and breakfast establishments, retirement homes, and the like) in which food handlers are employed in the manufacture, preparation, sale or supply of food.

- Under the Food Safety Act 1990, the word food includes drink and all articles and substances which are used for human consumption (even if of no nutritional value). It also includes chewing gum and other products of a like nature and use, and articles and substances used as ingredients in the preparation of food (*ibid*; section 1).

- A person working in a food handling area who —

  (a) knows or suspects that he (or she) is suffering from, or that he is a carrier of a disease (such as typhoid, paratyphoid or any other salmonella infection) likely to be transmitted through food; or

  (b) is afflicted with an infected wound, a skin infection, sores, diarrhoea, or with any analogous medical condition,

  in circumstances where there is any likelihood of him directly or indirectly contaminating any food with pathogenic micro-organisms, must report that knowledge, suspicion or affliction to the proprietor of the food business at which he is working (Regulation 5, The Food Safety (General Food Hygiene) Regulations 1995 (SI 1995/1763).

- Any person known, or suspected to be, suffering from (or to be the carrier of, or to be afflicted by) any of diseases or conditions referred to in the previous paragraph must not be permitted to work in any food handling area in any capacity (ibid; Schedule 1, Chapter VIII). Furthermore, the proprietor or manager of the relevant food business must notify the food authority without delay and report the matter to the district medical officer of health.

- The obligation to report certain infections likely to cause food poisoning therefore applies to factory operatives, chefs, cooks, kitchen porters, counter attendants, waiters, waitresses, barmaids and barmen — indeed to any person employed in a food factory, canteen, restaurant, cafeteria, public house, hotel, boarding house, hospital, school etc; whose duties involve him (or her) in the preparation or handling of food or drink for human consumption. If the employer, proprietor or manager is himself (or herself) suffering from food poisoning or a related infection, or knows himself to be a carrier, he too must report his condition to the district medical officer of health without delay.

- If an employee neglects or omits to notify his (or her) employer that he is either a sufferer from or a carrier of an infectious disease, he is guilty of an offence and liable to a fine not exceeding £5,000, and/or to imprisonment for a term not exceeding two years. The employer is similarly liable if he (or she) fails to take all reasonable steps to secure compliance by any person employed by him or under his control, or if he continues to employ a person known to be infected or afflicted by, or the carrier of, a food-borne infection (*ibid;* Reg. 29(2)).

Measures by local authority

- If a medical officer of health is of the opinion that a person is suffering from, or the carrier of, food poisoning or a food-related infection, he must inform the local authority without delay. For its part, the local authority may serve written notice on that person directing him to refrain from any occupation connected with food until such time as the risk of causing infection is removed. If the person is already employed in an occupation connected with food, a copy of the notice will also be sent to his employer (Reg. 8(2) and Schedule 5, The Public Health (Infectious Diseases) Regulations 1968 [SI 1968/1366]).

Statutory sick pay

- If an employee (such as a waitress, cook, etc.) is known to be the carrier of one or other of the infections referred to earlier in this section, or of an infection likely to cause food poisoning, he or she will (as we have seen) ordinarily be ordered to refrain from working until the risk is removed. At such times, the employee is deemed to be incapacitated for work (even if not actually ill) and, subject to the usual conditions, will qualify to be paid statutory sick pay during the period of absence.

Duty of medical practitioners

- If a doctor becomes aware, or suspects, that one of his (or her) patients is suffering from a notifiable disease or from food poisoning, he must immediately send a certificate to the medical officer of health for that district, stating:

  (a)   the name, age and sex of the patient;
  (b)   the patient's address or present location (e.g. a hospital);
  (c)   particulars of the disease or, as the case may be, the food poisoning from which the patient is, or is suspected to be, suffering, and the date, or approximate date, of its onset; and
  (d)   if the patient has been admitted to hospital, the date of his admission and whether or not, in his opinion, the disease or poisoning was contracted in hospital.

- A copy of the doctor's certificate must be forwarded on to the local authority by the medical officer of health on the day of its receipt (if possible) and in any case not later than 48 hours after receipt (section 48, Health Services and Public Health Act 1968).

Suspected carriers in food trade

- A local authority may serve notice on the employer or responsible manager, of any trade or business connected with food or drink, requesting his (or her) cooperation in permitting one or other of his employees to be examined by the medical officer of health or a medical officer acting on his behalf, and the responsible manager shall give to the medical officer of health all reasonable assistance in the matter (paragraph 2, Schedule 5, The Public Health (Infectious Diseases) Regulations 1968 (*q.v.*)).

DUTIES OF EMPLOYEES

- If a food handler (factory operative, canteen assistant, cook, kitchen porter, barmaid or waiter) is suffering from, or the carrier of, food poisoning or food borne infections, he (or she) would be well-advised to come forward. Indeed, he has a clear legal duty to do so. If he, or a member of his family, has already consulted a doctor, like as not the wheels will already have been set in motion, as explained in the text above. If the employee qualifies for statutory sick pay, well and good. But if, for one reason or another, he does not, his employer may well consider it a sensible precaution to ensure that the employee is not penalised financially during his enforced absence from work. To do otherwise, might deter others from coming forward, knowing that they too will forfeit pay if, as seems likely, they are sent home until the risk of infection is removed.

FOOD SAFETY & HYGIENE

Key points

- Premises in which food or drink is handled, prepared, sold or supplied for human consumption, whether for profit or not, are subject to the requirements of the Food Safety Act 1990 and Regulations made under (or saved by) that Act.

Food Safely Act 1990

- Most of the provisions of the Food Safety Act 1990 came into force on 1 January 1991. Section 1 of the Act defines food as meaning any item of food or drink intended for human consumption, including articles and substances used as ingredients in the preparation of food (whether or not such articles or substances have any nutritional value).

- The 1990 Act has served to 'tighten-up' legislation on the manufacture, storage, delivery, preparation, presentation and sale of food, and to strengthen existing legal powers and penalties. But, the 1990 Act is very largely an 'enabling Act'. Many of the technical details and rules governing the preparation, storage, presentation and sale of food (and related matters) are to be found in subordinate legislation, the most important of which, in the present context, are the Food Safety (General Food Hygiene) Regulations 1995 (SI 1995/1763)

Compulsory registration of food businesses

- Every food business in Great Britain must nowadays be

registered with their local food authority (usually the Environmental Health Department of the district or borough council in which the premises are situated). Furthermore, Application Forms for Registration must be completed and returned to the food authority at least 28 days before the premises in question are brought into first use as a food business.

• These provisions are to be found in the Food Premises (Registration) Regulations 1991 (SI 1991/2825, as amended) and apply to any business which handles, prepares, sells or supplies food for human consumption on five or more days (whether consecutive or not) in any period of five consecutive weeks. Any unregistered food business is liable to prosecution and a fine of up to £400, and a court order prohibiting the continued use of the premises as a food business.

• The purpose of registration is to enable local authorities to identify the types and numbers of food businesses within their areas and to take speedy and effective action to enforce compliance with the 1990 Act and its attendant Regulations. There is no fee to pay for registration and (as explained above) the owners or occupiers need do no more than complete a simple form.

Training of food handlers?

• The 1990 Act is policed and enforced by the food authorities (i.e., the borough, district or county councils). So far as the training of food handlers is concerned, Chapter X of Schedule 1 to the 1995 Regulations imposes a duty on the proprietors of food businesses to ensure that food handlers are supervised and instructed and/or trained in food hygiene matters commensurate with their work activities. A food authority may provide (or approve) training courses in food hygiene for persons who are, or intend to be, involved in food businesses, whether as proprietors or employees or otherwise. Alternatively, they may contribute towards the expenses incurred by any other such authority, or towards expenses incurred by any other person in providing such courses (*ibid*; section 23).

Note: A number of organisations (and local authorities) provide (or sponsor) a range of food hygiene courses for food handlers. These organisations include:

The Chartered Institute of Environmental Health (CIEH)

Chadwick Court, 15 Hatfields, London SE1 8DJ
Telephone: 0171 928 6006

The Royal Institute of Public Health & Hygiene (RIPHH)
28 Portland Place, London W1N 4ED
Telephone: 0171 580 2731

The Royal Society of Health (RSH)
38A St George's Drive, London, SW1V 4BH
Telephone: 0171 630 0121

The Royal Environmental Health Institute of Scotland (REHIS)
3 Manor Place, Edinburgh EH3 7DH
Telephone: 0131 225 6999

Society of Food Hygiene & Technology
PO Box 37, Lymington, Hants SO41 9WL
Telephone: 01590 671979

FOOD SAFETY REQUIREMENTS

- Under the 1990 Act, it is an offence for any person to sell, or possess for sale, any food:

  (a)   which is, or has been rendered, harmful to health (e.g., by having been improperly prepared or cooked);
  (b)   which is putrid or toxic;
  (c)   which is so contaminated that it would be unreasonable to expect any person to eat it.

  It is also an offence:

  (d)   to sell food which is not of the nature, substance or quality demanded (e.g., haddock sold as cod; stewing steak, as sirloin; stew with too little meat in it; and so on);
  (e)   to describe or present food in a way which is false or misleading.

  Enforcement officers have the right to enter and inspect any part of a food business when the premises are open for business or food is being prepared. They may examine the premises, inspect food to see if it is safe, order the production of records, ask questions, copy documents, seize and remove samples of food for later analysis, take photographs or use a video camera, require improvements to be made to unhygienic premises and, in extreme cases, order such premises to be closed down.

- It is a very serious offence to deny an enforcement officer access to food premises or to obstruct him in the cause of his inspection or investigations.

DEALING WITH UNSATISFACTORY FOOD PREMISES

Improvement notices

- A local authority enforcement officer may serve an improvement notice on any food business which is not complying with food safety requirements. The notice gives the proprietor a specified period within which to comply with those requirements or face prosecution.

Prohibition orders

- If the proprietor of a food business is convicted of an offence under food safety legislation (including failure to comply with an improvement notice), the court may make a prohibition order. Such an order may prohibit the continued use of a particular process or treatment, or the use of particular equipment, or the continued use of the premises in question as a food business. In serious cases, the proprietor or manager of the business may be banned from owning or managing any food business.

Emergency prohibition notices

- If a local authority enforcement officer is satisfied that a food business poses an imminent risk of injury to health, he may serve an emergency prohibition notice on the proprietor ordering the immediate closure of all, or part, of the premises in question. Within three days, the enforcement authority must apply to the magistrates' court for an emergency prohibition order, failing which the prohibition notice will cease to have effect and the proprietor of the business will be entitled to compensation for any loss suffered.

- If the magistrates' court upholds the emergency notice, it will make an emergency prohibition order (superseding the notice). The order will remain in force until such time as the enforcement authority issue a certificate to the effect that they are satisfied that the proprietor has taken steps sufficient to secure that his food business no longer presents an imminent risk of injury to health.

Emergency control orders

As a rule, emergency control orders (so-called) will be issued by the Government acting on the advice of the Department of Health. The purpose of an emergency control order is to require a firm (such as a food manufacturer or distributor) to take the necessary steps, for example, to prevent the further distribution or sale of contaminated food, thus removing any wider threat to public health.

Appeals procedure

- Any person who disagrees with the imposition of an improvement notice, or who is unhappy with the refusal of the enforcement authority to issue a certificate lifting a prohibition order or an emergency prohibition order, may appeal to a magistrates' court to have the notice or order lifted.

- The procedure for lodging an appeal (and the time limits for doing so) will be explained by the enforcing officer at the material time.

Penalties under the Food Safety Act 1990

- The penalties for any breaches of food safety legislation are quite severe. For most offences, a Crown Court may impose an unlimited fine and/or imprisonment for a period of up to two years. Magistrates' courts, for their part, may impose fines of up to £5,000 and imprisonment for up to six months. For more serious offences, such as:

  o   rendering food injurious to health; or

  o   selling (offering, exposing, advertising, possessing or preparing for sale) food which is unfit for human consumption, or has been rendered injurious to health, or is contaminated; or

  o   selling (to the purchaser's prejudice) any food, which is not of the nature or substance or quality demanded;

  the court can impose a fine of up to £20,000. The courts will also impose heavy penalties on persons convicted of obstructing an enforcement officer in the exercise of his duties.

FOOD SAFETY (GENERAL FOOD HYGIENE) REGS 1995

- The Food Safety (General Food Hygiene) Regulations 1995 (SI 1995/1763) lay down requirements for the structure, cleanliness and maintenance of food premises and of the equipment used in such premises; the hygienic handling of food; the cleanliness of persons engaged in the handling of food or drink, and of their clothing, and the action to be taken where they *suffer* from or are the carriers of certain infections likely to cause food poisoning; the provision of a clean and wholesome water supply and washing facilities; rules about personal hygiene; the disposal of waste materials; the temperatures at which certain foods are to be kept; and so on.

Cleanliness of premises,

- No food business may be carried on at any unsanitary premises or place, the condition, situation or construction of which is such that food is exposed to the risk of contamination. All articles and equipment which comes into contact with food intended for human consumption must be kept clean and in good order, repair and condition.

- The layout, design, construction and size of food premises must permit adequate cleaning and/or disinfection. Furthermore, they must be such as to protect against the accumulation of dirt, contact with toxic materials, the shedding of particles into food, and the formation of condensation or undesirable mould on surfaces. They must facilitate good food hygiene practices, including protection against cross-contamination between and during operations, by foodstuffs, equipment, materials, water, air supply or personnel, and external sources of contamination such as pests. Finally, the design, etc. of food premises must provide, where necessary, suitable temperature conditions for the hygienic processing and storage of food and food products.

- The floors and wall surfaces of rooms (other than dining areas) in which food is prepared, treated or processed must be maintained in a sound condition, must be easy to clean and/or disinfect, and must be kept clean. To that end, they must be coated (or covered) with an impervious, non-absorbent, washable and non-toxic material. Ceilings (and overhead fixtures) must be designed, constructed and finished to prevent the accumulation of dirt and reduce condensation, the growth of undesirable moulds and the shedding of particles.

- Windows must likewise be constructed to prevent the accumulation of dirt and, if they can be opened to the outside environment, must be fitted with insect screens which can be easily removed for cleaning. If open windows are likely to result in the contamination of foodstuffs (whether or not fitted with insect screens), they must be kept closed and fixed during food production. Doors must be coated with smooth and non-absorbent surfaces and must be easy to clean and, where necessary, disinfect. Work surfaces and the surfaces of equipment in contact with food must be maintained in a sound condition and be easy to clean and, where necessary, disinfect. This will require the use of smooth, washable and non-toxic materials, unless the proprietor of the food business can satisfy an environmental health officer (the food authority) that other materials used are appropriate. See also **Cleanliness of premises** elsewhere in this handbook).

Cleanliness of work tools and equipment

- Adequate facilities must be provided for the cleaning and disinfecting of work tools and equipment. These facilities must be constructed of materials resistant to corrosion and must be easy to clean and be equipped with an adequate supply of hot and cold water.

- All articles, fittings and equipment which come into contact with food must not only be kept clean, but must also be kept in good order, repair and condition. With the exception of non-returnable containers and packaging, they must be so constructed as to enable them to be kept thoroughly cleaned and, where necessary, disinfected, sufficient for the purposes intended. Furthermore, they must be installed in such a way as to allow adequate cleaning of the surrounding area.

Ventilation of food premises

- There must be suitable and sufficient means of natural or mechanical ventilation in food rooms. Mechanical air flow from a contaminated area to a clean area must be avoided. Ventilation systems must be so constructed as to enable filters and other parts requiring cleaning or replacement to be readily accessible. All sanitary conveniences within food premises must be provided with adequate natural or mechanical ventilation.

Facilities for washing food

- An adequate number of sinks and other facilities must be provided for any necessary washing of food. Those sinks and facilities must be equipped with an adequate supply of potable (that is to say, drinking) water, and must be kept clean.

Food waste

- Food waste and other refuse must not be allowed to accumulate in food rooms, except so far as is unavoidable for the proper functioning of the business. Food waste must be deposited in closable containers, which latter must be kept in sound condition and be easy to clean and disinfect. Adequate provision must be made for the removal and storage of food waste, which must be kept in a refuse store which must be kept clean and so designed as to protect against access by pests.

Washbasins and toilets

- Sanitary conveniences (i.e., WCs, toilets, lavatories or loos) situated in, or regularly used in connection with, any food premises must be kept clean and in efficient working order, and must be so situated that no offensive odours are capable of penetrating into any food room. All toilet accommodation must be well-ventilated and lit, and must be connected to an effective drainage system. A room which contains a toilet must never be used as a food room (whether for food storage or otherwise); nor may a food room communicates directly with a room or other place which contains a toilet. A notice should be placed on the inside door of every toilet used by persons engaged in the handling of food (waiters, waitresses, cooks, kitchen porters, still-room workers, etc.) warning them to wash their hands after using the convenience.

- Suitable and sufficient wash-hand basins for cleaning hands must be provided for the use of all persons engaged in the preparation and handling of food intended for human consumption. These facilities must be conveniently accessible and be equipped with an adequate supply of hot and cold (or appropriately mixed) running water, an adequate supply of soap or other suitable detergent, nail-brushes and clean towels or other suitable drying facilities (such as a hot-air dryer). The wash basins must be kept clean and in good working condition and must not be used for any purpose other than for securing the personal cleanliness of the user.

- Washbasins situated in a food preparation area (such as a kitchen or still-room) must be suitably located and designated for cleaning hands. To avoid the risk of cross-contamination, hand- washbasins must not be used for washing food; nor should sinks and other facilities for washing food be used for cleaning hands.

Water supply

- A supply of potable (that is to say, drinkable) water must be provided at all food premises in which food or drink intended for sale or sold for human consumption is prepared, stored or presented. This potable water must be used whenever necessary to ensure that foodstuffs are not contaminated. Where appropriate, ice must be made from potable water and must be used whenever necessary to ensure foodstuffs are not contaminated. It must be made, handled and stored under conditions which protect it from all contamination.

- Steam used directly in contact with food must not contain any substance which presents a hazard to health, or is likely to contaminate the product. Water unfit for drinking, which is used for the generation of steam, refrigeration, fire control and other similar purposes not related to food, must be conducted in separate systems, readily identifiable and having no connection with, nor any possibility of reflux into, the potable water systems. See also **Drinking water** elsewhere in this handbook.

Personal hygiene

- Persons working in food handling areas must maintain a high degree of personal cleanliness. They must have clean hands and fingernails (which they should wash frequently under running water — at the beginning of, and during, each shift, and after eating, smoking or using the toilet); must not drink, smoke or spit while handling open food or when present in a food handling area; must keep cuts and sores covered with waterproof and distinctive (e.g., blue) antiseptic dressings; must keep their hair clean and tied back (or covered); must not wear false nails or jewellery [other than plain wedding bands and sleeper earrings], while engaged in the handling of food; and must wear suitable and clean protective clothing.

- Furthermore, a person working in a food handling area who —

    (a) knows or suspects that he (or she) is suffering from, or the carrier of, a food-borne disease (such as typhoid, paratyphoid or any other salmonella infection); or

    (b) is afflicted with an infected wound, a skin infection, sores, diarrhoea, or with any analogous medical condition,

    in circumstances where there is any likelihood of him directly or indirectly contaminating any food with pathogenic micro-organisms, must report that knowledge, suspicion or affliction to the proprietor of the food business at which he is working .

- Any person known, or suspected to be, suffering from (or to be the carrier of, or to be afflicted by) any of diseases or conditions referred to in the previous paragraph must not be permitted to work in any food handling area in any capacity. Furthermore, the proprietor or manager of the relevant food business must notify the food authority without delay and report the matter to the district medical officer of health. For further particulars, please turn to the previous section: **Food poisoning**).

    A publication titled *Industry Guide to Good Food Hygiene: Catering Guide* (ISBN 0 11 321899 0), which includes advice on training and the 'rules of hygiene' for food handlers, is available from The Stationery Office (see page 328), price: £3.00

Accommodation for clothing

- Suitable and sufficient accommodation for the storage of outer clothing (or outer clothing and footwear not being worn during working hours) must be provided for use by persons engaged in the handling of food. Furthermore, if such accommodation is situated in a food room (a kitchen, still-room, canteen, or whatever), it must be in the form of lockers or cupboards. Changing rooms must also be provided where necessary. See also **Accommodation for clothing** elsewhere in this handbook.

Lighting of food rooms

- Suitable and sufficient means of lighting must be provided in every food room, and every such room must be suitably and sufficiently lighted (see also **Lighting in workplaces** elsewhere in this handbook).

FURTHER INFORMATION

- A useful booklet titled *The Food Safety Act 1990 & You* (Ref. PB 2507) summarises the legal duties of employers, managers and owners of food businesses under the 1990 Act. Copies of the booklet and information about other food safety publications can be obtained by contacting MAFF Publications, London SE99 7TP, or by telephoning 0645 556000. For other general enquiries, the MAFF Helpline Number is 0645 335577.

HSE BOOKS

The HSE publications listed throughout this handbook
are available from:

HSE Books. PO Box 1999. Sudbury. Suffolk. CO10 6FS

Telephone: 01787 881165
Fax: 01787 313995

STATIONERY OFFICE PUBLICATIONS CENTRE
(Mail, fax and telephone orders only)

PO Box 276. London. SW8 5DT

Telephone orders: 0171 873 9090
Fax orders: 0171 873 8200
General enquiries: 0171 873 0011

Stationery Office Bookshops

49 High Holborn
London WC1V 6HB
Telephone: 0171 873 0011
(*General enquiries only*)
Fax: 0171 831 1236

9-21 Princess Street
Manchester M60 8AS
Telephone: 0161 834 7201
Fax: 0161 833 0634

68/69 Bull Street
Birmingham B4 6AD
Telephone: 0121 236 9696
Fax: 0121 236 9699

16 Arthur Street
Belfast. BT1 4GD
Telephone: 01232 238451
Fax: 01232 235401

33 Wine Street.
Bristol BS1 2BQ
Telephone: 0117 9264306
Fax: 0117 9294515

71 Lothian Road
Edinburgh EH3 9AZ
Telephone: 0131 479 3141
Fax: 0131 479 3142

The Stationery Office Oriel Bookshop
The Friary
Cardiff CF1 4AA
Telephone: 01222 395548 Fax: 01222 38437

H

HAZARDOUS SUBSTANCES

Preamble

- Every employer has a duty under section 2 of the Health & Safety at Work etc. Act 1974 to do all that is reasonably practicable to ensure the health, safety and welfare at work of his employees. To comply with that duty, adds section 2(2)(b), he must (amongst other things) see to it that his employees are not exposed to risk when using, handling, storing or transporting substances. A "substance", for these purposes, is any natural or artificial substance, whether in solid or liquid form or in the form of a gas or vapour (*ibid*; section 53(1)).

- An employer who fails to discharge his duty under section 2 of the 1974 Act is guilty of an offence and liable on summary conviction to a fine of up to £20,000. If he is convicted on indictment, the court could impose a much heavier fine (*ibid*; section 33(1)(a) & (1A)).

Recent legislation

- In recent years, an employer's general duty under section 2 of the 1974 Act has been reinforced by more specific duties under a variety of health and safety regulations (most of which implement related provisions in relevant EC Directives). So far as hazardous substances are concerned, the most notable of recent legislation has been —

  (a) the Control of Substances Hazardous to Health Regulations 1994 (SI 1994/3246), which came into force on 16 January 1995 — re-enacting, with minor modifications, the Control of Substances Hazardous to Health Regulations 1988 (SI 1988/1657), as variously amended — hereinafter referred to as the COSHH Regulations 1994 or, simply, COSHH; and

  (b) the Chemicals (Hazard Information & Packaging for

Supply) Regulations 1994 (SI 1994/3247), which came
into force on 31 January 1995 — commonly referred to
by the acronym 'CHIP 2 '(to distinguish them from the
1993 CHIP Regulations now revoked and replaced).

A failure to comply to comply with the provisions of these and
related health and safety regulations is a fine of up to £2,000 or,
if a conviction is obtained on indictment, a fine of an
unspecified maximum amount. If the offender has contravened
any requirement or prohibition imposed by an improvement or
prohibition notice served on him by a health and safety
inspector, he could be fined up to £20,000 *and* be sent to prison
for up to six months.

EMPLOYER'S DUTIES UNDER COSHH

Key points

- It is perhaps as well to point out at this stage that the COSHH
  Regulations apply not only factories, chemical works, foundries,
  machine shops, and to related trades and industries (in which
  hazardous substances are likely to be present in quantity) but
  also to so-called 'low risk' operations (offices, banks, insurance
  companies, finance houses, small shops, department stores,
  hotels, restaurants, guest houses, schools, libraries, etc). It may
  not take long for an employer running an office or shop to carry
  out the 'risk assessment' required by the 1994 Regulations, or to
  comply with his other duties under COSHH; but comply with
  them he must.

- Given that the manufacturers, suppliers and importers of
  "substances and preparations dangerous for supply" are
  nowadays required by CHIP 2 to correctly classify, label and
  package their products *before* they sell them or offer them for
  sale; and, given also that they have a duty to provide every
  customer with an up-to-data *safety data sheet* every time a
  purchase or delivery is made, it is nowadays much easier for
  employers who buy such substances or preparations for use in
  connection with their work activities to comply with their duties
  under COSHH. For more information about CHIP 2, please turn
  to the section titled **Dangerous chemicals and preparations**.

Duties summarised

- To comply with his duties under the 1994 COSHH Regulations, an employer must —

  (a)   identify each and every hazardous substance (if any) which is manufactured, stored, processed, packaged or re-packaged, handled or used (or purchased for use) in connection with his business;

  (b)   assess the risk to the health of his employees arising out of their use of or exposure to such substances;

  (c)   decide what precautions he needs to take to prevent or control that risk;

  (d)   ensure that all control measures are used and that the relevant equipment is properly maintained and the correct procedures observed;

  Where there is the potential for serious risks to health, the employer must

  (e)   monitor the exposure of his employees to the substance or substances in question, introduce a health surveillance programme (including, where necessary, regular medical examinations), and maintain health records for at least five and, in some circumstances, at least 40 years.

  Finally, the employer must

  (f)   inform, instruct and train his employees about the risks to their health created by their possible exposure to a hazardous substance, and the precautions which they should take.

RISK ASSESSMENT

- Regulation 6 of COSHH warns that an employer must not carry on any work which is liable to expose any employees to any substance hazardous to health unless he has made a suitable and sufficient assessment of the risks created by that work and of the steps that need to be taken to prevent or adequately control that exposure.

- If an employer's assessment of the risks confronting his employees is to be in any way comprehensive, he must first identify every substance introduced, stored, manufactured, or used on his premises which has the potential to cause harm. His investigations (accompanied by a perusal of the *Approved Supply List* and a review of the relevant *safety data sheets* provided by manufacturers and suppliers) will also show how that harm might be caused, viz; by ingestion, inhalation, absorption through the skin, injection, or contact with the skin or eyes. He will know (or have learnt) that some substances have immediate harmful effects, while others have the capacity to produce a long-term deterioration in an employee's state of health. Some, such as tar, pitch, bitumen or mineral oil, may cause cancer; others, dermatitis; others, pneumoconiosis or byssinosis. Still others may damage the human reproductive system.

- Whether or not a hazardous substance currently in use presents a risk to members of the workforce will depend in large part on the effectiveness of existing control measures. The employer's familiarity with production processes, working practices and the design of plant and equipment will enable him (in concert with his production and engineering teams, safety advisers and employee representatives) to evaluate those control measures and the extent to which employees are or may be exposed to risk.

- His accident and occupational health records will reveal or confirm that people may be exposed to a hazardous substance in a number of ways:

  o **directly** — because they actually handle that substance or are exposed to dusts, fumes or vapours given off in the manufacturing process;

  o **indirectly** — because they happen to be working in areas or departments adjacent to those in which the substance is handled, manipulated, stored, produced or discharged;

  o **inadvertently** — if they are in the neighbourhood when there is an accidental spillage, discharge or sudden release of the substance;

o **deliberately or negligently** — if they refuse to wear the protective clothing or equipment provided; if they indulge in skylarking or horseplay; if they are in the habit of entering enclosed areas without suitable protection; or if they are given to removing machine guards, local exhaust ventilation, and the like, in order to speed up the production process.

A systematic approach will enable the employer to assess the risks posed by exposure to a hazardous substance. Is that exposure incidental or occasional, routine or constant, or somewhere in between? One of the best ways of determining this is to observe the work being done and to ask the employees concerned. Where dusts, fumes and gases are involved, he may need to carry out atmospheric sampling and measurements (if he is not already doing so) using the techniques described or referred to in HSE Guidance Note EH40/97 (*'Occupational Exposure Limits 1997'*). The Guidance Note (see below) also provides a comprehensive listing of other HSE Guidance Notes, Toxicity Reviews and some 60+ titles in the MDHS (*'Methods for the determination of hazardous substances'*) series.

- To be 'suitable and sufficient', the risk assessment exercise must lead to a decision about the steps to be taken if exposure to hazardous substances is to be prevented or adequately controlled. The assessment must also determine what new or additional control measures are required; how those measures are to be used (or applied) and the frequency with which they are to be maintained, examined and tested; what changes (if any) need to be made to existing working practices and how those changes are to be enforced; what procedures are to be introduced to monitor the exposure of employees to hazardous substances; which employees must submit to routine health surveillance; and what further information, instruction and training needs to be provided in order to acquaint employees with the health risks associated with their exposure to hazardous substances and the precautions which should be taken.

- In small organisations or in those in which exposure to hazardous substances is minimal or incidental, the employer need not prepare a written account of the results of the risk assessment exercise — so long as he can satisfy the health and safety inspectorate that he has carried out the assessment and that he has complied with his obligations under COSHH. However, in those organisations (large or small) in which exposure to hazardous substances is, or could be, significant, the risk assessment exercise is unlikely to be accepted as either 'suitable' or 'sufficient' unless the results are recorded and kept readily accessible to ensure continuity and accuracy of knowledge among all those who may need to know those results.

MEANING OF 'HAZARDOUS SUBSTANCE'

- What then is a 'hazardous substance'? According to COSHH, a substance hazardous to health is any natural or artificial substance, whether in solid or liquid form or in the form of a gas or vapour (including a micro-organism) which is —

(a)   a substance listed in Part I of the *Approved Supply List and database – CHIP 96* (see below) and for which the indication of danger, as specified in `Part V of that list is 'very toxic', 'toxic', 'harmful', 'corrosive', or 'irritant';

(b)   a substance specified in Schedule 1 to the COSHH Regulations (see **Table 1** overleaf) or for which the Health & Safety Commission has approved an occupational exposure standard (OES);

(c)   a biological agent (that is to say, a micro-organism, cell culture, or human endoparasite, including one which has been genetically modified) which may cause an infection, allergy or toxicity, or otherwise create a hazard to human health;

(d)   dust of *any* kind, when present at a substantial concentration in air;

(e)   a substance not mentioned in paragraphs (a) to (d) which creates a hazard to the health of any person which is comparable with the hazards mentioned in those paragraphs.

In other words, the COSHH Regulations 1994 apply to virtually every substance or preparation which is potentially harmful to health. They do *not* apply to work and processes involving exposure to lead, asbestos, ionising radiations or substances below ground in mines as these activities are covered by their own legislation.

Table 1
COSHH Regulations 1994
Schedule 1
SUBSTANCES ASSIGNED MAXIMUM EXPOSURE LIMITS

Acrylamide
Acrylonitrile
Arsenic & compounds
    except arsine (as As)
Benzene
Beryllium and beryllium
    compounds (as Be)
Bis (chloromethyl) ether
Buta-1, 3-diene
2-Butoxyethanol
Cadmium & cadmium
    compounds except
    cadmium oxide fume
    cadmium sulphide and
    cadmium sulphide pigments
    (as Cd)
Cadmium oxide fume (as Cd)
Cadmium sulphide and
    cadmium sulphide pigments
    (respirable dust as Cd)
Carbon disulphide
Chromium (Vl) compounds
        (as Cr)
Cobalt and cobalt compounds
        (as Co)
1,2-Dibromoethane
        (Ethylene dibromide)
1,2-Dichl oroethane
        (Ethylene dichloride)
Dichloromethane
2,2'-Dichloro 4,4'-methylene
    dianiline (mboca)

1 -Chloro-2,3-epoxypropane
    (Epichlorohydrin)
2-Ethoxyethanol
2-Ethoxyethyl acetate
Ethylene oxide
Formaldehyde
Grain dust
Hydrogen cyanide
Isocyanates, all (as-NCO)
Man-made mineral fibre
2-Methoxyethanol
2-Methoxyethyl acetate
4, 4'-Methylenedianiline
Nickel and its
    inorganic compounds
    except nickel carbonyl):
    water-soluble nickel
    compounds (as Ni)
    nickel and water-insoluble
    nickel compounds (as Ni)
2-Nitropropane
Rubber process dust
Rubber fume
Silica, respirable crystalline
Styrene
1, 1, 1 - Trichlorethan
Trichloroethylene
Vinyl chloride
Vinylidene chlonde
Wood dust (hard wood)

Approved Supply List

• The *Approved Supply List & database – CHIP 96,* referred to earlier, is the list titled *Information Approved for the Classification & Labelling of Substances & Preparations Dangerous for Supply* approved by the Health & Safety Commission (HSC) for the purposes of the CHIP 2 Regulations referred to earlier. There are six Parts to the *List*, as follows:

Part I contains a list of the names and index numbers of substances characterised as "dangerous for supply" (There are several hundred of these).

Part II contains a list of the names and index numbers of the substances for which the HSC has approved information.

Parts III and IV contains numbered lists of the "risks phrases" and "safety phrases" to be used on safety data sheets, labelling and packages.

Part V describes the classification, the labelling data (including the EEC number) and any concentration limits which the HSC has approved to classify preparations containing a dangerous substance.

Part VI provides a list of the conventional oral toxicity (LD_{50}) values which the HSC has approved in relation to the classification of pesticides.

The list of substances classified as "dangerous for supply" in the *Approved Supply List* is far too long to include in a handbook of this size. An employer who uses relatively few hazardous substances should be able to rely on the information given on the labels and (more importantly) in the accompanying safety data sheets necessarily provided by the relevant manufacturers and suppliers. If he manufactures dangerous chemicals or preparations containing mixtures of such chemicals (or purchases them in bulk and repackages them for onward sale or supply) he would be well-advised to purchase a copy of the *Approved Supply List* (see *FURTHER INFORMATION* below). He must also familiarise himself with the requirements and prohibitions imposed by the CHIP 2 Regulations (discussed elsewhere in this handbook in the section titled *Dangerous chemicals & preparations*).

PREVENTING OR CONTROLLING EXPOSURE

- "Every employer shall ensure that the exposure of his employees to substances hazardous to health is either prevented or, where this is not reasonably practicable, adequately controlled" (*ibid*; Reg. 7(1)).

- The one obvious way of preventing exposure to a hazardous substance is to eliminate that substance altogether. An employer should ask himself the question: Is there a substitute product or substance which is either harmless or rather less hazardous and which will do the job equally well? If the answer to that question is 'Yes', and it is reasonably practicable to introduce that other substance, the substitution must be made.

- Adequately controlling exposure to a hazardous substance is the prescribed alternative to prevention. Nowadays, many processes yielding or using hazardous substances are capable of being totally enclosed or partially enclosed (with the addition of local exhaust ventilation). The adoption of plant, processes and systems of work which minimise the generation of hazardous dusts, fumes and harmful micro-organisms is one way of limiting contamination in the event of spills and leaks.

- Efficient local exhaust ventilation may be all that is needed to control the exposure of employees to hazardous substances emitted or produced in the course of manufacturing processes or related activities. In other work situations, an employer may need to do no more than improve the general level of ventilation in a workshop or factory department.

Occupational Exposure Standards (OES)

- Some substances have been assigned a so-called 'occupational exposure standard'(OES). These are standards approved by the Health & Safety Commission for some 700 and more substances listed in HSE Guidance Note EH40/97 available from HSE Books (see *FURTHER INFORMATION* below).

- Regulation 7(5) of COSHH allows that where there is exposure to a substance for which an occupational exposure standard has been approved, the control of exposure to that substance by inhalation will be treated as being adequate if, but only if, the OES for that substance is not exceeded or, if it is exceeded, the employer identifies the reasons and takes appropriate action to remedy the situation as soon as is reasonably practicable.

Hazardous substances (other than carcinogens or biological agents)

- Preventing (or adequately controlling) the exposure of an employee to a substance hazardous to health *must* be secured by measures other than the provision of personal protective equipment (unless the substance in question is a carcinogen or a biological agent.). In other words, an employer should not issue respirators, masks, goggles, gloves, barrier creams, or whatever, as a way of preventing or minimising the exposure of his employees to hazardous substances unless all other prevention and control measures have failed or have not been wholly successful.

Exposure to carcinogens

- If it is not reasonably practicable to prevent exposure to a carcinogen by using an alternative substance or process, the employer must —

    (a)   totally enclose the process and handling systems (if it is reasonably practicable to do so);

    (b)   use plant, processes and systems of work which minimise the generation of (or suppress and contain) spills, leaks, dust, fumes and vapours of carcinogens;

    (c)   limit the quantities of a carcinogen present in the workplace;

    (d)   keep to a minimum the number of persons who might be exposed to a carcinogen;

    (e)   prohibit eating, drinking and smoking in areas that may be contaminated by carcinogens;

    (f)   provide hygiene measures including adequate washing facilities and the regular cleaning of walls and surfaces;

    (g)   designate areas and installations which may be contaminated by carcinogens, and post suitable and sufficient warning signs; and

    (h)   see to it that carcinogens are safely stored, handled and disposed of, and use closed and clearly-labelled containers.

- If none of the control measures adopted by an employer succeeds in preventing or adequately controlling exposure to a hazardous substance or carcinogen, then, *in addition to measures,* he must provide his employees with such personal protective equipment as will adequately control that exposure.

Exposure to biological agents

- The precautions to be taken by an employer to protect his employees against risks to their health (whether immediate or delayed) arising from exposure to biological agents in the course of their employment are explained at some length in Schedule 9 to the COSHH Regulations 1994. However, the relevant particular are included in HSE publication L5 titled *General COSHH ACOP and Carcinogens ACOP and Biological Agents ACOP [1996 Edition]: Control of Substances Hazardous to Health Regulations 1994,* copies of which are available from HSE Books. (See *FURTHER INFORMATION* below).

- Suffice to say, that where there is a risk of exposure to a biological agent and it is not otherwise reasonably practicable for an employer to prevent that exposure, he must (in the light of the results of the risk assessment he will already have carried out) apply *all* of the following measures to ensure that exposure to that agent *is* adequately controlled, namely by —

  (a)   keeping as low as practicable the number of employees exposed or likely to be exposed to the biological agent;

  (b)   designing work processes and engineering control measures so as to prevent or minimise the release of biological agents into the place of work;

  (c)   displaying the biohazard sign (see page 341) and other relevant warning signs;

  (d)   drawing up plans to deal with accidents involving biological agents;

  (e)   specifying appropriate decontamination and

disinfection procedures;

(f)   instituting means for the safe collection, storage and disposal of contaminated waste, including the use of secure and identifiable containers, after suitable treatment where appropriate;

(g)   making arrangements for the safe handling and transport of biological agents, or materials that may contain such agents, within the workplace;

(h)   specifying procedures for taking, handling and processing samples that may contain biological agents;

(i)   providing collective protection measures and, where exposure cannot be adequately controlled by other means, individual protection measures including, in particular, the supply of appropriate protective clothing or other special clothing;

(j)   where appropriate, making available effective vaccines for those employees who are not already immune to the biological agent to which they are exposed or are liable to be exposed; and

(k)   instituting hygiene measures compatible with the aim of preventing or reducing the accidental transfer or release of a biological agent from the workplace, including, in particular—

    (i)   the provision of appropriate and adequate washing and toilet facilities, and

    (ii)   the prohibition of eating, drinking, smoking and the application of cosmetics in working areas where there is a risk of contamination by biological agents.

The word "appropriate" in relation to the clothing and hygiene measures referred to above means appropriate for the risks involved and the conditions at the place where exposure to the risk may occur.

Other substances known to be 'hazardous'

- Ordinary cane sugar is a good example of a natural substance which is not generally recognised as being hazardous in the same way that an acid is hazardous. But to people working in sugar mills and in the manufacture of jams, confectionery and biscuits, regular exposure to sugar can and does cause health problems — particularly to employees who are prone to dermatitis. The revocation by the earlier COSHH Regulations 1988 (as amended) of (amongst others) the Bakehouses Welfare Order 1927, the Biscuit Factories Welfare Order 1927 and the Sugar Factories Welfare Order 1931 may have relieved employers of their duty to display the Official Cautionary Notice concerning dermatitis (Form SHW 355) on the walls of their premises. But the revocations do not make sugar any the less hazardous. In future, such employers will need to do rather more than issue factory operatives with barrier cream or see to it that their bath water is 'at a temperature as near as may be of 100 degrees Fahrenheit'. The outdated Sugar Factories Welfare Order 1931 seemingly tolerated 'hot, sticky or dirty processes'. Under COSHH, an employer will need to satisfy a health and safety inspector that he has taken all reasonably practicable steps to prevent or adequately control the exposure of his employees to sugar in the first place.

- Other substances — such as lemon and orange peel, flour, phenols, synthetic resins, mineral oils and certain types of dust — have been known to cause (respectively) skin, lung and associated problems. With the revocation of the related Welfare Orders (some of which dated back to the early 1900s) employers will not necessarily comply with their obligations under COSHH simply by issuing their employees with waterproof aprons, face masks, gloves, and whatever. Protective clothing and equipment should only be used as a last resort, *after* the employer has assessed the risks and taken all appropriate measures to prevent or adequately control exposure to such substances in the first place. If those measures are inappropriate or inadequate, then (and only then) should he consider issuing suitable protective clothing.

Dusts and fumes, etc.

- Dust, fumes and other agents, which are known to cause or promote asthma, provide yet another example of substances rightly classified as 'hazardous' under the COSHH Regulations. These include:

  o   isocyanates — used for making plastic foams, synthetic inks, paints and adhesives;

  o   platinum salts — likely to affect people working in laboratories or in the refining of platinum;

  o   acid anhydride and amine hardening agents (including epoxy resin curing agents— used in the manufacture of plastics, adhesives, moulding resins and surface coatings);

  o   fumes from rosin as a soldering flux — mainly encountered by workers in electronics factories;

  o   proteolytic enzymes — used in the baking, fish, silk and leather industries, and in the manufacture of biological washing powders; and

  o   dusts arising from wheat, barley, oats, flour, etc. — encountered by people working in flour mills, bakeries, and the like; and on farms.

  Employers in such industries will ordinarily be familiar with the hazardous properties of the raw materials, chemicals, products and by-products introduced, handled, stored and produced in their premises. Most will long since have taken steps to eliminate or minimise exposure to those substances.

- The fact that certain inhalable substances have not been assigned approved MELs or OESs does not necessarily mean that those substances are safe. In such cases, the exposure of employees to those substances must be controlled to a level to which nearly all the population could be exposed, day after day, without adversely affecting their health. If in doubt about the health risks associated with exposure to some substances , the employer should contact the manufacturer or supplier or, if those substances are produced as a by-product, get in touch with his own industry association or seek expert and professional advice.

- Certain substances are capable of causing health problems by ingestion, absorption through the skin or mucous membranes, or contact with the skin or mucous membranes — perhaps resulting in chemical burns, microbial infection or (as we have seen) dermatitis. The Approved Code of Practice (see *FURTHER INFORMATION* below) points out that exposure to such substances must be controlled to a standard such that nearly all the population could be exposed repeatedly without any adverse health effect.

Hazardous substances in 'low-risk' premises

- In offices, shops catering premises, and the like, a 'risk assessment' may reveal that the only hazardous substances present or used in the premises are substances and preparations such as lime scale removers, scouring agents, carpet cleaners, oven cleaning preparations, and the like (most of which are used manually). The control measures to be applied in such cases will ordinarily require the use of suitable protective clothing, such as gloves, face masks, safety spectacles, aprons, coveralls, suitable footwear, applicators, and the like — supported by rules (e.g., such as a prohibition on eating, drinking or smoking, etc.) based on the information necessarily included in the *safety data sheet* provided by the manufacturer or supplier of those substances or preparations. It is the employer's responsibility to supply (and pay for) all such protective clothing and equipment, to inspect them at regular intervals for evidence of damage, and to replace them as often as may be necessary. A failure to do so is an offence under the 1974 Health & Safety at Work Act, the penalty for which is a fine of up to £2,000 (or higher, in some circumstances).

- The typist who uses correcting fluid to mask her (or his) typing errors is exposed (albeit insignificantly) to a hazardous substance. Whether or not she is at risk depends on how often she uses the fluid and how she uses it. If she knows that the fluid contains 1,1,1,-Trichlorethan, which is "harmful' if swallowed or inhaled, she can control the risk to her health simply by following the directions on the bottle. Similar hazard/risk situations arise in other jobs not normally regarded as dangerous. Does the cloakroom attendant know that the bleach he employs to disinfect washbasins and toilets contains sodium hypochlorite, which is an 'irritant'? Is he aware also that a toxic gas is released if bleach is allowed to come into contact with Spirits of Salts (often used to remove hard water stains from porcelain)? Has the trainee operator in the Print Room been told that the product he uses to reduce the viscosity of lithographic inks may contain high boiling hydrocarbons and that he should wear chemically resistant gloves when doing so? Is the kitchen porter familiar with the corrosive properties of some commercial machine dish washing liquids and that such liquids must not to be used on aluminium or galvanised surfaces? And does the maintenance worker fully understand the risks if he eats, drinks or smokes while using paint stripper?

- Hazardous substances such as these, and there are a great many others in everyday use — paints, solvents, printing inks, coatings, adhesives, disinfectants, descalers, preservatives, pesticides, cleaning materials, etc. — are just as likely to be found in office buildings, warehouses, hotels, restaurants, print rooms and maintenance workshops as they are in factories, laboratories, workshops, construction sites, factories and industrial complexes. The only difference lies in the extent to which employees are exposed to risk.

- It could very well be that the health risks in certain establishments are minimal. However, it is a far greater risk for an employer to assume that he has no hazardous substances on his premises or that the COSHH Regulations do not apply to him. Some businesses may indeed have very little to do in order to comply with COSHH. Others have a great deal to do.

MAINTENANCE OF CONTROL MEASURES

- The effectiveness of all engineering control measures must be closely monitored. If there is a change in working methods or a new substance is introduced, the risk assessment exercise must be repeated and the appropriate modifications made. Such control measures as are used in a particular working environment must be maintained, examined and tested at regular intervals.

- Local exhaust ventilation must be examined and tested at least once every 14 months or, if used in conjunction with:

  o   processes in which blasting is carried out in or incidental to the cleaning of metal castings, in connection with their manufacture — once every month;

  o   processes, other than wet processes, in which metal articles (other than of gold, platinum or iridium) are ground, abraded or polished using mechanical power, in any room for more than 12 hours in any week — once every six months;

  o   processes giving off dust or fume in which non-ferrous metal castings are produced — once every six months; and

  o   jute cloth manufacture — once every month.

  An employer must keep a suitable record of every test and examination or local exhaust ventilation and respiratory protective equipment, and of all repairs carried out as a result of those examinations and tests.

INFORMATION, INSTRUCTION AND TRAINING

5. Information, instruction & training

- Regulation 12(1) of COSHH states that *any* employer "who undertakes work which may expose any of his employees to substances hazardous to health shall provide that employee with such information, instruction and training as is suitable and sufficient for him (or her) to know—

  (a)   the risks to health created by such exposure; and
  (b)   the precautions which should be taken".

  An employee has the right to be informed about the nature and degree of the risks he (or she) may face when carrying out his duties, and any factors or conduct on his part that may enhance that risk. He also has the right to be informed about the control measures that have been put in place, why they have been adopted and how to use them properly. If he is required to wear or use protective clothing and equipment, he must be left in no doubt as to when that clothing and equipment must be worn or used, and the consequences if he should refuse or fail to do so. He must be informed also of the steps taken to monitor his exposure to hazardous substances and of his right to be told if and when the maximum exposure limits or occupational exposure standards for certain substances have been exceeded. His employer must also explain to him his duty to submit to routine health surveillance, the possible consequences of his refusal or failure to do so, and his right of access to the resultant health record.

- The duty to inform, instruct and train employees applies as much to employers engaged in allegedly low-risk activities as it does to employers in large high-risk industrial complexes. If any employee (such as a cleaner, cook, maintenance work or shop assistant) is exposed to a hazardous substance, relevant training and information *must* be provided.

- An employer would do well to keep a record of all such training. He should also update his disciplinary rules — leaving employees in no doubt that they will be dismissed if they wilfully disregard those rules. In larger organisations, in which a great many hazardous substances are used in quantity, health surveillance is also desirable.

- One way to reinforce an employee's awareness of the hazardous substances to which he (or she) may be exposed in the course of his employment is to provide a 'health and safety' supplement to the standard job description (or a document couched in similar terms), a suggested version of which appears in **Table 2** on pages 348 to 350.

- Those responsible for the recruitment and selection of new employees should be provided with amended and updated job descriptions and man specifications. People applying for work involving exposure (or possible exposure) to hazardous substances may have health problems (e.g., asthma, a history of dermatitis) which could or should militate against selection. Requests for pre-employment medical examinations, and their accompanying questionnaires or check-lists, should also defer to the conditions and the hazardous substances likely to be encountered by job applicants if and when selected for employment.

MONITORING EXPOSURE AT THE WORKPLACE

- In situations in which the failure or deterioration of control measures could result in a serious health effect to the employees concerned, the employer has a duty to use valid and suitable occupational hygiene techniques in order to estimate the exposure of those employees to substances hazardous to health. If airborne contaminants are likely to be present, he must carry out the periodic or continuous sampling of the atmosphere in the workplace. Such monitoring should take place at least once every 12 months to ensure that the maximum exposure limits (MELs) or occupational exposure standards (OESs) specified in HSE Guidance Note EH40/97 are not exceeded.

- In the case of possible exposure to vinyl chloride monomer, the monitoring must be continuous. If vapour or spray is given off from vessels in which an electrolytic chromium process is carried on (except trivalent chromium), sampling of the atmosphere must be carried out at least once every 14 days. For further details, the reader is commended to the appropriate HSE publications listed at the end of this section.

HEALTH SURVEILLANCE

- Regulation 11 of COSHH states that an employee must be placed under suitable health surveillance:

  (a) by an employment medical adviser or appointed doctor (at least once every 12 months) if he (or she) is exposed to one of the substances and is engaged in a process specified in Schedule 5 to the Regulations (not reproduced here, but involving the manufacture, formation or use of certain chemicals)—unless that exposure is not significant; or

  (b) by a company doctor or occupational health nurse (as often as may be necessary) if he(or she) is engaged in work which involves exposure or possible exposure to a substance which is known to give rise to an identifiable disease or adverse health effect (e.g., dermatitis, asthma,

Table 2
XYZ Company Limited
JOB SPECIFICATION
Part 2: Health & Safety Supplement

JOB TITLE:	Cleaner
DEPARTMENT:	Cleaning & General Maintenance
LOCATION:	Head Office. London. EC1
REPORTING TO:	Maintenance Foreman

H1 Principal duties:
(Consult Job Description for further details)

Briefly: The occupant of this job is one of a team of four cleaners responsible for the cleanliness of the reception area, offices, hallways, staircases, kitchen (including work surfaces, floors, ovens and food preparation equipment), staff canteen, washrooms and toilets, and for the collection and hygienic disposal of waste material.

H2 Likely exposure to hazardous substances:

(List here any 'substance hazardous to health' which may be used or encountered by the employee in the course of his or her employment. Write 'NONE' as appropriate).

Item (1)	Active Ingredient (2)	Exposure (3)	SDS No. (4)
Disinfectant	Chlorinated phenol	S	H25
Descaler	Phosphoric acid	S	H28
			(Cont.)

Table 2 (Cont.)			
Oven Cleaner	Sodium Hydroxide	S	H29
Bleach	Sodium Hypochlorite	S	H30
Stain Remover	Methylene Chloride	O	H31
Paint Remover	Dichloromethane & Methanol & Trichloro-ethylene	I	H26

Column 3: S = Significant O = Occasional I = Infrequent

Column 4: Copies of the relevant safety data sheets (SDS) *must* be attached to this Job Specification.

Important: The list above must be updated when new substances are introduced and/or when suppliers provide revised safety data sheets.

H4 Protective clothing and equipment

The employee *must* wear the gloves, goggles and/or face masks prescribed by the relevant Safety Data Sheets (SDS) when using the substances listed in paragraph H2 above. Coveralls will be worn at all times.

H5 Health problems or disabilities not acceptable:

Any person with a physical disability which in the view of the occupational health nurse severely limits mobility and/or the ability of that person to carry out cleaning and maintenance activities without risk to his/her health and safety.

Persons with a history of dermatitis and related skin conditions/allergies.

(Cont.)

Table 2 (Cont.)

H6 Information/instruction/training required?

(All safety instruction and training must be logged on the employee's personal file).

Standard induction training. Employee to be supplied
with a copy of the Company's Health & Safety
Handbook, plus a copy of each of the safety data
sheets listed in paragraph H2 above.

Instruction and training in fire prevention &
evacuation procedures — to be provided by the
General Maintenance Foreman.

On-the-job instruction concerning the risks to
health created by exposure to the substances listed
in paragraph H2 above, and the precautions which
must be taken.

H7 Pre-employment health examination?

Yes - by the Company Occupational Health Nurse

Routine health surveillance?

Reactive surveillance only. All accidents/incidents
to be recorded in the employee's health record and
investigated.

---

carcinomas, byssinosis, pneumoconiosis, etc.) — so long as
there are valid techniques for detecting indications of the
disease or the effect.

Health records must be maintained in a form approved by the
Health & Safety Executive (there are examples in the Approved
Code of Practice referred to at the end of this section) and must
be kept for a minimum period of 40 years from the date of the
last entry in each of them. Employees are entitled to inspect
their health records on demand (provided they give their
employers reasonable notice) and may appeal to the Health &
Safety Executive if aggrieved by a decision, including

suspension from work on medical grounds, recorded in those health records by an employment medical adviser or appointed doctor. If an employer ceases to trade, he must write to the Health & Safety Executive offering his health surveillance records to them for safekeeping.

See also the sections titled **Asbestos at Work, Dangerous chemicals & preparations, Ionising radiation**, and **Lead at work**.

FURTHER INFORMATION

• The following HSE publications are available from HSE Books at the address given on page 328.

Approved Supply List & codes of practice

L76
Approved Supply List and database — CHIP 96 [1996]
ISBN 0 7176 1116 7   £17.00

L5
General COSHH ACOP and Carcinogens ACOP and Biological Agents ACOP [1996 Edition]: Control of Substances Hazardous to Health Regulations 1994 [1997]
ISBN 0 7176 1308 9   £7.50

L8
The prevention or control of legionellosis (including legionnaire's disease). Approved Code of Practice [1995]
ISBN 0 7176 0732 1   £4.75

L9
The safe use of pesticides for non-agricultural purposes. Control of Substances Hazardous to Health Regulations 1994. Approved Code of Practice (Rev) [1991]
ISBN 0 7176 0542 6   £6.95

L11
A guide to the Asbestos (Licensing) Regulations 1983 [1991]
ISBN 0 11 885728 2   £3.50

L29
A guide to the Genetically Modified Organisms (Contained Use)

Regulations 1992, as amended in 1996 (Rev)   [1996]
ISBN 0 7176 1186 8   £10.50

L60
Consolidation of COSHH in the Potteries [1995]
ISBN 0 7176 0849 2   £5.00

L62
Safety datasheets for substances and preparations dangerous for supply. Guidance on regulation 6 of the CHIP Regulations 1994. Approved Code of Practice   [1995]
ISBN 0 7176 0859 X   £3.95

L63
Approved guide to the classification & labelling of substances dangerous for supply — CHIP 2   [1995]
ISBN 0 7176 0860 3   ££6.50

L67
Control of vinyl chloride at work [1994 Edition]. Control of Substances Hazardous to Health Regulations 1994. Approved Code of Practice [1995]
ISBN 0 7176 0894 8   £3.95

L86
Control of substances hazardous to health in fumigation operations. Approved Code of Practice: COSHH 94   [1996]
ISBN 0 7176 1195 7   £8.50

L88
Approved requirements and test methods for the classification and packaging of dangerous goods for carriage [1996]
ISBN 0 7176 1221 X   £12.75

Environmental hygiene

EH40/97
Occupational exposure limits [1997]
ISBN 0 7176 1315 1   £6.95

EH40/95
Workplace air and biological monitoring database: instrument enhanced — developed by HSE using d-Base lll. Available on 3.5 and 5.25 inch diskettes (both sorts provided as part of package)

[1995]
ISBN 0 71 76 0902 2   £220.00 + VAT

EH 63
Vinyl chloride: toxic hazards and precautions [1992]
ISBN 0 11 885730 4 £2.50
Note: To be read in conjunction with the COSHH Approved
Codes of Practice: L5 (see above)

EH 64
Summary criteria for occupational exposure limits 1996 [1996]
(This combines all current EH64 summaries into one loose-leaf
binder which will be updated annually. The availability of
updates will be notified to customers who have purchased
copies of EH64 directly from HSE Books)
ISBN 0 7176 1085 3   £19.50

EH 65/1
Trimethylbenzenes: criteria document for an OEL   [1992]
ISBN 0 11 886351 7 £10.00

EH 65/2
Pulverised fuel ash: criteria document for an OEL [1992]
ISBN 0 11 886391 6 £10.00

EH 65/3
N-N-dimethylacetamide: criteria document for an OEL   [1992]
ISBN 0 11 886392 4 £10.00

EH 65/4
1,2-dichloroethane: criteria document for an OEL   [1993]
ISBN 0 11 882082 6 £10.00

EH 65/5
4-methylene dianiline: criteria document for an OEL   [1993]
ISBN 0 11 882083 4 £10.00

EH 65/6
Epichlorohydrin: criteria document for an OEL [1993]
ISBN 0 11 882084 2 £10.00

EH 65/7
Chlorodifluoromethane: criteria document for an OEL [1994]
ISBN 0 7176 0760 7 £10.00

EH 65/8
Cumene: criteria document for an OEL   [1994]
ISBN 0 7176 0767 4   £10.00

EH 65/9
1,4 Dichlorobenzene: criteria document for an OEL   [1994]
ISBN 0 7176 0766 6   £10.00

EH 65/10
Carbon tetrachloride: criteria document for an OEL   [1994]
ISBN 0 7176 0765 8   £10.00

EH 65/11
Chloroform: criteria document for an OEL   [1994]
ISBN 0 7176 0764 X   £10.00
EH 65/13

Kaolin: criteria document for an OEL   [1994]
ISBN 0 7176 0762 3   £10.00

EH 65/14
Paracetamol: criteria document for an OEL   [1994]
ISBN 0 7176 0761 5   £10.00

EH65/15
1,1,1,2-tetrafluoroethane hfc 134a: criteria document for an OEL
[1995]
ISBN 0 7176 0947 2   £10.00

EH65/16
Methyl methacrylate: criteria document for an OEL   [1995]
ISBN 0 7176 0945 6   £10.00

EH65/17
p-Aramid respirable fibres: criteria document for an OEL   [1995]
ISBN 0 7176 0941 3   £10.00

EH65/18
Propanol: criteria document for an OEL   [1995]
ISBN 0 7176 0 944 8   £10.00

EH65/19
*Mercury and its inorganic divalent compounds: criteria document for
an OEL*   [1995]

EH65/20
Ortho-toluidine: criteria document for an OEL [1996]
ISBN 0 7176 1057 8 £10.00

EH65/21
Propylene oxide: criteria document for an OEL [1996]
ISBN 0 7176 1056 X ££10.00

EH65/22
Softwood dust: criteria document for an OEL [1996]
ISBN 0 7176 1087 X £10.00

EH65/23
Antimony and its compounds: criteria document for an OEL [1996]
ISBN 0 7176 1054 3 £10.00

EH65/24
Platinum metal and soluble platinum salts: criteria document for an OEL [1996]
ISBN 0 7176 1055 1 £10.00

EH65/25
Iodomethane: criteria document for an OEL [1996]
ISBN 0 7176 1052 7 £10.00

EH65/26
Azodicarbonamide: criteria document for an OEL [1996]
ISBN 0 7176 1092 6 £10.00

EH65/27
Dimethyl and diethyl sulphates: criteria document for an OEL [1996]
ISBN 0 7176 1058 6 £10.00

EH65/28
Hydrazine: criteria document for an OEL [1996]
ISBN 0 7176 1099 3 £10.00

EH65/29
Acid anhydrides: criteria document for an OEL [1996]
ISBN 0 7176 1059 4 £10.00

EH65/30
Review of fibre toxicology: criteria document for an OEL [1996]
ISBN 0 7176 1205 8 £10.00

Other guidance

HS(G)28
Safety advice for bulk chlorine installations   [1986]
ISBN 0 11 883872.5   £7.50

HS(G)30
Storage of anhydrous ammonia under pressure in the UK: spherical and cylindrical vessels   [1986]
ISBN 0 11 883884 9   £8.50

HS(G)40
Chlorine from drums and cylinders   [1987]
ISBN 0 7176 1006 3   ££2.50

HS(G)70
The control of legionellis including legionnaire's disease (3rd Edition)
[1993]
ISBN 0 7176 0451 9   £4.95

HS(G) 77
COSHH and peripatetic workers [1992]
ISBN 0 11 885733 9 £4.00

HS(G) 97
A step by step guide to COSHH assessment [1993]
ISBN 0 11 886379 7 £5.00

HS(G)110
Seven steps to successful substitution of hazardous substances
[1994]
ISBN 0 7176 0695 3   £6.50

HS(G)117
Making sense of NONS: a guide to the Notification of New Substances Regulations 1993   [1994]
ISBN 0 7176 0774 7 £9.75

HS(G)126
CHIP 2 for everyone [1995]
ISBN 0 7176 0857 3   £6.75

Health surveillance under COSHH: guidance for employers [1990]
ISBN 0 7176 0491 8 £3.00

COSHH: guidance for schools [1989]
ISBN 0 11 885511 5   £2.00

COSHH guidance for universities, polytechnics and colleges of further and higher education [1990]
ISBN 0 11 885433 X   £2.00

COSHH — its application in the foundry [1991]
ISBN 0 11 885591 3   £4.00

The application of COSHH to plastics processing: a health at work guide [1990]
ISBN 0 11 885556 5   £4.00

COSHH in the rubber industry. Guidance on the Control of Substances Hazardous to Health Regulations 1988 [1992]
ISBN 0 11 85610 3   £5.00

Free leaflets (Telephone: 01787 881165)

AS 28
COSHH in Agriculture

AS 30
COSHH in forestry

IACL 42
COSHH — printers

IACL 48
COSHH in the paper and board industry

IACL 62
COSHH assessment in potteries

INDG 136
COSSH: the new brief guide for employers (Rev)
ISBN 0 7176 1189 2
Single leaflet free. £5.00 per pack of 10 leaflets, etc.

HEALTH & SAFETY AT WORK
(General duties of employers, self-employed persons & employees)

Key points

- Section 2 of the Health & Safety at Work etc. Act 1974 imposes a duty on *every* employer to ensure, so far as is reasonably practicable, the health, safety and welfare at work of *all* his employees.

Meaning of "Employee"

- Under the 1974 Act, the term "employee" applies not only to persons recruited, employed and paid by the employer himself. It also covers casual workers, temporary staff, and (this is particularly important) trainees or students accepted by an employer on 'work placement', 'work experience' and similar schemes. The rule relating to students and trainees is to be found in the Health & Safety (Training for Employment) Regulations 1990 (SI 1990/1380), which came into force on 8 August 1990, amending and updating the Health & Safety (Youth Training Scheme) Regulations 1983, which contained similar provisions.

GENERAL DUTIES OF EMPLOYERS

- Section 2(2) of the 1974 Act adds that an employer must:

    (a)   provide and maintain plant, machinery, equipment, tools, appliances and systems of work, which are, so far as is reasonably practicable, safe and without risk to the health of his employees;

    (b)   arrange, so far as is reasonably practicable, that employees are not at risk (and not exposed to risk) in connection with the use, handling, storage and transport of articles and substances (including chemicals, cleaning agent, dusts, vapours, etc.);

    (c)   provide as much information, instruction, training and supervision as is necessary to ensure, so far as is reasonably practicable, the health and safety at work of his employees;

(d) ensure, so far as is reasonably practicable, that the buildings, workrooms, offices, and other areas in which his employees are (or may be) expected to work, do not pose a risk to their health or safety;

(e) provide and maintain safe means of access to and egress from all parts of his premises; and

(f) provide and maintain a working environment for his employees which is, so far as is reasonably practicable, not only safe and healthy for them to use but also adequate as regards facilities and arrangements for their welfare at work (viz; adequate space, heating, light, seating, ventilation, sanitary and washing facilities, cloakroom accommodation, and so on).

An employer must not require an employee to pay for any item of protective clothing or equipment (whether by a deduction from his pay or by other means) or any other article or welfare facility (such as drinking water, soap, towels, showers, coveralls, etc.) provided in compliance with a specific requirement in health and safety legislation (*ibid*; section 9).

Safety policy

* If an employer has five or more persons in his employ (including any student or trainee), he must produce and distribute a written statement which not only outlines his general policy regarding the health and safety of his employees but which also explains what steps he has taken to ensure that his policy is carried out.(*ibid*; section 2(3)).

Consultations with safety representatives

* Under the provisions of the Safety Representatives & Safety Committees Regulations 1977 (SI 1977/500) or, as appropriate, those of the Health & Safety (Consultations with Employees) Regulations 1996 (SI 1996/1513) an employer must consult with trade union-appointed safety representatives or with elected *representatives of employee safety* on matters impacting, or likely to impact, on the health and safety of the employees they have been appointed or elected to represent. For further details, please turn to the section in this handbook titled **Safety**

representatives. See also **Competent persons**.

Duty to persons other than employees

- Employers are duty-bound also to conduct their businesses or undertakings in a way that will not put the health and safety of visitors, customers, clients, members of the public and passers-by at risk. That duty clearly devolves on the owners or occupiers of department stores, shops, restaurants, hotels, hospitals, schools, and the like, and on the occupiers of factories, workshops, garages, or whatever who routinely have visitors, tradesmen and the like on the premises. That same duty devolves on self-employed persons whose trailing electric cables, paint pots, faulty scaffolding, or whatever, could present a source of danger to people in the immediate vicinity (*ibid*; section 3).

Duty in relation to emissions into the atmosphere

- Persons having control of business premises must use the best practicable means for preventing the emission into the atmosphere of noxious or offensive substances and for rendering harmless or inoffensive any such substances as may be emitted (*ibid*; section 5). For further information, please consult the section in this handbook titled **Emissions of noxious or offensive substances**.

General duties of manufacturers and suppliers

- People and organisations who (or which) design, manufacture, import or supply "articles for use at work" or any article of fairground equipment have a duty in law to ensure, so far as is reasonably practicable, that the article will be safe and without risks to health at all times when it is being set, used, cleaned or maintained by a person at work. To that end, the manufacturer or supplier must carry out all appropriate tests and examinations before selling or offering to supply that article, and must provide the purchaser with whatever information he needs (technical drawings, safety manuals, operating handbooks, etc.) to enable him to use that machine safely, as to which see **Machinery safety** and **Work equipment** elsewhere in this handbook (*ibid*; section 6).

- If a machine is likely to expose an employee to a daily personal noise exposure of 85dB(A) or above, or to a level of peak sound pressure of 200 pascals, the manufacturer or supplier must provide the purchaser or hirer of that machine with adequate information about the noise likely to be generated by the machine during normal operations (*ibid*; as modified by Regulation 12 of the Noise at Work Regulations 1989 (SI 1989/1790)). See **Noise at work** elsewhere in this handbook.

- A similar duty extends to the manufacturers, importers and suppliers of substances. A "substance", for these purposes, is any natural or artificial substance, whether in solid or liquid form or in the form of a gas or vapour (*ibid*; section 53(1)) — a duty reinforced by the Chemicals(Hazard Information & Packaging for Supply) Regulations 1994 (SI 1994/3247), discussed elsewhere in this handbook in the section titled **Dangerous chemicals & preparations**.

GENERAL DUTIES OF EMPLOYEES AT WORK

- Section 7 of the 1974 Act cautions every employee that he (or she) must take reasonable care not only for his own health and safety but also for that of his workmates and any other persons who may be affected by his acts or omissions at work. Furthermore, he must cooperate with his employer so far as is necessary to enable him to comply with the requirements and prohibitions imposed on him by health and safety legislation. Finally, he must not recklessly or intentionally interfere with (or misuse) anything provided in the interests of health, safety and welfare (*ibid*; sections 7 & 8).

ENFORCEMENT AND PROSECUTION

- A person (whether employer, a self-employed person, or a person having control of premises) who fails to discharge a duty to which he is subject by virtue of sections 2 to 7 of the 1974 Act (summarised above) is guilty of an offence and is liable on summary conviction to a fine of up to £20,000. If he is convicted on indictment, he could be ordered to pay whatever fine the court considers appropriate in the circumstances (*ibid*; section 33(1)(a) & (1A)).

- If an employer contravenes any requirement or prohibition

imposed on him by an improvement or prohibition notice served on him by a health and safety (or local authority) inspector, he will not only be liable to a fine of up to £20,000 but could also be sent to prison for up to six months (two years, if convicted on indictment) (*ibid*; section 33(1)(g) & (2A)).

FURTHER INFORMATION

- The following publications are available from HSE Books at the address given on page 328.

Free leaflets (Telephone: 01787 881165)

HSC 2
Health & Safety at Work etc. Act 1974: The Act outlined

HSC 6
Writing a safety policy: Advice to employers

HSC13
Health and safety regulations: a short guide

HSE27
Your health and safety - a guide. This English version is an *extremely basic* guide for employers which is translated into the following language versions:

HSE27B: Bengali
HSE27G   Gujarati
HSE27H   Hindi
HSE27P   Punjab
HSE27U   Urdu

INDG 132
5 steps to successful health and safety management

Guidance notes

HS(G) 65
Successful health and safety management [1991]
ISBN 0 7176 0425 X   £10.00

HEALTH & SAFETY COMMISSION AND EXECUTIVE

Key points

* The Health and Safety Commission (HSC) and the Health and Safety Executive (HSE) were established as bodies corporate under the provisions of section 10 of the Health and Safety at Work etc. Act 1974, and came into being on 1 October 1974, and 1 January 1975, respectively.

* The HSC consists of a chairman and not less than six (nor more than nine) other members appointed by the Secretary of State. Three members of the Commission are selected from organisations representing employers; three from organisations representing employees; and three are 'independents' drawn from other bodies such as local authorities and professional organisations. One of the members holds the post of deputy chairman of the Commission.

* The HSE comprises three persons, one of whom is appointed director of the Executive by the HSC (with the approval of the Secretary of State); and the others appointed by the Commission with the like approval after consultation with the director.

General duty of the HSC

* It is the general duty of the Commission "to do such things and make such arrangements as it considers appropriate for the general purposes of Part I of the Health and Safety at Work etc. Act 1974", to which end the Commission will:

  (a) assist and encourage persons (such as employers, trade unions, etc.) in their observance of and compliance with their duties and obligations in relation to the health, safety and welfare of employees and members;

  (b) conduct research into aspects of health and safety; provide training and information in that connection to others;

  (c) prepare and submit proposals for the amendment and

revocation of existing health and safety legislation, and/or the introduction of new regulations.

(d)   confer functions on the Executive as the body responsible for enforcing the *relevant statutory provisions;*

(e)   direct investigations and inquiries into any accident, occurrence, or other matter whatsoever which the Commission thinks it necessary or expedient to investigate for any of the general purposes of the Health and Safety at Work etc. Act 1974 or direct the HSE or authorise any other person to investigate and make a special report on any such matter;

(f)   approve and issue such Codes of Practice (whether prepared by it or not) as in its opinion are suitable for providing practical guidance with respect to the duties of employers in relation to the health, safety and welfare at work of persons employed.

Duties of the HSE

- The HSE for its part, will:

(a)   exercise on behalf of the Commission such of the Commission's functions as the Commission directs it to exercise;

(b)   give effect as the *enforcing authority* to any directions given to it by the Commission;

(c)   appoint inspectors (of factories, mines and quarries, etc.) to carry into effect the *relevant statutory provisions* within their respective fields of responsibility;

(d)   confer powers on those inspectors in the exercise of their responsibilities under Part I of the Health and Safety at Work etc. Act 1974;

(e)   indemnify those inspectors against the whole or part of any damages and costs or expenses which they may have been ordered to pay or may have incurred in consequence of any action brought against them in the execution, or purported execution of any of the *relevant statutory provisions;*

(f)   receive such information from employers and other bodies as may have been ordered by the HSC in the exercise of its functions; and

(g)   make adequate arrangements for the enforcement of the *relevant statutory provisions* except to the extent that some other authority or class of authorities has been made responsible by regulations for their enforcement.

Meaning or 'relevant statutory provisions'

• The expression *relevant statutory provisions* means in effect the entire body of health and safety legislation (including statutes and regulations which impose prohibitions and requirements in relation to the health and safety at persons at work). For a list of existing enactments which are *relevant statutory provisions* (not all of which are of particular or immediate interest to the readers of this handbooks) please turn to page 426.

ENFORCING AUTHORITIES

• Under the Health and Safety (Enforcing Authority) Regulations 1989 (SI 1989/1903) responsibility for enforcing health and safety legislation (or, to use the correct term, the *relevant statutory provisions*) is shared between the HSE itself and local authorities. Enforcement of the Fire Precautions Act 1971, and the issuing of Fire Certificates, is a matter for the Home Office and, at a local level the fire authorities, (except for so-called 'special premises'). For further particulars, please turn to the sections titled **Fire certificate** and Fire precautions, elsewhere in this handbook.

• As a rule of thumb, HSE inspectors (still referred to as factory inspectors, explosives inspectors, mines inspectors, and the like) 'take care of' heavy and light manufacturing industry: factories, workshops, construction sites, engineering works, etc. and activities which involve the use and/or storage of highly flammable liquids and substances, explosive materials, and so on. In short, HSE inspectors enforce health and safety legislation in premises and workshops which are not otherwise assigned to local authority inspectors (except that local authority inspectors are not permitted to 'police' themselves or any premises or activities under their control — such as the police and fire services, hospitals, and so on).

- Local authority inspectors are responsible for enforcing compliance with health and safety legislation in premises where the main activities are:

  o the sale or storage of goods for retail or wholesale distribution (with exceptions);

  o office activities;

  o catering services (cafes, restaurants, pubs, fast food establishments, and the like);

  o the provision of permanent or temporary residential accommodation (hotels, guest houses, bed-and-breakfast establishments, residential clubs, retirement homes, caravan parks, camping sites, and similar);

  o some consumer services provided in shop premises (except dry cleaning or radio and television repairs);

  o coin-operated units in launderettes and similar cleaning premises;

  o premises in which cosmetic or therapeutic services are provided (with exceptions);

  o leisure centres (other than those under the control of the local authority itself), cinemas, theatres, sports clubs, health and fitness studios, and other premises providing cultural or recreational facilities and activities;

  o hiring of boats and pleasure craft on inland waters;

  o the display or demonstration of goods and services at exhibitions;

  o premises in which animals are cared for, treated, accommodated or exhibited (with exceptions);

o funeral parlours and similar (except the activities of embalming or coffin-making); and

o churches, chapels and other places used for worship or religious meetings.

A full list (including information about excepted premises) is to be found in the Schedule to the 1989 Regulations, copies of which can be found in reference libraries or purchased from The Stationery Office (see page 328) (quoting SI 1989/1903).

• Any employer or occupier of premises, who is uncertain whether his premises are 'policed' by the local authority or by the HSE, should contact his local authority Environmental Health Department or his nearest area office of the HSE for further advice. The addresses of all twenty-one HSE area offices are listed overleaf.

Obstruction of inspectors

• Health and safety inspectors have considerable powers and can enter any premises within their areas of responsibility without having to obtain the permission of the owner or occupier. Although unannounced visits do take place (usually during normal opening hours), the standard procedure is for an inspector to contact the owner or occupier to advise that he wishes to inspect the premises and to arrange a convenient time and date.

• It is, of course, a serious offence to obstruct an inspector in the exercise or performance of his powers or duties. It is an offence also to make false statements or falsify entries in any register, book, notice or other document required by or under health and safety legislation. The penalty for these and related offences is a fine of up to £2,000 or, if the offender is convicted on indictment, a fine of such amount as the court considers appropriate in the circumstances.

See also **Improvement notice, Inspectors, powers of, Offences & penalties**, and **Prohibition notice**, elsewhere in this handbook.

Health & Safety Executive (HSE)
HEADQUARTERS AND AREA OFFICES

Head Office
Daniel House
Trinity Road
Bootle L20 7HE

Telephone: 0151 - 951 4000

Area office   **Local authority areas covered**

London North

Maritime House 1 Linton Road Barking Essex IG 11 8HF	Barking and Dagenham Barnet Brent Camden Ealing Enfield
Tel: 0181 235 8000 Fax: 0181 235 8001	Hackney Haringey Harrow Havering
Chancel House Neasden Lane London NW10 2UD	Islington Newham Redbridge Tower Hamlets Waltham Forest
Tel: 0181 459 8855 Fax: 0181 459 2131	

London South

1 Long Lane London SE1 4PG Tel: 0171 556 2100 Fax: 0171 556 2200	Bexley, Bromley, City of London, Croydon, Greenwich, Hammersmith and Fulham, Hillingdon, Hounslow, Kensington & Chelsea, Kingston, Lambeth, Lewisham, Merton, Richmond, Southwark, Sutton, Wandsworth, Westminster

South

Priestley House
Priestley Road
Basingstoke
RG24 9NW

Tel: 0125 640 4000
Fax: 0125 640 4100

Berkshire
Dorset
Hampshire
Isle of Wight
Wiltshire

South East

3 East Grinstead House
London Road
East Grinstead
West Sussex
RH 19 1 RR

Tel: 01342 334200
Fax: 01342 334222

Mid Sussex
Surrey
East Sussex
West Sussex

South west

Inter City House
Mitchell Lane
Victoria Street
Bristol
BS1 6AN

Tel: 0117 929 0681
Fax: 0117 926 2998

Avon,
Cornwall, **Devon,**
Gloucs,
Somerset,
Isles of Scilly

East Anglia

39 Baddow Road
Chelmsford
CM2 OHL

Tel: 01245 706 200
Fax: 01245 706 222

Essex (except parts of Essex covered
by London North)
Norfolk,
Suffolk

Northern Home Counties

14 Cardiff Road
Luton,
Beds.
LU1 1PP

Tel: 01582 444 200
Fax: 01582 444 320

Bedfordshire
Buckinghamshire
Cambridgeshire
Hertfordshire

East Midlands

5th floor
Belgrave House
1 Greyfriars,
Northampton
NN1 2BS

Tel: 0160 4738 300
Fax: 0160 4738 333

Leicestershire
Northamptonshire
Oxfordshire
Warwickshire

West Midlands

McLaren Building
2 Masshouse Circus
Oueensway
Birmingham
B4 7NP

Tel: 0121 607 6200
Fax: 0121 607 6349

West Midlands

Wales

Brunel House
2 Fitzalan Road
Cardiff
CF2 1 SH

Tel: 01222 263 000
Fax: 01222 263120

Clwyd,
Dyfed,
Gwent
Gwynedd,
Mid Glamorgan
Powys
South Glamorgan
West Glamorgan

Marches

Marches House
Midway,
Newcastle under Lyme,
Staffs
ST5 1 DT

Tel: 01782 602 300
Fax: 01782 602 400

Hereford and
Worcester,
Shropshire,
Staffordshire

North Midlands

The Pearson Building
55 Upper Parliament St.
Nottingham
NG1 6AU

Tel: 0115 971 2800
Fax: 0115 971 2802

Derbyshire
Lincolnshire,
Notts

South Yorkshire

Sovereign House
110 Queen Street
Sheffield
S1 2ES

Humberside,
South Yorkshire

Tel: 0114 291 2300
Fax: 0114 291 2379

West and North Yorkshire

8 St Paul's Street
Leeds
LS1 2LE

North Yorkshire,
West Yorkshire

Tel: 0113 283 4200
Fax: 0113 283 4296

Greater Manchester

Quay House
Quay Street
Manchester
M3 3JB

Greater
Manchester

Tel: 0161 952 8200
Fax: 0161 952 8222

Merseyside

The Triad
Stanley Road
Bootle
Merseyside
L20 3PG

Cheshire,
Merseyside

Tel: 0151 479 2200
Fax: 0151 479 2201

North West

Victoria House
Ormskirk Road
Preston
PR1 1HH

Cumbria,
Lancashire

Tel: 01772 836 200
Fax : 01772 836 222

North East

Arden House
Regent Centre
Regent Farm Road
Gosforth
Newcastle-upon-Tyne
NE3 3JN

Cleveland,
Durham,
Northumber-land,
Tyne and Wear

Tel: 0191 202 6200
Fax: 0191 202 6300

Scotland East

Belford House
59 Belford Road
Edinburgh
EH4 3UE

Borders
Central
Fife
Grampian
Highland
Lothian
Tayside
and the island areas of Orkney and
Shetland

Tel: 0131 247 2000
Fax: 0131 247 2121

Scotland West

375 West George
Street
Glasgow
G2 4LW

Dumfries and Galloway
Strathclyde
and the Western Isles

Tel: 0141 2753000
Fax: 0141 275 3100

HEALTH SURVEILLANCE

Key points

- For many years, it has been commonplace for large factories and
  industrial complexes to have their own health departments
  employing one or more full-time occupational health nurses
  and, occasionally, a resident doctor — their roles being to carry
  out pre and post-employment medical examinations (or simple
  health checks in the case of junior personnel and job applicants)
  and to maintain a 'watching brief' on the health of employees
  whose duties routinely bring them into contact with known
  hazardous substances. Other organisations will have a fully-

equipped first aid room and at least one factory nurse on standby to deal with minor cuts, burns, abrasions, etc. However, it has never been the function of resident doctors in factories and large office complexes to do more than diagnose health problems and (if there are worrying symptoms) to encourage employees to talk to their own GPs.

- There is also, of course, the Employment Medical Advisory Service (EMAS) which is part of the Field Operations Division of the Health & Safety Executive. EMAS is staffed by doctors and nurses ('Employment Medical Advisers') whose job it is to monitor health hazards and medical problems in all branches of industry, and to advise the Secretary of State for Employment, the Health and Safety Commission, Careers Officers, School Medical Officers, young people (and their parents), employers, employees, trade unions, and the like, on precautions and environmental controls required to minimise health risks in employment.

- EMAS doctors and nurses have powers similar to those enjoyed by HSE inspectors. They may enter an employer's premises at any reasonable time to investigate suspected instances of occupational disease, may demand to see and inspect registers and other documents, and may interview managers and employees in all aspects of the working environment. EMAS also advises employers on the suitability of first-aid facilities and on the names of organisations which offer EMAS-approved first-aid training courses.

Management of Health & Safety at Work Regulations 1992

- In recent years, health surveillance (so-called) has been put on a stronger statutory footing. For example, Regulations 3 and 5 of the Management of Health & Safety at Work Regulations 1992 (SI 1992/2051, as amended by SI 1994/2865) — which apply to *every* situation in which people are employed to work (but not to the masters or crews of sea-going ships) — requires employers to assess the risks to health and safety to which their employees are exposed while they are at work and to provide "such health surveillance as is appropriate", having regard to risks (if any) identified by that assessment.

- The Approved Code of Practice which accompanies the 1992 Regulations adds that the primary objective of health surveillance must be to detect adverse health effects at an early stage (e.g., dermal effects commonly associated with work with certain substances), thereby affording the employer an opportunity to identify employees who are most at risk and to protect them from further damage.

- The minimum requirement under the 1992 Regulations is for employers to maintain individual health records, complemented, where appropriate, by —

    (a)   inspection of readily detectable conditions by one or more responsible persons (acting within the limits of their training and experience);

    (b)   enquiries by a qualified person (such as an Occupational Health Nurse) about symptoms, accompanied by routine inspections and examinations;

    (c)   medical surveillance by an appropriately qualified practitioner (which may include clinical examination and measurements of physiological and psychological effects);

    (d)   biological effect monitoring (that is to say, measurement and assessment of early biological effects such as [to give one example] diminished lung functions in workers exposed to zinc chromate, calcium chromate or strontium chromate in their pure forms);

    (e)   biological monitoring, i.e., the measurement and assessment of workplace agents or their metabolites either in tissues, secreta, excreta, expired air or any combination of those in exposed workers.

Just how often employees should submit to the health surveillance procedures described here will depend in large part on current industry guidelines and (in doubtful cases) on the advice of qualified practitioners and/or organisations such as EMAS. Affected employees, says the code of practice, should be invited to comment on the proposed frequency of health surveillance procedures and be given access to an appropriately qualified practitioner for his (or her) advice on the matter.

- Copies of the Approved Code:

  L21
  Management of Health and Safety at Work Regulations 1992:
  Approved code of practice [1992]
  ISBN 0 7176 041 2 8   £5.00

can be obtained from HSE Books (see page 328).

OTHER LEGISLATION

- Industry-specify legislation on the health surveillance of
  employees exposed to lead, asbestos, ionising raditions and
  specified hazardous substances, is to be found in —

  o   the Control of Lead at Work Regulations 1980 (SI
       1980/1248, as amended);

  o   the Ionising Radiations Regulations 1985 (SI
       1985/1333);

  o   the Control of Asbestos at Work Regulations 1987 (SI
       1987/2115, as amended); and

  o   the Control of Substances Hazardous to Health
       Regulations 1994 (SI 1994/3246),

  which latter came into force on 16 January 1995.

Control of Lead at Work Regulations 1980

- Employers engaged in activities which expose employees to
  lead (in a form in which it is liable to be inhaled, ingested or
  otherwise absorbed) must ensure that each of those employees
  is under medical surveillance (including biological tests) by an
  employment medical adviser or appointed doctor if either —

  (a)   the exposure of that employee to lead is significant; or

  (b)   an employment medical adviser or appointed doctor
        certifies that the employee should be under medical
        surveillance.

  Adequate records must be kept of all medical surveillance and biological tests. Furthermore, the results of all such tests and examinations must be kept on file and be made available for inspection by the individuals concerned for a minimum period of two years. If the results of any test or examination are unsatisfactory, the individual in question must be informed of that fact immediately.

• Employees must make themselves available for clinical examinations and/or biological tests during normal working hours when and as asked to do so (*ibid*; Reg. 16(2)). A refusal to comply (subject to the usual warnings) would undoubtedly provide grounds for dismissal.

• If an employment medical adviser or appointed doctor certifies that an employee should be suspended from work which exposes him (or her) to lead, the employer must either transfer him to suitable alternative employment (if such work is available) or pay him his normal wages or salary for the period of the suspension or for 26 weeks, whichever is the greater. An employee who has been suspended from work on medical grounds may present a complaint of unfair dismissal to an industrial tribunal as to which, see **Suspension on medical grounds** elsewhere in this handbook. For information about the availability of the 1980 Regulations and their accompanying Approved Code of Practice, see *FURTHER INFORMATION* below.

Note: The term "appointed doctor" means a registered medical practitioner who is appointed in writing by the Health & Safety Executive for the purposes of Regulation 16 of the 1980 Regulations.

Ionising Radiations Regulations 1985

• Employees who are "classified persons" (within the meaning of the Ionising Radiations Regulations 1985) and persons whom an employer intends to "classify" must be under adequate medical surveillance by an employment medical adviser or appointed doctor. The same applies to unclassified persons who have received an overexposure, and to persons who have been suspended from work with ionising radiations on medical grounds.

• Health records must be maintained for at least 50 years, and must be kept available for inspection by employees on demand. An employee who is suspended from work with ionising radiations, at the direction of an employment medical adviser or appointed doctor, has the right to be paid his normal wages or salary until such time as the 'suspension order' is lifted (subject to a maximum of 26 weeks' pay), unless he (or she) unreasonably refuses an offer of suitable alternative employment. For further information, please turn to the sections titled **Ionising radiation** and **Suspension on medical grounds** elsewhere in this handbook.

Control of Asbestos at Work Regulations 1987

- There are similar provisions in the Control of Asbestos at Work Regulations 1987. Employees exposed to asbestos *must* present themselves for medical examination by an employment medical adviser or appointed doctor when and as requested to do so (during normal working hours). The health record of every person subjected to medical surveillance must be kept on file for at least 40 years (*ibid;* Reg. 16). More detailed guidance on the provisions of the 1987 Regulations is to be found in the following HSE publications which are available from HSE Books at the address given on page 328:

L27
The Control of Asbestos at Work. Control of Asbestos at Work Regulations 1987: Approved code of practice [2nd Edition, 1993]
ISBN 0 11 882037 0   £5.00

L28
Work with asbestos insulation, asbestos coating and asbestos insulating board. Control of Asbestos at Work Regulations 1987: Approved code of practice [2nd Edition, 1993]
ISBN 0 11 882038 9   £5.00

See also the section titled **Asbestos at work** elsewhere in this handbook.

COSHH Regulations 1994

- Under the COSHH Regulations 1994, which came into force on 16 January 1995 (revoking and re-enacting, with minor modifications, the Control of Substances Hazardous to Health Regulations 1988), employees whose work exposes them to specified hazardous substances (or to substances which have been known to cause identifiable diseases or adverse health effects) must submit to routine health surveillance and medical examinations when and as instructed to do so by an employment medical adviser or appointed doctor.

• Employers must monitor the exposure of their employees to hazardous substances to ensure that the measures they have taken to adequately control that exposure are having the desired effect. Monitoring must take place as frequently as circumstances and common sense dictate. The exposure of employees who work with vinyl chloride monomer must be monitored continuously (in accordance with procedures approved by the Health & Safety Executive) and at least once every 14 days when employees are, or may be, exposed to vapours or sprays given off from vessels at which an electrolytic chromium process (except trivalent chromium) is carried on.

• An employee who is suspended from work by reason of his exposure to specified hazardous substances is entitled to be paid his (or her) usual "remuneration" during the period of suspension or for 26 weeks, whichever is the greater, For further particulars, please turn to the section titled **Suspension on medical grounds**.

More detailed guidance on the provisions of the 1994 Regulations is to be found in the following HSE publications which are available from HSE Books at the address given on page 328:

L5
The Control of Substances Hazardous to Health Regulations 1994 (COSHH): Approved Code of Practice
ISBN 0 7176 0819 0   £6.75

L60
Control of substances hazardous to health in the production of pottery. The Control of Substances Hazardous to Health Regulations 1994. The Control of Lead at Work Regulations 1980. Approved Code of Practice.
ISBN 0 7176 0849 2   £5.00

See also **Hazardous substances** elsewhere in this handbook.

HIGHLY FLAMMABLE LIQUIDS
(and liquefied petroleum gases)

Key points

- Rules for protecting employees from the risk of fire or explosion (or, indeed, asphyxiation) in factories and other workplaces in which quantities of highly flammable liquids or liquefied petroleum gases are used or stored for the purposes of a trade, business or undertaking are laid down in the Highly Flammable Liquids & Liquefied Petroleum Gases Regulations 1972 (SI 1972/917).

- For the purposes of the 1972 Regulations, a "highly flammable liquid" is any liquid, liquid solution, emulsion or suspension (other than aqueous ammonia, liquefied flammable gas and liquefied petroleum gas) which, when tested in accordance with Part III of Schedule 1 to the Chemicals (Hazard Information & Packaging for Supply) Regulations 1994, has a flash point of less than 32° Celsius (see **Table 1** on page 383 below); and which, when tested in the manner specified in Schedule 2 to the 1972 Regulations (not reproduced here because of its length), supports combustion. "Liquefied petroleum gas" means commercial butane, commercial propane, or a mixture of those two gases.

STORAGE & RELATED REQUIREMENTS

- Unless the amount of highly flammable liquid present in a workplace is small (in other words, the minimum amount needed to support manufacturing and related activities), all highly flammable liquids must be stored —

  (a)   in suitable fixed storage tanks in safe positions; or

  (b)   in suitable closed vessels kept in a safe position in the open air and, where necessary, protected against direct sunlight; or

  (c)   in suitable closed vessels kept in a storeroom which is either in a safe position or is a fire-resisting structure; or

(d)   in the case of a workroom, where the aggregate quantity stored does not exceed 50 litres, in suitable closed vessels kept in a fire-resisting cupboard or bin.

Except in the case of tanks and vessels which have already been emptied and made free of vapour, all openings (other than air vents) in cupboards, bins, tanks and vessels used for the storage of highly flammable liquids must be kept closed except for access. Furthermore, all reasonably practicable steps must be taken to ensure that leakages and spills of highly flammable liquids are either neutralised and made safe, or drained off to a suitable container.

Explosion pressure relief

• Storerooms, workrooms, cabinets or enclosures necessarily provided for the storage or use of highly flammable liquids must not only be fire-resisting and constructed of non-combustible materials, but must also incorporate suitable explosion pressure reliefs so arranged as to ensure that the pressure released by an explosion is vented to a safe place.

Hazard warning signs

• Every storeroom, cupboard, bin, tank and vessel used for the storage of a highly flammable liquid must be clearly and boldly marked with the words "Highly Flammable", or "Flashpoint below 32°C, or "Flashpoint in the range of 22°C to 32°C" or otherwise with an appropriate indication of flammability.

• The rule about marking storage cupboards, vessels and the like with the words "Highly flammable" (or whatever) does not apply to storerooms, cupboards etc., which are used for the storage of whisky, gin, vodka and other spirits intended for human consumption. Nor does it apply to the fuel tanks of cars, trucks, tractors, and the like; or to small canisters or similar containing a half-litre or less of highly flammable liquid, or to aerosol canisters in which the amount of any highly flammable liquid is no more than 45 per cent by weight of the total contents, or 250 grammes in weight.

Conveyance of highly flammable liquids

• Highly flammable liquids should not be conveyed from one

part of a factory or workplace to another part of that same workplace other than through a leak-proof and totally-enclosed system, such as a pipeline.

- All drums and containers used to transport such liquids must be so designed and constructed as to avoid the risk of spilling. Accidental spillages and leakages of highly flammable liquids must be contained or made safe without delay, or be drained off to a suitable container or a safe area. Empty tanks and drums (or similar) must be returned to their original storage area (or fire-proof cupboard or bin) and, unless made free of vapour, must be kept closed.

Sources of ignition

- No matches, lighters, naked lights, radiant heaters or similar may be permitted in any storeroom or other area (such as a production department) in which there is likely to be a dangerous concentration of vapours from a highly flammable liquid. By a "dangerous concentration" is meant a concentration greater than the lower flammable limit of the vapours in question. It follows that no employee should be permitted to smoke in any factory or place in which any highly flammable liquid is present. To that end, the occupier must display clear and bold "No Smoking!" notices both at the entrance to his factory or premises and at suitable locations elsewhere within the premises (other than in those areas which have been safely set aside as smoking areas).

Fire precautions

- Factories and workplaces in which highly flammable liquids are present must have adequate and safe means of escape in the case of fire. A sufficient quantity of fire fighting appliances (extinguishers, etc.) must be provided and maintained, and be readily available for use in the event of an emergency.

- Cotton waste, cleaning rags and the like, which are contaminated with highly flammable liquids and could ignite spontaneously, must immediately be deposited in a covered metal container or be removed to a safe place without delay.

- Extreme care must be taken to prevent any solid residue resulting from a highly flammable liquid containing cellulose nitrate being deposited on a surface which is liable to attain a temperature of 120° Celsius. The implements used to remove such residues must not be of iron or steel. Steps should be taken also to prevent the deposit or formation of any other solid waste residue resulting from a process or operation involving a highly flammable liquid. Such deposits as do occur must be removed to a safe place as often as may be necessary to avoid the risk of fire.

Preventing the escape of vapours

• All practicable steps (including the installation and maintenance of an adequate exhaust ventilation system) must be taken to prevent vapours from highly flammable liquids escaping into the general atmosphere of a workroom. All ducts, trunks and casings used in connection with an exhaust ventilation system must be fire-resisting structures. For obvious reasons, electric motors used to power exhaust ventilation systems must not be sited in the path of highly flammable vapours. Furthermore, the vents through which such vapours are discharged into the atmosphere must be fitted with suitable and efficient flame arrestors.

• If it is reasonably practicable for a particular process or operation (which gives rise to a dangerous concentration of highly flammable vapours) to be carried on in a fire-resistant, cabinet or other suitable enclosure, the work must be carried in just such a cabinet or enclosure — which must be equipped with its own powered exhaust. ventilation system designed to prevent the escape of those vapours into any workroom. However, natural ventilation will suffice in the case of a batch-loaded, box-type oven used to evaporate highly flammable liquid if the oven has a capacity of less than one-and-a-half cubic metres.

Ignition and burning of highly flammable liquids

• A highly flammable liquid must not be ignited (whether as part of a production process or in order to dispose of it) except in plant or apparatus specifically designed and properly used for that purpose. If the sole purpose is to dispose of any highly flammable liquid as waste, it must be burnt either in the plant or apparatus referred to or by a competent person in a safe manner and in a safe place.

- These requirements do not, however, apply if a highly flammable liquid is burnt by a competent person as part of a fire-fighting training exercise, so long as the training is carried out under the direct and continuous supervision of a competent person.

DUTIES OF EMPLOYEES

- Persons employed in factories and other places to which the 1972 Regulations apply must not intentionally or recklessly interfere with any plant, equipment or appliance provided by their employer in compliance with those Regulations. Given the

---

Table 1

METHODS FOR THE DETERMINATION OF FLASH POINT

The Chemicals (Hazard Information & Packaging for Supply Regulations 1994 (SI 1994/3247)
Schedule 1, Part III

1. For the purpose of classifying a substance or preparation dangerous for supply in accordance with Part I of this Schedule the flash point shall be determined —

(a) by one of the equilibrium methods referred to in paragraph 3, or

(b) by one of the non-equilibrium methods referred to In paragraph 4, except that when the flash point so determined falls within one of the following ranges, namely:-

    (i)   - 2°C to + 2°C
    (ii)   19°C to 23°C, or
    (iii)   53°C to 57°C.

that flash point shall be confirmed by one of the equilibrium methods referred to in paragraph 3 using like apparatus

2. The use of any method or apparatus referred to in paragraphs 3, 4 and 5 is subject to the conditions specified in the appropriate standard particularly having regard to the nature of the substance (eg viscosity) and to the flash point range and also to the advice provided in paragraphs 21 to 25 of the approved classification and labelling guide.

(Continued overleaf)

Table 1 (Continued)

---

3. The equilibrium methods referred to in paragraph l(a) are those defined in the following standards, namely, International Standards ISO 1516, ISO 3680, ISO 1523 and ISO 3679.

4. The non-equilibrium methods referred to in paragraph 1(b) use the apparatus referred to below in accordance with the following standards namely —

(a) Abel Apparatus —

    (i)   British Standard BS 2000 Part 170,
    (ii)   French Standard NF M07– 011,
    (iii)   French Standard NF T66 – 009:

(b) Abel-Pensky Apparatus —

    (i)   German Standard DIN 51755. Part I (for temperatures from 5 to 65 degrees C),
    (ii)   German Standard DIN 51755. Part 2 (for temperatures below 5 degrees C),
    (iii)   French Standard NF M07~136.
    (iv)   European Standard EN 57:

(c) Tag Apparatus —

    (i)   American Standard ASTM D-56;

(d) Pensky-Martens Apparatus —

    (i)   British Standard BS 6664 Part 5,
    (ii)   International Standard ISO 2719,
    (iii)   American Standard ASTM D-93.
    (iv)   French Standard NF M07-019.
    (v)   German Standard DIN 5175S,
    (vi)   European Standard EN 11.

5. To determine the flash point of viscous liquids (paints, gums and similar) containing solvents, only apparatus and test methods suitable for determining the flash point of viscous liquids may be used namely —

International Standards ISO 3679, ISO 3680, ISO 1523, and German Standard DIN 53213. Part 1.

---

hazards associated with the storage and use of LPG and highly flammable liquids, employees must cooperate fully with their employers' efforts to prevent or minimise any risk to their health and safety.

- Employees must not smoke (or carry matches or lighters) in designated 'No Smoking' areas. Furthermore, they have a duty in law notify their immediate supervisor or manager immediately if they discover any defect in the plant, equipment and appliance provided for their use and/or protection

LIQUEFIED PETROLEUM GAS

- Quantities of liquefied petroleum gas (or LPG) must be stored either below ground in suitable reservoirs or tanks (the upper surfaces of which must be wholly or mainly in the open air) or in suitable fixed storage tanks or fixed storage vessels safely situated out of doors. LPG may also be kept in any pipeline or pump forming part of a totally enclosed pipeline system. Cylinders containing LPG should ordinarily be stored in safe positions out of doors or, if that is not reasonably practicable, in a fire-resistant cupboard or storeroom constructed specifically for that purpose.

  Note: For these purposes "cylinder" means a cylinder which complies with the relevant provisions in the Pressure Systems & Transportable Gas Containers Regulations 1989 (SI 1989/2169) as to which see the section titled **Pressure systems and transportable gas containers** elsewhere in this handbook.

- In most other respects the rules relating to the storage of LPG are the same as those which apply to highly flammable liquids (rules about minimum quantities, aerosol dispensers, LPG in the fuel tanks of vehicles, and so on), except that tanks, bins, cupboards, cylinders and the like in which LPG is stored must be marked with the words "Highly Flammable — LPG"

- Cylinders containing LPG should only be removed from the cupboard or place in which they are stored in the quantities needed at the time (e.g., one at a time). Empty cylinders should be returned promptly after use and refilled without delay.

PETROLEUM SPIRIT

- Any person, employer or otherwise, who wishes to store more than 15 litres of petroleum spirit on his premises (that is to say petroleum having a flash point of less than 21°C), must obtain a licence from his local authority.

- The law regulating the keeping, storage, labelling and transport of petroleum spirit is laid down in the Petroleum

(Consolidation) Act 1928, as modified by the Health & Safety (Miscellaneous Provisions) (Metrication etc.) Regulations 1992 (SI 1992/1811).

FURTHER INFORMATION

• The following HSE publications are available from HSE Books at the address given on page 328:

Notices/Posters

F.2440
Highly flammable liquids etc
ISBN 0 7176 0434 9   £2.98 + VAT

Legal

COP 6
Plastic containers with nominal capacities up to 5 litres for petroleum spirit: Requirements for testing and marking or labelling (in support of SI 1982/830) [1982]
ISBN 0 11 883643 9   £2.00

Guidance notes

CS 4
Keeping LPG in cylinders and similar containers [1986]
ISBN 0 7176 0631 7   £3.25

CS 8
Small scale storage and display of LPG at retail premises [1985] ISBN 0 11 883614 5   £2.50

CS 15
Cleaning and gas freeing of tanks containing flammable residues [1985]
ISBN 0 11 883518 1   £2.50

Liquefied petroleum gas storage & use: open learning pack [1993]
ISBN 0 7176 0649 X   £14.50

HS(G) 34
Storage of LPG at fixed installations [1987]
ISBN 0 11 883908 X   £6.00

HS(G) 41
Petrol filling stations: construction and operation [1990]
ISBN 0 7176 0461 6 £6.00

HS(G) 50
The storage of flammable liquids in fixed tanks (up to 10,000 m³ total capacity) [1990]
ISBN 0 11 885532 8 £4.50

HS(G) 51
The storage of flammable liquids in containers [1990]
ISBN 0 7176 0481 0 £4.50

HS(G) 52
The storage of flammable liquids in fixed tanks (exceeding 10,000 m³) total capacity) [1991]
ISBN 0 11 885538 7 £4.50

GS 40
Loading and unloading of bulk flammable liquids and gases at harbours and inland waterways [1986]
ISBN 0 7176 1230 9   £5.00

Guidance on health and safety monitoring in the petroleum industry [1992]
ISBN 0 11 886376 2 £2.50

Guidance on multi-skilling in the petroleum industry [1992]
ISBN 0 11 886319 3   £2.00

Guidance on permit-to-work systems in the petroleum industry [1997]
ISBN 0 7176 1281 3   £8.50

Free leaflets (Telephone 01787 881165)

INDG 50
Safe use of petrol in garages (pocket card)

INDG 78
Transport of LPG cylinders by road

INDG 104
Petrol filling stations

HOISTS & LIFTS

Key points

- Every hoist or lift — whether used for carrying passengers or goods — must be of good mechanical construction, sound material and adequate strength, and must be properly maintained (section 22(1), Factories Act 1961).

- Furthermore, every hoist or lift must be thoroughly examined by a competent person at least once in every period of six months, and a written report containing the results of the examination produced within 28 days of the date on which the examination took place. The report should be attached to the General Register (Form F31, F35 or F36, as appropriate) and must be produced for inspection by a health and safety inspector on demand. The report may be stored on computer so long as a 'hard copy' can be produced at short notice.

  Note: A lifting machine or appliance, which does not have a platform or cage, and the direction of movement of which is restricted by a guide or guides, is not a hoist or lift for these purposes *(ibid;* section 25(1)). A continuous hoist or lift need only be examined once in every period of 12 months *(ibid,* section 25(2)).

- The particulars to be included in the report are those required by the Lifting Plant & Equipment (Record of Test & Examination etc.) Regulations 1992 (SI 1992/195), as described in **Table 1** on page 390 *(ibid;* section 22(2)).

- If the six-monthly thorough examination (and accompanying report) reveal that the hoist or lift cannot continue to be used with safety unless certain repairs are carried out immediately or within a specified time, the person who authenticated and signed the report (the owner or occupier of the premises in question) must see to it that his nearest area office of the Health & Safety Executive (see pages 368 to 372) is sent a copy of the report not later than 28 days after the date on which the examination was carried out.

- The six-monthly (or more frequent) examinations of hoists and lifts should ordinarily be undertaken by a qualified engineer. Nowadays, it is commonplace for such examinations to be carried out by the manufacturer or supplier under the terms of a maintenance agreement. However it is for the factory occupier in each case to ensure that his hoists or lifts are properly maintained and examined, that reports of every thorough examination are kept on file, and that copies are sent to the HSE when urgent repairs are recommended.

Passenger-carrying lifts

- Lifts and hoists used to carry passengers (whether accompanied by goods or otherwise) must be fitted with efficient automatic devices designed to prevent the cage or platform overruning. Lift or cage doors giving access to the various stages or landings must be designed to prevent the lift moving upwards or downwards when the doors are open. Modern lifts and hoists (constructed or reconstructed after 29 July 1937), which are suspended by ropes or chains, must be supported by at least two ropes or chains separately connected, each capable of carrying the whole weight of the platform or cage and its maximum working load. Efficient devices must also be provided and maintained which will support the platform or cage with its maximum working load should the supporting chains or ropes (or their attachments) suddenly break (*ibid*; section 23.

- The Safe Working Load (SWL) or passenger-carrying capacity of every hoist and lift must be conspicuously marked inside or adjacent to the lift itself.

Exemptions

- The Hoists Exemption Order 1962 (SI 1962/715) lists some 14 types of hoists and lifts which are exempted from some or all of the requirements of sections 22 to 25 of the Factories Act 1961, subject to such conditions or limitations (if any) as are laid down in the Schedule to the Order (copies of which are available from HMSO).

Building operations, etc.

- For Regulations concerning the construction, installation, maintenance and examination of hoists used on construction sites, and at works of engineering construction, see **Construction work** elsewhere in this handbook.

Table 1

PARTICULARS REQUIRED IN RECORDS TO BE MADE FOLLOWING THE THOROUGH EXAMINATION OF A LIFTING APPLIANCE
as prescribed by the Lifting Plant & Equipment (Records of Test & Examination etc.) Regulations 1992
(SI 1992/195)

1. Description, identification mark and location of the equipment referred to.

2. Date of the last thorough examination and number of the record of such thorough examination.

3. The safe working load (or loads) and (where relevant) corresponding radii.

4. The date of the most recent test and examination or test and thorough examination and the date and number of other identification of the record of it.

5. Details of any defects found and, where appropriate, a statement of the time by when each defect shall be rectified.

6. Date of completion of the thorough examination.

7. Latest date by which the next thorough examination should be carried out.

8. A declaration that the information is correct and that the equipment has been thoroughly examined in accordance with the appropriate provisions and is found free from any defect likely to affect safety, other than any recorded by virtue of item 5 above.

9. Name and address of the owner of the equipment.

10. Name and address of the person responsible for the thorough examination.

11. Date the record of the thorough examination is made.

12. Name and address of the person authenticating the record.

13. A reference number or some other means of identifying the record.

Note: Form F2530 ('*Record of thorough examination of lifting plant*') available from HSE Books, see *FURTHER INFORMATION* below may be used for this purpose, but there is no obligation to do so.

Offices, shops and railway premises

- Hoists or lifts in use in premises to which the Offices, Shops and Railway Premises Act 1963 applies (whether those lifts, etc. are used for the carriage of persons or goods, or both) must be properly maintained, and must be examined by a competent person at least once in every period of six months.

- The particulars to be included in the report of every thorough examination of a hoist or lift installed in premises to which the 1963 Act are those listed in **Table 1** opposite. Every such report and its accompanying results must be produced within 28 days and kept on file for inspection on demand by a local authority health and safety inspector. If the report calls for immediate or urgent repairs, a copy of the report must likewise be forwarded to the relevant local authority within 28 days.

  See also the section titled **Chains, ropes & lifting tackle** and the summary on page 141 *et seq.* of the principal provisions of the Construction (Lifting Operations) Regulations 1961 (notably in relation to the maintenance and routine tests and examinations of cranes and other lifting machines).

FURTHER INFORMATION

- The following leaflets and publications are available from HSE Books at the address given on page 328.

  HS(R)26
  Guidance on the legal and administrative measures taken to implement the European Community Directives on Lifting and Mechanical Handling Appliances and Electrically Operated Lifts [1987]
  ISBN 0 11 883962 4   £3.50

  PM 7
  Lifts: thorough examination and testing [1982]
  ISBN 0 11 883546 7   £2.50

  PM 24
  Safety at rack and pinion hoists [1981]
  ISBN 0 11 883398 7   £2.50

PM 26
Safety at lift landings [1981]
ISBN 0 11 883383 9   £2.50

PM 63
Inclined hoists used in building and construction work [1987] ISBN 0
11 883945 4   £2.50

HOLIDAYS, ANNUAL
(and the 'Working Time Directive')

Key points

- Under current UK legislation, employees have no statutory right to annual holidays (paid or otherwise). However, every employee has the statutory right, under section 1 of the Employment Rights Act 1996, to receive a written statement from his (or her) employer explaining the terms and conditions of his employment — including his contractual right (if any) to paid annual holidays. If a particular employee has no entitlement to annual holidays, that fact must be mentioned in the statement. A 'Nil Return' on this issue is unacceptable.

- The law relating to annual holidays is set to change. With the coming into operation, on 23 November 1996, of EU Council Directive 93/104/EC 'concerning certain aspects of the organisation of working time' (commonly referred to as the 'Working Time Directive'), a reluctant British Government must now take steps to adopt the measures contained in the Directive — including the right to paid annual holidays (see next paragraph) — by introducing appropriate national legislation. Until that happens, the measures contained in the Working Time Directive prevail and are arguably already enforceable in UK tribunals and courts, not to mention the European Court of Justice [ECJ])(but see *Transitional period* below).

  Note: Strictly speaking, the Working Time Directive already applies to persons (such as civil and public servants) who are employed by 'emanations of the State' (Government departments, local authorities, and the like). For workers in the private sector, an employer's failure to follow the terms of the directive (compounded, perhaps, by the UK Government's dilatoriness in introducing appropriate national legislation) could be challenged before UK tribunals and courts (and ultimately the European Court of Justice).

- Article 7 of the Directive requires every Member State of the European Union to introduce legislation designed to ensure that *every* worker receives a minimum of four weeks' paid annual holidays "in accordance with the conditions for entitlement to, and granting such, leave laid down by national legislation and/or practice". Furthermore, a worker's entitlement to those four weeks may not lawfully be replaced by a payment in lieu except when the worker resigns or is dismissed from his employment. It should, perhaps, be pointed out that the Working Time Directive makes no distinction between part-time and full-time employees. Each will have the right to four weeks' paid annual holiday, regardless of the length of the working week.

Transitional period

- Point 1(b)(ii) of Article 18 does, however, provide the option of a 'breathing space' or transitional period. In short, the UK Government (and other Member States) need not adopt Article 7 of the Directive in full until 23 November 1999, *subject to the proviso* that every worker must, in the meantime, be allowed a minimum of three weeks' paid annual holidays (which, as with the full four-week entitlement, cannot lawfully be replaced by a payment of money in lieu). Whether the UK Government plans to take advantage of the transitional period will become clear when the draft new legislation is laid before Parliament (mid-1997?)

Advice for employers (pending new legislation)

- In the meantime, employers whose employees are already entitled to a minimum of four weeks' paid annual holidays need do no more than check that there is nothing in their contracts of employment which allows them to convert some or all of that annual entitlement into cash (for example, should they choose either to take no holidays at all in a particular holiday year or to take only some of those holidays). Given that the Working Time Directive was introduced (controversially) as a 'health and safety measure' under Article 118a of the Treaty of Rome, it is contrary to the spirit of the Directive for employees to be permitted (or to be 'persuaded') to forfeit their annual holidays in return for a cash payment. Nor should they be allowed to 'roll-over' a particular year's holiday entitlement into the next or any subsequent holiday year.

- Employers who allow their workers fewer than three weeks' paid annual holidays (or, exceptionally, allow them no annual holidays at all) would be well-advised to amend the contract of employment of every person in their employ to ensure that it complies fully with Article 7 of the Working Time Directive and with legislation shortly to be introduced by the UK Government. Should those same employers decide to 'sit tight', they might well face challenges before an industrial tribunal (or before the ECJ) and the possibility (perhaps likelihood) of being ordered to pay compensation (backdated to 23 November 1996).

Written particulars of terms of employment

- As was indicated in the preamble to this section, section 1 of the Employment Rights Act 1996 requires employers to issue every employee (part-time as well as full-time) with a written statement outlining the terms and conditions of his (or her) employment. In addition to information about the employee's job title, rate of pay, sickness benefits, and the like, the statement must explain the employee's entitlement (if any) to holidays, including public holidays (paid or unpaid) — which information must be sufficiently detailed so as to enable the employee to calculate his entitlement to accrued holiday pay on the termination of his employment (*ibid*; section 1(4)(d)(i)).

- Furthermore, that information must be given in the "principal statement" itself. It is no longer permissible for an employer to refer an employee to a collective agreement or some other document for information about his holiday entitlement — however accessible that other document may be (*ibid*; section 2(4)). Bearing in mind that the Working Time Directive must soon be imported into UK legislation, employers have little to gain by denying paid annual holidays. As was suggested earlier, that legislation might well be back-dated to 23 November 1996 — although this is by no means certain..

- If an employee is not entitled to annual holidays (paid or otherwise), the statement *must* say so in as many words (*ibid*; section 2(1)). If it makes no mention of holidays, and the employer refuses to amend it, the employee has the right, effectively, to invite an industrial tribunal to re-write the statement for him. If this happens, the particulars about holidays and holiday pay inserted by the tribunal will be 'read into' the employee's contract of employment — to be enforced by a tribunal or court if the employer refuses to comply (*ibid*; section 11). It should be emphasised that an employee has the right to refer his (or her) employer's intransigence to an industrial tribunal while he is still employed. He does not have to resign in order to do so, nor (as is demonstrated in the next paragraph) can he lawfully be dismissed for exercising that right.

- If an employee is dismissed (either for questioning his [or her] employer's failure to comply with section 1 of the 1996 Act or for referring the matter to an industrial tribunal), that dismissal will be held to have been unfair and compensation will be awarded (*ibid*; section 104). An employee may present a complaint of unfair dismissal in such circumstances (including a claim for damages arising out of any breach of contract), regardless of his age or length of service at the time of his dismissal. But the complaint must be presented within three months of the effective date of termination. If the complaint is upheld, the employer will be ordered to pay compensation.

Note: Section 21(3)(b)(i) of the Shops Act 1950 (which was repealed on 1 December 1994 by sections 23 and 24 of the Deregulation & Contracting Out Act 1994, per SI 1994/3037) stated that shop assistants employed under the so-called Catering Trade Scheme — that is to say, wholly or mainly in connection with the sale of food or drink (including alcohol) for consumption on their employer's premises — had to be allowed at least 32 whole weekdays as holidays in every calendar year; six of which had to be consecutive and on full pay. Their employer could spread the remaining 26 days (which could be unpaid) over the rest of the year — on days other than Sundays — so long as at least two of those days fell within the currency of each month. Although the 1950 Act has been repealed, staff recruited before 1 December 1994 still enjoy the contractual (if not the strict statutory right) to those 32 days each year — given that the conditions of employment laid down in Part II of the 1950 Act were imported into their contracts of employment and *remain* part of their terms and conditions of employment.

See also **Canteens & rest rooms, Meals for employees, Pregnant employees & nursing mothers**, and **Working hours** elsewhere in this handbook.

HUMID FACTORIES

Key points

- A 'humid factory' is one in which atmospheric humidity is artificially produced by steaming or other means in connection with any textile process (section 176(1), Factories Act 1961).

- Before producing artificial humidity on his premises for the first time, the occupier of a factory must write to his nearest area office of the Health & Safety Executive (see pages 368 to 372) informing them of his intentions (*ibid*; section 68(1)).

- He must also provide and maintain two hygrometers (and a thermometer close to each hygrometer) in every workroom in which artificial humidity is produced — one at the centre of the room, and the other at the side; and both clearly visible to the people working in the room. Readings from each hygrometer and thermometer must be taken between ten and eleven o'clock in the morning on every day that persons are employed in the room in the morning, and between three and four o'clock in the afternoon on every day that persons are employed in the room in the afternoon, and at such other times as the health and safety (or factory) inspector may direct. The records of all temperature readings must be retained for at least two years from the date on which each of those readings was taken, and must immediately be made available for examination by any employee who asks to see them, together with any additional information the employee needs to enable him (or her) to interpret them (*ibid*; section 68(3) & (4)).

- There must be no artificial humidity in any room at any time when the reading of the wet bulb thermometer exceeds 22.5 degrees Celsius (72.5 degrees Fahrenheit) or, in the case of a room in which cotton, merino or cashmere is spun by the French or dry process (or in which wool is spun or combed by that same process), 27 degrees Celsius (80 degrees Fahrenheit). Nor may artificial humidity be produced if at any time the difference between the readings of the dry and wet bulb thermometers is less than 2 degrees Celsius (4 degrees Fahrenheit). However, the occupier of the factory may notify the factory inspectorate that the atmospheric humidity in one or more nominated workrooms will never be greater than that needed to maintain a difference of at least 2 degrees Celsius between the readings of the wet and dry bulb thermometers. So long as that difference is maintained, the morning and afternoon readings and the accompanying records referred to in the previous paragraph need not be taken or retained (*ibid*, section 68(8)).

Note: A factory inspector may approve the fixing of only one hygrometer in a workroom. But such approval must be sought and given in writing.

- Water which is likely to pose a health risk, or yield effluvia, must not be used for artificial humidification. For these purposes, any water which absorbs (from an acid solution of permanganate of potash in four hours at 16 degrees Celsius) more that half a grain of oxygen per gallon of water (or 7 milligrams of oxygen per litre) will deemed injurious to health (*ibid*; section 68(6)).

Special Regulations

- Similar provisions are to be found in the following Special Regulations still in force for certain textile factories in which artificial humidity is employed in certain processes. These are:

  o   the **Flax & Tow (Spinning & Weaving) Regulations 1906** (SR & O 1906/177) — Regulations 4, 5 & 6;

  o   the **Hemp Spinning & Weaving Regulations 1907** (SR & O 1907/660) — Regulations 6 (hygrometer and thermometer to be positioned adjacent to one another, and readings to be taken between 11 and 12 am and between 4 and 5 pm);

  o   the **Cotton Cloth Factories Regulations 1929** (SR & O 1929/300) — Regulations 3 & 4 (two hygrometers and a thermometer positioned adjacent to each hygrometer, plus one extra hygrometer and thermometer for every 500 looms [or part of 500 looms in excess of 700], and readings to be taken between 15 and 30 minutes from the time work commences and, again between 11 am and 12 noon and [except on Saturdays] between 4 pm and 5 pm); and

  o   the **Jute (Safety, Health & Welfare) Regulations 1948** (SI 1948/1696) — Regulations 17 & 18 (a hygrometer and thermometer [close to the hygrometer] in the centre of the room and, at the direction of a health and safety inspector, a similar arrangement either at the side of the room in such other position as the inspector directs).

Note: Under the 1948 Regulations (*q.v.*), there must be no artificial humidification in any room at any time when the reading of the wet bulb thermometer in that room exceeds 22.5 degrees Celsius, or the difference between the reading of the wet bulb thermometer and the reading of the dry bulb thermometer is less than 2 degrees Celsius, If the reading of the wet-bulb thermometer in any room exceeds 24 degrees Celsius while work is going on in that room, all available means of ventilation and of reducing the temperature must be put into operation and kept in operation until the reading falls to 22.5 degrees Celsius.

See also **Temperature in workrooms** elsewhere in this handbook.

I

IMPROVEMENT NOTICES
(Health & Safety)

Key points

- After conducting a routine inspection of a workplace, a health and safety inspector may quietly draw certain matters to the attention to the owner or occupier (e.g., a slippery floor, faulty electrical equipment, filthy toilets, overcrowding, poor ventilation or light, an unguarded machine, an obstructed fire door, and so on). On a second occasion, if there is still evidence of a breach of health and safety legislation, the inspector will very likely serve an improvement notice on the employer or person having control of the premises effectively ordering him "to put matters to rights" (within a maximum period of 21 days) or face prosecution. (see *Notes* below).

- Any person on whom an improvement notice has been served has 21 days within which to lodge an appeal to an industrial tribunal. Doing so has the effect of suspending the operation of the notice until the appeal is finally disposed of or, if the appeal is withdrawn, until the withdrawal of the appeal.

- An appeal must be in writing and contain the following particulars:

  (a)   the name of the appellant and his address for the service of documents

  (b)   the date of the improvement notice appealed against and the address of the premises or place concerned;

  (c)   the name and address of the respondent;

  (d)   particulars of the requirements or directions appealed against; and

  (e)   the grounds for the appeal.

- Once completed, the appeal should be sent to the Secretary of the Tribunals at one or other of the following addresses:

  England & Wales
  Central Office of the Industrial Tribunals
  Southgate Street
  BURY ST EDMUNDS
  Suffolk
  IP33 2AQ

  Telephone: 01284 762300
  Fax: 01284 766334

  Scotland
  Central Office of the Industrial Tribunals
  St Andrew's House
  141 West Nile Street
  GLASGOW
  G1 2RU

  Telephone: 0141-331 1601
  Fax: 0141-332 3316

- Upon receipt of the notice of appeal, the Secretary of the Tribunals will enter the relevant particulars in a register and will send a copy to the relevant enforcing authority (viz. the HSE or local authority whose inspector issued the Improvement Notice in the first place). In due course, both parties will be informed of the time, date and place fixed for the hearing. Either party may produce witnesses and documents, and may be represented by counsel or by a solicitor or any other person whom they have elected to represent them (including, in the case of the appellant, a representative of a trade union or employer's association).

- At the appeal hearing, either party is entitled to make an opening statement, to give evidence on his own behalf, to call witnesses, to cross-examine any witnesses called by the other party, and to address the tribunal.

- The decision of the tribunal (which normally consists of a chairman and two lay members) may be taken by a majority and will be recorded in a document signed by the chairman and containing the reasons for the decision. An appeal from the decision of the industrial tribunal will be heard by the Court of Appeal.

- A full outline of the rules of procedure in such cases is to be found in the Industrial Tribunals (Constitution & Rules of Procedure) Regulations 1993 (SI 1993/2687) (ISBN 0 11 033137 0), available from The Stationery Office (see page 328), price £6.75 net. The power of an inspector to issue an improvement notice, and the question of appeals, are described in sections 21, 23 and 24 of the Health and Safety at Work, etc., Act, 1974.

  Note: When hearing an appeal against the service of either a prohibition notice or an improvement notice, the tribunal in question may appoint one or more assessors (specialists) to assist in the deliberations (*ibid*; section 24(4)).

Notes

- A health and safety inspector will serve an improvement notice if he is of the opinion that a person has contravened one or more of the *relevant statutory provisions* or in circumstances that make it likely that the contravention will continue or be repeated.

- The expression *relevant statutory provisions* refers to the Health & Safety at Work etc. Act 1974 and statutes and regulations made under or saved by that Act. In short: any current health and safety legislation which imposes duties on employers.

Offences and penalties

- It is an offence for a person to contravene any requirement imposed by an improvement notice (including any such notice as modified on appeal). The penalty, on summary conviction, is a fine of up to £20,000 and/or imprisonment for a term not exceeding six months; or, on conviction on indictment, a fine of an unlimited amount and/or imprisonment for a term not exceeding two years (section 33(1)(g) and (2A), Health and Safety at Work, etc., Act 1974).

  See also **Inspectors, Powers of, Offences & penalties** and **Prohibition Notices** elsewhere in this handbook.

INDUSTRIAL INJURIES *(Social Security Benefits)*

Key points

- Before the Employers' Statutory Sick Pay (ESSP) Scheme was introduced (April 1983), an employee disabled as a result of an accident at work or who had contracted a prescribed industrial disease, would qualify to receive Industrial Injury Benefit from the State.

- The Benefit, which was non-contributory (in the sense that it was not funded by employers' and employees' NI contributions) was payable for a maximum period of 26 weeks from the date of the industrial accident or the development of the industrial disease. If an employee was still incapable of work at the end of 26 weeks, the Injury Benefit would have been supplanted by Sickness Benefit, Invalidity Benefit or non-contributory Invalidity Pension. In the appropriate circumstances, he would also have received a Disablement Benefit.

ACCIDENTS AND DISEASES ON OR AFTER 6 APRIL 1983

- Industrial Injury Benefits (so-called) are no longer payable. Nowadays, any employee who is incapacitated for work because of ill health, injury or disease will ordinarily qualify to be paid statutory sick pay (SSP) by his (or her) employer for up to 28 weeks in any one period of incapacity for work. If, for one reason or another, he does not qualify for SSP (or he has exhausted his entitlement), his employer will issue him with a so-called 'changeover form' (form SSP 1) which, on presentation to the DSS, will entitle him to received the State Sickness Benefit (even if he has not paid sufficient [or any] National Insurance contributions. If he is still incapacitated for work at the end of 28 weeks, he will automatically qualify for Invalidity Benefit and will also qualify for Industrial Injuries Disablement Benefit. As is explained below, just how much he will receive will depend to a large extent on the severity of his disability.

SOCIAL SECURITY SICKNESS BENEFIT

- Social Security Sickness Benefit is payable for a maximum period of 28 weeks (168 days, excluding Sundays) in a period of interruption of employment, or — in circumstances where a sick or disabled employee has received SSP from his employer within the preceding eight weeks and his employer's liability to pay SSP has ended — for a maximum 20 weeks (120 days, excluding Sundays).

- The State Sickness Benefit is not normally paid for the first three days (called "waiting days") in a period of interruption of employment or if an employee is off work for less than four consecutive days (excluding Sundays). However, the question of "waiting days" and "Nil Benefit" for the first four days does not arise if the employee has recently received SSP from his employer. For a more exhaustive treatment of the subject, the reader is urged to obtain a copy of DSS Booklet NI16: *SSP and Sickness Benefit.*

- The current weekly rates of Sickness Benefit are listed in DSS leaflet NI 196 (copies of which are available on request from local offices of the DSS).

INVALIDITY BENEFIT

- Invalidity Benefit — payable if an employee is still incapacitated for work at the end of 28 weeks after injury or the onset of a prescribed industrial disease — consists of an Invalidity Pension, plus an Invalidity Allowance, the amount of which depends on the age of the employee at the time of his incapacity. For further particulars, see DSS Leaflet FB 28.

INDUSTRIAL INJURIES DISABLEMENT BENEFIT

- Industrial Injuries Disablement Benefit is payable (in addition to Invalidity Benefit) unless the claimant is self-employed. Disablement Benefit is a weekly pension or lump sum gratuity payable to an employee who has suffered any loss of physical or mental faculty as a result of an accident at work or the onset of a prescribed industrial disease (the meanings of which expressions are examined later in this section). Disablement Benefit is not payable until 15 weeks (90 days, excluding Sundays) have elapsed since the date of the accident or the date of onset of the disease.

- The expression "loss of physical or mental faculty" means some impairment of the employee's ability to enjoy a normal life and includes disfigurement even though this may have caused no bodily handicap or prevented the employee from carrying out his normal duties in his job. The loss of faculty is assessed by an independent medical board by comparing the employee's condition with the condition of a normal healthy person of the same age and sex.. The assessment is expressed in percentage terms. Thus, a 100 per cent assessment implies serious disablement (such as total loss of sight), whereas, to quote an example, the loss of an index finger has been assessed as a 14 per cent disablement. A person whose disability is assessed as less than 14 per cent will not qualify for the Benefit.

- To find out how to claim Industrial Injuries Disablement Benefit, an employee who has been injured at work or who has contracted a work-related disease should first obtain a copy of DSS leaflet NI6 (*Industrial Injuries Disablement Benefit*) which will tell him which form he needs to complete to progress his claim. There are different forms for different diseases (e.g., one for pneumoconiosis or byssinosis, another for chronic bronchitis and/or emphysema, still others for work-related deafness, asthma, asbestosis and so on).

- Once completed, the claim form should be despatched to: Department of Social Security. Aldershot Benefits Office. Hippodrome House. Birchett Road. Aldershot .Hants GU11 1NP. It will then be for an independent medical board to decide whether the claimant has suffered a loss of faculty as a result of the accident or disease and, if so, to assess the amount of disablement benefit and for how long.

Amount of disablement benefit

- When an assessment has been made, the local Social Security Insurance Officer will decide the rate and period for which the Disablement Benefit will be paid. The assessment of the medical board may be for life if there is permanent disability and little chance of recovery, or for a limited period (subject to review) if the employee is likely to make a full recovery. A provisional assessment may also be made for a limited period, at the end of which time the employee will be re-examined with a view to a further assessment.

- A summary of State Sickness and Disability Benefits, and the circumstances in which those benefits are payable, is provided by DSS Leaflet FB28, copies of which are usually to be found in post offices and libraries or can be obtained by telephoning the nearest Social Security office. Social Security benefit rates are reviewed every year and are listed in DSS leaflet NI 196.

MEANING OF 'ACCIDENT AT WORK'

- For industrial injuries benefit purposes, an employee is deemed to have suffered an accident at work if he was injured in the course of his employment, unless there is evidence to the contrary. For example, an employee will not normally be considered to have been injured in the course of his employment if he was travelling to or from his place of work at the material time (unless travelling in a vehicle provided by his employer).

- An accident will be treated as having happened at an employee's place of work if it occurred while the employee was doing something he was employed to do, or because his employment exposed him to a special risk, or if it occurred whilst he was providing help and assistance in an emergency (such as an outbreak of fire).

- If, at the time of the accident, an employee was doing something prohibited by his employer (or by law), he (or she) will nonetheless qualify for benefit — provided that what he was doing at the time was for the purpose of his employer's business and was within the scope of his job (e.g. operating a machine without a guard). In exceptional circumstances, an employee may qualify for benefit if he was injured while skylarking with his workmates, if he was working at the time and his injuries occurred through no fault of his own.

MEANING OF "PRESCRIBED INDUSTRIAL DISEASE"

- There are some 60 prescribed industrial diseases (i.e. diseases contracted in the course of employment and attributable to that employment) which would qualify a sufferer to receive Industrial Injuries Disablement Benefit. These range from angiosarcoma of the liver (arising out of work with vinyl chloride monomer) to miner's nystagmus (work in mines) and viral hepatitis (close and frequent contact with human blood and human blood products). A complete list of those diseases (and the occupations from which each is likely to arise) is given in The Social Security (Industrial Injuries)(Prescribed Diseases)

Regulations 1985 (SI 1985/967)(as amended) and in associated leaflets provided by the DSS.

- See **the Tables** on pages 407 to 424 for the current list of prescribed industrial diseases.

DEATH BENEFIT

- If an employee is killed as a result of an accident arising out of or in the course of his (or her) employment, or dies in consequence of his having contracted a prescribed industrial disease (since 4 July 1948), his dependants may be entitled to be paid industrial death benefit. This consists of a widow's pension (for the first 26 weeks and, thereafter, at a higher permanent or lower permanent rate, depending on age and circumstances at the time of her husband's death), allowances for dependent children, a widow's allowance, benefits for close relations, etc. and a widower's allowance (if permanently incapacitated at the time of his wife's death and his wife had been contributing more than the cost of his upkeep); and so on. A claim form for industrial death benefit can be obtained from the local Social Security office (details also in leaflet Nl 10 available from the same source).

REPORTING OF INDUSTRIAL ACCIDENTS

- If an employee is injured in the course of his (or her) employment, he must report the matter immediately to his supervisor or manager. If his employer maintains an Accident Book (obligatory in premises in which 10 or more people are employed), the relevant particulars must be entered in that book. If details of the accident have not been reported or recorded, the employee's claim to benefit may be delayed pending the outcome of an investigation into the circumstances (see **Accident book** elsewhere in this handbook).

REPORTING A CASE OF DISEASE

- Under the provisions of the Reporting of Injuries, Diseases & Dangerous Occurrences Regulations 1995 (SI 1995/3163), an employer has a duty in law to notify the "enforcing authority" immediately if any employee of his has been diagnosed AS suffering from one or other of the diseases specified in Schedule 2 to the Regulations (as to which see **Diseases, Reportable** elsewhere in this handbook.

- Accordingly, if an employee hands in a sick note from his doctor stating that he (or she) has contracted a reportable diseases (or the same diagnosis is made by an Employment Medical Adviser or 'appointed doctor' in the course of routine health surveillance), he must complete Form F2508A (ISBN 0 7176 1078 0), available from The Stationery Office — see page 328 for further details — and send it to the "relevant enforcing authority" without delay. A failure to do so is an offence under the 1985 Regulations, for which the penalty on conviction is a fine of up to £2,000.

Social Security (Industrial Injuries)
(Prescribed Diseases)
Regulations 1985 (SI 1985/967)
(as amended)
LIST OF PRESCRIBED DISEASES
AND THE OCCUPATIONS FOR WHICH THEY ARE
PRESCRIBED

Prescribed disease or injury	Occupation
A. *Condition due to physical agents*	
A1. Inflammation, ulceration or malignant disease of the skin or subcutaneous tissues or of the bones, or blood dyscrasia, or cataract, due to electro-magnetic radiations (other than radiant heat), or to ionising particles.	Any occupation involving exposure to electro-magnetic radiations (other than radiant heat) or to ionising particles.
A2. Heat cataract.	Any occupation involving frequent or prolonged exposure to rays from molten or red-hot material.

(Continued overleaf)

Prescribed Diseases (Cont.)

A3. Dysbarism, including decompression sickness, barotrauma and osteonecrosis.	Any occupation involving subjection to compressed or rarefied air or other respirable gases or gaseous mixtures.
A4. Cramp of the hand or forearm due to repetitive movements.	Any occupation involving prolonged periods of handwriting, typing or other repetitive movements of the fingers, hand or arm.
A5. Subcutaneous cellulitis of the hand (beat hand).	Any occupation involving manual labour causing severe or prolonged friction or pressure on the hand.
A6. Bursitis or subcutaneous cellulitis arising at or about the knee due to severe or prolonged external friction or pressure at or about the knee (beat knee).	Any occupation involving manual labour causing severe or prolonged external friction or pressure at or about the knee.
A7. Bursitis or subcutaneous cellulitis arising at or about the elbow due to severe or prolonged external friction or pressure at or about the elbow (beat elbow).	Any occupation involving manual labour causing severe or prolonged external friction or pressure at or about the elbow.
A8. Traumatic inflammation of the tendons of the hand or forearm, or of the associated tendon sheaths.	Any occupation involving manual labour, or frequent or repeated movements of the hand or wrist.
A9. Miner's nystagmus.	Any occupation involving work in or about a mine.
A10. Sensorineural hearing loss amounting to at least 50 dB in each ear, being the average of hearing losses at 1, 2 and 3 kHz frequencies, and being due in the case of at least one ear to occupational noise (occupational deafness).	Any occupation involving: (a) the use of powered (but not hand-powered) grinding tools on cast metal (other than weld metal) or on billets or blooms in the metal producing industry, or work

Prescribed Diseases (Cont.)

wholly or mainly in the immediate vicinity of those tools whilst they are being so used; or

(b) the use of pneumatic percussive tools on metal, or work wholly or mainly in the immediate vicinity of those tools whilst they are being so used; or

(c) the use of pneumatic percussive tools for drilling rock in quarries or underground or in mining coal, or work wholly or mainly in the immediate vicinity of those tools whilst they are being so used; or(

d) work wholly or mainly in the immediate vicinity of plant (excluding power press plant) engaged in the forging (including drop stamping) or metal by means of closed or open dies or drop hammers; or

(e) work in textile manufacturing where the work is undertaken wholly or mainly in rooms or sheds in which there are machines engaged in weaving man-made or natural (including mineral) fibres or in the high speed false twisting of fibres; or

(f) the use of, or work wholly or mainly in the immediate vicinity of, machines engaged in cutting, shaping or cleaning metal nails; or

(g) the use of, or work wholly or mainly in the immediate vicinity of,

(Continued)

Prescribed Diseases (Cont.)

plasma spray guns engaged in the deposition of metal: or

(h) the use of, or work wholly or mainly in the immediate vicinity of, any of the following machines engaged in the working of wood or material composed partly of wood, that is to say; multicutter moulding machines, planing machines, automatic or semi-automatic lathes, multiple cross-cut machines, automatic shaping machines, double-end tenoning machines, vertical spindle moulding machines (including high speed routing machines), edge banding machines, bandsawing machines with a blade width of not less than 75 millimetres and circular sawing machines in the operation of which the blade is moved towards the material being cut; or

(i) the use of chain saws in forestry.

A11. Episodic blanching, occurring throughout the year, affecting the middle or proximal phalanges or in the case of a thumb the proximal phalanx, of—

(a) in the case of a person with 5 fingers (including thumb) on one hand, any 3 of those fingers, or

(b) in the case of a person with only 4 such fingers, any 2 of those fingers. or

c) in the case of a person with less than 4 such fingers, any one of those fingers or. as the case may be, the (one remaining finger (vibration white finger).

Any occupation involving:

(a) the use of hand-held chain saws in forestry; or

(b) the use of hand-held rotary tools in grinding or in the sanding or polishing of metal, or the holding of material being ground, or metal being sanded or polished, by rotary tools; or

(c) the use of hand-held percussive metalworking tools, or the holding of metal being worked; upon by percussive tools, in riveting,

Prescribed Diseases (Cont.)

	caulking, chipping, hammering, fettling or swaging; or
	(d) the use of hand-held powered percussive drills or hand-held powered percussive hammers in mining, quarrying, demolition, or on roads or footpaths, including road construction: or
	(e) the holding of material being worked upon by pounding, machines in shoe manufacture.
A12. Carpal tunnel syndrome	Any occupation involving the use of hand-held vibrating tools
B. *Conditions due to biological agents*	
B1. Anthrax.	Contact with animals infected with anthrax or the handling (including the loading or unloading of transport) of animal products or residues.
B2. Glanders.	Contact with equine animals or their carcasses.
B3. Infection by leptospira.	(a) Work in places which are, or are liable to be, infested with rats, field mice or voles, or other small mammals; or
	(b) work at dog kennels or the care or handling of dogs; or
	(c) contact with bovine animals or their meat products or pigs or their meat products.
B4. Ankylostomiasis	Work in or about a mine.

(Continued)

Prescribed Diseases (Cont.)

B5. Tuberculosis	Contact with a source of tuberculous infection.
B6. Extrinsic allergic alveolitis (including farmer's lung).	Exposure to moulds or fungal spores or heterologous proteins by reason of employment in:—
	(a) agriculture, horticulture, forestry, cultivation of edible fungi or malt-working; or
	(b) loading or unloading or handling in storage mouldy vegetable matter or edible fungi: or
	(c) caring for or handling birds: or
	(d) handling bagasse.
B7. Infection by organisms of the genus brucella	Contact with—
	(a) animals infected by brucella, or their carcasses or parts thereof, or their untreated products; or
	(b) laboratory specimens or vaccines of, or containing, brucella.
B8. Viral hepatitis.	Any occupation involving: contact with –
	(a) human blood or human blood products; or
	(b) a source of viral hepatitis.
B9. Infection by Streptococcus suis.	Contact with pigs infected by Streptococcus suis, or with the carcasses, products or residues of pigs so infected.
B10(a). Avian chlamydiosis	Contact with birds infected with chlamydia psittaci, or with the remains or

Prescribed Diseases (Cont.)

	untreated products of such birds.
B10(b). Ovine chlamydiosis	Contact with sheep infected with chlamydia psittaci, or with the remains or untreated products of such sheep.
B11. Q fever	Contact with animals, their remains or their untreated products.
B12. Orf.	Contact with sheep, goats or with the carcasses of sheep or goats.
B13. Hydatidosis.	Contact with dogs.
C. Conditions due to chemical agents	
C1. Poisoning by lead or a compound of lead.	The use or handling of, or exposure to the fumes, dust or vapour of lead or a compound of lead, or a substance containing lead.
C2. Poisoning by manganese or a compound of manganese.	The use or handling of, or exposure to the fumes, dust or vapour of, manganese or a compound of manganese, or a substance containing manganese.
C3. Poisoning by phosphorus or an inorganic compound of phosphorus or poisoning due to the anti-cholinesterase or pseudo anti-cholinesterase action of organic phosphorus compounds.	The use or handling of, or exposure to the fumes, dust or vapour of, phosphorus or a compound of phosphorus, or a substance containing phosphorus.
C4. Poisoning by arsenic or a compound of arsenic.	The use or handling of, or exposure to the fumes, dust or vapour of, arsenic or a compound of arsenic, or a substance containing arsenic.
C5. Poisoning by mercury or a compound of mercury.	The use or handling of, or exposure to the fumes, dust

(Continued)

Prescribed Diseases (Cont.)

---

	or vapour of, mercury or a compound of mercury, or a substance containing mercury.
C6. Poisoning by carbon bisulphide.	The use or handling of, or exposure to the fumes or vapour of, carbon bisulphide or a compound of carbon bisulphide, or a substance containing carbon bisulphide.
C7. Poisoning by benzene or a homologue of benzene.	The use or handling of, or exposure to the fumes of, or vapour containing benzene or any of its homologues.
C8. Poisoning by a nitro- or amino- or chloroderivative of benzene or of a homologue of benzene, or poisoning by nitrochlorbenzene.	The use or handling of. or exposure to the fumes of, or vapour containing, a nitro- or amino- or chloro-derivative of benzene, or of a homologue of benzene, or nitrochlorbenzene.
C9. Poisoning by dinitrophenol or a homologue of dinitrophenol or by substituted dinitrophenols or by the salts of such substances.	The use or handling of, or exposure to the fumes of, or vapour containing, dinitrophenol or a homologue or substituted dinitrophenols or the salts of such substances.
C10. Poisoning by tetrachloroethane.	Any occupation involving the use or handling of, or exposure to the fumes of, or vapour containing, tetrachloroethane.
C11. Poisoning by diethylene dioxide (dioxan).	Any occupation involving the use or handling of, or exposure to the fumes of, or vapour containing, diethylene dioxide (dioxan).
C12. Poisoning by methylene bromide.	Any occupation involving the use or handling of, or exposure to the fumes of, or vapour containing, methyl bromide.

Prescribed Diseases (Cont.)

C13. Poisoning by chlorinated naphthalene.

Any occupation involving the use or handling of, or exposure to the fumes of, or dust or vapour containing, chlorinated naphthalene.

C14. Poisoning by nickel carbonyl.

Any occupation involving exposure to nickel carbonyl gas.

C15. Poisoning by oxides of nitrogen.

Any occupation involving exposure to oxides of nitrogen.

C16. Poisoning by gonioma kamassi (African boxwood).

Any occupation involving the manipulation of gonioma kamassi or any process in or incidental to the manufacture of articles therefrom.

C17. Poisoning by beryllium or a compound of beryllium.

Any occupation involving the use or handling of, or exposure to the fumes of, dust or vapour of, beryllium or a compound of beryllium, or a substance containing beryllium.

C18. Poisoning by cadmium.

Any occupation involving exposure to cadmium dust or fumes.

C19. Poisoning by acrylamide monomer.

Any occupation involving the use or handling of, or exposure to, acrylamide monomer.

C20. Dystrophy of the cornea (including ulceration of the corneal surface) of the eye.

Any occupation involving:

(a) The use or handling of, or exposure to, arsenic tar, pitch, bitumen, mineral oil (including paraffin), soot or any compound, product or residue of any of these substances, except quinone or hydroquinone: or

(b) exposure to quinone or hydro-quinone during their manufacture.

(Continued)

Prescribed Diseases (Cont.)

C21. (a) Localised new growth of the skin, papillomatous or keratotic; (b) squamous-celled carcinoma of the skin.	Any occupation involving the use or handling of, or exposure to, arsenic, tar, pitch, bitumen, mineral oil (including paraffin), soot or any compound, product or residue of any of these substances, except quinone or hydro-quinone.
C22. (a) Carcinoma of the mucous membrane of the nose or associated air sinuses; (b) primary carcinoma of a bronchus or of a lung.	Any occupation involving work in a factory where nickel is produced by decomposition of a gaseous nickel compound which necessitates working in or about a building or buildings where that process or any other industrial process ancillary or incidental thereto is carried on.
C23. Primary neoplasm (including papilloma, carcinoma-in-situ and invasive carcinoma) of the epithelial lining of the urinary tract (renal pelvis, ureter, bladder and urethra)	Any occupation involving: (a) work in a building in which any of the following substances is produced for commercial purposes:— (i) alpha-naphthylamine, betanaphthylamine or methylenebisorthochloroaniline; (ii) diphenyl substituted by at least one nitro or primary amino group or by at least one nitro and primary amino group (including benzidine); (iii) any of the substances mentioned in sub-paragraph (ii) above if further ring substituted by halogeno, methyl or methoxy groups, but not by other groups;

Prescribed Diseases (Cont.)	

	(iv) the salts of any of the substances mentioned in sub-paragraphs (i) to (iii) above;
	(v) auramine or magenta; or
	(b) the use or handling of any of the substances mentioned in sub-paragraph (a)(i) to (iv), or work in a process in which any such substance is used, handled or liberated; or
	(c) the maintenance or cleaning of any plant or machinery used in any such process as is mentioned in sub-paragraph (b) or the cleaning of clothing used in any such building as is mentioned in sub-paragraph (a) if such clothing is cleaned within the works of which the building forms a part or in a laundry maintained and used solely in connection with such works. (d) exposure to coal tar pitch volatiles produced in aluminium smelting involving the Soderberg process (that is to say the method of producing aluminium by electrolysis in which the anode consists of a paste of petroleum coke and mineral oil which is baked in situ).
C24. (a) Angiosarcoma of the liver: *(b)* osteolysis of the terminal phalanges of the fingers; (c) non-cirrhotic portal fibrosis.	Any occupation involving: (a) work in or about machinery or apparatus used for the polymerization of vinyl chloride monomer, a process which, for the purposes of this provision,
	(Continued)

Prescribed Diseases (Cont.)

	comprises all operations up to and including the drying of the slurry produced by the polymerization and the packaging of the dried product; or
	(b) work in a building or structure in which any part of that process takes place.
C25. Occupational vitiligo	Any occupation involving the use or handling of, or exposure to, para-tertiary-butylphenol, para-tertiary-butylcatechol, para-amyl-phenol, hydroquinone or the monobenzyl or monobutyl ether of hydroquinone.
C26. Damage to the liver or kidneys due to exposure to Carbon Tetrachloride.	Any occupation involving the use of or handling of, or exposure to the fumes of, or vapour containing, Carbon Tetrachloride.
C27. Damage to the liver or kidneys due to exposure to Trichloromethane (Chloroform).	Any occupation involving the use of or handling of, or exposure to the fumes of, or vapour containing, Trichloromethane (Chloroform).
C28. Central nervous system dysfunction and associated gastro-intestinal disorders due to exposure to Chloromethane (Methyl Chloride).	The use of or handling of, or exposure to the fumes of, or vapour containing, Chloromethane (Methyl Chloride).
C29, Peripheral neuropathy due to exposure to n-hexane or methyl n-butyl ketone.	The use of or handling of, or exposure to the fumes of, or vapour containing, n-hexane or methyl n-butyl ketone.
D. *Miscellaneous Conditions*	
D1. Pneumoconiosis.	Any occupation— (a) set out in Part 11 of this Schedule (see below); (b) specified in regulation *2(b)(ii).*

Prescribed Diseases (Cont.)

D2. Byssinosis.	Any occupation involving: work in any room where any process up to and including the weaving process is performed in a factory in which the spinning or manipulation of raw or waste cotton or of flax, or the weaving of cotton or flax, is carried on.
D3. Diffuse mesothelioma (primary neoplasm of the mesothelium of the pleura or of the pericardium or of the peritoneum).	Any occupation involving: a) The working or handling of asbestos or any admixture of asbestos; or
	(b) the manufacture or repair of asbestos textiles or other articles containing or composed of asbestos, or
	(c) the cleaning of any machinery or plant used in any of the foregoing operations and of any chambers, fixtures and appliances for the collection of asbestos dust; or
	(d) substantial exposure to the dust arising from any of the foregoing operations.
D4. Allergic rhinitis due to exposure to any of the following agents:	Exposure to dust, liquid or vapour — such as may occur in food processing and metal plating industries, in laboratories, grain processing, drug manufacture, washing powder manufacture, hair dressing, the electronics industry, amongst welders, in dye manufacture, and in tea and coffee processing.
(a) isocyanates;	
(b) platinum salts;	
(c) fumes or dusts arising from the manufacture, transport or use of hardening agents (including epoxy resin curing agents) based on phthalic anhydride, tetrachlorophthalic anhydride, trimellitic anhydride or triethylene-tetramine;	
(d) fumes arising from the use of rosin as a soldering flux;	

(Continued)

Prescribed Diseases (Cont.)

(e) proteolytic enzymes;

(f) animals, including insects and other anthropods used for the purposes of research or education, or in laboratories;

(g) dusts arising from the sowing, cultivation, harvesting, drying, handling, milling, transport or storage of barley, oats, rye, wheat, etc; or the handling, milling, transport or storage of meal or flour made from meal;

h)   antibiotics;

(i)   cimetidine;

(j)   wood dust;

(k) ispaghula;

(l)   castor bean dust;

(m) ipecacuanha;

(n) azodicarbonamide;

(o) animals including insects and other anthropods or their larval forms used for the purposes of pest control or fruit cultivation, or the larval forms of animals used for the purposes of reasearch or education, or in laboratories;

(p) glutaraldehyde;

(q) persulphate salts or henna;

(r) crustaceans or fish or products arising from these in the food processing industry;

(s) reactive dyes;

(t) soya bean;

(u) tea dust;

(v) green coffee bean dust;

Prescribed Diseases (Cont.)

(w) fumes from stainless steel
welding;

D5. Non-infective dermatitis of external origin (iexcluding dermatitis due to ionising particles or electro-magnetic radiations other than radiant heat).	Exposure to dust, liquid or vapour or any other external agent [except chromic acid, chromates or bi-chromates] capable of irritating the skin (including friction or heat but excluding ionising particles or electro-magnetic radiations other than radiant heat).
D6. Carcinoma of the nasal cavity or associated air sinuses (nasal carcinoma).	Any occupation involving: (a) attendance for work in or about a building where wooden goods are manufactured or repaired; or (b) attendance for work in a building used for the manufacture of footwear made wholly or partly of leather or fibre board, or (c) attendance for work at a place used wholly or mainly for the repair of footwear made wholly or partly of leather or fibre board.
D7. Occupational asthma	For further particulars, see DSS Leaflet NI 237.
D8. Primary carcinoma of the lung where there is accompanying evidence of one or both of the following:— (a) asbestosis (b) bilateral diffuse pleural thickening.	Any occupation involving: (a) the working or handling of asbestos or any admixture of asbestos; or (b) the manufacture or repair of asbestos textiles or other articles containing or composed of asbestos; or (c) the cleaning of any machinery or plant used in any of the foregoing

(Continued)

Prescribed Diseases (Cont.)	
	operations and of any chambers, fixtures and appliances for the collection of asbestos dust; or
	(d) substantial exposure to the dust arising from any of the foregoing operations.
D9. Bilateral diffuse pleural thickening.	As D8 above, See DSS Leaflet NI 272 for further particulars.
D10.—Primary carcinoma of the lung.	Any occupation involving:
	(a) work under ground in a tin mine; or
	(b) exposure to bis(chloremethyl)ether produced during the manufacture of chloromethyl methyl ether; or
	(c) exposure to zinc chromate, calcium chromate or strontium chromate in their pure forms.
D11. Primary carcinoma of the lung where there is accompanying evidence of silicosis.	Any occupation involving exposure to silica dust in the course of—
	(a) the manufacture of glass or pottery,
	(b) tunnelling in or quarrying sandstone or granite;
	(c) mining metal ores;
	(d) slate quarrying or the manufacture of artefacts from slate;
	(e) mining clay;
	(f) using siliceous materials as abrasives;
	(g) cutting stone;

Prescribed Diseases (Cont.)	
	(h) stonemasonry; or
	(i) work in a foundry.
D12. Chronic bronchitis or emphysema	For further particulars, see DSS Leaflet NI7 (*People who have worked underground in a coal mine for 20 years*).

Part II
OCCUPATIONS FOR WHICH PNEUMOCONIOSIS IS 'PRESCRIBED'
(See D1 above)

1. Any occupation involving—

(a) the mining, quarrying or working of silica rock or the working of dried quartzose sand or any dry deposit or dry residue of silica or any dry admixture containing such materials (including any occupation in which any of the aforesaid operations are carried out incidentally to the mining or quarrying of other minerals or to the manufacture of articles containing crushed or ground silica rock);

(b) the handling of any of the materials specified in the foregoing sub-paragraph in or incidental to any of the operations mentioned therein, or substantial exposure to the dust arising from such operations;

2. Any occupation involving the breaking, crushing or grinding of flint or the working or handling of broken, crushed or ground flint or materials containing such flint, or substantial exposure to the dust arising from any of such operations;

3. Any occupation involving sand blasting by means of compressed air with the use of quartzose sand or crushed silica rock or flint, or substantial exposure to the dust arising from sand and blasting.

4. Any occupation involving work in a foundry or the performance of, or substantial exposure to the dust arising from, any of the following operations:—

(a) the freeing of steel casting from adherent siliceous substance;

(b) the freeing of metal castings from adherent siliceous

substance—

(i) by blasting with an abrasive propelled by compressed air, by steam or by a wheel or

(*Continued*)

Part II (Cont.)

(ii) by the use of power-driven tools.

5. Any occupation in or incidental to the manufacture of china or earthenware (including sanitary earthenware, electrical earthenware and earthenware tiles), and any occupation involving substantial exposure to the dust arising therefrom.

6. Any occupation involving the grinding of mineral graphite, or substantial exposure to the dust arising from such grinding.

7. Any occupation involving the dressing of granite or any igneous rock by masons or the crushing of such materials, or substantial exposure to the dust arising from such operations.

8. Any occupation involving the use, or preparation for use, of a grindstone, or substantial exposure to the dust arising therefrom.

9. Any occupation involving—

(a) the working or handling of asbestos or any admixture of asbestos;
(b) the manufacture or repair of asbestos textiles or other articles containing or composed of asbestos;
(c) the cleaning of any machinery or plant used in any foregoing operations and of any chambers, fixtures or appliances for the collection of asbestos dust;
(d) substantial exposure to the dust arising from any of the foregoing operations.

10. Any occupation involving—

(a) work underground in any mine in which one of the objects of the mining operations is the getting of any mineral;
(b) the working or handling above ground at any coal or tin mine of any minerals extracted therefrom, or any operation incidental thereto;
(c) the trimming of coal in any ship, barge, or lighter, or in any dock or harbour or at any wharf or quay;
(d) the sawing, splitting or dressing of slate, or any operation incidental thereto.

11. Any occupation in or incidental to the manufacture of carbon electrodes by an industrial undertaking for use in the electrolytic extraction of aluminium from aluminium oxide, and any occupation involving substantial exposure to the dust arising therefrom.

12. Any occupation involving boiler scaling or substantial exposure to the dust arising therefrom.

Note: For factories, workshops and industrial premises, the relevant enforcing authority is the nearest area office of the Health & Safety executive (see pages 368 to 372). For offices, shops, hotels, restaurants, schools, hospitals, department stores, etc; it is the local authority for the district in which the premises are situated. For further details, please turn to the section titled Health & Safety Commission & Executive elsewhere in this handbook.

NOTIFICATION TO HEALTH AND SAFETY INSPECTORATE

- Employers are reminded that they have a duty in law to notify the "relevant enforcing authority" if an accident at work results in the death of, or "major injury" to, one or other of his employees, or if such an accident incapacitates an employee for more than three days (excluding Sunday and the day on which the accident occurred). Details of such accidents must also be recorded in a register. For further particulars, see **Accidents at work** elsewhere in this handbook.

  See also **Accident book, Accidents at work, Care, Common duty of, Defective equipment, Food poisoning,** and **Insurance, Compulsory** elsewhere in this handbook.

INSPECTORS, POWERS OF
(Health and Safety Legislation)

Key points

- Health and safety inspectors are responsible for 'policing' and enforcing Part I of the Health and Safety at Work etc. Act 1974, as well as an employer's compliance with his duties under the *relevant statutory provisions* (see below) — including Regulations made under (or saved by) the 1974 Act. For non-industrial undertakings (offices, shops, hotels, restaurants, etc.), the enforcing authority is the local authority for the area in which those premises are situated.

  Note: The expression "local authority" means (a) in relation to England and Wales, a district council, a London borough council, the Common Council of the City of London, the Sub-Treasurer of the Inner Temple, the Under-Treasurer of the Middle Temple or the Council of the Isles of Scilly; and (b) in relation to Scotland, an islands or district council (*ibid;* Regulation 2(1)).

- For a more comprehensive picture, the reader is commended to a recent HSE publication titled *Review of new health and safety enforcement procedures* (ISBN 0 7176 1275 9), copies of which are available from HSE Books, price £15.00. For further details, please turn to page 328.

RELEVANT STATUTORY PROVISIONS

- The *relevant statutory provisions* referred to here and throughout this handbook is the term used to describe the totality of health and safety legislation; that is to say, Part I of the Health & Safety at Work, etc. Act 1974, Regulations made under section 15 of that Act, pre-1974 Regulations and Orders saved by the 1974 Act (many of which are gradually being replaced by more up-to-date legislation (much of it prompted by EC Directives); and specified provisions in the following statutes:

Explosives Acts 1875 & 1923
Boiler Explosions Act 1890
Revenue Act 1909
Anthrax Prevention Act 1919
Employment of Women, Young Persons & Children Act 1920
Celluloid & Cinematograph Film Act 1922
Public Health (Smoke Abatement)Act 1926
Petroleum (Consolidation) Act 1928
Hours of Employment (Conventions) Act 1936
Petroleum (Transfer of Licences) Act 1936
Hydrogen Cyanide (Fumigation) Act 1937
Ministry of Fuel & Power Act 1945
Coal Industry Nationalisation Act 1946
Radioactive Substances Act 1948
Fireworks Act 1951
Agriculture (Poisonous Substances) Act 1952
Emergency Laws (Miscellaneous Provisions) Act 1953
Mines & Quarries Act 1954
Agriculture (Safety, Health & Welfare Provisions) Act 1956
Factories Act 1961
Public Health Act 1961
Pipe-lines Act 1962
Offices, Shops & Railway Premises Act 1963
Nuclear Installations Act 1965
Mines & Quarries (Tips) Act 1969
Mines Management Act 1971
Employment Medical Advisory Service Act 1972

Many of the statutes listed above are mere shadows of their former selves. Most (save for those outlined in bold) are unlikely to be of particular or immediate relevance to the readers of this handbook.

Appointment of inspectors

• The relevant enforcing authority, may appoint as inspectors such persons having suitable qualifications as it thinks necessary for carrying into effect the relevant health and safety legislation within its field of responsibility. However, an inspector may exercise only those powers as are specified in his or her instrument of appointment (or 'warrant'). When exercising, or seeking to exercise, any power conferred on him by the local authority (e.g. his power to enter and inspect any premises within his field of responsibility), an inspector must produce his warrant card on demand (*ibid*; section 19).

Powers of inspectors

• An inspector may enter any premises within his field of responsibility at any reasonable time (or, in a situation which in his opinion is or may be dangerous, *at any time*) for the purposes of carrying out his duties of inspection and enforcement. Furthermore, he may

(a) take with him a police constable, if he has reason to apprehend any serious obstruction in the execution of his duty;

(b) take with him any other person (such as a boiler engineer or lighting expert) duly authorised by the local authority and any equipment or other materials necessary for the conduct of an inspection of the premises or an examination of plant and machinery;

(c) direct that the premises, or part of the premises, be left undisturbed until he has completed his inspection or examination;

(d) take such measurements, photographs or recordings as he thinks appropriate in the circumstances;

(e) take samples of any articles or substances found on the premises, or of the atmosphere in and about the premises;

(f) cause any dangerous, or potentially dangerous, article or substance to be dismantled or subjected to any process or test, but not so as to destroy it unless absolutely necessary to ensure compliance with the law;

(g)   take possession of any article or substance, either with a view to arranging further examinations and analysis, or to ensure that it is not tampered with and, therefore, available as evidence in any subsequent legal proceedings;

(h)   interview or cross-examine any person (including any employee), if he believes that person may have information of use to him in the conduct of his inspection or examination of the premises;

(i)   inspect and, if need be, take copies of documents relevant to his investigations;

(j)   require the occupier or owner of the premises to provide him with such facilities as may be necessary (e.g. an office equipped with a desk and chair) for the purposes of interviewing persons, examining documents, making notes, etc. and may do whatever is necessary, within the limits of his authority, to ensure compliance with the relevant legislation *(ibid.,* section 20).

Improvement and Prohibition Notices

- If an inspector is of the opinion that the occupier of premises (factory, office, shop, hotel, cinema, or whatever) is in breach or contravention of his duties under the Health and Safety at Work, etc., Act 1974 or under any of the *relevant statutory provisions*, and is likely to do so again, he may serve an improvement notice on that person requiring to remedy the situation within such period (not exceeding 21 days) as may be specified in the notice *(ibid.;* section 21) (see **Improvement notices** elsewhere in this handbook) .

- If, on the other hand, an inspector is of the opinion that the activities carried on, or about to be carried on, at a particular premises (or in part of those premises) involves or will involve a risk of serious personal injury, he may serve a prohibition notice on the occupier directing a cessation of those activities until such time as the matters specified in the notice (and any associated contraventions of health and safety provisions) have been remedied (*ibid;* section 22) (see **Prohibition Notices** elsewhere in this handbook).

Power to deal with cause of imminent danger

- If an inspector has reasonable cause to believe that any article or substance found by him in premises which he is empowered to enter is a cause of imminent danger of serious personal injury, he may seize it and cause it to be rendered harmless (whether by destruction or otherwise). Before doing so (and if practicable for him to do so) the inspector must take a sample of that article or substance and give it to a responsible person (such as the manager or owner of the premises) — the sample to be marked or labelled in a manner sufficient to identify it. Once he has seized and rendered harmless any such article or substance, the inspector must prepare a report in writing giving particulars of the circumstances in which the article or substance was seized and rendered harmless. A copy of the report must be given to the owner or occupier as appropriate. If the occupier of the premises is not also the owner, a further copy of the report must be sent to the owner (*ibid;* section 25).

Offences & penalties

- It is an offence for a person:

  (a) to contravene any requirement imposed by a health and safety inspector in the exercise of his powers of entry and inspection of premises;

  (b) to prevent or attempt to prevent any person (such as an employee) from appearing before an inspector or from answering any question to which an inspector may require an answer;

  (c) to contravene any requirement or prohibition imposed by an improvement notice or a prohibition notice (including any such notice as modified on appeal);

  (d) intentionally to obstruct an inspector in the exercise or performance of his power or duties;

  (e) intentionally to make a false entry in any register, book or other document required to be kept, served or given under existing health and safety legislation; or

(f)   falsely to pretend to be an inspector.

- A person guilty of an offence under paragraphs (a), (b), (d) or (f) is liable on summary conviction to a fine not exceeding f2,000. A person guilty of an offence under paragraph (c) or (e) is liable to a fine on summary conviction of a maximum £2,000 or, on conviction on indictment, a fine of an unlimited amount. If, on the other hand, an offence under paragraph (c) consists of contravening a requirement or prohibition imposed by a prohibition notice, he is liable, on summary conviction, to a fine of up to £20,000 and/or imprisonment for up to six months; or,

  if convicted on indictment, to a fine of an unlimited amount, to imprisonment for a term not exceeding two years, or both (*ibid*; section 33).

See also **Health & safety at work, Health & Safety Commission and Executive, and Offences & Penalties** elsewhere in this handbook.

INSURANCE, COMPULSORY

".. every employer carrying on any business in Great Britain shall insure, and maintain insurance, under one or more approved policies with an authorised insurer or insurers against liability for bodily injury or disease sustained by his employees, and arising out of and in the course of their employment in Great Britain in that business".. (section 1, Employers' Liability (Compulsory) Insurance) Act 1969).

Key points

- If an employee is injured or contracts a disease in the course of his (or her) employment, as a direct consequence of his employer's negligence or breach of a statutory duty, he would ordinarily be prompted to bring a civil action for damages in the ordinary courts. It is against this contingency that statute law has long since required employers to take out appropriate insurance cover.

- Before 1 January 1995, every employer was duty-bound to take out (and maintain) a minimum of £2 million in insurance cover in respect of claims lodged by one or more of his employees (arising out of any one occurrence). This meant that a holding company would not only have to maintain £2 million in insurance cover for itself but £2 million also for each of its subsidiary companies which employed staff.

- However, that has now changed. With the coming into force on 1 January 1995, of the Employer's Liability (Compulsory Insurance) General (Amendment) Regulations 1994 (SI 1994/3301), a holding company need only take out a policy covering itself and all its subsidiaries, so long as that policy provides a minimum cover of £2 million.

  Note: In a Press Notice issued on 22 December 1994 (in which he heralded the amending legislation), the Employment Minister pointed to the then recent decision by the insurance industry to cease offering unlimited cover. This means, he said, that companies with one or more subsidiaries are placed in the impossible position of being unable to comply with their obligations under the Employers' Liability (Compulsory Insurance) Act 1969. From 1 January 1995 that will no longer be a problem. The Minister added that he intends to review the legislation during the early part of 1995 to ensure that the legislation provides an acceptable level of protection for injured employees in the event of a foreseeable accident; that it is consistent with the cover the insurance market is able to deliver; that it avoids any employers having to take out unnecessarily expensive cover; that it sets clear understandable requirements; and that it avoids unnecessary bureaucracy. "All aspects of the existing legislation", he concluded, "will be examined with a view to achieving these objectives in the most effective way. I will be discussing the details with the Health & Safety Commission and will make a further announcement shortly".

- The insurance cover prescribed by the 1969 and its attendant Regulations must be effected with an authorised insurer, i.e. a person or body of persons lawfully carrying on in Great Britain insurance business of any class relevant for the purposes of Part II of the Companies Act 1967 (as amended). A list of authorised insurers is given in The *Insurance Business Annual Report* (published by the Department of Trade & Industry and available from HMSO).

- Furthermore, the policy document, or a copy of that document, must be kept available for inspection by an HSE or local authority inspector. A copy of the Certificate of Insurance must also be displayed at the employer's place of business so as to be easily seen and read by all his employees. These certificates are routinely supplied by the insurance companies.

- The 1969 Act is enforced by the Health and Safety Executive (HSE). Any employer who is not insured, or has not taken out the prescribed minimum amount of insurance cover, is guilty of an offence and liable, on summary conviction, to a fine of up to £500. The employer who does not display a copy of his Certificate of Insurance, or who hinders an inspector in the course of his duties, is liable, on summary conviction, to a fine of up to £200.

- An employer is not obliged to insure employees who are also members of his family, i.e., husband, wife, father, mother, grandfather, grandmother, stepfather, stepmother, son, daughter, grandson, granddaughter, stepson, stepdaughter, brother, sister, half-brother or half-sister.

Note: The Health & Safety Executive may serve notice on an employer requiring him to send the certificate of insurance, or a copy of it, to the offices of the Executive specified in the notice. The penalty for non-compliance is a fine of up to £1,000.

See also **Care, Common duty of** and **Defective equipment** elsewhere in this handbook.

IONISING RADIATION

Key points

- Basic safety standards for the protection of employees whose work exposes them to ionising radiation (including exposure to the "short-lived daughters of radon 222") are to be found in the Ionising Radiations Regulations 1985 (SI 1985/1333)). As the Regulations are lengthy and complicated, the following is a summary only of their principal requirements and prohibitions. For more detailed advice, the reader is commended to the HSE's Approved Code of Practice (COP 16) and several related publications listed at the end of this section.

- "Ionising radiation" means gamma-rays, X-rays or corpuscular radiations which (directly or indirectly) are capable of producing ions. Over-exposure to such radiation can, of course, be extremely damaging to health. It is for this reason that the 1985 Regulations not only require employers to take all necessary steps to restrict so far as reasonably practicable the extent to which his employees and other persons are exposed to ionising radiation but also impose strict limits on the doses which they and other persons may receive in a calendar year (see **Table 1** overleaf). A "radioactive substance" is any substance having an activity concentration of more than 100 Bag⁻¹ and any other substance which contains one or more radio nuclides whose activity cannot be disregarded for the purposes of radiation protection. The term also includes a radioactive substance in the form of a sealed source.

- Although there are exceptions, most employers intending to undertake work with ionising radiation for the first time must notify their nearest Area Offices of Health & Safety Executive (HSE) (see pages 368 to 372) at least 28 days beforehand. Advance notification is not, however, necessary if the only work to be undertaken is work involving exposure to the "short-lived

  daughters of radon 222". Even so, the employer in question must inform the HSE as soon as that work begins.

DUTIES OF EMPLOYER

- Before considering any other option, an employer must restrict the exposure of his employees to ionising radiation by means of engineering controls and design features (which include shielding, ventilation, and containment of radioactive substances) *and* by the provision and use of safety features and warning devices.

- Unless the nature of the work or the circumstances in which it is done makes it impracticable to do so, an employer must further restrict the exposure of his employees to ionising radiation by developing safe systems of work and by providing suitable personal protective equipment (including suitable respirators) to those of his employees (and other persons) whose work takes them into a "controlled" or "supervised" area. Such protective clothing and equipment as is provided must be thoroughly examined at suitable intervals and must be properly maintained. In the case of respiratory protective equipment, a suitable record of every such examination must be made and kept for at least two years and must include a statement as to the condition of the equipment at the time of the examination. The employer must also provide an appropriate facility or room in which employees can store personal protective equipment when it is not being worn.

Table 1
IONISING RADIATIONS REGULATIONS 1985
Schedule 1

Part I
Dose limits for the whole body

The dose limit for the whole body resulting from exposure to the whole or part of the body, being the sum of the following dose quantities resulting from exposure to ionising radiation, namely the effective dose equivalent from external radiation and committed effective dose equivalent from that year's intake of radio nuclides, shall in any calendar year be

(a)	for employees aged 18 years or over	50 mSv
(b)	for trainees aged under 18 years	15 mSv
(c)	for any other person	5 mSv

Part II
Dose limits for individual organs and tissues

Without prejudice to Part I of this Schedule, the dose limit for individual organs or tissues, being the sum of the following dose quantities resulting from exposure to ionising radiation, namely the dose equivalent from external radiation, the dose equivalent from contamination and the committed dose equivalent from that year's intake of radionuclides averaged throughout any individual organ or tissue (other than the lens of the eye) or any body extremity or over any area of skin, shall in any calendar year be

(a)	for employees aged 18 years or over	500 mSv
(b)	for trainees aged under 18 years	150 mSv
(c)	for any other person	50 mSv

In assessing the dose quantity to skin whether from contamination or external radiation, the area of skin over which the dose quantity is averaged shall be appropriate to the circumstances but in any event shall not exceed 100 cm^2.

Part III
Dose limits for the lens of the eye

The dose limit for the lens of the eye resulting from exposure to ionising radiation, being the average dose equivalent from external and internal radiation delivered between 2.5 mm and 3.5 mm behind the surface of the eye, shall in any calendar year be —

(a)	for employees aged 18 years or over	150 mSv
(b)	for trainees aged under 18 years	45 mSv
(c)	for any other person	15 mSv

(Continued opposite)

Table 1 (Cont.)

Part IV
Dose limit for the abdomen of a woman
of reproductive capacity

The dose limit for the abdomen of a woman of reproductive capacity who is at work, being the dose equivalent from external radiation resulting from exposure to ionising radiation averaged throughout the abdomen, shall be 3 mSv in any consecutive three month interval.

Part V
Dose limit for the abdomen of a pregnant woman

The dose limit for the abdomen of a pregnant woman who is at work, being the dose equivalent from external radiation resulting from exposure to ionising radiation averaged throughout the abdomen, shall be 10 mSv during the declared term of pregnancy.

Note: A "controlled area" is an area or part of the workplace in which doses of ionising radiation are likely to exceed three-tenths of the specified dose limit for employees aged 18 and over. A "supervised area", on the other hand, is an area in which an employee is likely to be exposed to ionising radiation to an extent which exceeds one-third of the extent to which he would otherwise be exposed in a controlled area.

- The only employees who should be permitted to enter or remain in a controlled area are those who have been designated as "classified persons" and employees aged 18 or over who do so under a 'permit-to-work' system or similar arrangement in writing — subject to the proviso that employees aged 18 or over must *not* receive in any calendar year a dose of ionising radiation exceeding three-tenths of the relevant dose limit. Any other person who enters of remains in a controlled area (under a permit-to-work system or similar arrangement) must not receive in any calendar year a dose of ionising radiation exceeding the relevant dose limit.

Note: A "classified person" is a person who is likely to receive a dose of ionising radiation which exceeds three-tenths of any relevant dose limit.

- Areas designated as "controlled" or "supervised" must be physically demarcated or delineated by some other means. Employers must draw up suitable safety rules and must make it clear to every member of the workforce that access to such areas is strictly restricted.

Other provisions

- In premises and work areas to which the 1985 Regulations apply, the employer must also

    o   make an adequate assessment of the nature and magnitude of the radiation hazard before allowing any employee or other person to carry on work with ionising radiation;

    o   see to it that those of his employees who are (or who are likely to be) engaged in work with ionising radiation receive as much information, instruction, training and supervision as is necessary to create an awareness and understanding of the dangers associated with such work and to enable them to carry out their duties safely;

    o   inform female workers "of reproductive capacity" of the possible hazard to the foetus in early pregnancy arising from work with ionising radiation and of the importance of informing him as soon as they discover that they have become pregnant;

    o   appoint one or more competent and qualified radiation protection advisers whose job it is to advise him about the requirements and prohibitions imposed by the Regulations and other health and safety-related issues;

    o   issue dosemeters and arrange for an HSE-approved dosimetry service to measure and assess the doses received by those of his employees who work with ionising radiations;

    o   ensure that no radioactive substance in the form of a sealed source is held in the hand or manipulated directly by hand unless the instantaneous dose rate to the skin of the hand does not exceed $75\mu Svh^{-1}$; and, so far as is reasonably practicable, that no unsealed radioactive substance (nor any article containing a radioactive substance) is held in the hand or directly manipulated by hand;

    o   arrange for the medical surveillance of classified workers, workers who have received an over-exposure, workers identified by an employment medical adviser or appointed doctor as being especially at risk, and workers suspended from work on medical grounds;

o   preserve an employee's health (Form F2067) record for at least 50 years from the date of the last entry in it;

o   test articles containing or embodying radioactive substances at least once every 26 months to detect evidence of leakage;

o   account for and keep records of the quantity and location of all radioactive substances which are involved in work with ionising radiation;

o   provide and maintain adequate washing and changing facilities for persons who enter or leave controlled or supervised areas;

o   ensure that respiratory protective equipment complies with UK legislation implementing any relevant Community Directive applicable to that item of equipment, or (in the absence of such legislation) that it is of a type or conforms to a standard, in either case, approved by the Health & Safety Executive;

o   monitor levels of ionising radiation in "controlled" and "supervised" areas (and keep records);

o   develop contingency plans for dealing with the consequences of any reasonably foreseeable accident, occurrence or incident in which one or more employees are likely to receive a dose of ionising radiation in excess of the relevant dose limit; and

o   notify the Health & Safety Executive immediately if more than a specified quantity of a radioactive substance has been (or is likely to be) released into the atmosphere as a gas, aerosol or dust, or has been spilled or otherwise released in such a manner as to cause significant contamination.

Suspension from work on medical grounds

- An employee who is suspended from work with ionising radiation at the direction of an employment medical adviser or appointed doctor must be paid his (or her) normal wages or salary for so long as the period of suspension lasts or for 26 weeks, whichever is the greater of those two periods — unless he unreasonably refuses an offer of suitable alternative work or fails to make himself available for work when asked to do so by his employer. The dismissal of an employee who is suspended from work in such circumstances is *prima facie* unfair and, so long as the employee had worked for his employer for at least one month, could prompt a complaint to an industrial tribunal (as to which, please turn to the section titled **Suspension on medical grounds** elsewhere in this handbook).

Offences & penalties

- An employer who fails to comply with his duties under the 1985 Regulations is guilty of an offence and liable on summary conviction to a fine of up to £2,000. If his offence is tantamount to a failure on his part to discharge a duty to which he is subject by virtue of sections 2 to 7 of the Health & Safety at Work etc. Act 1974, he could be ordered to pay a fine of up to £20,000 (perhaps more, if convicted on indictment). In certain circumstances, he could be sent to prison for up to 2 years. See **Offences & penalties** elsewhere in this handbook.

DUTIES OF EMPLOYEES

- Employees who are engaged in work with ionising radiation must not knowingly expose themselves or other persons to ionising radiation to a greater extent than is reasonably necessary, and must exercise reasonable care when carrying out such work.

- Employees must not eat, drink, smoke, take snuff or apply cosmetics in any area which their employer has designated as a "controlled" or "supervised" area — except that an employee may drink from a drinking fountain which is constructed in a way that prevents the water becoming contaminated.

- Female employees engaged in work with ionising radiations must inform their employer if they become pregnant (given the possible danger to the foetus in early pregnancy).

- An employee engaged in work with ionising radiation must allow himself (or herself) to be medically examined by an employment medical adviser or HSE-appointed doctor as an when directed to do so by his employer. Furthermore, he must provide as much information about his health as the employment medical adviser or appointed doctor may reasonably require.

- Employees are duty-bound to wear the respirators and other equipment provided for their protection, and must take reasonable steps to return that equipment to the designated storage area after use.

GENERAL DUTIES OF MANUFACTURERS, ETC.

- The manufacturers, importers and suppliers of articles for use in work with ionising radiation must ensure that the article is so designed and constructed as to restrict so far as is reasonably practicable the extent to which employees and other persons are or are likely to be exposed to ionising radiation (section 6, Health & Safety at Work, etc. Act 1974, as modified by Regulation 32 of the 1985 Regulations (*q.v.*)).

- Any person who erects or installs an article intended for use at work with ionising radiation, must (together with a radiation protection adviser) undertake a critical examination of the way in which the article was erected or installed to ensure, in particular, that the safety features and warning devices operate correctly and that it provides sufficient protection from exposure to ionising radiation. He must also provide the employer with adequate information about the proper use, testing and maintenance of that article.

Other relevant legislation

- Other relevant legislation (which is of little immediate relevance to the readers of this handbook) includes —

  Mines & Quarries Act 1954
  Radioactive Substances Act 1960
  Nuclear Installations Act 1965

See also **Dangerous chemicals & preparations** and **Hazardous substances** elsewhere in this handbook.

FURTHER INFORMATION

- The following HSE publications are available from HSE Books at the address given on page 328:

F2067
Ionising radiation health record
ISBN 0 7176 0816 6   £5.00 (10 copies)

COP 16 (see also L7)
Protection of persons against ionising radiation arising from any work activity: The Ionising Radiations Regulations 1985: Approved code of practice [1985]
ISBN 0 7176 0508 6   £6.00

COP 23
Exposure to radon: the Ionising Radiations Regulations 1985: Approved code of practice [1988]
ISBN 0 11 883978 0   £2.00

L7
Dose limitation - restriction of exposure: Additional guidance on Regulation 6 of the Ionising Radiations Regulations 1985: Approved code of practice, Part 4 [1991]
ISBN 0 11 885605 7   £2.25

L49
Protection of outside workers against ionising radiations [1993] ISBN 0 7176 0681 3   £5.00

L58
The protection of persons against ionising radiation arising from any work activity (1994)
ISBN 0 7176 0508 6   £6.00

PM 77
Fitness of equipment used for medical exposure to ionising radiation [1992]
ISBN 0 11 886313 4   £2.50

HS(G) 49

The examination and testing of portable radiation instruments for external radiations [1990]
ISBN 0 11 885507 7 £4.00

HS(G) 91
A framework for the restriction of occupational exposure to ionising radiation [1992]
ISBN 0 1, 886324 X £3.50

HS(G) 94
Safety in the use of gamma and electron irradiation facilities [1993]
ISBN 0 7176 0647 3 £4.25
F.2067
Ionising radiation health record
ISBN 0 11 883864 4 £5.00 for 10 copies

CRR 64
Exposure to u/v radiation
ISBN 0 7176 0749 0 £20.00

CRR66
A critique of recommended limits of exposure to UV radiation with particular reference to skin cancer [1994]
ISBN 0 7176 0749 6   £20.00

L

LADDERS

Key points

- Employees and other pedestrians in a workplace should not have to use ladders or steep stairs to gain access to the upper or lower floors of a building. Fixed ladders or steep stairs may be installed in premises where a conventional staircase cannot be accommodated — but these must only be used by people who are capable of using them safely and any loads to be carried can be safely carried.

- Where a ladder over six metres long is needed for window-cleaning or related purposes, there must be suitable points for tying or fixing the ladder at its uppermost point (Regulation 16, Workplace (Health, Safety & Welfare) Regulations 1992 [SI 1992/3004]). An employer's duties in relation to work equipment (which expression includes ladders) are to be found in Regulations 1 to 10 of the Provision & Use of Work Equipment Regulations 1992 (as to which, see **Work equipment** elsewhere in this handbook).

Fixed ladders

- Fixed ladders are usually to be found in pits, tanks and similar structures where it would be inappropriate to install a regular stairway. A "fixed ladder" is a type of stairway (albeit steep) which a person ascends or descends facing the treads or rungs (*ibid*; Reg. 13).

- All fixed ladders must be soundly constructed, properly maintained and securely fixed. The rungs must be horizontal and provide an adequate foothold. They must not depend solely for their support upon nails, screws or similar fixings. The stiles of the ladder should protrude at least 1100mm above any landing served by the ladder (or the highest rung used to step or stand on).

- Fixed ladders installed in workplaces after December 31, 1992, with a vertical distance of more than six metres, should normally have a landing or other adequate resting place at every six-metre point. If these are impracticable, the ladders should only be used by specially trained and proficient people. If a fixed ladder passes through a floor, the opening must be as small as possible, fenced as far as possible, and be fitted with a gate to prevent falls.

- Fixed ladders which are more than 2.5 metres high and set at an angle of less than 15 degrees to the vertical must be fitted with safety hoops at 900mm intervals (or less). The bottom hoop must be 2.5 metres above the base and the top, in line with the top of the fencing on the platform served by the ladder. However, a hoop need not be provided at the top if the top of the ladder passes through a fenced hole in a floor.

- For further information, the reader should consult BS 5395:1985 (*Code of Practice for the design of industrial type stairs, permanent ladders and walkways*) and BS 4211:1987 (*Specification for ladders for permanent access to chimneys, other high structures, silos and bins*). European and British Standards (BS or BSen) are available from the British Standards Institution. 389 Chiswick High Road. London. W4 4AL (Telephone: 0181 996 70000).

- Ladders are also discussed elsewhere in this handbook (on pages 132 & 133) in the section titled **Construction work.**

LEAD AT WORK

Key points

- Legislation concerning the protection of employees (and self-employed persons) whose work may expose them to lead is to be found in the Control of Lead at Work Regulations 1980 (SI 1980/1248).

- "Lead" means lead (including lead alloys, any compounds of lead, and lead as a constituent of any substance or material) which is liable to be inhaled, ingested or otherwise absorbed by persons except where it is given off from the exhaust system of a vehicle on the road within the meaning of section 196(1) of the Road Traffic Act 1972.

- Under the 1980 Regulations and their accompanying Approved Code of Practice employers and self-employed persons are duty bound to assess the risk to their employees (or to themselves) before putting them to work (or starting work) on any activity or process (such as handling, movement, storage, processing, disposal, repairing, maintenance, etc.) which could conceivably expose them to lead —

  (a) in the form of lead dust, fume or vapour which is liable to be inhaled;

  (b) in any form which is liable to be ingested, e.g., lead powder, dust, paint or paste;

  (c) in the form of lead compounds which are liable to be absorbed through the skin, e.g., concentrated lead alkyls.

  It follows that the Regulations do not apply to work with substances or materials (such as articles of pottery) if the lead is present in a form which cannot be inhaled, ingested or absorbed.

  Note: Employers (and self-employed persons) should not only assess the risks to their own employees (and themselves) but also the risks to other persons working or living nearby who may be affected by the emission of dusts, fumes and vapours or by lead dust carried home by employees on their shoes and clothing. Indeed, paragraph 73 of the Approved Code of Practice reminds employers (and self-employed persons working with lead) that if they have reason to suspect that lead workers' families and other members of the public may be affected by lead arising from work activities, they must liaise closely with local authorities who have wide responsibilities for maintaining public health.

- The exposure of employees to lead must be considered significant if they are exposed to levels of airborne lead which are, or are liable to be, in excess of half the *lead-in-air standard* (see *Note* below); or if there is a substantial risk of ingesting lead; or if there is a risk of skin contact with concentrated lead alkyls. If biological monitoring (carried out as part of the risk-assessment exercise) reveals a blood-lead level of greater than 40 µg per 100 ml or, in the case of a worker exposed to lead alkyls, a urinary-lead level of greater than 120 µg/litre, the worker concerned should also be considered as significantly exposed to lead.

- If a person's exposure to lead is intermittent (e.g., for just a few hours a week) but in excess of half the *lead-in-air standard*, that exposure may be regarded as insignificant so long as it is below the lead-in-air standard and below half the lead-in-air standard when averaged over a notional 40-hour week.

Note: The standard for lead in air is an 8-hour time-weighted average concentration of 0.15 mg/m^3 (except for tetraethyl lead) and 0.10mg/m^3 of air for tetraethyl lead. For further particulars, the interested reader is commended to HSE publication COP2 which is available from HSE Books (see *FURTHER INFORMATION* at the end of this section)

DUTIES OF EMPLOYER

- An employer's (and self-employed person's) duties under the 1980 Regulations can be summarised as follows. Having assessed the extent to which his employees are (or may be) exposed to lead as they carry out their duties, an employer must —

  (a) provide those employees with as much **information, instruction and training** as they will need to ensure that they are aware of the risks and of the safe working methods and controls introduced for their protection;

  (b) adopt one or more of the following **control measures**, namely: substitution by lead-free materials or low solubility inorganic lead compounds; the use of lead or lead compounds in emulsion or paste form; the use of temperature controls to control the temperature of molten lead to below 500°C; the containment of lead in totally-enclosed plant and in enclosed containers such as drums or bags; an effective exhaust ventilation system [if total exposure is not reasonably practicable]; the exclusion of non-essential workers from the area when an accident is likely to lead to a substantial increase in exposure to lead (in which event, the workers remaining must be issued with and wear suitable protective clothing and respirators); and wet methods.

  (c) if the control measures referred to in (b) do not provide adequate protection against airborne lead, issue the employees concerned with suitable **respiratory protective equipment**;

(d)   unless the exposure is not significant, issue **protective clothing** to every employee who is liable to be exposed to lead — which clothing, including the respiratory protective equipment referred to in (c), must comply with the relevant Community Directive listed in Schedule 1 to the Personal Protective Equipment at Work Regulations 1992 (SI 1992/2966);

(e)   provide adequate **washing facilities (including hot showers or baths, soap, nailbrushes, towels, etc.)**, adequate **changing facilities**, adequate **storage facilities** for respiratory protective equipment and protective clothing put off at the end of the working day or shift, and separate and adequate **accommodation for personal clothing** not worn during working hours.

The control measures described in (b) above must be properly used or applied, as the case may be, and must be maintained in an efficient state, efficient working order and good repair. The same rule applies to the respiratory protective equipment and the protective clothing referred to in paras (c) and (d).

An employer must also see to it that his employees do not eat, drink or smoke in any place which is (or is liable to be) contaminated by lead. Furthermore, he must set aside a room or similar facility (such as a restroom or canteen) in which they can take their meals or smoke.

• Where an employee is liable to be exposed to lead, the employer must take adequate steps to secure the cleanliness of floors, workbenches, external plant surfaces, washing and changing facilities, rest rooms and eating areas (at least once a day), respiratory protective equipment (at the end of every shift or work period), protective clothing (washed, cleaned or renewed at least once a week). Advice on suitable cleaning methods and on the appointment of a responsible person to supervise cleaning procedures is to be found in the Approved Code of Practice referred to earlier and in *FURTHER INFORMATION* at the end of this section.

Air monitoring

• Every employer engaged in work with lead must use air sampling and biological testing to measure the concentrations of airborne lead in the breathing zone of employees and in the general workplace atmosphere. The general requirements for air monitoring and the associated procedures are explained at length in the Approved Code of Practice referred to earlier.

Medical surveillance and biological tests

- Every employee who is employed on work which exposes him (or her) to lead must submit to medical surveillance — *if* his exposure to lead is significant or if an employment medical adviser or appointed doctor certifies that the employee should be kept under medical surveillance. Such employees must present themselves for medical examination and biological tests when and as asked to do so by their employer (but during normal working hours).

- If an employment medical adviser or appointed doctor certifies that, in his opinion, an employee should not be employed on work which exposes him (or her) to lead or that he should only work under the conditions specified in the certificate, the employer will be left with no option but to transfer the employee to suitable alternative work or (if no such work is available) dismiss him. If, on the other hand, an employee is simply suspended from work (e.g., pending the outcome of biological tests or to enable further tests to be made), the employer must either transfer him to suitable alternative work or pay him his normal wages or salary for a minimum period of 26 weeks or until the employment medical adviser or doctor certifies that it is safe for the employee to resume his normal duties, whichever occurs sooner . For further particulars, please turn to the section titled **Suspension on medical grounds** elsewhere in this handbook.

Pregnant employees and women 'of reproductive capacity'

- "In order to safeguard a developing foetus, a woman of reproductive capacity who is employed on work which exposes her to lead and is subject to medical surveillance ..... (a) should be suspended from work which exposes her to lead when her blood level concentration exceeds 40μg/100 ml; (b) should notify her employer as soon as possible if she becomes pregnant; (c) once pregnancy has been notified and the employment medical adviser/appointed doctor informed, should on the advice of the employment medical adviser/appointed doctor .... be suspended from work which exposes her to lead" (per regulation 16 of the 1980 Regulations and para. 118 of the accompanying Approved Code of Practice). For further particulars, please turn to the section titled **Suspension on maternity grounds**.

Restrictions on employment of women and young persons

- Sections 74 and 128 of the Factories Act 1961 caution that no woman or young person may be employed in certain processes connected with lead manufacture. These include: work at a furnace where zinc or lead ores are reduced or treated; work involving ashes containing lead, the desilverising of lead, the melting of scrap lead or zince, the manufacture of lead carbonate, sulphate, chromate, acetate, nitrate, silicate or oxie; the manufacture of solder or alloys containing more than 10 per cent of lead; mixing or pasting in connection with the manufacture or repair of electric accumulators; and the cleaning of workrooms where any of these processes are carried on. For these and other restrictions on the employment of women and young persons, please turn to the section titled **Women & young persons, Employment of** elsewhere in this handbook.

Note: It should be pointed out that an employer's refusal to employ a woman of whatever age in compliance with sections 74 and 128 of the 1961 Act (and related legislation) is *not* unlawful discrimination on grounds of sex and is *not* actionable under the Sex Discrimination Act 1975 (section 4, Employment Act 1989).

Records

- An employer must keep adequate records of the risk assessments, maintenance activities, air monitoring, medical surveillance and biological tests required by the 1980 Regulations and, when asked to do so, must produce those records (other than the health records of identifiable individuals) for inspection by his employees.

- All records must be kept for at least two years from the date of the last entry in them.

  See also **Clay works & potteries, Health surveillance** and **Risk assessment** elsewhere in this handbook.

FURTHER INFORMATION

- The following publications are available from HSE Books at the address given on page 328:

COP 2
Control of lead at work: approved code of practice [Revised June 1985] (in support of SI 1980/1248)
ISBN 0 11 883780 X   £3.90

COP 41
Control of substances hazardous to health in the production of pottery. The Control of Substances Hazardous to Health Regulations 1988. The Control of Lead at Work Regulations 1980. Approved code of practice [1990]   ISBN 0 11 885530 1
£4.50

EH 28
Control of lead: air sampling techniques and strategies [1986]
ISBN 0 11 883555 6   £2.50

MDHS 7
Lead and Inorganic Compounds of Lead in Air. Laboratory method using X-ray fluorescence spectrometry [1987]
ISBN 0 11 885914 5   £2.50

EH 29
Control of lead: outside workers [1981]
ISBN 0 11 883395 2   £2.50

Silica and lead: control of exposure in the pottery industry [1992]
ISBN 0 11 882044 3   £6.00

EH 33
Atmospheric pollution in car parks [1982]
ISBN 0 11 883550 5   £2.50

Free leaflets (Telephone 01787 881165)

IACL 24
The control of lead in the printing industry

IACL 63
Lead assessment in potteries

LEGIONNAIRES' DISEASE

Key points

- Sections 2 and 3 of the Health & Safety at Work etc. Act 1974 impose a general duty on employers (as the owners or occupiers of business premises) to take such steps as are reasonably practicable to ensure the health, safety and welfare of their employees and to identify and prevent (or minimise) any risk to a member of the public from the way in which they conduct their businesses. It is as well to point out that section 3 also applies to self-employed persons (for example, the owners or managers of guest houses, bed-and-breakfast establishments, nursing homes, retirement homes, aerobics clubs, squash courts, leisure facilities, sports centres, etc.).

- The general duty imposed by the 1974 Act is underlined and reinforced by legislation such as the Workplace (Health, Safety & Welfare) Regulations 1992 (SI 1992/3004) and by the Control of Substances Hazardous to Health Regulations 1994 (SI 1994/3246) (the "COSHH Regulations").

  Note: The term "workplace", as used in the 1992 Regulations, refers to any premises or part of premises which is made available to a person as a place of work, and includes any place within those premises to which a person has access while at work (including storerooms, lobbies, corridors, staircases, washrooms, toilets, changing rooms, etc).

- An employer or self-employed person who fails to discharge a duty to which he (or she) is subject by virtue of sections 2 to 7 of the 1974 Act is guilty of an offence and liable on summary conviction to a fine of up to £20,000. If the offender is convicted on indictment, he (or she) could be fined whatever amount the court considers appropriate. The penalty for an offence under the COSHH Regulations is a fine of up to £2,000 or a much higher fine if the offender is convicted on indictment.

- Any employee or member of the public who is injured as a direct consequence of an employer's (or any other person's) negligent failure to comply with his common law and statutory duty to protect the health and safety of his employees and members of the public can pursue a civil action for damages in the ordinary courts. The occupier or owner of business premises may insure against liability for bodily injury or disease sustained by one of his employees or a member of the public, but he cannot insure himself against his criminal liabilities under the 1974 Act or under health and safety regulations made under (or saved by) that Act.

Legionellae pneumophila

- Legionnaires' disease is a form of pneumonia (sometimes fatal) caused by the inhalation of fine droplets of water containing viable legionellae pneumophila bacteria. Those bacteria are undoubtedly hazardous to health. They thrive and multiply in water at a temperature of between 20 and 45 degrees Celsius and are likely to proliferate within any plumbing system contaminated by rust, algae, slime, sludge, organic particulates, and related sedimentary deposits.

- Although the legionellae organisms are commonly associated with water-cooled air conditioning systems and rooftop cooling towers, the bacteria have also been found in storage tanks, calorifiers, and in hot and cold water supply systems. The danger of contracting Legionnaires' disease arises when legionellae-contaminated water is released into the atmosphere in the form of a fine mist or spray.

Duties of employers and others

- Regulation 6 of the COSHH Regulations 1994 imposes a duty on employers (and on persons having control of business premises) to identify and assess the risk of legionellosis from work activities and water sources, and to take appropriate measures to eliminate or minimise that risk.

- The assessment should identify and evaluate all potential sources of risk. If water systems, plant or systems of work could (or are likely to favour) the proliferation of legionella and other micro-organisms, a written (specific and detailed) risk control scheme must be prepared. This should include an up-to-date plan of the premises showing the location and layout of water systems, cooling plant, etc; a description of their safe and correct operation, and the precautions to be taken.

- Measures to prevent the proliferation of legionella in water systems and reduce exposure to water droplets and aerosol sprays should include:

(a)   minimisation of the release of water spray;

(b)   avoidance of water temperatures and conditions that favour the proliferation of legionella and other micro-organisms;

(c)   avoidance of water stagnation;

(d)   avoidance of the use of materials that harbour bacteria and other micro-organisms, or provide nutrients for microbial growth;

(e)   maintenance of the cleanliness of the system and the water in it;

(f)   use of water treatment techniques; and

(g)   action to ensure the correct and safe operation and maintenance of the water system and plant.

The prevention scheme should identify what measures are to be taken, at what intervals, and by whom. To ensure compliance with Regulation 6, any scheme aimed at avoiding risk to employees and members of the public (such as guests in a hotel, guest house, bed-and-breakfast establishment or club, or patients in a hospital or nursing home) from exposure to legionellae must be implemented and properly managed. The scheme itself must be reviewed and updated — the more so if there are any modifications to (or expansion of) the water systems and their associated plant.

Note: For further information, the reader is urged to obtain copies of the approved code of practice and guidance notes referred to at the end of this section.

Selection, training and competence of personnel

* The COSHH Regulations also impose a duty on employers and on the occupiers of business premises to appoint one or more 'competent persons' (who might well be external consultants) to advise them on health and safety matters (and on their duties and responsibilities under the law) and to supervise the implementation of the prevention scheme. An employer or owner may appoint himself to be the 'competent person'. But the appointee must have the ability, experience, information, training

and resources to enable him (or her) to carry out his tasks competently and safely. In the present context, a competent person must be aware of the dangers and must be able to pinpoint those parts of the water systems and control plant which could be a source of danger to guests, customers and employees alike. To pay 'lip service' to the COSHH Regulations by appointing a person who is not truly competent is an offence under the 1974 Act which could lead to prosecution and the attendant heavy penalties if a conviction is obtained.

- If the owner or occupier of business premises does not have the resources to employ a qualified engineer (or someone with the necessary knowledge and skills) to undertake a risk assessment and draw up and implement a prevention scheme, he should contact his local water company who will gladly give advice on water sampling and treatment and on materials suitable for construction which comply with water byelaws. Indeed, all water companies will nowadays provide a maintenance and prevention service (including an initial survey, prevention plan, etc.) or will recommend the organisations best qualified to do so.

Maintenance of plant and equipment

- Regulation 5 of the Workplace (Health, Safety & Welfare) Regulations 1992 (SI 1992/3004) requires employers and the occupiers of premises (including self-employed persons) to clean and maintain the plant and systems to which the Regulations apply (water delivery systems, showers, mechanical ventilations systems, etc.) to ensure that they are in good working order and in good repair. So far as air conditioning systems, cooling towers, evaporative condensers and the like are concerned, this means taking positive steps (regular cleaning and disinfection, routine sampling etc.) to prevent or minimise the risks associated with exposure to legionella.

Cooling towers and evaporative condensers

- Under the Notification of Cooling Towers & Evaporative Condensers Regulations 1992 (SI 1992/2225) every person who has, to any extent, control of non-domestic premises *must* (if he or she has not already done so) immediately notify his local authority if he has (or is about to install) a cooling tower or evaporative condenser on his premises. A local authority should supply a form for this purpose. But if no such form is yet available, the following information must be supplied:

(a)   the address of the premises where the cooling tower or evaporative condenser is to be situated.

(b)   the name, address and telephone number of a person who has, to any extent, control of the premises in question.

(c)   the number of cooling towers and evaporative condensers referred to in (a) above.

(d)   the location on the premises of each of the relevant cooling towers and evaporative condensers.

If the manufacturer of a cooling tower or evaporative condenser has to any extent control of the premises in which they are to be installed, the local authority need only be given the address of the premises in question, and the name and telephone number of the person who (to any extent) has control of those premises.

- Following notification, the owners or managers of business premises must again notify the local authority within one month of any change in the information given in the original notification. The local authority must also be informed in writing when such equipment ceases to be operational.

- A "cooling tower" is a device whose main purpose is to cool water by direct contact between that water and a stream of air. An "evaporative condenser" is a device whose main purpose is to cool a fluid by passing that fluid through a heat exchanger which is itself cooled by contact with water passing through a stream of air.

- Knowledge of the whereabouts of cooling towers and evaporative condensers is intended to help local authority health and safety inspectors 'police' compliance with the law and to investigate the possible source of an outbreak of legionnaires' disease which is why the Regulations were introduced in the first place.

FURTHER INFORMATION

- The reader is commended to the following HSE publications which are available from HSE Books (see page 328):

L8
The prevention or control of legionellosis (including legionnaires disease): Approved code of practice [1995]
ISBN 0 7176 0732 1 £4.75

HS(G) 70
The control of legionellosis including legionnaire's disease. 3rd Edition [1993]
ISBN 0 7176 0451 9 £4.95

- The following documents on legionnaires' disease and related topics are also available — either from The Stationery Office (where indicated) (see page 328) or from the institutions and associations mentioned. Some of these publications may have been updated.

The control of legionellae in health care premises: A Code of Practice
Department of Health [1989]
HMSO
ISBN 0 11 321208 9

CIBSE Technical Memorandum (TM13): *Minimising the risk of legionnaires' disease*
Chartered Institution of Building Services Engineers [1987]
ISBN 0 90 095334 9

British Association for Chemical Specialities: *A Code of Practice: The control of legionellae by the safe and effective operation of cooling systems 1989* Sutton 1989
ISBN 0 95 149500 3

British Standard 6700: 1997: *Specificabon for the design, installation, testing and maintenance of services supplying water for domestic use within buildings and their curtilages.*
Available from: British Standards Institution. 389 Chiswick High Road. London. W4 4AL (Telephone: 0181 996 7000).
Swimming Pool and Allied Trades Association: *Standards for commercial spas: installation, chemicals and water treatment*
Caterham 1986
ISBN 0 94 882401 8

See also **Air conditioning** and **Ventilation** elsewhere in this handbook.

LIFTING MACHINES

Key points

- The fixed and movable parts and working gear of every lifting machine (crane, crab, winch, teagle, pulley block, gin wheel, tranporter or runway, including associated anchoring and fixing appliances) must be of good construction, sound material and adequate strength. Furthermore, they must be free from patent defect and properly maintained (section 27, Factories Act 1961, as amended).

14-monthly thorough examinations

- All such parts and working gear must be thoroughly examined by a competent person at least once in every period of 14 months. A record of the results of every such *thorough examination* must be kept and must contain the particulars prescribed by the Lifting Plant & Equipment (Records of Test & Examination etc.) Regulations 1992 (SI 1992/195)) — as to which, see **Table 5** on page 150 of this handbook. Form F2530 may be used for this purpose (see page 165)

- If a thorough examination of a lifting machine reveals that it is unsafe and must be repaired immediately or within a specified period, a copy of the test results (or Form F2527, if preferred) must be despatched to the nearest area office of the Health & Safety Executive within 28 days of the date on which the examination took place.

- No lifting machine may be taken into use in a factory for the first time unless it has been tested and its parts and working gear thoroughly examined by a competent person. A record of every such test and thorough examination (containing the particulars listed in **Table 4** on page 146 of this handbook. Form F2531 may be employed for this purpose but its use is strictly optional (see again page 165).

Travelling cranes, etc.

- The rails on which a travelling crane moves and the track on which a transporter carriage or runway moves must have an even running surface and be strong enough for the machines in question. All such rails and track must be properly laid, adequately supported (or suspended) and properly maintained.

- To avoid danger to any person working on or near the wheel-track of an overhead travelling crane, the owner or occupier of the factory in question must establish an effective procedure for warning the driver of the presence of that person so as to ensure that the crane does not approach within 6 metres of the place in which that person is working. Persons working above floor level, in a place where they are liable to be struck by an overhead travelling crane or by a load suspended from the crane, must also be warned of the approach of the crane. Again, it is up to the employer or owner of the premises in question to ensure that such warnings are given.

Safe working loads

- Every lifting machine must be plainly marked with its safe working load (or loads). Jib cranes, whose safe working loads can be varied by lowering or raising the jib, must either display an automatic indicator of safe working loads or have attached to it (in a place where it can be easily seen) a table showing the safe working loads at corresponding inclinations of the jib or corresponding radii of the load.

   Note: In a consultative document titled *Proposals for Reform of Health & Safety Poster and Notice Requirements*, the Health & Safety Executive has indicated (November 1994) that it intends to review the requirement for the marking of safe working loads on cranes, winches, pulleys, etc. and will very likely propose the revocation of that requirement in a consultative document on lifting equipment planned for 1997.

FURTHER INFORMATION

- Further information about the requirements of the Lifting Plant & Equipment (Records of Test & Examination etc) Regulations 1992 (*q.v.*), notably in relation to the installation and use of lifting machines/appliances on building sites and works of engineering construction (although the requirements are basically the same) is given on pages 141 to 151 of this handbook in the section titled **Construction work**.

   See also **Hoists & lifts**.

LIGHTING IN WORKPLACES

Key points

- An employer's general duty under section 2 of the Health & Safety at Work etc. Act 1974, "to ensure, so far as is reasonably practicable, the health, safety and welfare at work of all his employees" includes a duty to ensure that no employee is exposed to risk by having to work (or operate a machine, or carry out precision work, or handle a dangerous substance, or negotiate a corridor of staircase) in poorly-lit surroundings.

- A failure to comply with that duty is a criminal offence for which the penalty on summary conviction is a fine of up to £20,000. If the offence consists of a contravention of any requirement or prohibition imposed by an improvement or prohibition notice served by a health and safety inspector, the offender will not only be ordered to pay a heavy fine but could be sent to prison for up to two years (*ibid*; section 33(1)(a) and (g), (1A) an (2A)).

- Any person injured as a direct consequence of his employer's breach of a statutory duty or of his common law (and implied contractual duty) to provide safe working conditions can sue for damages in the ordinary courts. Although an employer can (indeed must) insure against liability for bodily injury or disease sustained by his employees in the course of their employment, he cannot insure against his criminal liabilities under the 1974 Act. See also **Insurance, Compulsory** elsewhere in this handbook.

- Regulations concerning the provision of lighting in workplaces are imprecise. Invariably, an employer (or occupier of business premises) is simply required to provide lighting which is "suitable and sufficient". See *FURTHER INFORMATION* below.

Workplace (Health, Safety & Welfare) Regulations 1992

- The Workplace (Health, Safety & Welfare) Regulations 1992 (SI 1992/3004) caution that *every* workplace must have "suitable and sufficient" lighting — not only in those parts of the premises in which they actually work but also in storerooms, and in the washrooms, toilets, cloakrooms, canteens and eating areas provided for their use (*ibid*; Regs 8 and 20 to 25).

Note: A "workplace" in this context is any premises (or part of premises) made available to one or more persons as a place of work. Contemporary health and safety legislation is no longer restricted to factories, offices, shops and railways premises. It quite literally applies to every workplace (schools, hospitals, hotels, cinemas, leisure centres, guest house, bed-and-breakfast establishment, etc).

- Stairs in particular should be well-lit so that shadows are not cast over the main part of the treads. Where necessary, local lighting should be provided at individual workstations and in areas and places such as staff or works car parks, doorways, loading bays, ramps, pedestrian walkways and traffic routes used by forklift trucks, and so on. Particular attention should be paid to the needs of disabled persons.

- In complying with his duties under the 1992 Regulations, an employer should (whenever possible) make the best use of natural daylight (*ibid*; Reg. 8(2)). To that end, he must see to it that windows and skylights are cleaned regularly and kept free from unnecessary obstructions (such as tall cabinets, stacked materials, etc.). Desks, benches and worktops should be sited to take advantage of the available natural light — unless windows have to be screened or covered for security reasons or the processes on which employees are engaged (e.g., film processing) necessitate particular lighting conditions.

- Light fittings must be suitable for their intended use to avoid dazzling lights and annoying glare. As with windows, light fittings must not be allowed to become obscured (by stacked materials, or whatever) in such a way that the level of lighting becomes insufficient. Light fittings, including light bulbs and fluorescent tubes, must be replaced, repaired or cleaned as often as may be necessary, before the level of lighting becomes insufficient. The fittings themselves must be replaced immediately if they become dangerous (electrically or otherwise) or if they pose an electrical, fire, radiation or collision hazard.

- Light switches in workrooms should be positioned so that they may be found and used easily, and without risk. Wrongly-positioned switches should be relocated, especially when a room or work area is partitioned or converted.

- Without prejudice to an employer's general duty to provide suitable and sufficient lighting, an employer must also provide adequate emergency lighting in every room in which the sudden and unexpected failure of artifical lighting would expose workers to danger (*ibid*).

- Emergency lighting (notably on staircases and in fire escape routes) is prescribed by the Fire Precautions Act 1971 (see below). It is also necessary in workrooms where a sudden power failure could put employees at risk, e.g., if they are engaged in a hazardous activity or process.

- Under Regulation 5 of the 1992 Regulations, every employer must take steps to ensure that his emergency lighting system is in efficient working order and in good repair. He must keep a written (or electronic) log showing when and by whom the system was tested and make that log available for inspection on demand by a health and safety inspector (or by the local fire authority).

Provision & Use of Work Equipment Regulations 1992

- There is a complementary requirement in the Provision & Use of Work Equipment Regulations 1992 (SI 1992/2932), Regulation 21 of which requires employers to provide suitable and sufficient lighting at any place where a person uses "work equipment" — that is to say, any machine, tool or appliance used in the course of his (or her) employment. The accompanying Approved Code of Practice (see *FURTHER INFORMATION* below) points out that special or local lighting may be needed in situations in which an employee is engaged in detailed assembly work or is carrying out precision measurements; or when normal lighting is inadequate for the safe and efficient operation of a machine. Additional lighting, says the code, should also be provided (perhaps in the form of a hand-held or portable lamp) when an employee is engaged in complicated maintenance or repair work or is working in a shaft or other confined space.

Occupiers' Liability Act 1957

- By section 2 of the Occupiers' Liability Act 1957 (as amended), the occupier of premises owes a common duty of care to all his visitors (including tradesmen, contractors' employees, guests and customers) to take such care as is reasonable to ensure that they will be reasonably safe in using the premises for the purposes for which they are invited or permitted by the occupier to be there.

- Implicit in that duty is an obligation to provide sufficient lighting to enable members of the public to move about the premises in safety. Once again, if a visitor, customer or guest stumbles and falls in an unlit passageway or on a badly-lit staircase, the proprietor or occupier of those premises may be sued for damages.

- The proprietor or occupier may also be prosecuted by a health and safety inspector for failing in his duty "to conduct his undertaking in such a way as to ensure .... that persons not in his employment who may be affected thereby are not thereby exposed to risks to their health and safety" (section 3, Health and Safety at Work, etc. Act 1974) . The penalty on summary conviction is a fine of up to £20,000 or, if the offender is convicted on indictment, a fine of an unlimited amount *(ibid.,* section 33(1)(a) and (1A)).

Food Safety (General Food Hygiene) Regulations 1995

- Chapter I of Schedule 1 to the The Food Safety (General Food Hygiene) Regulations 1995 (SI 1995/1763) stipulates that food premises must have adequate natural and/or artificial lighting. The term "food premises" means any business or undertaking in which food or drink intended for human consumption is manufactured, processed, handled, prepared, stored, sold or supplied, whether or not for profit. For further particulars, please turn to the section in this handbook titled **Food safety & hygiene**.

Fire Precautions Act 1971

- A fire certificate issued under the Fire Precautions Act 1971 will ordinarily specify the maintenance of adequate artificial lighting over steps, ramps and passageways as well as the provision of an emergency lighting system and lighting points capable of illuminating all stairways, exit routes, and exit and directional signs. Section 9A of the 1971 Act warns that premises which do not require a fire certificate must nonetheless be equipped with *adequate* means of escape in case of fire.

- A system of emergency lighting should be from a source entirely independent of the normal lighting source and arranged either to come into operation automatically (on the failure of the mains supply) or kept operating at times when natural lighting is insufficient to enable people to leave premises with safety in event of fire. The independent power source will ordinarily consist of a central battery or individual battery-operated system, or an automatic self-starting engine-driven generator.

- Emergency lighting will not normally be required in small shops, restaurants, cafeterias or public-houses, which consist of ground floor premises only and are designed to accommodate fewer than 100 persons — provided there is a sufficient number of suitable exits to enable a rapid evacuation of customers and patrons into the street or other approved dispersal area. If the occupier of business premises is in any doubt about what comprises suitable and sufficient lighting, he should contact his local fire authority.

FURTHER INFORMATION

Recommended illumination levels

- The Lighting Division of the Chartered Institution of Building Services Engineers (CIBSE) has published a *Code of practice for interior lighting* (1994 Edition, price £52.00) which can be purchased by writing to, or telephoning, CIBSE, Delta House, 222 Balham High Road, London SW12 9BS (Telephone 0181-675 5211). The Institution has also prepared a series of *Lighting Guides* (Numbered 1 to 8), plus two further lighting publications, giving more detailed requirements for factories, offices, shops, catering premises, and the like.

- The following HSE publications are available from HSE Books at the address given on page 328:

L22
Work equipment. Provision and Use of Work Equipment Regulations 1992. Guidance on Regulations [1992]
ISBN 0 7176 0414 4   £5.00

L24
Workplace health, safety and welfare. Workplace (Health, Safety and Welfare) Regulations 1992: Approved code of practice and guidance [1992]
ISBN 0 7176 0413 6   £5.00

HS(G) 38
Lighting at work [1987]
ISBN 0 7176 0467 5   £4.00

M

MACHINERY SAFETY
(Duties of employers, manufacturers and suppliers)

Key points

- Legislation concerning the safety of machinery is to be found in
  —

  o sections 2 and 6 of the Health & Safety at Work etc.
     Act 1974, which set out, in general terms, the duties of
     employers and the duties of manufacturers, importers
     and suppliers of machines and their components;

  o the Provision & Use of Work Equipment Regulations
     1992 (SI 1992/2932) which are of particular relevance to
     employers; and in

  o the Supply of Machinery (Safety) Regulations 1992 (SI
     1992/3073), as amended by the Supply of Machinery
     (Safety) (Amendment) Regulations 1994 (SI 1994/2063),
     which implement into UK law the EC Machinery Directive
     (89/392/EEC), as amended by Directives 91/368/EEC and
     93/44/EEC, and the 'CE Marking' Directive (93/68/EEC).

HEALTH & SAFETY AT WORK ETC. ACT 1974

- Section 2 of the Health & Safety at Work etc. Act 1974 imposes a
  general duty on every employer to provide and maintain plant
  and systems of work that are, so far as is reasonably practicable,
  safe and without risks to health. A failure to discharge that duty
  is an offence punishable by a fine of up to £20,000 or (if the
  offender is convicted on indictment) a fine of an unlimited
  amount.

Duties of manufacturers and suppliers, etc.

- The designers, manufacturers and suppliers of machinery

intended for use at work have a general duty to ensure (so far as is reasonably practicable) that every machine they design, sell or supply is safe and without risks to health when used in the way in which it is intended to be used. To that end, the manufacturer or supplier must not only carry out suitable tests and examinations but must also conduct (or instigate) whatever research is necessary to enable him and the designer to identify potential health and safety risks and to eliminate or minimise those risks (*ibid*; section 6).

- Furthermore, when selling or supplying machinery for use at work, the manufacturer, importer or agent is duty-bound to provide his customers with adequate and up-to-date information (handbooks, technical data, operating instructions, etc.) about the use for which the particular machine or item of equipment has been designed or tested and about any conditions necessary to ensure that it will be safe and without risks to health while being set, used, cleaned or maintained by a person at work (*ibid*; section 6(1)(c) and (d)).

- Indeed, unless a supplier can produce a certificate issued by the manufacturer (or designer) to the effect that a particular machine or appliance has been exhaustively tested and examined, and that it is safe when properly used, the importer or agent who supplies or sells such a machine must either test and examine the machine himself or engage the services of a competent person or organisation do so on his behalf (*ibid*; section 6(1)(a) and (b) and (6)). But, see the paragraph headed *SUPPLY OF MACHINERY (SAFETY) REGULATIONS 1992* later in this section.

- The manufacturer, importer, supplier or agent who fails to comply with his duty under section 6 of the 1974 Act is guilty of an offence and liable, on summary conviction, to a fine of up to £20,000; or, if convicted on indictment, a fine of an unlimited amount (*ibid*; section 33(1)(a) and (1A)(a) and (b)).

PROVISION & USE OF WORK EQUIPMENT REGS 1992

- Under the reinforcing provisions of the Provision & Use of Work Equipment Regulations 1992 (*q.v.*) any machine provided for first use in a workplace after 31 December 1992 must not only comply with current health and safety legislation or BSI standards relating to the design and construction of such machines but (where appropriate) must also comply with

Regulations implementing any relevant Community Directive listed in Schedule 1 to the 1992 Regulations (and reproduced, together with their UK-implementing Regulations, in HSE publication L22 (See page 279 for further details).

- Employers and self-employed persons must ensure that every machine provided for the use of their employees or for their own use is so constructed or adapted as to be suitable for the purpose for which it is used or provided. When selecting a machine, an employer (or self-employed person) must take account of the conditions and circumstances in which the machine is to be used (bearing in mind, for example, that some machines are neither designed nor intended for use in wet, humid or flammable atmospheres, or in confined spaces).

- Every machine must be maintained in an efficient state, in efficient working order and in good repair. To that end, an employer is duty-bound to introduce a programme of routine and planned preventive maintenance. If a machine *has* a maintenance log, it must be kept up to date.

Note: Legislation requiring a record to be obtained, kept or made following the test and examination of specified lifting plant and equipment is discussed elsewhere in this handbook in the section titled **Hoists and lifts**.

- If a machine is beyond repair and no longer capable of safely doing the work it was designed or adapted to do, it must either be taken out of service or replaced. Employers must encourage their employees to report any defective or faulty machine and should be wary of disciplining or dismissing any employee for bringing such matters to their attention. Indeed, machine operators and the like have a specific duty under Regulation 12 of the Management of Health & Safety at Work Regulations 1992 (SI 1992/2051) to inform their supervisors or appointed safety officers of any work situation which they reasonably consider to represent a serious and immediate danger to health and safety.

Note: Sections 44 and 100 of the Employment Rights Act 1996 warn employers that it is *prima facie* unlawful to victimise an employee (safety representative, etc) or to dismiss him (or her) or to select him for redundancy for drawing their attention to circumstances connected with his work which he reasonably believes to be harmful or potentially damaging to health or safety. For further details, please turn to the section in this handbook titled **Dismissal or victimisation**.

- People who supervise or manage the use of machinery, as well as machine operators and maintenance workers, must have ready access to *written* information and instructions about the conditions in which, and the methods by which, a particular machine may be used — including advice about any foreseeable abnormal situations and the action to be taken if such a situation were to occur. All such information and instructions must be reinforced by appropriate induction training, reinforced by supervised on-the-job training to ensure that an employee whose job it is to operate, clean, lubricate and maintain machines can do so competently — without putting himself (or herself) at risk or exposing other people to danger See also **Dangerous Machines** and **Fencing & guarding** elsewhere in this handbook.

- Regulations 11 to 24 (the so-called "hardware provisions") of the 1992 Regulations contain comprehensive rules concerning the fencing and guarding of the dangerous parts of machines, protection against specific hazards, the capabilities, positioning and marking of 'Stop-Start' and emergency controls, the isolation of machinery from sources of energy, ambient lighting, the location of warning signs, and so on. For further particulars, please turn also to the sections in this handbook titled **Fencing and guarding, Lighting, Safety and warning signs** and **Work Equipment.**

- The hardware provisions of the 1992 Regulations (referred to in the previous paragraph) do *not*, however, apply to a machine which has been designed and constructed in compliance with standards laid down in current UK legislation implementing the relevant Community (or EC) Directive for that machine. Nor do they apply to relevant machines sold or supplied within the EC which have been manufactured in accordance with 'transposed harmonised standards' (i.e., standards developed by the European Standardisation Bodies and adopted in the UK by the British Standards Institution). Most machines placed on the market from 1 January 1993 must bear the CE marking and be accompanied either by an EC Declaration of Conformity or by an EC Declaration of Incorporation (which matters are discussed later in this section)(*ibid*; Regulation 10).

Note: The Health & Safety Executive (HSE) has published a 64-page booklet giving general guidance on the Provision & Use of Work Equipment Regulations 1992. For details, please see *FURTHER INFORMATION* at the end of this section.

SUPPLY OF MACHINERY (SAFETY) REGULATIONS 1992

- The Supply of Machinery (Safety) Regulations 1992, as amended by the Supply of Machinery (Safety) (Amendment) Regulations 1994 (*q.v.*) came into force on 1 January 1993. The Regulations, which implement Council Directive 89/392/EEC (as variously amended) on the approximation of the laws of the Member States relating to machinery, do *not* apply —

  (i)   to the machinery listed in Tables 1 and 2 of **Appendix I** ((pages 637 to 639) to this handbook ;

  (ii)   to machinery previously used in the European Community or first supplied in the European Community before 1 January 1993;

  (iii) to machinery supplied for use outside the European Community, so long as it does not carry CE marking;

  (iv)   to machinery in respect of which the health and safety risks are wholly covered by other Directives applicable to that machinery (as to which, see Schedule 1 to the PUWER Regulations 1992 — not reproduced here, but listed in pages 43 to 47 of HSE publication L22 (see page 279 of this handbook);

  (v)   to machinery covered by the Low Voltage Electrical Equipment (Safety) Regulations 1989 (SI 1989/728) where the risks are mainly of electrical origin;

  All other machinery is *relevant machinery* and must comply with the 1992 Regulations.

- At the option of the manufacturer or supplier of *relevant machinery*, the 1992 Regulations (as amended) do not apply to a safety component or machinery for the lifting or moving of persons which is first supplied in the European Economic Area (EEA) before 1 January 1977, provided that it complies with national regulations in force on 14 June 1993 when second amending Directive (93/44/EEC) was adopted.

  Note (1): A *safety component* is a component which is supplied separately to fulfil a safety function when in use — the failure or malfunctioning of which endangers the safety or health of exposed persons. *Note (2):* The EEA comprises the 15 Member States of the EEC, plus Iceland and Norway.

Meaning of "machinery"

Regulation 4 of the 1992 Regulations defines "machinery" as

(a)   "an assembly of linked parts or components, at least one of which moves, including, without prejudice to the generality of the foregoing, the appropriate actuators, control and power circuits, joined together for a specific application, in particular for the processing, treatment, moving or packaging of a material;

(b)   an assembly of machines, that is to say, an assembly of items of machinery as referred to in paragraph (a) above which, in order to achieve the same end, are arranged and controlled so that they function as an integral whole notwithstanding that the items of machinery may themselves be relevant machinery and accordingly severally required to comply with these Regulations; or

(c)   interchangeable equipment modifying the function of a machine which is supplied for the purpose of being assembled with an item of machinery as referred to in paragraph (a) above or with a series of different items of machinery or with a tractor by the operator himself save for any such equipment which is a spare part or tool".

General requirements

- The Supply of Machinery (Safety) Regulations 1992 (as amended) are a little too complicated (not to mention lengthy) to allow of more than cursory treatment in a handbook of this size. Fortunately, the Department of Trade & Industry (DTI) has produced two excellent explanatory booklets, which the interested reader can obtain free of charge by telephoning the DTI's **Business in Europe Hotline** on **0117 944 4888** (see also *FURTHER INFORMATION* at the end of this section).

- The 1992 Regulations state that a manufacturer or distributer may not supply *relevant machinery* for use within the European Community *unless* —

(a) it satisfies those provisions of the *essential health and safety requirements* which apply to it (as listed in Annexes B and A, respectively, of the DTI booklets referred to in the previous paragraph);

(b) the appropriate *conformity assessment procedure* has been carried out, either by the manufacturer himself or by his authorised representative in the EC;

(c) the manufacturer (or his authorised representative in the EC) has issued either an *EC Declaration of Conformity* or, as appropriate, a *Declaration of Incorporation* in respect of that machinery;

(d) the *CE marking* has been properly affixed to the machinery; and unless

(e) it is in fact safe (that is to say, safe when properly installed, maintained and used for its intended purpose — there being no risk (or, at best, a minimal risk) of its being the cause or occasion of death or injury to persons or domestic animals, or of it causing damage to property.

These requirements also apply to *relevant machinery* constructed by a manufacturer for his own use.

Conformity assessment procedure

- The manufacturer or importer of *relevant machinery* (other than *Schedule 4 machinery*) will satisfy the *conformity assessment procedure* for that machinery if he can assemble a technical file.

- The *technical file* (which must be in English, if it is drawn up in the UK, and in at least one other Community language) is a file which contains detailed drawings of the machinery in question (including drawings of the control circuits), calculation notes, a list of the *essential health and safety requirements*, standards complied with, other technical specifications, technical reports or certificates obtained from a competent body or laboratory, instructions for the machinery; and so on. The requirements are explained more fully in the DTI booklets referred to earlier.

Table 1
UK APPROVED BODIES
Schedule 4 machinery

The following is a consolidated list of organisations which have been appointed to be United Kingdom Approved Bodies for the purposes of the Supply of Machinery (Safety) Regulations 1992 (SI 1992/3073, as amended by SI1994/2063) **as at 28 February 1997**. They have been notified to the European Commission and other Member States and are able to undertake type-examination and other related activities under the terms of the EC Machinery Directive 89/392/EEC (as amended) within the scope indicated below; as to which, see Table 2 on page 478.

AEA Technology
Thomson House
Risley
WARRINGTON
Cheshire
WA3 6AT

Tel: 01925 254349
Fax: 01925 254109

Scope: **Items 1 - 17**
and **Items B1 - 5** of Schedule 4
to the Regulations.

Identification No. 0466

AMTRI Veritas
Hulley Road
MACCLESFIELD
Cheshire
SK10 2NE

Tel: 01625 425421
Fax: 01625 434964

Scope: **Items A1 - 11 and 15**
and **Items B1 - 3** of Schedule 4
to the Regulations.

Identification No. 0463

BSI Testing
Unit 5
Finway Road
HEMEL HEMPSTEAD
Herts
HP2 7PT

Tel: 01442 233442
Fax: 01442 232442

Scope: **Items A1 - 11 and 16**
and **Items B1 - 5** of Schedule 4
to the Regulations.

Identification No. 0630

ERA Technology
Cleeve Road
Leatherhead
Surrey
HT22 7SA

Tel: 01372 367000 (ext. 2415)
Fax: 01372 367099

Scope: **Items A1 - 17** (excluding equipment for working with meat and analagous materials) and **Items B1 - 5** of Schedule 4 to the Regulations.

Identification No. 0524

(Continued opposite)

Table 1 (Continued)

Lloyds Register of Shipping
Lloyds Register House
29 Wellesley Road
CROYDON
CR0 2AJ

Tel: 0181 681 4040
Fax: 0181 681 6814

Scope: **Items A1 - 17** and **Items B1 - 5** of Schedule 4 to the Regulations.

Identification No. 0038

National Vulcan Engineering
Insurance Group Limited
St Mary's Parsonage
MANCHESTER
M60 9AP

Tel: 0161 834 8124
Fax:0161 681 2394

Scope: **Items 9 - 11 and 15 - 16** and **Items B1 - 5** of Schedule 4 to the Regulations.

Identification No. 0040

Plant Safety
Parklands
825a Wilmslow Road
Didsbury
MANCHESTER
M20 8RE

Tel: 0161 446 4600
Fax: 0161 446 2506

Scope: **Items A1 - 11 and 13 - 17** and **Items B1 - 5** of Schedule 4 to the Regulations.

Identification No. 0041

Powered Access Certification
Ltd
PO Box 27
Carnforth
Lancashire
LA6 1GA

Tel: 01524 782792
Fax: 01524 781301

Scope: **Items A16** of Schedule 4 to the Regulations.

Identification No. 0545

SGS (UK) Limited
Johns Lane
TividalWarley
West Midlands
B69 3HX

Tel: 0121 520 6454
Fax: 0121 520 4117

Scope: Items A1 - 12, 14 - 16 and Items B1 - 3 of Schedule 4 to the Regulations.

Identification No. 0353

Note: Under the Supply of Machinery (Safety) Regulations, type-examination is required only for machinery specified in Schedule 4 (as amended) (see pages 478 to 479) which is not manufactured in accordance with transposed harmonised standards.

Conformity assessment procedures for Schedule 4 machinery

- The conformity assessment procedure for *Schedule 4 machinery* (i.e; machinery which poses special problems, see **Table 2** on pages 478 to 479 below) is a little different. Before supplying such a machine, the manufacturer or his authorised representative in the EC must —

  (a)   draw up the technical file as described earlier and forward it to an *approved body* (see **Table 1** on pages 470 and 471) for their retention (receipt will be acknowledged); or

  (b)   submit the technical file to the *approved* body for a *certificate of adequacy*; or

  (c)   submit the technical file to an *approved* body for an *EC Type Examination certificate.*

  Again, these requirements are explained in detail in the DTI booklets referred to earlier and listed at the end of this section.

EC Declaration of Conformity

- An *EC Declaration of Conformity* (see example on page 475) is a declaration by the manufacturer (or by his authorised representative established within the EC) to the effect that the machine to which the declaration refers complies with all the *essential health and safety requirements* applying to it (as to which, please consult the DTI booklets listed at the end of this section).

Declaration of Incorporation

- A *Declaration of Incorporation* (see example on page 476) is required for *relevant machinery* which is intended for incorporation into, or assembly with, other machinery (so long as it is not interchangeable equipment and cannot function independently of that machinery).

CE Marking

- The CE marking, so-called, is a form of identification (see below) which must be affixed to a machine in respect of which the manufacturer or supplier has issued an EC *Declaration of*

Conformity. So long as it has been lawfully applied, the CE marking indicates that the machine in question meets all the requirements of the Machinery Directive.

- The CE marking must be affixed in a distinct, visible, legible and indelible manner. It is an offence for any person to affix CE marking to machinery unless it satisfies the essential health and safety requirements and is safe. It is an offence also to affix a mark to machinery which may be confused with the correct CE marking.

  If the CE marking is reduced or enlarged, the proportions given in the drawing above must be respected. The various components of the CE marking must have substantially the same vertical dimension, which may not be less than 5mm.

- With the coming into force on 1 January 1995 of the Supply of Machinery (Safety) (Amendment) Regulations 1994 (*q.v.*) the 'CE marking' affixed to relevant machinery need no longer be followed by the last two figures of the year in which it was affixed — so long as the year or manufacture or construction appears elsewhere on the machinery.

- The manufacturers or importers of machinery which was supplied or made available for supply in the EEA before 1 January 1997, and which already carries the 'old-style' CE marking (e.g., 'CE 93') prescribed by the 1992 Regulations *before* they were amended, may continue to supply that machinery until stocks are exhausted. It follows that individuals and organisations which have already purchased that machinery may continue to use it without fear of prosecution.

Offences & penalties

- Failure to comply with the requirements of the Supply of Machinery (Safety) Regulations 1992 (as amended) will not only mean that the machinery in question cannot legally be supplied in the UK but could also result in prosecution. The penalty on conviction is a fine of up to £5,000 (or £2,000 in Northern Ireland) and/or imprisonment for up to three months.

See also the sections titled **Dangerous machines, Defective equipment, Fencing & guarding** and **Machinery safety** elsewhere in this handbook.

EC DECLARATION FORMS

The sample 'EC Declaration of Conformity', 'Declaration of Incorporation' and 'EC Declaration of Conformity for Safety Component'
illustrated on pages 475, 476 and 477 overleaf
comply with the requirements of the Supply of Machinery (Safety) Regulations 1992, as amended by the Supply of Machinery (Safety) (Amendment) Regulations 1994,
and can be purchased from:

CHANCELLOR FORMECON
Gateway
Crewe
CW1 1YN
Telephone 01270 500800

The company also supplies
poly-carbonate 'CE marking' labels (in three sizes)
with 467MP Hi-Performance adhesive.

$C\epsilon$ In accordance with The Supply of Machinery (Safety) Regulations 1992
and The Supply of Machinery (Safety) (Amendment) Regulations 1994

EC DECLARATION OF CONFORMITY $C\epsilon$

See Chancellor 'Guidance for Machinery Suppliers'

COMPLETION OF THIS DECLARATION
Please complete by hand using BLOCK CAPITALS or by typewriter and in the same language as the machinery. See translations overleaf

Responsible person is ☐ **Manufacturer** *(complete Manufacturer only)* ☐ **Importer** *(also complete name and address of Manufacturer)*

MANUFACTURER *(Business name and full address)*

IMPORTER *(Business name and full address)*

DESCRIPTION OF THE MACHINERY
Make, model, type and style:

MACHINERY COMPLIES WITH EC DIRECTIVES, TRANSPOSED HARMONISED STANDARDS, NATIONAL STANDARDS AND TECHNICAL SPECIFICATIONS AS FOLLOWS

Date of manufacture:

Serial number:

Modification number:

Other relevant descriptive information:

* Machinery conforms with the example to which
this EC type-examination certificate relates

THIS SECTION APPLICABLE ONLY TO MACHINERY IN SCHEDULE 4 OF THE REGULATIONS

APPROVED BODY *(name, address and/or identification ref.no.)*

Technical Construction File forwarded - Date:	
EC Type-Examination Certificate *	Dated:
	Cert. Number:
Machinery (or example) granted Certificate of Adequacy	Dated:
	Cert. Number:

IMPORTANT NOTE:
Signature of this EC Declaration of Conformity authorises the manufacturer, or his authorised representative in the Community, to affix the CE mark to the machinery.

The above machinery, taking into account the state of the art, complies with, or is designed and constructed so far as is possible to comply with, the relevant health and safety requirements as indicated in the Technical File.

For and on behalf of the Manufacturer

Name

Status

Date   Signature

For and on behalf of the Importer into European Community

Name

Status

Date   Signature

CHANCELLOR FORMECON

FS.430
J869/001

$C\epsilon$

Reproduced by courtesy of Chancellor Formecon, from whom supplies can be purchased - Tel. 01270 500800

EC **DECLARATION OF INCORPORATION**

In accordance with The Supply of Machinery (Safety) Regulations 1992 and The Supply of Machinery (Safety) (Amendment) Regulations 1994

See Chancellor 'Guidance for Machinery Suppliers'

COMPLETION OF THIS DECLARATION
Please complete by hand using BLOCK CAPITALS or by typewriter and in the same language as the machinery. See instructions which accompany the machinery. See translations overleaf.

Responsible person is ☐ Manufacturer *(complete Manufacturer only)* ☐ Importer *(also complete name and address of Manufacturer)*

MANUFACTURER *(Business name and full address)*

IMPORTER *(Business name and full address)*

DESCRIPTION OF THE COMPONENT MACHINERY
Make, model, type and style:

THIS COMPONENT MACHINERY COMPLIES WITH THE TRANSPOSED HARMONISED STANDARDS AS FOLLOWS

Date of manufacture:

Serial number:

Modification number:

Other relevant descriptive information:

* Machinery conforms with the example to which this EC type-examination certificate relates

The component machinery which is the subject of this declaration of incorporation must not be put into service until the machinery into which it is to be incorporated has been declared in conformity with the provisions of the Supply of Machinery (Safety) Regulations 1992 / Machinery Directive.

THIS SECTION APPLICABLE ONLY TO MACHINERY IN SCHEDULE 4 OF THE REGULATIONS

APPROVED BODY *(name, address and/or identification ref.no.)*

Technical Construction File forwarded - Date:	
EC Type-Examination Certificate *	Dated:
	Cert. Number:
Machinery (or example) granted Certificate of Adequacy	Dated:
	Cert. Number:

IMPORTANT NOTE -
CE marking must **not** be affixed to the component machinery which is the subject of this declaration.

The above component machinery, taking into account the state of the art, complies with, or is designed and constructed so far as is possible to comply with, the relevant health and safety requirements as indicated in the Technical File.

For and on behalf of the Manufacturer

Name

Status

Date   Signature

For and on behalf of the Importer into European Community

Name

Status

Date   Signature

CHANCELLOR FORMECON

FS.431

J870/001

Reproduced by courtesy of Chancellor Formecon, from whom supplies can be purchased - Tel. 01270 500800

In accordance with The Supply of Machinery (Safety) Regulations 1992 and The Supply of Machinery (Safety) (Amendment) Regulations 1994

See Chancellor 'Guidance for Machinery Suppliers'

EC DECLARATION OF CONFORMITY FOR SAFETY COMPONENT

COMPLETION OF THIS DECLARATION
Please complete by hand using BLOCK CAPITALS or by typewriter and in the same language as the instructions which accompany the machinery. See translations overleaf.

Responsible person is ☐ Manufacturer *(complete Manufacturer only)* ☐ Importer *(also complete name and address of Manufacturer)*

MANUFACTURER *(Business name and full address)*

IMPORTER *(Business name and full address)*

DESCRIPTION OF THE SAFETY COMPONENT
Make, model, type and style:

SAFETY COMPONENT COMPLIES WITH TRANSPOSED HARMONISED STANDARDS, NATIONAL STANDARDS AND TECHNICAL SPECIFICATIONS AS FOLLOWS

Date of manufacture:

Serial number:

Modification number:

Other relevant descriptive information:

Details of the safety function fulfilled by this safety component (if not self explanatory from the description given above)

* Machinery conforms with the example to which this EC type-examination certificate relates

THIS SECTION APPLICABLE ONLY TO MACHINERY IN SCHEDULE 4 OF THE REGULATIONS

APPROVED BODY *(name, address and/or identification ref.no.)*

Technical Construction File forwarded - Date:	
EC Type-Examination Certificate *	Dated:
	Cert. Number:
Machinery (or example) granted Certificate of Adequacy	Dated:
	Cert. Number:

IMPORTANT NOTE - CE marking must **not** be affixed to the safety component which is the subject of this declaration.

The above safety component, taking into account the state of the art, complies with, or is designed and constructed so far as is possible to comply with, the relevant health and safety requirements as indicated in the Technical File.

For and on behalf of the Manufacturer

Name

Status

Date   Signature

For and on behalf of the Importer into European Community

Name

Status

Date   Signature

Reproduced by courtesy of Chancellor Formecon, from whom supplies can be purchased - Tel. 01270 500800

Table 2
Schedule 4 Machinery
TYPES OF MACHINERY & SAFETY COMPONENTS
SUBJECT TO SPECIAL ATTESTATION PROCEDURES

A. Machinery

1.   Circular saws (single or multi-blade) for working with wood or meat.

1.1.   Sawing machines with fixed tool operation, having a fixed bed with manual feed of the workpiece or with a demountable power feed.

1.2   Sawing machines with fixed tool during operation, having a manually operated reciprocating saw-bench or carriage.

1.3   Sawing machines with fixed tool during operation, having a built-in mechanical feed device for the workpieces, with manual loading and/or unloading.

1.4   Sawing machines with movable tool during operation, with a mechanical feed device and manual loading and/or unloading.

2.   Hand-fed surface planing machines for woodworking.

3.   Thicknessers for one-side dressing with manual loading and/or unloading for woodworking.

4.   Band-saws with a fixed or mobile bed or carriage and bandsaws with a mobile carriage, with manual loading and/or unloading for working with wood and analogous materials or meat and analogous materials.

5.   Combined machines of the types referred to in 1 to 4 and 7 for woodworking.

6.   Hand-fed tenoning machines with several tool holders for woodworking.

7.   Hand-fed vertical spindle moulding machines.

8.   Portable chain saws for woodworking.

9.   Presses, including press-brakes, for the cold working of metals, with manual loading and/or unloading, whose movable working parts may have a travel exceeding 6 mm and a speed exceeding 30 mm/s.

10.   Injection or compression plastics-moulding machines with manual loading or unloading.

11.   Injection or compression rubber-moulding machines with manual loading or unloading.

Table 2 (Continued)

12. Machinery for underground working of the following types:

    o   machinery on rails: locomotives and brake-vans.
    o   hydraulic-powered roof supports.
    o   internal combustion engines to be fitted to machinery for underground working.

13. Manually-loaded trucks for the collection of household refuse incorporating a compression mechanism.

14. Guards and detachable transmission shafts with universal joints.

15. Vehicle-servicing lifts.

16. Machines for lifting persons involving a risk of falling from a vertical height of greater than 3 metres.

17. Machines for the manufacture of pyrotechnics.

B   **Safety components**

1. Electro-senisitive devices designed specifically to detect persons in order to ensure their safety (non-material barriers, sensor mats, electromagnetic detectors, etc).

2. Logic units which ensure the safety functions of bi-manual controls.

3. Automatic movable screens to protect the presses referred to in items 9, 10 and 11 above.

4. Roll-over protective structures (ROPS).

5. Falling-object protective structures (FOPS).

FURTHER INFORMATION

- The following booklets published by the Department Of Trade & Industry (DTI) can be obtained free of charge by telephoning the DTI's **Business in Europe Hotline** on **01179 944888**.

  Product standards: Machinery
  (UK Regulations April 1993)
  Stock code MA-V00; and

  Product standards: Machinery Update
  (UK amending Regulations October 1994)

Stock code MA-V02

- Copies of the Supply of Machinery (Safety) Regulations 1992 Regulations and of the eponymous 1994 (Amendment Regulations (SIs 1992/3073 and 1994/2063) are available from HMSO bookshops and accredited agents, or from the HMSO Publications Centre (Tel: 0171 873 9090 or Fax: 0171 872 8200).

- The complete texts of Council Directives 89/392/EEC, 91/368/EEC, 93/44/EEC, and the CE Marking Directive (93/68/EEC) were published in the Official Journal (OJ) of the European Communities (Nos L183 of 29.6.89, L198 of 22.7.91, L175 of 19.7.93, and L220 of 30.8.93, respectively). Copies of those texts can be obtained from The Stationery Office and from UK-based European Information Centres and European Documentation Centres. The addresses of those Centres (which may impose a modest charge for their services) are given in the DTI's booklet '*Contacts*', also available from the Business in Europe Hotline on 01179 944 8988.

MAINTENANCE OF PLANT & EQUIPMENT

Key points

- Section 2(2)(a) of the Health & Safety at Work etc. Act 1974 imposes a duty on every employer to provide and maintain plant and systems of work that are, so far as is reasonably practicable, safe and without risks to health.

- An employer cannot expect to comply with his general duty under the 1974 Act or his more specific duties under the Workplace (Health, Safety & Welfare) Regulations 1992 (SI 1992/3004) if the back-up systems (devices and equipment) which provide the ventilation, heating, lighting, power, water, etc. in his premises are not kept in an efficient state, efficient working order, and in good repair.

- For that reason, regulation 5 of the 1992 Regulations requires the owner or occupier of every workplace to inspect, test, adjust, lubricate, and clean all systems, plant and equipment in the workplace to ensure that maintenance and remedial work is carried out regularly. If potentially dangerous defects cannot be remedied immediately, he must see to it that warning notices are posted around the danger area and that access is restricted until repairs are effected. If repairs are not carried out promptly (if, for example, a flushing mechanism in a WC is left unrepaired for longer than is strictly necessary), the employer or occupier will very soon be in breach of his duties under the Regulations and could be prosecuted (or served with an improvement or prohibition notice).

- Finally, employers should keep a written record of their maintenance and repair programme and activities. This will not only ensure that the programme is properly implemented but will enable him to validate its success and highlight inefficiencies. Health and safety inspectors will want to inspect the maintenance log to satisfy themselves that the employer (owner or occupier) is complying with the provisions of Regulation 5.

- An employer who fails to discharge a duty to which he is subject under section 2 of the 1974 Act is guilty of an offence and liable to a fine of up to £20,000 or, if he is convicted on indictment, a fine of an unlimited amount. If he ignores a health and safety inspector's warnings and subsequently contravenes a requirement or prohibition imposed by an improvement or prohibition notice, he is not only liable to a very heavy fine but could be sent to prison for up to two years. The penalty for a contravention of the 1992 Regulations is a fine of up to £2,000 (or a higher amount, if the offender is convicted on indictment) (*ibid;* section 33).

See also **Air conditioning, Accommodation for clothing, Lighting in workplaces, Machinery safety, Toilet facilities, Washing facilities, Ventilation,** and **Work equipment** elsewhere in this handbook.

MANAGING HEALTH & SAFETY AT WORK

Key points

- Section 2 of the Health & Safety at Work etc Act 1974 imposes a general duty on every employer to ensure (so far as is reasonably practicable) the health, safety and welfare at work of all his employees. To that end, an employer must (again, so far as is reasonably practicable) —

    (a) provide safe plant and systems of work;

    (b) make arrangements for safety and the absence of risks to health in connection with the use, handling, storage and transport of articles and substances;

    (c) see to it that his employees are given as much information, instruction, training and supervision as they may require to enable them to carry out their duties safely;

    (d) maintain the workplace in a condition that is safe and without risks to health (including safe means of access and egress);

    (e) provide and maintain a working environment that is safe, without risks to health and adequate as regards facilities and arrangements for the welfare of his employees.

    Any employer who fails to discharge that general duty is guilty of an offence and, if prosecuted, could face a fine of up to £20,000. If he is convicted on indictment, the court is free to impose a much higher fine (*ibid*; section 33(1)(a) and (1A)).

Management of Health & Safety at Work Regulations 1992

- An employer's general duties under section 2 of the 1974 Act have been interpreted in more specific terms by the Management of Health & Safety at Work Regulations 1992 (SI 1992/2051) — as amended by the Management of Health & Safety at Work (Amendment) Regulations 1994 (SI 1994/2865) — which came into force on 1 January 1993 (or, in the case of the Amendment

Regulations, 1 December 1994).

- In the Approved Code of Practice which accompanies the 1992 Regulations (see *FURTHER INFORMATION* below), the Health & Safety Commission (HSC) make the point that, because of their wide-ranging nature, the duties of employers under the 1992 Regulations summarised in this section will very often overlap with the duties imposed by regulations such as the Control of Lead at Work Regulations 1980 (SI 1980/1248), the Control of Asbestos at Work Regulations 1987 (SI 1987/2115), the Control of Substances Hazardous to Health Regulations 1994 (SI 1994/3246), the Health & Safety (Display Screen Equipment) Regulations 1992 (SI 1992/2792), the Provision & Use of Work Equipment Regulations 1992 (SI 1992/2932); and so on — all of which are discussed elsewhere in this handbook under the appropriate suibject heads.

- "Where duties overlap", say the HSC, "compliance with the duty in the more specific regulations will normally be sufficient to comply with the corresponding duty in the Management of Health & Safety at Work Regulations".

- The Management of Health & Safety at Work Regulations 1992 are *not* industry-specific. In other words, they apply to *every* workplace (other than sea-going ships) in which people are employed to work. In short, they are no less applicable to the owner/manager of Ye Olde Corner Tea Shoppe than they are to the Chairman and Board of Directors of a multi-national corporation employing several thousand people in the UK. The only difference is that an employer running a corner shop (or small office or workshop), with fewer than five people 'on the payroll', should not find his duties under 1992 Regulations quite so onerous or time-consuming as might the new pharmaceutical company on the outskirts of town.

RISK ASSESSMENT

- Under the 1992 Management Regulations, an employer must identify and assess the risks (if any) to which his employees are (or may be) exposed while they are at work as well as the risks facing visitors and members of the public arising out of, or in connection with, the way he conducts his business or undertaking (e.g., a faulty appliance or machine in an office or factory, hazardous substances, a frayed stair carpet in a hotel, an unlit passageway, a slippery patch on a supermarket floor; and so on).

Risk assessment and new or expectant mothers

If he employs women of child-bearing age, he must also (in the course of that risk assessment exercise) determine whether any employee of his who is pregnant or breastfeeding, or has given birth to a child within the previous six months, is engaged in work which (because of her condition) could involve risk to her health and safety (or that of her child) from any processes or working conditions, or physical, biological or chemical agents (as to which, see **Pregnant employees & nursing mothers**, elsewhere in this handbook).

If there is nothing an employer can do to avoid the risks confronting a new or expectant mother, he must either alter her working hours or conditions of employment or, if that is not reasonably practicable, suspend her from work (on full pay) until the danger has passed. Furthermore, if a new or expectant mother works at night and produces a certificate signed by her doctor (or a registered midwife) to the effect that she should be taken off night work for a specifed period, in the interests of her health and safety, her employer must either offer to employ her in suitable alternative work during the day or suspend her from work on full pay for the period specified in the notice. For further particulars, please turn to the section titled **Suspension on maternity grounds** elsewhere in this handbook.

Risk assessment and young persons under 18

- The 1992 Regulations also contains provisions relating to the employment of school leavers and young persons under 18. Regulation 13D(1) reminds employers that young persons under 18 may not be fully matured, Furthermore, they are likely to be inexperienced, and are often inclined to be somewhat cavalier in their approach to (and acceptance of) health and safety risks in the workplace.

Note: Regulation 13D was inserted by regulation 2(6) of the Health & Safety (Young Persons) Regulations 1997 (SI 1977/135) which came into force on 3 March 1997. The new Regulations give effect in Great Britain to Articles 6 and 7 of Council Directive 94/33/EC (OJ No. L216, 20.8.94, p. 12) on the protection of young people at work.

- From 3 March 1997, employers may not employ any young person under 18 without first reviewing their risk assessments to determine the particular risks facing young persons in the light of their relative immaturity, lack of experience, and unfamiliarity with the workplace. When doing so, an employer must take particular account of the fitting and layout of the workplace; the machines, plant and equipment in use in the workplace; the amount of training young persons can expect to receive before they are put to work; and the risks they are likely to face if ther are to be engaged in work involving (amongst other things) the handling of equipment for the production, storage or application of compressed liquefied or dissolved gases; or in work involving high-voltage electrical hazards; or in work the pace of which is determined by machinery and involving payments by results. See also **Risk assessment** and **Women & young persons, Employment of** elsewhere in this handbook.

Records

If the employer has five or more people 'on the payroll', he must keep a record of the significant findings of the assessment and identify (by name or job title) which group or groups of employees are especially at risk. See also **Risk assessment** elsewhere in this handbook.

Preventive and protective measures

- The employer's next step is to develop and implement a plan of action to eliminate or (if that is not possible) to minimise the risks identified during the risk assessment exercise — bearing in mind the type of undertaking in which he is engaged, the machinery and equipment installed in his premises, the chemicals and substances he uses, the cleanliness and condition of the workplace, his general duties under section 2 of the 1974 Act (summarised at the beginning of this section), and the requirements or prohibitions imposed by industry-specific or related health and safety regulations (as discussed thoughout this handbook).

- A failure to carry out a risk assessment or to develop and implement a plan of action to prevent or adequately control the risks confronting employees (and members of the public) will not only invite the attentions of a health and safety inspector (whether because of an accident or dangerous occurrence, or in the course of a routine visit) but could lead to criminal prosecution.

HEALTH AND SAFETY ARRANGEMENTS

* Regulation 4 of the 1992 Regulations requires every employer to make and give effect to such arrangements as are appropriate (given the nature of his activities and the size of his undertaking) for the effective planning, organisation, control, monitoring and review of the preventive and protective measures introduced as a consequence of the 'risk assessment' exercise summarised in the previous paragraph.

* In short, an employer must identify priorities, set objectives for the elimination or minimisation of risks, develop a plan of action and timetable, appoint responsible people at all levels to put that plan of action into effect, and make it plain to them that they will be held accountable for any delays or mismanagement.

* Any employer with five or more people in his employ must keep a written (or computer-stored) record of those arrangements and should make it available for inspection on demand by a health and safety inspector.

Safety policy statements

* Section 2(3) of the Health & Safety at Work etc. Act 1974 has long since required employers (other than those with fewer than five employees) to prepare (and, as often as may be appropriate, revise) a written statement of their general policy with respect to the health and safety at work of their employees, and the organisation and arrangements for the time being in force for carrying out that policy. Furthermore, every employer must bring that policy statement to the attention of all his employees (either by displaying on his notice board or, better still, seeing to it that every employee receives a copy. New recruits and temporary employees should have the policy statement explained to them as part of their induction training programme.

* In the consultative document which heralded the 1992 Regulations the Health & Safety Commission remarked that *good* written safety policy statements should demonstrate that the appropriate control measures have been determined and applied. "Unfortunately, HSE inspectors all too often find that a

structured, well though-out approach to health and safety is lacking, in organisations of all sizes. Many health and safety policy statements" concluded the Commission, "are either inadequate or, while adequate on paper, do not reflect reality".

- Regulation 4 of the 1992 Regulations (and the relevant parts of the Approved Code of Practice) emphasise the need for improvement in employers' arrangements for health and safety.

HEALTH SURVEILLANCE

- Every employee in every workplace, whose work activities pose a risk to his (or her) health and safety must be provided with such health surveillance as is appropriate having regard to that risk (*ibid*; Reg. 5).

- The assessment of risk necessarily carried out by an employer in compliance with Regulation 3 of the 1992 Regulations will (or should have) identified circumstances in which health surveillance is mandatory under industry-specific health and safety legislation. Other risks, however, will not be covered by such legislation (e.g., the risk of dermatitis associated with work with raw sugar). For further information, please turn to the sections titled **Diseases, Reportable, Employment Medical Advisory Service, Hazardous substances, Health surveillance** and **Industrial injuries** elsewhere in this handbook.

HEALTH & SAFETY ASSISTANCE

- Regulation 6 imposes a duty on every employer (whatever the size or nature of his business or undertaking) to appoint one or more 'competent persons' to help him comply with the requirements and prohibitions imposed upon him by (or under) health and safety legislation. For further particulars, please turn to the section titled **Competent persons, Appointment of** elsewhere in this handbook.

PROCEDURES FOR SERIOUS AND IMMINENT DANGER

- Every employer must establish and, where necessary, give efect to appropriate procedures to be followed by his employees in the event of serious or imminent danger. Furthermore, he must nominate a sufficient number of competent persons to put those procedures into effect, to evacuate the premises and to 'shepherd' employees and visitors to a place of safety. He must also see to it that the only employees permitted to remain in a dangerous or hazardous area are trained personnel who have specific tasks to carry out (such as shutting down plant that might otherwise compound the danger).

For more detailed advice on the development and implementation of procedures for dealing with situations involving serious and imminent danger, the reader is commended to the Approved Code of Practice referred to in *FURTHER INFORMATION* at the end of this section. See also **Dangerous occurrences** elsewhere in this handbook.

Control of industrial major accident hazards

- There are cognate provisions in the Control of Industrial Major Accident Hazards Regulations 1984 (SI 1984/1902), as amended by the ditto (Amendment) Regulations 1988 (SI 1988/1462). Under those Regulations, any manufacturer having control of installations, in which specified processes (such as alkylation, esterification, sulphonation, distillation, etc.) are used for the production, processing or treatment of organic or inorganic chemicals, must be able to demonstrate to the relevant enforcing authority that he has identified major accident hazards, has taken appropriate steps to prevent or limit the consequences of any major accident, and has provided suitable information, training and equipment for those of his employees who are working on the site. He must also report any major accident to the Health & Safety Executive (HSE) which, in its turn, is duty-bound to relay that information to the Commission of the European Communities.

- The manufacturer is also required to prepare and keep up to date an on-site emergency plan detailing how major accidents will be dealt with on the site. The local authority for the district in which the installation is situated is also duty-bound to prepare and keep up to date an off-site emergency plan on the basis of the information to be supplied to it by the manufacturer after consulting him, the HSE and "any other appropriate person". The manufacturer must also inform persons outside the installation, who may be affected by a major accident occurring on the premises, of the nature of the hazard, and of the safety measures and steps to be taken should such an accident occur. HSE publications HS(R)21 and HS(G)25, which explain the requirements and prohibitions imposed by the 1984 Regulations are to be found at the end of this section under *FURTHER INFORMATION*.

Employment Rights Act 1996

- Sections 44 and 100 of the Employment Rights Act 1996 caution employers that it is unfair to victimise an employee, dismiss him (or her) or select him for redundancy for leaving or proposing to leave his place of work in circumstances of danger which he reasonably believed to be serious and imminent, or for refusing to return to his workstation [or to the dangerous part of the workplace] until the danger had passed. For further particulars, please turn to the section titled **Dismissal or victimisation** elsewhere in this handbook.

COOPERATION & CO-ORDINATION

- When two or more employers share the same building or workplace (whether temporarily or otherwise) they should get together to discuss common health, safety and welfare issues (e.g., cleanliness of premises, removal of obstructions from corridors, fire escape routes and evacuation procedures, whether the activities of one employer pose a risk to other employees working in the same area; and so on. Very much the same approach must be adopted by self-employed persons who are just as liable to prosecution under the 1974 Act as are employers in the mainstream (*ibid*; Reg. 9).

- If there are several employers occupying the same premises, the Code of Practice suggests that a health & safety co-ordinator be elected from among their number to agree joint arrangements and, if need be, to discuss common health and safety issues with the owner of the premises.

'TEMPS' AND CONTRACTORS' EMPLOYEES

- When carry out their risk assessments, employers must consider the interests of 'agency temps', contractors' employees, self-employed tradesmen and the like who, from time to time, will be present in the workplace carrying out maintenance and repair work, cleaning duties, security patrols, etc. If there *are* health and safety rules to be obeyed or danger areas to be avoided, such people must be informed as if they were the employees of the host employer (*ibid*; Reg. 10).

INFORMATION & TRAINING FOR EMPLOYEES

- Every employer must provide his employees with comprehensible and relevant information on any risks to their health and safety as identified by the risk assessment exercise carried out in compliance with Regulation 3 of the 1992 Regulations. He must also see to it that they are made aware of the preventive and protective measures that have been put in place to eliminate or minimise those risks, and of the procedures that have been put in place and the names of the 'competent persons' whose job it is to evacuate them from the premises in the event of fire (or a bomb scare) or any other situation which presents serious and imminent danger (*ibid*; Reg. 8).

- When recruiting employees (and when transferring employees from one section or department to another), an employer must take into account their knowledge, capabilities and experience. Before putting them to work, he must provide comprehensive induction and supervised on-the-job training in safe working methods (evacuation procedures, and the like). All such training must be repeated whenever new plant or equipment is installed (or existing plant and equipment is modified), or when hazardous substances are introduced, or when new working methods are adopted. 'Refresher training' courses should also be provided if there is any suggestion (e.g., a rise in the number of accidents or 'near misses') that employees are not taking their responsibilities for health and safety seriously (*ibid*; Reg. 11).

- Employers would be well-advised to maintain a written (or computerised) record of all health and safety training given to their employees, if only to satisfy a health and safety inspector that the extent and quality of training provided is sufficient for the purposes of the 1992 Regulations. See also **Training of employees** elsewhere in this handbook.

DUTIES OF EMPLOYEES

- Employees must not use any machinery, equipment, dangerous substance, transport equipment, means of production or safety device unless and until they have been given suitable and sufficient training by their employer and have received any instructions relating to the use of that equipment in compliance with the requirements and prohibitions imposed upon their employer by or under the relevant health and safety legislation (*ibid*; Reg. 12(1)).

- If an employee has an accident with a machine (or known hazardous substance), and an investigation by a health and safety inspector reveals that he (or she) had not been comprehensively trained in safe working methods or had not been made aware of the risks or the precautions to be taken, the employer is liable to be prosecuted under the Health & Safety at Work etc. Act, with the attendant heavy penalties if he is convicted. See **Offences & penalties** elsewhere in this handbook.

- An employee is duty-bound to inform his employer (through his immediate supervisor or manager, or the 'competent person' appointed to advise his employer on health and safety matters) of any work situation which a competent and experienced employee would reasonably consider represented a serious and imminent danger to health and safety. He should also report any shortcoming in his employer's protection arrangements for health and safety (although he would be well-advised to discuss his suspicions with the 'competent person' or with his supervisor before taking the matter further) (*ibid*; Reg. 12(2)). See also **Dismissal or victimisation** elsewhere in this handbook.

FURTHER INFORMATION

- The following HSE publications are available from HSE at the address given on page 328:

Code of practice

L21
Management of Health and Safety at Work Regulations 1992: Approved code of practice [1992]
ISBN 0 7176 0412 8   £5.00

Guidance

HS(R)21 (Rev)
A guide to the Control of Industrial Major Accident Hazards Regulations 1984 [1990]
ISBN 0 11 885579 4   £5.00

HS(G)25
*Control of Industrial Major Accident Hazard Regulations 1984
(CIMAH): further guidance on emergency hazards* [1985]
ISBN 0 11 883831 8   £3.00

Health & safety management in schools [1995]
ISBN 0 7176 0770 4   £5.95
HS(G)65

Successful health and safety management
ISBN 0 7176 0425 X   £10.00

Essentials of health and safety at work [1994]
ISBN 0 7176 0716 X   £5.95

Essentials of health and safety at work (Welsh language version)
ISBN 0 7176 0838 7   £5.95

HS(G)96
The costs of accidents at work
ISBN 0 7176 0439 X   £8.50

*Health and safety management in higher and further education:
guidance on inspection, monitoring and auditing* [1992]
ISBN 0 11 886315 0   £3.00

The management of occupational health services for healthcare staff
[1993]
ISBN 0 11 882127 X   £4.50

Free leaflets (Telephone 01787 881165)

INDG123
101 tips to a safer business

INDG 132
5 steps to successful health and safety management

INDG 173
Officewise

MANUAL HANDLING OF LOADS
(Lifting and carrying)

Key points

- The Manual Handling Operations Regulations 1992 (SI 1992/2793) supplement an employer's general duties under section 2 of the Health & Safety at Work etc. Act 1974 by requiring every employer, so far as is reasonably practicable, to avoid the need for his employees to have to undertake any manual handling activity which involves a risk of their being injured. If he cannot eliminate those activities altogether, he must take appropriate steps to reduce the risk of injury to the lowest level reasonably practicable.

- A health and safety inspector has the right to enter an employer's premises, observe the work being done, talk to employees engaged in manual handling operations, examine accident records, and remind the employer about his duties under the 1992 Regulations. If he believes that some employees are particularly at risk, he may invite an employment medical adviser or appointed doctor to intervene or may warn the employer that he is dissatisfied with the way in which certain manual handling operations are being carried on. In a more serious situation, he may serve an improvement or prohibition notice on the employer effectively requiring him to 'set matters to rights' within a stated period or cease a particular activity altogether. A failure to comply with any requirement or prohibition imposed by an improvement or prohibition notice is a very serious offence, for which the penalty on summary conviction is a fine of up to £20,000 and/or imprisonment for a term not exceeding six months.

Meaning of 'manual handling'

- Manual handling means using one or both hands, or a degree of physical force, to lift, move, carry, put down, throw, push or pull a load. The 1992 Regulations do not define the word "load" except to say that it *includes* a person (such as a hospital patient) and an animal (for example, in a veterinary surgery). Otherwise, a load can be taken to include boxes, cartons, sacks, drums, cylinders, bundles of loose materials, and so on — indeed, any discrete moveable item or object — which an employee may be expected to lift, move, carry (etc.) in the course of his or her employment. However, a tool or appliance does not constitute a load so long as it is being used for its intended purpose.

Guidance on the 1992 Regulations

- The Health & Safety Executive (HSE) have published comprehensive guidance on the 1992 Regulations in conjunction with those Regulations. The 48-page booklet gives a great deal of practical advice on 'risk assessment' and the steps which should be taken to eliminate or minimise the risk of injury arising out of manual handling operations. For information about that and related HSE publications, see *FURTHER INFORMATION* at the end of this section.

Duties of employer

- To comply with his duties under the 1992 Regulations, an employer must make a list of every manual handling operation carried on within his business or undertaking. That done, he must then determine which of those operations presents a risk of injury to the persons engaged in them (What does his accident book tell him? What do the employees think?). He must then do something about eliminating or minimising those risks. Can a particular manual handling operation be avoided altogether, e.g., by having raw materials and other supplies palletised by the supplier and loaded directly onto forklift trucks at the point of delivery? Can the amount of effort expended be minimised by issuing employees with mechanical aids such as hand-powered hydraulic hoists, trolleys, lift tables and roller conveyors? In small premises (such as a shoe shop accepting deliveries of large cartons at the rear entrance), it may be wholly impracticable to introduce mechanical aids (if only because of restrictions on space). In such a situation, the employer would be expected to lay down rules which may, for instance require a minimum of two employees to lift or carry a 'largish' carton or to break open the carton at the loading bay or other point of delivery and remove the contents piecemeal.

- One novel feature of the 1992 Regulations is the duty imposed on employers to provide those of their employees who are necessarily engaged in manual handling operations with a general indication (or, where practicable, precise information) about the weight of each and every load and the heaviest side of any load whose centre of gravity is not positioned centrally. This will undoubtedly require a degree of cooperation between employers and their suppliers, and manufacturers and their customers.

- When assessing the risk associated with manual handling operations, an employer must take account of the factors and questions specified in Schedule 1 to the 1992 Regulations (reproduced on page 498). Furthermore, the 'risk assessment' exercise must be repeated if there is reason to suspect that it is no longer valid or if there has been a significant change in the manual handling operations to which the original assessment relates (e.g., a change in packaging methods or the size of loads, or in the number of employees assigned to carry out manual handling operations previously classified as 'low risk').

- Notwithstanding the 1992 Regulations, every employer (whatever the nature of his business) has an overriding statutory duty to ensure the health, safety and welfare at work of his employees. Section 2(2)(b) of the Health and Safety at Work, etc. Act 1974 adds that the matters (amongst others) to which that duty extends include arrangements for ensuring safety and absence of risks to health in connection with the use, storage and transport of articles and substances. To avoid prosecution and the attendant heavy penalties (let alone a civil action for damages at the suit of an injured employee), an employer would be well-advised to lay down ground rules for those of his employees who may be required to lift or carry heavy loads in the course of their duties.

Duty and rights of employees

- The Regulations stress that employees also have a duty to make use of any system of work provided for their protection — including machinery and other aids provided for the safe handling of loads.

- An employee has the right to challenge his (or her) employer's failure or refusal to provide him with help in lifting, carrying or moving a load which he considers to be too heavy or unwieldy to lift or carry alone. Indeed, he may refuse to carry out any manual handling operation which he genuinely believes is likely to cause him injury. However, before doing so, he would be well-advised to seek the advice of his immediate supervisor, or his safety representative, or the 'competent person' necessarily appointed by his employer in accordance with Regulation 6 of the Management of Health & Safety at Work Regulations 1992 (SI 1992/2051).

Note: Sections 44 and 100 of the Employment Rights Act 1996 warn that it is *prima facie* unfair to victimise an employee (or to dismiss him or select him for redundancy) for bringing to his employer's attention, by reasonable means, circumstances connected with his (or her) work which he believes or reasonably believes to be harmful or potentially harmful to his health and safety. An employee victimised or dismissed for that reason may present a complaint to an industrial tribunal regardless of his (or her) age or length of service at the material time.

Strength and stamina, and sex discrimination

- Section 7(2)(a) of the Sex Discrimination Act 1975 cautions that physical strength or stamina is not a "genuine occupational qualification" for a job. In other words, it is unlawful for an employer to refuse to employ a woman for a particular job on grounds only that she lacks the strength or stamina to do the work. If he has any doubt about the capabilities of job applicants, he should apply (and be able to demonstrate that he applied) the *same* criteria to *all* applicants, male *and* female (e.g., by asking each to show what he or she can do).

Information, instruction and training

- Regulation 8 of the Management of Health & Safety at Work Regulations 1992 (*q.v.*) imposes a duty on every employer to provide his employees with "comprehensive and relevant" information on any risks to their health and safety which they are likely to encounter in the course of their employment and on the measures which have been introduced to eliminate or minimise those risks.

- Regulation 11 (*ibid.*) warns that, when entrusting tasks to new recruits and inexperienced employees (including temporary employees and employees transferred from one department or section of the business to another), employers must take into account individual capabilities of those employees and provide them with adequate health and safety training *before* they are put to work.

- In short, induction training is nowadays a 'must' in every workplace in which new recruits are required to carry out work (including manual handling operations) which could put their health and safety at risk. The original training session must be reinforced by 'on-the-job' training and supervision, which must be repeated whenever there is a change in working methods or when new products or processes are introduced. Employers would be well-advised to keep a record of all training provided, and be prepared to make it available for inspection by a health and safety inspector.

See also **Care, Common duty of, Children, Employment of** and **Women & young persons,** elsewhere in this handbook

FURTHER INFORMATION

* The following HSE publications are available from HSE Books at the address given on page 328:

L23
Manual handling. Manual Handling Operations Regulations 1992. Guidance on regulations [1992]
ISBN 0 7176 0411 X   £5.00

HS(G) 115
Manual handling — solutions you can handle
ISBN 0 7176 0693 7   £7.95

Manual handling in drinks delivery
ISBN 0 7176 0731 3   £5.00

Manual handling and lifting: An information and literature review with special reference to the back [1985]
ISBN 0 11 883778 8   £5.50

Manual handling of loads in the health service [1992]
ISBN 0 7176 0430 6   £4.00

Free leaflets (Telephone 01787 881165)

IACL 86
Manual handling assessment in paper and board mills

INDG 109
Lighten the load — employers: guidance for employers on musculoskeletal disorders

INDG 110
Lighten the load — employees: guidance for employees on musculoskeletal disorders

INDG 143
Getting to grips with manual handling: a short guide for employers

Table 1 **The Manual Handling Operations Regulations 1992** **(SI 1992/2793)**	
FACTORS TO WHICH THE EMPLOYER MUST HAVE REGARD AND QUESTIONS HE MUST CONSIDER WHEN MAKING AN ASSESSMENT OF MANUAL HANDLING OPERATIONS	
Column I *Factors*	**Column 2** *Questions*
1. **The tasks**	Do they involve: holding or manipulating loads at distance from the trunk? unsatisfactory bodily movement or posture, especially twisting the trunk, stooping, reaching upwards? excessive movement of loads, especially: excessive lifting or lowering distances? excessive carrying distances? excessive pushing or pulling of loads? risk of sudden movement of loads? frequent or prolonged physical effort? insufficient rest or recovery period? a rate of work imposed by a process? *(Continued opposite)*

Table 1 (Cont.)	
2. **The loads**	**Are they:** heavy? bulky or unwieldy? difficult to grasp? unstable, or with contents likely to shift? sharp, hot or otherwise potentially damaging? *(Continued overleaf)*
3. **The working environment**	**Are there:** space constraints preventing good posture? uneven, slippery or unstable floors? variations in level of floors or work surfaces? extremes of temperature or humidity? conditions causing ventilation problems or gusts of wind? poor lighting conditions?
4. **Individual capability**	**Does the job:** require unusual strength, height, etc? create a hazard to those who might reasonably be considered to be pregnant or to have a health problem? require special information or training for its safe performance?
5. **Other factors**	Is movement or posture hindered by personal protective equipment or by clothing?

MEAL AND REST BREAKS
(Statutory Provisions)

Key points

- UK employees have no general statutory right to be allowed time off work for meal and rest breaks (paid or otherwise). Most of the legislation restricting the working hours and periods of employment of women and young persons (and, in some instances, men) in industry and commerce was repealed some years ago by the Employment Act 1989. Before the appearance of the European Community's Working Time Directive, (see below) the only other protection afforded to UK employees was and is to be found in the Road Traffic Act 1968 and, for drivers of vehicles of 3.5 tonnes and over, the relevant EC Regulations (as to which, please turn to the section titled **Working hours** elsewhere in this handbook).

Note: Legislation restricting the working hours and periods of employment of airline pilots, deep sea divers, and persons employed in specialist occupations will be familiar to employers in the industries in question and is beyond the scope of this handbook.

WORKING TIME DIRECTIVE

- Articles 3, 4, 5, 6, 8 and 16 of the 'Working Time Directive' (EU Council Directive 93/104/EC), which came into force on 23 November 1996, obliges each of the 15 Member States to take the measures necessary to ensure (among other things) that —

  (a)   every worker is entitled to a minimum daily rest break of 11 consecutive hours in every period of 24 hours;

  (b)   employees working more than six hours a day have a rest break (of an unspecified length) during the working day, the duration of which must either be a matter for negotiation and agreement between both sides of industry (either at a local or national level) *or* be prescribed in the appropriate legislation;

  (c)   over a working week of a maximum *average* 48 hours (including overtime) — averaged over a period of not more than four months (or six months in certain circumstances) — workers be allowed a minimum rest period of 24 hours (averaged over a period of not more that 14 days), *in addition to* the minimum 11-hour break referred to in (a) above.

Article 18 of the Directive affords Member States the option not to apply the maximum 48-hour working week for a period of seven years until 23 November 2003 — so long as the appropriate measures are put in place during the intervening period to ensure the health and safety of workers who *expressly agree* to work hours in excess of that maximum. For further particulars, please turn to the section titled **Working hours** elsewhere in this handbook.

Night work

• Night workers, says the Directive, should not be required to work for more than an *average* eight hours in any 24-hour period — averaged over a yet-to-be determined period — unless engaged in hazardous or physically (or mentally) demanding work (as defined by national legislation); in which latter case, the actual number of hours worked at night *must not* exceed eight.

Note: A *night worker* is a person who routinely works at least three hours of his (or her) daily work time during a period of not less than seven hours — which includes the period between midnight and 5:00 a.m. — or who regularly work a certain proportion of his annual working time at night (as defined by national legislation).

Shift workers

• The Directive contains similar provisions for the protection of shift workers, that is to say, workers employed on a pattern of shifts (including rotating or continuous shifts, and work at night) over a given period of days or weeks. Patterns of shift work must take account of the general principle of adapting work to the worker with a view, in particular, to alleviating monotonous work and work at a predetermined work rate. Suitable rest breaks must also be permitted.

Derogations

• The restrictions summarised above need not apply to directors, senior managers and others in decision-making roles (who generally work flexible hours), or to family workers (or to priests, vicars, nuns, monks and others officiating at religious ceremonies in churches and religious communities) so long as the hours they *do* work do not pose a risk to their health and safety.

- Derogations are also permissible in the case of doctors, nurses and other hospital or care workers, security guards, caretakers, prison workers, dock and airport workers, police officers, ambulance men (and women), fire fighters, refuse collectors, people employed in continuous process industries (including workers in the gas, electricity and water industries), press and media workers, farm workers; and so on — so long as the workers concerned "are afforded equivalent periods of compensatory rest". A "foreseeable surge of activity" (e.g., in agriculture, tourism or the postal service) will also justify a temporary lifting of the restrictions on working hours and periods of employment laid down in the Directive. Such derogations will be a matter for national legislation or collective agreement. In the UK, legislation is the more likely method of enforcement.

Note: Given that the Directive was introduced under Article 118a of the Treaty of Rome, and that its challenge has been rejected by the European Court of Justice, the British Government has no choice but to implement the Working Time Directive (which also contains strictures relating to paid annual holidays) and is currently in consultations with both sides of industry concerning its likely impact on employment and current working practices. Draft legislation is expected by mid-1997. The requirement to provide employees with a rest break if their working day exceeds six hours is unlikely to make a great deal of difference to current working arrangements in UK industry and commerce — given that employees generally (let alone the trade unions) will not long tolerate a situation in which they are denied regular meal and rest breaks during the course of the normal working day. Most UK employees also enjoy at least one day a week off work and, unless they work at night, an overnight break of at least 11 hours.

What to do now?

- Arguably, employers in the UK should already be looking to put their houses in order, if the terms and conditions on which their employees are employed do not tally with the corresponding provisions of the Working Time Directive. Public sector workers (that is to say, people employed by 'emanations of the State') already have recourse to UK tribunals and courts to enforce their rights under the Directive. Private sector employees, on the other hand, may have to take a more circuitous route. In short, they may have to obtain a ruling from the European Court of Justice (ECJ) in order to enforce those same rights under the Directive — the more so if the UK Government is somewhat dilatory in introducing implementing legislation, or if it decides not to implement the Directive in full, or if the legislation it *does* introduce is not intended to have retrospective effect.

WRITTEN PARTICULARS OF TERMS OF EMPLOYMENT

- Notwithstanding the foregoing, employers have a duty under Part I (sections 1 to 7) of the Employment Rights Act 1996 to issue a written statement of terms of employment to every person in their employ who is employed under a contract of employment. The statement must include particulars of any terms and conditions relating to hours of work (including any particulars relating to normal working hours, which, by definition, should include information about intervals for meals and rest — whether paid or unpaid). Furthermore, if there *are* no particulars to be included under the heading of working hours, the statement must say as much.

- If an employer refuses or fails to provide his employees with a written statement, or issues a statement which does not comply fully with Part I of the 1996 Act, an employee has every right to refer the matter to an industrial tribunal (and cannot lawfully be dismissed for exercising that right). If the employer remains uncooperative, the tribunal may determine what particulars ought to be included in the written statement — which particulars will form part of the terms and conditions of his (or her) employment and will be enforced, if need be, by a tribunal or court.

HEALTH & SAFETY LEGISLATION

- Although the Health & Safety at Work, etc. Act 1974 makes no mention of meal or rest breaks as such, section 2(1) of that Act nonetheless imposes a general duty on every employer to ensure, so far as is reasonably practicable, the health, safety and welfare at work of all his employees. If an employee is injured or killed in the course of his employment, and an investigation by a health and safety inspector reveals that the employee was required to work long hours without a break for meals or rest, the employer could be prosecuted and, if convicted, could be fined up to £20,000.

- The notion that employees must be allowed meal and rest breaks in the interests of their health, safety and welfare is reinforced by Regulation 25 of the Workplace (Health, Safety & Welfare) Regulations 1992 (SI 1992/3004) — regulation 25 of which imposes a duty on every employer to provide suitable and sufficient rest facilities for his employees, including suitable and sufficient facilities for eating meals, where meals are regularly eaten in the workplace.

- Indeed, there are safety regulation concerning work with prescribed dangerous or hazardous substances which forbid employees to eat or drink in workrooms or to wear work clothing during their meal breaks. In such circumstances, the employer is required to set aside a place where employees can take their meals in relative comfort. The Regulations in question are:

  the Control of Lead at Work Regulations 1980
  (SI 1980/3004) (Regulation 10);

  the Ionising Radiations Regulations 1985
  (SI 1985/1333) (Regulation 6(6));

  the Control of Asbestos at Work Regulations 1987
  (SI 1987/2115) (Regulation 14(4)); and

  the Control of Substances Hazardous to Health
  Regulations 1994 (SI 1994/3246) (Regulation 7(3)).

  For further particulars, please turn to the section titled **Canteens and rest rooms** and **Dangerous chemicals** elsewhere in this handbook. See also the next section: **Meals for employees**.

Pregnant employees and nursing mothers

- Regulation 25 of the 1992 Workplace Regulations (see previous paragraph) requires employers to provide suitable rest facilities for use by any employee who is pregnant or a nursing mother. Again, the implication is that an employer should think twice before denying a pregnant or breastfeeding mother (or any woman who has given birth within the previous six months) time off during the working day to make use of the rest facilities which he is duty-bound to provide for just such a contingency.

- Common sense will dictate what is *suitable* in relation to one workplace, and what is unsuitable in relation to another. In a large factory, office block, hotel or department store, an employer would be expected to set aside a small, well-ventilated room equipped with (or adjacent to) a toilet and washbasin, and furnished with one or more day beds or reclining chairs. In a smaller establishment, employing just a handful of employees, a small curtained-off area, furnished with a comfortable reclining chair, would undoubtedly satisfy the requirement. If not equipped with a toilet or washbasin, the rest area must be situated as near as possible to the washrooms and toilets used by other (female) employees.

- A failure to provide sutiable rest facilities for new or expectant mothers could lead to prosecution and the imposition of a fine of up to £2,000; as to which see **Inspectors, Powers of** and **Offences & Penalties** elsewhere in this handbook. See also the sections titled **Suspension on maternity grounds** and **Pregnant employees and nursing mothers**.

MEALS FOR EMPLOYEES

Key points

- There is no law which requires an employer to provide a full or partial catering service for his employees. However, if employees regularly eat their meals in the workplace, their employer must provide them with suitable and sufficient eating facilities (Regulation 25, Workplace (Health, Safety & Welfare) Regulations 1992 [SI 1992/3004]).

- This means that employees must be able to eat their meals while seated and in relative comfort, in a place where they are not likely to be seen or disturbed by members of the public. There must also be a suitable surface on which to place food, and a facility for preparing or obtaining a hot drink (such as an electric kettle, a vending machine or a canteen). If there is no sandwich bar, cafeteria or snack bar in, or reasonably near to, the workplace, the employer must also provide his employees with the means for heating their own food (e.g. a small oven with a hotplate, or a microwave oven). This is particularly important for shift workers and others whose working hours may not coincide with the opening hours of local shops, sandwich bars and other fast food establishments.

- If a dedicated canteen or simple rest room *is* provided, it must be cleaned regularly to a satisfactory standard of hygiene. Furthermore, a person must be nominated to see to it that it is kept clean.

Hazardous occcupations

- There are safety regulations concerning work with prescribed dangerous or hazardous substances which specifically forbid employees to eat or drink in workrooms or to wear work clothing (overalls, protective clothing, etc.) during their meal breaks. In such circumstances, the employer is duty-bound to set aside a place where his employees can take their meals in relative comfort. For further particulars, please refer to the previous section titled Meal & rest breaks. See also **Canteens & restrooms** elsewhere in this handbook.

MEDICAL REPORTS, ACCESS TO

Key points

- An employer will often ask an employee — or a job applicant — for permission to approach his (or her) family doctor (or GP) for a report on his recent medical history and current state of health. In some large firms, pre and post-employment medical examinations are carried out by the company's own medical team or by independent consultants appointed for that purpose.

- Although it has always been an employee's (or job applicant's) prerogative to refuse to allow his (or her) employer (or putative employer) to make any direct approach to his doctor, this will not usually stand him in good stead if he is anxious to obtain employment or eager to hold on to the job he already occupies. However, the Access to Medical Reports Act 1988 (reviewed below) does give an employee (or job applicant) certain statutory rights in the matter.

HEALTH SURVEILLANCE

- As has been demonstrated elsewhere in this book, contemporary health and safety legislation often includes provision for the routine health surveillance of employees who are engaged in work which exposes (or could expose) them to hazardous substances or to substances known to cause adverse health conditions in certain people.

- Thus, Regulation 5 of the Management of Health & Safety at Work Regulations 1992 imposes a duty on *every* employer to provide his employees with such health surveillance as is appropriate having regard to the type of work they have been employed to do and the substances and processes to which they are exposed in the course of their employment. Paragraph 30 of the accompanying Approved Code of Practice adds that health surveillance procedures may well call for medical examinations (including laboratory tests, X-rays, biological effect monitoring, and so on) by an appropriately qualified practitioner.

- Similar provisions are to be found in the Control of Lead at Work Regulations 1980 (SI 1980/1248), the Ionising Radiations Regulations 1985 (SI 1985/1333), the Control of Asbestos at Work Regulations 1987 (SI 1987/2115), and the Control of Substances Hazardous to Health (COSHH) Regulations 1994 (SI 1994/3246).

- Any employee who is engaged in work which involves exposure to lead, ionising radiation, asbestos or "a substance hazardous to health" within the meaning of Regulation 2 of the COSHH Regulations 1994, has a duty in law to present himself (or herself) for health surveillance procedures (including medical examinations by an Employment Medical Adviser or appointed doctor) when and as required to do so by his employer. If he refuses to cooperate, he may leave his employer with no choice but to dismiss him.

- Employees who are subject to compulsory health surveillance under the Regulations referred to earlier have the right to inspect any and all health records kept on them by their employer.

ACCESS TO MEDICAL REPORTS ACT 1988

- Since 1 January 1989, when the Access to Medical Reports Act 1988 came into force, the whole business of seeking and obtaining a report on an employee's state of health (other than for statutory health surveillance purposes) has been put on a statutory footing.

- In broad terms, the Act gives any person applying for a job, and any person already in work, the right:

(a) to refuse his (or her) employer (or prospective employer) permission to approach his doctor for a medical report on his state of health;

(b) intercept any medical report prepared by his doctor for employment purposes;

(c) to challenge the accuracy or relevance of any of the information given in the medical report;

(d) to attach a statement of his own views to the medical report (if, in the event, his doctor refuses to amend it) before it is sent to the employer;

(e) to refuse to allow the medical report to be sent to the employer; and

(f) to be given access to any medical report supplied for employment purposes during the previous six months.

Meaning of 'Medical Report'

- Under section 2(1) of the Act, a *medical report* is a report on the physical or mental health of an individual prepared by a doctor or physician who is or has been responsible for his or her clinical care. In this context, the word *care* means any "examination, investigation or diagnosis for the purposes of, or in connection with, any form of medical treatment" (*ibid*).

- For most people in employment, their family doctor or GP is the doctor normally responsible for their clinical care. Company doctors, employment medical advisers, factory doctors and other doctors appointed by the Health & Safety Executive or specifically nominated by an employer, may carry out routine or occasional medical examinations of employees when asked to do so by the employer or in compliance with health and safety legislation. But they are not responsible for the clinical care of the employees they examine. If they diagnose a health problem in a particular employee (or job applicant) they will urge that person to seek treatment from his or her own doctor.

- It follows that a medical report prepared by a company doctor will not normally fall within the scope of the Access to Medical

Reports Act 1988. An employee or job applicant will have no statutory right of access to that report and no right to stop the report being sent forward to his or her employer or would-be employer.

- An employer cannot compel an employee (or job applicant) to submit to a medical examination for employment purposes. But he can refuse to engage any person who refuses to attend a pre-employment medical examination. Indeed, he may have no choice but to dismiss an existing employee who unreasonably refuses to be medically examined either by his or her own doctor or one nominated by (and paid for) by the employer.

The contents of medical reports

- While the Access to Medical Reports Act 1988 accepts that an employer may have good reason for wanting a medical report on an employee's state of health, it recognises also that some medical reports may contain information which could prejudice a person's chances of finding and keeping work.

- Does an employer really need to be told that a job applicant is homosexual or that he once had a sexually-transmitted disease? Should a doctor tell an employer that one of his staff has the HIV virus or an alcohol or drug-related problem?

- In the final analysis, it is up to an employee's (or job applicant's) own doctor to decide whether such information should be supplied — given the nature of the employee's job and the questions raised by the employer. What the 1988 Act does is give an employee the right to intercept his (or her) doctor's medical report, to challenge the relevance or accuracy of some of the information contained in the report, to ask his doctor to remove any prejudicial or irrelevant information, to add his own comments and, as a last resort, to refuse to allow the report to go forward.

Procedure

- In the text which follows, the expression *employee* should be taken to include job applicant and the expression employer to include *prospective employer*.

- If an employer wishes to apply to an employee's own doctor for a report on his recent medical history and current state of health he must:

(a)   notify the employee in writing that he wishes to make the application;

(b)   obtain the employee's written consent (reminding him at the same time that he (or she) has the right to withhold that consent);

(c)   advise the employee (again in writing) that he has the right also to see the medical report before it is supplied (even if he has previously indicated that he does not wish to see it); to ask his doctor to amend any part of the report which he considers to be inaccurate, misleading or irrelevant; to attach his own written comments to the report if his doctor is unwilling to alter the report; and (in the final analysis) to refuse to allow the report to go forward.

Finally he must:

(d)   make sure that the employee understands that it is his responsibility (and his alone) to approach his doctor and arrange with him to see or take a copy of the medical report before it is sent forward — emphasising that he must do so within 21 days after the date of the employer's application.

• When applying to an employee's doctor for a medical report, the employer should not only confirm that the employee has consented to his doing so, but must also indicate whether the employee wishes to be given access to the report before it is sent.

• If the employee does not exercise his (or her) statutory right to see the report within 21 days after his employer's application to his doctor, the doctor need wait no longer and can send the report to the employer. If the doctor has been told that the employee does *not* wish to preview the report, he (or she) is free to send it as soon as it is ready. The employee can change his mind about not wanting to see the report. But he will need to act swiftly if he is to have any chance of intercepting the report before his doctor mails it to the employer.

Exceptions

- The 1988 Act recognises that a doctor may be reluctant to show some parts of his medical report to a patient if doing so would cause him distress. The medical report may, for example, indicate that the man or woman is suffering from an incurable illness or that major surgery is required. In those circumstances, the doctor may either withhold the report from the employee altogether or allow him or her to see only parts of it. If he adopts either course, he must write to the employee explaining what he has done and his motives for doing so. At this point the employee may refuse to allow the report to go forward.

Enforcement of the 1988 Act

- If an employee or job applicant is denied (or seems likely to be denied) his (or her) statutory rights under the 1988 Act, he may apply to the county court (or sheriff's court in Scotland) for an order directing his employer or doctor to comply with the relevant requirement of the Act. A refusal to comply with the terms of any such court order would be a contempt of court.

  See also **Employment Medical Advisory Service, Health surveillance** and **Managing health & safety at work** elsewhere in this handbook.

NO SMOKING!

Key points

- Smoking is strictly prohibited in the premises or situations referred to in the following Regulations:

Celluloid (Manufacture etc.) Regulations 1921 (SR & O 1921/1825)

"No person shall be allowed to smoke in any room in which celluloid is manufactured, manipulated or stored" (Reg. 7).

Manufacture of Cinematograph Film Regulations 1928 (SR & O 1928/82)

"No open fire or light, nor any smoking materials or matches ... shall be allowed in any storeroom or in any room in which cinematograph film is manufactured, repaired, manipulated or used. Suitable arrangements shall be provided for the temporary reception outside such rooms of smoking materials, matches and similar articles" (Reg. 10).

Cinematograph Film Stripping Regulations 1939 (SR & O 1939/571)

"No open light or fire, nor any smoking materials or matches ... shall be allowed in any part of the premises. Suitable arrangements shall be provided for the temporary reception outside the premises of smoking materials, matches and similar articles" (Reg. 13).

Testing of Aircraft Engines & Accessories Special Regulations 1952 (SI 1952/1689)

" ..... no smoking shall be allowed, and no person shall smoke in any room, department or place, even in the open air, where testing of aircraft engines or accessories is done, and no person shall strike a light or spark in or introduce a naked flame into any such room, department or place. Notices shall be kept prominently affixed, particularly in or immediately outside each test room, clearly stating that smoking is prohibited in such rooms, departments or places as aforesaid" (Reg. 20).

Food Safety (General Food Hygiene) Regs 1995 (SI 1995/1763)

Guidance notes interpreting the personal hygiene provisions of the 1995 Regulations state that persons engaged in the handling of food or drink intended for human consumption must not smoke (or spit) while doing so or while working in a room in which there is open food.

Highly Flammable Liquids & Liquefied Petroleum Gases Regulations 1972 (SI 1972/917)

"No person shall smoke in any place in which any highly flammable liquid is present and the circumstances are such that smoking would give rise to a risk of fire" and shall display "a clear and bold notice indicating that smoking is prohibited in that place" (Regulation 14)

Control of Lead at Work Regulations 1980 (SI 1980/1248)

"Every employer shall take such steps as are adequate to secure that ... his employees do not eat, drink or smoke in any place which is or is liable to be contaminated by lead"; and that "suitable arrangements are made for such employees to eat, drink or smoke in a place which is not liable to be contamin-ated by lead)" (Reg. 10)

Ionising Radiations Regulations 1985 (SI 1985/1333)	"No employee shall eat, drink, smoke, take snuff or apply cosmetics in any area which the employer has designated as a controlled area ..." (Reg. 6(6)).
Control of Asbestos at Work Regulations 1987 (SI 1980/1248)	"Every employer shall take steps to ensure that his employees do not eat, drink or smoke in any area designated as an asbestos area or a respirator zone" (Reg. 14(4)).
Control of Substances Hazardous to Health Regulations 1994 (SI 1994/3246)	If it is not reasonably practicable "to prevent exposure to a carcinogen by using an alternative substance or process, the employer shall apply all the following measures", including "(e) the prohibition of eating, drinking and smoking in areas that may be contaminated by carcinogens" (Reg. 7(3)).

- For obvious reasons, similar prohibitions apply in mines, on drilling rigs and in premises to which the Explosives Acts 1875 and 1923, and the Fireworks Act 1951, apply (not otherwise reviewed in this handbook).

PASSIVE SMOKING

- The regulations listed above prohibit smoking in the workplaces to which they apply because of the risk of an explosion or fire or because of the risks associated with smoking in workrooms and areas contaminated by dangerous dusts, vapours and fumes. In other words, there is no legislation as yet which prohibits smoking in every workplace on the grounds that smoking is dangerous *per se* or because of the damaging effects of passive smoking on the comfort or health of other people.

- However, there is movement in that direction. Regulation 25(3) of the Workplace (Health, Safety & Welfare) Regulations 1992 (SI 1992/3004) states that the rest rooms or equivalent facilities necessarily provided by employers for the use of their employees must in future "include suitable arrangements to protect non-smokers from discomfort caused by tobacco smoke". Paragraph 239 of the accompanying Approved Code of Practice (see below) warns that, to achieve this, employers will either have to provide separate areas or rooms for smokers and non-smokers *or* ban smoking in rest rooms and rest areas altogether.

FURTHER INFORMATION

• The following publications are available from HSE Books at the address given on page 328:

Code of practice

L24
Workplace health, safety and welfare. Workplace (Health, Safety and Welfare) Regulations 1992: Approved code of practice and guidance [1992]
ISBN 0 7176 0413 6   £5.00

Free leaflet (Telephone 01787 881165)

IND(G) 63
Passive smoking at work
ISBN 0 7176 0882 4   £5.00 per pack of 10 leaflets. Larger quantity discounts

See also **Asbestos at work, Canteens & restrooms, Celluloid & cinematograph film, Food safety & hygiene, Hazardous substances, Highly flammable liquids, Ionising radiation,** and **Lead at work.**

NOISE AT WORK

Key points

- An employer's first duty under the Noise at Work Regulations 1989 (SI 1989/1790, as amended) is to see to it that his employees are not exposed to a level of noise which is likely to damage their hearing.

Noise assessment

- If an employer suspects (see next paragraph) that one or more of his employees may be exposed to noise at or above the *first action level* (or at or above the *peak action level*) he must appoint a "competent person" (e.g., a professional acoustic consultant) to carry out a noise assessment. The assessment must identify the individuals who are exposed to that level of noise, indicate where the noise is coming from (machines, tools, processes, etc.) and provide the employer with sufficient information to enable him to comply with his duties under the 1989 Regulations (*ibid* Regulation 4).

   Note: See **Table 1** opposite for the meaning of the expressions *first action level, peak action level* and *second action level* used in this section.

- In a report titled *Essential elements of noise at work assessments*, published by Sandy Brown Associates (see *FURTHER INFORMATION* below), the authors state that noise assessment is usually needed wherever people have to shout or have difficulty in being heard clearly by someone about two metres away, or wherever they find it difficult to talk to each other.

- If the noise assessment reveals that one or more employees are exposed to the *second action level* or above, or to the peak action level or above, the employer must do all that he reasonably can (by means other than the provision of personal ear protectors) to minimise the exposure of those employees to that noise (*ibid* Regulation 7).

Ear protection

- If, in spite of the employer's efforts to reduce noise levels, an employee's daily personal noise exposure is still likely to be between 85 and 90 dB(A), the employee has the right to be provided with ear protectors for his (or her) personal use — but only if he asks for them (*ibid* Regulation 8(1).

- If, on the other hand, an employee is likely to be exposed to the *second action level* or above, or to the *peak action level* or above, he must not only be issued with personal ear protectors (whether he has asked for them or not) but *must* wear them (*ibid* Regulations 8(2) and 10(2))). When properly worn, the ear protectors issued in these circumstances must be capable of reducing the risk of damage to the employee's hearing to below that arising from exposure to the *second action level* or, as the case may be, to the *peak action level*. An employee who refuses to wear the personal ear protectors necessarily issued to him in accordance with Regulation 8(2) runs the risk of being dismissed for a breach of his statutory duty under Regulation 10(2) of the 1989 Regulations.

Table 1
NOISE AT WORK REGULATIONS 1989
Definitions

FIRST ACTION LEVEL means a daily noise exposure of 85 d(B)A

PEAK ACTION LEVEL means a level of peak sound pressure of 200 pascals

SECOND ACTION LEVEL means a daily personal noise exposure of 90 d(B)A

Ear protection zones

- Any part of a workplace in which employees are routinely exposed to the second action level or above, or the peak action level or above, must be designated an "ear protection zone". The employer must demarcate and identify every ear protection zone in the workplace with one or more of the safety signs (colour-coded white against a blue background) of the size and type specified in paragraph A.3.3 of Appendix A to Part I of BS 5378 ('This is an ear protection zone. Ear protectors must be worn'). Furthermore, the employer must make it known that none of his employees may enter an ear protection zone unless he (or she) is wearing personal ear protectors (*ibid* Regulation 9).

Note: For the names of a selection of organisations which supply safety signs to the required standards, please turn to pages 306 and 307.

Other duties

*   An employer must also —

    (a)   ensure that noise-reduction devices or components fitted to machines are properly used and maintained

    (b)   ensure that personal ear protectors are maintained in an efficient state, in efficient working order and in good repair and

    (c)   see to it that those of his employees who are likely to be exposed to noise at the *first action level* or above (or at the *peak action level* or above) receive adequate information, instruction and training on the damage that can be caused by regular exposure to those noise levels, the steps they can take to minimise the risk, whom they should see to obtain personal ear protectors, and the circumstances in which they must use the personal ear protectors provided for their use.

An employee should also remind his employees that they are duty-bound to report any defect in the personal ear protectors and other protective devices issued or provided for their use.

Exemptions

*   The Health & Safety Executive will, in certain circumstances, exempt an employer from his obligation under Regulation 7 to use methods (other than the provision of personal ear protectors) to reduce the exposure of employees at or above the *second action level*. See *FURTHER INFORMATION* below and the first publication in the accompanying list.

Duties of manufacturers and suppliers

*   Under section 6 of the Health & Safety at Work etc. Act 1974 (as modified by Regulation 12 of the Noise at Work Regulations 1989) the designers, manufacturers and suppliers of any machine

intended for use at work, which is likely to expose an employee to noise at or above the *first action level* (or at or above the *peak action level),* must not only ensure that the machine will be safe when properly used but must also provide their customers with adequate information about the noise likely to be generated by that machine when it is being used.

Note: Machinery sold or supplied within the UK on or after 1 January 1995 must comply with the Supply of Machinery (Safety) Regulations 1992, one of whose requirements is that "machinery must be so designed and constructed that risks resulting from the emission of airborne noise are reduced to the lowest level, taking account of technical progress and the availability of means of reducing noise, in particular at source" (*ibid* Schedule 3, para. 1.5.8).

- The HSE has produced a number of leaflets and guidance notes on the 1989 Regulations. Some of the most important of these are listed below under *FURTHER INFORMATION.*

ENVIRONMENTAL PROTECTION ACT 1990

- If a local authority is satisfied that any noise emitted from industrial, trade or business premises is prejudicial to health or a nuisance to, local residents, it may serve an "abatement notice" on the occupier of the premises in question requiring him to abate the nuisance and to execute such works and take such steps as may be necessary for that purpose. If a person on whom an abatement notice is served, without reasonable excuse, contravenes or fails to comply with any requirement or prohibition imposed by the notice, he shall be guilty of an offence and liable, on summary conviction, to a fine of up to £20,000 (Part III, Environmental Protection Act 1990).

FURTHER INFORMATION

- The following publications are available from HSE Books at the address given on page 328:

Form F2381
Record of octave band sound
ISBN 0 11 885488 7   £3.00

Noise in the workplace: a select bibliography [1990]
ISBN 0 11 885577 8   £3.25

Noise at work: the Noise at Work Regulations 1989 [1989]
Guide No. 1: legal duties of employers to prevent damage to hearing.

Guide No. 2: legal duties of designers, manufacturers, importers and suppliers to prevent damage to hearing.
ISBN 0 7176 0454 3   £3.50

HS(G) 56
Noise at work. Noise assessment, information and control. Noise guides 3 to 8 [1990]
ISBN 0 11 885430 5   £3.00

HS(G) 138
Sound solutions: techniques to reduce noise at work [1995]
ISBN 0 7176 0791 7   £10.95

PM 56
Noise from pneumatic systems [1985]
ISBN 0 11 883529 7   £2.50

Noise in the workplace: a select bibliography [1990]
ISBN 0 11 885577 8   £3.25

Noise reduction at buckle folding machines [1986]
ISBN 0 11 883849 0   £2.50

Noise reduction at web-fed presses [1988]
ISBN 0 11 883972 1   £4.90

Noise control in the rubber industry [1990]
ISBN 0 11 885550 6   £8.50

Contract research report

CRR 63
Noise and the foetus
ISBN 0 7176 0728 3   £25.00

Free leaflets (Telephone 01787 881165)

INDG 75
Introducing the Noise at Work Regulations: a brief guide to the requirements for controlling noise

Note: Information about other free leaflets dealing with noise in the workplace is to be found in HSE Books List of Free Publications.

Other recommended publications

Report NAW 9102
Essentials elements of noise at work assessments
(by Kyriakides and Galbraith)
ISBN 1 873865 00 7   £9.30

available from Sandy Brown Associates. 1 Coleridge Gardens.
London NW6 3QH (Telephone 0171 624 6033).

O

OCCUPIER OF PREMISES *(Duty to Visitors, etc.)*

Key points

- The Occupiers' Liability Act 1957 (as amended by the Occupiers'
  Liability Act 1984) regulates the common duty of care which an
  occupier of premises owes to his visitors in respect of dangers
  due to the state of his premises or to things done or omitted to be
  done on those premises. The common duty of care is a duty to
  take such care as in all the circumstances of the case is
  reasonable to see that the visitor will be reasonably safe in using
  the premises for the purposes for which he is invited or permitted
  by the occupier to be there (*ibid* section 2 (2)).

- Thus, if a visitor to a factory, a client in an office, a customer in a
  shop, a guest in guest in a hotel, etc. is injured as a direct
  consequence of the owner or occupier's negligence, he (or she)
  may bring an action for damages in the ordinary courts. The
  occupier of business premises (to which members of the public
  are invited to resort) will nowadays take out public liability
  insurance. In the case of employees, such insurance is, of course,
  compulsory (as to which, see **Insurance, Compulsory** elsewhere
  in this handbook).

Avoidance of liability for negligence

- Section 2 (1) of the Unfair Contract Terms Act 1977 cautions that "a person cannot, by reference to any contract term or to a notice given to persons generally or to particular persons, exclude or restrict his liability for death or personal injury resulting from negligence". Further, a person's agreement to or awareness of such a contract term or notice is not of itself to be taken as indicating his voluntary acceptance of any risk (*ibid* section 2(3)). While it is open to the occupier of business premises to display a notice warning visitors and members of the public that they enter the premises or use his facilities at their own risk, such a notice will be of no consequence if, in the event, one of his customers is injured. The occupier may be sued and, if negligence is proven, will have to pay damages — notice or no notice.

Duty to children

- When considering the overall safety of his premises, an occupier must be prepared for children to be less careful than adults (section 2 (3), Occupiers' Liability Act 1957). A "Keep Out" notice will not necessarily prevent a child from wandering into dangerous areas within a factory, office block, supermarket, hospital, or whatever. Injuries sustained by a trespassing child will not preclude a civil action for damages in respect of injuries sustained by a wandering child.

Duty to contractors and tradesmen

- On the other hand, the occupier of business premises is entitled to assume "that a person, in the exercise of his calling, will appreciate and guard against any special risks ordinarily incident to it, so far as the occupier leaves him free to do *so*" (*ibid* section 2(3)(b)). For example, a plumber may be presumed to know better than to drill into a wall without first checking for buried electric cables. On the other hand, it would be reasonable to expect the occupier to warn tradesmen of unforeseen or unlikely hazards, such as an unlit staircase, an open kier, a faulty ladder, frayed carpeting, slippery floors, loose fittings, etc. If a tradesman or contractor is injured while undertaking work on business premises, it will be for the court to decide whether or not there had been negligence on the part of the occupier. See also **Accidents to customers, visitors, etc.** elsewhere in this handbook.

Negligence by third party

- If a visitor is injured due to the faulty execution of any work of construction, maintenance or repair by an independent contractor employed by the occupier of the premises in question, the occupier need not be held answerable for those injuries if he had acted reasonably in entrusting the work to an independent contractor and had taken the elementary precaution of satisfying himself that the contractor was competent and that the work had been properly done (*ibid* section 2 (4) (*b*)). For example, if a cafe proprietor has had his premises rewired "on the cheap" by an unqualified electrician, he will almost certainly be liable to pay damages if, in the event, a customer is injured because of faulty workmanship. If, on the other hand, he had engaged the services of a reputable firm of electrical contractors, and had satisfied himself that the work had been carried out in a competent and professional manner, he may escape liability or, at worst, seek his own remedy from the contractor in question.

Health and Safety at Work etc. Act 1974

- Section 3 of the Health and Safety at Work etc. Act 1974 imposes a general duty on employers and self-employed persons to conduct their undertakings in such a way as to ensure, so far as is reasonably practicable, that members of the general public are not needlessly exposed to risk to their health and safety. If a health and safety inspector is of the opinion that premises are unsafe and a risk to members of the public, he may serve an improvement or prohibition notice on the proprietor or occupier of those premises requiring him to set matters to rights or face prosecution (*ibid.*, sections 21 and 22). A person who fails to discharge his duty under section 3 of the Act, or who contravenes any requirement of an improvement notice, is guilty of an offence and liable, on summary conviction, to a fine of up to £20,000 and, on conviction on indictment, a fine of an unlimited amount (*ibid* section 33 (1)(*a*) and (1A)). If the offence consists of a contravention of a requirement or prohibition imposed by a prohibition notice, the person convicted will not only be liable to a heavy fine but could be sent to prison for up to two years (*ibid* section 33(1)(g) and (2A))

- For further related particulars, please turn to the sections titled **Access to premises, Car parks, Care, Common duty of, Fire**

certificate, Fire precautions, Improvement notices and
Prohibition notices, elsewhere in this handbook.

OFFENCES & PENALTIES

Key points

- Any person (employer, self-employed person, company,
  authority or 'corporate body') who fails to comply with the
  requirements or prohibitions imposed upon him by health and
  safety legislation is guilty of an offence and liable to
  prosecution under the Health & Safety at Work etc. Act 1974.

Who pays the penalty?

- A man (or woman) who runs his own business, with just a
  handful of employees, is easily identifiable as the employer
  when a prosecution is pending. Unless he (or she) can show
  that the offence was due to the fault of some other person, he
  will have to pay the fine imposed by the court and, in extreme
  cases, could be sent to prison for up to two years. A large
  corporation or public limited company may be able to find the
  funds to pay a heavy fine, but a 'corporate body' cannot so
  readily be sent to prison.

- The answer is to be found in section 37 of the Health & Safety
  at Work etc. Act 1974 which points out that "Where an offence
  under any of the relevant statutory provisions committed by a
  body corporate is proved to have been committed with the
  consent or connivance of, or to have been attributable to any
  neglect on the part of any director, manager, secretary or other
  similar officer of the body corporate or a person who was
  purporting to act in any such capacity, he as well as the body
  corporate shall be guilty of the offence and shall be liable to be
  proceeded against and punished accordingly".

- The enforcement provisions of the 1974 Act are summarised in
  the Table opposite.

Prosecution by health and safety inspector

- A health and safety inspector will not normally prosecute an employer (self-employed person, or whomever) for an alleged offence under the 1974 Act or associated health and safety legislation without first warning him (or her) that he is in breach of a particular statutory duty and that he runs the risk of being prosecuted unless he 'puts matters to rights', and quickly. The next option open to an inspector is to serve the offending employer with an improvement notice or, if there is an imminent risk of serious personal injury, a prohibition notice. A refusal or failure to comply with the terms laid down in either form notice is a very serious matter and will inevitably lead to prosecution without further warning.

NATURE OF OFFENCE	PENALTY
A failure on the part of an employer, self-employed person, occupier of premises, manufacturer, importer of supplier to discharge a duty imposed by sections 2 to 6 of the 1974 Act (*ibid* section 33(1)(a)).	A fine of up £20,000 (or a fine of an unlimited amount if convicted on indictment) (*ibid* section 33(1A)).
Intentional or reckless interference with (or misuse of) anything provided in the interests of health, safety or welfare in compliance with health and safety legislation (*ibid* sections 8 and 33(1)(b)).	On summary conviction, a fine not exceeding £2,000 (*ibid* section 33(2)).
Charging an employee for items of protective clothing or equipment provided in accordance with a specific requirement of health and safety legislation (or permitting such a charge to be levied) (*ibid* sections 9 and 33(1)(b)).	On summary conviction, a fine not exceeding £2,000 on conviction on indictment, a fine [of an unspecified amount] (*ibid* section 33(3)(a) and (b)(ii)).
Failure to comply with health and safety regulations or with any requirement or prohibition imposed by such regulations (*ibid* sections 15 and 33(1)(c)).	On summary conviction, a fine not exceeding £2,000 on conviction on indictment, a fine [of an unspecified amount] (*ibid* section 33(3)(a) and (b)(ii)) — but see *Note* below.
Refusal to cooperate with the Health & Safety Commission (HSC) in the conduct of its legitimate investigations or to obstruct any person in the exercise of his powers under the Health & Safety Inquiries (Procedure) Regulations 1975 (SI	On summary conviction, a fine not exceeding £2,000 (*ibid* section 33(2)).

1975/335) (*ibid* sections 14 and 33(1)(d)).

Contravention of any requirement imposed by a health and safety inspector in the course of an investigation under sections 20 or 25 of the 1974 Act (*ibid* section 33(1)(e)).	On summary conviction, a fine not exceeding £2,000 (*ibid* section 33(2)).
Preventing or attempting to prevent any other person from appearing before a health and safety inspector or from answering any questions put to that person by the inspector (*ibid* sections 20(2) and 33(1)(f)).	On summary conviction, a fine not exceeding £2,000 (*ibid* section 33(2)).
Contravention of any requirement or prohibition imposed by an improvement or prohibition notice served by a health and safety inspector (*ibid* sections 21, 22 and 33(1)(g)).	(a) On summary conviction, imprisonment for a term not exceeding six months, or a fine not exceeding £20,000, or both (b) on conviction on indictment, imprisonment for a term not exceeding two years, or a fine, or both (*ibid* section 33(2A)).
Intentionally to obstruct a health and safety inspector in the exercise or performance of his powers or duties (*ibid* section 33(1)(h)).	On summary conviction, a fine not exceeding £2,000 (*ibid* section 33(2)).
A refusal or failure to provide information in the form and manner, and within the time limits specified in a notice served on a person by the Health & Safety Commission (*ibid* sections 27(1) and 33(1)(i)).	On summary conviction, a fine not exceeding £2,000; on conviction on indictment, a fine [of an unspecified amount] (*ibid*; section 33(3)(a) and (b)(ii)) — but see *Note* below.
To use or to disclose to unauthorised persons information obtained or relayed in confidence by the Health & Safety Commission in the course of its enquiries or investigations (*ibid*; sections 27(4), 29 and 33(1)(j)).	On summary conviction, a fine not exceeding £2,000; on conviction on indictment, a fine [of an unspecified amount] (*ibid*; section 33(3)(a) and (b)(ii)) — but see *Note* below.
To make a false statement to the HSC or HSE in purported compliance with a requirement to provide certain information to the enforcing body or for the purposes of obtaining a certificate or document under	On summary conviction, a fine not exceeding £2,000; on conviction on indictment, a fine [of an unspecified amount] (*ibid*; section 33(3)(a) and (b)(ii)) — but see *Note* below.

any health and safety regulations (*ibid*; section 33(1)(k)).

Intentionally to make a false entry in any register, book, notice or other document required by health and safety legislation to be kept, served or given; or, with intent to deceive, to make use of any such entry knowing it to be false (*ibid*; section 33(1)(l)).	On summary conviction, a fine not exceeding £2,000; on conviction on indictment, a fine [of an unspecified amount] (*ibid*; section 33(3)(a) and (b)(ii)) — but see *Note* below.
With intent to deceive, to use a document issued (or authorised to be issued) under health and safety legislation, or required for any purpose under that legislation, or to make or possess a document so closely resembling any such document as to be calculated to deceive (*ibid*; section 33(1)(m))	On summary conviction, a fine not exceeding £2,000; on conviction on indictment, a fine [of an unspecified amount] (*ibid*; section 33(3)(a) and (b)(ii)) — but see *Note* below.
Falsely to pretend to be a health and safety inspector (*ibid*; section 33(1((n)).	On summary conviction, a fine not exceeding £2,000 (*ibid*; section 33(2)).
Failure of a person convicted of an offence under health and safety legislation to comply with a court order to remedy the matters specified in the order (*ibid*; section 33(1)(o)).	(a) On summary conviction, imprisonment for a term not exceeding six months, or a fine not exceeding £20,000, or both; (b) on conviction on indictment, imprisonment for a term not exceeding two years, or a fine, or both (*ibid*; section 33(2A)).

Note: The penalty (on conviction on indictment) for an offence under section 33(1)(j) or for an offence under sections 33(1)(c), (i), (k), (l) or (m) consisting of doing something for which a licence is required under health and safety legislation, without the benefit of such a licence; or contravening a term or condition attached to such a licence; or acquiring or attempting to acquire, possessing or using an explosive article or substance in contravention of the relevant health and safety legislation concerning that article or substance (*ibid*; section 33(3)(b)(ii) and (4)).

See also **Health & Safety Commission and Executive and Inspectors, Powers of** elsewhere in this handbook.

P

POWER PRESSES

Key points

- Most factory legislation relating to the fencing and guarding of the dangerous parts of machines (as well as subordinate legislation relating to the safety of woodworking machines, horizontal milling machines, bottling plant, self-acting mules, and an assortment of agricultural machinery) have been repealed or revoked by the Provision & Use of Work Equipment (PUWER) Regulations 1992 (SI 1992/2932), discussed elsewhere in this handbook in the sections titled **Fencing & guarding** and **Machinery safety**.

- Although the Power Presses Regulations 1965 (SI 1965/1441), as amended by the ditto (Amendment) Regulations 1972 (SI 1972/1512), have survived the depredations of the PUWER Regulations relatively unscathed, it should be pointed out that Regulations 5 to 12, 23 and 24 of the 1992 Regulations will nonetheless apply to power presses as they do to all other items of machinery and work equipment installed and used in workplaces.

- The 1965 Regulations contain comprehensive (and, to a degree, more stringent) rules for the appointment of competent persons to prepare power presses for use; the routine examination and testing of power presses and safety devices; the inspection, testing, identification and marking of safety devices; maximum permissible flywheels speeds; the maintenance of registers; and so on.

  See also **Fencing & guarding** and **Machinery safety** elsewhere in this handbook.

FURTHER INFORMATION

- Because of their specialist nature, the 1965 Regulations are not discussed here in any detail. The interested reader is commended to the following HSE publications, all of which are available from HSE Books at the address given on page 328:

L2
Power presses. The Power Presses Regulations 1965 and 1972
[1991]
ISBN 0 11 885534 4   £3.50

Power press safety: press tool design. Part 1: safety in manipulation: standards [1981]
ISBN 0 11 883423 1   £2.60

Power press safety: safety in material feeding and component ejection systems: standards [1984]
ISBN 0 11 883743 5   £2.60

Power press safety: standards [1979]
ISBN 0 11 883248 4   £3.00

Press brakes [1984]
ISBN 0 11 883784 2   £3.20

F.2258
Power presses placard
ISBN 0 11 883323 5   £1.50

PREGNANT EMPLOYEES & NURSING MOTHERS
(Provision of facilities for)

Key points

- In future, every employer must provide suitable rest facilities for those of his employees who are pregnant or nursing mothers, including (where necessary) the facility to lie down. Common sense will dictate what is suitable in relation to one workplace, and what is unsuitable in relation to another. In a large factory, office block, hotel or department store, an employer would be expected to set aside a small, well-ventilated room equipped with a toilet and washbasin and furnished with one or more beds or reclining chairs. In a small establishment, employing just a handful of employees, a small curtained-off area with a comfortable reclining chair would probably satisfy the requirement. However grand or modest, the room or facility must either be equipped with a toilet or washbasin or be conveniently situated in relation to the staff washrooms and toilets (Regulation 25(4), Workplace (Health, Safety & Welfare) Regulations 1992 (SI 1992/3004)).

- For workplaces brought into first use as such before 1 January 1993, this requirement does not come into force until 1 January 1996. For new workplaces (i.e., workplaces brought into first use as such on or after 1 January 1993), the requirement is already in force and must be complied with now.

Management of Health & Safety at Work Regulations 1992

- Under the Management of Health & Safety at Work Regulations 1992 (SI 1992/2051), as amended by the Management of Health & Safety at Work (Amendment) Regulations 1994 (SI 1994/2865), the 'risk assessment exercise' necessarily carried out by *every* employer must include an assessment of the risk to the health and safety of new or expectant mothers (or to that of their babies) arising out of their working conditions, the type of work in which they are engaged (e.g., manual handling of loads, noise, vibration hot or humid conditions, etc.), or their exposure to physical, biological or chemical agents. If there *is* a risk, the employer must either transfer a pregnant employee or new mother to suitable alternative employment or suspend her from work on full pay until that risk has passed (*ibid*; Regulation 13A). See also *Night work* below.

  Note: The expression "new or expectant mother" means an employee who is pregnant; who has given birth within the previous six months; or who is breastfeeding.

- There are similar provisions in the Control of Lead at Work Regulations 1980 (SI 1980/1248) and in the Ionising Radiations Regulations 1985 (SI 1985/1335), both of which require the suspension of a pregnant employee in specified circumstances. Indeed, under the Ionising Radiations Regulations a "woman of reproductive capacity" (that is to say, a woman who is capable of bearing a child, but not necessarily pregnant at the time) may have to be suspended from work involving exposure to ionising radiation, on the advice of an employment medical adviser or HSE-appointed doctor, if the radiation dose limit for her abdomen is likely to be (or has been) exceeded. See **Ionising radiation** and **Lead at work** elsewhere in this handbook.

Note: The right of a new or expectant mother to be paid her normal wages or salary while suspended from work on maternity grounds is laid down in sections 66 to 68 of the Employment Rights Act 1996. Any woman denied her statutory rights in this respect may obtain redress by presenting a complaint to an industrial tribunal.

Night work

- If a doctor or registered midwife certifies that a particular employee who is pregnant or breastfeeding (or has given birth to a child within the previous six months) should not work at night, her employer must either offer her suitable alternative work on the day shift or, if that is not reasonably practicable, suspend her from work on full pay until the danger has passed (Regulation 13A, Management of Health & Safety at Work Regulations 1992 (*q.v.*)).

  For further details, please turn to the sections in this handbook titled **Managing health & safety at work, Suspension on maternity grounds and Women & young persons, Employment of.**

FURTHER INFORMATION

- The following HSE publication is available from HSE Books at the address given on page 328.

  New and expectant mothers at work
  ISBN 0 7176 0826 3   £6.25

PRESSURE SYSTEMS
(and transportable gas containers)

Key points

- Safety requirements with respect to pressure systems and transportable gas containers used (or intended for use) at work are to be found in the Pressure Systems & Transportable Gas Containers Regulations 1989 (SI 1989/2169), as amended by the Carriage of Dangerous Goods (Classification, Packaging & Labelling) & Use of Transportable Pressure Receptacles Regulations 1996 (SI 1996/2092).

- The Regulations, which revoked outdated sections 32, 33, 35 and 36 of the Factories Act 1961 (relating to the construction, maintenance, examination and use of steam boilers and air receivers), impose duties both on the manufacturers, importers and suppliers of pressure systems and transportable gas containers (other than transportable pressure receptacles), and on the occupiers and owners of premises in which those systems and containers are installed or used.

Steam boilers — restrictions on entry

- Section 34 of the 1961 Act (which survived the depredations visited upon its immediate neighbours by the 1989 Regulations) remains in force. It states that no person may enter or be in any steam boiler, which is one of a range of steam boilers, unless all related steam or hot water inlets have been disconnected; or all valves controlling the entry of steam or hot water are closed and securely locked. If the boiler has a blow-off pipe in common with the other boiler (or boilers) in the range, it must be constructed so that it can only be opened by a key which cannot be removed until the valve or tap is closed and is the only key in use for that set of blow-off valves or taps.

The 1989 Regulations — summary of requirements

- The term "pressure system" applies to a system comprising one or more pressure vessels of rigid construction and associated pipework and protective devices. It also applies to pipework and protective devices for connection to gas cylinders, and pipework and devices which contain (or may contain) steam or a fluid (including any gas or liquid which readily forms a gas when released into the atmosphere) at a pressure greater than 0.5 bar above atmospheric pressure. A "transportable gas container" is, in effect, a gas cylinder.

- In essence, the manufacturers, importers and suppliers of pressure systems and transportable gas containers must ensure that their products are designed and constructed in such a way as to be safe when properly installed and used. Pressure vessels must be visibly, legibly and indelibly marked with the manufacturer's name, the serial number, date of manufacture, standard to which the vessel was built, maximum design pressure, and the design temperature.

- People who install pressure systems must do so in a way that does not give rise to danger. Employers must likewise ensure that any employee of theirs who is charged with the responsibility of modifying or repairing a pressure system or gas container is suitably qualified and has the necessary technical data to hand to carry out his (or her) duties safely.

- The Regulations contain detailed rules concerning the provision of information about safe operating limits (notably in relation to mobile pressure systems); written schemes for the periodic examination of specified components; the conduct of examinations by competent persons; the action to be taken in the event of imminent danger; maintenance schedules; the keeping of records; the pressurisation of certain vessels; design standards for transportable gas containers (including 'EC Verification Certificates'); the filling, examination, repair and modification of containers; the re-rating of cylinders; and so on.

- The requirements and prohibitions imposed by the 1989 Regulations are a little too detailed for inclusion in a handbook of this type. However, practical and comprehensive guidance is provided in the publications listed at the end of this section under *FURTHER INFORMATION*.

SIMPLE PRESSURE VESSELS (SAFETY) REGULATIONS 1991

- The Simple Pressure Vessels (Safety) Regulations 1991 (SI 1991/2749, as amended by SI 1994/3098) came into force on 31 December 1991, implementing Council Directive 87/404/EEC (as amended by Directive 90/488/EEC) on the harmonisation of the laws of the Member States relating to simple pressure vessels.

- A "simple pressure vessel" is a welded vessel intended to contain air or nitrogen at a gauge pressure greater than 0.5 bar, not intended for exposure to flame, whose components are made either of non-alloy quality steel, or of non-alloy aluminium, or of non-age hardening aluminium alloy. It consists either of two co-axial outwardly dished ends or of a cylindrical component with circular cross-section, closed at each end, each end being either outwardly dished or flat and being also co-axial with the cylindrical component. For the purposes of the Regulations, a simple pressure vessel has a maximum working pressure of not more than 30 bar, and PS.V of not more than 10,000 bar.litres. The maximum working temperature is not lower than minus 50°C and not higher than 300°C (in the case of steel vessels) or 100°C (in the case of aluminium or aluminium alloy vessels).

* Fire extinguishers, vessels for nuclear use, vessels intended for export outside the EC, and vessels designed for use as part of a ship or aircraft's propulsion system, are excluded from the Regulations. All other simple pressure vessels must meet the essential safety requirements laid down in the Directive referred to above. Certain pressure vessels must carry the 'CE marking' (see pages 472 *et seq.*); others must be manufactured in accordance with accepted EC practice. All must be safe. Documents relating to manufacture, certificates of EC-type approval, technical data, associated reports, etc. must be retained for 10 years. Offences relating to misuse of the CE marking, failure to retain documents, etc. render the offender liable to a fine of up to £5,000.

FURTHER INFORMATION

* The following codes of practice and guidance notes are available from HSE Books at the address given on page 328:

COP 37
Safety of pressure systems. Pressure systems and Transportable Gas Containers Regulations 1989: Approved code of practice. [1990]
ISBN 0 11 885514 X   £4.50

COP 38
Safety of transportable gas containers. Pressure Systems and Transportable Gas Containers Regulations 1989: Approved code of practice [1990]
ISBN 0 11 885515 8   £4.00

HS(R)30
A guide to the Pressure Systems and Transportable Gas Containers Regulations 1989 [1990]
ISBN 0 11 885516 6   £4.50

Pressure Systems and Transportable Gas Containers Regulations 1989: an open learning course [1994]
ISBN 0 7176 0687 2   £16.00

A free leaflet titled *Safe pressure systems* (INDG27) is also available. For a copy, telephone 01787 881165.

PROHIBITION NOTICES
(Risk of serious personal injury)

Key points

- If a health and safety inspector is of the opinion that the activities carried on at a particular workplace (factory, office, shop, building site, warehouse, hotel, school, hospital, workshop, etc.) involve, or are likely to involve, a risk of serious personal injury, he may serve a *prohibition notice* on the owner or occupier of those premises (section 22, Health and Safety at Work etc. Act 1974).

- A prohibition notice is, in effect, a directive instructing the person on whom it has been served to remedy the matters specified in the notice either immediately or within a specified period. A prohibition notice will have immediate effect if the inspector who issued it is of the opinion, and states it, that the risk of serious personal injury is imminent (*ibid*; section 22(4)).

- If a person contravenes any requirement or prohibition imposed by a prohibition notice, he is guilty of an offence and liable, on summary conviction, to a fine of up to £20,000 and/or imprisonment for a term not exceeding six months. If he is convicted on indictment, the court may impose a fine of an unlimited amount and/or may send the offender to prison for up to two years (*ibid*; section 33(1)(g) and (2A)).

- A prohibition notice will —

  (a) state the opinion of the inspector concerning the risk of serious personal injury;

  (b) specify the matters which in his opinion give, or as the case may be, will give rise to the said risk;

  (c) where in his opinion any of those matters involves or, as the case may be, will involve a contravention of a duty imposed by or under the 1974 Act and/or existing health and safety legislation, state that he is of that opinion, specify the relevant enactment or regulations as to which he is of that opinion, and give particulars of the reasons why he is of that opinion; and

(d)   direct that the activities to which the notice relates must not be carried on by or under the control of the person on whom the notice is served until the matters specified in the notice in pursuance of paragraph (b) above, and any associated contraventions so specified in pursuance of paragraph (c) above have been remedied (*ibid*; section 22(3)).

- A prohibition notice may (but need not) include directions as to the measures to be taken to remedy any contravention or matter to which the notice relates; and any such directions may refer the proprietor or occupier of the particular establishment to the terms of an approved code of practice; or may, on the other hand, afford him a choice between different ways of remedying the contravention or matter (*ibid*; section 23(1)).

Note: If a prohibition notice involves the taking of measures to improve the means of escape from fire from the premises in question, the local authority inspector will first of all consult with the fire authority (*ibid*; section 23 (4)).

- If a prohibition notice is not intended to take immediate effect (e.g., if the occupier of a factory, office block, etc. has been given 14 days to repair a potentially dangerous item of equipment), the notice may be withdrawn by the issuing inspector if satisfied that the matters specified in the notice have been fully remedied (*ibid*; section 23 (5) (a)).

Appeal against prohibition notice

- A person on whom a prohibition notice has been served has 21 days within which to appeal to an industrial tribunal and, on such an appeal, the tribunal may either cancel or affirm the notice and, if it affirms it, may do so either in its original form or with such modifications as the tribunal may in the circumstances think fit. The bringing of an appeal against the service of a prohibition notice does *not* have the effect of suspending the notice unless the appellant applies to have the notice suspended and the tribunal gives a direction to that effect (*ibid*; section 24 (3) (b)).

- The procedure for bringing an appeal against the service of a prohibition notice is explained in the notice itself. The rules are explained in greater detail in the Industrial Tribunals

((Constitution & Rules of Procedure) Regulations 1993 (SI 1993/2687) (ISBN 0 11 033137 0), available from The Stationery Office (see page 328), price £6.75 net. The power of an inspector to issue a prohibition notice, and the question of appeals, are described in sections 22, 23 and 24 of the Health and Safety at Work, etc., Act, 1974.

Note: When hearing an appeal against the service of either a prohibition notice or an improvement notice, the tribunal in question may appoint one or more assessors (specialists) to assist in the deliberations (*ibid*; section 24(4)).

See also **Improvement notices** and **Inspectors, Powers of** elsewhere in this handbook.

PROTECTIVE CLOTHING & EQUIPMENT
(Duties of Employer)

Key points

- Legislation concerning the supply and use of personal protective equipment (PPE) is laid down in —

    (a)   the Personal Protective Equipment at Work Regulations 1992 (SI 1992/2966, as amended); and in

    (b)   the Personal Protective Equipment (EC Directive) Regulations 1992 (as amended by the Personal Protective Equipment (EC Directive)(Amendment) Regulations 1993 and 1994 (SIs 1993/3074 and 1994/2326)

    implementing Council Directive 89/686/EEC of 21 December 1989 (as amended by Council Directive 93/95/EEC of 29 October 1993) on the approximation of the laws of the Member States relating to personal protective equipment. Both sets of regulations came into force on 1 January 1993.

Meaning of 'personal protective equipment'

- The term "personal protective equipment" (or PPE) means all equipment (including clothing designed to afford protection against the weather) which is intended to be worn or held by a person at work and which protects him (or her) against one or more risks to his health and safety, and any addition or accessory designed to meet that objective.

Note: Article 1 of Council Directive 89/686/EEC (referred to above) defines PPE as meaning "any device or appliance designed to be worn or held by an individual for protection against one or more health and safety hazards".

PERSONAL PROTECTIVE EQUIPMENT AT WORK REGS 1992

- The PPE Regs 1992 do *not* apply to uniforms whose sole or primary purpose is to present a corporate image or to coveralls, smocks, etc. supplied by an employer to prevent an employee's street clothing from becoming dirty.

- Nor do the Regulations apply to PPE supplied or worn in compliance with the provisions of the following regulations so long as the equipment in question provides adequate protection against all the risks likely to be encountered and has been designed, manufactured and supplied in compliance with the Personal Protective Equipment (EC Directive) Regulations 1992 (*q.v.*) summarised later in this section.

Control of Lead at Work Regulations 1980 (SI 1980/1248)	Respiratory protective equipment and overalls (Regs 7 & 8)
Ionising Radiations Regulations 1985 (SI 1985/1333)	Respiratory protective equipment (Regs 6 & 23)
Control of Asbestos at Work Regulations 1987 (SI 1987/2115)	Respiratory protective equipment (Reg. 8)
Noise at Work Regulations 1989 (SI 1989/1790)	Personal ear protectors (Reg. 8)
Construction (Head Protection) Regulations 1989 (SI 1989/2209)	Safety helmets ('hard hats')
Control of Substances Hazardous to Health (COSHH) Regulations 1994 (SI 1994/3246)	Respiratory protective equipment (Regs 7 & 8)

- Accordingly, the PPE Regulations 1992 apply to PPE (other than that provided in compliance with the Regulations listed above (although the effect is similar) whose purpose it is to provide —

    o   head protection (safety helmets, scalp protectors);

o eye protection (e.g., safety goggles, face shields, welding filters, etc. designed to guard against impact hazards, splashes from chemicals or molten metals, dusts, gases, welding arcs, non-ionising radiation, laser beams, etc.)

o foot protection (safety boots, clogs, foundry boots, wellington boots, anti-static footwear, etc.);

o hand and arm protection (e.g., gloves designed to provide protection against the risks associated with manual handling, vibration, construction and outdoor work, hot and cold materials, electricity, contact with toxic or corrosive substances, the handling of radioactive substances, etc.);

o body protection (in the form of coveralls, chemical suits, vapour suits, splash-resistant suits, dust and fibre-exclusion suits, flame-retardant clothing, cold and wet-weather clothing; and so on).

Duties of employer

• The following is a summary only of the principal provisions of the 1992 Regulations. More comprehensive coverage is provided by the HSE publications listed at the end of this section.

• Regulation 4 of the PPE Regulations 1992 requires every employer to issue suitable PPE to those of his employees who are exposed to a risk to their health and safety *EXCEPT* where and to the extent that those risks have been adequately controlled by other means which are equally or more effective. That same duty applies to self-employed persons.

• In other words, PPE should only be issued as a 'last resort'; that is to say, *after* engineering controls, local exhaust ventilation, the total enclosure of hazardous substances and other control measures have been tried and found wanting. If an employer's only response to work-related risks is to issue his employees with protective clothing and equipment (in the pious hope that they will use or wear it responsibly), he is simply 'side-stepping' his primary duty under the Health & Safety at Work etc. Act 1974 and associated legislation to identify workplace hazards and to use the best practicable means to eliminate any associated risks to the health and safety of his workforce. If he has not even considered alternative control measures, he is guilty of an offence and liable to criminal prosecution — with the attendant heavy penalties if he is convicted.

- Before choosing PPE, an employer must first identify the types of hazard against which the equipment is intended to provide protection. He should then talk to the manufacturers or suppliers of such equipment who are duty-bound to give the correct advice and to supply a suitable form of PPE from the current range of 'CE marked' equipment (see page 473), i.e., equipment which satisfies the relevant provisions of Directive 89/686/EEC and has either been EC type-examined or carries an EC type-approval certificate (*ibid*; Reg. 6).

Compatibility of PPE

- Such PPE as is necessarily issued to an employee to enable him to carry out his duties in safety must be compatible. If, for instance, an employee is expected to wear or use one or more items of protective clothing or equipment at the same time (e.g., a safety helmet as well as a respirator), his employer must see to it that the effectiveness of the one is not cancelled-out or undermined by the intrusion of the other, perhaps because it cannot be properly worn or adjusted (or does not provide adequate protection) when worn or used in concert with the other item of PPE.

Maintenance and replacement of PPE

- PPE must be maintained in an efficient state and in good working order. It must be tested and examined regularly for evidence of defects, should (where appropriate) be stripped-down, cleaned, disinfected and repaired; and must be discarded and replaced when it is beyond its useful life and can no longer provide the degree of protection for which it was designed. Some equipment (such as respirators, fall-arrest systems, and the like) must be checked at regular intervals consistent with the number of times it is used and the manufacturer's instructions. The results of all such tests and examinations should be recorded in a written log (kept both for the employer's benefit and for perusal on demand by a health and safety inspector) (*ibid*; Reg. 7).

Accommodation for PPE

- PPE must be stored in a safe place either after use or when it is not in use. This will not only facilitate routine tests, examination, cleaning and repair but will also ensure that the equipment is not misplaced or damaged by exposure to damp, sunlight or other contaminants. Special storage arrangements will be necessary when the PPE is itself contaminated by hazardous substances (such as asbestos). As a rule of thumb (the more so if there is a risk of cross-contamination), protective clothing and equipment put off at the end of the working day or shift should not be stored in the same room or facility made available for the storage of employees' street clothing (*ibid*; Regulation 8).

Information, instruction and training

- Before issuing his employees with PPE the employer must see to it that they are provided with adequate information, instruction and training about the purpose of the equipment and the measure of protection it affords, the risks to which they would be exposed if they neglected to wear the equipment, the correct way of using or wearing it, and the steps they must take to ensure that the equipment remains in good working order and in an efficient state of repair (*ibid*; Regulation 9).

Duties of employees

- Employees should be given to understand in no uncertain terms that they have a duty in law to make full and proper use of the protective clothing and equipment issued to them in the interests of their health and safety at work. They must also report any loss of, or damage to, that equipment and must return it to the designated storage area at the end of their working day or shift (*ibid*; Regulations 10 & 11).

   Note: An employer's disciplinary rules and procedures should (advisedly) make it an offence (punishable by dismissal or a transfer to another department) for any employee to refuse to use the PPE issued to him by his employer.

Charging employees for PPE

- It is as well to point out that it is an offence under section 9 of the Health & Safety at Work etc. Act 1974 for an employer to charge an employee for any PPE necessarily issued in the interests of health and safety at work. It is an offence to withhold any PPE (or to refuse to replace PPE which has become damaged or lost) pending receipt of a payment. The penalty, on summary conviction, is a fine of up to £2,000, or, if the offender is convicted on indictment, a fine of an unlimited amount (*ibid*; section 33(1)(b) and (3)).

Offences & penalties

- The employer (or self-employed person) who fails to comply with his duties under the 1992 Regulations is liable to prosecution under the 1974 Act and could be fined up to £2,000 (higher, if he is convicted on indictment). If his offence consists of a refusal or failure to comply with the terms of an improvement or prohibition notice served on him by a health and safety inspector) he could face a fine of up to £20,000 and/or imprisonment for up to six months (two years, if convicted on indictment).

PRODUCT STANDARDS FOR PPE

- The manufacturers, importers and suppliers of "articles intended for use at work" (which expression includes PPE) have a duty under section 6 of the 1974 Act to ensure that every such article will be safe when used in the way in which it is intended to be used. To that end, they must carry out all necessary research (supported by tests and examinations) and must provide as much technical data, handbooks, instructions etc. as will enable the customer or 'end user' to make the right selection and to use and maintain the equipment correctly. A failure to comply with section 6 is a criminal offence for which the penalty on summary conviction is a fine of up to £20,000 (or higher, if the offender is convicted on indictment).

- In recent years, the general duties of manufacturers, importers and suppliers of PPE have been reinforced by the more precise requirements of the Personal Protective Equipment (EC Directive) Regulations 1992, as amended by the ditto (Amendment) Regulations 1994 (*q.v.*). The Regulations implement in the UK the current EC Directive (89/686/EEC, as amended by Council Directive 93/95/EEC) on the approximation of the laws of the Member States relating to personal protective equipment.

- When purchasing (or making enquiries about) PPE for use by their employees, employers should look for the 'CE marking' (there is an example on page 473) which, if lawfully affixed to the PPE in question, means that it satisfies the basic health and safety requirements laid down in the Schedule to the 1992 Regulations and (if of 'complex design') that it has been issued with an EC type-examination certificate (by an EC-approved examining body) and is subject to ongoing production surveillance. Simple PPE must also bear the 'CE marking' but need only be accompanied by an EC Declaration of Conformity (effectively, a declaration by the manufacturer or his authorised representative in the EC that the equipment satisfies the design and manufacturing requirements laid down in the PPE Directive).

FURTHER INFORMATION

• The following publication is available from HSE Books at the address given on page 328:

L25
Personal Protective Equipment at Work Regulations 1992.
Guidance on Regulations [1992]
ISBN 07176 0415 2   £5.00

EH 27
Acrylonitrile: personal protective equipment [1981]
ISBN 0 11 883381 2   £2.50

EH 53
Respiratory protective equipment for use against airborne radioactivity
[1990]
ISBN 0 11 885417 8   £2.50

HS(G) 53
Respiratory protective equipment: a practical guide for users [1990]
ISBN 0 11 885522 0   £4.00

Respiratory protective equipment: legislative requirements and lists of HSE approved standards and type approved equipment. [3rd Edition, 1992]
ISBN 0 11 886382 7   £3.25

Free leaflets (Telephone 01787 881165)

IACL 56
Ceramics: personal protective equipment

INDG 111
Personal protective equipment in the chemical industry

INDG 174
Personal protective equipment at work

R

RISK ASSESSMENT

Key points

- Regulation 3 of the Management of Health & Safety at Work Regulations 1992 (SI 1992/2051) imposes a duty on *every* employer (and on every self-employed person) to make a "suitable and sufficient assessment" of the risks to which (he or) his employees are exposed while they are at work and of any risks to members of the public (customers, clients, visitors, guests, passers-by) who may be affected by the way in which he conducts his business or undertaking.

- Risk assessment is also mandatory under —

  (a) the Control of Lead at Work Requlations 1980
       (SI 1980/1248);
  (b) the Ionising Radiations Regulations 1985
       (SI 1985/1333);
  (c) the Control of Asbestos at Work Regulations 1987
       (SI 1987/2115);
  (d) the Electricity at Work Regulations 1989
       (SI 1989/635);
  (e) the Noise at Work Regulations 1989
       (SI 1989/1790);
  (f) the Health & Safety (Display Screen Equipment) Regulations 1992 (SI 1992/2792);
  (g) the Personal Protective Equipment at Work Regulations 1992 (SI 1992/2966);
  (h) the Manual Handling Operations Regulations 1992

(SI 1992/2793); and
(i) the Control of Substances Hazardous to Health
Regulations 1994 (SI 1994/3246).

all of which are reviewed/summarised in this handbook under the appropriate subject heads. See also *FURTHER INFORMATION* below.

Note: There are similar provisions in the Diving Operations at Work Regulations 1981 (SI 1981/399, as amended) and in the Docks Regulations 1988 (SI 1988/1655). New legislation currently under consideration by the Home Office will soon require the owners and occupiers of workplaces to assess the risks to life and limb presented by an outbreak of fire and to develop a clear plan of action to eliminate or minimise those risks.

Meaning of 'risk assessment'

- Risk assessment is nothing more or less than a systematic general examination of workplace activities, environmental factors and working conditions which will enable the employer (or self-employed person) to identify the risks posed not only by working methods, machines, tools and equipment, processes, noise, electricity, ionising radiation, flammable liquids and gases, dusts, fumes and vapours, and a seemingly endless list of prescribed hazardous substances (including lead and asbestos) but also by factors such as temperature, humidity, poor lighting and ventilation, the inadequacy of the means of access to (and egress from) premises, obstructions in corridors and walkways, the condition of floors, floor coverings, and so on. It is only when he has assessed the hazards and determined the degree of risk, that an employer can hope to take the steps he is required to take in law to eliminate or minimise those risks. Indeed, the whole tenor of the 1992 Regulations (and of the hazard-specific regulations listed above) is that employers (and self-employed persons) cannot realistically expect to comply with their general duties (to employees and members of the public) under the Health & Safety at Work etc. Act 1974) unless they *do* carry out a risk assessment and make a genuine effort to eliminate the risks uncovered by that assessment.

Risk assessment and new or expectant mothers

If he employs women of child-bearing age, he must also (in the course of that risk assessment exercise) determine whether any employee of his who is pregnant or breastfeeding, or has given birth to a child within the previous six months, is engaged in work which (because of her condition) could involve risk to her health and safety (or that of her child) from any processes or working conditions, or physical, biological or chemical agents (as to which, see **Pregnant employees & nursing mothers,** elsewhere in this handbook).

If there is nothing an employer can do to avoid the risks confronting a new or expectant mother, he must either alter her working hours or conditions of employment or, if that is not reasonably practicable, suspend her from work (on full pay) until the danger has passed. Furthermore, if a new or expectant mother works at night and produces a certificate signed by her doctor (or a registered midwife) to the effect that she should be taken off night work for a specifed period, in the interests of her health and safety, her employer must either offer to employ her in suitable alternative work during the day or suspend her from work on full pay for the period specified in the notice. For further particulars, please turn to the section titled **Suspension on maternity grounds** elsewhere in this handbook.

Risk assessment and young persons under 18

- The 1992 Regulations also contains provisions relating to the employment of school leavers and young persons under 18. Regulation 13D(1) reminds employers that young persons under 18 may not be fully matured. Furthermore, they are likely to be inexperienced, and are often inclined to be somewhat cavalier in their approach to (and acceptance of) health and safety risks in the workplace.

  Note: Regulation 13D was inserted by regulation 2(6) of the Health & Safety (Young Persons) Regulations 1997 (SI 1977/135) which came into force on 3 March 1997. The new Regulations give effect in Great Britain to Articles 6 and 7 of Council Directive 94/33/EC (OJ No. L216, 20.8.94, p. 12) on the protection of young people at work.

- From 3 March 1997, employers may not employ any young person under 18 without first reviewing their risk assessments to determine the particular risks facing young persons in the light of their relative immaturity, lack of experience, and unfamiliarity with the workplace. When doing so, an employer must take particular account of the fitting and layout of the workplace; the machines, plant and equipment in use in the workplace; the amount of training young persons can expect to receive before they are put to work; and the risks they are likely to face if ther are to be engaged in work involving (amongst other things) the handling of equipment for the production, storage or application of compressed liquefied or dissolved gases; or in work involving high-voltage electrical hazards; or in work the pace of which is determined by machinery and involving payments by results. See also **Women & young persons, Employment of** elsewhere in this handbook.

Maintenance of records

- To ensure compliance, employers with five or more employees must keep written (or computerised) records of the significant findings of their 'risk assessment' exercises and must keep those records available for inspection by a health and safety inspector. Nor is risk assessment a one-off exercise. The Regulations make it clear that the assessment must be repeated whenever there is a change in working methods, or if new machines, substances or processed are introduced into the workplaces; or if there is an increase in the number of accidents, dangerous occurrences and 'near misses' occurring in the workplace.

- In small workplaces and allegedly 'low-risk' establishments (such as offices, shops, cinemas, schools, hotels, boarding houses, and the like) it should not be too difficult for the employer or occupier to identify the hazards and the likelihood of injury to employees and members of the public should those hazards be realised. Gas heaters, electrical appliances, power tools, kitchen equipment, lighting, ventilation, escape routes, carpeting, the conditions of floors, stair, handrails, the presence of chemicals, solvents and flammable liquids and gases must all be included on the list and all subject to scrutiny.

FURTHER INFORMATION

- The following codes of practice and guidance notes published by the Health & Safety Executive (HSE) provide a great deal of practical advice on the form and content of risk assessments. These are available from HSE Books at the address given on page 328:

L21
Management of Health and Safety at Work Regulations 1992:
Approved code of practice [1992]
ISBN 0 7176 041 2 8   £5.00

L22
Work equipment. Provision and Use of Work Equipment
Regulations 1992. Guidance on Regulations [1992]
ISBN 0 7176 0414 4   £5.00

L23
Manual handling. Manual Handling Operations Regulations 1992.
Guidance on Regulations [1992]
ISBN 0 7176 0411 X   £5.00

L24
Workplace health, safety and welfare. Workplace (Health, Safety and
Welfare) Regulations 1992: Approved code of practice and guidance
[1992]
ISBN 0 7176 0413 6   £5.00

L25
Personal Protective Equipment at Work Regulations 1992.
Guidance on Regulations [1992]
ISBN 07176 0415 2   £5.00

L26
Display screen equipment work. Health and Safety (Display
Screen Equipment) Regulations 1992. Guidance on Regulations
[1992]
ISBN 0 7176 0410 1   £5.00

L21 -26
Also available as a pack (6 vols.)
ISBN 0 7176 0420 9   £30.00

L27
The Control of Asbestos at Work. Control of Asbestos at Work
Regulations 1987: Approved code of practice [2nd Edition,
1993] ISBN 0 11 882037 0   £5.00

COP 2
Control of lead at work: approved code of practice [Revised June
1985] (in support of SI 1980/1248)
ISBN 0 11 883780 X   £3.90

COP 16 (see also L7 below)
Protection of persons against ionising radiation arising from any work

activity: The Ionising Radiations Regulations 1985: Approved code of practice [1985]
ISBN 0 7176 0508 6   £6.00

COP 25
Safety in docks: Docks Regulations 1988: Approved code of practice with Regulations and guidance [1988]
ISBN 0 11 885456 9   £7.50

HS(R)25
Memorandum of guidance on the Electricity at Work Regulations 1989 [1989]
ISBN 0 11 883963 2   £4.00

L1
A guide to the Health and Safety at Work etc. Act 1974 [4th Edition, 1990]
ISBN 0 7176 0441 1   £4.00

L5
The Control of Substances Hazardous to Health Regulations 1994 (COSHH): Approved Code of Practice
ISBN 0 7176 0819 0   £6.75

L6
Diving operations at work. The Diving Operations at Work Regulations 1981 as amended by the Diving Operations at Work (Amendment) Regulations 1990 [1991]
ISBN 0 11 885599 9   £4.25

L28
Work with asbestos insulation, asbestos coating and asbestos insulating board. Control of Asbestos at Work Regulations 1987: Approved code of practice [2nd Edition, 1993]
ISBN 0 11 882038 9   £5.00

L49
Protection of outside workers against ionising radiations [1993]
ISBN 0 7176 0681 3   £5.00

L55
Preventing asthma at work
ISBN 0 7176 0661 9   £6.25

L56
The Gas Safety (Installations & Use) Regulations 1994:
Approved Code of Practice
ISBN 0 7176 0797 6   £5.75

L58
The protection of persons against ionising radiation arising from
any work activity (1994)
ISBN 0 7176 0508 6   £6.00

L60
Control of substances hazardous to health in the production of pottery.
The Control of Substances Hazardous to Health Regulations 1994.
The Control of Lead at Work Regulations 1980. Approved Code of
Practice.
ISBN 0 7176 0849 2   £5.00

Quantified risk assessment: its input to decision making [1989] ISBN
0 11 885499 2   £4.00

Risk assessment of notified new substances (loose leaf pack and
disks)
ISBN 0 7176 0758 5   £55.00

EH 58
The carcinogenicity of mineral oils [1990]
ISBN 0 11 885581 6   £2.50

HS(G) 55
Health and safety in kitchens and food preparation areas [1990] ISBN
0 11 885427 5   £4.00

HS(G) 60
Work-related upper limb disorders: a guide to prevention [1990]
ISBN 0 11 885565 4   £3.75

HS(G) 61
Surveillance of people exposed to health risks at work [1990] ISBN 0
11 885574 3   £3.25

Free leaflet (Telephone 01787 881165)

INDG 163
5 steps to risk assessment

Telephone HSE Books on 01787 881165 for the latest catalogue of HSE publications.

ROOF WORK

Key points

- Under Regulation 13 of the Workplace (Health, Safety & Welfare) Regulations 1992 (SI 1992/ 3004), employers are duty-bound to take suitable and sufficient measures to prevent any person falling a distance likely to cause personal injury. Paragraphs 127 to 131 of the accompanying Approved Code of Practice point out that the dangers associated with work on roofs are well known. If employees are required to work on a roof top (whether routinely or occasionally), their employer must see to it they are provided with crawling boards and with physical safeguards to prevent them falling through or from the edge of the roof. The roof must be inspected beforehand to ensure that it has not become fragile because of corrosion. Glazed roofs and those clad with asbestos sheeting or similar should be treated as being fragile unless there is firm evidence to the contrary.

- The Construction (Health, Safety & Welfare) Regulations 1996 (SI 1996/1592) contain specific requirements in relation to work on fragile materials; as to which, please turn to the section titled **Construction work** elsewhere in this handbook (specifically, pages 128 to 130. There is also a British Standard (BS 6399: Part 3:1988 titled *Design loading for buildings: code of practice for imposed roof loads* available from the British Standards Institution. 389 Chiswick High Road. London. W4 4AL (Telephone: 0181 996 7000).

- Copies of the Approved Code of Practice referred to above may be obtained from HSE Books at the address given on page 328. The particulars are as follows:

L24
Workplace health, safety and welfare. Workplace (Health, Safety and Welfare) Regulations 1992: Approved code of practice and guidance [1992]
ISBN 0 7176 0413 6   £5.00

ROOM DIMENSIONS & SPACE

Key points

- Regulation 10 of the Workplace (Health, Safety & Welfare) Regulations 1992 (SI 1992/3004) states that employees have the right to sufficient floor area, height and unoccupied space to enable them to carry out their duties safely and efficiently, without risk to their health. This means, in effect, that employees should be able to get to and from their desks or workbenches (machines or whatever) with ease; to stand up and stretch; and to move about the workroom without having to 'duck and weave' around filing cabinets, machines, stacked goods, raw materials, etc.

- According to the accompanying Approved Code of Practice (see below), the minimum average amount of unoccupied space available to each employee in a workroom should be 11 cubic metres — ignoring any space which is more than 3 metres above floor level and the space taken up by desks, workbenches, cabinets, machinery, stacked goods, raw materials, and the like. In a typical office or workroom, with a 2.4 metre high ceiling, this means that the average amount of floor space available to each employee should be some 4.6 square metres (or 3.7 square metres in a workroom where the ceiling is 3 metres high or higher).

- Locating 10 employees in a workroom with a net volume of 110 cubic metres may give each employee an average floor space of 4.6 square metres. But doing so will not necessarily satisfy Regulation 10 — the more so if the layout of the room and the type of activity carried on in that room means that some of those employees have significantly less floor space than others. In short, the room may be too small to accommodate 10 employees and the employer must either consider changing the layout or move those 10 employees to a larger workroom.

Note: In factories brought into first use as such before 1 January 1993, the cubic volume of a workroom may include any space up to 4.2 metres (14 feet) from the floor — not 3 metres as is now the case with other workplaces and new workplaces (including factories) brought into first use after 31 December 1992. This means that pre-1993 factories which satisfy the requirements of section 2 of the Factories Act 1961 will be deemed to comply with Regulation 10 now and after January 1, 1996. But any conversion or extension to a pre-1993 factory must satisfy Regulation 10 when it is brought into use, so long as the work was begun on that extension or conversion after 31 December 1992.

- The following Approved Code of Practice, referred to earlier in this section, is available from HSE Books at the address given on page 328:

  L24
  Workplace health, safety and welfare. Workplace (Health, Safety and Welfare) Regulations 1992: Approved code of practice and guidance [1992]
  ISBN 0 7176 0413 6   £5.00

S

SAFETY COMMITTEES

Key points

- It is an employer's duty to establish a safety committee if two or more appointed safety representatives write to him asking him to do so. The function of such a committee will be monitor the measures the employer has introduced to ensure the health and safety at work of his employees (section 2(7), Health and Safety at Work etc. Act 1974).

  Note: An independent trade union, which is recognised by an employer as having negotiating rights in respect of some or all of his workforce, has the right to appoint safety representatives from amongst those employees to represent their interests in consultations with the employer on health and safety matters (*ibid*; section 2 (4)).

- Once an employer has received a request in writing to establish a safety committee, he must do so within three months of the date on which that request was made. In determining the composition of the safety committee, the employer must consult with the safety representatives who made the request and with the representatives of recognised trade unions whose members work in or about the premises in which it is proposed that the committee will function. Once agreement has been reached, the employer must post a notice stating the composition of the committee and the workplace or workplaces to be covered by it, in a place where it may be easily read by the employees (Regulation 9, Safety Representatives and Safety Committees Regulations 1977 (SI 1977/500).

Objectives and functions of safety committees

- In keeping with its function of monitoring measures taken by an employer to ensure the health and safety at work of his employees, a safety committee should consider the drawing up of agreed objectives or terms of reference.

- Guidance Notes issued by the Health and Safety Commission (as a companion document to the Safety Representatives and Safety Committees Regulations 1977 (*q.v.*)) urge that one of the first objectives of a safety committee should be the promotion of co-operation between employers and employees in the development and implementation of a health and safety action programme.

- Within the agreed basic objectives, certain specific functions are likely to be defined. These, say the Guidance Notes, might include:

  (a) the study of accidents and notifiable diseases, statistics and trends, so that reports can be made to management on unsafe and unhealthy conditions and practices, together with recommendations for corrective action;

  (b) examinations of safety audit reports on a similar basis;

  (c) consideration of reports and factual information provided by HSE or local authority health and safety inspectors;

  (d) consideration of reports which safety representatives may wish to submit;

(e)   assistance in the development of safety rules and safe systems of work;

(f)   a watch on the effectiveness of the safety content of employee training;

(g)   a watch on the adequacy of safety and health communication and publicity in the workplace; and

(h)   the provision of a link with the health and safety inspectorate.

On occasion, a safety committee may consider it useful to carry out its own inspection of the premises. Although it is management's ultimate responsibility to have adequate arrangements for regular and effective checking for health and safety precautions, the safety committee has a useful role to play in supplementing those arrangements.

Membership of safety committees

- The membership and structure of a safety committee will be settled in consultation between the employer and the trade union representatives concerned. The aim should be to ensure adequate representation of all employees. The number of management representatives on the committee should not exceed the number representing employees.

- It should be the practice for membership of safety committees to be regarded as part of an individual's normal work. As a consequence, he or she should suffer no loss of pay through attendance at committee meetings/inspections.

Conduct of safety committees

- Safety committees should meet as often as necessary. The frequency of meetings will depend on the volume of business, which in turn is likely to depend on local conditions, the size of the premises, numbers employed, the kind of work carried out and the degree of risk inherent in that work.

- The minutes of every meeting should be displayed on notice boards, or, made available to employees by other means. A copy should be sent to the senior executive in charge of the premises with a view to ensuring speedy decisions on the committee's recommendations.

• Essential to the effective working of any safety committee is good communications between management and the committee. In addition, there must be a genuine desire on the part of management to tap the knowledge and experience of employees, and an equally genuine desire on the part of employees to improve the standards of health and safety at their place of work. The effectiveness of a safety committee will likewise depend on the regularity of meetings, the enthusiasm of committee members, the degree to which employees are involved and the speed with which its recommendations are translated into action.

Guidance notes

• The Health and Safety Commission has published a booklet titled *Safety representatives and safety committees* which contains Guidance Notes (referred to earlier in this section) and a Code of Practice (See *FURTHER INFORMATION* below).

> *Note:* An employer whose employees are not members of a recognised independent trade union is under no obligation to establish a safety committee to represent the interests of his employees on issues affecting their health and safety at work. Health and Safety Commission leaflet HSC 8 provides practical guidance for employers in such circumstances who are nonetheless anxious to establish safety committees on their premises. Copies of the leaflet are available from HSE Books (see *FURTHER INFORMATION* below). In organisations in which there is no trade union representation or recognition, the employees nonetheless have the legal right to be consulted by their employer on health and safety issues and the right also to elect one or more of their number to be *representatives of employee safety*; as to which, please turn to the next section which is titled Safety representatives.

Offences and penalties

• An employer who ignores a request by two or more appointed safety representatives to establish a safety committee, is guilty of an offence and liable on summary conviction to a fine of up to £2,000 or, on conviction on indictment. a fine of an unlimited amount (section 33 (1) (c) and (3), Health and Safety at Work, etc., Act 1974). See also **Competent persons** and **Safety representatives** elsewhere in this handbook.

FURTHER INFORMATION

- The following HSE publications are available from HSE Books at the address given on page 328:

  COP 1
  Safety representatives and safety committees [1988] (The Brown Book)
  ISBN 0 11 883959 4   £2.50

Free leaflet (Telephone 01787 881165)

  HSC 8
  Safety committees: Guidance to employers whose employees are not members of recognised independent trade unions

---

| **SAFETY REPRESENTATIVES** |
| *and representatives of employee safety* |

Key points

- For the purposes of this section, there are two types of safety representive. The one is the trade union appointed representative; the other is the representative of employee safety elected by his (or her) fellow-employees in circumstances in which there is no trade union recognition or representation on the employer's premises.

- Under the Safety Representatives and Safety Committees Regulations 1977 (SI 1977/500 ("the 1977 Regulations"), an independent trade union, recognised by an employer as having negotiating rights in respect of some or all of his employees, has the right to appoint one or more safety representatives to represent the interests of those employees in matters affecting their health and safety at work.

- Under the Health & Safety (Consultation with Employees) Regulations 1996 (SI 1996/1513) (the 1996 Regulations"), any group of employees who are *not* represented by trade union-appointed safety representatives under the 1977 Regulations have the right to elect one or more of their colleagues to represent their interests in consultations with their employer. Such persons are referred to as *representatives of employee safety*. For the most part, they enjoy the same statutory rights as their trade union-appointed contemporaries, including the right to paid time off work to carry out their functions and/or to attend appropriate safety training courses (see below).

TRADE UNION-APPOINTED SAFETY REPRESENTATIVES

- A trade union-appointed safety representative should either have worked with his (or her) employer for two or more years preceding his appointment or have had at least two years' experience in similar employment *(ibid;* Regulation 3 (4), 1977 Regulations).

  Note: Guidance Notes (see below) issued by the Health and Safety Commission explain that the requirement of two years' service (or at least two years' experience in similar employment) is intended to ensure that those who are appointed as safety representatives have the kind of experience and knowledge of their particular type of employment necessary to enable them to make a responsible and practical contribution to health and safety in their employment. Circumstances will, of course, arise where it will not be reasonably practicable for an appointed safety representative to have such experience (e.g., where the employer is newly-established, or where work is of short duration, or where there is a high labour turnover).

- Trade unions should enter into consultations with employers to reach agreement on the number of safety representatives to be appointed in a particular situation. When the number of recognised trade unions is high relative to the number of persons employed, officials of those unions should consider the possibility of a safety representative representing more than one group or groups of employees (e.g., in a small workplace or within an organisation with several branches in the same geographical area).

Functions of safety representatives

- Once an employer has been notified in writing by (or on behalf of) a trade union of the names of the persons appointed as safety representatives, each of those representatives will enjoy the right:

  (a) to investigate potential hazards and dangerous occurrences at the workplace (whether or not they are drawn to his attention by the employees he represents) and to examine the causes of accidents at the workplace;

(b)   to investigate complaints by an employee he represents relating to that employee's health, safety or welfare at work;

(c)   to make representations to the employer on matters arising out of (a) and (b) above;

(d)   to make representations to the employer on general matters affecting the health, safety or welfare at work of the employees at the workplace;

(e)   to carry out inspections of the workplace at least once in every period of three months, or more frequently as necessary (always provided that the safety representative gives reasonable notice in writing to his employer of his intention to carry out an inspection);

(f)   to carry out inspections following notifiable accidents, dangerous occurrences and diseases, provided it is safe for such inspections to be carried out and he has notified his employer of his intentions;

(g)   to represent the employees he was appointed to represent in consultations at the workplace with health and safety inspectors (and/or fire authority inspectors);

(h)   to attend meetings of safety committees, where he attends in his capacity as safety representative in connection with any of the above functions.

- Although a trade union-appointed safety representative has a right to investigate potential hazards and dangerous occurrences at the workplace (see (f) above), he (or she) cannot neglect his normal duties at a moment's notice to carry out a less urgent or *ad hoc* inspection of his employer's premises. Under normal circumstances, he would be expected to liaise with his supervisor or other member of management to agree arrangements for workplace inspections, etc.

Access to relevant information and documents

- A trade union-appointed safety representative has the legal right to inspect and take copies of any document relevant to the workplace or to the employees he (or she) has been appointed to represent — being documents which his employer is required to keep under existing health and safety legislation (e.g. under the Reporting of Injuries, Diseases & Dangerous Occurrences Regulations 1995). However, the safety representative must give his employer reasonable notice of his wish to inspect and take copies of any such documents (*ibid;* Regulation 7 (1)).

Note: A safety representative has no right to see any document consisting of, or relating to, any health record of an identifiable individual. Nor can he oblige his employer to make available any information relating specifically to an individual (unless he has consented to its being disclosed); any information the disclosure of which would, for reasons other than its effect on health, safety or welfare at work, cause substantial injury to the employer's business; or any information obtained by the employer for the purpose of bringing, prosecuting or defending any legal proceedings (*ibid;* Regulation 7 (3)). Furthermore, an employer need not produce or allow inspection of any document or part of a document which is not related to health, safety or welfare (*ibid;* Regulation 7 (3)).

Facilities and assistance to safety representatives

- An employer's general duty to consult safety representatives about his health and safety arrangements is reinforced by a list of more precise duties under Regulation 4A of the 1977 Regulations — inserted by Regulation 17 and the Schedule to the Management of Health & Safety at Work Regulations 1992 (SI 1992/2051). In short, an employer must consult safety representatives in good time with regard to —

  (a) the introduction of any measure at the workplace which may substantially affect the health and safety of the employees the safety representatives concerned represent;

  (b) his arrangements for appointing or, as the case may be, nominating one or more competent persons in accordance with Regulations 6(1) and 7(1)(b) of the 1992 Regulations referred to above;

  (c) any health and safety information that he will be relaying to the employees represented by those safety representatives in accordance with health and safety legislation;

(d) the planning and organisation of any health and safety training he is required to provide to the employees the safety representatives concerned represent by or under the relevant statutory provisions; and

(e) the health and safety consequences to the employees they represent of the introduction (including the planning thereof) of new technologies into the workplace.

- Finally, an employer must see to it that his safety representatives have the facilities and assistance they need (or may reasonably require) to carry out their functions, including such facilities as they may need to enable them to carry out workplace inspections or investigations following a notifiable accident or dangerous occurrence. Even so, an employer does have the right to accompany a safety representative during such inspections (*ibid;* Regulations 4A(2) and 6 (2)).

Note: An approved code of practice (COP 1) titled *Safety Representatives and Safety Committees* (The Brown Book) (ISBN 0 11 883959 4) is available from HSE Books at the address given on page 328. The price is £2.50.

REPRESENTATIVES OF EMPLOYEE SAFETY

- Under the 1996 Regulations, any employee standing for election as a *representative of employee safety* has the right to be permitted a reasonable amount of paid time off work, during his (or her) normal working hours so as to enable him "to perform his functions as such a candidate" (*ibid;* reg. 7(2)). Just what the functions of such a candidate are is not explained. It must be assumed that he has the right to be allowed a reasonable amount of paid time off work to canvass votes from his fellow employees.

Note: Although employees have the right to elect one or more of their number to represent their interests in consultations with their employer, they are not bound to do so. If there *is* no elected representative, it devolves on the employer to consult the employees directly, and in good time, on matters relating to their health and safety at work.

- When consulting *representatives of employee safety*, the employer must make available to those representatives such information as is necessary to enable them both to participate fully in the consultation and to carry out of their functions under the 1996 Regulations. He must also make available information contained in any record he is required to keep by regulation 7 of the

Reporting of Injuries, Diseases & Dangerous Occurrences Regulations 1995, subject to the proviso that he need only allow access to information/documents which relate/s to the workplace or to the group of employees represented by those representatives.

Note: As is the case with trade union-appointed safety representatives, a *representative of employee safety* has no right to see any document consisting of, or relating to, the health record of an identifiable individual. Nor can he (or she) oblige his employer to make available any information relating specifically to an individual (unless that individual has consented to its being disclosed). The same is true of information the disclosure of which would, for reasons other than its effect on health, safety or welfare at work, cause substantial injury to the employer's business; or any information obtained by the employer for the purpose of bringing, prosecuting or defending any legal proceedings (*ibid;* Regulation 7(3)). Furthermore, an employer need not produce or allow inspection of any document or part of a document which is not related to health, safety or welfare (*ibid;* Regulation 7 (3)).

- If an employer who has been consulting representatives of employee safety changes his mind and decides to consult employees directly, he must inform the employees *and* the representatives of that fact. If an employer chooses to consult with employees directly, he must make available to those employees such information as is necessary to enable them to participate fully and effectively in the consultation process (1966 Regulations, regulations 4(4) and 5(1)).

Functions of representatives of employee safety

- During consultations with his (or her) employer on health and safety issues, a representatives of employee safety has the right to make representations on potential hazards and dangerous occurrences at the workplace which affect, or could affect, the group of employees he represents. He also has the right to make representations on general matters affecting the health and safety at work of the employees he represents and, in particular, on —

  (a)   the introduction of measures which may substantially affect the health and safety of those employees;

  (b)   the employer's arrangements for appointing or, as the case may be, nominating one or more 'competent persons' in accordance with regulations 6(1) and 7(1)(b) of the Management of Health & Safety at Work Regulations 1992 (as to which, see **Competent persons** elsewhere in this handbook);

(c) any health and safety information the employer is required to make known to those employees by or under relevant health and safety legislation;

(d) the planning and organisation of any health and safety training, the employer is required to provide under existing health and safety legislation (as to which, see Training of employees elsewhere in this handbook); and

(e) the health and safety consequences for those employees when new technologies are introduced (or are planned to be introduced) into the workplace.

In the course of consultations, a *representative of employee safety* also has the right to attend workplace consultations with health and safety inspectors and to make representations to those inspectors on behalf of the employees or group of employees he (or she) has been elected to represent.

Training and facilities

- Finally, an employer who consults with elected *representatives of employee safety* must see to it that those representatives have the facilities and assistance they need (or may reasonably require) to carry out their lawful functions (e.g; access to a desk, telephone, photocopier and/or secretarial assistance). He must see to it also that each representative receives such training in health and safety matters as is reasonable to enable him (or her) to carry out his functions effectively. To that end, the employer must meet any reasonable costs associated with such training (including travel and subsistence costs) (*ibid*; reg 7).

OFFENCES & PENALTIES

- An employer who refuses or fails to comply with his duties under the 1977 or 1966 Regulations is guilty of an offence under the Health & Safety at Work etc. Act 1974 and is liable, on summary conviction, to a fine of up to £2,000; or, if convicted on indictment, to a fine of an unlimited amount (*ibid*; section 33(1)(c) and (3)); as to which, see **Offences & penalties** elsewhere in this handbook..

TIME OFF WORK

- Trade union-appointed safety representatives and elected *representatives of employee safety* have the right not only be consulted on health and safety issues but the right also —

  (a)   to be permitted by their employer to take a reasonable amount of paid time off work (during normal working hours) to enable them to function effectively.

  They are also entitled —

  (b)   to be allowed a reasonable amount of paid time off work (again during normal working hours) to attend appropriate health and safety training courses (arranged or approved by their employer).

- An employee standing as a candidate for election as a *representative of employee safety*, is similarly entitled to be permitted a reasonable amount of paid time off work to perform his functions as such a candidate (reg. 7(2), 1996 Regulations).

COMPLAINT TO INDUSTRIAL TRIBUNAL

- A safety representative or *representative of employee safety* may complain to an industrial tribunal that—

  (a)   his (or her) employer has failed to permit him to take time off work for the purposes of performing his functions or undergoing training in aspects of those functions; or

  (b)   that his employer has failed to pay him his normal remuneration on such occasions.

Such a complaint must be presented within three months of the date when the failure occurred. If the tribunal finds the complaint well-founded, it will make a declaration to that effect and will order the employer to pay compensation of such amount as the tribunal considers just and equitable in all the circumstances. If a tribunal finds that the employer has failed to pay the employee the whole or part of the remuneration due to him (or her), it will likewise order the employer to pay the employee the amount in question

RIGHT NOT TO BE VICTIMISED OR DISMISSED

- Safety representatives (whether trade union-appointed or elected by their peers) have the right not to be victimised, penalised or 'subjected to any detriment' by their employer for carrying out (or attempting to carry out) their legitimate functions. They have the right also not to be dismissed or selected for redundancy for asserting their statutory rights or for challenging their employer's failure to allow them to carry out their legitimate functions. It is as well to point out her that an employee who has been victimised (that is to say, disciplined or subjected to some other detriment) for exercising or proposing to exercise those functions has no need to resign in order to present a complaint to an industrial tribunal. For further particulars, please turn to the section titled **Dismissal or victimisation (in health and safety cases)** elsewhere in this handbook.

CODE OF PRACTICE

- A Code of Practice (L87) titled *Safety Representatives & Safety Committees (The Brown Book) 3rd Edition. Approved Code of Practice and guidance on the regulations* [1996] ISBN 0 7176 1220 1 is available from HSE Books (see page 328). The price is £5.75 per copy (1 - 9 copies). Other quantity discounts available.

See also **Competent persons** elsewhere in this handbook.

SAFETY SIGNS & SIGNALS

Key points

- As has been demonstrated time and again throughout this handbook, the whole thrust of modern health and safety legislation is to impose a duty on employers (and self-employed persons) to identify workplace hazards, to determine the extent of the risks associated with those hazards, and to take positive action to eliminate or minimise those risks. For example, the Personal Protective Equipment at Work Regulations 1992 remind employers that personal protective equipment should only be issued as a 'last resort'; that is to say, only *after* engineering controls, local exhaust ventilation, the total enclosure of hazardous substances, and other control measures, have been tried and found wanting. A similar cautionary note is sounded in the Noise at Work Regulations 1989 and (amongst others) in the all-embracing Management of Health & Safety at Work Regulations 1992.

- And so it is with safety signs. A health and safety inspector is unlikely to be impressed by a picture gallery of safety signs if the premises in which they are deployed or displayed are noisy, dusty, fume-filled, dark, overcrowded, wet underfoot, equipped with unguarded machinery of uncertain vintage, and stacked to the rafters with an Aladdin's cave of dangerous chemicals.

- As is the case with other recent legislation, the Health & Safety (Safety Signs & Signals) Regulations 1996 (SI 1996/341) first remind employers that they have a duty under regulation 3(1)of the Management of Health & Safety at Work Regulations 1992, to carry out a risk assessment exercise. Regulation 4(1) points out that if the risk assessment made under the 1992 Regulations indicates that an employer cannot avoid or adequately control risks to his employees, except by providing safety signs — in spite of his having adopted all appropriate techniques (methods, measures and procedures) — then safety signs must be provided.

Note: The risks identified by the risk assessment exercise referred to above will be treated as having been adequately reduced (thereby eliminating the need for safety signs) if, but only if, the techniques, measures, methods or procedures adopted by an employer to avoid or control those risks have been successful to the extent that they are no longer significant — having regard to the magnitude and nature of the risks identified by that assessment (*ibid.*).

Fire safety signs

- It should be pointed out that fire safety signs *must* be provided and maintained — regardless of an employer's success in eliminating or minimising workplace risks — if such signs are required under the provisions of the Fire Precautions Act 1971 (or under related or subordinate legislation). The expression "fire safety sign" means a sign (including an illuminated sign or an acoustic signal) which provides information on escape routes and emergency exits in case of fire; which provides information on the identification or location of fire-fighting equipment; or which gives a warning in case of fire.

Purpose and definition of "safety signs"

- The pupose of safety signs (which expression includes illuminated signs, acoustic signals, verbal communications and hand signals) is to warn or instruct employees (as well as tradesmen, visitors, contractors, etc.) of the nature of the risks present in the workplace and the measures to be taken to protect against those risks.

- A "safety sign" is a sign referring to a specific object, activity or situation which provides information or instructions about health or safety at work by means of a signboard, a safety colour, an illuminated sign, an acoustic signal, a verbal communication or a hand signal.

  Note: "acoustic signals" are coded sound signals (hooters, klaxons, bells, etc.) released and transmitted by a device designed for that purpose. A "verbal communication" is a predetermined spoken message communicated by a human or artificial voice. A "hand signal" is a movement or position of the arms or hands (or a combination of hands and arms), in coded form, for guiding persons who are carrying out manoeuvres which create a risk to the health and safety of persons at work.

Application of the 1996 Regulations

- The 1996 Regulations repeal and replace the Safety Signs Regulations 1980 and came into force on 1 April 1996. They impose requirements in relation to the provision and use of safety signs and signals and, as respects Great Britain, implement Council Directive 92/58/EEC on the minimum requirements for the provision of safety and/or health signs at work.

  Note: The Regulations apply in Great Britain and to and in relation to premises and activities outside Great Britain (such as offshore platforms). They do not, however, extend to Northern Ireland.

- The 1996 Regulations do *not* apply —

  (a) to signs used in connection with the supply of any dangerous substance, preparation, product or equipment *except* to the extent that any enactment (statutes, regulations and orders) specifically refers to them;

  (b) to dangerous goods being transported by road, rail, inland waterway, ea or air;

  (c) to signs used for regulating road, rail, inland waterway, sea or air traffic — unless it is appropriate to provide safety signs at a workplace because of the risk to the health and safety of employees and pedestrians in connection with the presence or movement of traffic in or about that workplace, so long as there is a sign in that connection prescribed under the Road Traffic Regulation Act 1984 and that sign is used, whether or not the 1984 Act applies to that place of work.

(d) to, or in relation to, the master or crew of a sea-going ship or to the employer of such persons in respect of normal ship-board activities of a ship's crew under the direction of the master (*ibid*; reg. 3(1)).

INFORMATION, INSTRUCTION AND TRAINING

* When safety signs — signboards, safety colours, illuminated signs, acoustic signals, verbal communications and/or a system of hand signals — are deployed or used in a place of work (in compliance with the 1996 Regulations), the employer in question has a duty to ensure that his employees know and understand what those signs, signals and communications mean and what steps they must take in connection with those safety signs and signals.

* To that end, the employer must see to it that each of his employees (and every new recruit) receives suitable and sufficient instruction and training in the meaning of safety signs and the measures to be taken in connection with those signs.

MINIMUM REQUIREMENTS FOR SAFETY SIGNS & SIGNALS

* The following is a summary only of the requirements of the 1996 Regulations in relation to safety signs and signals. For more comprehensive coverage (including illustrations and examples, which are beyond the scope of a handbook of this size), the reader is commended to the HSE publications listed at the end of this section.

* If safety signs and signals (other than hand signals and verbal communications) are required to be provided or use in a workplace, they must comply with the requirements of Parts I to VII of Schedule 1 to the 1996 Regulations. Hand signals and verbal communications must comply with the requirements of

Parts I, VIII and IX of that Schedule.

- When signboards and illuminated signs are required or installed, it is the employer's duty to ensure that they are correctly located and properly maintained (e.g., by ensuring that they are visible at all times and are repaired or replaced promptly when damaged or mislaid).

- There are two types of signs: permanent signs and occasional signs.

Permanent signs

- Permanent signboards must be used for signs relating to prohibitions, warnings and mandatory requirements (see below), and for the location and identification of emergency escape routes and first-aid facilities. Signboards and/or a safety colour must be used to mark permanently the location and identification of fire-fighting equipment.

- The rules relating the placement of of signboards on containers and pipes state that containers used at work for dangerous substances or preparations (defined in Directives 67/548/EEC and 88/379/EEC) and containers used for the storage of such substances or preparations, (together with the visible pipes containing or transporting dangerous substances and preparations) must be labelled (pictogram or symbol against a coloured background) in accordance with those Directives. The labels may be replaced by warning signs, using the same pictograms or symbols or they may be supplemented by additional information (such as the name and/or formula of the dangerous substance or preparation, and details of the hazard). Labels used on pipes must be positioned visibly and at reasonable intervals in the vicinity of the most dangerous points, such as valves and joints. Signs must be mounted on the visible sides of containers or pipes and be in unpliable, self-adhesive or painted form.

- If containers are to be transported at the workplace, the labels on them may also be supplemented or replaced by signs applicable throughout the European Community for the transport of dangerous substances or preparations.

- Places where there is a risk of falling, or of colliding with obstacles, must be permanently marked with a safety colour and/or a signboard. Traffic routes likewise must be permanently marked with a safety colour.

Occasional signs

- Illuminated signs, acoustic signals and/or verbal communication must be used when the occasion requires, taking into account the possibilities for interchanging and combining signs (see below) to signal danger, to call persons to take a specific course of action, and for emergency evacuations. Hand signals and/or verbal communications must be used when the occasion requires to guide persons carrying out hazardous or dangerous manoeuvres.

Interchanging and combining signs

- Any one of the following signs may be used if equally effective:

  — a safety colour or a signboard to mark places where there is an obstacle or a drop,
  — illuminated signs, acoustic signals or verbal communication,
  — hand signals or verbal communication.

- Some signs may be used together:

  — illuminated signs and acoustic signals (e.g., flashing lights and hooters),
  — illuminated signs and verbal communication (e.g., flashing lights and tannoy announcements),
  — hand signals and verbal communication.

- The instructions in the following Table apply to all signs incorporating a safety colour.

Colour	Meaning or purpose	Instructions and information
RED	Prohibition sign	Dangerous behaviour
	Danger alarm	Stop Shutdown, Emergency cut-out devices Evacuate
	Fire-fighting equipment	Identification and location
YELLOW or AMBER	Warning sign	Be careful Take precautions Examine
BLUE	Mandatory sign	Specific behaviour or action Wear personal protective equipment
GREEN	Emergency escape First aid sign	Doors Exits Routes Equipment
	No danger	Return to normal

MINIMUM GENERAL REQUIREMENTS FOR SIGNBOARDS

- The shape and colours of signboards determine their specific purpose (a prohibition, a warning, a mandatory action, an escape route, an emergency, or fire-fighting equipment). The pictograms used on signboards must be as simple as possible and contain only essential details. The pictograms used by various manufacturers may differ slightly from, or be more detailed than those illustrated in Schedule 1, Part II of the 1996 Regulations (not reproduced here), provided that they convey the same meaning and that the difference or adaptation does not obscure that meaning. Signboards must be made of shock and weather-resistant materials suitable for the surrounding environment. Furthermore, their dimensions and colorimetric and photometric features must be such that they can be easily seen and understood.

Conditions of use

• In principle, signboards must be installed at a suitable height and in a position appropriate to the average person's line of sight. In practice, their positioning must take account of any obstacles, either at the access point to an area in the case of a general hazard, or in the immediate vicinity of a specific hazard or object, and in a well-lit, easily accessible and visible location. Phosphorescent colours, reflective materials or artificial lighting should be used where the level of natural light is poor. Finally, a signboard must be removed when the situation to which it refers ceases to exist.

Approved signs

• There are five approved types of signs — prohibitory signs, warning signs, mandatory signs, emergency escape or first-aid signs, and fire-fighting signs — as follows:

    o   ***prohibitory signs*** (circular with a red border and diagonal crossbar over a black pictogram on a white background — the red part to take up at least 35% of the area of the sign).

        For example: 'No smoking', 'Smoking and naked flames forbidden', No access for pedestrians', 'Do not extinguish with water', 'Not drinkable', 'No access for unauthorised persons', 'No access for industrial vehicles', ' Do not touch'.

    o   ***warning signs*** (black-edged triangular shape with a black pictogram on a yellow background — the yellow part to take up at least 50% of the area of the sign).

        For example: 'Flammable material or high temperature', 'Explosive material', 'Toxic material', 'Corrosive material', 'Radioactive material', 'Overhead load', 'Industrial vehicles', 'Danger: Electricity', 'General Danger', 'Laser beam', 'Oxidant material', 'Non-ionizing radiation'.

    o   ***mandatory signs*** (circular with a white pictogram on a blue background — the blue part to take up at least 50% of the area of the sign).

For example: 'Eye protection must be worn', 'Safety helmet must be worn', 'Ear protection must be worn', 'Respiratory equipment must be worn', 'Safety boots must be worn', 'Safety gloves must be worn', 'Pedestrians must use this route', etc.

o   *emergency escape or first-aid signs* (rectangular or square shape, with a white pictogram on a green background — the green part to take up at least 50% of the area of the sign).

For example: 'Emergency exit/escape route', 'This way' (supplementary information sign), 'First-aid post', 'Stretcher', 'Safety shower', 'Eyewash', 'Emergency telephone for first-aid or escape'.

o   *fire-fighting signs* (square or rectangular shape with a white pictogram on a red background — the red part to take up at least 50% of the area of the sign).

For example: 'Fire hose', 'Ladder', 'Fire extinguisher', 'Emergency fire telephone', 'This way' (supplementary information sign).

OBSTACLES, DANGEROUS LOCATIONS & TRAFFIC ROUTES

- The 1996 Regulations also lay down minimum requirements governing signs used for obstacles and dangerous locations, and for marking traffic routes.

- Places where there is a risk of colliding with obstacles, or of falling, or of objects falling, should be marked with alternating yellow and black stripes, or red and white stripes in built-up zones in the undertaking, to which workers have access during their work. The dimensions of the markings must be commensurate with the scale of the obstacle or dangerous location in question. The yellow and black (or red and white) stripes must be at an angle of approximately 45° and must be of more or less equal size.

Marking of traffic routes

- Where the movement of fork lift trucks, palletisers and other vehicles in or about a room or place of work pose a risk to workers, the routes used by such vehicles must be clearly identified by continuous stripes in a clearly visible colour, preferably white or yellow (taking into account the colour of the surrounding floor surface or ground).

- The stripes must be located in such a way as to indicate the necessary safe distance between the vehicles and any nearby object, and between pedestrians and vehicles. Permanent traffic routes in built-up areas out-of-doors must, so far as is reasonably practicable, be similarly marked, unless they are provided with suitable barriers or pavements.

MINIMUM REQUIREMENTS FOR ILLUMINATED SIGNS

- When an illuminated sign is used, the light emitted by the sign must produce a luminous contrast appropriate to the environment in which it is located, but without producing glare or an excessive amount of light or poor visibility as a result of insufficient light. The luminous area which emits a safety sign may be of a single colour or contain a pictogram on a specified background (e.g., a white pictogram against a blue background) — as to which, see the specifications for *Approved signs* above.

- If an illuminated sign is capable of emitting both continuous (or steady) and intermittent (flashing) signs, the latter should be used only to signal a higher level of danger or a more urgent need for the requested (or imposed) intervention or action (e.g; the immediate evacuation of premises). If a flashing sign is used instead of, or at the same time as, an acoustic signal, identical codes must be used. Devices for emitting flashing signs, used in the event of an emergency or grave danger, must be under special surveillance or be fitted with an auxiliary lamp.

MINIMUM REQUIREMENTS FOR ACOUSTIC SIGNALS

- Where acoustic signals are used in a workplace, they must have a sound level considerably higher than the level of ambient noise so that they are audible without being excessive or painful to the ear. Acoustic signals must also be easily recognisable, particularly in terms of pulse length and the interval between pulses or groups of pulses. Furthermore, the sound emitted by an acoustic signal must be clearly distinguishable from the sound emitted by any other acoustic signal and ambient noises. If a device can emit an acoustic signal at variable and constant frequencies, the variable frequency should be used to indicate a higher level of danger or a more urgent need for action — subject to the proviso that the signal for evacuation must be continuous.

MINIMUM REQUIREMENTS FOR VERBAL COMMUNICATION

• Verbal communications, whether delivered face to face, or by tannoy or other broadcast means, which are used to issue safety instructions, or to indicate or warn of risks to health and safety must be short, simple, direct and readily understandable. In some situations, a coded form of words may need to be used (e.g; so as not to alarm visitors, customers, etc).

• Persons (managers, foremen, supervisors, safety officers, or whoever) whose function it is to issue safety instructions or make safety announcements (whether face to face, or by tannoy, or otherwise) should have a good command of the English language (or of the language used at the time) and be able to articulate and pronounce words in a way which will not be misunderstood by their listeners.

• If verbal communication is used instead of, or together with, gestures, code words such as the following should be used:

— start	to indicate the start of a command
— stop	to interrupt or end a movement
— end	to stop the operation
— raise	to have a load raised
— lower	to have a load lowered
— forwards	to be co-ordinated
— backwards	with the
— right	corresponding
— left	hand signals
— danger	for an emergency stop
— quickly	to speed up a movement for safety reasons

MINIMUM REQUIREMENTS FOR HAND SIGNALS

• Hand signals (commonly used to direct the drivers of heavy goods vehicles, fork lift trucks, travelling platforms, etc.) must be precise, simple, expansive, and easy to make and understand. They must be clearly distinguisable from other such signals (including everyday gestures). If both arms are used simultaneously, they must be moved symetrically and be used for giving one sign only.

• The person (the 'signalman') using hand signals to give manoeuvring instructions to an operator (e.g., HGV driver, winchman, etc.) must be in a position to monitor all manoeuvres visually and without endangering himself (or herself) or others working nearby. If this is not possible, two or more signalmen should be deployed. When a signalman is giving hand signals, he (or she) must do so to the exclusion of all other activities — until the relevant manoeuvres are completed. If a driver or operator is confused by the signals he (or she) is receiving, or feels that he cannot safely comply with a particular hand signal, he must stop what he is doing and ask for fresh instructions.

- A driver or operator should have no difficulty in recognising the signalman deployed to help him with his manoeuvres. To that end, the signalman must either wear one or more brightly-coloured items (such as a jacket, helmet, sleeves or armbands) or carry bats.

Coded hand signals

- The 1996 Regulations contain a set of coded hand signals (with accompanying illustrations — which latter are not reproduced here for technical and other reasons).

CODED HAND SIGNALS
per Para. 3, Part IX of Schedule 1 to
the Health & Safety (Safety Signs & Signals) Regulations 1996
(SI 1996/341)

Meaning	*Description*
A. General Signals	
START Attention Start of Command	Both arms are extended horizontally with the palms facing forwards.
STOP Interruption End of movement	The right arm points upwards with the palm facing forwards. (The left arm is kept to the side of the body)
END of the operation	Both hands are clasped at chest height.
B. Vertical movements	
RAISE	The right arm points upwards with the palm facing forward and slowly makes a circle. (The left arm is kept to the side of the body)

LOWER	The right arm points downwards (at an angle of roughly 30° away from the body) with the palm facing inwards and slowly making a circle. (The left arm is kept to the side of the body)
VERTICAL DISTANCE	The hands indicate the relevant distance.

C. Horizontal movements

MOVE FORWARDS	Both arms are bent with the palms facing upwards, and the forearms making slow movements towards the body.
MOVE BACKWARDS	Both arms are bent with the palms facing downwards, and the forearms making slow movements away from the body.
RIGHT to the signalman's	The right arm is extended more or less horizontally, with the palm facing downwards and slowly making small movements to the right. (The left arm is kept to the side of the body)
LEFT to the signalman's	The left arm is extended more or less horizontally, with the palm facing downwards and slowly making small movements to the left. (The right arm is kept to the side of the body)
HORIZONTAL DISTANCE	The hands indicate the relevant distance.

D. Danger

DANGER Emergency stop	Both arms point upwards with the palms facing forwards.

E. Other

QUICK	All movements faster.
SLOW	All movements slower.

Alternative coded signals for agricutural operations, the safe use of cranes, and for rescue operations involving the fire service, are to be found in the following standards issued by the British Standards Institution:

BS 6736: 1986 Hand Signals for Agricultural Operations
BS 7121: 1989 Code of Practice for safe use of cranes

and in Appendix C of the Fire Service Training Manual.

The British Standards referred to above are available from BSI

standards. 389 Chiswick High Road, London W4 4AL. The Fire
Service Training Manual can be purchased from The Stationery
Office (see page 328) quoting ISBN 0 11 341091 3.

EMPLOYER'S DUTY

- It is the responsibility of the employer, that is to say, the person
  or organisation having control of a place of work to ensure that
  the safety signs (including acoustic signals, verbal communication
  and hand signals) displayed or used in that workplace comply
  with the 1996 Regulations. He or she must also see to it that
  signboards, illuminated signs etc. are correctly situated and
  maintained, and that they are repaired or replaced as necessary
  (or removed, when no longer relevant). Where appropriate, that
  duty also extends to premises occupied by a self-employed
  person.

ENFORCEMENT

- Inspectors appointed by the Health & Safety Executive (HSE) are
  responsible for 'policing' and enforcing compliance with the 1996
  Regulations (as they are in respect of most health and safety
  legislation). For non-industrial undertakings (offices, shops,
  hotels, schools, hospitals, etc.), the enforcing authority is the
  local authority for the area in which those premises are situated.
  The enforcing authority in relation to the deployment of *fire safety
  signs* will ordinarily be the fire authority, except in relation to
  premises to which the Fire Certificates (Special Premises)
  Regulations 1976 (SI 1976/2003) apply, for which latter the HSE
  retains responsibility, as they do for offshore sites (oil platforms,
  etc.). For further particulars, please turn to the sections titled **Fire
  certificate, Inspectors, Powers of** and **Offences & penalties**
  elsewhere in this handbook.

FURTHER INFORMATION

Safety signs prescribed by the 1996 Regulations and which
comply with the relevant BS (or transposed harmonised
standards) are nowadays readily available from organisations
such as RoSPA, Chancellor Formecon, Stocksigns Limited, etc.,
as to which, please turn to pages 306 and 307.

SEATS OR CHAIRS FOR EMPLOYEES

Key points

- Employees who are able do all or part of their work sitting down must be provided with suitable seats or chairs. By "suitable" is meant suitable for the people using them and suitable for the type of work they are doing — bearing in mind that an employee must be at a suitable height in relation to the work surface in front of him and be able to carry out his duties without undue bending or stretching. Seats or chairs must provide adequate support for the lower back and (if employees cannot comfortably place their feet flat on the floor) must be equipped with footrests (Regulation 11, Workplace (Health, Safety & Welfare) Regulations 1992 [SI 1992/3004]). See also **Accommodation for clothing**, and **Canteens and rest rooms** elsewhere in this handbook.

- Changing rooms should be furnished with adequate seating (usually benches). Rest rooms, canteens and mess-rooms should likewise contain a sufficient number of chairs or seats with backrests (as well as tables). By 'sufficient' is meant sufficient for the number of people likely to use those facilities at any one time (*ibid*; Regulations 24 & 25).

- People (such as machine operators, shop assistants, receptionists, waitresses and waiters, forecourt attendants, hospital porters, teachers, nurses, assembly-line workers, warehousemen etc.) who spend most of their working hours standing should be able to sit down whenever circumstances permit — e.g., when there are no customers about, or when there is a temporary interruption in the flow of work, or if they are required to remain in the workroom during tea or coffee breaks. To that end, their employer should provide a sufficient number of suitable seats with backrests or chairs (*Regulation 25*).

Users of display screen equipment

- Chairs used by people operating display screen equipment (desktop computers with monitors) must be stable and must allow the operator or user easy freedom of movement and a comfortable position. The height of the seat must be capable of being adjusted as must that of the seat back. The latter must also be capable of being tilted forward or backwards. If a computer operator asks to be supplied with a footrest, it must be provided (*vide* Regulation 3 and The Schedule to the Health & Safety (Display Screen Equipment) Regulations 1992, SI 1992/2792). For further details, see also **Visual Display Units (VDUs)** elsewhere in this handbook.

STACKING & RACKING

Key points

- Badly-stacked goods and materials, and overloaded or unstable racking, are liable to collapse or fall and cause serious injury. An employer must satisfy himself that the racking he uses for the storage of raw materials or finished goods (or work-in-progress) is strong and stable enough to accommodate any load likely to be placed on it — not forgetting its vulnerability to damage by passing vehicles or heavy plant and machinery (Regulation 13, Workplace (Health, Safety & Welfare) Regulations 1992 (SI 1992/3004).

- The accompanying Approved Code of Practice cautions that the appropriate precautions in stacking and storage must include:

  o safe palletisation;

  o banding or wrapping to prevent individual articles falling out;

  o ensuring the stability of stacked materials by limiting the height of stacks;

  o inspecting stacks and racks regularly to detect and remedy unsafe stacking or overloaded or unstable racking;

  o instructing and training employees in safe methods for stacking and racking and, in particular, the handling and storage of irregularly-shaped objects.

There is further useful advice in the HSE publication *Health & Safety in retail and wholesale warehouses* (HS(G)76) (ISBN 011

885731 2), available from HSE Books at the address given on page 328 (price £7.50).

STAIRS & STAIRCASES

Key points

- All stairs and staircases, including banisters and handrails, must be kept clean and in a good state of repair. Spillages of any liquid or substance must be removed promptly; loose or damaged treads and frayed stair carpeting, made good; and so on. Banisters or handrails should be set to a height of 900mm or higher and, if there are no uprights, must be fitted with one or more lower rails to eliminate or minimise the risk of people (especially children) falling through the gaps.

- On steep stairs and staircases, of the type often found in factories, where there is a particular risk of falling or there are narrow treads, there should be a handrail with lower guard rails) on both sides. On wide staircases, commonly found in department stores and theatres (both of which are 'workplaces'), there should be an additional handrail down the centre, with upward-moving and downward traffic directed to the left. Building and fire regulations will also apply in such cases (Regulations 12 & 17, Workplace (Health, Safety & Welfare) Regulations 1992 [SI 1992/3004]).

- All stairs and staircases must be well-lit in such a way that shadows are not cast over the main part of the treads. Emergency lighting should also be provided at suitable intervals to facilitate safe and rapid evacuation in the event of a power failure, fire or other emergency (*ibid*; Regulation 8).

- Guardrails or handrails should also be provided at every edge or opening where a person is likely to fall a distance of two metres or more. In such cases, there should also be a lower rail with the gap between filled in to prevent people falling through the gap. See also **Falls & falling objects**.

SUSPENSION ON MATERNITY GROUNDS

Key points

- An employee who is suspended from work on maternity grounds is entitled to be paid her normal wages or salary during her enforced leave of absence — so long as she has not unreasonably refused an offer of suitable alternative work made to her by her employer before the suspension period began (*per* sections 66 to 68 of the Employment Rights Act 1996).

- Section 66 of the 1996 Act explains that an employee is to be treated as suspended from work on maternity grounds if, in consequence of any requirement imposed by health and safety legislation (or of any recommendation in a code of practice issued or approved under section 16 of the Health & Safety at Work etc. Act 1974), she is suspended from work by her employer on the ground that she is pregnant or breastfeeding, or has given birth to a child within the previous six months.

Health and safety legislation

- Health and safety legislation in the UK has long restricted the employment (or continued employment) of pregnant women in occupations which could expose them or their unborn children to risk. For example: paragraph 118 of the code of practice accompanying the Control of Lead at Work Regulations 1980 (SI 1980/1248) states that any woman of reproductive capacity, who is employed in work which exposes her to lead, must notify her employer if she becomes pregnant and must be suspended from such work if an employment medical adviser or appointed doctor certifies that it would be unsafe for her to continue doing that work — at least for the time being. There are similar provisions in the Ionising Radiations Regulations 1985. For further details, please see **Table 1** on pages 585 to 587 below.

- On 1 December 1994, the Suspension from Work (on Maternity Grounds) Order 1994 (SI 1994/2930), gave effect in Great Britain to Articles 5(2) and 7(2) of Council Directive 92/85/EEC "on the introduction of measures to encourage improvements in the safety and health at work of pregnant workers and workers who have recently given birth or are breastfeeding". The directive is commonly referred to as 'the Pregnancy Directive'.

Note: The 1994 Order specifies the requirements imposed by the Management of Health & Safety at Work Regulations 1992 (SI 1992/2051) as amended by the Management of Health & Safety at Work (Amendment) Regulations 1994 (SI 1994/2865)(collectively referred to as "the 1992 Regulations"). If an employee is suspended from work in consequence of such requirements, she will have the right under section 67 of the Employment Rights Act 1996 to be offered suitable alternative work and the right under section 68 (*ibid*) to be paid her normal wages or salary during the suspension period— if no offer of suitable alternative work is forthcoming or she has not unreasonably refused such an offer.

- In future, any new or expectant mother doing a job which could expose her (or her baby) to risk — because of her condition — must either be transferred to more suitable work or be offered different working conditions and hours, or (if such measures are impracticable or unlikely to be effective) be suspended from work for so long as is necessary to avoid that risk. The risk may be related to her working conditions (e.g., a hot or humid atmosphere), or to the type of work in which she is engaged (e.g., lifting and carrying) , or to the physical, biological or chemical agents (including those specified in Annexes I and II of the Pregnancy Directive) to which she is or may be exposed when doing her normal job (as to which, see **Tables 2, 3 & 4** on pages 588, 589 & 590 below).

Note: Regulation 2(2) of the 1992 Regulations (see previous *Note*) defines "new or expectant mother" as meaning an employee who is pregnant, or who has given birth within the previous six months, or who is breastfeeding. "Given birth" means delivered a living child or, after 24 weeks of pregnancy, a stillborn child. Regulation 3 of the 1992 Regulations requires every employer to make a suitable and sufficient assessment of the risks to the health and safety of his employees to which they are exposed while they are at work. Furthermore, if his workforce includes women of child-bearing age, the assessment must include an assessment of the risks to the health and safety of a new or expectant mother (or to that of her baby)(*ibid*; Reg. 13A).

Prohibition on night work

- If a new or expectant mother works at night and produces a certificate signed by a doctor (or by a registered midwife) stating that night work could be detrimental to her health or safety, her employer must either transfer her to daytime work or, if this is impracticable, suspend her from work on full pay for the period specified in the certificate — unless she has unreasonably refused an offer of suitable alternative work. As is explained below, any dispute about an employee's right or otherwise to be paid during a period of maternity suspension may have to be resolved by an industrial tribunal (*ibid*; Regulation 13B).

Employer's duty to offer suitable alternative work

- An employee who would otherwise be suspended from work on maternity grounds has the right to be offered suitable alternative work by her employer *if* he has such work available. Furthermore, the offer must be made *before* the suspension period is due to begin. If he fails to do so, or makes an offer of work which the employee considers unsuitable, she may complain to an industrial tribunal. Her complaint must be presented within three months of the first day of the suspension period or within such further period as the tribunal considers reasonable in the circumstances. Unless satisfied that the employer had no suitable alternative work for the employee to do (or that the work he did offer her *was* suitable), the tribunal will order him to pay the employee a "just and equitable" amount of compensation — having regard to the infringement of the employee's right to be offered suitable alternative work and to any loss attributable to that infringement (section 67(1), Employment Rights Act 1996)).

Meaning of "suitable alternative work"

- "Suitable alternative work" means work of a kind which is both suitable in relation to the employee and appropriate for her to do in the circumstances — bearing in mind the type of work she normally does and her status, qualifications, skills and experience. Furthermore, the terms and conditions applicable to that alternative work must not be substantially less favourable to her than the corresponding terms and conditions applicable to the work she normally performs under her contract of employment (*ibid*; section 67(2)).

Right to remuneration on suspension

- Section 68 of the 1996 Act states that an employee suspended from work on maternity grounds must be paid her normal wages or salary during the period of her suspension, unless (as was indicated earlier) she has unreasonably refused an offer of suitable alternative work (see above). However, any payment made to her under her contract of employment in respect of that same period can be offset against that statutory entitlement, and vice versa.

- An employee can complain to an industrial tribunal that her employer has failed to pay her normal wages or salary during her suspension on maternity grounds. The complaint must be presented within three months of the day on which payment was withheld, although a tribunal *may* consider a complaint presented 'out of time' if satisfied that it was not reasonably practicable for her to have acted sooner. If such a complaint is upheld, the tribunal will order the employer to pay the employee the amount of remuneration which it finds is due to her (*ibid;* section 70).

Dismissal for asserting a statutory right

- An employee who is dismissed by her employer for asserting her statutory rights in relation to a period of suspension on maternity grounds, or for having complained to an industrial tribunal about his infringement of those rights, will be treated in law as having been unfairly dismissed (regardless of her length of service or working hours at the material time) and will be compensated accordingly (*ibid;* section 105)

See also **Pregnant employees & nursing mothers** elsewhere in this handbook.

Table 1

UK HEALTH & SAFETY PROVISIONS CONCERNED WITH THE PROTECTION OF WOMEN WHO ARE PREGNANT OR OF 'REPRODUCTIVE CAPACITY'

Regulations & Orders	Provision
Control of Lead at Work Regulations 1980 (Reg. 16 and **para. 118 of the accompanying Approved Code of Practice).** (SI 1980/1248)	"In order to safeguard a developing foetus, a woman of reproductive capacity who is employed on work which exposes her to lead and is subject to medical surveillance .... (a) should be suspended from work which exposes her to lead when her blood lead concentration exceeds 40µg/100 ml; (b) should notify her employer as soon as possible if she becomes pregnant; (c) once pregnancy has been notified and the employment medical adviser or appointed doctor informed, should, on the advice of the employment medical adviser/appointed doctor ... be suspended from work which exposes her to lead."

Ionising Radiations Regulations 1985
(Regulation 16(6) and
Schedule 1, Parts IV and V)

(SI 1985/1333)

"Where the employment medical adviser or appointed doctor has certified in the health record of an employee .. that in his professional opinion that employee should not be engaged in work with ionising radiation or that he (*or she*) should only be so engaged under conditions he has specified in the health record, the employer shall not permit that employee to be engaged in work with ionising radiation except in accordance with the conditions, if any, so specified".

The dose limit for the abdomen of a female employee of reproductive capacity, who is exposed to ionising radiation, is 13mSv in any consecutive three month interval. In the case of a pregnant employee, the dose limit averaged throughout the abdomen is 10mSv during the declared term of pregnancy.

Air Navigation Order 1985
(Article 20(8))

(SI 1985/1643)

A member of a flight crew who has reason to believe she is pregnant must notify her employers in writing without delay. Once her pregnancy is confirmed, she is deemed to be suspended from work and may only resume her duties during the initial stages of her pregnancy if it is considered safe for her to do so. But she will not be permitted to return to work as a member of a flight crew after her pregnancy has ended until she has been medically examined and pronounced fit to do so.

Merchant Shipping (Medical Examination) Regulations 1983
(Reg. 7)

(SI 1983/808)

Restrictions imposed on the employment (or continued employment) of women as laid down in Parts X (so far as relating to gynaecological conditions) and XI of the Merchant Shipping Notice No. M 1331.

Management of Health & Safety at Work Regulations 1992(Regulations 13A & 13B)

(SI 1992/2051, as amended by SI 1994/2865)

"(1)(a) Where the persons working in an undertaking include women of child-bearing age; and (b) the work is of a kind which could involve risk, by reason of her condition, to the health and safety of a new or expectant mother, or to that of her baby, from any processes or working conditions, or physical, biological or chemical agents, including those specified in Annexes I and II of Council Directive 92/85/EEC (*see Tables 2, 3 & 4 overleaf*) ... the assessment required by regulation 3(1) shall also include an assessment of such risk."

"(2) Where, in the case of an individual employee, the taking of any other action the employer is required to take under the relevant statutory provisions would not avoid the risk referred to in paragraph (1)(a) would not avoid such risk, the employer shall if it is reasonable to do so, and would avoid such risks, alter her working conditions or hours of work."

(3) If it is not reasonable to alter the working conditions or hours of work or if it would not avoid such risk, the employer shall ... suspend the employee from work for so long as is necessary to avoid such risk."

(Table 2 overleaf)

Table 2
Annex I (EC Directive 92/85/EEC
Measures to encourage improvements in the safety and health at
work of pregnant workers and workers who have recently given
birth or are breastfeeding
NON-EXHAUSTIVE LIST OF AGENTS,
PROCESSES & WORKING CONDITIONS

A1. *Physical agents*

where these are regarded as agents causing foetal lesions and/or
likely to disrupt placental attachment, and in particular:

(a)   shocks, vibration or movement;
(b)   handling of loads entailing risks, particularly of
           a dorsolumbar nature;
(c)   noise;
(d)   ionising radiation;
(e)   non-ionising radiation;
(f)   extremes of cold or heat;
(g)   movements and posture, travelling — either inside or outside
           the establishment — mental and physical fatigue and other
           physical burdens concerned with the activity of the worker
           within the meaning of Article 2 of the Directive.

A2. *Biological agents*

Biological agents of risk groups 2,3 and 3 within the meaning of
Article 2(d) numbers 2, 3 and 4 of Directive 90/679/EEC, in so far as it is
known that these agents or the therapeutic measures necessitated by such
agents endanger the health or pregnant women and the unborn child and in
so far as they do not yet appear in Annex II.

A3. *Chemical agents*

The following chemical agents in so far as it is known that they
endanger the health or pregnant women and the unborn child and in so far
as they do not yet appear in Annex II:

(a)   substances labelled R40, R45, R46, and R47 under Directive
           67/548/EEC in so far as they do not yet appear in Annex II;
(b)   chemical agents in Annex I to Directive 90/394/EEC;
(c)   mercury and mercury derivatives;
(d)   antimitotic drugs;
(e)   carbon monoxide;
(f)   chemical agents of known and dangerous percutaneous
           absorption.

B.   *Processes*

Industrial processes listed in Annex I to Directive 90/394/EEC
(See Table 4 below)

C.. *Working conditions*:   Underground mining work.

Table 3
Annex II (EC Directive 92/85/EEC
Measures to encourage improvements in the safety and health at work of pregnant workers and workers who have recently given birth or are breastfeeding.
NON-EXHAUSTIVE LIST OF AGENTS, PROCESSES & WORKING CONDITIONS

A. Pregnant workers within the meaning of Article 2(a)

1(a) Physical agents

Work in hyperbaric atmosphere, e.g., pressurised enclosures and underwater diving.

1(b) Biological agents

The following biological agents
— toxiplasma,
— rubella virus,
unless the pregnant workers are proved to be adequately protected against such agents by immunisation.

1(c) Chemical agents

Lead and lead derivatives in so far as these agents are capable of being absorbed by the human organism.

2. Working conditions

Underground mining work.

B. Workers who are breastfeeding within the meaning of article 2(c)

1(a) Chemical agents

Lead and lead derivatives in so far as these agents are capable of being absorbed by the human organism.

2. Working conditions

Underground mining work

(Table 4 overleaf)

Table 4
Annex I to Directive 90/394/EEC
on the protection of workers from the risks relating to
exposure to carcinogens at work
PROCESSES LIKELY TO POSE A RISK TO THE HEALTH
AND SAFETY OF NEW AND EXPECTANT MOTHERS

1. Manufacture of auramine.

2. Work involving exposure to aromatic polycyclic hydrocarbones present in coal soots, tar, pitch, fumes or dust.

3. Work involving exposure to dusts, fumes and sprays produced during the roasting and electro-refining of cupro-nickel mattes.

4. Strong acid process in the manufacture of isopropyl alcohol.

SUSPENSION ON MEDICAL GROUNDS

Key points

- An employee who is suspended from work on medical grounds under apposite health and safety legislation (or any associated code of practice) must be paid his (or her) normal wages or salary while he is so suspended — for a period not exceeding 26 weeks (*per* section 64, Employment Rights Act 1996).

- There are currently three sets of health and safety regulations which provide for suspension from work on medical grounds as a consequence of routine health surveillance (*ibid*; Schedule 1). Other regulations (and codes of practice) may follow. Under those regulations, an HSE-appointed doctor or employment medical adviser has the right to suspend an employee on medical grounds *if* there is evidence that the employee's continued exposure to certain hazardous substances or processes is likely to be detrimental to his (or her) health. The regulations in question are :

(a)   the **Control of Lead at Work Regulations 1980** (SI

1980/1248), which contain provisions relating to exposure to lead (including lead alloys, any compounds of lead, and lead as a constituent of any substance or material) which is liable to be inhaled, ingested or otherwise absorbed by persons, except where it is given off from the exhaust system of a vehicle on the road within the meaning of section 196(1) of the Road Traffic Act 1972;

(b)   the **Ionising Radiations Regulations 1985** (SI 1985/1333), which apply to exposure to electro-magnetic or corpuscular radiation capable of producing ions and emitted from a radioactive substance or from a machine or apparatus that is intended to produce ionising radiation or in which charged particles are accelerated by a voltage of not less than five kilovolts; and

(c)   Regulation 11 of the **Control of Substances Hazardous to Health Regulations 1994** (SI 1994/3246), which deals with the health surveillance of employees engaged in processes which could give rise to exposure to one or other of the following substances listed in Schedule 5:

Vinyl chloride monomer (VCM)
Nitro or amino derivatives of phenol and of
        benzene or its homologues
Potassium or sodium chlorate or dichromate
1-Napthylamine and its salts
Orthotolidine and its salts
Dianasidine and its salts
Dichlorobenzidine and its salts
Auramine
Magenta
Carbon disulphide
Disulphur dichloride
Benzene, including benzol
Carbon tetrachloride
Trichloroethylene
Pitch

Employers to whom the above regulations apply must develop and maintain suitable arrangements for the routine health surveillance of their employees and must keep comprehensive health records.

Note: Regulations 3 and 5 of The Management of Health & Safety at Work Regulations 1992 (SI 1992/2051), as amended by the ditto (Amendment) Regulations 1994 (SI 1994/2865), which apply to all employment situations (other than the ship-board activities of a ship's crew under the direction of the master) require every employer to assess the risks to which his employees are exposed while at work and to introduce health surveillance if that assessment shows that there is an identifiable disease or adverse health condition related to the work they do.

- An employee will usually be suspended from work because of the risks associated with his (or her) exposure to one or other of the hazardous substances listed above. He will not be ill or incapacitated for work in the accepted sense, but may well be showing signs of fatigue (headaches, etc.) or have other potentially disabling symptoms. Indeed, an employment medical adviser or HSE-appointed doctor may decide to suspend an employee for a short or 'longish' period simply to enable further tests to be carried out. Until the employee receives the 'all clear', there can be no good reason why he should not be transferred to less hazardous work elsewhere in the same factory or workshop.

Qualifying conditions

- To qualify to be paid his (or her) normal wages or salary during a period of suspension on medical grounds, the employee —

    (a) must have been continuously employed for a period of one month or more ending with the day before that on which the suspension begins (see *Note* below); but not if employed under a contract for a fixed term of three months or less, or under a contract made in contemplation of the performance of a specific task which is not expected to last for more than three months, unless he (or she) has been continuously employed for a period of more than three months ending with the day before that on which the suspension begins (1996 Act, section 65(1) & (2))

    (b) must not otherwise be incapable of work by reason of disease or bodily or mental disablement (*ibid*; section 65(3)); and

    (c) must not have unreasonably refused an offer of suitable alternative work — whether or not work of a kind which he is employed under his contract to do; *or*, if his employer has nothing to offer immediately, must remain on standby (e.g., at home or by a telephone) in case his employer *does* find something else for him to do (*ibid*; section 65(4)).

• Medical suspension will not be appropriate if an employee is already incapacitated for work because of illness or injury (whether or not related to the hazardous nature of his work). Such an employee would either qualify for statutory sick pay (SSP) or be entitled to Social Security Sickness or Invalidity benefits — as to which, please turn to the section titled **Industrial injuries** elsewhere in this handbook.

Complaint to an industrial tribunal

• An employee suspended from work on medical grounds (who satisfies the conditions explained earlier) may present a complaint to an industrial tribunal that his (or her) employer has not paid him the whole or part of the wages or salary due to him while he was suspended. An employee need not resign in order to pursue his statutory rights, but must present his complaint (using Form IT1, available from local offices of the Employment Service) within three months of the day on which the expected payment was withheld. If the employee's complaint is upheld, the industrial tribunal will order the employer to pay the disputed amount (*ibid*; section 70).

• An employee who is dismissed for asserting his right to be paid his normal wages or salary during a period of suspension on medical grounds (or for questioning his employer's refusal to pay him) may complain to an industrial tribunal regardless of his (or her) age or length of service at the material time (*ibid*; 104). If a complaint of unfair dismissal is upheld, the employer will be ordered either to reinstate or re-engage the complainant or pay compensation. See also **Dismissal or victimisation** and **Suspension on maternity grounds** elsewhere in this handbook.

T

TEMPERATURE IN WORKROOMS

Key points

- The temperature in indoor workrooms should be comfortable — neither too hot nor too cold. Where a reasonable temperature is impractical, because of hot, cold or humid processes, the employer should take all reasonable steps to achieve as comfortable a working temperature as is possible in the circumstances (Regulation 7, Workplace (Health, Safety & Welfare) Regulations 1992 [SI 1992/3004]).

- In most indoor workrooms, the temperature should normally be at least 16° Celsius. For people engaged in strenuous physical work, the temperature should be at least 13 ° Celsius.

- Some employees will feel uncomfortably hot seated or working next to hot pipes or radiators or within a few yards of a furnace or autoclave (or beside an unshaded window on a sunny day); others will feel uncomfortably cold working in the middle of an office or workshop or adjacent to a draughty doorway. The steps an employer might consider to achieve a comfortable working temperature could include:

  o increasing the ventilation

  o providing local heating or cooling (fans or portable heaters)

  o insulating hot plants or pipes

  o shading windows with blinds or curtains

  o siting workstations away from places subject to radiant heat

  o fitting draught excluders to existing doors or installing self-closing doors at entrances and exits

- Insulated duckboards or other floor coverings should be provided where workers have to stand for long periods on cold floors, unless they have been issued with special footwear which prevents discomfort. If, in spite of everything, workers are still exposed to uncomfortably high or low temperatures, their employer should issue suitable protective clothing and use a job rotation or similar system to ensure a limit on the length of time any worker is exposed to uncomfortable temperatures. Regular breaks in a nearby restroom would also be helpful.

- An employer's duty to provide a comfortable working temperature (13° or 16° Celsius, as appropriate) does not apply to rooms where it is impractical to maintain those temperatures—for example, rooms necessarily open to the outside, chill rooms (where processed food or other products have to be kept at low temperatures), and workrooms in which a close, humid atmosphere is necessary.

Thermometers

- Employers must provide a sufficient number of dry bulb thermometers in accessible places throughout the workplace (not necessarily in every office or workroom) which employees can borrow and use to measure the temperature in their workrooms (*ibid*).

- In an office block, there should be at least one dry bulb thermometer on each floor. In a small workshop, just the one should do. In a sprawling factory complex, several may be needed. The point is that employees should not have to walk too far to obtain a thermometer to measure the temperature in their workrooms.

Temperatures in changing rooms, washrooms, etc.

- Washrooms, toilets, changing rooms, messrooms, canteens and storerooms, should be both dry (or as dry as circumstances permit) and well-ventilated. The temperature in such rooms should be reasonable in all the circumstances including the length of time people are likely to be there. Changing rooms and shower rooms should not be cold.

See also **Humid factories** elsewhere in this handbook.

FURTHER INFORMATION

- The following publication is available from HSE Books at the address given on page 328:

  L24
  Workplace health, safety and welfare. Workplace (Health, Safety and Welfare) Regulations 1992: Approved code of practice and guidance [1992]
  ISBN 0 7176 0413 6   £5.00

TOILET FACILITIES

Key points

- The occupier or owner of every workplace must provide a suitable and sufficient number of 'sanitary conveniences' (lavatories, toilets, water closets, WCs, loos, urinals — whichever the preferred expression) and washbasins close enough to the workplace to enable employees to use them without undue delay (Regulations 20 & 21, Workplace (Health, Safety & Welfare) Regulations 1992 (SI 1992/3004)).

- Separate toilet accommodation with washbasins must be provided for men and women unless each toilet is in a separate room (fitted with its own washbasin, soap and towel) the door of which is capable of being secured from the inside.

- Toilets and urinals, and the accommodation which houses them, must be adequately ventilated and lit, and must be kept in a clean and orderly condition. Each WC should be in its own cubicle capable of being secured from the inside, and contain a coat hook and sufficient supply of toilet paper in a holder or dispenser.

Sanitary dressings, facilities for disposal of

- In toilet accommodation used only by women, suitable means (e.g., an electric furnace or an enclosed container) must be provided for the hygienic disposal of sanitary dressings.

Table 1		
TOILET FACILITIES		
(1) **Number of** **people** **at work**	**(2)** **Number of WCs**	**(3)** **Number of** **Washbasins**
1 to 5	1	1
6 to 25	2	2
26 to 50	3	3
51 to 75	4	4
76 to 100	5	5
100+	(See *Note* below)	(See *Note* below)

Note: One additional WC and one extra washbasin should be provided for every 25 (or fraction of 25) people above 100.

Each WC should be in its own cubicle, capable of being secured from the inside. There should also be a coat hook in every cubicle plus a sufficient supply of toilet paper in a suitable holder or dispenser.

Washbasins must be in the immediate vicinity of WCs and should be equipped with hot and cold (or warm) running water, soap (or other suitable cleaning aid) and towels (or other suitable method for drying hands).

Privacy for persons using toilets

- In the interests of privacy and decorum, it should not be possible for any passer-by to see into any part of the interior of the room housing WCs, urinals or washbasins when the door is open. This is usually achieved by erecting a partition parallel to the wall containing the doorway and set at a convenient distance from that doorway. For the same reason, windows in toilet blocks should be of frosted glass (or the equivalent) unless they are set high enough in the wall to make it impossible for any person to see inside the toilet block.

Table 2
MEN'S TOILETS
when urinals also provided

(1) Number of men at work	(2) Number of WCs	(3) Number of urinals
1 to 15	1	1
16 to 30	2	1
31 to 45	2	2
46 to 60	3	2
61 to 75	3	3
76 to 90	4	3
91 to 100	4	4
100+	(see *Note* below)	(see *Note* below)

Note: One additional WC and one additional urinal for every 50 men (or fraction of that number) above 100.

A urinal may either be an individual urinal (screened from its neighbours) or a section of urinal space which is at least 600 mm long.

The expression 'men at work' in Column 1 above refers to the maximum number of men (including visitors and members of the public likely to be in the workplace at any one time.

Alternative when urinals also provided

• **Table 1** on the previous page shows the number of WCs and washbasins which must be provided in a workplace. The number of people at work shown in column (1) refers to the maximum number of people (including, where appropriate, visitors and members of the public) likely to be in the workplace at any one time. Where separate toilet accommodation is provided for a group of workers (e.g., men, women, office staff or manual workers) a separate calculation must be made for each group. **Table 2** above applies if Gents' Toilets are equipped with urinals as well as WCs.

Exception for certain factories

- Factories first established as such before 1 January 1993, need *not* comply with Regulation 20 of the Workplace Regulations summarised here so long as there is at least one WC for every 25 female employees, and at least one for every 25 males (any fraction over and above 25 being treated as 25) (*ibid*; Schedule 1, Part II).

Maintenance and repair

- All plumbing systems serving toilets, washrooms, drinking water taps, showers, baths, etc. must be kept in sound working order and good repair. They must be tested and inspected at regular intervals, and the findings recorded in a log. In the interests of health and hygiene, and to ensure that the prescribed minimum number of toilets and urinals are available and working efficiently, faulty flushing mechanisms must be reported and repaired as soon as possible (*ibid*; Regulation 5*)*.

  See also **Food safety & hygiene** and **Washing   facilities** elsewhere in this handbook.

FURTHER INFORMATION

- For further information, the reader is commended to the following publication available from HSE Books at the address given on page 328:

  L24
  Workplace health, safety and welfare. Workplace (Health, Safety and Welfare) Regulations 1992: Approved code of practice and guidance [1992]
  ISBN 0 7176 0413 6   £5.00

TRAFFIC & TRAFFIC ROUTES IN WORKPLACES

Key points

- Section 2(2)(d) of the Health & Safety at Work etc. Act 1974 imposes a duty on every employer to maintain the workplace under his control in a condition that is safe and without risks to health.

- Reinforcing provisions are to be found in the Workplace (Health, Safety & Welfare) Regulations 1992 (SI 1992/3004) which state (inter alia) that every workplace must be organised in such a way that pedestrians and vehicles can circulate in a safe manner. Traffic routes must be suitable for the persons or vehicles using them. They must be clearly marked, sufficient in number and size, and suitable for their intended purpose.

- The expression 'traffic routes' applies not only to routes taken by HGVs, lorries, company cars, fork lift trucks and palletisers when moving in and about a factory, warehouse or loading bay. It also refers to the routes — corridors, walkways, paths, steps, stairs — taken by pedestrians (usually employees) when walking to and from their workstations (desks, workbenches, or whatever) or when going about their normal duties.

- Traffic routes, whatever their purpose, must be well-defined, and well-lit and signposted (particularly at crossroads, pedestrian crossing points, sharp bends and dangerous or concealed exits). Sensible speed limits should be set and clearly displayed on vehicle routes except those used by slow-moving vehicles. Speed retarders (such as humps) will serve to slow down larger vehicles and should be installed where necessary. But they should not be installed on routes used by fork trucks unless they are of a type which can negotiate speed humps safely.

Condition of floors and traffic routes

- Employers must take appropriate measures to ensure that the surfaces of every 'traffic route' are free from obstruction and from any article or substance which may cause a person to slip, trip or fall. Floor surfaces must be even, well-drained and in a good state or repairs (free from holes or slopes). The accompanying code of practice specifically mentions the risks from snow and ice and cautions employers to make arrangements to minimise those risks — by gritting, snow-clearing or closing badly affected routes, including ladders and walkways on roofs.

FURTHER INFORMATION

- Practical advice for employers on the implications of the 1992 Regulations is to be found in the accompanying Approved Code of Practice and in the following publications available from HSE Books at the Address given on page 328:

L24
Workplace health, safety and welfare. Workplace (Health, Safety and Welfare) Regulations 1992: Approved code of practice and guidance [1992]
ISBN 0 7176 0413 6   £5.00

GS9(Rev)
Road transport in factories and similar workplaces
(ISBN 0 11 885732 0)

HS(G)6(Rev)
Safety in working with lift trucks
ISBN 0 11 886395 9)

Free leaflet (Telephone 01787 881165)

IND(G)22L
Danger! Transport at work

TRAINING OF EMPLOYEES

Key points

- Implicit in every contract of employment is the employer's duty to provide his employees with training sufficient to enable them to carry out their duties safely and efficiently. If an employee is injured as a direct consequence of his (or her) employer's negligence (including any failure to provide the proper degree of training necessary to minimise risks of injury), he may sue his employer for damages in the ordinary courts.

- Section 2(2)(c) of the Health & Safety at Work etc. Act 1974 has long since put that implied contractual duty onto a statutory footing by stating that every employer has a duty in law to provide his employees with such information, instruction, training and supervision as is necessary to ensure, so far as is reasonably practicable, their health, safety and welfare at work. A failure to discharge that duty is an offence for which the penalty, on summary conviction, is a fine of up to £20,000.

- Although there is a great deal of complementary and industry-specific legislation on the question of training (see below), section 2 of the 1974 Act is all-embracing in its scope and applies as much to employers engaged in supposedly low-risk trades and activities as it does to foundries, steel mills, cracking plants, chemical works, building sites, etc., all too often mistakenly identified as the prime (if not the only) targets of health and safety legislation.

Management of Health & Safety at Work Regulations 1992

- The Management of Health & Safety at Work Regulations 1992 (SI 1992/2051) apply to *every* premises or part of premises (other than a sea-going ship) in which one or more persons are employed to work. Regulation 3 imposes a duty on every employer, whatever the size or nature of his trade or business, to assess the risks to the health and safety of his employees (and to members of the public) arising out of the way in which he manages or conduct his business. If the risk assessment reveals that there *are* workplace hazards, the measures necessarily taken by the employer to eliminate or adequately control those risks must include training — whose purpose it is to educate employees about the risks associated with such hazards, the measures their employer has put in place to eliminate or minimise those risks, and the procedures the employees must themselves follow to protect themselves from injury.

- Before putting an employee to work, an employer must satisfy himself that the person in question is competent to carry out his (or her) duties safely — taking into account the extent of his previous knowledge, training and experience. Regulation 11 states that new recruits must not be put to work in any job involving a risk to their health and safety without first receiving induction training (supported, where necessary, by supervised 'on-the-job' training). The same applies when an employee is transferred from one part of his employer's business to another, if the transfer is likely to expose that employee to new or increased risks. Training must also be provided when new plant and equipment, new processes, new technology or unfamiliar chemicals and substances are introduced to the workplace for the first time. 'Refresher' training should also form part of an employer's safety strategy, the more so if an increase in accidents, dangerous occurrences or 'near misses' suggests that the workforce do not fully appreciate the dangers to which they are exposed or are too lax or complacent about complying with their employer's health and safety rules (*ibid*; Regulation 11).

Provision & Use of Work Equipment (PUWER) Regulations 1992

- Under Regulation 16 of the PUWER Regulations 1992 (SI 1992/2932), every employer must ensure that those of his employees who use work equipment (plant, machinery, tools or appliances) have received adequate training in safe working methods, the risks involved in using such equipment, and the precautions to be taken to avoid injury to themselves and other people. Managers, supervisors and chargehands, whose job it is to oversee the use of work equipment, should not be appointed to such posts unless they too are familiar with the work equipment under their control and have received the same degree of training.

Health & Safety (Display Screen Equipment) Regulations 1992

- Regulation 6 of the Health & Safety (Display Screen Equipment) Regulations 1992 (SI 1992/2792) imposes a duty on employers to ensure that those of their employees who habitually use display screen equipment (VDUs) as a significant part of their normal work receive adequate health and safety training in the risks (musculoskeletal, visual and mental) associated with the use of the workstations upon which they are or may be required to work. A "workstation" for these purposes is an assembly comprising display screen equipment (or VDU) and its accessories: keyboard, mouse, disk drive, telephone, modem, printer, document holder, work chair, work desk, work surface; and the immediate environment around the display screen equipment.

Manual Handling Operations Regulations 1992

- Although the Manual Handling Operations Regulations 1992 (SI 1992/2793) do not mention training as such, regulation 4(1)(b)(ii) does require employers to take appropriate steps to minimise the risk of injury to those of their employees who are engaged in manual handling operations. The accompanying HSE Guidance Notes (L23) remind employers of their duties under section 2 of the 1974 Act, and under Regulations 8 and 11 of the Management of Health & Safety at Work Regulations 1992 (*q.v.*) to provide their employees with health and safety information and training. That information and training, says the Guidance Notes, should be supplemented as necessary with more specific information and training on manual handling injury risks and prevention.

Fire Precautions Act 1971

- A fire certificate issued under the aegis of the Fire Precautions Act 1971 will ordinarily impose a duty on the occupier or owner of the relevant premises to provide each of his employees with instruction and training appropriate to his responsibilities in the event of an emergency. Records of training provided (giving dates and names) must be maintained and kept available for inspection by an inspector of the fire authority (see **Fire certificate** and **Fire precautions** elsewhere in this handbook).

First aid

- For details of first-aid training requirements, see **First aid** elsewhere in this handbook.

MISCELLANEOUS LEGISLATION

There are similar provisions in —

(a) Regulation 5 of the **Control of Lead at Work Regulations 1980** (SI 1980/1248);

(b) Regulation 12 of the **Ionising Radiations Regulations 1985** (SI 1985/1333);

(c) Regulation 7 of the **Control of Asbestos at Work Regulations 1987** (SI 1987/2115); and in

(d) Regulation 12 of the **Control of Substances Hazardous to Health (COSHH) Regulations 1994** (SI 1994/3246);

as well as in —

(e) Regulation 4 of the **Power Presses Regulations 1965** (SI 1965/1441, as amended) (training of employees whose job it is to set, re-set, adjust or try out the tools on a power-press, or install or adjust any safety device (preparatory to production or die proving), or inspect or test any such safety device);

(f) Regulation 9 and the Schedule to the **Abrasive Wheels Regulations 1970** (SI 1970/535) (training and appointment of persons to mount abrasive wheels);

(g) Regulation 13 of the **Woodworking Machines Regulations 1974** (SI 1974/903) (no person to be employed on any kind of work at a woodworking machine without sufficient training and instruction)

(h) Regulation 7(1) of the **Diving Operations at Work Regulations 1981** (SI 1981/399, as amended by SI 1990/996) (certificate of training for divers);

(i) Regulation 15 of the **Work in Compressed Air Regulations 1996** (SI 1996/1656) (the compressed air contractor to ensure that adequate information, instruction and training has been given to any person who works in compressed air so that he (or she) is aware of the risks arising from such work and the precautions which should be observed.

(i) Regulation 11 of the **Pressure Systems & Transportable Gas Containers Regulations 1989** (SI 1989/2169) (adequate and suitable instructions for persons operating pressure systems);

(j) Regulation 15 of the **Carriage of Dangerous Goods by Rail Regulations 1996** (SI 1996/2089) (information, instruction and training for train crew members and employees of infrastructure controllers);

(k) Regulations 17 & 18 of the **Carriage of Explosives by**

Road Regulations 1996 (SI 1996/2093) (information and instruction of drivers and attendants);

(l)   **Carriage of Dangerous Goods by Road (Driver Training) Regulations 1996 (SI 1996/2094);**

This list is not exhaustive.

FOOD HYGIENE

- As might be expected, the Food Safety (General Food Hygiene) Regulations 1995 (SI 1995/1763) impose a great many duties on food manufacturers, and on the proprietors, supervisors, licensees and employees in food businesses (restaurants, cafes, dining-rooms, pubs, bars, kitchens, hospitals, schools and the like, where food or drink intended for human consumption is prepared, processed, manufactured, stored, transported, distributed, handled, sold or supplied (whether or not for profit).

- Thus food and drink must be protected from contamination. Food and drink handlers (such as factory operatives, bar staff, waiters and waitresses, chefs, cooks, kitchen porters, still room employees, storemen, etc.) must observe a high standard of personal cleanliness; must refrain from smoking (and spitting) while carrying out their duties; must cover or bandage open cuts and abrasions; must inform their supervisor or manager if they are suffering from (or are the carriers of) certain infections; must wash their hands after using the lavatory; and so on. All of which imposes a heavy responsibility, not only on the employees themselves, but more particularly on the management of the establishment in which they are working. It is the manager's duty to ensure that they receive adequate instruction and training, and that they are familiar with their obligations under the 1995 Regulations (*ibid*; Schedule 1, Chapter X).For further particulars, please turn to the section titled **Food safety & hygiene** elsewhere in this handbook..

- Regulation 4 (*ibid*) cautions that a person carrying on a "food business" will be guilty of an offence if he fails to ensure that the preparation, processing, manufacturing, packaging, storing, transportation, distribution, handling, sale or supply of food is carried out in a hygienic way. The penalty for contravening regulation 4 is a fine of up to £5,000. If a conviction is obtained on indictment, the penalty is a fine of an unlimited amount and/or imprisonment for a term not exceeding two years.

See also **Asbestos at work, Care, Common duty of, Dangerous chemicals, Dangerous machines, Hazardous substances, Health & safety at work, Lead at work, Machinery safety** and **Risk assessment** elsewhere in this handbook.

| **VENTILATION OF WORKPLACES** |

Key points

- Section 2(2)(e) of the Health & Safety at Work etc. Act 1974 imposes a duty on every employer to provide and maintain a safe working environment for all his employees.

- Under the reinforcing provisions of the Workplace (Health, Safety & Welfare) Regulations 1992 (SI 1992/3004), an employer must ensure that every enclosed workplace under his control is ventilated by a sufficient quantity of fresh and purified air — the intention being to replace stale air, and air which is hot or humid, at a reasonable rate (that is to say, between 5 and 8 litres per second, per occupant of every workroom) (*ibid*; Regulation 6).

- The accompanying Approved Code of Practice (see *FURTHER INFORMATION* below) points out that, although windows, skylights and other openings will provide sufficient ventilation in a great many workplaces, a mechanical ventilation system may have to be installed to ensure that stale air, and air which is hot or humid, is replaced at the rate referred to in the previous paragraph.

- Air which is recirculated by mechanical means must be adequately filtered to remove impurities. To avoid air becoming unhealthy, purified air should have some fresh air added to it before being recirculated. Reasonable steps should also be taken to minimise smells coming in from outside.

- If the failure of any plant or air conditioning system (such as a 'dilution ventilation' system) is likely to cause health and safety problems, the plant or system should be equipped with a device which gives a visible or audible warning of any failure.

- For rules about the ventilation of "food premises", please turn to the section titled **Food safety & hygiene** elsewhere in this handbook.

Avoidance of draughts

- Employers should ensure that no member of the workforce is seated or working in an uncomfortable draught, whether coming from an open doorway or window or from a mechanical ventilation system. If the draught cannot be eliminated, the affected workstations must either be re-sited or screened to eliminate or minimise the discomfort (*ibid*).

Humid atmospheres

- In some workplaces, it will not always be practicable to provide the sort of ventilation required by the 1992 regulations. There are certain activities and processes which require humid atmospheres (e.g., the textile industry, or the growing of mushrooms). In such cases, the employer must see to it that his employees are allowed 'adequate' breaks in a well-ventilated place (*ibid;* Regulation 7).

Welfare facilities

- Non-work areas such as cloakrooms, changing rooms, washrooms and toilets must also be well-ventilated.

Maintenance and repair

- All ventilation plant and equipment must be kept in good working order and must be routinely inspected, tested, lubricated, cleaned and (if damaged or defective) repaired (as quickly as possible). The owner or occupier of a workplace must keep a log book confirming the existence and implementation of a well-planned maintenance programme.

EXHAUST VENTILATION

- Regulation 6 does not apply to local exhaust ventilation fitted to machines, etc. as one of the measures necessarily adopted by employers to control the exposure of employees to asbestos, lead, ionising radiation and other substances known to be dangerous or hazardous to health — as to which, see **Asbestos at work, Hazardous substances, Ionising radiation** and **Lead at work** elsewhere in this handbook.

CONFINED SPACES

- An owner or occupier's duty to ensure that every enclosed workplace under his control is sufficiently well ventilated does *not* extend to 'confined spaces' (chambers, tanks, vats, pipelines, silos, etc.) which employees may called upon to enter for the purposes of cleaning, maintenance or repair.

- Rules about entry into, and work in, confined spaces (where breathing apparatus may be necessary) are to be found in section 30 of the Factories Act 1961; Regulations 49 to 52 of the Shipbuilding and Ship-Repairing Regulations 1960 (SI 1960/1932); the Construction (Health, Safety & Welfare) Regulations 1996 (SI 1996/1593); and Regulation 18 of the Docks Regulations 1988 (SI 1988/1655). See also **Confined spaces** elsewhere in this handbook.

FURTHER INFORMATION

- The following publications are available from HSE Books at the address given on page 328:

L24
Workplace health, safety and welfare. Workplace (Health, Safety and Welfare) Regulations 1992: Approved code of practice and guidance [1992]
ISBN 0 7176 0413 6   £5.00

EH 22 (Rev)
Ventilation of the workplace [1988]
ISBN 0 11 885403 8   £2.50

HS(G) 37
Introduction to local exhaust ventilation [1993]
ISBN 0 11 882134 2   £4.50

HS(G) 54
The maintenance examination and testing of local exhaust ventilation
[1990]
ISBN 0 11 885438 0   £3.00

VISUAL DISPLAY UNITS
(Work with visual display screen equipment)

Key points

- Legislation on the minimum health and safety requirements for work with display screen equipment (VDUs) is contained in the Health & Safety (Display Screen Equipment) Regulations 1992 (SI 1992/2792). The Regulations, which came into force on 1 January 1993, implement the substantive provisions of Council Directive 90/270/EEC (OJ No. L156, 21.6.90, p.14). These cover issues such as workstation design, ergonomic requirements, hardware and keyboard design, space, eye and eyesight effects and so on.

- Although the 1992 Regulations do not contain detailed technical specifications for lists of approved equipment, they do set general objectives (covering issues such as display screen and keyboard design, work desks and chairs, space requirements, the elimination of reflections and glare, radiation protection, and the interface between the computer and the operator or user).

Definitions

- The term "display screen equipment" means any alphanumeric or graphic display screen, regardless of the display process involved.

- A "user" is an employee who *habitually* uses display screen equipment as a significant part of his (or her) normal work. The use of the word *habitually* implies that people such as hotel receptionists, librarians, bank tellers, clerks at airline check-in desks, and others similarly engaged, who use display screen equipment simply to retrieve or input information, are not *users* within the meaning of the 1992 Regulations — although employers will be expected to use their judgement in such cases.

- A self-employed person, who habitually uses display screen equipment provided by a client employer (on the employer's premises) is referred to in the Regulations as an "operator". Employers who provide workstations (see next paragraph) for the use of *operators* must assess the health and safety risks associated with those workstations as if those *operators* were his own employees (i.e., *users*).

- A "workstation" is an assembly comprising —

  (a) display screen equipment (whether provided with software determining the interface between the equipment and its user or operator, a keyboard or any other input device);

  (b) any disk drive, telephone, modem, printer, document holder, work chair, work desk, work surface or other item peripheral to the display screen equipment; and

  (c) the immediate work environment around the display screen equipment.

  Note: The 1992 Regulations do *not* apply to drivers' cabs or control cabs for vehicles or machinery; display screen equipment on board a means of transport (lorries, trains, planes, ferries, ships, etc); display screen equipment mainly intended for public operation (e.g., in public libraries, on railway concourses, coach stations, etc.); portable systems (such as 'lap-top' computers) not in prolonged use; calculators, cash registers or any equipment having a small data or measurement display required for direct use of the equipment; or to 'window' typewriters.

DUTIES OF EMPLOYERS

- The Regulations state that employers must:

  o Analyse VDU workstations and assess and reduce the risks to which *users* and *operators* are likely to be exposed when using those workstations. This means that an employer must look at the computer hardware itself, the environment in which VDU users and operators work, and factors specific to the individuals using the equipment. If there are any associated risks, the employer must take steps to reduce those risks (*ibid*; Regulation 2).

  o Ensure that workstations meet minimum requirements. Workstations (whether new or second-hand) first put into service in an employer's undertaking on or after 1 January 1993, must comply immediatelywith the minimum requirements for workstations laid down in the Schedule to the Regulations (see *FURTHER INFORMATION* below) (*ibid*; Regulation 3(1)).

Note: Workstations brought in service (or first use) before 1 January 1993, should by now have been modified or adapted to comply with the Regulations. The final date for compliance was 31 December 1996(*ibid*; Regulation 3(2)).

o   Organise the work of VDU *users* and *operators*, so that they can have breaks or changes of activity. The need for breaks will depend on how intensely and for how long the individual employee (or self-employed person) is required to use his or her VDU. But short, frequent breaks are better than longer, less frequent ones. Ideally, the VDU worker should be relied upon to use his (or her) own discretion concerning the frequency and timing of rest breaks (*ibid*; Regulation 4).

o   On request, arrange eye and eyesight tests for *users* and would-be *users* (but not *operators*), and provide and pay for special spectacles if prescribed by an optometrist or doctor. VDU users can ask their employer to provide and pay for an eye or eyesight test carried out by an optometrist or by a doctor with an ophthalmic qualification. The employer must comply with that request "as soon as (is) practicable" and likewise with any request for repeat tests (usually on the recommendation of the optometrist who carried out the first test). If a VDU *user* experiences (or continues to experience) visual difficulties — whether or not he or she has already had an eyesight test — the employer must again comply with any request for a further test (*ibid*; Regulation 5).

Note: If an optometrist (or doctor) prescribes special spectacles or lenses for VDU work — to correct vision defects at the viewing distance or distances used specifically for the display screen work concerned (where the spectacles or contact lenses normally needed or already worn by the user cannot be used) — the employer must pay for those special appliances. However, he is not required to pay more than the cost of the basic appliance. If an employee chooses a more costly appliance (e.g., with designer frames), he or she will have to pay the extra costs involved.

Information, instruction and training

- Regulation 6 of the 1992 Regulations states that an employer must provide adequate health and safety training for the VDU *users* in his employ. This should be designed to enable *users* to identify and avoid the physical (musculoskeletal), visual and stress-related risks associated with VDU work. Training should cover correct posture, the use of adjustment mechanisms on seating and on the workstation itself, how to avoid glare, cleaning of screens, how to take advantage of rest breaks, sources of further advice and information, and so on. Repeat training should be provided as often as may be necessary, the more so if the *user's* workstation is modified for any reason (*ibid*; Regulation 6).

- For the benefit of both *users* and *operators,* the employer should explain what action he has taken to comply with his duties under the Regulations, his policy in relation to rest breaks, and provide them with adequate information about all aspects of health and safety relating to their workstations (*ibid*; Regulation 7).

Do VDUs give out harmful levels of radiation?

- The HSE free leaflet INDG 36 (see *FURTHER INFORMATION* below) addresses the questions that are most commonly asked about VDUs and health and is a useful desk-top companion for all VDU *users* and *operators.*

- As to whether VDUs give out harmful levels of radiation, the short answer given in the leaflet is "No". "VDUs", it says, "give out both visible light (which enables us to see the screen) and other forms of electromagnetic radiation which can be harmful above certain levels. However, the levels emitted from VDUs are well below the safe levels set out in international recommendations". Employers, it concludes, do not have to check radiation levels from VDUs; nor do people working with VDUs need special devices such as protective spectacles, screens or aprons.

Are pregnant employees at risk?

- Employees, says the leaflet, do not need to stop working with VDUs when they become pregnant. "There has been some concern about reports of higher levels of miscarriage and birth defects among some groups of VDU workers. Many scientific studies have been carried out which, taken as a whole, do not show any link between miscarriages or birth defects and working with VDUs". If any pregnant employee is anxious about working with VDUs (or about work generally during pregnancy), she should contact her doctor or talk to someone who is well-informed of current authoritative scientific information and advice on VDUs.

FURTHER INFORMATION

* The following publications are available from HSE Books at the address given on page 328:

L26
Display screen equipment work. Health and Safety (Display Screen Equipment) Regulations 1992. Guidance on regulations [1992]
ISBN 0 7176 0410 1   £5.00

HS(G) 90
VDUs: an easy guide to the Regulations
ISBN 0 7176 0735 6   £5.00

Working with VDUs
ISBN 0 7176 0808 5   £3.50 for 10; £6 for 20; £13 for 50; £20 for 100; £75 for 500

HS(G) 38
Lighting at work [1987]
ISBN 0 7176 0467 5   £4.00

HS(G) 57
Seating at work [1991]
ISBN 0 11 885431 3   £2.25

HS(G) 60
Work-related upper limb disorders: a guide to prevention [1990]
ISBN 0 7176 0475 6   £3.75

Free leaflets (Telephone 01787 881165)

INDG 36
Working with VDUs

INDG 90
Ergonomics at Work [1990]

| **WASHING FACILITIES**
(Washbasins, etc.) |

Key points

- Every employer has a duty in law to provide "suitable and sufficient" washing facilities for his employees. This duty, which extends to *every* workplace is imposed by Regulation 21 of the Workplace (Health, Safety & Welfare) Regulations 1992 (SI 1992/3004).

  Note: For the purposes of the 1992 Regulations ("the Workplace Regulations"), the expression "workplace" refers to any premises or part of premises (other than domestic premises) which are made available to any person as a place of work. Accordingly, the Regulations apply not only to offices, shops, factories, workshops, department stores, supermarkets, restaurants, public houses, and the like, but also to schools, hospitals, hotels, guest houses, nursing homes, prisons, theatres, places of entertainment; and so on. However, they do *not* apply to construction sites, docks, mines, quarries, oil drilling sites or (with the exception of Regulation 13) to operational road vehicles, trains or aircraft; or to operational ships, boats and hovercraft — all of which have their own industry-specific legislation.

- Employers who already provide "suitable and sufficient" washing facilities (in compliance with the related, but since repealed, provisions of the Factories Act 1961 or the Offices, Shops & Railway Premises Act 1963), need not engage in expensive rebuilding in order to comply with the Workplace Regulations. The purpose of the latter is to consolidate and 'rationalise' existing UK legislation (much of which is outdated) and to expand the definition of "workplace" to encompass not only premises within the scope of the 1961 and 1963 Acts, but any and all premises (other than domestic premises) "which are made available to any person as a place of work".

- Pre-1993 employers who equipped their premises in compliance with the 1961 and 1963 Acts should nonetheless consider whether the arguably outdated facilities they currently provide are suitable for use by disabled persons (see below) and whether they should now install showers for the benefit of employees engaged in strenuous or dirty work, or in work which exposes them to materials or substances which could promote dermatitis and other skin diseases (see *Showers or baths?* below).

SUITABILITY OF WASHING FACILITIES

- To be "suitable", washing facilities must be well-ventilated and lit, must be kept in a clean and orderly condition, and must be readily accessible to those wishing to use them. They must be situated in the immediate vicinity of toilets and changing rooms; and should be sited in the same building as that containing the workplace, if not in the workplace itself. The accompanying Approved Code of Practice (see *FURTHER INFORMATION* below) makes the point (for the benefit, undoubtedly, of shopkeepers, small workshops, and the like) that "the use of public facilities is only acceptable as a last resort, where no other arrangement is possible". Pre-1993 washroom facilities which made no special provision for disabled workers, should already have been modified or adapted to comply with the 1992 Regulations. The deadline for doing so expired on 31 December 1995.

Showers or baths?

- Workers engaged in particularly strenuous or dirty work (or in work involving exposure to harmful or offensive materials or substances), must be provided with showers or baths for use both at the end of their working day or shift and during normal working hours. All washbasins, showers, etc. must be plumbed into a supply of clean hot and cold (or warm) running water, as well as with soap and clean towels (or other suitable means of cleaning and drying — such as soap dispensers and wall-mounted electric hand-dryers). If showers are fed by both hot and cold water, they should be fitted with a thermostatic mixer valve (or the equivalent) to prevent users being scalded.

Note: On remote or temporary building sites, where there is no access to running water, the employer must nonetheless provide a sufficient supply of water in containers.

Cleanliness of wall, floors and fittings

- The floors and walls of washrooms should have surfaces suitable for regular wet cleaning (e.g., ceramic tiles or plastic-coated materials). Just how often washrooms (and their fittings and fixtures) should be cleaned or washed-down will depend in large part on the frequency of use, bearing in mind that "washing facilities shall *not* be suitable unless .... they and the rooms containing them are kept in a clean and orderly condition". The Code of Practice cautions employers that they should not only make arrangements for the routine cleaning of washing facilities but should also ensure that the responsibility for the cleaning function is "clearly established". In buildings (such as large office blocks), in which washrooms and toilets are shared by a number of tenants, the responsibility for providing suitable and sufficient washing facilities and for keeping those facilities clean (and supplied with soap, towels, etc.) ordinarily devolves on the owner. If in any doubt, tenant employers should discuss the issue with the owner rather than assume that he is aware of his responsibilities (and liabilities) under the 1992 Regulations.

Separate facilities for male and female employees

- Separate washing facilities must be provided for men and women unless the facilities that *are* provided are intended only for washing the hands, forearms and face. In other words, separate male and female washrooms must be provided (whatever the size of the employer's business) if washing facilities necessarily include showers or baths or if employees working in hot and dusty conditions would normally need to strip to the waist when using wash-basins.

- In small business premises, with just a handful of employees, the same washing facilities (including a WC) may be used by both male and female employees, so long as the door to the washroom (and toilet) is capable of being locked or otherwise secured from the inside. Such an arrangement would not, however, be appropriate or acceptable in a larger establishment where the provision of just one washroom and toilet would cause undue delays for other workers. See *SUFFICIENCY OF WASHING FACILITIES* below.

Wash-basins, troughs, showers or baths?

• In offices, shops, hotels, restaurants and the like, the employers (or owners) need only provide wash-basins — provided each is large enough to enable an employee to wash his (or her) hands, face and forearms in relative comfort. In factories, workshops, warehouses, packaging plants, etc., troughs or fountains are acceptable alternatives to wash-basins (given the number of people employed), so long as the section of trough or fountain intended for use by one person is sufficient (that is to say, large enough) for that one person. As was indicated earlier, showers or baths *must* be provided in workplaces in which any employee is engaged in hot, dirty and dusty work, or whose duties involve exposure to potentially harmful substances (cutting oils, coal and coal dust, grease, sugar, flour, chromic acid, and the like).

Note: In *Reid v. Westfield Paper Company Ltd* [1957] SC 218, the Court of Session held that an employee was entitled to recover damages from his employer if he could show that the dermatitis he had contracted arose out of his employer's failure to provide "suitable" washing facilities.

• The rule, that washing facilities must be situated in the immediate vicinity of toilets and changing rooms, applies even if the employer has provided separate washrooms in other parts of his premises (e.g., adjacent to the staff or works canteen).

SUFFICIENCY OF WASHING FACILITIES

• Just how many washbasins, troughs, fountains, or showers are needed will depend on the number of employees in the workplace at any one time, bearing in mind that most will want to use the washroom before meal-breaks and at the end of their working day or shift, especially if intending to use the showers or baths. To avoid queues and delays, the code of practice states that the ratio of "wash-stations" (i.e., basin, or section of trough or fountain) to the number of people at work should be as described in **Table 1** opposite.

OTHER RELEVANT LEGISLATION

• Certain industry or hazard-specific regulations, dealing with the provision of suitable washing facilities, will remain in force alongside the 1992 Regulations. These include:

o   the Control of Lead at Work Regulations 1980

(SI 1980/1248);
o the Ionising Radiations Regulations 1985
   (SI 1985/1333);
o Control of Asbestos at Work Regulations 1987
   (SI 1987/2115); and the
o Control of Substances Hazardous to Health (COSHH)
   Regulations 1994 (SI 1994/3246).

each of which are discussed elsewhere in this handbook under the appropriate subject heads.

Table 1
MINIMUM NUMBER OF WASH-STATIONS
Workplace (Health, Safety & Welfare) Regulations 1992
Approved Code of Practice (Para. 201)

NUMBER OF PEOPLE AT WORK (Men or women, as appropriate)	NUMBER OF WASH-STATIONS
1 to 5	1
6 to 25	2
26 to 50	3
51 to 75	4
76 to 100	5

NOTES

An additional wash-station (i.e., wash-basin, section of trough or fountain) should be provided for every 25 people (or fraction of 25 people) above 100.

If work activities result in heavy soiling of the face, hands and forearms, the number of wash-stations should be increased to one for every 10 people (or fraction of 10 people) at work up to 50 people; and one extra for every additional 20 people (or fraction of 20 people).

If washrooms are used by both employees and members of the public, the number of wash-stations should be increased as necessary to ensure that employees can use the washing facilities without undue delay.

If showers (or baths) are provided in compliance with Regulation 21(1), there must be a sufficient number of them to enable the employees for whom they are intended to use them without undue delay.

SOAP AND TOWELS

- Washrooms and communal showers and bathing areas should be equipped with soap (or soap dispensers), nail brushes (where required) and towels (or hot air dryers) for the use of employees. These items should be replenished or replaced and, in the case of towels, laundered or replaced as often as may be necessary. Employers may not charge employees for supplying these items.

FOOD SAFETY REGULATIONS

- Under the Food Safety (General Food Hygiene) Regulations 1995 (SI 1995/1763) an adequate number of washbasins must be made available, suitably located and designated for cleaning hands. Such washbasins must be provided with hot and cold (or appropriately mixed) running water, materials for cleaning hands (soap, nail brushes, etc.) and for hygienic drying. Every such washbasin (and the washroom in which it is situated) must be kept clean and in good working order, and must not be used for any purpose other than for securing the personal cleanliness of the user. See also **Food safety & hygiene** and **Toilet facilities** elsewhere in this handbook.

FURTHER INFORMATION

- The full text of the 1992 Regulations and their accompanying Approved Code of Practice is to be found in HSE booklet L24 *'Workplace health, safety and welfare'* (ISBN 0 7176 0413 6) which is available, price £5.00 net, from HSE Books at the address given on page 328.

WINDOW CLEANING

Key points

- If the windows and skylights in a workplace cannot be cleaned from the ground or for some other suitable and safe position, they must be designed and constructed in a way which enables them to be cleaned safely (Regulation 16, Workplace (Health, Safety & Welfare) Regulations 1992 (SI 1992/3004).

- There are several types of windows and several methods which can be installed/adopted to eliminate or minimise the risks associated with cleaning windows, especially those above ground level or on roofs. These include:

  o fitting windows (such as pivoting windows) both surfaces of which can be cleaned safely from the inside

  o fitting suspended cradles or other types of access equipment, or travelling ladders with an attachment for a safety harness

  o providing adequate access for mobile access equipment (including ladders up to 9 metres long) and a firm level surface in a safe place on which to stand it. Suitable points must be provided for tying or fixing any ladder over 6 metres long

  o fixing suitable and suitably placed anchorage points for safety harnesses worn by window cleaners.

Glare, Reduction of

- The windows and skylights in every workplace must be cleaned regularly to admit maximum daylight. They must also be kept free from unnecessary obstructions, such as filing cabinets and stacked materials. By the same token, employees should not be exposed to excessive heat or glare. This means that windows and skylights must be capable of being shaded when the need arises. Another option is to reposition work-benches, desks and other work surfaces so that employees can take maximum advantage of natural daylight without being discomforted by excessive glare (*ibid*; Regulation 8 & 16).

See also the section titled **Doors & other openings**.

FOOD PREMISES

- Windows in food rooms and other premises regulated by the Food Safety (General Food Hygiene) Regulations 1995 (SI 1995/1763) must beconstructed in such a way as to prevent accumulations of dirt. If they are capable of being opened to the outside environment, they must be fitted with insect screens which can be easily removed for cleaning. If open windows are likely to result in the contamination of foodstuffs (whether or not they are fitted with insect screens), they must be closed and must remain closed while food intended for human consumption is being prepared, processed or handled. For further particulars, please turn to the section titled Food safety & hygiene elsewhere in this handbook.

FURTHER INFORMATION

- The following publications are available from HSE Books at the address given on page 328:

L24
Workplace health, safety and welfare. Workplace (Health, Safety and Welfare) Regulations 1992: Approved code of practice and guidance [1992]
ISBN 0 7176 0413 6   £5.00

GS 25 (Rev)
Prevention of falls to window cleaners [1991]
ISBN 0 11 885682 0   £2.50

PM 30
Suspended access equipment [1983]
ISBN 0 11 883577 7   £2.50

WOMEN & YOUNG PERSONS
(Restrictions on employment of)

Key points

- Most of the legal restrictions on the employment of women and young persons have long since been repealed or revoked, either by the Sex Discrimination Act 1986 or, more recently, by the Employment Act 1989. Those which remain (see **Table 1** below) are primarily concerned with the protection of women and young persons in occupations which (for one reason or another) are viewed as potentially damaging to their health. It should be noted that an employer's refusal to employ a woman of whatever age (or a young woman under 18), in compliance with one or other of the provisions listed below, is *not* unlawful discrimination on grounds of sex and does *not* provide grounds for action under the Sex Discrimination Act 1975 (section 4, Employment Act 1989).

- Restrictions on the employment of young persons under 18 are still to be found in the Licensing Act 1964 and in the Licensing (Scotland) Act 1976, both of which statutes prohibit their employment in the bar of licensed premises when that bar is open for the sale or consumption of intoxicating liquor. The prohibition on the employment of a young person under 18 "in the effecting of any betting transaction or in a licensed betting office" also remains (per section 21, Betting, Gaming & Lotteries Act 1963).

The Management of Health & Safety at Work Regulations 1992

- Further restrictions on the employment of young persons under 18 are to be found in the Management of Health & Safety at Work Regulations 1992 (SI 1992/2051), regulation 13D(1) of which imposes a duty on every employer to ensure that young persons under 18 employed by him are protected at work from any risks to their health and safety which are a consequence of their lack of experience, of absence of awareness of existing or potential risks or the fact that young persons have not yet fully matured.

Note: Regulation 13D was inserted by regulation 2(6) of the Health & Safety (Young Persons) Regulations 1997 (SI 1977/135) which came into force on 3 March 1997.

- Regulation 13(D)(2) cautions that no employer may employ a young person under 18 for work which —

(a) is beyond his physical or psychological capacity;

(b) involves harmful exposure to agents which are toxic or carcinogenic, cause heritable genetic damage or harm to the unborn child or which in any other way chronically affect human health;

(c) involves harmful exposure to radiation;

(d) involves the risk of accidents which it may reasonably be assumed cannot be recognised or avoided by young persons owing to their insufficient attention to safety or lack of experience or training; or for work

(e)   in which there is a risk to health from extreme cold or heat, noise, or vibration;

unless the work is necessary for the young person's training in circumstances in which he (or she) is supervised by a competent persons and the risks associated with that work are reduced to the lowest level that is reasonably practicable.

Table 1
RESTRICTIONS ON THE EMPLOYMENT OF WOMEN AND YOUNG PERSONS

Statutory provision	Prohibition/restriction
Public Health Act 1936 (Section 205)	No **woman or girl** may be employed in a factory or workshop within four weeks after she has given birth to a child.
Factories Act 1961 (Section 20)	"A **young person** shall not clean any part of a prime mover or of any transmission machinery while the prime mover or transmission machinery is in motion, and shall not clean any part of any machine if the cleaning thereof would expose the young person to risk of injury from any moving part either of that machine or of any adjacent machinery."
Factories Act 1961 (sections 74 and 128)	No **woman or young person** may be employed in certain processes connected with lead manufacture. These include: work at a furnace where zinc or lead ores are reduced or treated; work involving ashes containing lead, the desilverising of lead, the melting of scrap lead or zince, the manufacture of lead carbonate, sulphate, chromate, acetate, nitrate, silicate or oxide; the manufacture of solder or alloys containing more than 10 per cent of lead; mixing or pasting in connection with the manufacture or repair of electric accumulators; and the cleaning of workrooms where any of these processes are carried on.

Factories Act 1961 (section 131)	**Women and young persons** under 18 must not be employed in painting any part of a building with a lead-based paint — except young males employed as apprentices in the painting trade and women and young persons employed in the execution of wall or ceiling paintings or any similar work of decorative design.
Lead Paint Manufacture Regulations 1907 (Reg. 3) (SR & O 1907/17)	No **woman, young person or child** may be employed in manipulating lead colour. This rule does *not* , however, apply to the employment of a woman in the packing of lead colour in parcels or kegs not exceeding 6 kilograms in weight (*ibid*; Preamble, para (2)).
Lead Smelting & Manufacture Regulations 1911 (Reg. 10) (SR & O 1911/752)	No **female of any age** may be employed in the smelting of materials containing lead, the manufacture of red or orange lead, or the manufacture of flaked litharge.
Indiarubber Regulations 1922 (Reg. 1) (SR & O 1922/329)	No **person under 16 years of age and no female under 18 years of age** may be employed in any lead process. Nor may any **woman or young person** be employed at mixing or incorporating rolls in the process of incorporating dry compound of lead with indiarubber.
Electric Accumulator Regulations 1925 (Reg. 1) (SR & O 1925/28)	No **person under the age of 18** may be employed in any lead process. **Women and young persons** under 18 must not be employed in any room in which the manipulation of raw oxide of lead or pasting is carried on.
Pottery (Health & Welfare) Special Regulations 1950 (Reg. 6(1), (3) & (4) and the First Schedule) (SI 1950/65)	**Women and young persons under 18** must not be employed in the stopping of biscuit ware with lead-based materials; or in the weighing-out, shovelling or mixing of unfritted lead compounds; or in the preparation or weighing-out of flow materials; or in the washing of saggars with a lead-based wash; or in the cleaning of boards in any

place where dipping, drying, ware-cleaning or glost placing is done (other than in a leadless glaze factory); or in the cleaning of mangles (or any part of a mangle), other than in a leadless glaze factory.

Young persons under 18 must not be employed or work as wheel turners at a press for pressing tiles; or in the making or mixing of frits or glazes containing lead or of colours; the preparation or weighing out of flow material; in colour blowing or in the wiping-off of colour after that process; in ground laying or colour dusting, or the wiping-off of colour after either of those processes; in colour grinding; in lithographic transfer making; or in any other processes in which any material, other than glaze, which contains more than 5 per cent of its weight of a soluble lead compound is used or handled in a dry state or in the form of a spray or in suspension in liquid other than oil or a similar medium.

Young persons under 16 must not be employed or work in the following processes when carried on in factories other than 'leadless glaze' factories: dipping or other process carried on in the dipping house; the application of majolica or other glaze by dipping, blowing or any other process; drying or ware-cleaning after the application of glaze by dipping, blowing or any other process; glost placing; or in any other process in which glaze is used or in which pottery articles treated with glaze are handled before glost firing.

Ionising Radiations Regulations 1985
(Parts IV and V of Schedule 1)

(SI 1985/1333)

Dose limits for the abdomen of **a pregnant woman or for that of a woman of reproductive capacity** (See page 435 of this handbook).

No person under the age of 18 may be designated as a 'classified person'(*ibid*; Regulation 9(3),

Air Navigation Order 1985 (Article 20(8)) (SI 1985/1643)	**A member of a flight crew** who has reason to believe she is pregnant must notify her employers in writing without delay. Once her pregnancy is confirmed, she is deemed to be suspended from work and may only resume her duties during the initial stages of her pregnancy if it is considered safe for her to do so. See also Table 1 on pages 585 to 587 of this handbook.
Merchant Shipping (Medical Examination) Regulations 1983 (Reg. 2) (SI 1983/808)	Restrictions imposed on the employment (or continued employment) of women as laid down in Parts X (so far as relating to gynaecological conditions) and XI of the Merchant Shipping Notice No. M 1331. Please turn to the section titled **Suspension on maternity grounds** elsewhere in this handbook.
The Maternity (Compulsory Leave) Regulations 1994 (Reg. 2) (SI 1994/2479)	"**An employee entitled to maternity leave** in accordance with Part VIII of the Employment Rights Act 1996 shall not work, or be permitted by her employer to work, during the period of two weeks which commence with the day on which childbirth occurs."

Note: The list above is not intended to be exhaustive, although it does include most subordinate legislation made under (or saved by) the Factories Act 1961 and still in force. It does not include industry-specific legislation on activities or work situations beyond the scope of this handbook (mines & quarries, carriage of explosives, off-shore installations, diving operations, etc.) which will be well-known to the employers concerned.

See also the sections titled **Children, Employment of** and **Suspension on maternity grounds** elsewhere in this handbook.

WORK EQUIPMENT

Key points

- "Work equipment" is the term used in the Provision & Use of Work Equipment (PUWER) Regulations 1992 (SI 1992/2932) to describe any machinery, appliance, apparatus or tool and any assembly of components which, in order to achieve a common end, are arranged and controlled so that they function as a whole. In short, the PUWER Regulations apply not only to machinery in the accepted sense (lathes, power presses, bottling plant, horizontal milling machines, guillotines, combine harvesters, woodworking machines, etc.) but also to tools and appliances (such as power drills, chain saws, chisels, hand-held saws, screwdrivers, hammers, ladders, vehicle hoists, bunsen burners, cookers, scalpels, knives, etc. etc.) which are made available for use by a person at work. The list is virtually endless.

- Rules concerning the construction, maintenance, fencing and guarding and use of machines (in the accepted sense) are reviewed elsewhere in this handbook in the sections titled **Fencing & guarding** and **Machinery safety**.

- All tools and appliances issued to employees for use in the workplace must not only be suitable for the purpose for which they are used or provided, but must be properly maintained. If a hammer has a loose head, it must be repaired. If a steel chisel has a splintered or mushroom top, it must be replaced. If a ladder has a loose rung, it must taken out of service until it has been repaired. And so on.

- Employees (new recruits and transferees) must be trained in the correct use of work equipment and be made aware of the circumstances and situations in which certain tools and appliances must *not* be used (e.g., in flammable atmospheres or confined spaces). Employees should be given to understand that work equipment must not be used other than for the purposes for which it was designed. Broken or damaged tools must be returned immediately to the maintenance workshop for repair or replacement. Defective equipment must be reported immediately to the supervisor or manager. See also **Training of employees** elsewhere in this handbook.

- An employer (or self-employed person) who disregards his duties under the 1992 Regulations is guilty of an offence under the 1974 Act and is liable to prosecution. If he has been served with an improvement or prohibition notice by a health and safety inspector, but fails to comply with the terms laid down in such a notice, he is liable to a fine of up to £20,000 and/or imprisonment for a period of up to six months. If he is convicted on indictment, he could be fined an unlimited amount and be sent to prison for up to two years. He also faces the prospect of being sued by any person (employee or otherwise) who is injured as a direct consequence of his negligence; as to which, see **Defective equipment** and **Insurance, Compulsory** elsewhere in this handbook.

- An employer who discourages employees from reporting broken or defective equipment, or who disciplines, punishes, dismisses (or selects such an employee for redundancy) for refusing to use potentially dangerous machines, tools or appliances, should be aware that any such action is *prima facie* unlawful under sections 44 and 100 of the Employment Rights Act 1996. Indeed he could be ordered by an industrial tribunal to pay a substantial amount of compensation to the employee or employees in question. For further details, please turn to the section titled **Dismissal or victimisation** elsewhere in this handbook.

FURTHER INFORMATION

- Comprehensive advice on the practical implications of the PUWER Regulations 1992 is to be found in the following 64-page publication produced by the Health & Safety Executive:

  L22
  Work equipment. Provision and Use of Work Equipment Regulations 1992. Guidance on Regulations 1992]
  ISBN 0 7176 0414 4   £5.00
  Copies are available from HSE Books at the address given on page 328.

WORKPLACE REGULATIONS

Key points

- The Workplace (Health, Safety & Welfare) Regulations 1992 (SI 1992/3004) reinforce an employer's general statutory duty under section 2(2)(2)(e) of the Health & Safety at Work etc. Act 1974 to provide and maintain a working environment for his employees that is, so far as is reasonably practicable, safe, without risks to health and adequate as regards arrangements and facilities for their welfare at work.

- The 1992 Regulations are reviewed throughout this handbook under the appropriate subject heads (**Accommodation for clothing, Canteens & rest rooms, Lighting, Temperature, Toilet facilities, Washing facilities, Ventilation**, etc).

Meaning of "workplace"

- It is as well to emphasise that the term "workplace" nowadays refers not only to factories, building sites, warehouses, offices and shops (and the like) but to *every* premises or part of premises which are made available to a person as a place of work (e.g., schools, hospitals, hotels, guest houses, bed-and-breakfast establishments, leisure complexes, 'keep fit' centres, cinemas, theatres, retirement homes, and so on, and so on). The list is endless.

FURTHER INFORMATION

- The following explanatory document is available from HSE Books at the address given on page 328:

  L24
  Workplace health, safety and welfare. Workplace (Health, Safety and Welfare) Regulations 1992: Approved code of practice and guidance [1992]
  ISBN 0 7176 0413 6   £5.00

WORKING HOURS
(Restriction on, on health & safety grounds)

Key points

- Until the appearance of Council Directive 93/104/EC "concerning certain aspects of the organisation of working time", commonly referred to as the 'Working Time Directive', there has been no general UK legislation regulating the working hours and periods of employment of UK employees. Nor is there any general statutory right in the UK to time off work for meal or rest breaks (paid or otherwise) — although most employees have a contractual right to time off for a meal break. Legislation restricting the working hours and periods of employment of women and young persons (and, in some instances, men) in industry and commerce has long since been repealed.

- The only other relevant legislation is to be found in the Road Traffic Act 1968 and, for drivers of vehicles of 3.5 tonnes and over, the relevant EC Regulations (reviewed later in this section). Legislation restricting the working hours of airline pilots, flight crews, deep sea divers, and those of persons employed in other specialist occupations (for example, work in compressed air) will be familiar to employers in the industries in question and is outside the scope of this handbook.

WORKING TIME DIRECTIVE

- The Working Time Directive referred to in the preamble was proposed under Article 118a of the Treaty of Rome (that is to say, as *a health and safety measure*) and was formally adopted by a qualified majority vote of the Member States on 23 November 1993. The Directive, vigorously but unsuccessfully challenged by the UK Government, includes measures for minimum daily and weekly rest periods, a minimum of four weeks' paid annual holidays, a limit of 48 hours on the average working week, and restrictions on night work.

- Although the British Government has yet to introduce the necessary implementing legislation , the Working Time Directive is arguably enforceable now and has been (certainly for public sector employees) since 23 November 1996. Private sector employees (or their representatives) need only bring a test case to the European Court of Justice for the Directive to be applied to all UK workers affected by its provisions. If the Government fails to bring forward the necessary legislation, such a case is not only inevitable, but its outcome predictable. In the meantime, employers would be well-advised to take the working-hours provisions on board and to comply with the transitional provisions summarised below.

Maximum weekly working time

- Article 6 of the Directive requires each of the Member States to take the measures necessary to ensure that, in keeping with the need to protect the safety and health of workers —

  (a) the period of weekly working time is limited by means of laws, regulations or administrative provisions or by collective agreements or agreements between the two sides of industry;

  (b) the average working time for each seven-day period, *including* overtime, does not exceed 48 hours.

The average working time referred to in (b) above may be calculated over a reference period not exceeding four months (*ibid;* Article 16).

The imposition of a maximum average 48-hour working week does not apply to managing executives or others with autonomous decision-taking powers. Nor does it apply to family workers. In any event, Article 6 is unlikely to be (indeed, need not be) enforced by the Member States until 23 November 2003 (*per* Article 18) (but see next paragraph).

Transitional provisions

- However, there are certain conditions attached to the seven-year transitional period described above. Until 23 November 2003, employees *must not* be required to work more than an *average* 48-hour week (including overtime) — calculated over a reference period of not more than four months (six months, in some situations)— unless their employer has first obtained their agreement. It is to be assumed that any such agreement must be given in writing. Nor may an employer victimise, penalise or dismiss any employee of his who withholds his (or her) of the weekly hours worked by their employees, including copies of the agreements obtained from those amongst them who have agreed to work more than an average 48-hour week.

• The records referred to in the previous paragraph must be kept up-to-date and must be produced on demand for inspection by the 'competent authority'. In the UK, the competent authority is likely to be the Health & Safety Inspectorate (although this is by no means certain). Whatever their provenance, inspectors will have the right not only to examine employee records but also to prohibit or restrict the working hours of any employee whose weekly working hours are likely to compromise his (or her) health and safety.

Restrictions on night work

• The Directive also imposes restrictions on night work. A *night worker* is a worker who works at least three hours a night or who works a certain proportion of his annual working time at night. The definition of *night time* will be left to the Member States, so long as it encompasses a period of not less than seven hours, including the period between midnight and 0500 hours.

• Article 8 cautions Member States that they must take the measures necessary to ensure that —

(a) normal hours of work for night workers do not exceed an average of eight hours in any 24-hour period (calculated over a reference period defined after consultation between both sides of industry or by collective agreement at national or local level);

(b) night workers whose work involves special hazards or heavy physical or mental strain do not work more than eight hours in any period during which they perform night work.

Technically, the Directive's restrictions on night work already apply (certainly to public sector employees), and can be enforced within the private sector (if not in the British tribunals and courts) by the European Court of Justice. Pending any challenge, it is incumbent on the UK Government to introduce the necessary implementing legislation without further delay. Unlike Article 6 (maximum weekly working time), Article 8 comes into force immediately.

- Work involving special hazards or heavy physical or mental strain must be defined by legislation and/or practice, or by collective agreements or agreements concluded between both sides of industry. Furthermore, night workers must be offered free health assessments before being assigned to such work and be given (unspecified) assurances about risks to their safety or health linked to night-time working and the protection and facilities to be put in place to eliminate or minimise those risks. Employer must keep records of all night work and must make those records available for inspection by the 'competent' authorities. Finally, night workers suffering from health problems (recognised as being linked to night work) must be transferred to day work whenever possible, so long as it is work to which they are suited.

- Member States may disapply Article 8 for specified categories of night work (so long as the workers concerned are afforded equivalent periods of compensatory rest). Such categories may include security and surveillance activities, services provided by doctors and nurses in hospitals and similar establishments, dock and airport workers, the emergency services (police, fire or ambulance), press and media workers, postal workers, gas, electricity and water workers, continuous process workers, farm workers, etc. — all of which must inevitably be defined in national legislation or (less likely in the UK) collective agreements at national or local level.

WRITTEN PARTICULARS OF TERMS OF EMPLOYMENT

- Every employee has the legal right to receive a written statement of particulars of employment. Those particulars *must* include information *about* "any terms and conditions relating to hours of work (including any terms and conditions relating to normal working hours and, by definition, time off for meals or rest)" (*per* section 1, Employment Rights Act 1996).

DRIVERS' HOURS

- The daily driving hours of drivers of goods and passenger vehicles operating in Great Britain are regulated by Part VI of the Road Transport Act 1968 (as amended). Whether or not the Working Time Directive reviewed earlier in this section will lead to amendments to the 1968 Act remains to be seen.

- The following is intended as a summary (no more) of the principal provisions of the 1968 Act. There are a great many subordinate regulations and orders containing exemptions, modifications and dispensations, which are beyond the scope of this book. Part VI is intended to secure "the observance of proper hours or periods of work by persons engaged in the carriage of passengers or goods by road and thereby protect the public in cases where the drivers of motor vehicles are suffering from fatigue" (*ibid*; section 95(1)).

    Note: The term *passenger vehicle* applies to public service vehicles and to motor vehicles (other than passenger service vehicles) constructed or adapted to carry more than 12 passengers (*ibid*; section 95(2)).

- Section 96 of that Act restricts a driver's working day to 11 hours, and the time he (or she) spends 'behind the wheel' to 10 hours a day. A driver must not drive a goods vehicle (or any passenger-transport vehicle) for more than five-and-a-half hours without a break of at least 30 minutes for rest and refreshment. In an 11-hour working day, this would entitle a driver to two half-hour meal and rest breaks.

- A driver of any vehicle to which the 1968 Act applies must be allowed an interval of at least 11 work-free hours between one working day and the next. He (or she) must not be on duty in any working week for more than 60 hours in the aggregate, and must be allowed an off-duty period of at least 24 uninterrupted hours in every period of seven consecutive days. The penalty for a contravention of the domestic drivers' hours code — whether by the driver or his employer, or both — is a fine not exceeding level 4 on the standard scale (currently £2,500).

- Section 97 of the 1968 Act (as substituted by the Passenger & Goods Vehicles (Recording Equipment) Regulations 1979 (SI 1979/1746)) states that a tachograph must be installed in a goods vehicle in compliance with Council Regulation EEC/3821/85, as amended. A tachograph automatically records a driver's driving hours and rest periods, and must be installed in the cab of any goods vehicle with a gross plated weight of more than 3.5 tonnes. Any person who contravenes this requirement is liable on summary conviction to a fine not exceeding level 5 on the standard scale (currently £5,000).

EC law

- The daily and weekly driving hours (and daily and weekly rest periods) for drivers operating heavy goods vehicles to and from other EC member states, are regulated by provisions laid down in EC Regulations 3820/85 and 3821/85. As a rule, the driver of any such goods vehicle having a gross plated weight of more than 3.5 tonnes must not drive his vehicle for more than four-and-a-half hours without a break of at least 45 minutes (in total or in the aggregate) during the course of, or at the end of, that driving period. Two or more shorter breaks are permitted during those four-and-a-half hours so long as no single break lasts for less than 15 minutes and they add up to a total of 45 minutes or more. Any break lasting less than 15 minutes does not count as a rest period for these purposes.

- UK drivers operating in and out of the European Community must not drive for more than nine hours a day or for more than 56 hours in any week (subject to a fortnightly driving limit of 90 hours). Within those limits, a driver's daily hours can increase to 10 hours on not more than two days a week. There must be an off-duty period of at least 11 consecutive hours in every 24-hour period, and a weekly rest period of 45 consecutive hours in every working week. The weekly rest period *can* reduce to 36 consecutive hours if taken at the driver's home base, or to 24 consecutive hours if taken elsewhere — subject to the proviso that *all* rest hours lost in this way must be taken in a single rest period within the ensuing three weeks.

Note: Drivers engaged in international operations outside the European Community, in and out of the UK, will normally need to comply with AETR as well as EC regulations.

See also the sections titled Canteens & rest rooms, Holidays, Annual, Meals for employees, Pregnant employees & nursing mothers, and **Suspension on maternity grounds** elsewhere in this handbook.

Appendix I

Table 1
EXCLUSION OF MACHINERY COVERED BY OTHER
DIRECTIVES
Supply of Machinery (Safety) Regulations 1992
(Regulation 9)

The 1992 Regulations do not apply to —

(a) roll-over protective structures as referred to in Article 1 of Council Directive 86/295/EEC on the approximation of the laws of the member States relating to roll-over protective structures (ROPS) for certain construction plant (as detailed in OJ No. L186 of 8 July 1986, page 1);

(b) falling-object protective structures as referred to in Article 1 of Council Directive 86/296/EEC on the approximation of the laws of the member States relating to falling-object protective structures (FOPS) for certain construction plant (see OJ No. L186 of 8 July 1986, page 10); or

(c) industrial trucks as referred to in Article 1 of Council Directive 86/663/EEC on the approximation of the laws of the member States relating to self-propelled industrial trucks,

which are supplied or put into service for the first time in the Community before 1 July 1995.

(2) On and after 1 July 1995, in respect of machinery mentioned in paragraph (1) above which is supplied or put into service for the first time in the Community on or before 31 December 1995, a supplier may comply with —

(a) the requirements of these Regulations (viz; the Supply of Machinery Regulations (Safety) Regulations 1992); or with

(b) the requirements of —

(i) in the case of roll-over protective structures, the Roll-over Protective Structures for Construction Plant (EEC Requirements) Regulations 1988 (SI 1988/363);

(ii) in the case of falling-object protective structures, the Falling-object Protective Structures for Construction Plant (EEC Requirements) Regulations 1988 (SI 1988/362); or

(iii) in the case of industrial trucks, in Great Britain, the Self-Propelled Industrial Trucks (EEC Requirements) Regulations 1988 (SI 1988/1736) as amended by the Self-Propelled Industrial Trucks (EEC Requirements) (Amendment) Regulations 1989 (SI 1989/1035), and in Northern Ireland, the Self-Propelled Industrial Trucks (EEC Requirements) Regulations (Northern Ireland) 1990 (SR 1990/172).

Note: OJ is the acronym for the Official Journal of the European Communities (copies of which are available from EC Information Centres and good reference libraries).

Table 2
EXCLUDED MACHINERY
Schedule 5, Supply of Machinery (Safety) Regs 1992
(SI 1992/3073)

The 1992 Regulations do *not* apply to the following machinery:

o   Machinery whose only power source is directly applied manual effort unless it is a machine used for lifting or lowering loads.

o   Machinery for medical use used in direct contact with patients.

o   Special equipment for use in fairgrounds and/or amusement parks.

o   Steam boilers, tanks and pressure vessels.

o   Machinery specially designed or put into service for nuclear purposes which, in the event of failure, may result in an emission of radioactivity.

o   Radioactive sources forming part of a machine.

o   Firearms.

o   Storage tanks and pipelines for petrol, diesel fuel,

inflammable liquids and dangerous substances.

o   Means of transport, that is vehicles and their trailers intended solely for transporting passengers by air on or road, rail or water networks, as well as means of transport in so far as such means are designed for transporting goods by air, on public road or rail networks or on water. Vehicles used in the mineral extraction industry shall not be excluded.

o   Seagoing vessels and mobile offshore units together with equipment on board such vessels or units.

o   Passenger lifts, cableways, rack and pinion railaways, mine winding gear, theatre elevators and construction site hoists.

o   Agricultural and forestry tractors, as defined in Article 1(1) of Council Directive 74/150/EEC of 4 March 1974 on the approximation of the laws of the member States relating to the type-approval of wheeled agricultural or forestry tractors, as last amended by Directive 88/297/EEC.

o   Machines specially designed and constructed for military or police purposes.

Index

Note: Page numbers printed in **bold** type point to the main reference in the text.